THE GREAT LANDOWNERS
OF GREAT BRITAIN AND IRELAND

THE VICTORIAN LIBRARY

THE GREAT LANDOWNERS
OF GREAT BRITAIN AND IRELAND

JOHN BATEMAN

WITH AN INTRODUCTION BY
DAVID SPRING

LEICESTER UNIVERSITY PRESS
NEW YORK: HUMANITIES PRESS
1971

First published in 1876
Fourth edition published in 1883
Victorian Library edition (reprinting 1883 text)
published in 1971 by
Leicester University Press

Distributed in North America by
Humanities Press Inc., New York

Introduction copyright © Leicester University Press

Printed in Great Britain by
Unwin Brothers Limited, The Gresham Press
Old Woking, Surrey

ISBN 0 7185 5013 7

THE VICTORIAN LIBRARY

There is a growing demand for the classics of Victorian literature in many fields, in political and social history, architecture, topography, religion, education, and science. Hitherto this demand has been met, in the main, from the second-hand market. But the prices of second-hand books are rising sharply, and the supply of them is very uncertain. It is the object of this series, THE VICTORIAN LIBRARY, to make some of these classics available again at a reasonable cost. Since most of the volumes in it are reprinted photographically from the first edition, or another chosen because it has some special value, an accurate text is ensured. Each work carries a substantial introduction, written specially for this series by a well-known authority on the author or his subject, and a bibliographical note on the text.

The volumes necessarily vary in size. In planning the newly-set pages the designer, Arthur Lockwood, has maintained a consistent style for the principal features. The uniform design of binding and jacket provides for ready recognition of the various books in the series when shelved under different subject classifications.

Recommendation of titles for THE VICTORIAN LIBRARY and of scholars to contribute the introductions is made by a joint committee of the Board of the University Press and the Victorian Studies Centre of the University of Leicester.

INTRODUCTION

I

That *The Times'* obituary for John Bateman omitted to
mention that he was the author of *The Great Landowners of
Great Britain and Ireland* is perhaps partly understandable.[1]
After all the book was not a literary work, being a statistical
compilation of British landowners in the 1870s; and in a sense
it was far from being wholly Bateman's work, having been
derived from those parliamentary papers known familiarly as
the New or Modern Domesday Book.[2] Nonetheless Bateman's
work was – and remains – significant. In its own day it made
easily accessible, and it corrected and amplified, one of the
most heroic of the Victorians' pioneering enterprises in
statistical inquiry. Today it may well find uses hitherto
undreamt of, as the historically minded turn more readily than
ever before to quantifying the past.

II

A proper understanding of Bateman's work must begin with an
account of the New Domesday Book and its origins. The idea
of a Domesday Book – that is, a national inventory of British
land – as well as the phrase itself were given currency by the
statistician, F. P. Fellows. Addressing the Statistical Section
of the British Association for the Advancement of Science in
August 1871, he dwelt on the utility of the Government's
having a detailed valuation of its property, and it was only
en passant – "the least important of my suggestions", as he

put it – that he proposed a Domesday Book of the nation's landed property as well.[3] It was the Land Question – that fruitful source of public controversy – which found for Fellows' modest proposal more enthusiastic and influential advocates.

The Land Question might equally well have been called the Aristocracy Question: anti-aristocrats were anti-landowners: they were especially against great landowners who wielded a large political and social influence. Radicals like John Bright thus deplored what they called "the practical monopoly of land" by which, it was charged, rural industry was impoverished, tenant farmers were made dependants and agricultural labourers made wretched, and small landowners were eaten up by a few large ones. To reduce landed power Radicals proposed, among other things, the abolition of primogeniture and strict family settlement, those legal and customary means by which aristocracy kept its landed estates intact. Because of the oddities of the 1861 Census Radicals were able to give statistical shape to their accusations. The Census reported that the total number of landowners amounted to no more than 30,000 – which figure John Bright and others seized on triumphantly to prove that landowners were dwindling in number, prey to the Leviathans among them, those "fewer than one hundred and fifty men" who Bright declared were owners of "half the land of England".[4]

Bright plainly suffered from no lack of statistics – but his opponents did. Accordingly the fifteenth earl of Derby, a landed aristocrat of much intelligence and great influence, took up with alacrity Fellows' proposal for a Domesday Book. He was the sort of nobleman who attended learned meetings, and had himself not long before addressed the British Association on the application and uses of the statistical method. "It is the statistical test employed on a large scale", he declared on that occasion, "which alone can be conclusive."[5]

In September 1871, shortly after the delivery of Fellows'
paper, Lord Derby faced an audience of farmers at a meeting of
the Manchester and Liverpool Agricultural Society, and to
them he unburdened himself about the vexations of the Land
Question – that grave question "which many have for years
past been discussing at public meetings", and which, he
supposed, was likely to come increasingly to the forefront of
public life.[6]

"What I most wish to point out", he said, "is the curious
uncertainty as to the facts of the case in which we are, and the
expediency of doing something to have that uncertainty
removed." The 1861 Census summed up for Derby the in-
adequacy of landed statistics in current use. That return, he
rightly argued, was highly misleading, being a return only of
those landowners who had chosen to designate themselves as
landowners, most of them having chosen some other designa-
tion; that half of them were women was proof enough of
something being wrong. In place of thirty thousand landowners
Derby guessed that ten times that figure was closer to although
still below the true one. He also guessed that the Radical case
for landed estates "constantly tending to become fewer in
number and bigger in size" was far from being proved. "My
belief is – though I give it only as a thing which seems to me
probable, not as a thing proved – that both very great and
very small properties are becoming fewer, and those of a
middle size more numerous. Poor landowners prefer 10 per
cent in trade to 2 per cent from land – they sell and go into
business; and on the other hand, there is a limit beyond which
most men do not desire to extend their holding of what is
essentially an unremunerative investment. But why should we
be left on this subject to mere speculation? Is it impossible to
get at the facts? Is a Domesday Book more difficult now than
in the days of the Conqueror?"[7]

Victorian obstacles to compiling a Domesday Book shortly proved surmountable. In the following February Derby raised the matter in the House of Lords. This time his surmises on landownership were in some respects different. He still held 30,000 to be an absurd global figure, and 300,000 much closer to the truth. But he was now silent about large owners being less numerous, and showed a change of mind about small owners being less numerous; he was not immune, in short, from a certain waywardness of opinion to which the Land Question gave rise in many minds, both Radical and Tory, both strong and weak. "It was true", he said, "that the class of peasant proprietors formerly to be found in the rural districts was tending to disappear – for the very good reason that such proprietors could, as a general rule, obtain from 40 to 50 years' purchase for their holdings and thereby vastly increase their incomes. In the place of that class, however, there was rapidly growing up a new class of small owners, who, dwelling in or near towns or railway stations, were able to buy small freeholds. He believed this new class would fully replace, and perhaps more than replace, the diminution in the other class to which he had referred."[8] As to the making of the New Domesday, Derby proposed that the Local Government Board undertake the collection of statistical data in the shape of a return which would include the name of every owner and the amount of his land. Lord Halifax, the Government spokesman in the Lords, could scarcely have been more agreeable. His views on the Land Question coincided with Derby's, and he declared the Government's readiness to publish a Domesday Book based on parish valuation lists.

Four years later the first fruits of this vast statistical undertaking appeared. Information had been gathered from 15,000 parishes and five million parochial assessments. This information was arranged by county, each owner within a county being listed alphabetically, together with his address, the extent of his land, and his estimated gross rental. Under Bedfordshire, for example, appeared the name of the Duke of Bedford, address Woburn Abbey, the owner of 33,589 acres at an estimated gross rental of £47,421; next to the Duke appeared one Robert Beechener, address Barton, the owner of slightly more than one acre at an estimated gross rental of £63. Efforts to aggregate this detailed information were curiously skimpy. The aggregate figure which drew most attention was that of the total number of English and Welsh landowners (excluding those of the Metropolis). This was estimated at 972,836, of which 269,547 were owners of one acre and upwards, and 703,289 were owners of less than an acre.

Three journals – *The Times*, *The Daily News* and *The Spectator* – set out the main lines of public reaction to the New Domesday Book. *The Times*, Tory in its politics, declared with evident satisfaction that "the legend of 30,000 landowners has been found to be as mythical as that of St. Ursula and her company of 10,000 virgins".[9] *The Daily News*, Liberal in its politics, complained that the aggregate figure of English and Welsh landowners was useless, that "persons who have theories or prejudices or interests concerning what is commonly called the 'land question' are not thinking of fragments of land of less than an acre".[10] *The Spectator*, also Liberal, and the most illuminating perhaps of the great weeklies, took the discussion furthest. The point of its first article was that "neither Mr. Bright nor Lord Derby is wholly in the wrong". On the one hand, "nearly a million of persons (972,836) in England and Wales outside London . . . own a freehold, be it only a house, or a garden, or a patch of building." On the other hand, by dint of some hasty researches in the New Domesday Book, *The Spectator* estimated that landowners "in the political sense – in the sense in which the word has always been present to Mr.

Bright's mind" – numbered only 43,000. These were owners of 100 acres and more – that is, they were persons of some political influence. Moreover, *The Spectator* argued, "this 43,000 is in practice influenced by a much smaller number, the great territorialists, who claim the right, usually conceded to them, to lead opinion in county districts."[11]

Some weeks later *The Spectator* described precisely who these "territorialists" were, publishing what it called "the true Libro d'Oro of England, a nominal roll of every man in England and Wales who possesses 5,000 acres in any one county and therefore belongs to the Territorial Aristocracy". These comprised 710 persons, titled and untitled, the "Seven Hundred". According to *The Spectator*, "the total result is a most extraordinary one, and one that would justify any club which interests itself in the repeal of the Land Laws, in expending a few hundreds in a short but thoroughly complete analysis of 'Domesday Book'. Whatever else is uncertain about the position of English landlords, this one fact is certain: *Seven hundred and ten individuals own more than a fourth of the soil of England and Wales*, exclusive of lakes, roads, rivers, London, waste spaces, and Crown property, and within a fraction of a fourth of the entire geographical area of the country. And those 710 own also, immediately or in reversion, one-seventh of the entire rental of the Kingdom, a proportion which, if London could be included, would be very greatly increased . . . Mr. Bright was undoubtedly wrong in believing that Englishmen have been divorced from the soil, . . . but he was as undoubtedly right in believing that a most limited number of gentlemen . . . wield still an enormous territorial and political influence. They own a fourth of the Kingdom – more, probably, than the same class in any country in Europe, unless it be Hungary or Bohemia."[12]

There was not much comfort in this for Lord Derby. Although

he was right about the number of landowners, he was wrong about the large ones: the unpalatable Thirty Thousand had been replaced by an even more unpalatable Seven Hundred. Not surprisingly, once the Domesday Book returns were published, Lord Derby kept his silence about counting landowners, although he was as quick as ever to defend the system of large estates.[13] Generally speaking, those on Lord Derby's side of the Land Question also kept silent about the fewness of large owners and the extent of their acreage – with one notable exception. *The Spectator* had advised the enemies of landed power to invest some of their money in bringing out a thorough analysis of Domesday Book along lines already laid down in its article on the Seven Hundred. But as it happened this work fell not to a follower of John Bright but to a Tory country gentleman, John Bateman.

III

Bateman was born in 1839, educated at Trinity College, Cambridge, and came of an established Staffordshire family. In the early 1870s, owing to the discomforts of life in an industrial county, he exchanged his ancestral acres for more bucolic surroundings in Essex, first briefly at Bromley, then permanently at Brightlingsea on the banks of the Colne where he acquired an estate of 1400 acres.

So far as the meagre record shows, Bateman's life at Brightlingsea Hall – until his death in 1910 – was mainly that of a conventional Victorian squire. He was an agricultural improver who experimented in forestry and tobacco growing and who had firm ideas about proper methods of ensilage. He was kindly to his dependants, to Nonconformist no less than to Anglican. And he bore his full share of public responsibility, being an original member of the Essex County Council, a member of the Brightlingsea Urban District Council, chairman

of the local branch of the Harwich Division Conservative and
Unionist Association, and chairman of the Lexden and Wins-
tree Bench. He died in harness, falling ill at a meeting of his
fellow Justices in Colchester.[14]

Being an author was quite another matter – less congenial to
squires than farming, good works and public office. Bateman's
Great Landowners appeared in 1876, and its successive editions
in 1878, 1879 and 1883. No other writings by him have come to
light, apart from a series of eight articles in the *Essex County
Standard*, September-December 1882, entitled "From the
Colne to the Plate". These described Bateman's journey to the
Argentine in May 1882, and were chiefly devoted to rapturous
accounts of his decimating the wild creatures along the River
Plate. Bateman found these delights exceeding even those
offered at Sandringham by the Prince of Wales: "Never did I
see such a sight or hear such a clangour – fowls at 6 ounces,
8 ounces, 10 ounces, 1 pound, 2 pounds, and so on, up to 18
pounds in weight were flying round us, at us, from us, each
talking their own peculiar fowl tongue . . . It was a day to be
marked in white stone."[15]

That the pleasure of slaughtering exotic birds might have
driven a Victorian squire to the unaccustomed labours of
provincial journalism is not impossible to imagine. But it is
less easy to imagine why Bateman became the author of
Great Landowners of Great Britain and Ireland. If, as *The
Spectator* had it, this was proper work for a Radical, Bateman
gave few signs of being one. He was no friend of John Bright:
the Thirty Thousand, as he put it, was "an absurd illusion".
Landowners, moreover, were not the oppressors but the
oppressed, victims of their own generosity and sense of social
obligation. Thus Bateman drew up an imaginary expense
account for an imaginary John Steadyman of Wearywork Hall
– a "typical £5000 a year squire" – showing how little of this

gross income remained for him to live on. It is true that among Bateman's slapdash opinions on the land laws may be found expressions of sympathy for greater freedom in the sale and transfer of land. But he was not alone in this: by 1880 many Tories saw advantages in such legislation. Bateman himself looked favourably on it, the better to encourage small landowners in whom he had found the makings of good Tory voters.[16]

Perhaps one should conclude that Bateman compiled his book for the simple reason that he found enjoyment in it. In migrating to Essex from Staffordshire he had searched for two years for a suitable property, thereby acquiring a good deal of knowledge about acreages, prices and rentals. This information – together with a curiosity about the acreages of his fellow squires – whetted his appetite for more. Being already something of an expert, it was not inappropriate to become an author, especially of a book that promised to be popular; Bateman had noticed that even the bulky volumes of Domesday Book provided a titillating diversion for country-house guests. Thus he might well describe his book as a "labour of love". Throwing landed statistics into various shapes became an absorbing hobby, so much so that he even furnished George Brodrick, a Radical writer, with a set of tables which illustrated the extent of monopoly in English landownership, despite the fact that Brodrick removed anti-Radical comments which had accompanied the tables.[17]

So in April 1876 Bateman "conceived the idea of making a list of those who held a substantial share of the land of England and Wales", this work being based on the initial instalment of Domesday Book.[18] The first step in this process was to decide how many of the English and Welsh landowners were to get into his book. Bateman claimed that this decision was made for him by his publisher who insisted on quick publication and therefore on eliminating all landowners with less than 3000 acres. The second step was to guess who these owners were, to hunt up their aggregate holdings in the various counties in Domesday Book, and to arrange them in alphabetical order. Bateman took it upon himself to correct and simplify the original returns, especially where the same owner was presented in a variety of guises, as when John Smith became J. Smith, or when the same John Smith was divided between several places of residence, or when part of his property was attributed to a son or a dowager. The third and final step was to add information not found in Domesday Book, such as the landowner's college, his club, and whether his family was to be found in Shirley's *Noble and Gentle Men of England*, this last indicating that the family had held land in the same county since the time of Henry VII in unbroken male line.

Bateman's book – the first edition was entitled *The Acre-Ocracy of England* – had a mixed reception from the journals of opinion, some of it severely critical. *The Spectator* was the most kindly: "Mr. John Bateman . . . has with great labour and ingenuity boiled down the Domesday Book of England into a kind of 'Peerage' . . . The work is as useful and handy as a Peerage, and might have as wide a sale, the original volumes being almost unmanageable, both from their bulk and the inherent defects of their arrangement."[19] But even *The Spectator* joined the critics: first, to find fault with the title – for which, it should be noted, Bateman had apologized – and to suggest a new one, something like the "Landowners of Great Britain"; and second, to find fault with "the would-be comic cover", the humour of which seems to have been as incomprehensible then as it is today. *The Saturday Review* objected to landowners being primarily classified by acreage: "it is a pity [Bateman] could not have made it three thousand acres *or* £3000 a year. As it is, he both excludes a large number of persons whose rent-roll is far above £3000 a year and includes a number, who, owning a large estate in forest or moor, have comparatively little in money".[20] *The Athenaeum* complained about the exclusion of Scottish and Irish landowners.[21] Finally, apart from *The Spectator* which was grateful for the reasonable accuracy of Bateman's facts, the reviewers generally deplored the many inaccuracies, of which they drew up sample lists, these being presumably but a faint shadow of the host of errors which stalked Bateman's pages.

Bateman humbly accepted most of these criticisms, and in 1878 brought out a much revised edition of his work which served as the model for the remaining editions. He changed the title to *The Great Landowners of Great Britain and Ireland*. He had the book bound in a cover more suited to its contents. He added the particulars of Irish and Scottish landowners to those of English and Welsh, thus increasing his list from roughly 1500 to 2500 persons. In seeking to exclude owners of large and unproductive estates in Irish bog and Scottish moor, Bateman now defined large landowners as those who possessed 3000 acres *and* £3000. He also provided further information about landowners' lives and careers: in addition to their colleges and clubs he gave such particulars as schools; dates of birth, succession, and marriage; service in Army, Navy and Diplomacy; and, in a precise way, Parliamentary service, indicating such things as whether landowners represented places on their own property. Most important, he had solicited corrections from all landowners – that is, corrections of Domesday Book – and now incorporated them in this (and successive) editions, the corrected information being specially marked. Finally, he drew up a list of impoverished peers, worth less than £3000 a year, and a set of tables arranging landowners in several classes according to acreage and income – an exercise which was to be more fully set out in the last edition.

The principal change in the next edition (1879) was the inclusion of a further set of owners. These were persons who, having failed to meet the definition of 3000 acres *and* £3000, nevertheless possessed 2000 acres *and* £2000. They amounted to an extra 1320 owners, each of them placed at the bottom of the page and separated from the larger owners by a heavy black line; for almost none of these was information offered beyond his acreage and rental. This edition also provided a far larger number of corrected returns than the previous edition, and these were more carefully marked than before to indicate the extent of correction and whether the owner had included the size of his woodland – this last being information which Domesday Book had not solicited and which was now offered at the expense of reducing (regrettably) some of the particulars previously given about Parliamentary service. Lastly the 1879 edition added some new tables, of which the most illuminating classified landowners according to their membership in London clubs. Bateman was happy to report that 856 great landowners belonged to Tory clubs, 348 to Liberal.

Apart from further corrections supplied by landowners, the fourth and last edition (1883) offered the least novelty. Its chief innovation comprised the tables – and what Bateman called "the dissertation thereon" – which had been written for Brodrick's *English Land and English Landlords* and was now incorporated with some revisions. These tables arranged British landowners, both globally and by county, in eight classes: peers, great landowners (commoners with 3000 acres and more), squires (with between 1000 and 3000 acres), greater yeomen (with between 300 and 1000 acres), lesser yeoman (with between 100 and 300 acres), small proprietors (with between 1 and 100 acres), cottagers (with less than an acre), and public bodies. Bateman paid special attention to the class of small proprietors whom he cherished politically. He estimated – somewhat arbitrarily, it would seem – that quadrupling them "would add greatly to the stability of our fatherland and its institutions"[22] and that more than quadrupling them would bring glut and ruin. Since in the very next breath he groaned about the depression in agriculture, it is not clear why he entertained such visions of Englishmen returning in swarms to the land.

IV

But Bateman was neither an agricultural economist nor, alas, a very thoughtful man. His strength lay in counting heads, in sifting and arranging the relatively raw facts of landownership which Domesday Book had provided. If Domesday had its imperfections, these were very much reduced by Bateman's labours.[23] Some sorts of improvement were, of course, impossible to make, as he himself recognized in expressing the hope that "if ever a revision of the Great Return of 1873 is made a separate volume will be given to all town properties".[24] Bateman recorded the Duke of Bedford's gross income as £141,793, aware that the Duke's London property was not included – a property which itself brought a gross income of £102,296 in 1880.[25] In such cases, especially in respect of income, Bateman was bound to be deficient. But in respect of acreages, especially where agricultural land was involved, he improved on Domesday Book and helped to provide a reasonably reliable guide to the structure of British landownership in the 1870s.

Since English landed society is now largely a thing of the past, and may at last be studied with less heat and more light than was once the case, our appreciation of Bateman's work is likely to be different from that of his own time. He has already provided the source for some scholarly speculation about nineteenth-century trends in the distribution of land.[26] Conceivably he might well become a major source for further investigation into the nature of English landed society. In this age of collective biography his compilation offers a tempting prospect. Suppose someone were to extract the owners of 1000–2000 acres from Domesday Book and add them to Bateman's list, the result would be something like the complete population of England's nobility and gentry. Once this was obtained, any number of useful questions might then be asked with the hope of obtaining precise answers. For example, what were the relations between English landed society and the professions, the business world, the armed services, etc.? Who were the political families? How were landed families educated? What was the extent of social mobility? In effect Bateman might provide the scaffolding for a sort of sociology of English landed society, an ironical fate for the hobby of a rustic squire, although congenial enough to modern historical interests.

David Spring
August 1970

NOTES

1. *The Times*, 13 October 1910.
2. Parliamentary Papers, 1874, LXXII, Parts I and II, Return of Owners of Land, 1872–3 (England and Wales), was the first instalment of this inquiry into landholding which did not in fact appear until 1876. Later instalments were 1874, LXXII, Part III (Scotland); and 1876, LXXX (Ireland).
3. F. P. Fellows, "On a Proposed Domesday Book, giving the value of the Governmental Property as a basis for a sound system of National Finance and Accounts", *Report of the British Association for the Advancement of Science* London, 1872).
4. G. Barnett Smith, *Life and Speeches of John Bright* (New York, 1881), p. 137. For a valuable discussion of the Land Question, see F. M. L. Thompson, "Land and Politics in England in the Nineteenth Century", *Transactions of the Royal Historical Society*, 1965.
5. Sir T. H. Sanderson and E. S. Roscoe, *Speeches and Addresses of Edward Henry XVth Earl of Derby* (London, 1894), I, 72.
6. *Ibid.*, I, 139.
7. *Ibid.*, I, 141.
8. *Hansard*, 3rd series, vol. 209, pp. 639–40, 19 February 1872.
9. *The Times*, 7 February 1876. *The Times* was mistaken: according to legend, St Ursula's companions numbered 11,000.

10. *The Daily News*, 16 February 1876.

11. *The Spectator*, 12 February 1876.

12. *Ibid.*, 4 March 1876. For a comparison of English and Hungarian landownership in the nineteenth century, see S. M. Eddie, "The Changing Pattern of Landownership in Hungary, 1867–1914", *The Economic History Review*, August 1967.

13. This statement is based on an examination of Lord Derby's public utterances, 1872–80, published in *The Times*, *Hansard* and his collected speeches.

14. *Essex County Chronicle*, 14 October 1910; *Walton Gazette*, 19 October 1910; J. Bateman, *The Great Landowners of Great Britain and Ireland* (1883), preface, p. xiv.

15. *Essex County Standard*, 9 December 1882.

16. For Bateman's opinions on Bright and the Land Question, see *Great Landowners* (1883), pp. 516 ff.

17. *Ibid.*, p. 515.

18. *Ibid.*, preface, p. xiv.

19. *The Spectator*, 26 August 1876.

20. *The Saturday Review*, 9 September 1876.

21. *The Athenaeum*, 9 September 1876.

22. *Great Landowners* (1883), pp. 527–8.

23. A rough measure of Bateman's corrections for Welsh landowners may be found in B. L. James, "The 'Great' Landowners of Wales", *The National Library of Wales Journal*, Summer 1966.

24. *Great Landowners* (1883), p. 527.

25. Bedford MSS., Bedford Estate Office, London.

26. F. M. L. Thompson, *English Landed Society in the Nineteenth Century* (London, 1963), pp. 27 ff; see also his "The Social Distribution of Landed Property in England since the Sixteenth Century", *The Economic History Review*, December 1966.

BIBLIOGRAPHICAL NOTE

The present volume reprints the fourth and last edition of *The Great Landowners of Great Britain and Ireland* by John Bateman. The work was first published in London in 1876 under the title *The Acre-Ocracy of England*. For the extensively revised and expanded second edition of 1878 Bateman adopted the new title which was retained in subsequent editions. The third edition of 1879 incorporated further corrections and additions to the lists of landowners and the tables. The fourth edition of 1883 includes Bateman's final corrections and, with revisions, the tables which he had contributed two years earlier to George Charles Brodrick's *English Land and English Landlords*.

J. L. Madden

THE GREAT LANDOWNERS OF

GREAT BRITAIN & IRELAND.

THE
GREAT LANDOWNERS

OF

Great Britain and Ireland.

A LIST OF ALL OWNERS OF

THREE THOUSAND ACRES AND UPWARDS,

WORTH £3,000 A YEAR;

ALSO, ONE THOUSAND THREE HUNDRED OWNERS OF

TWO THOUSAND ACRES AND UPWARDS,

IN

ENGLAND, SCOTLAND, IRELAND, & WALES,

Their Acreage and Income from Land,

CULLED FROM

THE MODERN DOMESDAY BOOK;

Also their Colleges, Clubs, and Services.

Corrected in the vast majority of cases by the Owners themselves.

BY

JOHN BATEMAN, F.R.G.S.,

With a Series of Tables originally compiled for "English Land and English Landlords," by HON. G. BRODRICK, *with a Dissertation thereon.*

———

4TH EDITION,
REVISED AND CORRECTED THROUGHOUT.

———

LONDON:
HARRISON, 59, PALL MALL, S.W.,
Bookseller to Her Majesty and H.R.H. the Prince of Wales.

———

1883.

LONDON :

HARRISON AND SONS, PRINTERS IN ORDINARY TO HER MAJESTY,
ST. MARTIN'S LANE.

PREFACE.

THAT the affairs of one's neighbours are of no little interest to men of every class of life has perhaps never been more strongly proved than by the production of and great demand for "The Modern Domesday Book." Not only have Mr. Frederick Purdy and others analyzed it, Mr. Lyulph Stanley abused it, Mr. John Bright moved its digestion in the House, and the "Spectator" and other London journals scathingly criticised it, but the immense herd of country newspapers have actually reproduced it, as far as their own neighbourhoods are concerned, in their columns, much, probably, to the satisfaction of the bulk of readers, to whom twenty-six shillings (the price of the English volumes alone) is prohibitory. As an example of this, I may mention, that having a small party in my house during one of those dubious weeks which come in 'twixt the close of the hunting and the beginning of the London season, I was saved all Marthean cares as to the amusement of my guests simply by leaving about on the table the two huge volumes of "The Modern Domesday," over which I found bowed with the utmost constancy two or more heads.

I heard from one of my guests that the copy of the work at the "Ultratorium" was reduced to rags and tatters within a fortnight of its arrival—a lesson which was not wasted on the library committee of my own club, who caused the book to be so bound as to defy anything short of a twelve-year-old school-boy.

Mr. Lyulph Stanley finds great fault with the carelessness of some of the entries in " Domesday,"—faults which, it must be admitted, are most perplexing to the compiler— faults in spelling, faults in description of residence, gross faults as to the initialling of names, not infrequent double entries of the same man, first as John, then as J., and in the same fashion through the alphabet; and not least, the almost invariable mixing up of a parson's glebe land, or possession in his public capacity of parish priest, with his private acreage, as what Sidney Smith dubbed a " squarson." One huge stumbling-block in the way of the work's perfection is the large number of double-barrelled (if I may use the term) names in England, such as Hart-Dyke, Leveson-Gower, and Vernon-Harcourt, to say nought of such perfect " mitrailleuses " as Rouse-Boughton-Knight and Butler-Clarke-Southwell-Wandesforde. This necessitates a search for acres under every one of the bracketed family names.

In Wales the difficulty lies in a very different direction, *i.e.*, in the almost desperate simplicity of names; in fact, it may be taken for granted that two-thirds of Wales is owned by the families of Jones, Davies, Evans, and Williams.

Would that for the wretched compiler's sake there had been a few more " Sir Watkins " in existence!

In a compilation of the sort I have attempted, mistakes must occur, but I have tried to minimize them by noting the most glaring and oft-recurring errors in the return, in order to be on guard against them. I may class these errors as follows :—

I. *Mixture of Vowels.*—Vowels I find in the return mean next to nothing. For instance, Sir H. Selwin-Ibbetson is returned as himself properly spelt, and in the same county as "Sir H. Ebbetson"; in the far north, the name of Lindow is spelt with the most perfect impartiality "Lindow," "Lindon," and "London"; in a Midland county, my good friend John Levett and his kinsfolk are put in as "Levitt," "Lovett," and "Lovatt," and unless a man knew or found out that no Lovett was ever squire of Wichnor and guardian of the hereditary flitch, he would grievously fail in judging the Levett acreage aright. In Derbyshire, again, the considerable family of Turbutt of Ogston is robbed of its entire patrimony (except a beggarly four acres), which is given to the mythical house of "Tinbutt," while to add further insult to the first injury, some property in Notts is said to appertain to one Tarbutt of "Hogstar"—a heavenly body till now unknown.

In Somerset one "Troate" usurps a goodly share of Mr. Troyte's domains. I might multiply these cases a hundredfold.

II. *Variation of Consonants.*—Even consonants, though not so bad as vowels, are muddled in a most arbitrary fashion; one main object of the rural authority who furnished the materials for "Domesday" being to spell his local landowners phonetically, the family possessions of the house of "Fazakerley" are distributed among the "Fazackerleys," "Fizackleas," "Phizackarleys," and "Phizackleas."

The half-educated Briton, especially the South Saxon,

is fond of adding to the length, if not to the dignity of a name, by adding a final "s"; the London mob invariably cheered the late champion of popular rights as "Odgers." This final "s" is in the "Domesday Book" very frequently added, so much so that in a similar compilation to the present for England alone, somewhat hastily done, I altogether failed to recognize as one and the same owner the head of the Bucks and Essex family of "Tower," who figures under the fourfold spellings of "Tower," "Towers," "Trower," and "Trowers." It is possible he may even be entered for a few acres as "Trousers," on some page which I have overlooked.

Mr. Pochin would probably hardly care to own an estate were the ownership coupled with the condition that he should change his name to "Poctim," yet so "Domesday" has it. Mr. Ellis Nanney perhaps thinks the return a most incorrect piece of work, and his estate lamentably understated, in which case I would advise him to look for his missing lands under "Vanney." Col. Gunter, of short-horn celebrity, might have been acquitted of any special proclivity for swine; he nevertheless figures as "Col. Grunter."

A small estate in Sussex is returned as belonging to one "Burdfmak"; what this appalling name is meant for quite outreaches all conjecture.

III. *Titles.*—Titles are a great trial. Englishmen are said to "love a lord," but that is hardly an excuse for giving two steps in the peerage, as is done in Lord Stafford's case, and some others, or for making the widows of knights into Lady Janes, Lady Bettys, and Lady Marys. I may mention that a Viscount seems to be a hopeless grievance to the compilers, who get out of the difficulty by sometimes using the simple letter V, and in other cases Vincent ; Lord Valentia, for instance, being entered as " V. Valentia."

In countrified parts one often hears of ladies who act the part of Lady Bountiful being described as " Ladies as is Ladies," but I was hardly prepared to find that this description had gained a footing in the parochial rate books and the parliamentary returns ; so it is, however, and I could mention several cases where plain " Mrs. A." is returned as "Lady A." A more excusable, but at the same time puzzling vagary, is to enter the numerous class of " Hon. Mesdames " as " Ladies." The letter V is not a prolific one, but two such cases occur in it, " Hon. Mrs. Vernon " and "Hon. Mrs. Vansittart " being entered as "Lady Vernon " and " Lady Vansittart." Titles, however, are no obstacle when, as seems to have been the case in some counties north of the Humber, the parochial authorities were of the Quaker persuasion, for there I find a man's title sometimes denied him *in toto.* Had the Prince been a Northern landowner, they would have possibly entered him as "Albert E. Guelph." Lord Houghton is re-converted in one county into a commoner, not as Monckton-Milnes, but as "Aaron " Houghton.

IV. *Addresses.*—The general orders of Government were that the rate collectors should give the addresses of the landowner, and not the name of the farm or farms he owned, or the name of the parish in which they lay. This has been done fairly well in some counties, notably the south-eastern, where, if they do not know an owner's address, they either leave it blank, with the name of the place in which the acreage is situate in brackets, or simply insert the address of the firm of lawyers who collect the rents, at No. ———, Lincoln's Inn.

In some parts of England the confusion is horrible; for instance, an owner, say Mr. J. T. P. Smith-Green, of Granby Hall, will be described as J. Smith, Little Pedlington—perhaps he only owns an outlying farm there; as J. T. Green Smith, of Granby Hall, his real abode; as John Thomas Plantagenet SMITH-GREEN, of 200, Portland Place, W.; as J. T. P. GREEN-SMITH, of the Fogies' Club, S.W.—the only error in this case being the putting the Green in front of the Smith, and giving his address at his club on the all-sufficient ground that he once dated a letter enclosing a cheque for rates from it; as J. G. Smith, of Aix-les-Bains, for same reason; or as J. T. P. Smythe-Green, of Boulevard, Paris—"Boulevard," "Paris," being all the _locus standi_ given to one owner whose popularity is undoubted, and whose acres are very broad. I have, therefore, had no scruple, where internal evidence is forthcoming in any case, in crediting a man with acres, whether his address be parochial, real country seat, London house, club, such-and-such a regiment, Lincoln's Inn, or any English or foreign watering-place where he may be making a temporary sojourn for economy, health, or any other cause.

The Scotch and Irish returns, as regards workmanship, compare most favourably with the English—the Scotch returns being, however, undoubtedly the best. It is curious to note, that while in England and Scotland a man is the unfortunate inmate of an asylum, the compilers discreetly conceal the fact by leaving the address blank; in Ireland, contrariwise, the name of the asylum is always given.

Even Scottish counties, like English ones, vary in degrees of goodness and badness; Kirkcudbrightshire being *facile princeps* in excellence, which is strange, as at low water it almost touches Cumberland, a badly done county, and next neighbour to Lancashire, which is out-and-out the worst done of all counties in England.

V. *Initials.*—These are not always to be trusted. F and T being particular sinners, so much so that I have in this work utterly disregarded the distinction between them, where the addresses are the same, or even in the same neighbourhood.

The following case, affecting two estates not far from my own, is a fair example :—

White, F. G. G., Wethersfield, acres 1,561, val. 2,491*l.*
White, T. G. G., Wethersfield, „ 3,576 „ 4,303*l.*

The facts of the case simply these :—

That Mr. White owned estates in two parishes or more. That in each case his address was correctly given. That one returning authority could not have written an over plain T, but that he gave T as the initial not a soul who knows Essex and remembers poor "Tom" White would for a moment doubt. These entries, I may say, occur, not side by side as I have put them, but on different sheets. The initial of a father's name is frequently given, while he may have been dead and his acres in the son's possession, say ten years.

Ten years, however, does not suffice for the eminently conservative county of Somerset, where in one case they "keep the memory of the dead man green" for eighteen years in the rate books, not troubling themselves to substitute the son's name for that of the father.

VI. *Miscellaneous Blunders.*—Such as the mixture of names and addresses ; the giving the name of the tenant as owner instead of that of the freeholder ; the too liberal use of trusteeships as substitutes for ownerships personal ; and lastly the " clerical error " pure and simple. As an instance of the first form of blunder I would mention the case of the late Col. Peers Williams, whose Anglesea estate is given to Col. T. Williams, of " Peers," " Menai Bridge." A curious attempt at the same thing is made in the case of the late Sir Digby Neave, of Dagenham Park, Essex, where the compiler of "Domesday " has tried to fuse the name and address Digby and Dagenham into a harmonious whole——result, " Neaves, Sir D., Bart., Digman Park, Sussex."

A fair example of the second class of error is that of Mr. Peckover, of Wisbeach, who is returned as owner of only about 2,000 acres in various counties—his estates amounting to well over 3,000 acres, partly entered in his tenants' names ; this sort of error is probably very common in England ; while in Ireland it is, excepting faulty addresses, almost the only grievous stumbling-block.

Of the third class Sir Walter Barttelot's is noteworthy, Sir Walter being owner of between 3,000 and 4,000 acres, while " Domesday " only allows him something short of 2,400 ; the balance being entered as the property of various trustees. The last class of blunders is the most hopeless. A mysterious " Mr. Jos. Rewes," in my county, troubled me not a little, being entered as an owner of some 6,000*l.* a-year in land. Thinking it odd I had never heard of him socially, politically, in the hunting field, or even on a subscription list, I wrote to friends in the close neighbourhood of his supposed estate ; they knew him not ! I then teased all the neighbouring rate collectors without effect, beyond discovering the existence of a clodhopper named " Reeves," who did not own much more than half an acre. In despair I attacked the Local Government Board, who very civilly investigated the matter, and informed me that " Jos. Rewes " was inserted by a clerical error for " Jas. Tabor," the head of an Essex family, seated in the same parish, who, if " Domesday " were to be trusted, would have had but a few hundreds a-year to live upon.

A few gentlemen, in cases of these gross errors, have been at considerable pains to clear them up ; some on the contrary nothing will induce them to answer, the consequence being that I have omitted a few acreages, which though exceeding 3,000 acres are palpably in error. Mr. Potts, for instance, of Chester, is down for 5,560 acres in Staffordshire, rented at 221_l._ a-year. Staffordshire marl is not exactly the same thing as Sutherland bog, as the noble owner of Trentham knows full well, and I may safely affirm that, except in the latter county, Wester Ross, County Mayo, or County Kerry, no such poverty-stricken estate could be found. All endeavours, however, have failed in the case of a " Revd. Scutt," of Bognor, whose existence is denied by the Sussex officials ; and of a mysterious estate in county Down, the ownership of which is bandied backwards and forwards by the Irish Local Government Board, Lord Clanwilliam, his second son, and every other " Meade " and " Mead " whose address could be discovered in print. (_see_ Clanwilliam.)

In arranging these pages I have drawn the line at 3,000 acres—the line must be drawn somewhere, how it came to be drawn at the double 3,000 was in this wise. Having lately been smoke-driven from my paternal acres, and forced to invest the proceeds of their sale in fields and pastures new, I had spent the greater part of two years in examining every middle-sized estate then in the market, and thus knew at the time much of the values and sizes of some scores of estates in the three kingdoms. The "Return of Landowners," published early in 1876, became naturally doubly interesting to me, and in April of that year I conceived the idea of making a list of those who held a substantial share of the soil of England and Wales. Seeing at once that as the size of the estates diminished, their number enormously increased, and as poor Pickering (kindest-hearted and most regretted of all publishers) had urged the publication before summer was past, I adopted 3,000 acres as a minimum, *i.e.*, about what could be accomplished in four months' work ;—as land in England and Wales is practically always worth at least one pound per acre, no rental qualification was fixed. My labours resulted in "The Acreocracy of England." Pickering, 1876.

Forthwith the papers began to criticize. Many shortcomings and errors were pointed out, and many suggestions good and bad were given—"The Athenæum" showed conclusively that nothing so marred the value of the book as the omission of Ireland and Scotland. I, therefore, in attempting a second work, drew the line at a minimum of 3,000 acres and 5,000*l.* a-year in each sister kingdom— which was designed to exclude the almost endless McMethuselahs and O'Doghertys who possess the uplands of Ross and the bogs of Donegal. But again Milesian critics were too strong for me, and I was told that 'twas "bhase injusthice" on the part of a "bhase Saxn" to make one rule for England and another for Ireland—poor McMethuselah meanwhile never uttering a word—and so I was forced to make a hard and fast line, applicable to all three kingdoms, of 3,000 acres and 3,000*l.* per annum in the first edition of "Great Landowners."

Burke's "Landed Gentry," Walford's "County Families," and Shirley's "Noble and Gentle Men of England," excellent work as each is in its own line, rather amuse some Philistines among us, by the insertion, in the first and third cases, of men with pedigrees long or splendid, who have perhaps but one dilapidated and moated grange (whence poor Mariana, unless pre-eminently moon-faced, might have in dowerless solitude gazed and sighed in vain), left to them as a relic of former greatness, the value of which may not reach 50*l.* per annum ; while Walford is, to say the very least of it, uncommonly catholic in his idea of what constitutes a "county family." Writing to one of my collaborateurs in the same field, and asking him where he "drew the line," I was much tickled to find that he drew it at "untitled supporters of the Tichborne claimant," the late Lord Rivers being tolerated because Peers could not be suppressed. The critics of the first stillborn Tory Reform Bill might have stigmatized even this as a "Fancy Franchise."

Many friends again urged that the line should be drawn at 3,000 acres *or* 3,000*l.* per annum ; but a careful test of the number of persons in one county (Lancashire), where the number of nearly landless individuals with a gross annual value put upon the few acres they had of 3,000*l.* and upwards, amounted to 142—convinced me that they, who were I presume chiefly mill-owners, plus all the Cheshire soapboilers, Stafford potters, Durham and Northumberland coal-masters, Warwick hardwaremen, Nottingham hosiers, Yorkshire clothiers, and Glamorganshire iron-masters, to say nothing of smaller trades, would form a quite unmanageable host. To quote the words of the reviewer in the " Broad Arrow," I stick to my original " clear cut rule, even if it be a rule of thumb, whereby we may distinguish the sheep from the goats, amongst those who would have us believe them to be cream upon the milk of English society ; in these days, when every man with a gardener in a drab coat and a cockade, aspires to be recorded among the Upper Ten Thousand, and to have his kith and kin enumerated amongst the county families."

Though 'tis hard for some old-established families, such as Bodenham, of Rotherwas, to be excluded because, as in his case, he lacks but a quarter of an acre, though his income therefrom amounts to about 6,000*l.* a-year, whilst Sir Goahead Scattercash, with his 3,001 acres, mortgaged for rather more than they are worth, duly appears as a " great landowner "; yet so it must be, and I can only assure Mr. Bodenham that if he can show me the additional quarter acre under some mis-spelling, he shall be duly entered in the next edition.

As some amends for this Medo-Persic exclusion, such persons as come within a minimum of 2,000 acres and 2,000*l.* rental value are arranged, like Peris outside the gate of Paradise, in sight of the blessed 3,000 sanctum, but barred out by a strong black line ; their possessions are massed, and not separated into counties.

I have also to mention that I have given, in every case

but that of Mr. T. Truesdale Clarke, Mr. Clarke-Thornhill, Mr. Sotheron-Estcourt, Lord Holmesdale, and one or two others, the son's acres to the father, the Dowager's property, in every case where it will probably go back to the main estate, to her eldest son, and the wife's property to the husband ; for instance, his Grace of Devonshire has added to his acreage some 5,000, which in the return are under Lord Hartington's name.

In case, however, an amalgamation of nominally different owners is made, I take care to mention it at the foot of the notice.

No notice is taken of parts of an acre, or of shillings and pence ; in every case, therefore, where a man owns in divers counties, his acres and income will be slightly greater. Some English families here entered do not enjoy the credit of anything like their real income and area, for three reasons : first, that that area may be in Lancashire, West Yorkshire, or Staffordshire, where the return sins grievously in giving incomes without area ; or that it may be in the Metropolitan District, which is not entered at all, or that it may lie in East Hereford, West Sussex, or other well wooded district, where one-third perhaps of the whole area is under timber ; at the date of the compilation of " Domesday " woods destitute of saleable underwood being still unrated.

The rent-roll pertaining to the houses of Bedford, Westminster, Portland, Maryon-Wilson, Cadogan, and Lowndes of Chesham, to mention only a few, would look more imposing by far were London included in the return.

In Scotland great misapprehension may arise from two causes. First, that only part of that kingdom is surveyed, and where done, well done; the result of the survey being to reduce in almost every case the supposed area of far northern estates. A recent trial between a laird and his game tenant exemplifies this. The laird had leased the moor as measuring say 20,000 acres; the tenant doubting this had it surveyed, when it was found to be about 13,000, and recovered a part of his rent. All the time the laird was acting in perfectly good faith, merely calling the place what it had always been called, viz., 20,000 acres.

Lord Southesk kindly warns me that "corrections" of acreage when sent by Highland lairds, should be received with caution, as the amount given in the blue-book would, unless the laird had bought lands in the meantime, be often nearer the truth than the corrected acreage.

A faint suspicion of this stamp of correction should be noted in the case of a Ross-shire baronet, who claims to hold over a quarter million of acres—the return giving him only 110,000; while another baronet in the highlands of Perthshire has added 30,000 acres to the total given him in the return. Recent purchases may, however, account for both corrections.

As to the second, Mr. Guthrie, a West Highland laird, sends me a most amusing homily, which I would fain have copied, but space forbids, on the emptiness and vexation of spirit entailed on a man who expects revenue from a Highland estate; he calls the rental therefrom a "delusion and a snare"; while Louisa, Lady Ashburton, tells me to erase it altogether, being something gravely past the point one might call "profitless."

In Ireland, the many complications of tenure and

custom made it difficult for the very painstaking officials who compiled the first Irish return (for there are two) to reduce chaos into order.

The instructions from London seem to have been that the compilers were to accept the poor-law valuation as a test of value. This valuation varies, as I am told, in various districts, being on an average 15 per cent. under letting value in Ulster, somewhat more in central Ireland, and even as much as 35 per cent. under the mark in Co. Kerry. This should be borne in mind where an Irish estate in this work remains without the asterisks, which mark a more or less complete correction. The lessees of lands for 99 years and upwards, a class common in Ireland, were ordered to be entered in the Irish return as "owners," as also were all such names as at the time showed on the poor-law valuation rolls. Now as every immediate lessor is treated in Ireland as owner for poor-law purposes, the confusion entailed is horrible, "middlemen" without end figuring in the return as owners. On Sir C. Domvile's estate eleven such cases occur, mulcting him of about half his property. What in the year of grace 1882 is the value of Irish property to those in whose veins the pure Celtic blood flows not, I leave others to answer. I should hardly think the extirpation of landlordism in Wales could long be delayed—after its extinction across St. George's Channel. Can Mr. Gladstone urge that his stock is pure native Welsh when he comes to plead for his family rights over the rapidly diminishing forests of Hawarden? War is brutal! say the modern illuminati; bag and baggage must the Turk be ousted from Europe—conquest being his only title to Turkey. Let us carry the principle further,—

the Saxons, under various English kings and Cromwell, conquered Ireland. The Saxon landlord is already all but driven away. Let the descendants of the ancient Briton, in the shape of the modern Welsh, then repossess themselves of England, and let the American Indian vindicate his claims to the domain of Yankeedom!

The second Irish return, published in August, 1876, is commonly called the "amended" return; two Ulster proprietors have referred me to it for a correct account of their possessions, the inference to be drawn being that they believed this return to be a great amendment on the first one.

A howl of indignation has, however, reached me from other parts of Erin, and owners in the three other provinces with one accord denounce the "amended" as far more untrustworthy than the original return.

As an instance, the first return makes Mr. R. Berridge, of Connemara, territorially the biggest owner in Ireland (he bought in 1872), while the amended return erases his name *in toto*, and gives his estates back to those who had sold them four years before; I have, therefore, put the "amended" Irish return on one side, using the other alone.

As it is interesting to know a man's religion and politics, and at the same time unusual to say what they are; I have added, where I can arrive at them, each landowner's college and club. From his college may be inferred the religion of his forebears, if not his own; though this inference is not so invariably true as of yore. Had this compilation been made twenty years ago, every Roman Catholic proprietor might have been "spotted" by the place of his education being given as Oscott, Ushaw, or Stonyhurst; now, on the contrary, at least fifteen per cent. of the heirs to Roman Catholic estates find their way to either Oxford or Cambridge. It is noticeable that among perverts from the Protestant to the Roman Catholic faith, though Oxford is responsible for far the greater number of cases among both laic small fry and the English clergy, the perversions of big-wigs from Cambridge more than equal those from Oxford. When a landowner's *alma mater* is given as " Edinburgh " or " Glasgow," it is, as far as I can judge, only evidence to the extent of about four to one in favour of his being a Presbyterian.

From a man's club may be pretty safely gathered his status, his politics and pursuits; for instance, in " Brooks's " one does not expect to find a violent radical; in "White's " a *nouveau riche;* in the "Athenæum " a sporting man ; in the " St. George's " a hot Orangeman ; in the " National " a henchman of Cardinal Manning ; in the " Raleigh " one of the straitest sect of the Pharisees ; in the " Turf " a great light of science ; or, I may add, in the " Travellers' " a Livingstone, a Speke, or a Baker ; though in justice to the " Turf," I should add that the fact of a man's membership is just as likely to mean that he is an accomplished whist player, as that he concerns himself in the smallest degree with the comparative speed of what Sir A. Lusk, in a recent attack on Queen's Plates, informed the House were nothing but " exaggerated greyhounds."

The conservative power of the soil on owners is a perpetual pill to the French extreme left ; they see it, admit it, but cannot understand it—why should a man, say they, who works 13 hours a day, and eats meat once a week, always vote for the *de facto* Government, because he owns 2½ acres of soil? while his easier worked, better fed, and better instructed kinsman in Paris will always vote for upsetting it.

Without for a moment putting English and French liberalism on the same level, it is curious to note how the ownership of land seems to drive the possessors into the Tory fold, high and low alike. The number of men in these pages who belong to one or other of the Tory clubs will be seen to vastly outnumber that of members of the Liberal ones, even if " Brooks's " be added (as in strictness it ought not) to the latter—*see* List of Clubs in Appendix. As to men of humbler standing—no county for its size contains anything like so many peasant holdings as Lancashire, yet a Liberal poet, who has not yet reached Tennysonian fame, writes of the general elections of 1868 and 1874—

" Frailty ! thy name is Lancashire !"

If the Party leaders would condescend to take the compiler's advice 'twould be thus given :—

To Sir S. N. At the risk of mortally offending every rising Parliamentary lawyer, insist on the simplification of all laws relating to land transfer.

To Mr. G. Pile on the agony ! Impose a new and crushing tax on every dealing in the soil.

In England mines vastly complicate the return, coal property being added to and mixed with the land, a most

unfair proceeding, as coal is capital, not in any sense
income, coal rents being in point of fact annual coal sales.
The canny Scot takes good care in every case to separate
between a man's above-ground and under-ground rental.
Again the cases of exaggerated incomes from the ground
landlord being credited with the whole rent, from building
property, which will eventually fall in to his grandchildren,
are very frequent, when estates impinge on large towns or
fashionable watering-places. The return takes care to
note five of the more glaring instances of this exaggera-
tion, viz., the Duke of Norfolk, at Sheffield, Lord Calthorpe, at Birmingham, Sir John St. Aubyn, at Plymouth,
Sir J. Ramsden, in Yorkshire, and Lord Haldon, at Torquay;
I have added notes to a few more cases that have come
within my own ken. In regard to other mineral property I
am much indebted to Mr. Jasper More, late Member for
South Salop, who has pointed out to me the incongruity of
entering incomes from coal, and not those from lead, tin,
and copper. Lead and other metallic mines, though now
rateable, were not so at the date of the English return,
and in consequence many Welsh and Cornish estates are
returned at but a tithe of their real value, for I need
hardly say that where, as in Lord Lisburne's case, a mine
proves "real jam," the owner is in no hurry to turn it into
a limited company.

One reviewer in his critique says plaintively that
"many who answer the requirements of Mr. Bateman's
3,000 acres and 3,000*l.* a-year, by no means as an actual
fact are in receipt of that income." True words, forsooth !
For the benefit of guileless fundholders who have not as

yet dabbled in land, I will give them what I consider a fair specimen of what a "landed income" of 5,000*l.* a-year means when analysed. My typical 5,000*l.* a-year squire shall be called—

STEADYMAN, JOHN, of Wearywork Hall, Cidershire.

	acres.	g. an. val.
b. 1825, s. 1860, m. 1851.	3,500 .	5,000

	£
Deduct for value in the rate-books put upon mansion, grounds, fishponds, &c.	220
Deduct also the value put upon cottages lived in rent free by old workmen and pensioners of the late Mr. Steadyman . .	30
	250
Leaving a clear rent roll of	£4,750

Now deduct as under :—

	£
His late father's two maiden sisters, Jane and Esther Steadyman, who each have a rent charge of 180*l.* per annum. (*N.B.*—Both these old ladies seem immortal)	360
His mother, Lady Louisa Steadyman, a rent charge of . . .	700
His sisters, Louisa, Marian, and Eva (all plain), each 150*l.* . .	450
His brother, Wildbore Steadyman, who was paid off and emigrated, but almost annually comes down on the good-natured head of the family for say	50
Mortgage on Sloppyside Farm and Hungry Hill (started when his father contested the county), interest	650
Do. on Wearywork End (started when his one pretty sister married Sir Shortt Shortt, Bart., and was paid off), interest . . .	150
His estate agent, Mr. Harrable, salary	150
Keep of a horse for do., 35*l.* ; house for do. 45*l.* . . .	80
Average of lawyer's bill (settlements, conveyances, &c.) . . .	60
Average cost of farm repairs, &c.	350
Draining tiles furnished gratis to the tenants	40
Repairs to the family mansion	70
Voluntary church rate, school at Wearywork, do. at Wearywork End, pensions, and purely local charities	175

(*N.B.*—If Mr. S. is a Roman Catholic, which I do not think he is, a private chaplain, chapel, school, &c., would increase this to at least 225*l.*)

Carried forward £3,285

		Brought forward .	.	.	£3,285
Subscription to county (Liberal or Tory) registration fund .			.	.	10
Do. to the Cidershire Foxhounds (25*l.*) and Boggymore Harriers (5*l.*).					30
Do. to the Diocesan—? (everything now-a-days is Diocesan, we shall soon be taking pills from Diocesan dispensaries) .			.	.	25
Other county subscriptions—hospitals, flower shows, races, &c. .				.	35
Returned 15 per cent. of rents in "hard times," averaging perhaps one year in five (would that we could say so now, 1882)			.	.	150
Loss on occasional bankrupt tenants (Mr. Harrable dislikes distraint), average			.	.	30
Arrears of rent, say annually 300*l.*, loss of interest thereon at 5 per cent.					15
Income-tax at 4*d.* in the pound on rents paid and unpaid .			.	.	83
Insurance on all buildings .			.	.	55
					£3,718

Leaving our worthy squire the magnificent annual sum of 1,032*l.* to live upon. The subscriptions, I think I may say, are hardly over painted—being, as folks say, "the least that can be expected from a person in Mr. S.'s position."

In conclusion, let me say that this compilation (partially attempted in 1876 for England alone) was undertaken by me simply as a labour of love, when no one else seemed disposed to attempt it; it is, no doubt, full of errors, but such errors would be tenfold were the process repeated by any one who, unlike myself, lacked a fair knowledge of who's who.

Also let me express my gratitude to many correspondents who have taken the trouble to correct their own notices, and to point out errors in those of their neighbours; I venture to hope that others will follow their good example, and where they find a mis-statement, will send me a correct one, noting in cases where they have added to their family acres by purchase, from whom those acres were bought, or in the unhappy case of a dwindling patrimony, to whom they were sold, so that in a fifth edition I may get my "Great Landowners" absolutely correct.

JOHN BATEMAN.

BRIGHTLINGSEA, COLCHESTER,
June, 1882.

NOTE ON ARRANGEMENT.

WHERE the letter ⚶ occurs after a name, it denotes that the person to whom it is attached, or his father, is noticed in Mr. Shirley's "Noble and Gentle Men of England" as being either head of, or head of a junior branch of, a family who held land in England since the time of Henry VII., in unbroken male line.

I am indebted to Mr. Shirley for having carefully gone over this list in 1879; his book, I may say, excludes all families which did not in Henry VII.'s time hold land enough to give what we now call the position of a "county family."

Some correctors, however, demur to my omission of the ⚶ in their cases, and being no genealogist myself, and unable to take up the genealogical cudgels for Mr. Shirley, I have inserted in a condensed form their claims.

 Attached to a name means that the corrector has added or included his woods.

*** 3 asterisks mean a careful or minute correction, or that the notice has been sent me as "correct" or "now correct."

** 2 asterisks mean that the notice has been returned me as "fairly right," "approximately true," or "not far from the mark," "roughly corrected," and so on, as well as in a few cases returned without remark, implying that all was about right; these last, however, are but few.

* 1 asterisk points to an unsatisfactory correction, either of acreage only (this is very common), or to a correction in part only of the figures, or to an admission (in three cases) that the figures were "not as far wrong as some the corrector had seen in 'Domesday.'"

To many landowners' names I have added a list of their services to the Queen or the Parliament, irrespective of such local services as are the usual penalties of local greatness— *i.e.*, Shrievalties, Lord and Deputy Lieutenancies, Militia and Volunteer commands, and Justiceships of the Peace. Almost every great landowner worthy of his salt (and not a few quite unworthy) have filled one or more of these posts ; had I inserted them the volume would have been far too bulky.

Where dates of succession of widows are given, these dates only refer in nine cases out of tento the year of their widowhood.

Where a father, a brother, a husband, or other predecessor had sent a correction for the edition of 1879, the present owner has not been teased for a further correction, personal details only being changed.

GREAT LANDOWNERS OF GREAT BRITAIN.

** ABDY, Sir William Neville, Bart., of Albyns, Stapleford Abbots, Romford.

		acres.	g. an. val.
Club. Carlton.	Essex . . .	2,903 .	3,990
b. 1844, s. 1877.	Berks . . .	170 .	220
	Surrey . . .	48	5,500
		3,121 .	9,710

Exclusive of the acreage of such parts of the Surrey estate as lie within the borough of Southwark.

** ABERCORN, Duke of, K.G., Baron's Court, Newtown Stewart, Co. Tyrone, &c.

		acres.	g. an. val.
Coll. Harrow, Ch. Ch. Ox.	Tyrone . . .	60,000 .	29,000
Club. Carlton, Travellers'.	Donegal . .	16,500 .	12,500
b. 1811, s. 1818, m. 1832.	Edinburgh . .	1,500 .	7,400
Served twice as Lord Lieut.	Renfrew . .	662 .	4,500
of Ireland.		78,662 .	53,400

*** ABERCROMBY, Lord, Airthrey Castle, Stirling, N.B., &c.

		acres.	g. an. val.
Club. St. James's, Brooks's.	Perth . . .	10,407 .	7,007
b. 1838, s. 1852, m. 1858.	Clackmannan .	3,707 .	5,199
	Stirling . . .	1,150 .	2,753
		15,264 .	14,959

ABERCROMBY, Sir Robert John, Bart., of Forglen House, Turriff, Banffshire.

		acres.	g. an. val.
Coll. Eton.	Banff . . .	8,053 .	6,290
Club. Carlton.	Aberdeen . .	1,942 .	1,669
b. 1850, s. 1872.	Kirkcudbright.	1,339 .	1,857
	Cork . . .	434 .	2,579
		11,768 .	12,395

** ABERDARE, Lord, Duffryn, Aberdare, S. Wales.

Club. Athenæum.   Glamorgan . .   3,950 .   12,113
b. 1815, s. 1872, m. 1st 1846, 2nd 1854.
  Served as Home Sec. and Ld. Pres. of the Council.   Sat for Merthyr Tydvil and Renfrew.

  This includes mineral royalties, which fluctuate greatly.

*** ABERDEEN, Earl of, Haddo House, Aberdeen, N.B., &c.

Coll. Univ. Oxon.   Aberdeen . .   62,422 .   44,112
Club. Windham, Science.
b. 1847, s. 1870, m. 1877.
  Served as Lord High Comr. to Gen. Ass. of the Kirk of Scotland.

ABERGAVENNY, Marquis of, Eridge Castle, Tunbridge Wells.

Coll. Eton.	Sussex . . .	15,364 .	12,752
Club. Carlton, Cons.,	Kent . . .	5,854 .	9,867
Beaconsfield.	Warwick . .	2,683 .	2,765
b. 1826, s. 1868, m. 1848.	Monmouth .	2,639 .	2,660
Served in 2nd Life Guards.	Worcester . .	1,664 .	1,859
	Hereford . .	319 .	300
	Norfolk . . .	11 .	32
		28,534 .	30,235

** ABINGDON, Earl of, Wytham Abbey, Oxford. $.

			acres.	g. an. val.
Coll. Eton, Trin. Cam.	Oxon	. . .	8,173 .	12,944
Club. Brooks's, White's, St.	Berks	. . .	7,738 .	10,261
James's.	Bucks	. . .	66 .	159
b. 1808, s. 1854, m. 1835.	Lancashire . .		4,695 .	4,670
Sat for Oxon and for	York	. . .	604 .	214
Abingdon.				

21,276 . 28,248

The two last properties (which do not include mine rents) belong to Lord Norreys, who has corrected this notice.

*** ABINGER, Lord, Inverlochie Castle, Kingussie, &c., N.B.

Coll. Eton, Trin. Cam.	Inverness . .	39,414 .	4,346
Club. Carlton, Guards, Uni.	Surrey . . .	1,005 .	689
Ser., Marlborough			
b. 1826, s. 1861, m. 1863.		40,419 .	5,035

Served in Scots Fus. Gds., is a Maj.-Gen.

*** ACLAND, Sir Thomas Dyke, Bart., of Killerton, Exeter, &c. $.

Coll. Harrow, Christ Ch.	Somerset . .	20,300 .	10,680
Oxon.	Devon . . .	15,018 .	19,225
Club. Athenæum.	Cornwall . .	4,578 .	4,880
b. 1809, s. 1871, m. 1st 1841,			
2nd 1856		39,896 .	34,785

Sat for W. Somerset, sits for N. Devon. Served as 2nd Church Estates Commr., unpaid.

ACTON, Lord, Aldenham Hall, Bridgnorth, Salop. $.

Coll. St. Mary's, Oscott.	Salop . . .	6,321 .	7,573
Club. Brooks's, Athenæum,	Middlesex . .	14 .	23
Travellers', Dev.			
b. 1834, s. 1837, m. 1865.		6,335 .	7,596
Sat for Carlow and Bridgnorth.			

ACTON, Thos., of West Aston. Wicklow . 4,845 . 2,729

* ADAIR, John George, of Rathdaire, Ballybrittas, Queen's Co.

			acres.		g. an. val.
Coll. Trinity, Dublin.	Donegal	. .	42,000	.	746
Club. Kildare St., Dublin,	Queen's Co.	.	9,655	.	3,719
Brooks's, Devonsh.	Kilkenny	. .	518	.	357
b. 1823, s. 1873, m. 1867.					
			52,173	.	4,822

The original Irish return gives Mr. Adair's Donegal property as 16,308 acres—the amended return at 28,209.

*** ADAM, Charles Elphinstone, of Blair Adam, Kinross, N.B.

Club. Brooks's.	Kinross	. . .	2,869	.	2,985
b. 1859, s. 1881.	Fife	. . . .	1,408	.	754
			4,277	.	3,739

Exclusive of 400*l.* for minerals.

ADEANE, Charles Robert Whorwood, of Babraham Hall, Cambridge.

Coll. Eton.	Cambridge	. .	3,157	.	4,564
b. 1863, s. 1870.	Suffolk	. . .	291	.	439
			3,448	.	5,003

Including property returned as belonging to his mother.

AFFLECK, Sir Robert, Bart., of Dalham Hall, Newmarket, Cambs.

b. 1805, s. 1854, m. 1850.	Suffolk	. . .	2,913	.	4,085
	Essex	. . .	734	.	552
	Cambridge	. .	113	.	132
	Hunts	. . .	4	.	7
			3,764	.	4,776

ADAMSON, W. R., of Rushton Park　Sussex　2,806　.　2,607

** AGNEW, Sir Andrew, Bart., of Lochnaw Castle, Stranraer, N.B.

			acres.	*g. an. val.*
Coll.	Harrow.	Wigtown . .	14,000 .	11,100

Club. Brooks's, Ar. and Na. b. 1818, s. 1849, m. 1846.

Served in 93rd Highlanders during the Rebellion in Canada in 1838, and in 4th Light Dragoons ; sat for Wigtownshire.

** VANS-AGNEW, Robert, of Barnbarroch, Wigtown, N.B.

Coll.	Eton.	Wigtown . .	6,777 .	6,696

Club. Carlton, Cons. b. 1817, s. 1842, m. 1852.

Served in Rifle Brigade ; sat for Wigtownshire.

AGNEW, William, of Kilwaughter Castle, Larne, Co. Antrim.

b. 1799, s. 1876. Antrim . . . 9,770 . 5,845

AILESBURY, Marquis of, Savernake, Marlborough, &c. $.

Coll.	Eton, Trin. Cam.	Wiltshire . .	37,993 .	40,334
Club.	White's, Trav., Ath.,	Yorkshire . .	15,502 .	17,897
	St. James's.	Berkshire . .	1,556 .	1,485

b. 1811, s. 1878, m. 1834.

55,051 . 59,716

Served as Lord of the Bedchamber to Will. IV., and Vice-Chamberlain of the Queen's Household. Sat for Marlborough.

***AILSA, Marquis of, Cassillis House, Maybole, N.B.

Coll.	Eton.	Ayrshire . .	76,015 .	35,825

Club. Guards. b. 1847, s. 1870, m. 1871.

Served in Coldstream Guards.

AINSLIE, Ainslie Douglas, of Delgaty Castle, Turriff, N.B.

Coll.	Balliol, Oxon.	Elgin . . .	3,140 .	1,896
b. 1838, s. 1866, m. 1865.		Aberdeen . .	2,882 .	1,768

Served in Diplomatic Ser.

6,022 . 3,664

AINSLIE, Robert, of Muirton House, Urray, Beauly, N.B., &c.

	Ross . . .	4,500 .	663
	Haddington .	1,480 .	3,362

5,980 . 4,025

AIRLIE, EARL OF, Cortachy Castle, Kirriemuir, N.B., &c.

				acres.		*g. an. val.*
Coll.	Eton.	Forfar	. . .	65,228	.	22,506
Club.	Guards, Marlb.	Perth	. . .	4,647	.	6,086
b. 1856, s. 1881.						
				69,875	.	28,592

Serves in 10th Hussars, was in Scots Guards. These figures include the lands of Craighead and Craignethie—since sold.

ALBEMARLE, EARL OF, Quiddenham Hall, Attleboro', Norfolk.

Coll.	Westminster.	Norfolk	. . .	7,340	.	7,292
Club.	Ath., Brooks's.	Leitrim	. . .	2,506	.	1,064
b. 1799, s. 1851, m. 1831.						
				9,846	.	8,356

Served in 14th Foot at Waterloo, Gen. Unatt., was Groom in Waiting, sat for E. Norfolk and Lymington.

**ALCOCK, HARRY, of Wilton Castle, Enniscorthy.

Club.	Kildare St., Dublin.	Co. Wexford	.	9,121	.	4,672
b. 1821, s. 1840.						

**ALDAM, WILLIAM, of Frickley Hall, Doncaster, &c.

Coll.	Trin. Camb.	York, W.R.	.	4,579	.	6,991
Club.	Oxf. and Cam.	Lincoln	. .	365	.	412
b. 1813, m. 1845.						
Sat for Leeds.				4,944	.	7,403

Inclusive of 1,476 acres belonging to his eldest son, Mr. WARDE-ALDAM.

ALDRIDGE, LT.-COL. JOHN, of St. Leonard's Forest, Horsham.

Coll.	Eton.	Sussex	. . .	5,739	.	3,164
Club.	Carlton.	b. 1832, s. 1871, m. 1863.				
	Served in 21st Foot.					

ALCOCK, W. N., of Aireville.	York	. . .	2,093	.	3,165
S. ALDERSEY, T., of Aldersey.	Cheshire.		2,340	.	3,132
ALDWORTH, R. O., of Newmkt.	Cork, Limk.		8,739	.	2,648

***ALEXANDER, Col. Claud, of Ballochmyle, Mauchline, N.B.

		acres.		g. an. val.
Coll. Eton, Ch. Ch. Oxon.	Ayr	4,339	.	4,359

Club. Gds., Carl., Army and
Navy, Uni. Ser.

b. 1831, s. 1861, m. 1863.

Served in Grenadier Guards
in the Crimea.
Sits for S. Ayrshire.

Exclusive of a fluctuating mineral
rent of over 6,000*l.*, and of all
feus.

ALEXANDER, Granville Henry Jackson, of Forkhill, Dundalk.

b. 1852, s. 1878, m. 1880.   Armagh . . . 8,324 . 5,151

Served in 83rd Foot.

ALEXANDER, Robert Jackson, of Portglenone House, Ballymena.

Coll. Harrow.	Antrim . . .	4,215	.	3,576
Club. Kild. St., Sackv. St.,	Londonderry .	2,866	.	1,518
Dublin.	Tyrone . . .	1,769	.	1,178
b. 1843, s. 1854.				
		8,850	.	6,272

** ALEXANDER, Robert Quin, of Acton, Poyntzpass, Co. Armagh.

Club. Sackv. St., Kild. St.,	Co. Dublin .	2,973	.	2,992
Dublin.	Armagh . .	192	.	200
b. 1816, m. 1840.				
		3,165	.	3,192

ALEXANDER, Samuel Maxwell, of Roe Park, Limavady, Co. Derry.

Club. Windham.	Londonderry .	5,229	.	3,843
b. 1834, s. 1854.	Donegal . .	504	.	393
		5,733	.	4,236

ALEXANDER, J., of Milford Ho. Carl., Antrim 2,375 . 2,809

* ALINGTON, Lord, Crichill, Wimborne.

		acres.	g. an. val.
Coll. Eton, Ch. Ch. Oxon.	Dorset . . .	14,756	. 21,140
Club. Carl., White's, Trav.,	Devon . . .	2,587	. 2,307
Beacsfd., Arln., Turf.	Hants . . .	81	. unstated
b. 1825, s. 1866, m. 1853.	Cambridge . .	42	. 67
Sat for Dorchester and	Herts . . .	34	. 90
Dorset.	Oxford . . .	unstated	. 20
		17,500	. 23,624

HAVELOCK-ALLAN, Sir Henry Marshman, Bart., C.B., V.C., of Blackwell Hall, Darlington, &c.

		acres.	g. an. val.
Club. Reform, U. Ser.	Durham . .	1,537	. 2,332
b. 1830, s. (estates) 1879,	York, N.R. .	1,476	. 3,444
m. 1865.		3,013	. 5,776

Is a Maj.-Gen. Served in Persian exp., Indian Mutiny, &c. Commanded 2nd Inf. Brigade at Aldershot.
Sat for Sunderland.

*** ALLCROFT, John Derby, of Stokesay Castle, Onibury, Salop.

		acres.	g. an. val.
Club. Cons., Carlton.	Salop . . .	5,636	. 8,100
b. 1822, s. 1867, m. 1st 1854,	Middlesex . .	61	. 265
2nd 1864.			
Sat for Worcester.		5,697	. 8,365

ALLEN, Henry Seymour, of Cresselly House, Pembroke.

		acres.	g. an. val.
Coll. Harrow.	Pembroke . .	2,860	. 2,667
b. 1847, s. 1861.	Carmarthen .	868	. 723
	Glamorgan .	926	. 294
	Ditto . . .	unstated	. 404
		4,654	. 4,088

Including his mother Lady Cath. Allen, who has acres 961, value 354*l.*

*** ALLAN, Alex., of Aros.	Argyll . . .	11,279	. 2,080
ALLEN, George, of Mt. Panther.	Down .	2,585	. 3,132
ALLEN, Henry, of Inchmartine.	Perth .	2,855	. 5,118

ALLGOOD, LANCELOT JOHN HUNTER, of Nunwick, Hexham.

		acres.		*g. an. val.*
Coll. Rugby.	Durham . .	306	.	264
Club. Arthur's, Ar. and Na.	Northumberland	15,773	.	8,584
b. 1823, s. 1854, m. 1854.				
Served in 13th Light Dragoons.		16,079	.	8,848

* CRACROFT - AMCOTTS, WESTON, of Hackthorn Hall, Lincoln.

		acres.		*g. an. val.*
Coll. Eton.	Lincolnshire .	6,847	.	9,630
Club. Brooks's, Uni. Ser.,	Notts . . .	2,753	.	3,642
Jun. Uni. Ser.	Northampton .	1,211	.	1,455
b. 1815, s. 1862, m. 1st 1844.				
2nd 1864.		10,811	.	14,727

Sat for Mid-Lincolnshire.

The two last properties are Mrs. C-Amcotts' for life ; they then go to her son, Mr. Nevile, of Wellingore.

AMHERST, EARL, Montreal Park, Sevenoaks, Kent.

Coll. Westminster, Ch. Ch.	Kent . . .	4,269	.	5,441
Oxon.	Warwick . .	1,789	.	1,861
Club. Carlton.	Sussex . . .	834	.	504
b. 1805, s. 1857, m. 1834.	Essex . . .	741	.	975
Sat for Kent.				
		7,633	.	8,781

The Sussex property is returned as Lady Amherst's.

AMHERST, LORD, *see* HOLMESDALE.

TYSSEN-AMHERST, WILLIAM AMHURST, of Didlington Hall, Brandon.

Coll. Eton, Ch. Ch. Oxon.	Norfolk . .	9,488	.	6,592
Club. Carl., Trav., Ath.	York, E.R. .	240	.	292
b. 1835, s. 1855, m. 1856.	Kent . . .	47	.	92
Sits for W. Norfolk.				
		9,775	.	6,976

ALSTON, W. CHARLES, of Elmdon.	Warwick	2,111	.	4,008
AMES, LOUIS ERIC, of Lindon.	Northum. .	2,996	.	2,449

HEATHCOAT-AMORY, Sir John Heathcoat, Bart., of Knightshaye's Court, Tiverton.

			acres.	*g. an. val.*
Coll. Uni. Coll. London.	Devonshire	.	5,202	. 11,057

Club. Reform, Brooks's, Devonsh. b. 1829, s. 1859, m. 1863.
Sits for Tiverton.

*** **ANCKETILL**, William, of Ancketill's Grove, Emyvale.

   Coll. Bath Prop. Sch. Monaghan . 7,754 . 4,600
   Club. Raleigh. b. 1851, s. 1872, m. 1875.

*** **ANDERSON**, Sir Charles Henry John, Bart., of Lea Hall, Gainsborough.

Coll. Oriel, Oxon.	York, E.R.	.	2,647	.	3,408
Club. Athenæum.	Lincoln	. .	2,153	.	3,218
b. 1804, s. 1846, m. 1832.	Nottingham	.	293	.	368
			5,093	.	6,994

ANDERSON, George, of Little Harle Tower, Newcastle-on-Tyne.

| *Coll.* Eton, Ch. Ch. Oxon. | Northumberland | 4,544 | . | 5,158 |

Club. Conservative. b. 1843, s. 1872.

ANGERSTEIN, William, of Weeting Hall, Brandon, &c.

Coll. Harrow, Ch. Ch. Ox.	Lincoln .	. .	11,669	.	13,815
Club. Travellers'.	Norfolk .	. .	7,235	.	3,342
b. 1811, s. 1866, m. 1842.	Suffolk .	. .	827	.	355
Sat for Greenwich.			19,731	.	17,512

    Mr. Angerstein holds a large property within the omitted Metropolitan area.

** **ANGLESEY**, Marquis of, Beaudesert Park, Lichfield.

Club. Carlton.	Stafford .	. .	17,441	.	91,304
b. 1835, s. 1880, m. 1st 1858	Anglesea	. .	9,620	.	9,784
2nd 1874	Derby .	. .	1,559	.	8,696
3rd 1880	Dorset .	. .	1,117	.	814
			29,737	.	110,598

    Lord A.'s agent does not profess to draw an exact balance between the Staffs. and Derby estates, but the total of both counties is right.

ANDERSON,T.W.,Gracedieu. Klk.,Cork,Wat. 3,690 . 2,739

*** ANNALY, Lord, Woodlands, Clonsilla, Dublin, &c.

			acres.	*g. an. val.*
Coll. Eton.	Longford . .		12,560 .	9,016
Club. Army and Navy.	Dublin . . .		3,954 .	5,745
b. 1829, s. 1873, m. 1853.				
			16,514 .	14,761

Served in 13th Lt. Dragoons, and as Lord of the Treasury. Sat for Co. Clare, Longford, and Kidderminster.

** ANNESLEY, Earl, Castle Wellan, Co. Down, &c. 🐚.

Coll. Eton, Trin. Dub.	Cavan . . .		24,221 .	8,802
Club. Carlton, White's, Gds.	Co. Down . .		24,350 .	19,131
b. 1831, s. 1874, m. 1877.	Queen's Co. .		2,489 .	1,606
			51,060 .	29,539

Served in Fusilier Guards and 43rd Foot in the Kaffir war of 1851 and Crimean campaign; severely wounded in each. Sat for Co. Cavan.

Out of the Co. Down property the Countess Dowager has 1,500*l.*

** LLOYD-ANSTRUTHER, James Hamilton, of Hintlesham Hall, Ipswich.

Coll. Sandhurst.	Suffolk . . .		3,612 .	4,539
Club. Jun. Uni. Ser. b. 1807, s. 1837, m. 1st 1838, 2nd 1847.				

Served in 46th Foot.

** ANSTRUTHER, Sir Robert, Bart., of Balcaskie, Pittenween, Fife, N.B.

Coll. Harrow.	Caithness . .		22,597 .	4,000
Club. Brooks's, Trav., Reform.	Fife		2,121 .	5,062
b. 1834, s. 1863, m. 1857.			24,718 .	9,062

Served in Grenadier Guards.   Sat for Fife.

*** ANSTRUTHER, Sir Windham Charles James Carmichael, Bart., of Carmichael House, Thankerton, Lanarkshire, N.B.

Club. Carlton, Arthur's, Wind.	Lanark . .		11,814 .	9,435
b. 1824, s. 1869, m. 1872.	Ayrshire . .		584 .	99
Hereditary Carver to the Royal Household in Scotland. Sat for S. Lanark.			12,398 .	9,534

🐚. ANNE, George, of Burghwallis   York .   2,473 •   3,745

✱✱ ANTRIM, Earl of, Glenarm Castle, Co. Antrim.

				acres.		*g. an. val.*
Coll.	Eton, Ch. Ch. Oxon.	Antrim . . .		34,292	.	20,837
Club.	St. James's, White's.	Londonderry .		112	.	73
b. 1851, s. 1869, m. 1875.						
				34,404	.	20,910

ANTROBUS, Sir Edmund, Bart., of the Abbey, Amesbury, Wilts. 🐍.

Coll.	Eton, St. John's, Cam.	Roxburgh . .	1,796	.	2,499
Club.	Uni. Univ.	Wilts . . .	8,374	.	9,193
b. 1818, s. 1870, m. 1847.		Cheshire . .	290	.	521
Sat for E. Surrey and Wilton.		Surrey . . .	100	.	750
		Derby . . .	113	.	261
			10,673	.	13,224

ANTROBUS, John Coutts, of Eaton Hall, Congleton. 🐍,

Coll.	Eton, St. John's, Cam.	Cheshire . .	1,371	.	3,651
Club.	Uni. Univ.	Stafford . .	1,680	.	2,155
b. 1829, s. 1861, m. 1st 1855,					
2nd 1865, 3rd 1875.			3,051	.	5,806

APPLETHWAITE, Edward Archer, of Pakenham Hall, Swaffham.

Coll.	Charterhouse.	Norfolk . . .	5,135	.	4,864
Club.	Boodles', Union. b. 1800, s. 1805, m. 1821.				

ARBUTHNOTT, Miss Helen Carnegy, of Balnamoon, Brechin.

s. 1871.	Forfarshire .	8,066	.	5,204

ARBUTHNOTT, Viscount, Arbuthnott House, Fordoun, N.B.

Club.	Carlton.	Kincardine .	13,560	.	13,036
b. 1806, s. 1860, m. 1837.					
Served in the Army. (Captain unattached.)					

ARBUTHNOT (late), of Invernethie. Aberd.	2,267	.	2,470

ARCHDALE, Mervyn Edward, of Castle Archdale, Lisnarick, Co. Fermanagh, &c.

		acres.	*g. an. val.*
Club. Carl., White's, Ar. and	Fermanagh .	27,410 .	13,517
Na., Kild. St., Dub.	Tyrone . . .	5,605 .	3,474
b. 1812, s. 1864, m. 1848.			
		33,015 .	16,991

Served in Inniskilling Drs.   Sat for Co. Fermanagh.

* ARCHDALE, William Humphrys, of Riversdale, Enniskillen.

Coll. Exeter, Oxon.	Fermanagh .	5,627 .	3,182

Club. Carlton. b. 1813, s. 1864, m. 1845.

Sits for Fermanagh.

Exclusive of a large amount of land on perpetual leases, which appears in tenants' names.

*** ARDEN, Richard Edward, of East Burnham House, Slough, &c.

Club. National, Thatched	Pembroke . .	3,254 .	1,677
House, Jun. Ath.	Carmarthen .	1,887 .	1,193
b. 1804, m. 1st 1832.	Middlesex . .	58 .	830
2nd 1839.	Bucks . . .	49 .	360
	Herts . . .	113 .	251
	Sussex . . .	17 .	25
		5,378 .	4,336

*** ARDILAUN, Lord, St. Anne's, Dublin, &c.

Coll. Eton, Trin. Dublin.	Co. Galway	27,111 .	3.564
Club. Carlton, Garrick, Nat.,	Mayo . . .	3,747 .	1,707
St. Ste., Kild. St.,	Dublin . . .	484 .	1,302
Univ., Dub. b. 1840, s. 1868, m. 1871.			
Sat for Dublin City.		31,342 .	6,573

ARCHER, E., of Trelaske. Cornwall . .	2,029 .	2,030
ARCHIBALD, R., of Davidstown. Kildare .	3,075 .	2,022

* ARGLES, FRANK AIKINSON, of Eversley, Milnthorpe.

		acres.	g. an. val.
Coll. Tonbridge H. Sch.	Westmorland	2,838	3,060
Club. Conservative.	Staffordshire .	1,199	1,562
b. 1816, m. 1858.	Lancashire .	162	197
	Cumberland .	52	74
	Cheshire .	16	30
	York, W.R. .	24	30
		4,291	4,953

ARGYLL, DUKE OF, K.T., The Castle, Inverary, N.B.

Club. Athenæum.	Argyll . . .	168,315	45,672
b. 1823, s. 1847, m. 1st 1844.	Dumbarton .	6,799	5,170
2nd 1881.			
		175,114	50,842

Served as Lord Privy Seal, Sec. State for India, and Post-master-General.   Is Keeper of the Great Seal of Scotland.

** ARKWRIGHT, JOHN HUNGERFORD, of Hampton Court, Leominster.

Coll. Eton, Ch. Ch. Oxon.   Herefordshire   10,559   .   14,972
Club. Carlton.   b. 1833, s. 1858, m. 1866.

*** ARKWRIGHT, WILLIAM PHILIP, of Sutton Scarsdale, Chesterfield.

Coll. Eton, Ch. Ch. Oxon.   Derbyshire   .   5,093   .   6,607
Club. White's, St. Geo.   b. 1857, s. 1866.

*** WRIGHT-ARMSTRONG, HENRY BRUCE, of Killylea House, Armagh.

Coll. Roy. Sch. Armagh,	Armagh . .	3,181	2,515
Trin. Cam.	Longford . .	1,949	894
Club. New Uni., Kild. St.,			
Dublin.		5,130	3,409

b. 1844, s. 1872.
    A portion of this property pays head rent to Trin. Coll., Dublin ; the sum payable is, however, deducted.

ARMSTRONG, SIR W. G.   Northum. . .   2,265   .   6,606

*** ARMYTAGE, Sir George, Bart, of Kirklees Park, Brighouse, Yorkshire.

			acres.	*g. an. val.*
Coll. Harrow, Oriel, Oxon.	York, W.R.	.	3,274	8,700

Club. Carlton, Garrick.   b. 1819, s. 1836, m. 1841.

* ARRAN, Earl of, K.P., Castle Gore, Mayo.

b. 1801, s. 1837, m. 1838.	Co. Mayo .	.	29,644	6,967
Served as Chargé d'Affaires	Donegal	.	6,883	3,145
at Buenos Ayres.				
			36,527	10,112

   Exclusive of 7,000 acres let on perpetual leases, fisheries, &c., and rental therefrom.

ARTHUR, Francis, of ——, Co. Clare.   (Residence, Dublin.)

	Co. Clare . •.	10,534	3,550

* ARUNDELL of WARDOUR, Lord, Wardour Castle, Tisbury, Wilts. 𝕾.

Coll. Stoneyhurst.	Wilts .	.	.	6,037	9,054
Club. Athenæum.	Cornwall	.	.	182	120
b. 1831, s. 1862, m. 1862.					
				6,219	9,174

   The Cornish acreage is rather overstated. The rental in that county does not include some reserved manorial rights, which (with the land) have been in the family since 12th of Edward I.

*** ASHBROOK, Viscount, The Castle, Durrow, Kilkenny.

Coll. Eton.	Kilkenny .	.	9,292	4,709
Club. Carlton, Ar. and Na.,	King's County		7,746	2,837
R.Y.S.	Queen's County		4,643	3,702
b. 1829, s. 1871, m. 1860,	Limerick .	.	860	959
div. 1877.	Dublin	.	509	1,704
Served in 52nd Foot.				
			23,050	13,911

ASHBURNHAM, Earl of, Ashburnham Place, Battle, &c. 𝕾.

Coll. Westminster.	Sussex .	.	14,051	13,069
Club. White's, St. James's,	Suffolk .	.	3,372	5,566
Travellers'.	Carmarthen	.	5,685	3,538
b. 1840, s. 1878.	Brecon .	.	1,381	1,963
			24,489	24,136

** ASHBURTON, Louisa, Lady, Melchet Park, Romsey, &c.

			acres.		*g. an. val.*
s. 1868, m. 1858.	Devon . . .		2,676	.	3,785
	Cornwall . .		1,872	.	1,737
	Hants . . .		190	.	480
	Ross-shire . .		28,556	.	valueless
			33,294	.	6,002

The Scotch property is of the nominal value of 1,885*l.*, but practically produces no income.

ASHBURTON, Lord, The Grange, Alresford, Hants, &c.

Coll. Ch. Ch. Oxon.	Hereford . .		6,583	.	11,523
Club. White's, Travellers'.	Hants . . .		15,330	.	13,289
b. 1835, s. 1868, m. 1864.	Wilts . . .		9,591	.	9,863
Sat for Thetford.	Essex . . .		4,207	.	5,414
	Somerset . .		1,061	.	6,596
			36,772	.	46,685

ASHLEY, Hon. Anthony Evelyn Melbourne, of Classybawn, Cliffany, Co. Sligo.

Coll. Harrow, Trin. Cam.	Sligo		12,436	.	5,801

Club. Brooks's. b. 1836, m. 1866.
   Served as Treasurer of County Courts; is Par. Sec. to the B. of Trade. Sat for Poole, sits for I. of Wight.

** ASHTOWN, Lord, Woodlawn, Galway, &c.

Coll. Eton.	York, W.R. .		6,386	.	7,753
b. 1868, s. 1880.	Limerick . .		11,273	.	5,214
	Galway . . .		8,310	.	5,570
	Waterford . .		9,435	.	7,397
	King's Co. . .		2,780	.	2,385
	Tipperary . .		4,526	.	3,795
	Roscommon .		841	.	1,347
	Dublin . . .		50	.	1,208
	Westmeath . .		42	.	20
			43,643	.	34,689

ASHTON, R. H., of Castleton. Che., Dby.	2,800	.	3,939

*** ASKEW, Watson, of Pallinsburn, Cornhill, Northumberland.

			acres.		*g. an. val.*
Coll.	Eton, Ch. Ch. Oxon.	Northumberland	4,390	.	7,821
Club.	Carl., Boodl., Oxford	Essex . . .	50	.	230
	and Cambridge.				
b. 1834, s. 1851, m. 1856.			4,440	.	8,051

*** ASSHETON, Ralph, of Downham Hall, Clitheroe. ⚑.

Coll.	Eton, Trin. Cam.	Lancashire . .	3,670	.	4,610
Club.	Carlton, Uni. Univ.	York, W.R. .	71	.	190
b. 1830, s. 1858, m. 1854.					
Sat for Clitheroe.			3,741	.	4,800

*** ASTLEY, The Misses (three), of Arisaig, Fort William, N.B., &c.

s. 1880.	Inverness . .	27,960 .	2,232
	Cheshire . .	1,140 .	4,219
		29,100 .	6,451

** ASTLEY, Sir John Dugdale, Bart., of Everley House, Marlborough, &c. ⚑.

Coll.	Eton, Ch. Ch. Oxon.	Lincoln . . .	10,000 .	17,000
Club.	Marlb., Arthur's,Turf,	Wilts	5,500 .	5,000
	Guards.	Hants . . .	67 .	57
b. 1828, s. 1873, m. 1858.			15,567 .	22,057

Served in Scots Guards in the Crimea; wounded at Alma (3 medals). Sat for N. Lincolnshire.

*** ATHLUMNEY, Lord, Somerville House, Navan, Co. Meath.

Coll.	Harrow.	Meath . . .	10,213 .	11,131
b. 1865, s. 1873.	Dublin . . .	274 .	233
		10,487 .	11,364

ASPINALL, R. J., of Standen.	Lanc., York	2,743	.	5,480
ASTLEY, J. N. F., of Ansley.	Warwick .	2,261	.	3,755
FRANKLAND-RUSSELL-ASTLEY, Mrs.,	of Chequers Ct.			
	Bucks . .	2,534	.	3,719

*** ATHOLE, Duke of, K.T., The Castle, Blair Athole, N.B.

		acres.	*g. an. val.*
Coll. Eton.	Perthshire .	201,640 .	42,030

Club. Carlton, Guards, Marl. b. 1840, s. 1864, m. 1863.
Served in Scots Guards.

ATHORPE, Rev. George Middleton, of Dinnington Hall, Rotherham.

Coll. Emman. Cam.	York,E.&W.R.	3,655 .	4,435
b. 1835, s. 1880.	Derbyshire .	253 .	226
		3,908 .	4,661

MARTIN-ATKINS, Edwin, of Kingston Lisle, Wantage.

b. 1870, s. 1875.	Berks . . .	2,635 .	3,192
	Surrey . . .	1,734 .	1,653
	Sussex . . .	56 .	30
		4,425 .	4,875

ATKINSON, Lieut.-Col. Ralph, of Angerton, Morpeth.

b. 1824, s. 1871.   Northumberland 3,484 .   3,420
Served in Grenadier Guards.

*** GODWIN-AUSTEN, Robert Alfred Cloyne, F.R.S., of Shalford House, Guildford.

Coll. Midhurst, Oriel,Oxon. Surrey . . .   4,100 .   4,858
Club. Athenæum. b. 1808, s. 1871, m. 1833.

AUSTIN, Charles, of Brandeston Hall, Wickham Market.

Coll. Eton.   Suffolk . . .   3,134 .   5,300
b. 1858, s. 1874.

** AVELAND, Lord, Normanton Park, Stamford, &c.

Coll. Harrow, Trin. Cam.	Lincoln . . .	17,637 .	27,082
Club. White's, Travellers',	Rutland . .	13,633 .	19,797
b. 1830, s. 1867, m. 1863.	Derby . . .	3 .	10
Serves as Dep. Lord Great	Huntingdon .	2 .	5
Chamberlain.			
Sat for Boston and Rutlandshire.		31,275 .	46,894

ATKINSON, W., of Ashton Heys. Ches. .	2,132 .	5,080
AUSTEN, J. F., of Capel. Kent, Sussex .	2,980 ,	6,802

AYLESFORD, Earl of, Packington Hall, Coventry, &c. ⚓.

		acres.	*g. an. val.*
Coll. Eton.	Warwick . .	12,453 .	19,653
Club. Carlton, Garrick.	Leicester . .	4,272 .	6,709
b. 1849, s. 1871, m. 1871.	Kent . . .	2,856 .	6,258
		19,581 .	32,620

Of this rental the return gives the Dowager Lady Aylesford 465*l.*

*** AYLMER, Sir Gerald George, Bart., of The Castle, Donadea, Co. Kildare.

Coll. Sandhurst.	Kildare . . .	15,396 .	6,890
Club. London Masonic,	Cumberland .	— .	500
R. St. G.Y.C., Kildare St.,			
Dublin. b. 1830, s. 1878, m. 1853.		15,396 .	7,390

AYLMER, Michael, of Courtown, Kilcock, Co. Kildare.

b. 1831, s. 1857, m. 1852.	Co. Kildare .	3,871 .	3,645
	King's County	732 .	414
	Co. Cork . .	9 .	30
		4,612 .	4,089

AYTOUN, Roger Sinclair, of Inchdairnie, Kirkcaldy, N.B.

Coll. Trin. Cam.	Renfrew . .	86 .	170
Club. Brooks's.	Fife	4,242 .	6,086
b. 1823.			
Sat for Kirkcaldy Burghs.		4,328 .	6,256

** BACON, Sir Hickman Beckett, Bart., of Thonock Hall, Gainsborough. ⚓.

Coll. Eton.	Lincoln . .	3,377 .	5,358
Club. Guards. b. 1855, s. 1872.			
Served in Grenadier Guards.			

*** BACON, Mrs. (the late), of Richill, Co. Armagh.

d. 1881.	Armagh . .	6,878 .	7,600

* BAGGE, Sir Alfred Thomas, Bart., of Stradsett Hall, Downham Market, Norfolk.

		acres.		g. an. val.
Coll. Royal Naval, Ox.	Norfolk . . .	3,769	.	6,285
b. 1832, s. 1881, m. 1872.				

BAGOT, John Lloyd Neville, of Ballymoe, &c., Co. Galway.

b. 1814, s. 1863, m. 1843.	Co. Galway .	19,303	.	7,067
	Co. Roscommon	104	.	56
		19,407	.	7,123

Much litigation took place about the succession to Aughrane, which forms the larger part of this property, between Mr. Bagot and his sister-in-law (now Mrs. Roberts), who takes a portion of the rental.

*** BAGOT, Lord, Blithfield House, Rugeley, &c. §.

Coll. Charterho., Mag.	Stafford . .	10,841	.	14,595
Cam.	Denbigh . .	18,044	.	7,200
Club. Carlton, White's,	Merioneth . .	1,658	.	417
Trav.				
b. 1811, s. 1856, m. 1851.		30,543	.	22,212

Served as Lord in Waiting.   Sat for Denbigh.

** BAGWELL, John, of Marlfield, Clonmel, &c.

Coll. Winchester.	Tipperary . .	3,519	.	8,480
Club. Reform, Kildare St.,	Co. Cork . .	509	.	568
Dublin.	Waterford . .	778	.	385
b. 1811, s. 1825, m. 1838.				
		4,806	.	9,433

Served as a Lord of the Treasury.   Sat for Clonmel.

BAGGE, J. H., of Monea.	Waterford . .	3,016	.	2,370
BAGGE, R., of Gaywood.	Norfolk . . .	2,891	.	6,978
BAGSHAWE, F. W., of The Oaks.	Derby .	2,050	.	2,800

BAILEY, Crawshay, of Maindiff Court, Abergavenny, &c.

		acres.	*g. an. val.*
b. 1841, s. 1872, m. 1863.	Monmouth .	4,078 .	6,432
	Glamorgan .	5,343 .	4,533
	Brecon . . .	2,076 .	295
	Essex . . .	1,332 .	1,183
	Carmarthen .	786	398
	Hereford . .	34 .	47
		13,649 .	12,888

** BAILEY, Sir Joseph Russell, Bart., of Glanusk Park, Crickhowell.

Coll. Har., Ch. Ch. Oxon.	Brecon . . .	21,979 .	19,367
Club. Carlton, Cons.	Hereford . .	4,838 .	4,803
b. 1840, s. 1858, m. 1861.	Radnor . . .	602 .	435
Sits for Herefordshire.	Bucks . . .	641 .	661
	Monmouth .	63 .	53
	Suffolk . . .	185 .	240
		28,308 .	25,559

BAILLIE, Evan, of Dochfour, Kingussie, N.B., &c.

Club. Carlton.	Inverness . .	68,148 .	10,231
b. 1798, m. 1st 1821,	Ross .	24,500 .	1,650
2nd 1823.		92,648 .	11,881

BAILLIE, Rt. Hon. Henry James, of Redcastle, Inverness, &c.

Coll. Eton.	Ross . . .	6,512 .	6,276
Club. Carlton, Trav.	Inverness . .	5,447 .	762
b. 1804, s. 1866, m. 1st 1840,			
2nd 1857. .		11,959 .	7,038

Served as Joint Sec. to Board of Control and as Under Sec. of State for India. Sat for Inverness.

BAILLIE, Sir W., Bart., of Polkemmet. Linl.	4,320 .	2,825
BAILLIE, W. Hunter, of Duntisbourne. Glo., Derby, Lanark	2,108 .	2,230
BAILWARD, T. H. M., of Horsingtn. Som., Gloc.	2,931 .	5,716

*** BAIRD, ALEXANDER, of Urie, Stonehaven, N.B.

			acres.		*g. aṅ. val.*
Coll. Harrow.	Kincardine	.	8,000	.	7,800
Club. Carlton, Cons.	Inverness	. .	1,662	.	2,550
b. 1849, s. 1870, m. 1873	Forfar .	. .	1,150	.	1,900
	Perth .	. .	206	.	380
			11,018	.	12,630

** BAIRD, GEORGE ALEXANDER, of Stichill Ho., Kelso, N.B., &c.

b. 1861, s. 1870.	Aberdeen	. .	17,243	.	11,813
	Roxburgh	. .	4,339	.	8,734
	Berwick	. .	1,500	.	2,532
	Dumfries	. .	59	.	120
			23,141	.	23,199

** BAIRD, JOHN, of Knoydart, Inverness, N.B., &c.

Coll. Harrow.	Inverness	. .	67,000	.	4,000
Club. Cons., St. James's.	Lanark .	. .	1,000	.	1,800
b. 1852, s. 1876, m. 1878.					
			68,000	.	5,800

* BAIRD, MRS., of Cambusdoon, Ayr, N.B.

s. 1876, m. 1859.   Ayr   19,599   .   8,043
       Exclusive of 1,000*l.* per annum for minerals.

BAIRD, WILLIAM, of Elie House, Fife, N.B.

Club. Conservative.   Fifeshire . .   3,575   .   8,815
b. 1848, s. 1864.

WINGFIELD-BAKER, DIGBY HANMER RICHARD, of Orsett Hall, Romford.

Club. Guards.   Essex . . .   8,545   .   11,791
b. 1838, s. 1880.

*** BAKER, WILLIAM ROBERT, of Bayfordbury, Hertford.

Coll. Eton, Ch. Ch. Oxon.   Herts . . .   3,911   .   6,631
b. 1810, s. 1813, m. 1838.

BAIRD, SIR D., Bart., of Newbyth, Hadd., Midlo.	2,771	.	8,354
BAKER, H. G., of Elemore. Durh.,York,Worc.	2,493	.	4,859
BAKER, T. LL. B., of Hardwicke Glo., Sal.	2,845	.	3,989

** CHILDE-BALDWYN, Rev. Edward George, of Kinlet Hall, Bewdley, &c. 🐟.

		acres.		g. an. val.
Club. Oxford & Cambridge.	Salop . . .	8,479	.	7,899
b. 18—, s. 1881, m. 1862.	Worcester . .	3,609	.	3,329
	Hereford . .	2,146	.	1,955
		14,234	.	13,183

** BALFE, Patrick, of South Park, Castlerea.

Coll. Trinity, Dublin.	Co. Roscommon	6,024	.	5,000
Club. Stephen's Green, Dub.	Co. Galway .	376	.	158
b. 1819, s. 1856, m. 1845.				
		6,400	.	5,158

*** BALFOUR, Arthur James, of Whittinghame, Preston-Kirk, N.B., &c.

Coll. Eton, Trin. Cam.	Ross	71,778	.	4,202
Club. White's, Trav., Carl.,	Haddington .	14,198	.	14,172
New Edin.	Berwick . .	1,220	.	1,459
b. 1848, s. 1856. Sits for Hertford.				
		87,196	.	19,833

This does not include the value of a deer forest in Mr. Balfour's own hands, formerly let at 2,000*l.* per annum.

BALFOUR, Blayney Townley, of Townley Hall, Drogheda, Co. Louth.

Coll. Harrow, Ch. Ch. Ox.	Louth . . .	3,139	.	3,048
Club. Trav., Sackville St.	Meath . . .	1,453	.	1,201
b. 1799, s. 1856, m. 1843.	Westmeath . .	1,623	.	1,246
Served as Lieut.-Governor	Armagh . .	645	.	827
of the Bahamas.	Tyrone . . .	76	.	144
	Down . . .	16	.	89
		6,952	.	6,555

** BALFOUR, David, of Balfour Castle, Kirkwall, N.B.

Coll. Edin. Univ.	Orkney . . .	30,000	.	9,000

Club. R.T.Y.C., Scientific, Cons., and New Edin. b. 1811, s. 1846, m. 1844.

** BALFOUR OF BURLEIGH, Lord,
Clackmannan, Perth, Stirling . . . 2,715 . 3,364

BALFOUR, JOHN, of Balbirnie, Markinch, Fife, N.B.

			acres.	*g. an. val.*
Club. Travellers'.	Fifeshire	. .	10,590	14,533
b. 1811, m. 1840.	Midlothian	.	10 .	185

With 530*l.* in addition for minerals.   10,600 . 14,718

BALFOUR, MRS., of Balgonie Castle, Markinch, Fife, N.B.

s. 1872, m. 1865.	Fifeshire	. .	2,327 .	4,529
	Berwick	. .	919 .	1,763
	Roxburgh	. .	318 .	780

With 573*l.* in addition for minerals.   3,564 . 7,072

BALL, THOMAS P. (reps. of), Castleblayney.

Co. Armagh . 5,085 . 4,071

** BANDON, EARL OF, Castle Bernard, Bandon, &c.

Coll. Eton.   Co. Cork . . 40,941 . 19,215
Club. Carlton, Jun. Carl., National. b. 1850, s. 1877, m. 1876.
   Exclusive of a large area of and rental from perpetually leased lands, returned in the names of the middlemen.

BANGOR, VISCOUNT, Castle Ward, Downpatrick.

Coll. Rugby, Sandhurst. Co. Down . . 9,861 . 13,156
Club. Union, Kild. St. and Berkshire . .   3 .   87
   U. Serv., Dub.
b. 1828, s. 1881, m. 1st 1854, 2nd 1874.

Served in 43rd Foot in Kaffir War 1851–3.   9,864 . 13,243

*** BANKES, WALTER RALPH, of Kingston Lacy,Wimborne, &c.

Coll. Harrow, Trin. Cam. Dorset . . . 19,228 . 14,985
Club. Carlton, Arth. St. Jam. b. 1853, s. 1869.
   MR. BANKES is by an ancient Royal Charter Lord High Admiral of Purbeck and Bishop of Wimborne Minster.

BALL, HON. MRS., of Fort Fergus. Clare,Kilk. 3,104 . 2,577
BANKES, MRS. H., of Trecwn. Pemb.   4,972 . 2,517

BANKES, WILLIAM MEYRICK, of Winstanley Hall, Wigan, &c.

		acres.		*g. an. val.*
b. 1835, s. 1881, m. 1876.	Ross . . .	69,800	.	2,463
	Lancashire . .	2,398	.	14,130
	Dorset . . .	755	.	618
	York, W.R. .	598	.	956
	Wilts . . .	314	.	405
		73,865	.	18,572

* BANNERMAN, MISS, of Elsick, Aberdeen, &c., N.B.

s. 1877.	Aberdeen . .	7,660	.	7,744
	Kincardine . .	500	.	702
		8,160	.	8,446

BANTRY, EARL OF, Macroom Castle, East Ferry, Co. Cork, &c.

Coll. Downing, Cam. Co. Cork . . 69,500 . 14,561
Club. Kild. St., Uni. Ser., Carlton. b. 1801, s. 1868, m. 1845.

** BARBOUR, ROBERT, of Bolesworth Castle, Chester.

Coll. Glasgow Cheshire . . 4,250 . 9,000
b. 1797, m. 1st 1827, 2nd 1836.

** BARCLAY, JOSEPH GURNEY, of Leyton, Essex, &c.

Club. City, City Liberal.	Suffolk . . .	2,383	.	2,523
b. 1816, s. 1853, m. 1st	Herts . . .	1,340	.	2,070
1842, 2nd 1857.	Bedford . .	23	.	51
	Norfolk . . .	5	.	122
	Essex . . .	65	. unstated
		3,816	.	4,766

* BARING, WILLIAM HENRY, of Norman Court, Salisbury.

Coll. Eton.	Hants . . .	5,234	.	6,449
Club. Guards, Turf.	Wilts . . .	3,644	.	437
b. 1820, s. 1873, m. 1850.				
Served in Coldstream Guards.		8,878	.	6,886

BARCHARD, F., of Horsted.	Sussex, Linc.	2,311	.	3,163
BARLOW, F., of Montagu Sq.	York, Notts.	2,204	.	2,243

RAYMOND-BARKER, Jno. Raymond, of Fairford Pk., Fairford.

		acres.	g. an. val.
Coll. Oriel, Oxon.	Gloucestershire	3,395 .	4,500

b. 1801, s. 1827, m. 1st 1823, 2nd 1841.

BARNE, Frederick, of Sotterley Hall, Wangford, &c.

Club. Arthur's.	Suffolk . . .	6,424 .	6,812
b. 1806, s. 1837, m. 1834.	Kent. . . .	1,218 .	2,659

Served in 12th Lancers.

Sat for Dunwich.	7,642 .	9,471

BARNEBY, William, of Saltmarsh Castle, Bromyard, &c. 🌞.

Coll. Eton, Trin. Cam.	Hereford . .	4,533 .	5,240
b. 1845, s. 1856 and 1871,	Monmouth .	667 .	667
m. 1870.	Worcester . .	435 .	461
	Cheshire . .	113 .	145
		5,748 .	6,513

** BARNES, Mrs., of Gilling Castle, York.

s. 1871, m. 1837.	York, N.R. .	3,659 .	3,500

** BARRINGTON, Sir Croker, Bart., of Glenstal, Murroe,
Co. Limerick.

Coll. Trinity, Dublin.	Limerick . .	9,485 .	4,999

Club. Junior Carl., Limerick County. b. 1817, s. 1872, m. 1845.

** BARRINGTON, Viscount, Becket House, Shrivenham.

Coll. Eton, Ch. Ch. Oxon.	Berkshire . .	3,477 .	7,193
Club. Carlton, White's, St.	York, W.R. .	1,635 .	2,040
Step.,Trav., Marlb.,	Northumberland	1,275 .	7,854
Garrick, Turf.			
b. 1824, s. 1867, m. 1846.		6,387 .	17,087

Served as Vice-Chamberlain of the Household.   Sat for Eye.

BARNARD, C. E. Gee, of Cave Castle	York	2,735 .	4,812
BARNARD, W., of Sawbridgworth	Herts, Ess.	2,133 .	3,644
🌞 BARNARDISTON, N. C., of The Ryes.			
Essex, Suffolk, Cambridge . . .		2,932 .	2,672
BARNES, T., of Farnworth, Lanc., Sal., Denb.		2,659 .	6,399
BARNEWALL, C., of Meadstown	Meath .	2,782 .	2,754
🌞 BARNSTON, H., of Farndon	Cheshire,		
Flintshire, Denbigh		2,184 .	3,403

BARRON, Sir Henry Page Turner, Bart., of Belmont Park, Waterford, &c.

		acres.		*g. an. val.*
Club. St. James's.	Waterford . .	6,281	.	3,625

b. 1824, s. 1872. Served as Attaché at Brussels, Sec. Leg. at Lisbon, Sec. Embassy at Constantinople, and Sec. Leg. at Brussels.

*** SMITH-BARRY, Arthur Hugh, of Fota Island, Queens-town, Co. Cork, &c.

Coll. Eton, Ch. Ch. Oxon.	Co. Cork . .	12,969	.	15,890
Club. Brooks's, Trav.	Tipperary . .	8,620	.	12,131
b. 1843, s. 1857, m. 1868.	Cheshire . .	3,124	.	6,910
Sat for Co. Cork.	Huntingdon .	2,079	.	2,348
		26,792	.	37,279

*** SMITH-BARRY, James Hugh, of ———, Co. Louth.

Coll. Eton, Ch. Ch. Oxon.	Co. Louth . .	6,273	.	6,050

Club. Junior Carlton.   b. 1845, s. 1862, m. 1874.
Served in Grenadier Guards.
The return makes these figures somewhat less.

SMITH-BARRY, Richard Hugh, of Ballyedmond, Middleton, Co. Cork.

Coll. Eton.	Co. Cork . .	8,137	.	5,460
Club. A.& N.,Carlton,R.Y.S.	Limerick . .	269	.	92
b. 1823, s. 1861, m. 1850.				
Served in 12th Lancers.		8,406	.	5,552

BARTON, Henry John Hope, of Stapleton Park, Pontefract.

b. 1873, s. 1876.	Lincoln . . .	3,404	.	5,926
	York, W.R. .	2,476	.	2,299
		5,880	.	8,225

** BARTON, Hugh Lynedoch, of Straffan House, Straffan, Co. Kildare.

Club. Junior Carlton.	Kildare . . .	5,044	.	5,096

b. 1824, s. 1867, m. 1855.   Served in 6th Inniskilling Dragoons.

** BARTON, Samuel Henry, of Grove, Fethard, Co. Tipperary.

		acres.	gr. an. val.
Coll. Harrow.	Tipperary . .	5,119 .	4,607

Club. Junior Carlton, Kil-
dare St. Dublin. b. 1817, s. 1871, m. 1862.

*** BARTTELOT, Sir Walter Barttelot, Bart., C.B., of
Stopham House, Pulborough, Sussex. ♒.

Coll. Rugby.   Sussex . . .   3,633 .   4,793
Club. Carlton, Jun. Uni. Ser.   b. 1820, s. 1872, m. 1st 1852,
2nd 1868.
Served in 1st Royal Dragoons.   Sits for West Sussex.

** BASKERVILLE, Walter Thomas Mynors, of Clyro Court,
Hay.

Coll. Eton, Ch. Ch. Oxon.	Radnor . . .	3,900	4,100
Club. Junior Carlton.	Wilts . . .	1,360 .	1,060
b. 1839, s. 1864, m. 1875.	Brecon . . .	97 .	110
	Hereford . .	1,040 .	1,080
		6,397 .	6,350

BASSET, Charles Henry, of Pilton House, &c., Barnstaple.

Club. Jun. Uni. Ser.   Devonshire .   6,968 .   6,062
b. 1834, s. 1880, m. 1858.   Somerset . .   5 .   43
Served in the R. Navy (with distinction),
during Crimean War.   6,973 .   6,105
Sat for Barnstaple.

BASSET, Gustavus Lambart, of Tehidy Park, Redruth, &c. ♒.

Coll. Eton.   Cornwall . .   16,969 .   32,854
b. 1833, s. 1870, m. 1869.   Served in 72nd Foot.

BASKERVILLE, J., of Crowsley Park, Oxon	2,392 .	2,926
BASS, Michael T., of Rangemore Staffs., Kent, Herts, Brec., Derby . .	2,283 .	17,317
BASSETT, W. W. J., of Bonvilstone, Glam. .	3,087 .	2,805

BASTARD, Baldwin John Pollexfen, of Kitley, Yealmpton,
&c. ♗.

		acres.	*g. an. val.*
Coll. Winch., Ball. Oxon.	Devon . . .	7,557 .	11,221
Club. Army and Navy.	Cornwall . .	82 .	38
b. 1830, s. 1856, m. 1861.			
Served in 9th Foot, in the Crimea.		7,639 .	11,259

** BATEMAN, John, of Brightlingsea, Colchester.

		acres.	*g. an. val.*
Coll. Trin. Cam.	Co. Mayo . .	2,997 .	135
Club. Carlton, National.	Essex . . .	1,413 .	2,910
b. 1839, m. 1865.			
		4,410 .	3,045

** BATEMAN, Lord, Shobdon Court, Leominster.

		acres.	*g. an. val.*
Coll. . Eton, Trin. Cam.	Hereford . .	7,200 .	12,000
Club. Boodle's, Carlton.	Suffolk . . .	53 .	101
b. 1826, s. 1845, m. 1854.			
Served as Lord in Waiting.		7,253 .	12,101

** BATES, Sir Edward, Bart, of Bellefield, West Derby, &c.

		acres.	*g. an. val.*
Club. Carl., Jun. Carl., Cons.	Hants . . .	4,100 .	5,000
b. 1816, m. 1st 1837,	Flint . . .	700 .	1,100
2nd 1844.	Lancashire .	17 .	300
Sat for Plymouth.	Wilts . . .	830 .	110
		5,647 .	6,510

ELLIOT-BATES, Mrs., of Milbourne Hall, Newcastle-on-Tyne.

		acres.	*g. an. val.*
s. 1878, m. 1843.	Northumberland	3,104 .	9,755

About 900 acres, here included, val. 4,170*l.*, are her husband's
property.

*** BATESON, Sir Thomas, Bart., of Belvoir Park, Belfast, &c.

		acres.	*g. an. val.*
Club. Carl., White's, Trav.	Co. Down . .	6,400 .	9,411
b. 1819, s. 1863, m. 1849.	Limerick . .	2,927 .	991
Served in 13th Lt. Dra-	Londonderry .	7,762 .	3,808
goons and as a Lord of the	Antrim . . .	284 .	678
Treasury. Sits for Devizes.			
Sat for Co. Derry.		17,373 .	14,888

Sir T. B. includes part of estates shared with Lords Strafford
and Londonderry and Lady Louisa Trench.

BATEMAN, Thomas, of Youlgreave. Derby 2,585 . 2,945

BATH, Marquis of, Longleat, Warminster. ♒.

			acres.		*g. an. val.*
Coll.	Eton, Ch. Ch. Oxon.	Monaghan . .	22,762	.	19,561
Club.	Carl.,Trav.,Boodle's,	Wilts . . .	19,984	.	29,325
	Jun. Carl.	Somerset . .	8,212	.	13,402
b. 1831, s. 1837, m. 1861,		Hereford . .	699	.	1,052
		Salop . . .	3,508	.	4,181
		Sussex . . .	409	.	494

			55,574	.	68,015

The return gives the Dowager Lady Bath a rental of 140*l.* in Wilts and the whole of the Sussex property.

*** BATHURST, Earl, Oakley Park, Cirencester.

Coll.	Eton, Trin. Cam.	Gloucester . .	10,320	.	17,700
Club.	White's,Car.,Trav.	Derby . . .	3,343	.	3,468
b. 1832, s. 1878, m. 1st 1862,					
	2nd 1874.		13,663	.	21,168
Sat for Cirencester.					

HERVEY-BATHURST, Sir Frederick Thomas Arthur, Bart., of Clarendon Park, Salisbury. ♒.

Coll. Eton.	Wilts. . . .	5,084	.	3,789
Club. Carlton.	Hants . . .	2,918	.	1,831
b. 1833, s. 1881, m. 1869.	Devon . . .	1,203	.	2,216
Served in Grenadier Gds.	Somerset . .	807	.	1,100
Sat for S. Wilts.				

		10,012	.	8,936

BATHURST, Charles, of Lydney Park, Gloucester.

b. 1836, s. 1877, m. 1864.	Gloucestershire	4,098	.	5,189

BATSON, Stanlake Henry, of Horseheath Lodge, Newmarket, Cambridge.

b. 1863, s. 1871.	Cambridge . .	2,284	.	2,809
	Oxford . . .	1,198	.	1,983
	Suffolk . . .	237	.	252

		3,719	.	5,044

BATT, Thos., of Rathmullan Donegal . .   4,337 . 2,176

BATT, Robert Narcissus, of Purdysburn, Belfast.

		acres.	*g. an. val.*
Coll. Harrow, Trin. Cam.	Co. Down .	12,010 .	6,535

Club. Junior Carlton. b. 1844, s. 1864, m. 1866.

BAYNING, The Lady, Honingham Hall, Norwich.

s. 1866, m. 1842. Norfolk . . . 4,323 . 5,419

* BAZLEY, Sir Thomas, Bart., of Eyford Park, Moreton-in-the-Marsh, &c.

Club. Reform, Brooks's.	Lancashire . left blank .	8,124
b 1797, m. 1828.	Gloucestershire 5,391 .	6,890

Served on various Royal Commissions.
Sat. for Manchester. Unstated . 15,014

His only son, Thos. Sebastian Bazley, of Hatherop Castle, Fairford, has in Gloucester a rental included in this total of 6,293*l.*

** HICKS-BEACH, Rt. Hon. Sir Michael Edward, Bart., of Williamstrip Park, Fairford, &c.

Coll. Eton, Ch. Ch. Oxon.	Wilts . . .	7,199 .	4,982
Club. Carlton, Arthur's, St.	Gloucester . .	4,135 .	5,485

Stephen's, Ath.
b. 1837, s. 1854, m. 1st 1864, 2nd 1874. 11,334 . 10,467
Served as Secretary Poor Law Board, Under Secretary Home Department, Chief Secretary for Ireland, and Secretary of State for the Colonies ; sits for East Gloucestershire.

*** BEACH, William Wither Bramston, of Oakley Hall, Basingstoke, &c.

Coll. Eton, Ch. Ch. Oxon.	Hants . . .	6,156 .	6,569
Club. Carlton, Boodle's.	Wilts . . .	895 .	2,123

b. 1826, s. 1856, m. 1857.
Sits for North Hants. 7,051 . 8,692

* BAXTER, Rt. Hon. W. E., of Kincaldrum			
Forfar		2,097 .	3,277
BAYLEY, E., of Rookwood	Ros.,Wmea.,Gal.	3,168 .	2,155
BAYLY, E. S., of Ballyarthur	Wic., Wmea.	3,685 .	2,011

** BEAMISH, Sampson, of Kilmalooda, Timoleague, Co. Cork.

		acres.		*g. an. val.*
b. 1802, s. 1876, m. 1836.	Co. Cork . .	6,626	.	3,130

** STEWART-BEATTIE, Miss, of Crieve, Lockerbie, N.B.

b. 1834, s. 1836.	Argyll . . .	9,354	.	915
	Dumfries . .	11,159	.	3,105
		20,513	.	4,020

BEAUCHAMP, Earl, Madresfield Court, Great Malvern.

Coll. Eton, Ch. Ch. Oxon.	Worcester . .	10,624	.	17,789
Club. Carlton.	Lincoln . . .	2,878	.	1,691
b. 1830, s. 1866, m. 1868 and	Gloucester . .	2,429	.	3,151
1878.	Warwick . .	959	.	1,218
	Hereford . .	744	.	1,092
		17,634	.	24,941

Served as Lord of the Admiralty and Lord Steward of the Household. Sat for Tewkesbury and West Worcestershire.

** PROCTOR-BEAUCHAMP, Sir Reginald William, Bart., of Langley Park, Norwich.

Coll. Eton, Trin. Cam.	Norfolk . . .	6,768	.	10,226
Club. Carlton, White's, Marl.	Essex . . .	378	.	408
b. 1853, s. 1874, m. 1880.				
		7,146	.	10,634

*** BEAUCLERK, Aubrey de Vere, Ardglass Castle, County Down.

Coll. Chelt., Trin. Cam.	Co. Down . .	3,474	.	5,560
Club. Gun, St. James's. b. 1836, s. 1862, m. 1858.				

BEARCROFT, Edward, of Mere Hall Worc.	2,857	.	3,640
BEARD, G. H., of Rottingdean Suss., Glo.	2,500	.	3,685
BEAUCHAMP, E. B., of Trevince Dev., Corn.	2,081	.	2,632

BEAUFORT, Duke of, K.G., Badminton, Chippenham.

		acres.	g. an. val.
Coll. Eton.	Monmouth .	27,299 .	24,582
Club. Carlton, Garrick,	Gloucester . .	16,610 .	21,220
Boodle's, Turf,	Brecon . . .	4,019 .	3,625
Travellers'.	Glamorgan .	1,218 .	4,356
b. 1824, s. 1853, m. 1845.	Wilts . . .	1,939 .	2,443
Served in 7th Hussars and as Master			
of the Horse. Sat for East Gloucester		51,085 .	56,226

*** BEAUMONT, Sir George Howland, Bart., of Cole-Orton
Hall, Ashby-de-la-Zouch.

Coll. Winch., Ch. Ch. Oxon.	Leicester . .	2,977 .	3,935
Club. Carlton, Garrick.	Essex . . .	378 .	484
b. 1828, s. 1845, m. 1st 1850,	Suffolk . . .	201 .	241
2nd 1872.			
		3,556 .	4,660

** BEAUMONT, Henry Frederick, of Whitley Beaumont,
Huddersfield, &c.

Coll. Eton, Trin. Cam.	York, W., N.,		
Club. Brooks's, Ref., Turf.	and E. R. .	5,306 .	12,022
b. 1833, s. 1857, m. 1858.	Sat for S.W. Riding of York.		

Though not mentioned in Mr. Shirley's work, some of these
lands have been in Mr. Beaumont's family since the Conquest.

** BEAUMONT, Lord, Carlton Hall, Selby.

Coll. Eton.	York, E.&W.R.	5,700 .	12,400
Club. Brooks's, St. James's,	Middlesex . .	24 .	11,000
Carlton, Marlbro',	Kent . . .	30 .	2,000
Guards. b. 1848, s. 1854.			
Served in 1st Life Guards.		5,754 .	25,400

The two latter properties are in London and Dover.

BEAUMONT, Wentworth Blackett, of Bretton Park, Wakefield, &c.

Coll. Harrow, Trin. Cam.	Northumberland	14,279 .	15,076
Club. Reform, Travellers',	York, W.R. .	9,015 .	18,634
White's, Brooks's,	Durham . .	804 .	960
St. James'.			
b. 1829, s. 1849, m. 1856.		24,098 .	34,670
Sits for S. Northumberland.			

WRIXON-BECHER, Sir Henry, Bart., Castle Hyde, Fermoy,
  Co. Cork, &c.   *acres.   g. an. val.*
Coll. Eton, Univ. Oxon.   Co. Cork . .   18,933 .   10,528
Club. Army and Navy.   Tipperary . .   358 .   295
b. 1826, s. 1850, m. 1878.
  Served in Rifle Brigade.   19,291 .   10,823

* BECKETT, Sir Edmund, Bt., Q.C., of Batch Wood, St. Alban's.
Coll. Eton, Trin. Cam.   Lincolnshire .   1,663 .   2,120
Club. Athenæum.   York, E. & W.R.   1,459 .   5,123
b. 1816, s. 1874, m. 1845.   Herts . . .   274 .   274
                                                   ———————   ———————
                                                   3,396 .   7,517
*** BECKETT, Miss, of Somerby Park, Gainsborough.
  s. 1872.   Lincoln . .   3,918 .   5,550
                                 York . . .   1,159 .   2,487
                                                   ———————   ———————
                                                   5,077 .   8,037
  The Lincoln property is shared with Lady Bacon, Miss
Beckett's sister.

BEDFORD, Duke of, Woburn Abbey, Bedford, &c. $.
Club. Ref., Brooks's, Trav.,   Beds . . .   32,269 .   45,687
          Uni. Ser.   Devon . . .   22,607 .   45,907
b. 1819, s. 1872, m. 1844.   Cambridge .   18,800 .   34,325
Served in Scots Fus. Gds.   Northampton .   3,414 .   4,049
  Sat for Bedfordshire.   Dorset . . .   3,412 .   3,996
                                 Bucks . . .   3,036 .   2,710
                                 Huntingdon .   1,334 .   2,536
                                 Cornwall . .   1,231 .   514
                                 Hants . . .   148 .   1,950
                                 Herts . . .   83 .   117
                                 Lincoln . . .   1 .   2
The Duke's large London property is   ———————— ————————
  unreturned.   86,335 . 141,793
** PASTON-BEDINGFELD, Sir Henry George, Bart., of
        Oxburgh Hall, Stoke Ferry, Norfolk. $.

Coll. Stonyhurst.   Norfolk . .   4,800 .   4,406
Club. Reform.   Warwick . .   838 .   1,438
b. 1830, s. 1862, m. 1859.   ———————   ———————
  Served in the Austrian Army.   5,638 .   5,844
  The Warwickshire rental is returned as the Dowager Lady
Bedingfeld's.

*** BEECH, JAMES, of Brandon Lodge, Coventry.

			acres.		*g. an. val.*
Coll.	Corpus, Oxon.	Stafford . .	2,351	.	3,141
Club.	Carlton.	Warwick . .	1,808	.	2,949
b 1813, s. 1828, m. 1843.					
			4,159	.	6,090

** BELHAVEN, Lord, Wishaw House, Motherwell, N.B.

		acres.		*g. an. val.*
b. 1822, s. 1868, m. 1877.	Lanarkshire .	2,078	.	4,674
	Midlothian .	965	.	359
		3,043	.	5,033

Exclusive of a rental of 19,621*l.* for minerals.

** BELL, HENRY, of Woolsington, Newcastle-on-Tyne.

Coll. Eton.	Northumberland	4,308	.	7,073

b. 1803, s. 1872, m. 1830.
Served in 29th and 36th Foot.

** BELL, MATTHEW, of Bourne Park, Canterbury.

Coll. Eton, Trin. Cam.	Kent . . .	3,573	.	4,444

Club. Carlton, Jun. Carlton. b. 1817, s. 1836, m. 1839.

BELL, REGINALD, of The Hall, Thirsk.

Club. Junior Carlton.	York, N.R. .	3,834	.	5,228

b. 1848, s. 1875, m. 1878.

BELLEW, Lord, Barmeath, Dunleer, Co. Louth. **S.**

		acres.		*g. an. val.*
Coll. Stonyhurst.	Louth . . .	4,110	.	4,988
Club. Brooks's, St. George's.	Meath . . .	204	.	104
b. 1830, s. 1866, m. 1853.				
		4,314	.	5,092

BEEVOR, SIR T., BART., of Hargham. Nfk.	2,386	.	2,193
BELDAM, V., of Royston. Cambs., Herts .	2,535	.	3,377
BELL, RICHARD, of Castleoer. Peeb., Dumf.	9,450	.	2,529
BELL, JOHN, of Enterkine. Ayr	2,256	.	2,950
BELLAMY, REV. JAMES, of Sellinge. Kent, Norfolk, Cambs.	2,024	.	2,913
S. BELLEW, J.F., of Stockleigh. Dev., Soms.	2,582	.	2,258

BELLINGHAM, Sir Alan Edward, Bart., of Castle Bellingham, Co. Louth.

			acres.		g. an. val.
Coll. Trinity, Dublin.	Louth	. .	4,186	.	4,291
Club. Carlton.	Co. Mayo	.	11,810		295
b. 1800, s. 1827, m. 1841.					
			15,996	.	4,586

*** BELMORE, Earl of, K.C.M.G., Castle Coole, Enniskillen.

Coll. Eton, Trin. Cam.	Co. Tyrone	.	14,388	.	7,541
Club. Carl., White's, Trav.,	Fermanagh		5,041	.	3,474
Ath., Sackville St.					
b. 1835, s. 1845, m. 1861.			19,429	.	11,015

Served as Un. Sec. for Home Dep., as Governor of New South
Wales, and as Com. of Education in Ireland.

Exclusive of lands let on leases for ever, and rents therefrom.

*** BELPER, Lord, Kingston Hall, Kegworth, Derby.

Coll. Harrow, Trin. Cam.	Notts	. .	2,950	.	5,532
Club. Brooks's, Athenæum.	Leicester	. .	2,030	.	4,250
b. 1840, s. 1880, m. 1874.	Derby	. .	246	.	1,520
Sat for E. Derbyshire and Berwick-on-Tweed.			5,226	.	11,302

BENCE, Mrs., of Thorington Hall, Saxmundham.

m. 1850, s. 1881.	Suffolk	. .	2,625	.	3,488
	York, W.R.	.	717	.	826
	Lancashire	.	412	.	487
	Cheshire	. .	168	.	356
	Norfolk	. .	7	.	7
			3,929	.	5,164

*** BENGOUGH, John Charles, of The Ridge, Wotton-under-
Edge.

Coll. Rugby, Oriel, Oxon.	Gloucester	.	4,930	.	7,000
b. 1829, s. 1865, m. 1857.	Hereford	. .	1,209		2,025
	Monmouth	.	536	.	520
			6,705	.	9,545

BENCE, E. R. S., of Kentwell.	Suffolk	. .	2,795	.	3,810
♗. BENDYSHE, Rev. R., of Barrington.	Cam.		2,253	.	3,687

** BENNET, Philip, of Rougham Hall, Bury St. Edmund's.

		acres.	g. an. va!.
Coll. Haileybury.	Suffolk . . .	3,949 .	4,892
b. 1862, s. 1875.			

** BENSON, Ralph Augustus, of Lutwyche Hall, Wenlock.

Coll. Winch., Ch. Ch. Salop . . . 4,300 . 4,000
Oxon.
Club. Carlton, St. James's. b. 1828, s. 1871, m. 1860. Was
a Metropolitan Police Magistrate.

** BENYON, Rev. Edward Richard, of Culford Hall, Bury
St. Edmund's.

Coll. St. John's, Cam.	Suffolk . . .	10,060 .	6,928
Club. Conservative.	Essex . . .	601 .	848
b. 1802, m. 1830.	Huntingdon .	3 .	8
		10,664 .	7,784

BENYON, Richard, of Englefield House, Reading.

Coll. Charterho., St. John's,	Berks . . .	10,129 .	13,303
Cam.	Essex . . .	3,438 .	5,163
Ciub. Boodle's, Carl., Cons.	Hants . . .	2,440 .	1,538
b. 1811, s. 1854, m. 1858.			
Sat for Berks.		16,007 .	20,004

BERENS, Richard Benyon, of Kevington, St. Mary Cray, Kent.

Coll. Westr.,Ch.Ch.Oxon.	Kent . . .	1,909 .	2,670
Club. Oxford and Cam.	Essex . . .	1,529 .	1,267
b. 1834, s. 1859, m. 1860.			
		3,438 .	3.937

BENNETT, F.V., of Thomastown. King's Co.	5,480 .	2,707
BENNETT (late), of Cadbury. Somerset .	2,494 .	5,502
BENNETT (late), T., of Castleroe. Derry,Ant.	2,776 .	2,443
ALDENBURG-BENTINCK, G. W. P., of Terrington. Norfolk	2,802 .	4,791

*** PACK-BERESFORD, Denis Robert, of Fenagh House,
  Bagenalstown, &c.   *acres.   g. an. val.*
b. 1864, s. 1881.   Carlow . . .   7,679 .   6,936

*** BERESFORD, John Barré, of Learmount Park, London-
  derry, &c.

Coll. Eton, Ch. Ch. Oxon.	Londonderry .	10,420 .	3,889
b. 1815, s. 1837, m. 1st	Co. Donegal .	1,342 .	446
1840, 2nd 1853.	Tyrone . . .	1,111 .	147

                                             12,873 .   4,482
      The rental of these properties in 1878 was 5,475*l.*

*** MASSY-BERESFORD, Very Rev. John Maunsell (Dean
  of Kilmore), St. Hubert's, Linaskea, Co. Fermanagh, &c.

Coll. Trin. Dublin.	Peebles . . .	3,875 .	2,899
Club. Uni. and R.St.G.Y.C.	Limerick . .	2,261 .	1,390
Dub., New Edin.	Fermanagh .	1,169 .	670
b. 1823, m. 1851.	Tipperary . .	488 .	522

                                             7,793 .   5,481

BERESFORD, Most Rev. Marcus Gervais (Archbishop of
  Armagh, in the disestablished Church of Ireland), of The
  Palace, Armagh.

Coll. Trin. Cam.	Co. Cavan . .	6,788 .	4,119
Club. Athenæum.	Tyrone . . .	273 .	294
b. 1801, s. 1862, m. 1st 1824,	Leitrim . . .	950 .	35
2nd 1850.	King's Co. . .	94 .	75
Served as Com. Ed. in	Meath . . .	21 .	31
Ireland, was B. of Kilmore.	Monaghan . .	23 .	5
209*l.* of the Co. Cavan rents are in his			
eldest son's name.		8,149 .	4,559

BERESFORD (late), J. D.	Cavan . . .	3,356 .	2,160
*** BERESFORD, Lord C.	Cavan, Leit.	11,060 .	2,974
DE LA POER-BERESFORD, Lady.	Argyll	5,198 .	2,804
BERIDGE, Rev. B., of Algarkirk.	Lin. .	2,182 .	4,234

** BERKELEY, ROBERT, of Spetchley Park, Worcester. ⚲

		acres.		g. an. val.
Coll. Oscott.	Worcestershire	4,811	.	7,750

Club. Travellers'. b. 1823, s. 1874, m. 1851.

*** BERNARD, COL. THOMAS, of Castle Bernard, Kinnetty, King's Co.

Coll. Winchester.	King's Co.	.	14,629	. 6,705

Club. Carlton. b. 1816, s. 1834.
Served in 12th Lancers.

BERNERS, JOHN, of Woolverstone Park, Ipswich.
b. 1800, m. 1832. Suffolk . . . 4,815 . 6,808

** BERNEY, GEORGE DUCKETT, of Morton Hall, Norwich. ⚲.

Coll. St. John's, Cam.	Norfolk	. .	5,429	. 6,977

b. 1813, s. 1869, m. 1864.

BERNEY, SIR HENRY HANSON, BART., of Barton Bendish (res. Woodlands, Windermere). ⚲.

Coll. Trin. Hall, Cam.	Norfolk .	. .	3,148	. 4,181

b. 1843, s. 1870, m. 1866.

BERRIDGE, RICHARD, of Clifden Castle, Connemara, County Galway.

Club. Reform.	Galway . . .	160,152	.	6,520
	Mayo . . .	9,965	.	2,222
	Middlesex . .	321	.	577
	Kent . . .	79	.	184
		170,517	.	9,503

Mr. Berridge is the largest landowner in Ireland.

*** BERRINGTON, ARTHUR VENDIGAED DAVIES, of Pant-y-Goitre, Abergavenny, &c.

Coll. Eton, Exeter, Oxon.	Glamorgan	.	3,264	. 4,385
b. 1833, s. 1871, m. 1st 1853,	Monmouth	.	693	. 1,117
2nd 1861.	Carmarthen	.	414	. 310
			4,371	. 5,812

BERKELEY, REV. W. COMYNS, of Cotheridge. Worcester. . . . . 2,301 . 3,701

** BERWICK, LORD, Attingham, Shrewsbury.

			acres.		g. an. val.
Coll. Rugby.	Salop . . .		5,553	.	10,461

Club. Carlton, Uni. Serv. b. 1802, s. 1861.
Served in the 87th Foot in the Burmese War, 1825–6.

*** BESSBOROUGH, EARL OF, Bessborough House, Piltown,
Co. Kilkenny, &c.

Coll. Harrow, Trin. Cam.	Leicester . .	694	.	902
b. 1815, s. 1880.	Kilkenny . .	23,967	.	15,484
	Carlow . . .	10,578	.	5,522
	Tipperary . .	200	.	467
	Waterford . .	1	.	9
		35,440	.	22,384

** BEST, THOMAS, of Red Rice, Andover.

Coll. Eton, Magd. Oxon.	Hants . . .	6,184	.	6,165
Club. Carlton.	Lincoln . .	34	.	45
b. 1827, s. 1880, m. 1858.				
Rental somewhat overstated.		6,218	.	6,210

BETHELL, WILLIAM, of Rise Park, Hull, &c.

Coll. Eton, Brase. Oxon.	York, E.R. .	13,395	.	17,234
b. 1847, s. 1879, m. 1880.				

*** BEVAN, ROBERT COOPER LEE, of Fosbury House, Hungerford.

Coll. Harrow, Trin. Oxon.	Wilts . . .	2,227	.	1,679
Club. National, Union.	Berks . . .	956	.	807
b. 1809, s. 1846, m. 1st 1836,	Middlesex . .	469	.	794
2nd 1856.	Herts . . .	47	.	136
	Hants . . .	214	.	160
		3,913	.	3,576

BERTIE, The LADY GEORGIANA.	Oxon, Berks	2,205	.	2,396
BERTRAM, W., of Kersewell.	Lanark .	5,863	.	2,893

** BEWES, Rev. Thomas Archer, of Beaumont House, Plymouth.

		acres.	g. an. val.
Coll. Westr., Exeter, Oxon.	Cornwall . .	3,700 .	2,772
b. 1803, s. 1857.	Devon . . .	1,011 .	2,670
		4,711 .	5,442

*** BEWICKE, Calverley, of Close House, Wylam-on-Tyne, &c.

Club. Northern	Northumberland	2,693 .	3,050
Counties.	Durham . . .	1,397 .	6,862
b. 1858, s. 1876, m. 1880.		4,090 .	9,912

MYDDELTON-BIDDULPH, Rd., of Chirk Castle, Ruabon, &c.

Coll. Eton.	Denbigh . . .	5,781 .	8,653
Club. Arthur's.	Hereford . .	1,372 .	2,585
b. 1837, s. 1872, m. 1862.	Merioneth . .	1,170 .	474
	Salop . . .	15 .	30
Served in 1st Life Guards.		8,338 .	11,742

FENWICK-BISSETT, Mordaunt, of Bagborough House, Taunton, &c.

Coll. Trin. Cam.	Aberdeen . .	2,682 .	2,585
Club. Army and Navy, Carl.	Somerset . .	2,180 .	2,665
b. 1825, s. 1858, m. 1851.	Northumberland	82 .	105
	Co. Donegal. .	5,005 .	959
Sits for W. Somerset.			
Served in 1st Dragoon Guards.		9,949 .	6,314

BLACKALL, Major Robert, of Coolamber Manor, Co. Longford.

b. 1834, s. 1871, m. 1867.	Longford . .	4,643 .	2,759
	Leitrim . . .	1,805 .	620
		6,448 .	3,379
Served in 30th Foot.			

YEATMAN-BIGGS, A. G., of Stockton House. Wilts, Leicester	2,995 .	3,048
BILLINGTON, J. W., of Kennington. Kent	2,069 .	3,345
BIRD, C. H., of Crookey. Lancashire . .	2,052 .	4,622

BLACKBURNE, COL. JOHN IRELAND, of Hale Hall, Widnes.

			acres.	*g. an. val.*
Coll.	Eton.	Lancashire .	3,148 .	8,490

Club. Boodle's, Carlton, Uni. Ser., St. Stephen's. b. 1817, s. 1874,
m. 1st, 1846, 2nd, 1857.
Sits for S. W. Lancashire.

BLACKETT, SIR EDWARD, BART., of Matfen Hall, Newcastle-
on-Tyne.

Coll.	Eton, Ch. Ch. Oxon.	Northumberland	15,354 .	13,832
Club.	Carlton, Boodle's,	York, N.R. . .	1,569 .	1,493
	Arthur's.	Durham . . .	553 .	858
b. 1805, s. 1816, m. 1st 1830,				
2nd 1851, 3rd 1875, 4th 1880.			17,476 .	16,183
Served in 1st Life Guards.				

BLAGRAVE, JOHN HENRY, of Calcot Park, Reading, &c.

Club.	Windham.	Berks . . .	2,041 .	4,385
b. 1811, s. 1867, m. 1st 1844,	Somerset . .	1,812 .	3,692
2nd, 1869.	Herts . . .	396 .	632

			4,249 .	8,709

The return gives the Herts property to MRS. BLAGRAVE.

HUNTER-BLAIR, SIR EDWARD, BART., of Blairquhan, Maybole, N.B.

Coll.	Edinb., Royal Naval.	Ayrshire . .	13,417 .	7,944
Club.	Carlton, Grafton.	Wigtown . .	8,255 .	4,948
b. 1818, s. 1857, m. 1850.				
Served in 93rd Highlanders.			21,672 .	12,892

The Wigtown rental, and 811*l.* of that in Ayrshire, is the
property of his eldest son, DAVID H.-BLAIR.

BLACHFORD, LORD.	Devon . . .	2,919 .	2,575
BLACKBURN, JOHN, of Killearn.	Stir. .	2,739 .	2,220
BLACKER, REV. R. S. C., of Woobrook, Wex.	5,624 .	2,489

** STOPFORD-BLAIR, EDWARD JAMES, of Penninghame, Newton-Stewart, N.B.

acres.   *g. an. val.*
Coll. Eton.   Wigtown . . 37,268 . 9,035
Club. Travellers', Carlton, Army and Navy.
b. 1826, s. 1868, m. 1853. Served in 13th Light Dragoons and 10th Hussars.

*** BLAIR, CAPT. WILLIAM FORDYCE, of Blair, Dalry, N.B.

Coll. Royal Naval.   Ayr . . . . 7,280 . 5,828
Club. United Ser., New Edin. b. 1805, s. 1841, m. 1840.
Served in Royal Navy at Navarino, capture of Morea Castle, Rangoon War (twice honourably mentioned), was Attaché to Marshal Bourmont at the taking of Algiers.
Exclusive of a mine rent of at least 2,000*l.*

BLAKE, ARTHUR MAURICE, of Danesbury, Welwyn.

Coll. Eton.	Herts . . .	1,414 .	2,282
b. 1852, s. 1875, m. 1881.	Leicester . .	1,266 .	2,213
Served in Gren. Guards.	Northampton .	964 .	1,403
	Derby . . .	382 .	875
	Rutland . . .	317 .	558
		4,343 .	7,331

BLAKE, MAURICE CHARLES JOSEPH, of Towerhill, Ballyglass, Co. Mayo, &c.

Coll. Stonyhurst.	Co. Galway .	7,690 .	2,191
Club. U. Ser., Dublin.	Co. Mayo . .	4,198 .	1,905
b. 1837, s. 1879, m. 1863.		11,888 .	4,096

BLAKE, WALTER MARTIN, of Ballyglunin Park, Athenry.
b. 1828, s. 1861.   Co. Galway . 10,452 . 3,968

** BLAKE, F. D., of Twizel.	Northum. .	2,083 .	4,726
BLAKE, T. M., of Frenchfort.	Galway . .	5,103 .	2,006
BLAKENEY, JOHN, of Abbert.	Galway .	7,504 .	2,579

** DAVISON-BLAND, Thomas, of Kippax Park, Castleford.

		acres.	g. an. val.
Coll. Eton, Ch. Ch. Oxon.	York, W.R. .	4,320 .	8,500

b. 1812, s. 1847, m. 1st 1848, 2nd 1860.

*** BLANTYRE, Lord, Erskine, Renfrewshire, N.B., &c.

		acres.	g. an. val.
Club. Travellers'.	Renfrew . .	4,449 .	8,503
b. 1818, s. 1830, m. 1843.	Dumbarton .	2,946 .	3,435
Served in Gren. Guards.	Haddington .	2,953 .	6,110
	Berwick . . .	2,878 .	1,395
	Lanark . . .	835 .	527
		14,061 .	19,970

Exclusive of 623*l.* for minerals and quarries.

*** BLATHWAYT, George William, of Dyrham Park, Chipping-Sodbury.

		acres.	g. an. val.
Club. Army and Navy.	Gloucester . .	2,306 .	4,335
b. 1824, s. 1871, m. 1856.	Somerset . .	5,043 .	4,370
Served in the 1st Dragoon Guards.		7,349 .	8,705

BLENNERHASSETT, Arthur, of Ballyseedy House, Tralee.

		acres.	g. an. val.
b. 1856, s. 1859.	Co. Kerry . .	12,621 .	4,159

** BLAND, F. C., of Derriquin. Kerry . . 25,576 . 2,500

BLANSHARD, R., of Fairfield. Essex,
Durham, Hants . . . . 2,469 . 6,140

BLAYNEY, Peerage (reps. of). Tipp. Ant.,
Midd. . . . . 2,074 . 2,323

BLENCOWE, J. George, of Bineham.
Sussex, Nottingham, Warwick . . . . 2,207 . 2,723

BLENNERHASSETT, Sir Rowland,
Bart., of Churchtown. Kerry . . . 8,393 . 2,145

BLISSET, Rev. H., of Letton Ct. Hfd., Glo. 2,243 . 4,335

*** BLOIS, Sir John Ralph, Bart., of Cockfield Hall, Sax-
mundham, &c. ♒.

		acres.	g. an. val.
Coll. Royal Naval.	Suffolk . . .	6,057 .	7,462
Club. Cons., Union, Gun.	Norfolk . . .	250 .	750

b. 1830, s. 1855, m. 1865.

Served in Royal Navy. 6,307 . 8,212

*** LYNCH-BLOSSE, Sir Robert, Bart., of Athavallie, Balla,
Co. Mayo, &c.

Coll. Rugby. Mayo . . . . 22,658 . 9,274
Club. Brooks's, Kild. St. Dub. b. 1825, s. 1840, m. 1853.

BLOUNT, John, of Mapledurham, Reading, &c. ♒.

b. 1833, s. 1881, m. 1881.	Oxon . . .	2,680 .	4,167
	Kent . . .	2,596 .	3,361

The Kentish property is Mrs. Blount's. 5,276 . 7,528

*** BLOUNT, Sir Walter de Sodington, Bart., of Sodington
Court, Bewdley, &c. ♒.

Club. Brooks's.	Worcester . .	2,622 .	2,553
b. 1833, s. 1881, m. 1870.	Salop . . .	2,861 .	2,516

5,483 . 5,069

** WELD - BLUNDELL, Thomas, of Ince-Blundell, Liver-
pool. ♒.

Coll. Stonyhurst, Paris Lancashire . 10,400 . 60,000
Univ.
Club. Brooks's, St. George's, Reform. b. 1808, s. 1841, m. 1859.

* BLUNT, Wilfrid Scawen, of Crabbet, Crawley.

Coll. Stonyhurst, Oscott.	Sussex . . .	4,116 .	3,295
Club. Trav.,Carl.,St.James's.	Durham . .	695 .	3,217

b. 1840, s. 1872, m. 1869.

Was in Diplomatic Service. 4,811 . 6,512

The Durham property is returned as Lady Anne Blunt's.

BLOOMFIELD, John C., of Castle Caldwell.
Fermanagh, Donegal. . . . . . . 4,899 . 2,354
BLUNDELL, N., of Crosby Hall. Lanc. . 2,128 . 6,138
BURN-BLYTH, R., of Woolhampton. Berks. 2,195 . 4,413

BOILEAU, Sir Francis George Manningham, Bart., of
    Ketteringham Park, Wymondham, &c.

			acres.	g. an. val.
Coll.	Eton, Ch. Ch. Oxon.	Norfolk . .	3,626 .	5,101
Club.	Brooks's, Travellers',	Suffolk . .	26 .	45
	Marlb., St. James's.			

b. 1830, s. 1869, m. 1860.   3,652 . 5,146

BOLINGBROKE, Viscount, Lydiard Park, Swindon. §.

Club.	White's.	Wilts . .	3,382 .	5,556

b. 1820, s. 1851.

** BOLITHO, Thomas Simon, of Penalverne, Penzance, &c.

Club.	Athenæum.	Cornwall . .	3,500 .	6,000

b. 1808, m. 1838.

BOLTON, Francis George, of Bective Lodge, Rahinstown,
    Co. Meath.

s. 1868.		Meath . .	3,516 .	3,034

*** BOLTON, George, of Nenagh, Co. Tipperary.

b. 1818, m. 1849 and 1869.	Tipperary . .	4,301 .	2,452
	Kildare . . .	618 .	400
	Limerick . .	303 .	316
	King's Co. . .	679 .	211
		5,901 .	3,379

BOLTON, Lord, Hackwood Park, Basingstoke, &c.

Club.	Carlton, Boodle's.	Hants . . .	13,808 .	13,728
b. 1818, s. 1850, m. 1844.	York, N.R. .	15,413 .	13,824
			29,221 .	27,552

§. BODENHAM, C. de la B., of Rotherwas.

		acres	g. an. val.
Hereford, Radnor, Gloucester . . .	2,999 .	5,926
BODKIN (late), R., of Annagh. Gal., Mayo	6,506 .	2,522
BOLLAND, Mrs., of Kettlewell. York. .	4,375 .	2,973
BOMFORD, G., of Oakley Park. Mea., Wmea.	2,879 .	2,418

BOND, James Willoughby, of Farragh, Longford.

		acres.	g. an. val.
b. 1837, s. 1875, m. 1864.	Longford . .	6,574 .	3,783
	Meath . . .	1,525 .	1,372
	Westmeath .	1,057 .	541
		9,156 .	5,696

BOND, Joshua Walter MacGeough, of Drumsill, Armagh, &c.

Coll. Chelt., Sandhurst.	Armagh . .	3,992 .	3,567
Club. Carlton, Army and	Westmeath .	995 .	892
Navy, Sackville	Co. Down . .	610 .	686
Street.	Louth . . .	27 .	33
b. 2831, s. 1866, m. 1856.			
Served in 49th Foot. Sat for Armagh.		5,624 .	5,178

*** BOND, Rev. Nathaniel, of Creech Grange, Wareham. ⚓.

Coll. Oriel, Oxon.	Dorset . . .	7,429 .	4,499
Club. Carlton.	Hants . . .	1,115 .	928
b. 1804, s. 1844, m. 1835.	Cardigan . .	250 .	187
		8,794 .	5,614

Inclusive of 998*l.* in Dorsetshire in his eldest son's name, and 2,560 acres of rough land, but exclusive of the rent of clay pits.

GRAHAM-BONTINE, William Cunninghame, of Ardoch, Cardross, N.B., &c.

Club. Brooks's, Army and	Stirling . . .	6,931 .	4,188
Navy.	Dumbarton .	1,940 .	2,561
b. 1825, s. 1845, m. 1851.	Perth . . .	2,009 .	1,498
Served in 2nd Dragoons.			
		10,880 .	8,247

Mr. Bontine's quarries are returned at an additional 115*l.*

** GORE-BOOTH, Sir Henry William, Bart., of Lissadell, Co. Sligo.

Coll. Eton.	Sligo . . .	31,774 .	16,774
Club. Windham.	Lancashire .	unstated .	572
b. 1843, s. 1876, m. 1867.			
		31,774 .	17,346

*** BOROUGH, John Charles Burton, of Chetwynd Park,
     Newport, Salop, &c. $.

			acres.	g. an. val.
Coll.	Eton, Ch. Ch. Oxon.	Shropshire . .	4,853 .	8,588
Club.	Carlton, Uni. Univ.	Derby . . .	1,324 .	1,963
b. 1810, s. 1838, m. 1848.		Stafford . . .	1,108 .	1,438
		York, W.R. .	8 .	15

                          7,293 . 12,004

** BORROWES, Robert Higginson, of Gilltown, Newbridge,
     Co. Kildare.

Coll.	Eton.	Kildare . . .	6,089 .	4,103

Club. Arth., Orleans, Kild. St. Dub.   b. 1826, s. 1850, m. 1859.
Served in 13th Light Dragoons.
     Mr. Borrowes has also house property in Dublin.

BORTHWICK, John, of Crookston House, Edinburgh.

Coll.	Edin. Univ.	Midlothian . .	5,239 .	4,366
Club.	Junior Carlton.	Berwick . .	4,484 .	1,484
b. 1825, s. 1846, m. 1854.				

                          9,723 . 5,850

BOSTON, Lord, Llanidan, Anglesea.

Coll.	Eton, Ch. Ch. Oxon.	Anglesea . .	9,507 ,	7,520
b. 1860, s. 1877.		Lincoln . . .	1,200 .	2,119
		Warwick . .	1,103 .	2,526
		Bucks . . .	562 .	1,683
		Carnarvon . .	98 .	1,323
		Berks . . .	4 .	1

                       12,474 . 15,172

BOSVILLE, Alexander Westworth Macdonald, of Thorpe
     Hall, Bridlington.

b. 1865, s. 1865.   York, E., W.,
                     and N.R. . 8,949 . 8,993

BORROWES, Sir E. D., Bart., of Barretts-
    town.   Kildare, Queen's County . . . 4,818 . 2,594
BOSANQUET, C. B. P., of Rock.   North-
    umberland, Essex . . . . 2,182 . 2,495
BOSANQUET, S. R., of Dingestow. Mon., Es. 2,668 . 2,557

HOUSTON-BOSWALL, Sir George Augustus Frederick, Bart., Blackadder, Chirnside, N.B., &c.

		acres.	*g. an. val.*
Club. Travellers', Uni. Ser.	Berwickshire .	5,309 .	8,746

b. 1809, s. 1842, m. 1847.
  Served in Grenadier Guards. Is a Colonel unattached.

BOSWELL, Lady, of Auchinleck House, Mauchline, N.B.

s. 1857, m. 1830.	Ayrshire . .	11,977 .	8,256

Also a mineral rent of 3,633*l.*

** GARNETT-BOTFIELD, Rev. William Bishton, of Decker Hill, Shiffnal, &c. $.

Coll. Shrew., Bras. Oxon.	Salop . . .	7,670 .	8,587
Club. Union.	Cheshire . .	353 .	651
b. 1816, s. 1863, m. 1st 1848,	Montgomery .	78 .	123
2nd 1872.			
		8,101 .	9,361

** BOUCHERETT, Miss, of Willingham Hall, Market Rasen.

b. 1821, s. 1877.	Lincolnshire .	5,834 .	7,823

FENTON-BOUGHEY, Sir Thomas Fletcher, Bart., of Aqualate Hall, Newport, Salop.

Coll. Eton, Ch. Ch. Oxon.	Stafford . .	10,505 .	15,849
b. 1836, s. 1880, m. 1864.	Derby . . .	270 .	328
	Salop . . .	153 .	538
	Cheshire . .	47 .	—
		10,975 .	16,715

The return describes the Cheshire acres as plantation and fallow.

*** ROUSE-BOUGHTON, Sir Charles Henry, Bart., of Downton Hall, Ludlow. $.

Coll. Harrow.	Salop . . .	5,456 .	7,645

Club. Junior United Service, Athenæum.
b. 1825, s. 1856, m. 1852. Served in 52nd Foot.

BOUCHER, Mrs., of Thornhill. Dor., Som.	2105 .	4,260

BOULTON, Matthew Piers Watt, of Haseley Court, Tetsworth, &c.

		acres.	g. an. val.
Club. Athenæum.	Oxford . . .	7,945 .	13,101
b. 1820, m. 1st 1845,	Warwick . . left blank .		211
2nd 1868.	Worcester . .	2 .	225
	Stafford . . .	291 .	644
	Lancashire . .	77 .	111
		8,315 .	14,292

** BOURNE, Robert, of Much Cowarne, Hereford (res. Grafton
Manor, Bromsgrove).

			acres.	g. an. val.
Coll. Westm.,Ch.Ch.Oxon.	Hereford . .	3,243 .	4,500
Club. Oxford County.	Oxon . . .	465 .	717
b. 1832, m. 1857.	Wilts . . .	115 .	281
Served in 54th Foot.	Worcester . .	62 .	116
		3,885 .	5,614

Nearly all the smaller properties belong to his father.

PLEYDELL-BOUVERIE, Rt. Hon. Edward, of East Lavington Manor, Devizes.

Coll. Harrow, Trin. Cam.   Wiltshire . .   3,349 .   4,811
Club. Brooks's, Reform.   b. 1818, m. 1842.
  Served as Under Sec. Home Department, Vice-Pres. Board of
Trade, and President of Poor Law Board.   Sat for Kilmarnock.

BOUVERIE, John Augustus Sheil, of Delapré Abbey, Northampton.

b. 1836, s. 1871, m. 1860.   Northampton .   3,188 .   8,676

** PLEYDELL-BOUVERIE, Philip, of Brymore, Bridgwater.

Coll. Harrow, Trin. Cam.   Somerset . .   3,470 .   3,367
Club. Travellers', Brooks's,   Leicester . .   612 .   724
b. 1821, s. 1872, m. 1847.
                                                4,082 .   4,091

BOURKE, Lady Susan, Coalstoun. Haddn.   2,702 .   4,843
BOUSTEAD, J., of Armathwaite. Cumb. .   2,648 .   2,495

*** BOWEN, James Bevan, of Llwyngwair, Newport, Pembroke.

			acres.		*g. an. val.*
Coll. King's, Lon., Wor.	Pembroke . .	3,035	.	3,027
Oxon.	Carmarthen .	2,290	.	1,355
Club. Univ., Carlton.	Cardigan . .	35	.	25
b. 1828, s. 1856, m. 1857.				
Sat for Pembrokeshire.		5,360	.	4,407

** BOWEN, Robert Cole, of Bowenscourt, Castletown Roche, Co. Cork.

Coll. Chelt., Trin. Dub.	Co. Cork . .	1,680	.	1,221
Club. Cork County.	Tipperary . .	5,060	.	2,574
b. 1830, s. 1842, m. 1860.				
Served in 87th Foot.		6,740	.	3,795

** BOWER, Frederick, of West Dean Park, Chichester.

b. 1827, m. 1852.	Sussex . . .	8,500	.	6,000

BOWES, John, of Streatlam Castle, Gateshead.

Club. Reform, Travellers',	York, N.R. .	34,887	.	5,283
Arthur's.	Durham . .	8,313	.	15,788
b. 1811, s. 1820, m. 1872 and 1877.				
Sat for S. Durham.		43,200	.	21,071

BOWYER, Sir George, Bart., of Radley House, Abingdon.

Club. Reform, St. Geo.,	Berks . . .	4,451	.	9,412
Oriental. b. 1811, s. 1860.				
Sat for Dundalk and for Wexford.				

** MORSE-BOYCOTT, Frederic Augustus, of Sennowe Hall, Fakenham, &c.

Coll. Hertford, Oxon.	Norfolk . .	5,257	.	8,290
Club. Ox. and Cam., Pall	Suffolk . . .	507	.	874
Mall.	Herts . . .	20	.	unstated
b. 1849, s. 1874, m. 1879.				
		5,784	.	9,164

BOWEN, C. E. H., of Kilnacourt.	Q. Co., Dub.	2,123	.	2,564
WEBB-BOWEN, C. W. T., of Camrose.	Pem.	2,637	.	2,036
BOYCOTT, Miss, of Rudge.	Salop, Staffs. .	2,367		4,096

BOYD, Rev. Sir Frederick, Bart., of The Mansion, Bally-
    castle, Co. Antrim.

		acres		g. an. val.
Coll. Chart., Univ. Oxon.	Co. Antrim .	5,304	.	3,501

Club. Cons., Garrick. b. 1820, s. 1876, m. 1st 1864, 2nd 1872.

*** ROCHFORT-BOYD, George Augustus, of Middleton
    Park, Castletown, Co. Westmeath.

Coll. Trin. Dub.	Co. Westmeath	16,397	.	9,730

Club. Carlton, Sackville St. b. 1817, s. 1836, m. 1843.

The last Government valuation of this estate is 10,249*l.*

** BOYD, Richard Keown, of Ballydugan, Downpatrick.

Coll. R.N.A.Gosport,Green-	Down . . .	4,249	.	5,238
wich.	Antrim . . .	70	.	83
Club. Junior Carlton.	Wicklow . .	57	.	unstated
b. 1850, s. 1877, m. 1875.				
Served in Royal Navy.		4,376	.	5,321

BOYLE, The Ladies Elizabeth and Charlotte Anne, of
    Courtmasherry, Bandon.

b. 1814, 1817.	Co. Cork . .	5,696	.	4,272

Each of these ladies is credited with exactly one-fourth of the
acreage and income ; *i.e.*, 1,424 acres and 1,068*l.* " Lady Boyle,"
of "Courtmasherry," is given 2,515 acres more, rented at 284*l.*—
probably a misprint for Ladies Boyle. Two sisters have died
since the return was published.

BOYNE, Viscount, Brancepeth Castle, Durham, &c.

Coll. Eton.	Durham . .	18,023	.	76,885
Club. Carlton.	Salop . . .	8,424	.	8,014
b. 1830, s. 1872, m. 1858.	York, N.R. .	439	.	235
	Radnor . . .	580	.	258
	Co. Meath . .	2,739	.	2,972
Lady Boyne has a rental (here				
included) of 25*l.* in Radnor.		30,205	.	88,364

BOYD, J. R., of Ballymacool.	Donegal	.	5,001	.	2,036
BOYLAN, T., of Hilltown.	Meath . .		2,914	.	2,970
BOYLE, David, of Shewalton.	Ayr .	.	2,358	.	2,708

** BOYNTON, Sir Henry Somerville, Bart., of Burton Agnes Hall, Hull. 🐚.

			acres.	g. an. val.
Coll. Cambridge.	York, E.R.	.	9,300	. 10,000

Club. Carlton. b. 1844, s. 1869, m. 1876.

** BOYSE, Henry Arthur, of Bannow House, New Ross, Co. Wexford.

b. 1848, s. 1880, m. 1872.	Wexford	. .	4,589	.	3,960
	Kilkenny	. .	2,372	.	1,995
	King's County		159	.	86
			7,120	.	6,041

BRABOURNE, Lord, Smeeth Paddocks, Ashford. 🐚.

Coll. Eton, Magd. Oxon.	Kent	. . .	4,173	.	5,646

Club. Brooks's, Uni. Univ., Empire.
Served as Lord of the Treasury, U. Sec. Home Dept., and U. Sec. Colonies. Sat for Sandwich.

* BRADFORD, Earl of, Weston Park, Shiffnal, &c.

Coll. Harrow, Trinity	Salop	. . .	10,883	.	15,686
Cam.	Stafford	. .	6,843	.	10,795
Club. Carlton, Trav.	Warwick	. .	1,906	.	5,276
b. 1819, s. 1865, m. 1844.	Lancashire	.	1,958	.	9,893
Served as Vice-Chamberlain	Westmorland	.	62	.	133
of the Household, Lord	Worcester	. .	13	.	23
Chamberlain, and Master	Montgomery	.	15	.	52
of the Horse. Sat for South	Leicester	. .	6	.	124
Salop.	Denbigh	. .	24	.	—
			21,710	.	41,982

BRADSHAW, Frank, of Lifton Park, Exeter, &c.

Club. Oxford and Cam-	Devon	. . .	6,642	.	7,840
bridge, Cons.	Herts	. . .	811	.	1,394
b. 1821, s. 1856 and 1877,	Somerset	. .	396	.	671
m. 1853.	Hants	. . .	270	.	367
	Sussex	. . .	3	.	70
			8,122	.	10,342

BRABAZON, Capt., of Brabazon Park. Mayo 6,857 . 2,081

*** BRAMSTON, COL. THOMAS HARVEY, of Skreens, Chelmsford.

		acres.		*g. an. val.*
Coll. Winchester.	Essex . . .	5,426	.	6,665

Club. Guards', Travellers', Turf.
b. 1831, s. 1871, m. 1864.
  Served in Rifle Brigade (and in Grenadier Guards), at the Cape, and in the Crimea.

** BRAND, HON. SIR HENRY BOUVERIE WILLIAM, G.C.B., of Glynde, Lewes.

Coll. Eton.	Sussex . . .	8,846	.	8,121

Club. Brooks's, Reform, Athenæum.   b. 1814, m. 1838.
  Served as a Lord of the Treasury, Secretary to the Treasury, and Keeper of the Privy Seal to the Prince of Wales, and is Speaker H. C.   Sat for Lewes; sits for Cambridgeshire.

*** BRASSEY, ALBERT, of Heythrop House, Chipping Norton.

Coll. Eton, Uni. Oxon.	Oxford . . .	4,275	.	5,100

Club. Nav. & Mil., Carl., Boodle's, Ox. & Cam., Jun. Univ.
b. 1844, m. 1871.   Served in 14th Hussars.

*** BRASSEY, HENRY ARTHUR, of Preston Hall, Maidstone.

Coll. Harrow, Uni. Oxon.	Kent . . .	4,061	.	11,253

Club. Oxford and Cambridge, Boodle's, City Lib., Dev.
b. 1840, m. 1866.   Sits for Sandwich.

** BRASSEY, SIR THOMAS, K.C.B., of Normanhurst, Battle, Sussex.

Coll. Rugby, Uni. Oxon.	Sussex . . .	3,544	.	3,681
Club. Reform, Uni. Univ.,	Cheshire . .	73	.	736
Brooks's, Athenæum.				
b. 1836, m. 1860. Serves as Lord of the Adm.		3,617	.	4,417

Sat for Devonport; sits for Hastings.

DUNBAR-BRANDER, J.B., of Pitgaveny. Elg.	3,121	.	2,823
BRANDRETH, H. C. G., of Houghton Hall. Cornwall, Beds	2,670	.	3,357
BRASIER, BROOKE R., of Ballyellis. Limk., Tipp., Cork	2,109	.	2,636

*** BRAYBROOKE, Lord, Audley End, Saffron Walden, &c.

			acres.		*g. an. val.*
Coll. Eton, Magd., Cam.	Essex . . .	9,820	.	13,160
Club. Trav., Carlton.	Berks . . .	3,691	.	5,013
b. 1823, s. 1861, m. 1849.				
		13,511	.	18,173

BRAYE, Lord, Stanford Park, Rugby.

		acres.		*g. an. val.*
Coll. Eton, Ch. Ch. Oxon.	Leicester . .	2,896	.	5,449
Club. Reform.	Northampton .	1,065	.	2,017
b. 1849, s. 1879, m. 1873.	Herts . . .	650	.	759
	Middlesex . .	47	.	92
		4,658	.	8,317

These properties come under seven heads in the return, viz., "Baroness Bray, execs. of," "Rev. Edgehill" (twice), "Baroness Bray, co-heiresses of," "Mr. Edgehill," and "Lady Bray." Curious that in one instance only could the compilers hit on the right spelling. Mr. Wyatt-Edgell is given about 2,400 of these acres.

** BREADALBANE, Earl of, Taymouth Castle, Aberfeldy, N.B., &c.

		acres.		*g. an. val.*
Coll. St. Andrew's.	Perth . . .	234,166	.	35,977
Club. White's, Marlb., Ref.	Argyll . . .	204,192	.	22,315
b. 1851, s. 1871, m. 1872.				
Served as a Lord in Waiting.		438,358	.	58,292

The total annual value is overstated by 2,600*l.*

*** STAPLETON-BRETHERTON, Hon. Mrs., of Lackham, Chippenham, &c.

		acres.		*g. an. val.*
s. 1856, m. 1st 1829,	Lancashire .	1,882	.	8,855
2nd 1848.	York, N.R . .	2,189	.	723
	Wilts . . .	577	.	2,094
		4,648	.	11,672

** BRIDGER, Harry, of Buckingham House, Shoreham.

		acres.		*g. an. val.*
b. 1828, s. 1872, m. 1850.	Sussex . . .	3,753	.	3,689

FRENCH-BREWSTER, R. A. B., of 22, Merrion Square. Dub., Carl., Rosc., Wick. 2,863 . 2,522

BRIGSTOCKE, Mrs., of Blaenpant. Carm., Pemb., Card. . . . . 2,684 . 2,070

** BRIDGES, Rev. Alexander Henry, of Beddington House,
      Croydon, &c.

			acres.		g. an. val.
Coll. Winch., Oriel, Oxon.	Aberdeen	. .	4,456	.	2,816
Club. Athenæum.	Surrey	. . .	453	.	2,341
b. 1811, s. 1861, m. 1848.	Essex	. . .	503	.	671
			5,412	.	5,828

*** BRIDGES, Rev. Sir Brook George, Bart., of Good-
      nestone Park, Wingham, Kent.

Coll. Oriel, Oxon.	Kent	. . .	4,365	.	7,848
Club. National.	Essex	. . .	1,606	.	1,894
b. 1802, s. 1875, m. 1832.					
			5,971	.	9,742

*** BRIDPORT, Viscount, Cricket St. Thomas, Chard, Som.

Club. Carlton, Uni. Ser.;	Somerset	. .	3,103	.	5,223
Travellers'.	Dorset	. . .	2,356	.	2,785
b. 1814, s. 1868, m. 1838.	Devon	. . .	53	.	90
			5,512	.	8,098

    Served in Scots Fusilier Guards, a General in the Army, was
Groom in Waiting, and Equerry to the Queen. Is Duke of
Brontë in Sicily, and a landowner there.

BRINKLEY, Richard Graves, of Fortland, Easkey, Co. Sligo.

Coll. Trinity, Dublin.	Sligo	. . . .	6,730	.	3,006
Club. R. St. Geo. Y., Dub.	b. 1823, s. 1855, m. 1845.				

**· BRISCO, Sir Robert, Bart., of Crofton Hall, Wigton, Cum-
      berland. ♣.

Coll. Midhurst School.	Cumberland	.	3,540	.	5,229
b. 1808, s. 1862, m. 1832.					

BRINCKMAN, Sir T. H., Bart., of St.					
Leonards. York, Midd., Linc., Berks	.	2,301	.	3,857
BRISBANE, C. T., of Brisbane. Ayr	. .	6,982	.	2,154

BRISCO, The MISSES, of Bohemia House, Hastings, &c.
s. 1878.

		acres.		*g. an. val.*
	Sussex . . .	4,390	.	6,608
	Lincoln . . .	1,280	.	1,813
	Montgomery .	530	.	3,048
		6,200		11,469

BRISTOL, MARQUIS OF, Ickworth Park, Bury St. Edmunds. $

Coll. Eton, Trin. Cam.	Suffolk . . .	16,981	.	20,011
Club. Trav., White's, Carl.	Lincoln . . .	13,745	.	19,429
b. 1834, s. 1864, m. 1862.	Essex . . .	1,131	.	1,557
Sat for W. Suffolk.	Sussex . . .	157	.	273
		32,014	.	41,270

* HARRISON-BROADLEY, WILLIAM HENRY, of Welton
Brough, Hull.
Coll. Rugby, Bras. Oxon.   York, E.R.   .   14,877 . 23,378
Club. Carlton, Uni. Univ.   b. 1820, s. 1829.
Sits for E. Riding of York.

*** BROADWOOD, HENRY FOWLER, of Lyne, Horsham.

Coll. Har., Trin. Cam.	Surrey . . .	2,962	.	2,137
Club. Oxf. and Cam.	Sussex . . .	2,090	.	1,021
b. 1811, s. 1864, m. 1840.				
		5,052	.	3,158

FITZ-HERBERT-BROCKHOLES, WILLIAM, of Claughton
Hall, Garstang.
Club. Junior Carlton.   Lancashire . .   4,600   .   6,033
b. 1851, s. 1875, m. 1876.

** BROCKLEBANK, Thomas, of Springwood, Allerton, Liverpool, &c.

b. 1814.	Cumberland .	2,753	.	2,930
	Cheshire . .	1,358	.	2,987
	Lancashire . .	168	.	970
		4,279	.	6,887

Acreage rather overstated in Cumberland—understated in the
other counties.

RUGGLES-BRISE, COL., of Spains. Essex	2,208	.	3,107
BRITTLEBANK, MRS., of Winster. Der.,Staf.	2,536	.	4,207
BROADWOOD, T., of Laugharne. Carm. .	2,144	.	2,581

*** BROCKLEHURST, Philip Lancaster, of Swythamley
Park, Macclesfield.

		acres.	g. an. val.
b. 1827.	Stafford .	4,641 .	3,542
	Cheshire . .	679 .	1,058
		5,320 .	4,600

BROCKMAN, Francis Drake, of Beachborough, Hythe.

b. 1851, s. 1876.	Kent . . .	3,864 .	4,882

** BRODIE, Alexander, of Lethen, Nairn, N.B., &c.

b. 1876, s. 1880.	Nairn . . .	22,378 .	4,947
	Elgin . . .	1,304 .	1,120
		23,682 .	6,067

BRODIE, Hugh Fife Ashley, of Brodie Castle, Forres, N.B.

Club. Trav., Carl., Ar. and	Nairn . .	4,407 .	2,586
Na., Jun. Carl.	Elgin . . .	4,728 .	2,172
b. 1840, s. 1873, m. 1868.			
Served in Royal Artillery.		9,135 .	4,758

BROKE, Miss, of Livermere Park, Bury St. Edmund's.

s. 1855.	Suffolk . . .	2,737 .	2,933
	Norfolk . . .	813 .	994
		3,550 .	3,927

* BROOK, Edward, of Hoddam Castle, Ecclefechan, N.B., &c.

b. 1825, m. 1863.	Dumfries . .	4,296 .	4,694
	York, W.R. .	70 .	177
		4,366 .	4,871

The Scottish estate was bought in 1877.

BROOK (late), Mrs., of Enderby.	Leic.,York	2,347 .	5,109
🌳. BROOKE, F. C., of Ufford.	Suffolk .	2,063 .	2,177
BROOKE, G. F., of Summerton.	Wexford .	5,797 .	2,676

BROOKE, Lord (*jure uxoris*), Easton Lodge, Dunmow.

		acres.		g. an. val
Coll. Ch. Ch. Oxon.	Essex . . .	8,617	.	10,482
Club. Carlton.	Leicester . .	4,411	.	7,931
Ld. B. b. 1853, m. 1881.	Northampton .	802	.	1,559
Ldy. B. b. 1861, s. 1865.	Cambridge . .	8	.	11
Sits for E. Somerset.	Middlesex . .	6	.	18
		13,844	.	20,001

*** BROOKE, Sir Richard, Bart., of Norton Priory, Runcorn. ♺.

		acres.		g. an. val
Coll. Eton.	Cheshire . .	4,898	.	10,358
Club. Travellers'.	Lancashire . .	1,400	.	2,984
b. 1814, s. 1864, m. 1st 1848,	Flint . . .	99	.	25
2nd 1871.				
Served in 1st Life Guards.		6,397	.	13,367

** BROOKE, Sir Victor Alexander, Bart., of Colebrooke, Co. Fermanagh.

Coll. Harrow.	Fermanagh . .	27,994	.	15,288
Club. Carlton. b. 1843, s. 1854, m. 1864.				

DE-CAPELL-BROOKE, Sir William, Bart., of Oakley Hall, Kettering.

Coll. Rugby, Bras. Oxon.	Northampton .	2,966	.	4,281
Club. Uni. University.	Rutland . .	533	.	889
b. 1801, s. 1858, m. 1829.	Leicester . .	61	.	486
	Co. Cork . .	2,132	.	2,171
	Tipperary . .	901	.	645
		6,593	.	8,472

BROOKSBANK, Rev. Edward Hawke, of Helaugh Hall, Tadcaster.

Coll. Queen's, Cambridge.	York, W. and N.R.	4,567	.	5,973
b. 1789, s. 1856, m. 1st 1825, 2nd 1848.				

This includes 847 acres in his son's name.

BROOKE, J. T., of Haughton Hall.	Salop .	2,467	.	4,084
BROOKE, Mrs. Jane.	York	2,179	.	2,916
BROOKS (late) S. of Manchester.	Ches., Lan.	2,488	.	14,663

BROUGHAM AND VAUX, LORD, Brougham, Penrith, &c.

			acres.	g. an. val.
Coll. Edin., Jesus, Cam.	Cumberland	.	1,369	.	905
Club. Wanderers'.	Westmorland	.	985	.	1,646
b. 1795, s. 1868, m. 1834.	Somerset	. .	2,716	.	4,580
	Hants	. . .	6	.	7

Sat for Southwark.   5,076 . 7,138

The two last properties belong to his eldest son, and appear in the return in SIR C. TAYLOR'S name.

BROUGHTON, SIR HENRY DELVES, of Doddington Park, Nantwich, &c. 🐍.

b. 1810, s. 1851, m. 1857.	Cheshire	. .	13,832	.	19,723
	Stafford	. .	1,320	.	2,049
	Salop	. . .	2	.	2

      15,154 . 21,774

GILPIN-BROWN, GEORGE, of Sedbury Park, Richmond, Yorkshire, &c.

Coll. Magd. Oxon.	York, N.R.	.	6,886	.	8,042
Club. Jun. Carlton, Ox. and Cam.	Durham	. .	72	.	227
b. 1815, m. 1847.			6,958	.	8,269

*** BROWN, MISS, of Lanfine House, Kilmarnock, N.B.

s. 1873.	Ayrshire	. .	9,713	.	6,378
	Lanark	. . .	1,161	.	145
			10,874	.	6,523

BROUGHTON (late), PETER, of Tunstall. Staff., Notts, Salop	. . . .	2,329	.	4,496
BROWN, DOUGLAS, of Arncliffe. York	. .	2,535	.	3,263
BROWN, W. T., of Tostock. Suffolk	. .	2,278	.	3,109
BROWN, SIR W. R., BART., of Astrop. Northampton	. . . .	2,087	.	4,925
GRAVER-BROWNE, Mrs., of Morley Hall, Norfolk	. . . .	2,053	.	3,941

BROWNE, ALEXANDER, of Acklington, Warkworth, &c.

		acres.		g. an. val.
Club. Carlton, Boodle's.	Northumberland	5,797	.	7,162

b. 1812, m. 1842.

This property consists of three estates, the largest of which (Calialy) belongs to his eldest son, Mr. A. H. BROWNE. It was bought in 1877, and is said by Sir H. Bedingfeld (trustee for sale) to be worth 800*l.* more than here stated.

*** BROWNE, ROBERT CLAYTON, of Browne's Hill, Carlow.

Coll. Eton, Ch. Ch. Oxon.	Carlow . . .	4,652	.	5,380
Club. Carlton, Kildare St.	Dublin . . .	265	.	530
b. 1799, s. 1840, m. 1834.	Queen's Co. .	277	.	578
		5,194	.	6,488

** BROWNE, THOMAS BEALE, of Crotta, Kilflynn, Co. Kerry, &c.

Coll. Oriel, Oxon.	Co. Kerry . .	2,064	.	2,051
b. 1810, s. 1850, m. 1840.	Gloucester .	2,064	.	2,767
		4,128	.	4,818

** BROWNE, THOMAS RICHARDSON, of Aughentaine Castle, Fivemiletown, Co. Tyrone.

Club. Wanderers', Kildare	Tyrone . . .	10,350	.	5,040
St., Dublin. b. 1811, s. 1847, m. 1839.				

** BROWNLOW, EARL, Belton House, Grantham, &c.

Coll. Eton.	Salop . . .	20,233	.	29,717
Club. Carlton, Guards.	Lincoln . . .	11,652	.	20,457
b. 1844, s. 1867, m. 1868.	Bucks . . .	11,785	.	15,450
	Herts . . .	8,551	.	12,760
	Beds . . .	2,968	.	3,009
	York, N.R. .	1,689	.	2,479
	Durham . .	920	.	1,204
	Berwick . .	536	.	1,340
	Flint . . .	1	.	10
Served in Gren. Gds. Sat for N. Salop.		58,335	.	86,426

BROWNE, Mrs., of Walkern Hall. Herts, Beds, Cambs.	2,784	.	4,499
BROWNE, T. B., of Newgrove. Clare . .	5,960	.	2,885
BROWNLOW, W., of Knapton Ho. Mghn. .	2,959	.	2,394

*** TYNDALL-BRUCE, ANDREW HAMILTON, of Falkland, N.B.

			acres.		g. an. val.
Coll.	Edin. Acad., Addis-	Fifeshire . .	7,058	.	9,992
	combe.	Haddington .	445	.	1,247
Club.	N. and M. b. 1842, s. 1874.				
	Served in 102nd Foot.		7,503	.	11,239
	Exclusive of 100*l.* mineral rental.				

** BRUCE, SIR HENRY HERVEY, BART., of Downhill, Coleraine.

Coll.	Trin. Cam.	Londonderry .	20,801	.	11,397
Club.	Junior Uni. Service.	Montgomery .	713	.	1,012
b. 1820, s. 1836, m. 1842.					
			21,514	.	12,409

Served in 1st Life Guards.   Sits for Coleraine.

*** BRUCE, JAMES, of Benburb (res. Thorndale, Belfast).

b. 1835, m. 1877.   Co. Tyrone   .   9,230   .   8,322

** BRUCE, HON. ROBERT PRESTON, of Broomhall, Dunfermline, N.B.

Coll.	Eton, Ball. Oxon.	Fifeshire . .	3,243	.	3,833
Club.	N. University. b. 1851. Sits for Fifeshire.				

* BRUEN, RT. HON. HENRY, of Oak Park, Carlow.

Club.	Carlton, Sackville St.	Carlow . . .	16,477	.	14,059
b. 1828, s. 1852, m. 1854.		Wexford . .	6,932	.	3,288
		Kildare . .	218	.	134

Sat for Co. Carlow.   23,627   .   17,481

** PRIDEAUX-BRUNE, CHARLES GLYNN, of Prideaux Place, Padstow. ⚓.

Coll.	Ch. Ch. Oxon.	Cornwall . .	5,746	.	6,038
Club.	U. University.	Hants . . .	1,739	.	3,209
b. 1821, s. 1875, m. 1846.		Dorset . . .	1,097	.	1,360
		Somerset . .	47	.	47
			8,629	.	10,654

BRUCE, H. S. B., of Ballyscullion. Derry, Ant.	4,000	.	2,107
BRUCE, W. A., of Symbister. Zetland . .	25,180	.	2,354
BRUNSKILL, W. F., of Polsloe. Devon .	2,926	.	5,043

*** BRYAN, Hon. George Leopold, of Jenkinstown, Kilkenny.

		acres.		g. an. val.
b. 1857, s. 1880.	Kilkenny . .	8,209	.	5,721
	Meath . . .	3,055	.	1,953
	Kildare . . .	1,627	.	1,223
Serves in 10th Hussars.		12,891	.	8,897

** BRYAN, Loftus Anthony, of Borrmount Manor, Enniscorthy, &c.

b. 1867, s. 1873.	Wexford . .	6,135	.	3,928

** JONES-BRYDGES, Sir Harford James, Bart., of Boultibrooke, Presteign.

Coll. Merton, Oxon.	Radnor . . .	1,476	.	2,074
Club. Athenæum.	Hereford . .	1,612	.	1,575
b. 1808, s. 1847, m. 1850.		3,088	.	3,649

** BRYMER, William Ernest, of Ilsington House, Dorchester.

Coll. Harrow, Trin. Cam.	Dorset . . .	4,831	.	5,152
Club. Carl., Ox. and Cam.	Somerset . .	415	.	1,039
b. 1840, s. 1870.				
Sits for Dorchester.		5,246	.	6,191

BUCCLEUCH and QUEENSBERRY, Duke of, K.G., Dalkeith Palace, Edinburgh, &c.

Coll. Eton, St. John's, Cam.	Northampton	17,965	.	26,531
Club. Carlton, Uni. Serv.,	Warwick . .	6,881	.	12,567
Trav., St. Stephen's.	Huntingdon .	1,065	.	1,312
b. 1806, s. 1819, m. 1829.	Bucks . . .	894	.	2,769
	Lancashire .	369	.	447
	Surrey . . .	7	.	708
	Dumfries . .	254,179	.	95,239
	Roxburgh . .	104,461	.	39,457
	Selkirk . . .	60,428	.	19,828
Served as Lord Privy Seal	Midlothian .	3,436	.	16,328
and as President of the	Lanark . . .	9,091	.	1,544
Council. Is Capt.-Gen. of	Kirkcudbright	1,000	.	100
the Queen's Bodyguard of	Peebles . .	272	.	318
Scottish Archers.	Fife . . .	60	.	15
		460,108	.	217,163

Lord Dalkeith has out of this total 77*l.* standing in his name. The Duke is also credited with minerals, quarries, &c., to the value of 4,091*l.* per annum, and with Granton Harbour, valued at 10,601*l.*

** CARRICK-BUCHANAN, David Carrick, C.B., of Drum-
pellier House, Coatbridge, N.B.

			acres.		*g. an. val.*
Coll. Trin. Cam.	Argyll	. .	18,000	.	2,575
Club. Army and Navy.	Lanark	. .	8,549	.	8,693
b. 1825, s. 1840, m. 1849.	Renfrew	. .	2,472	.	3,406
	Linlithgow	. .	1,345	.	706
	Stirling	. .	868	.	350
	Dumbarton	.	97	.	140

Served in the Scots Greys.   31,331 . 15,870
Exclusive of 16,424*l.* for minerals.

** LEITH-BUCHANAN, Sir George Hector, Bart., of Dry-
grange, Melrose, N.B., &c.

Club. Army and Navy, Gun,	Dumbarton	.	1,778	.	1,416
New Edin.	Roxburgh	. .	1,315	.	1,724
b. 1833, s. 1842, m. 1st 1856,	Stirling	. .	1,314	.	422
2nd 1861.	Berwick	. .	128	.	275

Served in 17th Lancers.   4,535 . 3,837

BUCKINGHAM and CHANDOS, Duke of, G.C.S.I., Stowe,
Buckingham, &c. ⚲

			acres.		*g. an. val.*
Coll. Eton, Ch. Ch. Oxon.	Bucks	. .	9,511	.	15,789
Club. Carlton, Athenæum.	Cornwall	. .	498	.	1,298
b. 1823, s. 1861, m. 1851.	Middlesex	. .	232	.	634
	Oxford	. .	236	.	351
	Somerset	. .	5	.	8

     10,482 . 18,080

Served as Pres. of Privy Council. Sec. of State for the Colonies,
was Governor of Madras. Sat for Buckingham.

BUCKINGHAMSHIRE, Earl of, Richmond Lodge, Sidmouth, &c.

Coll. Westminster, Brase-	Co. Limerick	.	2,082	.	2,200
nose, Oxon.	Bucks	. .	3,113	.	3,509
b. 1793, s. 1849, m. 1816,	Devon	. .	8	.	181
2nd 1826.					

     5,203 . 5,890

BUCHAN, Miss, of Auchmacoy.	Aberdeen	3,408	.	2,972
BUCHANAN, A., of Auchentorlie.	Dumb.	2,014	.	2,820

BUCKLEY, Sir E., Bart., Assignees of.

	acres.	g. an. val.
Merioneth . .	8,737 .	3,924
Montgomery .	2,170 .	584
York, W.R. .	287 .	329
Lancashire .	91 .	10,144
Cheshire . .	1 .	9
	11,286 .	14,990

Large portions of these estates were in the market, and some (query, nearly all) are sold.

BUCKLEY, Nathaniel, of Ryecroft, Ashton-under-Lyme, &c.

Club. Reform.	Tipperary . .	13,260 .	3,585
b. 1823.	Limerick . .	7,563 .	1,208
	Lancashire .	62 .	230
	Cheshire . .	2 .	1,299
	Derby . . .	11 .	504
Sat for Stalybridge.		20,898 .	6,826

BUCKWORTH, Everard Theophilus, of Cockley Cley Hall, Swaffham.

b. 1866, s. 1873.	Norfolk . . .	3,614 .	1,728
	Lincoln . . .	2,701 .	5,246
	Middlesex . .	1 .	162
		6,316 .	7,136

WILLIAMS-BULKELEY, Sir Richard Mostyn Lewis, Bart., of Baron Hill, Beaumaris.

b 1833, s. 1875, m. 1st, 1857,	Anglesea . .	16,516 .	17,997
2nd 1866.	Carnarvon . .	13,362 .	3,141
Served in Royal Horse Guards.		29,878 .	21,138

BULLER, John Francis, of Morval, Liskeard. ♨.

Coll. Magd. Oxon.	Cornwall . .	3,617 .	3,756
b. 1818, s. 1849.	Devon . . .	977 .	1,258
		4,594 .	5,014

BUDDICOM, W. B., of Penbedw. Den., Fl. 2,511 . 2,284

** BULLER, Col. Redvers Henry, C.B., C.M.G., V.C., of
Downes, Crediton. ♣.   *acres.*   *g. an. val.*
Coll. Eton,   Devon . . .   2,942 .   7,001
Club. Arthur's, A. and N., Cornwall . .   2,147 .   7,136
N. & M., Windham.   ─────────────────
b. 1839, s. 1874.   5,089 . 14,137
Served in 60th Rifles in Chinese and Ashantee wars, Red River
Expedition, Kaffir war of 1878, and in Zulu war ; is A.D.C. to the
Queen.

***TROYTE-BULLOCK, George, of Sedghill House, Shaftesbury.
Coll. Eton, Ch. Ch. Oxon. Dorset . . .   2,899 .   3,370
Club. Boodle's.   Somerset . .   800 .   1,926
b. 1829, m. 1st 1856,   ─────────────────
2nd 1860.   3,699 .   5,296

** BULWER, William Earle Gascoyne, of Quebec House,
East Dereham, &c.
Coll. Winchester.   Norfolk . . . 8,943 . 10,885
Club. Union, Hanover Sq.   Kent. . . .   108 .   142
b. 1829, s. 1877, m. 1855.   ─────────────────
                                             9,051 . 11,027
Served in Scots Guards in the Crimea; severely wounded at Alma.

** BUNBURY, Sir Charles James Fox, Bart., of Barton Hall,
Bury St. Edmunds. ♣.

Coll. Trin. Cam.   Suffolk . . .   9,831 . 11,924
Club. Athenæum.   b. 1809, s. 1860, m. 1844.

** BURDETT, Col. Sir Francis, Bart., of Ramsbury Manor,
Westbury, &c. ♣.
Coll. Charterho., Tr. Cam. Derby . . .   5,923 . 12,065
Club. U. Ser., Carlton.   Berks . . .   6,541 .   6,243
b. 1813, s. 1880, m. 1st 1842, Wilts . . . 3,958 .   4,514
2nd 1867. Leicester . .   2,258 .   2,880
Warwick . .   1,885 .   2,994
Stafford . . .   419 .   689
                                            ─────────────────
Served in 17th Lancers.   20,984 . 29,385

♣. BULLER, J. H., of Down Hall. Cor., Sur. 2,005 . 7,151
BULLOCK, W. H., of Faulkbourne. Essex.   2,865 . 4,661

* BURDON, Rev. John, of Castle Eden, Ferryhill, Durham.

		acres.	g. an. val.
Coll. Univ. Oxon.	Durham . .	4,000 .	5,000

b. 1811, s. 1875, m. 1847.

BURGES, John Ynyr, of Parkanaur, Dungannon.

Coll. Brasenose, Oxon.	Tyrone . . .	2,485 .	1,958
Club. Carlton.	Armagh . . .	729 .	742
b. 1798, s. 1838, m. 1833.	Co. Down . .	430 .	525
	Essex . . .	896 .	2,975
		4,540 .	6,200

** BURKE, Sir Henry George, Bart., of Marble Hill, Loughrea, Co. Galway.

Coll. Oscott.	Galway . .	25,258 .	7,564
b. 1859, s. 1880.	Roscommon .	2,230 .	775
		27,488 .	8,339

** PEGGE-BURNELL, Col. Edward Strelley, of Winkbourn Hall, Southwell, Notts.

Coll. Eton, Ch. Ch. Oxon.	Notts . . .	3,188 .	3,903
Club. Carlton, Guards.	Derby . . .	1,541 .	1,936
b. 1835, s. 1878.	Lincoln . .	818 .	1,153
Serves in Coldstream	York, W.R. .	332 .	307
Guards.			
		5,879 .	7,299

*** BURNETT, Sir Robert, Bart., of Crathes, Aberdeen.

Coll. Edinb. Ch. Ch.	Kincardine .	12,025 .	5,006
Oxon.	Aberdeen . .	84 .	108
Club. Arthur's, Trav.			
b. 1833, s. 1876, m. 1864.		12,109	5,114

BURGOYNE, Sir J. M., Bart., of Sutton.	Beds.	2,375 .	3,547
BURNETT, Rev. A. G., of Kemnay.	Aber.	4,486 .	2,719
BURNETT, J. C., of Monboddo.	Kincardine.	3,013 .	2,542

*** BURNS, JOHN WILLIAM, of Kilmahew, Cardross, N.B., &c.

		acres.	*g. an. val.*
Coll. Trinity, Cambridge.	Dumbarton	5,568	8,026
b. 1837, s. 1871, m. 1861.			

Exclusive of mine rents amounting to 1,963*l.*, and of some house property in Glasgow.

** BURR, DANIEL HIGFORD DAVALL, of Aldermaston Ct., Reading.

Coll. Eton, Ch. Ch. Oxon.	Gloucester	1,200	2,200
Club. Carlton.	Berks	2,778	3,054
b. 1811, s. 1836, m. 1839.	Hereford	500	750
Sat for Hereford.	Hants	51	37
	Monmouth	6	12
		4,535	6,053

BURRELL, SIR WALTER WYNDHAM, BART., of West Grinstead Park, Horsham, &c.

Club. Carlton.	Sussex	9,294	9,367
b. 1814, s. 1876, m. 1847. Sits for Shoreham.			

*** BURROUGHES, HENRY RANDALL, of Burlington Hall, Norwich, &c.

Coll. Harrow.	Norfolk	7,414	13,244
b. 1863, s. 1872.			

995*l.* of this rental is returned as belonging to his mother.

** BURROWES, ROBERT JAMES, of Stradone House, Cavan.

b. 1845, s. 1881, m. 1876.	Co. Cavan	9,572	5,426
Served in 1st Dragoon Guards.			

BURTON, FRANCIS NATHANIEL VALENTINE, of Carrigaholt Castle, Kilrush, &c.

b. 1842, s. 1867, m. 1866.	Co. Clare	9,169	4,392
Served in 18th Foot.			

BURRELL, B., of Broompark.	Nhd., Som.	2,208	3,444
TRAILL-BURROUGHS, GEN., of Rousay.	Orkney	6,693	2,116
S. BURTON, JOHN, of Longner.	Salop	2,244	4,653

** BURTON, WILLIAM FITZ-WILLIAM, of Burton Hall, Carlow.

		acres.	g. an. val.
Coll. Eton.	Carlow . . .	5,964 .	4,057
Club. Kildare St. Dublin.	Kildare . . .	577 .	411
b. 1826, s. 1844, m. 1848.	Queen's Co. .	155 .	117
Served in 4th Light	Dublin . . .	55 .	115
Dragoons.	Wicklow . .	32 .	40
	King's Co. .	587 .	265
		7,370 .	5,005

* BUTE, MARQUIS OF, K.T., Mount Stuart, Rothesay, N.B., &c.

		acres.	g. an. val.
Coll. Harrow, Ch. Ch. Ox.	Glamorgan .	21,402 .	100,000
Club. Car., White's, Marlb.,	Durham . .	1,953 .	5,424
Trav., St. Stephen's.	Bedford . .	72 .	256
b. 1847, s. 1848, m. 1872.	Brecon . . .	59 .	170
	Monmouth .	12 .	19
	Ayrshire . .	43,734 .	22,756
	Bute . . .	29.279 .	19,574
	Wigtown . .	20,157 .	2,936

Exclusive of 2,506*l.* for minerals in
Ayrshire.   116,668 . 151,135

Nearly all the Glamorgan estate stands in the name of the late Lord Bute's trustees, and is credited in the return with some 80,000*l.* per annum more than it really produces, viz., 180,286*l.*

*** BUTLER, THE MISSES ANNA, SOPHIA, and HENRIETTA, of Castle Crine, Sixmilebridge.

		acres.	g. an. val.
s. 1857.	Tipperary . .	465 .	185
	Co. Clare . .	11,389 .	3,859
		11,854 .	4,044

*** BUTLER, SIR THOMAS PIERCE, BART., of Ballin Temple, Tullow, Co. Carlow.

Coll. Cheltenham.	Co. Carlow .	6,538 .	4,310

Club. Junior Carlton, Kildare St. Dublin.
b. 1836, s. 1862, m. 1864.
Served in 56th and 24th Foot in the Crimea.

BURTON, W. SCHOOLCROFT, of Fogga-thorpe. York, Berks, Beds	2,085 .	2,694
BUSHE, G. P., of Glencairn. Kilk., Watfd.	2,366 .	2,051
BUSTARD, E., of Belville. Donegal . .	10,249 .	2,576

** BUTTER, Archibald, of Faskally, Pitlochry, N.B.

			acres.	g. an. val.
Coll.	Edin. H. S. & Univ.	Perth . . .	17,586 .	5,670

Club. New Edin. b. 1805, s. 1805, m. 1834.

BUXTON, Sir Robert Jacob, Bart., of Shadwell Lodge, Thetford.

Coll.	Eton, Ch. Ch. Oxon.	Norfolk . .	9,309 .	5,373
Club.	Car., St. Jas., Bood.,	Wilts . . .	801 .	1,727
	St. Stephen's.	Suffolk . . .	80 .	160

b. 1829, s. 1842, m. 1865.
Sits for S. Norfolk.

		10,190 .	7,260

* BUXTON, Sir Thomas Fowell, Bart., of Warlies, Waltham Abbey, Essex.

Coll.	Harrow, Trin. Cam.	Norfolk . . .	2,152 .	2,809
Club.	Brooks's, Uni. Univ.	Essex . . .	1,008 .	1,960

b. 1837, s. 1858, m. 1862.
Sat for King's Lynn.

		3,160 .	4,769

BYNG, Col. Alfred Molyneux, of Quendon Hall, Bishop Stortford.

Club.	Guards', Trav.	Essex . . .	2,081 .	2,935
b. 1840, s. 1881, m. 1870.		Cumberland .	1,670 .	669

Served in Gren. Guards.

		3,751 .	3,604

MOIR-BYRES, George, of Tonley House, Aberdeen, N.B., &c.

Coll.	Edinb. Univ.	Aberdeen . .	4,623 .	3,527

Club. Northern, Aberd. b. 1813, s. 1881, m. 1854.

CADDELL, Robert O'Ferrall, of Harbourstown, Balbriggan.

Coll.	Stonyhurst	Co. Sligo . .	3,464 .	1,153
Club.	Arthur's, Windham.	Roscommon .	3,341 .	1,652
b. 1810, s. 1856.		Co. Meath . .	1,372 .	1,375
		Co. Dublin. .	7 .	10

		8,184 .	4,190

BUTLER, A., of Ballyline. Clare . . . . 7,460 . 2,390

BYRON, E., of Coulsdon. Surrey, Middlesex 2,130 . 2,496

BYRON, Hon. Mrs., of Langford Grove.
    Essex, Notts . . . . 2,196 . 3,729

CADMAN, Mrs., of Crosshouse. York., Linc. 2,099 . 3,364

CAITHNESS, EARL OF, Barrogill Castle, Wick, N.B.

		acres.	*g. an. val*
Coll. Magd. Cam.	Caithness . .	14,460 .	4.478
b. 1858, s. 1881.	Herts . . .	613 .	973
		15,073 .	5,451

CALCRAFT, WILLIAM MONTAGU, of Rempstone Hall, Wareham.

Coll. Trin. Cam.	Dorset . . .	4,569 .	4,503
Club. Arthur's.	Kent . . .	285 .	1,907
b. 1834, s. 1880.			
		4,854 .	6,410

** CALEDON, EARL OF, Caledon, Tyrone, &c.

Coll. Harrow,Ch.Ch.Oxon.	Tyrone . .	29,236 .	16,518
Club. Carlton, Sackv. St.	Armagh . . .	2,877 .	3,236
Dublin.	Herts . . .	1,947 .	2,567
b. 1846, s. 1855.			
Served in 1st Life Guards.		34,060 .	22,321

The English property belongs to the Dowager Countess.

CALLANDER, GEORGE FREDERICK WILLIAM, of Ardkinglas, Cairndow, Glasgow.

Coll. Eton.	Argyll . . .	51,670 .	5,626
b. 1848, s. 1851, m. 1876.	Stirling . . .	601 .	1,885
		52,271 .	7,511

** CALLANDER, HENRY, of Preston Hall, Edinburgh.

b. 1862, s. 1865.	Midlothian .	4,869 .	6,810
	Haddington .	919 .	2,169
	Stirling . . .	95 .	313
		5,883 .	9,292

Mr. CALLANDER's minerals are valued at 337*l.* per annum.

CALDECOTT, C. M., of Holbrook. North-ampton, Warwick, Oxon.	2,382 .	5,424

CALLEY, THOMAS CHARLES PLEYDELL, of Burderop Park, Swindon.

		acres.		*g. an. val.*
Coll. Harrow,Ch.Ch.Oxon. Wiltshire	. .	3,444	.	4,970

Club. White's, Arthur's. b. 1856, s. 1881.
 Serves in 1st Life Guards.

CALTHORPE, LORD, Elvetham Park, Winchfield.

				acres.		*g. an. val.*
Coll. Eton.		Warwick	. .	2,073	.	113,707
Club. Brooks's,White's,Tra.,		Norfolk .	. .	2,559	.	3,306
Garrick.		Hants	. .	1,390	.	4,404
b. 1826, s. 1868.		Suffolk .	. .	235	.	310
		Stafford	. .	197	.	857
		Worcester .	.	16	.	44
				6,470	.	122,628

 Sat for E. Worcestershire.

This (Warwickshire) is one of the cases specially referred to in the Return, the "ground landlord" being credited with the whole rental. Lord C. is Lord of the Manor of Edgbaston, the Belgravia of Birmingham, which fully accounts for the enormous rental of 113,000*l.*

CAMDEN, MARQUIS, Wilderness Park, Sevenoaks.

				acres.		*g. an. val.*
b. 1872, s. 1872.		Kent	. . .	7,214	.	9,836
		Brecon .	. .	6,430	.	3,470
		Sussex .	. .	3,755	.	3,073
				17,399	.	16,379

** CAMERON, DONALD ("Lochiel"), of Achnacarry Castle, Fort William.

				acres.		*g. an. val.*
Coll. Harrow.		Inverness	. .	109,574	.	7,830
Club. Carlton,White's,Trav.		Argyll	. .	16,000	.	2,462
b. 1835, s. 1858, m. 1875.		Bucks .	. .	434	.	429
				126,008	.	10,721

 Served as Attaché in China and at Berlin; was a Groom in Waiting. Sits for Inverness-shire.

HOLLWAY-CALTHROP, H. C.,ofStanhoe.

		acres.		*g. an. val.*
Norfolk		2,033	.	2,512
CALVERLEY, E., of Oulton Hall. York .		2,401	.	8,334

*** CAMMELL (late), CHARLES, of Norton Hall, Sheffield, &c.

		acres.	g. an. val.
d. 1879.	Derby . . .	4,860	3,780
	Hants . . .	1,482	1,902
	Sussex . . .	193	122
	York, W.R. .	28	121
		6,563	5,925

These estates have been split up among his sons.

** CAMOYS, LORD, Stonor, Henley-on-Thames. 🐚.

b. 1856, s. 1881, m. 1881.	Oxford . . .	4,500	5,000
	Bucks . . .	900	1,000
	Stafford . . .	300	1,321
	Leicester . .	810	1,268
	Warwick . .	230	240
		6,740	8,829

CAMPBELL, SIR ARCHIBALD CAMPBELL, BART., of Blythswood House, Renfrew, &c.

Club. Carlton, Guards.
b. 1835, s. 1868, m. 1864.
Served in Scots Fus. Gds.
in the Crimean War.
Sat for Renfrewshire.

Argyll . . .	14,032	2,361
Renfrew . .	1,854	4,094
	15,886	6,455

Exclusive of 1,906*l.* for minerals.

** CAMPBELL, COLIN GEORGE, of Stonefield, Tarbert, N.B.

b. 1811, s. 1857, m. 1839.   Argyll . . . 35,186 . 5,813

** CAMPBELL, DUNCAN, of Lochnell, Bonaw, N.B.

Coll. Harrow.   Argyll . . . 35,000 . 6,801
Club. Uni. Ser., Ed.   b. 1806, s. 1855.
Served in H.E.I.C. Civil Service.

PICKARD-CAMBRIDGE, H., of Bloxworth. Gloucester, Dorset	3,932	2,202
CAMERON, MRS., of Barcaldine. Argyll .	20,000	2,078
CAMERON, MAJOR T. M., of Garth. Zetld.	24,363	2,035
CAMPBELL, C., of Colgrain. Dumbarton .	2,124	2,429

** GARDEN-CAMPBELL, Francis William, of Troup House, Banff, N.B., &c.

			acres.	g. an. val.
Coll. Eton.	Banff	. .	9,547 .	5,794
Club. Army and Navy.	Perth	. .	10,516 .	1,620

b. 1840, s. 1848.
Served in Scots Fus. Guards.   20,063 . 7,414

FLETCHER-CAMPBELL, Capt. Henry John, C.B., of Bol-quhan House, Stirling, N.B.

Club. U. Ser., New, Edin.	Stirling	. .	5,679 .	3,185
b. 1837, s. 1877.	Perth	. .	5 .	97

Served in the Royal Navy, in the Baltic
(1854–5), and with the Naval Brigade   5,684 . 3,282
during the Zulu War.

** HUME-CAMPBELL, Sir Hugh, Bart., of Marchmont House, Dunse, N.B.
Coll. Eton, Trin. Cam.   Berwick . . 20,180 . 17,976
Club. Carl., Travellers'.
b. 1812, s. 1833, m. 1st 1834, 2nd 1841.
Sat for Berwickshire.

*** CAMPBELL, James Alexander, of Stracathro, Brechin, N.B.

Coll. Glas. H. Sch. & Uni.	Forfar	. . .	3,846 .	5,901
Club. Carlton.	Lanark	. . .	2 .	4,956

b. 1825, s. 1876, m. 1854.
Sits for Glasgow and Aberdeen Universities.   3,848 . 10,857
The Lanark property is entirely situate in Glasgow.

*** CAMPBELL, John, of Strachur Park, Cairndow, N.B.
Club. New, Edin.   Argyll . . . 24,593 . 3,376
b. 1848, s. 1874, m. 1876.

** CAMPBELL, John Livingston, of Achalader, Blairgowrie, N.B.
Club. Carlton.   Perth . . . 4,150 . 3,140

CAMPBELL, Adm. C., of Barbreck.   Argyll 10,369 . 2,461
CAMPBELL, Lt.-Col. D., of South Hall.
  Argyll, York . . . . 19,842 . 2,351
CAMPBELL, Jas., of Jura.   Argyll . . . 55,000 . 2,914
CAMPBELL, Duncan, of Inverneil.   Argyll 11,810 . 2,977
CAMPBELL, John, of Kilberry.   Argyll . 20,000 . 2,173

*** CAMPBELL, LADY (of Succoth), of Garscube, Glasgow, N.B.

		acres.	g. an. val.
m. 1858, s. 1874.	Argyll . . .	6,787 .	1,216
	Dumbarton .	2,478 .	6,098
	Stirling . . .	906 .	1,620
	Midlothian .	233 .	1,649
	Lanark . . .	197 .	725
		10,601 .	11,308

Exclusive of 6,608*l.* for mines.

** CAMERON-CAMPBELL, MRS., of Fassifern, Fort William
(res. Inverawe, Oban, N.B.)

s. 1869, m. 1844.	Inverness . .	74,000 .	4,827
	Argyll . . .	9,500 .	831
		83,500 .	5,658

CAMPBELL, ROBERT, of Buscot Park, Farringdon.

Club. Reform, Union, City.	Berkshire . .	4,183 .	8,398
b. 1811, m. 1835.	Wilts . . .	144 .	580
		4,327 .	8,978

Sat for Helston.

CAMPERDOWN, EARL OF, Camperdown House, Dundee,
N.B., &c.

Coll. Eton, Balliol, Oxon.	Forfar . . .	6,770 .	8,241
Club. St. James's, Brooks's.	Perth . . .	7,122 .	3,479
b. 1841, s. 1867.		13,892 .	11,720

Served as Lord in Waiting and as a Lord of the Admiralty.

*** CAMPION, WILLIAM HENRY, of Danny Park, Hurstpier-
point.

Coll. Eton.	Sussex . . .	3,468 .	4,124
b. 1836, s. 1869, m. 1869.	Essex . . .	1,975 .	2,099
	Kent	1,389 .	1,668
Served in 72nd and 53rd Foot in the			
Crimea, and during Indian Mutiny.		6,832 .	7,891

CAMPBELL, R. F. F., of Craigie.	Ayr . .	2,099 .	3,770
CAMPBELL, R. M., of Auchmannoch.	Ayr	3,928 .	2,914

*** CANTERBURY, Viscount, Witchingham Hall, Norwich,&c.

		acres.		*g. an. val.*
Coll. Har., Magd. Cam.	Norfolk . . .	5,177	.	8,399

Club. Marlb., White's. b. 1839, s. 1877, m. 1872.

Served as Private Secretary to his father when Governor of Trinidad and of Victoria.

*** CAPRON, Rev. George Halliley, of Southwick Hall, Oundle.

Coll. St. John's, Cam.	Northampton .	3,846	.	4,795

b. 1816, s. 1872, m. 1853.

CARBERY, Lord, Castle Freke, Rosscarbery, Co. Cork, &c.

b. 1810, s. 1845, m. 1852.	Cork . . .	13,692	.	6,179
	Queen's Co. .	2,919	.	1,344
	Limerick . .	2,724	.	2,992
	Northampton .	1,667	.	1,985
	Dorset . . .	244	.	350
		21,246	.	12,850

** CARDEN, Sir John Craven, Bart., of Templemore Abbey, Tipperary.

Coll. Eton. Trin. Cam.	Tipperary . .	7,850	.	9,500

b. 1854, s. 1879.

** CARDIGAN, Countess of (Countess de Lancastre of Portugal), Deane Park, Wandsford, &c.

s. 1868, m. 1st 1858,	Northampton .	7,210	.	9,561
2nd 1873.	Leicester . .	2,931	.	5,238
	York, W.R. .	5,583	.	20,558
		15,724	.	35,357

GORDON-CANNING, P., of Hartpury. Glou.	2,813	.	4,438
CANNON, W. J., of Castlegrove. Gal., Mayo	5,973	.	2,958
CARDEN, A. M., of Barnane. Tipperary .	2,709	.	2,001

** CARDROSS, Lord, Amondell, Broxburn, Linlithgow, N.B.

			acres.		*g. an. val.*
Coll.	Harrow.	Linlithgow . .	2,995	.	5,693
Club.	Carlton, White's.	Midlothian . .	76	.	65
b. 1850, m. 1876.					
			3,071	.	5,758

Lord Cardross has also minerals to the annual value of 3,635*l.*

CARDWELL, Viscount, Ellerbeck Hall, Chorley.

Coll.	Winch., Ball. Oxon.	Lincolnshire .	2,523	.	3,574
Club.	Athenæum, Reform.	Lancashire . .	1,317	.	3,799
b. 1813, m. 1838.		Warwickshire .	717	.	1,488
			4,557	.	8,861

Served as President of the Board of Trade, Chief Secretary for Ireland, Chancellor of the Duchy of Lancaster, and Secretary of State for the Colonies and for War. Sat for Clitheroe, Liverpool, and Oxford (city).

*** CAREW, Edmund Geo., of Crowcombe Court, Taunton, &c.

Coll.	Eton.	Somerset . .	4,577	.	4,654
Club.	Uni. Eton and Har.	Salop . . .	1,165	.	1,547
b. 1860, s. 1874.		Pembroke . .	1,249	.	1,557
			6,991	.	7,758

* CAREW, the Misses E. A. and B., of Haccombe, Buckfastleigh, Devon.

s. 1874.	Devon . . .	10,889	.	15,148

** CAREW, Lord, Castleborough, Enniscorthy. ♨.

b. 1860, s. 1881.	Wexford . .	17,830	.	9,070
	Waterford . .	2,038	.	2,130
	Queen's Co. .	1,098	.	662
		20,966	.	11,862

This rental was in 1878 somewhat higher.

* POLE-CAREW, William Henry, of Antony, Devonport.

Coll.	Charterho, Oriel, Ox.	Cornwall . .	4,288	.	6,401

Club. Carlton. b. 1811, s. 1835, m. 1838. Sat. for E. Cornwall.

CARINGTON, LORD, Wycombe Abbey, High Wycombe.

			acres.	g. an. val.
Coll.	Eton, Trin. Cam.	Bucks . . .	16,128 .	26,805
Club.	White's, Bood., Turf,	Lincoln . .	9,656 .	15,418
	Brooks's, Gar., Ref.	Beds . . .	25 .	31
b. 1843, s. 1868, m. 1878.				
			25,809 .	42,254

Is Capt. Hon. Corps of Gentlemen at Arms and Joint Hereditary Lord Great Chamberlain.

Served in Royal Horse Guards. Sat for Wycombe.

The return gives the DOWAGER LADY C. out of this total a rental of 2,154*l.* in Bucks.

CARLINGFORD, *see* WALDEGRAVE.

CARLISLE, EARL OF, Castle Howard, York, &c. ♲.

b. 1808, s. 1864.	Cumberland .	47,730 .	16,850
	Northumberland	17,780 .	18,249
	York, N.R. .	13,030 .	14,502
		78,540 .	49,601

CARLYON (infant son of Horatio), of Place Ho., Falmouth.

b. 187–, s. 1876.	Cornwall . .	4,962 .	5,279

This estate will be found inserted under "Spry."

** CARLYON, MAJOR, of Tregrehan, Par Station, Cornwall.

Coll.	Ch. Ch. Oxon.	Cornwall . .	3,050 .	4,047
Club.	Boodle's, Army and	Middlesex . .	200 .	400
	Navy, R.Y.S. b. 1822, s. 1854.			
Served in 3rd Dragoon Guards.			3,250 .	4,447

** THOMSON-CARMICHAEL, MAURICE, of Eastend, Lanark, N.B., &c.

Club.	Jun. Uni. Ser., New	Ayr	1,812 .	1,628
	Edinburgh.	Lanark . . .	2,125 .	2,058
b. 1841, s. 1875, m. 1871.				
Served in 92nd Highlanders.			3,937 .	3,686

Exclusive of 339*l.* mine rents in Ayrshire, which with the rest of the property in that county stands in his mother's name.

GIBSON-CARMICHAEL, Rev. Sir William Henry, Bart.,
  Castle Craig, Dolphinton, N.B., &c.

			acres.		*g. an. val.*
Coll. Peterhouse, Cam.	Peebles	. .	8,756	.	5,795
Club. Oxford and Cam.	Midlothian	.	732	.	4,624
b. 1827, s. 1855, m. 1858.					
			9,488	.	10,419

** CARNARVON, Earl of, Highclere Castle, Newbury, &c.

Coll. Eton, Ch. Ch.	Somerset	. .	12,800	.	6,654
Oxon.	Hants	. . .	9,340	.	6,500
Club. Trav., Ath., Carl.,	Wilts	. . .	8	.	96
St. Stephen's.	Notts	. . .	13,247	.	23,825
b. 1831, s. 1849, m. 1861	Devon	. . .	68	.	36
and 1879.	Derby	. . .	120	.	100
Served as Sec. of State for the Colonies.					
			35,583	.	37,211

*** CARNEGIE, David, of Stronvar House, Lochearnhead,
  N.B., &c.

Coll. Eton.	Middlesex	. .	466	.	887
Club. Carlton.	Herts	. . .	314	.	404
b. 1813, m. 1st 1839,	Perth	. . .	22,205	.	3,558
2nd 1845.	Selkirk	. . .	9	.	10
			22,994	.	4,859

Exclusive of the value of a house on each English property.

** LINDSAY-CARNEGIE, Henry Alexander, of Boysack,
  Arbroath, N.B.

b. 1836, s. 1860, m. 1862.   Forfarshire . 3,670 . 5,171
  Served in Bengal Engineers during Indian Mutiny.

** CARNEGY, Patrick Alexander Watson, of Lour, Forfar,
  N.B.

Coll. Harrow.   Forfarshire . 4,206 . 5,024
Club. Ar. and Na., Boodle's,
          New Edinburgh. b. 1836, s. 1838, m. 1865.
Served in Queen's Bays and 15th Hussars during the Indian Mutiny.

** CARPENTER, Hon. Walter Cecil, of Kiplin Park,
  Northallerton. 🐟.

Coll. Harrow.   York, N.R. . 4,186 . 6,785
Club. Carlton, Uni. Ser. b. 1834, s. 1868, m. 1869.
Sat for Co. Waterford.   Served in Royal Navy during the
Russian War, at the taking of Kinburn and the Straits of Yenikale.

CARRUTHERS, WILLIAM, of Dormont, Lockerbie, N.B.

		acres.		g. an. val.
b. 1867, s. 1878.	Dumfries . .	6,355	.	4,698
	York, W.R. .	491	.	116
		6,846	.	4,814

CARTER, HENRY TILSON SHAEN, of Watlington Park, Oxfordshire.

Coll. Eton, Sandhurst.	Oxford . . .	537	.	569
b. 1845, s. 1875, m. 1867.	Co. Meath . .	166	.	151
	Co. Westmeath	1,137	.	669
	Co. Mayo . .	40,698	.	2,764
Served in the 17th Lancers.		42,538	.	4,153

BONHAM-CARTER, JOHN, of Adhurst, St. Mary's, Petersfield.

Coll. Trin. Cam.	Hants . . .	5,621	.	6,258
Club. Brooks's, Athenæum.	Sussex . . .	1	.	2
b. 1817, s. 1838, m. 1st 1848,				
2nd 1864.		5,622	.	6,260

Served as a Lord of the Treasury and Chairman of Committees in the House of Commons. Sat for Winchester.

** CARTWRIGHT, RICHARD AUBREY, of Edgcote, Banbury.

Coll. Charterhouse.	Northampton .	2,587	.	4,544
Club. Arthur's, Trav.	Oxford . . .	415	.	891
b. 1811, s. 1856, m. 1848.				
Served in the Royal Navy.		3,002	.	5,435

CARTWRIGHT, WILLIAM CORNWALLIS, of Aynhoe, Brackley.

Club. Brooks's, Athenæum.	Northampton .	4,396	.	9,155
b. 1826, s. 1850, m. 185–.	Oxford . . .	1,140	.	2,413
Sits for Oxfordshire.		5,536	.	11,568

CARROLL, T., of Mitchelstown. Limerick, Tipperary, Cork	2,492	.	2,026
CARRUTHERS, J.B., of The Gondra. Mon.	2,142	.	2,325
LESLIE - MELVILLE - CARTWRIGHT, T.R.B., of Melville House. Fife, Oxon.	2,464	.	3,703

*** CARYSFORT, Earl of, K.P., Glenart Castle, Arklow, &c.

		acres.		*g. an. val.*
Coll. Eton, Trin. Cam.	Hunts . . .	3,972	.	7,497
Club. Kildare St.,Dublin,	Northampton .	2,270	.	3,553
White's, Brooks's.	Co. Wicklow .	16,674	.	10,375
b. 1836, s. 1872, m. 1860.	Dublin . . .	1,250	.	8,123
	Kildare . . .	1,748	.	1,527
		25,914	.	31,075

CASTEJA, Marquis de, Scarisbrick Hall, Ormskirk.
b. 1805, s. 1872, m. 1835. Lancashire . 14,764 . 27,284

*** CASTLEMAINE, Lord, Moydrum Castle, Athlone, &c.

Club. Carlton, Sackv. St.	Westmeath .	11,444	.	8,669
b. 1826, s. 1869, m. 1857.	Roscommon .	597	.	250
Served in 41st Foot.		12,041	.	8,919

** CASTLESTUART, Earl of, Stuart Hall, Stewartstown, Co. Tyrone, &c.

b. 1837, s. 1874, m. 1866.	Tyrone . . .	32,615	.	11,768
	Cavan . . .	2,260	.	1,345
		34,875	.	13,113

The return gives the Cavan estate to his aunt, the Dowager Countess (Emmeline) of Castlestuart.

*** CASTLETOWN, Lord, Lisduff, Templemore, Queen's Co.

Coll. Eton.	Queen's Co. .	22,510	.	15,006
Club. Brooks's, Trav., Kild.	Sussex . . .	633	.	752
St., Sackv. St., Dub.				
b. 1809, s. 18—, m. 1830.		23,143	.	15,758

Served in the Army. Sat for Queen's Co.

** CATHCART, Earl, Thornton-le-Street, Thirsk.

Coll. Scottish Mil. Acad.	York, N. and			
Club. Carlton, Uni. Ser.	W R. . . .	4,114	.	6,491
b. 1828, s. 1859, m. 1850.	Stafford . . .	1,352	.	1,571
	Renfrew . .	88	.	567
Served in 23rd Foot.		5,554	.	8,629

CASEMENT, T., of Ballee. Ant., Lderry . 2,339 . 2,333

** CATHCART, Sir Reginald Archibald Edward, Bart., of Killochan Castle, Girvan, N.B., and (*jure uxoris*) of Cluny.

		acres.	g. an. val.
Coll. Harrow.	Ayrshire . .	13,118 .	7,000

Club. Guards, J. U. Service.
b. 1838, s. 1878, m. 1880.
    Served in Coldstream Guards and 68th Foot.

	acres.	g. an. val.
Aberdeen . .	20,395 .	13,713
Inverness . .	84,404 .	8,954
Nairn . . .	3,635 .	2,536
Banff . . .	2,735 .	2,724
Midlothian . .	701 .	2,116
Berwick . . .	484 .	1,145
	125,472 .	38,188

    The last six properties belong to Lady Cathcart, and are uncorrected.

*** CATOR, Albemarle, of Woodbastwick Hall, Norwich, &c.

		acres.	g. an. val.
Coll. Trin. Hall, Cam.	Norfolk . . .	2,463 .	2,820
Club. Carlton.	Kent . . .	1,673 .	16,476
b. 1836, s. 1868, m. 1859.		4,136 .	19,296

CAULFIELD, St. George Francis, of Donamon Castle, Co. Roscommon.

		acres.	g. an. val.
Club. Carlton.	Roscommon .	6,632 .	3,487
b. 1806, s. 1810, m. 1830.	Galway . . .	4,604 .	2,170
	Kilkenny . .	1,514 .	738
	Tipperary . .	824 .	682
	Tyrone . . .	558 .	344
		14,132 .	7,421

*** CAVE, Charles Daniel, of Cleeve Hill, Bristol, &c.

		acres.	g. an. val.
Coll. Exeter, Oxon.	Devon . . .	5,522 .	7,169
b. 1832, s. 1880, m. 1859.	Gloucester . .	1,154 .	2,516
	Somerset . .	270 .	575
		6,946 .	10,260

CAULFIELD, G., of Copeswood.	Lim. .	3,350 .	2.513
CAVAN, Earl of.	Mayo, Som., Herts. .	2,731 .	2,099

CAVENDISH, Henry Sheppard Hart, of Thornton Hall, Stony Stratford.

		acres.		*g. an. val.*
b. 1876, s. 1878.	Denbigh. . .	1,447	.	327
	Bucks . . .	3,379	.	6,066
	Stafford . . .	2,204	.	4,630
		7,030	.	11,023

CAWDOR, Earl of, Stackpoole, Pembroke, &c.

Coll. Eton, Ch. Ch. Oxon.	Carmarthen .	33,782	.	20,780
Club. Carlton, White's, Tra.	Pembroke . .	17,735	.	14,207
b. 1817, s. 1860, m. 1842.	Cardigan . .	21	.	55
Sat for Pembrokeshire.	Nairn . . .	46,176	.	7,882
	Inverness . .	3,943	.	1,738
		101,657	.	44,662

CAYLEY, Sir Digby, Bart., of High Hall, Brompton, York.

Coll. Trin. Cam.   York, N. and
Club. Carlton.   W.R. . . .   8,459 . 9,126
b. 1807, s. 1857, m. 1830.
 1,284*l.* of this amount is returned as Lady Cayley's.

*** SCOTT-CHAD, Joseph Stonehewer, of Thursford Hall, East Dereham, &c.

Coll. Harrow, Trin. Cam.   Norfolk . . .   6,242 . 9,364
Club. United University, United Eton and Harrow.
b. 1829, s. 1855 and 1873, m. 1856.

*** CHAFY-CHAFY, Rev. William Kyle Westwood, of Rous Lench Court, Evesham.

Coll. Ch. Ch. Oxon.	Worcester . .	3,001	.	5,289
Club. Junior Carlton.	Dorset . . .	284	.	318
b. 1841, s. 1864, m. 1862.	Somerset . .	181	.	311
	Suffolk . . .	463	.	511
		3,929	.	6,429

CHADWICK, J. de H. M., of Mavesyn.
 Stafford, Lancaster, Warwick . . . .   2,197 . 9,323

CHAINE, James, of Ballycraigy, Co. Antrim.

		acres.		g. an. val.
Club. Conser., Carlton, St.	Co. Antrim. .	5,010	.	4,972

Stephen's, Kild. St., and Sackv. St., Dublin.
b. 1841, m. 1863.   Sits for Co. Antrim.

CHALMERS, Patrick, of Aldbar Castle, Brechin, N.B.

			acres.		g. an. val.
b. 1841, s. 1868, m. 1871.	Forfar . . .	3,844	.	3,893

Served in 59th Foot.

CHALONER, Admiral Thomas, C.B., of Longhull Hall, Guisborough.

Club. United Service.	York, N.R. .	3,551	.	5,949

Served in the Royal Navy.   b. 1815.

** CHAMBERLAYNE, Tankerville, of Cranbury Park, Winchester, &c.

Coll. Eton, Magd. Oxon.	Hants . . .	11,000	.	16,788
b. 1840, s. 1876.	Leicester . .	1,350	.	2,199
	Oxon . . .	13	.	13
		12,363	.	19,000

** CHAPLIN, Henry, of Blankney Hall, Sleaford.

Coll. Har., Ch. Ch. Oxon.   Lincolnshire .   23,370 .   30,517
Club. Carlton, St. Stephen's.   b. 1840, s. 1859, m. 1876.
Sits for Mid-Lincolnshire.

** CHAPMAN, Sir Benjamin James, Bart., of Killua Castle. Clonmellon, Co. Westmeath.

Coll. Trinity, Dublin.	Westmeath .	9,516	.	6,532
Club. Reform, Kildare St.	Meath . . .	241	.	217
b. 1810, s. 1852, m. 1849.	Mayo . . .	3,600	.	50
Sat for Co. Westmeath.				
		13,357	.	6,799

CHALMERS (late), A., of Cluny. Banff .	3,009	.	2,505
INGLES - CHAMBERLAYNE, H., of Maugersbury. Glou., Ches.	2,803	.	3,450
CHAMPAGNÈ, A. H., of River Lyons. King's Co., Queen's Co., Corn., Sussex . . .	2,333	.	2,369
CHAMPERNOWNE, A., of Dartington. Dev.	2,385	.	3,388

** CHAPMAN, WILLIAM, of Southill, Delvin, Co. Westmeath.

			acres.	g. an. val.
Club.	Reform, Kildare St.,	Westmeath .	5,042 .	3,398
	Dublin.	Co. Meath .	1,386 .	1,217
b. 1812, m. 1841.		Co. Mayo . .	2,664 .	88
			9,092 .	4,703

CHARLEMONT, EARL OF, K.P., Roxburgh Castle, Moy, Co. Tyrone, &c.

			acres.	g. an. val.
Coll.	Trin. Cam.	Armagh . .	20,695 .	18,591
Club.	Bro., Ref., Trav., Ath.	Tyrone . . .	5,903 .	7,043
b. 1820, s. 1863, m. 1856.	Dublin . . .	222 .	700
Sat for Armagh.				
			26,820 .	26,334

** CHARLESWORTH, ALBANY HAWKE, of Chapelthorpe Hall, Wakefield, &c.

			acres.	g. an. val.
Coll.	Eton, Trin. Cam.	York,N.&W.R.	2,169 .	7,126
Club.	Cons., Oxf. and Cam.	Worcester . .	1,000 .	1,600
b. 1854, s. 1880.	Salop . . .	300 .	400
			3,469 .	9,126

CHARLEVILLE, COUNTESS OF, Charleville Forest, Tullamore.

s. 1875, m. 1854.   King's Co.   .   20,032 .   10,052

** CHARLTON, WILLIAM OSWALD, of Hesleyside, Bellingham.
b. 1850, s. 1880, m. 1873.   Northumberland 21,200   .   6,200
Is in the Diplomatic Service.

CHARTERIS, LADY MARGARET, of The Lodge, Cahir, Co. Tipperary.

		acres.	g. an. val.
b. 1834, m. 1858.	Peebles . . .	10 .	17
	Tipperary . .	16,616 .	11,635
	Huntingdon .	3 .	10
		16,629 .	11,662

CHAPMAN, E., of Hillend.   Chesh., York.   2,860 .   3,937
CHAYTOR, SIR W., BART., of Clervaux.
York., Durham . . . .   2,902 .   4,225
CHAYTOR, H., of Wilton Castle.   Durham   2,401 .   9,803

CHEAPE, George Clerk, of Wellfield, Strathmiglo, N.B.

		acres.	g. an. val.
Club. Union, New Edin. Fifeshire	. .	5,230	. 8,885

b. 1801, s. 1861, m. 1845.

*** CHEARNLEY, Henry Philip, of Salterbridge, Cappoquin, Co. Waterford.

Coll. Eton.	Waterford .	.	18,165	.	7,621

Club. Royal Irish.
b. 1852, s. 1879, m. 1879.

** CHESHAM, Lord, Latimer, Chesham, Bucks. ⚓.

Coll. Eton.	Bucks . . .	2,868	.	4,203
Club. Brooks's, Travellers'.	Huntingdon .	3,787	.	3,643
b. 1815, s. 1863, m. 1849.	Lancashire . .	2,365	.	3,654
	Lincoln . . .	1,688	.	3,093
	Herts . .	775	.	1,014
	Sussex . . .	1	.	12
	Northampton .	3	.	6

Served in 10th Royal Hussars.
Sat for Peterborough and for Bucks.   11,487 . 15,625

** CHESTER, Col. Charles Anthony, of Chicheley Hall, Newport Pagnell. ⚓.

b. 1816, s. 1879.   Bucks . . .   3,129 . 4,000

** CHESTERFIELD, Countess Dowager of, Bretby Park, Burton-on-Trent.

m. 1830, s. 1866.	Derby . . .	5,209	.	10,717
	Stafford . . .	8	.	43
		5,217	.	10,760

CHENEY, E., of Badger Hall. Salop, Essex	2,009	.	5,696
CHENEY, E. H., of Gaddesby. Leic., Staff.	2,723	.	4,348
CHERRY, G. C., of Denford House. Berks, Oxon	2,033	.	2,890
CHESTER, F., of Williamstown. Louth, Limerick, Meath	2,166	.	2,110
CHESTER, Miss, of Cartown. Louth, Mea.	2,412	.	2,046

* CHETWODE, Sir George, Bart., of Oakley Hall, Market Drayton, &c. 🐍.

		acres.	g. an. val.
Coll. Eton.	Stafford . . .	1,158 .	1,730
Club. Army and Navy.	Cheshire . .	1,617 .	3,361
b. 1823, s. 1873, m. 1868.	Salop . . .	917 .	1,345
Served in 8th Hussars in	Bucks . . .	413 .	635
Crimean War and Indian			
Mutiny.		4,105 .	7,071

CHETWODE, Mrs., of Chilton House, Thame.

m. 1st 18—, 2nd 1868.	Bucks . . .	6,241 .	8,816
	Glamorgan . .	5,399 .	4,820
	Oxford . . .	9 .	36
		11,649 .	13,672

CHETWYND, Sir George, Bart., of Grendon Hall, Atherstone. 🐍.

Club. Carlton, Gun.	Warwick . .	4,139 .	8,699
b. 1849, s. 1869, m. 1870.	Monmouth . .	1,066 .	1,063
	Stafford . . .	833 .	1,509
	Leicester . .	479 .	987
	Cheshire . .	109 .	187
		6,626 .	12,445

** CHICHESTER, Sir Arthur, Bart., of Youlston, Barnstaple. 🐍.

Coll. Eton.   Devon . . . 7,022 . 6,051
Club. Arthur's, Jun. Uni. Ser.   b. 1822, s. 1842, m. 1847.
  Served in 7th Hussars.

** CHICHESTER, Earl of, Stanmer, Lewes. 🐍.

Coll. Westminster, Trin.   Sussex . . . 16,232 . 13,650
  Cam.
Club. U. Ser., U. Uni.   b. 1804, s. 1826, m. 1828.
  Served in Royal Horse Guards, and as First Church Estates
Commissioner.

CHEVERS, M. J., of Killyan.	Gal., Mayo .	6,380 .	2,469
CHEYNE, Mrs., of Lismore.	Arg., Midlon.	2,402 .	2,052

CHICHESTER, Lady, of Arlington Court, Barnstaple. ♇.

		acres.	g. an. val.
s. 1881, m. 1865.	Devonshire .	5,317 .	4,737
	Montgomery .	597 .	553
	Cardigan . .	100 .	53
		6,014 .	5,343

*** CHICHESTER, Robert, of Hall, Barnstaple. ♇.

Coll. Eton, Worc. Oxon.	Devon . . .	4,426 .	4,293
b. 1804, s. 1835, m. 1826.	Cornwall . .	1,551 .	1,153
		5,977 .	5,446

** CHILDERS, John Walbanke, of Cantley Hall, Doncaster.

Coll. Eton, Ch. Ch. Oxon.	Cambridge .	7,402 .	12,587
Club. Reform.	York, W.R. .	5,709 .	5,711
b. 1798, m. 1st 1824,	Lincoln . .	222 .	471
2nd 1866.			
Sat for Cambridgeshire and for Malton.		13,333 .	18,769

*** CHISHOLM, The (James Sutherland), of Erchless Castle, Inverness, &c., N.B.

b. 1806, s. 1859, m. 1861.	Inverness . .	94,328 .	6,567
	Ross . . .	18,927 .	2,111
	Midlothian . .	1 .	180
		113,256 .	8,858

** CHOLMELEY, Sir Hugh Arthur Henry, Bart., of Easton Hall, Grantham, &c. ♇.

Coll. Harrow.   Lincolnshire .   11,452 .   15,723
Club. Brooks's, Boodle's, Guards.   b. 1839, s. 1874, m. 1874.
Served in Grenadier Guards.   Sat for Grantham.

CHILD, Sir S., Bart., of Stallington. Staff.	2,057 .	5,152
♇. CHOLMELEY, T. C., of Brandsby Ha. Yo.	2,320 .	2,761

*** CHOLMONDELEY, Marquis of, Cholmondeley Castle,
     Nantwich, &c. 🐍.   *acres.*   *g. an. val.*

				acres		g. an. val.
Coll.	Eton, Ch. Ch. Oxon.	Cheshire	. .	16,992	.	29,213
Club.	National.	Norfolk	. . .	16,995	.	11,960
b. 1800, s. 1870, m. 1825.		Devon	. . .	4	.	115

Sat for Castle-Rising and for S. Hants.
Is Joint Hereditary Great Chamberlain.   33,991 . 41,288

Inclusive of game rents, also of 150 acres in Cheshire let on
building leases, but exclusive of house and park in Norfolk.

** CHOLMONDELEY, Reginald, of Condover Hall, Shrews-
     bury. 🐍.

Coll.	Rugby, Trin. Cam.	Salop	. . .	5,525	.	8,599
Club.	Cosmopolitan, St. Stephen's.	b. 1827, s. 1864, m. 1867.				

CHRISTIE, Hugh, of Melbourne Hall, Pocklington.

b. 1853, m. 1879.	York, E.R.	.	5,527	.	6,126

*** CHRISTIE, William Langham, of Glyndebourne, Lewes.

Coll.	Eton, Trin. Cam.	Sussex	. . .	5,043	.	6,575
Club.	Carlton, Ox. and Cam.,	Lincoln	. .	1,203	.	2,656
	St. Stephen's.	Devon	. . .	5,368	.	4,151
b. 1830, s. 1861, m. 1855.						
Sits for Lewes.				11,614	.	13,382

CHRISTMAS, Miss Octavia, of Whitfield, Waterford (res.
     Cheltenham).

s. 1868.	Waterford	. .	4,026	.	3,171
	Kilkenny	. .	579	.	302
			4,605	.	3,473

*** CHURCHER, Emanuel, of Bridgmary House, Gosport.

b. 1821, s. 1868, m. 1848.	Hants	. . .	282	.	1,071
	Co. Galway	.	7,823	.	2,427
	Co. Mayo	. .	1,633	.	804
	Co. Roscommon	1,400	.	562
			11,138	.	4,864

CHRISTIE, J., of Cowden.	Perth, Lnk., Kinr.	2,808	.	2,747
CHRISTIE, Robert, of Durie.	Fife	. .	2,134	.	4,691

CHURCHILL, LORD, Cornbury Park, Charlbury, Oxon, &c. ♣.

			acres.		g. an. val.
Club. Travellers', St. Ste-	Oxfordshire	.	5,352	.	6,239
phen's, White's.	Wiltshire	. .	3,760	.	5,304
b. 1802, s. 1845, m. 1849.					
Served as Attaché at Vienna and Lisbon.			9,112	.	11,543

CHURSTON, LORD, Lupton House, Brixham. ♣.

Club. Guards', Carl., Salis.	Devon	. . .	5,326		6,277
b. 1846, s. 1871, m. 1872.	Cornwall	. .	4,786	.	4,225
	Stafford	. .	791	.	962
Served in Scots Guards.			10,903	.	11,464

*** WIGGETT-CHUTE, CHALONER WILLIAM, of The Vyne, Basingstoke.

Coll. Eton, Balliol, Oxon.	Hants	. . .	3,416	.	4,010
b. 1838, s. 1879, m. 1875.					

CLAGETT, MAJOR (and HARBOROUGH, COUNTESS OF), of Stapleford Park, Melton Mowbray.

Club. Jun. U. Service.	Leicester	. .	4,521	.	7,037
Major C., b. 1818, m. 1864.	Essex	. . .	597	.	599
Lady H., s. 1859, m. 1st	Rutland.	. .	5	.	19
1843, 2nd 1864.					
Served in the Madras Cavalry.			5,123	.	7,655

CLANCARTY, EARL OF, Garbally, Ballinasloe.

Coll. Chelt., Trin. Cam.	Co. Galway	.	23,896	.	11,724
Club. Carlton, Sackv. St.,	Roscommon	.	1,614	.	1,093
Kild. St., Dublin.					
b. 1834, s. 1872, m. 1866.			25,510	.	12,817

* CLANMORRIS, LORD, Creg Clare, Ardrahan, Co. Galway.

Coll. Eton.	Mayo	. . .	12,337	.	6,210
Club. Carl., Marlb., A. & N.,	Galway	. . .	5,774	.	2,053
Falconry, N. & M.,					
Kild. St., Dublin.			18,111	.	8,263
b. 1852, s. 1876, m. 1878.					
Serves in Rifle Brigade, late 28th Foot.					

CHURCHILL, GEORGE, of Alderholt.	Dor.	2,210	.	2,283
CHUTE, F. B., of Chute Hall.	Kerry . .	10,328	.	2,627

*** CLANRICARDE, Marquis of, Portumna Castle, Galway.

		acres.	g. an. val.
Coll. Harrow.	Co. Galway .	56,826 .	24,358
Club. Travellers', Reform, St. James's.			

b. 1832, s. 1874.
Served as Attaché and Sec. of Leg. at Turin. Sat for Co. Galway.

CLANWILLIAM, Earl of, Gill Hall, Dromore.

Coll. Eton.	Co. Down .	3,584 .	4,305
Club. Carl., Trav. b. 1832, s. 1879, m. 1867.			

Is a Vice-Admiral, served in the Baltic 1854-5, and at the capture of Canton, was Naval A.D.C. to the Queen, and a Lord of the Admiralty. Commands the Flying Squadron.

In the Irish return, "Trustees of Hon. R. Meade" are credited with over 13,000 acres, worth 13,700*l.* per annum. Mr. Meade disclaims the ownership. The Irish Local Government Board reaffirms it, and the late Lord Clanwilliam calls this notice "very incorrect."

*** ATKINSON-CLARK, George Dixon, of Belford Hall, Northumberland.

Coll. Chart., Univ. Oxon.	Northumberland	3,273 .	5,536
Club. Carl., Marl., Pratt's.	Perthshire . .	1,800 .	404
b. 1836, s. 1880, m. 1874.			
		5,073 .	5,940

*** CLARKE, Rev. Sir Charles, Bart., of Worlingham Hall, Beccles.

Coll. Charterhouse, Trin.	Suffolk . . .	3,071 .	3,650
Cam. b. 1812, s. 1857, m. 1838.			

$ CLARENDON, Earl of. War., Herts .	2,298 .	3,741
CLARINA, Lord. Limerick	2,012 .	2,497
CLARK, J. J., of Largantogher. Ldy., Tyr.	5,994 .	2,611
CLARKE, G. J., of The Steeple. Antrim .	2,422 .	2,313
CLARKE, R. C., of Noblethorpe. York. .	2,310 .	5,404
CLARKE, Thomas, of Knedlington. York .	2,417 .	5,596
CLARKE, William, of Farrans. Cork . .	5,679 .	2,588

*** CLARKE, DAVID, of Bushy Park, Borrisokane, Co. Tipperary.

		acres.		*g. an. val.*
Coll. Macclesfield, G.S.	Tyrone . . .	760	.	117
b. 1820, m. 1839.	Tipperary . .	5,873	.	3,513
	Chester . .	103	.	761
	Salop . . .	208	.	510
	Montgomery .	406	.	335
		7,350	.	5,236

** CLARKE, THOMAS TRUESDALE, of Swakeleys, Uxbridge, &c.

Coll. Harrow, Oriel, Oxon.	Norfolk . . .	3,087	.	3,968
Club. Oxford and Cam.	Middlesex . .	980	.	2,235
b. 1802, s. 1840, m. 1826.	Essex . . .	405	.	600
		4,472	.	6,803

For his eldest son, *see* CLARKE-THORNHILL.

** CLAVERING, SIR HENRY AUGUSTUS, BART., of Axwell Park, Blaydon-on-Tyne. §.

Coll. Royal Naval Coll.	Durham . .	5,179	.	6,794
Club. Army and Navy, Uni.	Northumberland	8,334	.	3,551
Service.	York, N.R. .	173	.	153
b. 1824, s. 1872, m. 1853.				
Served in Royal Navy.		13,686	.	10,498

** CLAYTON, JOHN, of The Chesters, Newcastle-upon Tyne, &c.

Coll. Uppingham.	Northumberland	9,579	.	11,167
Club. Carlton.	Cumberland .	349	.	276
b. 1792, s. 1832.	Durham . .	186	.	488
	Westmoreland	113	.	387
	Surrey . . .	777	.	895

Mr. CLAYTON has also property in London.   11,004 . 13,213

** BROWNE-CLAYTON, RICHARD CLAYTON, of Carrigbyrne Lodge, Enniscorthy, &c.

Coll. Harrow, Bras. Oxon.	Co. Wexford .	3,191	.	1,441
Club. Athen., Bur. Fine	Kilkenny . .	3,063	.	2,122
Arts	Lancashire . .	800	.	2,000
b. 1807, s. 1845, m. 1830.	Cheshire. . .	132	.	417
		7,186	.	5,980

** CLAYTON, Sir William Robert, Bart., of Harleyford
      Manor, Great Marlow, &c.

		acres.	g. an. val:
Coll. Sandhurst, Clare, Cam.	Surrey . . .	6,505 .	5,637
Club. Carlton, St. Stephen's,	Bucks . . .	2,067 .	3,292
Pratt's, R.T.Y.C.	Carmarthen .	1,502 ..	1,433
b. 1842, s. 1866, m. 1872.	Norfolk . . .	1,039 .	1,568
	Berks . . .	32 .	180
	Sussex . . .	20 .	16

11,165 . 12,126

CLELAND, James, of Tobar Mhuire, Crossgar, Co. Down, &c.

b. 1819, s. 1857, m. 1858.   Co. Down . .   3,544 .   4,230

CLELAND, John, of Stormont Castle, Dundonald, Co. Down.

Coll. Eton.   Co. Down . .   4,385 .   6,174
b. 1836, s. 1842, m. 1859.

** CLEMENTS, Henry Theophilus, of Ashfield, Cootehill,
      Co. Cavan, &c.

Club. Carlton, Sackv. St.,	Cavan . . .	3,908 .	2,924
Dublin.	Leitrim . . .	22,790 .	9,753
b. 1820, s. 1843 and 1878,	Waterford . .	174 .	96
m. 1868.	Galway . . .	18,145 .	870
	Kildare . . .	487 .	600

45,504 . 14,243

** CLENNELL, Percival Fenwick, of Harbottle Castle, Mor-
      peth.

b. 18—, s. 1848, m. 18—.   Northumberland 9,300 .   5,474

CLERK, Sir George Douglas, Bart., of Penicuik House,
      Edinburgh.

Coll. Exeter, Oxon.	Midlothian .	12,696 .	8,919
Club. Carl., New Edin.	Peebles . . .	500 .	74
b. 1852, s. 1870, m. 1876.			
Served in 2nd Life Guards.		13,196 .	8,993

Exclusive of 2,421*l.* for mines.

CLEMENTS, T. H., of Rathkenny. Cav., Meath 3,058 .   2,190

*** CLERMONT, Lord, Ravensdale Park, Newry, &c. ♠.

		acres.	g. an. val.
Coll. Exeter, Oxon.	Co. Louth . .	20,369 .	15,262
Club. Brooks's, Trav.	Armagh. . .	758 .	522
b. 1815, m. 1840.			
Sat for Co. Louth.		21,127 .	15,784

Exclusive of 8,500 acres in both counties let on perpetual leases at 764*l.*

CLEVELAND, Duke of, K.G., Raby Castle, Darlington, &c. ♠.

Coll. Eton, Oriel, Oxon.	Durham . .	55,837 .	29,219
Club. Trav., Athenæum, Ref.	Salop . . .	25,604 .	32,605
b. 1803, s. 1864, m. 1854.	Sussex . . .	6,025 .	6,491
Served as Sec. Legation at	Somerset .	4,784 .	8,062
Stockholm.	Northampton .	3,482 .	5,190
	Wilts . . .	2,397 .	3,165
	Kent . . .	2,449 .	2,002
	Cornwall . .	2,520 .	5,001
	Stafford. . .	unstated .	3,970
	Devon . . .	1,085 .	1,684
	Gloucester . .	11 .	9
		104,194 .	97,398

Sat for S. Durham and for Hastings.

The Return gives out of this total a rental 1,643*l.* to the Duchess Dowager, in Wilts and Cornwall, and a rental of 3,087*l.* to her jointly with Lord Sandwich, in Devonshire ; this last is omitted.

** CLIFDEN, Viscount, Gowran Castle, Kilkenny.

Coll. Eton.	Northampton .	4,774 .	7,087
b. 1863, s. 1866.	Bucks . . .	2,976 .	4,076
	Somerset . .	2,537 .	1,197
	Oxford . . .	1,107 .	1,379
	Middlesex . .	36 .	855
	Kilkenny . .	35,288 .	20,793
	Dublin . . .	821 .	2,286
	Kildare . . .	978 .	877
	Meath . . .	500 .	365
The English estates are not corrected.		49,017 .	38,915

*** CLIFFE, ANTHONY JOHN, of Belle Vue, Wexford.

			acres.		*g. an. val.*
Coll.	Brasenose, Oxon.	Wexford . .	4,459	.	3,489
Club.	St. George's.	Kilkenny . .	2,465	.	1,054
b. 1822, s. 1878, m. 1858.		Cork . . .	947	.	1,700
		Meath . . .	375	.	301
			8,246	.	6,544

** CLIFFORD OF CHUDLEIGH, LORD, Ugbrooke Park, Chudleigh, &c. ☘.

			acres.		*g. an. val.*
Coll.	Stonyhurst, Lon. Un.	Devon . . .	4,416	.	4,500
Club.	Devonshire.	Warwick . .	1,562	.	2,000
b. 1851, s. 1880.		Somerset . .	896	.	1,079
		Bucks . . .	858	.	1,530
		Cornwall . .	128	.	—
			7,860	.	9,109

The Cornish property (mining) in 1879 paid nothing.

** CLIFTON, HENRY ROBERT, of Clifton Hall, Nottingham.

Coll.   Har., Ch. Ch. Oxon.   Notts . . .   4,288   .   8,682
Club.   Jun. Carlton, Garrick.   b. 1833, s. 1869, m. 1860.

** CLIFTON, JOHN TALBOT, of Lytham Hall, Lytham, Preston, &c. ☘.

b. 1868, s. 1882.   Lancashire .   15,802   .   41,965

** CLINTON, LORD, Heanton Satchville, Beaford, Devon, &c. ☘.

			acres.		*g. an. val.*
Coll.	Eton, Ch. Ch. Oxon.	Devon . . .	14,431	.	11,685
Club.	Carlton, Travellers'.	Cornwall . .	3,690	.	6,700
b. 1834, s. 1866, m. 1st 1858,		Aberdeen . .	6,730	.	4,760
2nd 1875.		Perth . . .	4,918	.	5,412
		Kincardine .	5,007	.	4,056
			34,776	.	32,613

Served as Un. Sec. Sta. for India and as a Charity Commissioner. Sat. for N. Devon.

LORD C. is returned as holding the Scotch properties in trust for his eldest son.

CLINTON, H. R., of Ashley Clinton.
  Hants, Salop   2,013   .   2,164

PELHAM-CLINTON, Lord Charles, of Warwick Square, S.W. ♣.

			acres.		g. an. val.
Coll. —, Oxford.	Gloucester	.	14	.	205
b. 1813, m. 1848.	Cork . . .		4,563	.	3,063

Served in 1st Life Gds. Sat for Sandwich.   4,577 . 3,268

*** STRACEY-CLITHEROW, Col. Edward John, of Hotham Hall, Brough, &c.

Coll. Harrow.	York, E.R.	.	2,555	.	3,836
Club. Guards.	Middlesex . .		548	.	1,914
b. 1820, m. 1846.	Norfolk . . .		1,170	.	1,800
	Bucks . . .		668	.	1,094
	Huntingdon	.	545	.	726
	Sussex . . .		265	.	495

Served in Scots Fusilier Guards.   5,751 . 9,865

** CLIVE, Charles Meysey Bolton, of Whitfield, Hereford. ♣.

Coll. Harrow, Balliol,	Hereford . .		7,000	.	6,750
Oxon.	Co. Louth . .		3,103	.	3,016
Club. Trav., Brooks's,	Co. Mayo . .		3,457	.	364
New University.					
b. 1842, s. 1878, m. 1867.			13,560	.	10,130

** CLIVE, Col. Edward Henry, of Perrystone Court, Ross, &c. ♣.

Coll. Harrow.	Hereford. . .		1,700	.	2,500
Club. Trav., Guards, U.	Tipperary . .		4,689	.	2,250
Ser.	Mayo . . .		35,000	.	1,500
b. 1837, s. 1880, m. 1867.					
Sat. for Hereford.			41,389	.	6,250

*** CLONBROCK, Lord, Clonbrock, Ahascragh, Co. Galway.

Coll. Ch. Ch. Oxon.   Co. Galway . 29,550 . 11,873
Club. Travellers', Arthur's, Sackville Street,
Dublin. b. 1807, s. 1826, m. 1830.

** CLONCURRY, LORD, Lyons, Hazelhatch, Kildare, &c.

			acres.		*g. an. val.*
Coll.	Eton, Balliol, Oxon.	Kildare . . .	6,121	.	6,202
Club.	Carlton, St. James's.	Limerick . .	5,137	.	2,563
b. 1840, s. 1869.		Dublin . . .	923	.	1,297
		Meath . . .	306	.	381
			12,487	.	10,443

*** CLONMELL, EARL OF, Bishop's Court, Straffan, Co. Kildare.

Coll.	Eton.	Tipperary . .	16,187	.	8,152
Club.	Carl., Gun, Kildare	Kildare . . .	1,958	.	2,218
	Street, Dublin.	Kilkenny . .	2,226	.	1,893
b. 1839, s. 1866.		Carlow . . .	3,300	.	1,934
Served in 1st Life Guards.		Monaghan . .	2,022	.	1,449
		Limerick . .	1,902	.	790
		Dublin . . .	51	.	704
			27,646	.	17,140

CLOSE, MAXWELL CHARLES, of Drumbanagher, Newry.

Coll.	Ch. Ch. Oxon.	Armagh . .	9,087	.	10,865
Club.	Carlton, Kildare St.,	Queen's Co. .	3,678	.	2,576
	Sackville St., Dublin.				
b. 1827, s. 1867, m. 1852.			12,765	.	13,441
Sits for Armagh.					

** COBBE, CHARLES, of Newbridge House, Donabate, Co. Dublin, &c.

Coll.	Chart., Ex., Oxon.	Co. Dublin .	9,948	.	3,206
Club.	Sackville St., Dublin.	Louth . . .	1,419	.	1,429
b. 1811, s. 1857, m. 1839.					
			11,367	.	4,635

CLOUGH, C. BUTLER, of Boughton. Norf., Hants, Flintshire, Cheshire	2,308	.	2,080
CLUTTON, HENRY, of Hartswood. Surrey	2,436	.	2,911
COATES, THOMAS, of Beelsby. Lincoln . .	2,045	.	2,959
COATES, WILLIAM C., of Knockinally, Kildare, Longford	2,236	.	2,104
COBURNE, P. C., of Shanganagh. Kild., Queen's County, Dublin	2,533	.	2,063

CODRINGTON, Sir Gerald William Henry, Bart., of
Dodington Park, Chipping Sodbury. ♨.

			acres.		g. an. val.
Coll.	Eton.	Gloucester . .	4,218	.	6,101
Club.	White's, Carlton,	Wilts . . .	805	.	1,100
	St. James's.				
b. 1850, s. 1864.			5,023	.	7,201

Inclusive of 126*l.* rental in his mother's name.

** COEY, Sir Edward, Kt., of Merville, Belfast, &c.

Club.	Pall Mall, Ulster.	Antrim . . .	5,257	5,183
b. 1805, m. 1836.				

COGHILL, Sir John Joscelyn, Bart., of Glen Barrahane,
Castle Townsend, Co. Cork.

Coll.	Rugby.	Kilkenny . .	4,564	.	2,622
Club.	Garrick, Kildare St.,	Meath . . .	1,269	.	1,108
	Dublin.	Co. Dublin .	472	.	822
b. 1826, s. 1850, m. 1851.					
Served in 59th Foot.			6,305	.	4,552

COLBY, Mrs., of Fynone, Newcastle-Emlyn.

s. 1874, m. 1841.	Pembroke . .	6,663	.	3,402
	Carmarthen .	2,557	.	1,707
	Cardigan . .	32	.	38
		9,252	.	5,147

*** ROSSBOROUGH-COLCLOUGH, Mrs., of Tintern Abbey,
New Ross, &c.

s. 1853, m. 1848.	Wexford . .	13,329	.	7,124

COCHRAN, A., of Balfour. Rox., Ab., Ayr.	3,003	.	2,024
CODDINGTON, H. B., of Oldbridge. Meath,			
Wicklow	3,737	.	2,925
PINE-COFFIN, J. R., of Portledge. Devon.	3,854	.	2,971
COGAN, Right Hon. W. H. F., of Tinode.			
Kildare, Carlow, Wicklow	4,086	.	2,937
COKE, Hon. E. Keppel Wentworth, of			
Longford. Derby, Lanc., Norfolk . .	2,442	.	4,959
COLDHAM, H. J., of Anmer. Nor., Suff. .	2,469	.	2,644

COLEBROOKE, Sir Thomas Edward, Bart., of Abington House, Lanark, N.B.

			acres.		g. an. val.
Coll. Eton.	Lanark . . .	29,604	.	9,282
Club. Athenæum.	Surrey . . .	419	.	704
b. 1813, s. 1838, m. 1857.				
		30,023	.	9,986

Sat for Taunton ; sits for N. Lanarkshire.

COLLEY, Henry Fitz-George, of Mount Temple, Clontarf.

Coll. Trin. Dub.	Kildare . . .	4,216	.	2,637
Club. Univ. Dub.	Co. Cork . .	603	.	487
b. 1827, s. 1879, m. 1858.				
		4,819	.	3,124

COLLINGWOOD, Rev. Robert Gordon (*ju. uxo.*), of Dissington Hall, Newcastle-on-Tyne.

s. 1866, m. 1856.	Northumberland	5,551	.	5,706
	Cumberland .	153	.	142
		5,704	.	5,848

*** COLLINS, Digby, of Truthan, Truro, &c.

Coll. Eton, Trin. Hall, Cam.	Cornwall . .	4,948	.	5,116

Club. St. Stephen's, Raleigh. b. 1836, s. 1870, m. 1881.

*** COLLUM, William, of Bellevue, Tamlaght, Enniskillen.

Coll. Trinity, Dublin.	Fermanagh .	5,100	.	3,500
Club. Jun. United Service.	Cavan . . .	487	.	350
b. 1837, s. 1875, m. 1864.				
		5,587	.	3,850

Served in 28th Foot and 94th Foot in the Crimea.

** COLQUHOUN, Sir James, Bart., of Rossdhu House, Luss, N.B., &c.

Coll. Harrow, Trin. Cam.	Dumbarton. .	67,041	.	12,845

Club. Arthur's, New University. b. 1844, s. 1873, m. 1875.

COLLINGWOOD, E. J., of Lilburn.	Nhbld.	2,995	.	5,523
COLLINGWOOD, J., of Cornhill.	Nhbld.	2,474	.	5,410

** CAMPBELL-COLQUHOUN, Rev. John Erskine, of Chart-
    well, Edenbridge, &c.

		acres.		g. an. val.
Coll. Rugby, Trin. Ox.	Kent . . .	752	.	964
Club. National.	Dumbarton .	2,019	.	4,555
b. 1831, s. 1872, m. 1860.	Lanark . . .	915	.	1,038
	Stirling . . .	193	.	403

    Exclusive of a mineral rent of 2,422*l.*   3,879 . 6,960

** COLSTON, Charles Edward Hungerford Athole, of
    Roundway Park, Devizes.

Coll. Eton, Ch. Ch. Oxon.	Somerset . .	2,409	.	3,700
Club. New University.	Gloucester . .	4,000	.	7,500
b. 1854, s. 1864, m. 1879.	Wilts . . .	1,955	.	2,526
		8,364	.	13,726

Sir G. Smythe is joint owner with Mr. Colston in Gloucester.

** COLTHURST, Sir George St. John, Bart., of Blarney
    Castle, Co. Cork, &c.

b. 1850, s. 1878, m. 1881.   Cork . . . 31,260 . 9,664
    Served in 43rd Foot.

COLTMAN, William Bacheler, of Blelack, Dennet, Aberdeen,
    N.B.

Coll. Eton, Trin. Cam.	Aberdeen . .	7,484	.	2,376
Club. Ath., Oxf. &. Cam.	Lincoln . . .	1,577	.	2,066
b. 1828, m. 1860.				
		9,061	.	4,442

COLYER, Edward, of Wombwell Hall, Northfleet, Gravesend.

b. 18—, s. 1874.   Kent . . . 4,802 . 9,594

COOKE-COLLIS, Rev. M. A., of Castle
    Cooke. Tipperary, Cork . . . . . 5,841 . 2,343
CRONIN-COLTSMAN, Daniel, of Flesk.
    Cork, Kerry . . . . 14,794 . 2,095
♯. COLVILE, C. R., of Lullington Hall. Der. 2,138 . 3,680

** COMBERMERE, Viscount, Combermere Abbey, Whitchurch, Salop, &c. 🐍.

			acres.	g. an. val.
Coll. Eton, Oxford.	Cheshire	. .	9,414	. 17,000
Club. Carlton, Bood., Uni.	Salop	. .	2,447	. 3,724
Ser.	Lancashire	. .	1,818	. 6,055
b. 1818, s. 1865, m. 1844.				
			13,679	. 26,779

Served in 1st Life Guards and in 7th Hussars. Sat for
Carrickfergus.

His eldest son, Hon. Robt. Cotton, has out of this the whole
Lancashire property, 2,930*l.* in Salop and 212*l.* in Cheshire.

Lord C. has also West India estates, annual value 4,000*l.*

** COMPTON, Henry, of Minstead Manor, Lyndhurst.

b. 1871, s. 1877.	Hants	. . .	1,864	. 2,704
	Dorset	. . .	3,012	. 3,707
			4,876	. 6,411

Mr. C. has minerals, annual value about 3,000*l.*

** CONANT, Edward Nathaniel, of Lyndon Hall, Oakham.

Coll. Rugby, St. John's,	Lincoln	. .	3,591	. 7,083
Oxford.	Rutland	. .	1,472	. 2,600
Club. Carlton, Jun. Carlton.				
b. 1820, s. 1862, m. 1844.			5,063	. 9,683

*** CONGREVE, Ambrose, of Mount Congreve, Kilmeaden,
Waterford.

Coll. Eton.	Kilkenny	. .	2,295	. 2,315
Club. Kildare St., Dublin,	Waterford	. .	2,016	. 3,006
Arthur's.	Cork	. . .	2,998	. 129
b. 1832, s. 1863, m. 1866.				
Served in 2nd Life Guards.			7,309	. 5,450

Exclusive of head-rents, annual value 167*l.*

COMBE, R. T., of Earnshill. Somerset	.	2,776	. 5,231
COMYN, F. L., of Woodstock. Clair, Mayo, Galway		12,881	. 2,174
CONGLETON, Lord. Queen's Co., Cheshire		4,426	. 2,674

CONNOLY, Thomas, of Castletown, Celbridge, Co. Kildare, &c.

		acres.	g. an. val.
b. 1870, s. 1876.	Donegal . .	22,736 .	6,283
	Kildare . .	2,605 .	3,346
	Dublin . . .	1,512 .	2,982
		26,853 .	12,611

** CONSETT, William Warcop Peter, of Brawith Hall, Thirsk, &c. (res. Château du Champ de Bataille, Neubourgh, Eure, France).

Club. Junior Carlton.   York N. & W. R.   4,793 . 8,600
b. 1833, s. 1860, m. 1864.

CLIFFORD-CONSTABLE, Sir Frederick Augustus Talbot Bart., of Burton Constable, Hull, &c. ♫.

Club. Carlton, Road.	York E. & N. R.	18,666 .	23,650
b. 1828, s. 1870, m. 186—.	Middlesex . .	15 .	6c8
	Durham . .	25 .	36
	Staffordshire .	8 .	87
		18,714 .	24,381

The Middlesex property is the Dowager Lady C.-Constable's.

** STRICKLAND-CONSTABLE, Henry, of Wassand Hall, Hull.

Coll. Trin. Cam.   York E. & W. R.   6,271 . 10,500
b. 1821, s. 1865, m. 1859.

ROWLEY-CONWY, Conwy Grenville Hercules, of Boddrhyddan, Rhyl.

Club. Carl., Garrick, U. Ser.   Flint . . . 5,526 . 6,995
b. 1841, s. 1869, m. 1869.   Served in 2nd Life Guards.

CONYERS, Lord, Oran House, Tadcaster.

Club. Carlton, Beaconsfd.,   York, N. & W. R.   3,460 . 8,538
     Jun. Uni. Ser.
b. 1827, s. 1859, m. 1860.
  Served in Royal Horse Guards, and in 21st Foot, and in 87th Foot in the Crimea.

CONSIDINE, H., of Derk.   Long., Lim.,Tip.   2,074 . 2,573
GOULTON-CONSTABLE, J., of Walcot.
   Lincoln . . . . 2,975 . 4,681

CONYNGHAM, Marquis, Bifrons, Canterbury, &c. ♆.

			acres.	g. an. val.
Coll.	Eton.	Kent . . .	9,737 .	17,432
Club.	White's, Uni. Ser.,	Donegal . .	122,300 .	15,166
	Carlton, Sack.	Co. Clare . .	27,613 .	10,808
	St. Dublin.	Co. Meath .	7,060 .	6,670
b. 1825, *s.* 1876, *m.* 1854.				
			166,710 .	50,076

Served in 1st Life Guards, is Extra Equerry to the Queen, and a Major-General in the Army.

** COODE, Edward, of Polapit Tamar, Launceston, &c.

Coll.	Trin. Cambridge.	Cornwall . .	5,632 .	7,192
b. 1821, *s.* 1865, *m.* 1850.		Devon . . .	2,108 .	1,547
			7,740 .	8,739

** DAVIES-COOKE, Philip Bryan, of Owston, Doncaster, &c.

Coll.	Ch. Ch. Oxon,	York, W.R. .	3,379 .	4,646
Club.	Travellers'.	Flint . . .	3,397 .	7,756
b. 1832, *s.* 1853, *m.* 1862.		Denbigh . .	86 .	338
			6,862 .	12,740

COOKE, Sir William Ridley Charles, Bart., of Wheatley Hall, Doncaster.

Coll.	Eton.	York, W.R. .	3,638 .	6,228

b. 1827, *s.* 1851, *m.* 1st, 1855, 2nd, 1871.
Served in 7th Hussars.

*** COOKSON, John, of Meldon Park, Morpeth.

Club.	Union.	Northumberland	6,463 .	6,506

b. 1808, *m.* 1837.

** COOPE, Octavius Edward, of Rochetts, Brentwood, &c.

Club.	Carlton, City, Burl.	Essex . . .	3,621 .	5,994
	Fine Arts. *b.* 1814, *m.* 1848.			

Sat for Yarmouth ; sits for Middlesex.

LENOX-CONYNGHAM, Sir W. Fitz-W.,
  of Springhill. Tyro, Londonderry . . 2,526 . 2,429

COOKE, Rev. C. R., of Semer. Suff., Norf. 2,329 . 3,342

COOPER, EDWARD HENRY, of Markree Castle, Colloony, Co. Sligo.

				acres.		*g. an. val.*
Coll.	Eton.	Co. Sligo	. .	34,120	.	11,548
Club.	Carlton, Guards, Kild. St., Dublin.	Limerick	. .	1,118	.	1,187
b. 1827, s. 1863, m. 1858.				35,238	.	12,735

Served in Gren. Guards and in 7th Hussars. Sat for Co. Sligo.

*** COOPER, WILLIAM AUGUSTUS, of Cooper Hill, Carlow.

Coll.	Trinity, Dublin	Queen's Co.	.	2,822	.	2,859
b. 1839, s. 1879.		Kildare	. .	417	.	323
				3,239	.	3,182

** COOPER, WILLIAM COOPER, of Toddington Manor, Dunstable.

Club.	Union.	Beds	. . .	3,388	.	5,026
b. 1810, s. 1860, m. 1831.						

COOTE, SIR CHARLES HENRY, BART., of Ballyfin, Montrath, Queen's Co.

Coll.	Eton, Trin. Dublin.	Queen's Co.	. .	47,451	.	18,007
Club.	Carlton.	Roscommon	.	1,017	.	286
b. 1815, s. 1864.		Kildare	. .	878	.	601
		Limerick	. .	340	.	361
				49,686	.	19,255

COOTE, EYRE, of Rockbourne West Park, Salisbury.

Coll.	Eton.	Wilts.	. . .	6,840	.	5,604
b. 1857, s. 1864.		Hants	. . .	1,811	.	2,838
		Co. Dublin.	.	3,107	.	2,830
		Queen's Co.	.	1,524	.	1,423
				13,282	.	12,695

COOPER, COL., of Dunboden. Wmeath, Cork	3,536	.	2,920
** COOTE, C. J., ALDWORTH, of Mount Coote. Limerick, Cork	2,840	.	3,050
PURDON-COOTE, C., of Ballyclough. Cork	4,510	.	2,894
COOTE, REV. ALGERNON. King's Co. . .	4,436	.	2,491

** COOTE, John Chidley, of 5, Hereford Gardens, Park Lane, W.

	acres.	*g. an. val.*
Club. Union. Roscommon .	10,348 .	5,628

b. 1816, m. 1855. Served in 43rd Foot.

** COPE, Francis Robert, of the Manor House, Loughgall, Co. Armagh.

Coll. Harrow, Jesus, Cam. Armagh. . . 9,367 . 12,463
Club. Junior Carlton, Royal St. George's Yacht Club.
b. 1853, s. 1858.

COPE, Rev. Sir William Henry, Bart., of Bramshill Park, Hartfordbridge, Hants. 🐍

Coll. Trin. Dub., Mag. H.	Hants . . .	3,833 .	3,616
Oxon.	Oxford . . .	1,120 .	2,399
b. 1811, s. 1851, m. 1st 1834,	Northampton .	231 .	480
2nd 1865.	Warwick . .	184 .	230
	Berks . . .	74 .	72
		5,442 .	6,797

* COPLEY, Sir Joseph William, Bart., of Sprotborough, Doncaster.

Coll. Har., Ch. Ch. Oxon.	York, W.R. .	3,783 .	5,228
Club. Travellers'.	Cornwall . .	2,159 .	2,392
b. 1804, s. 1838, m. 1831.			
		5,942 .	7,620

CORBALLY, Hon. Mrs., of Corbalton Hall, Tara, Co. Meath.

s. 1870, m. 1842. Meath . . . 5,033 . 5,220

*** CORBET, Henry Reginald, of Adderley Hall, Market Drayton.

Coll. Harrow, Mag. Oxon.	Salop . . .	8,856 .	13,842
Club. Carlton, Boodle's.	Cheshire . .	127 .	166
b. 1832, s. 1877, m. 1855.			
		8,983 .	14,008

Inclusive of 600*l.* of tithes.

COPLAND, C., of Colliston. Dmfrs., Kirkt.	3,268 .	2,367
CORBALLIS, J. R., of Rosemount. Meath.	2,136 .	3,185

** CORBET, Rev. John Dryden, of Sundorne Castle, Shrewsbury.

		acres.	g. an. val.
Coll. Westm., Ch. Ch. Oxon.	Salop . . .	8,500 .	11,808

b. 1808, s. 1864.

** CORBET, Sir Vincent Rowland, Bart., of Acton Reynald Hall, Shrewsbury. 🐟.

Club. A. & N., Carl., Boodle's.	Salop . . .	7,080 .	8,548

b. 1821, s. 1855, m. 1854.   Served in Royal Horse Guards.

** CORBETT, Col. Edward, of Longnor Hall, Shrewsbury.

Coll. Eton.	Salop . . .	4,000 .	4,050
Club. Carlton.	Montgomery .	40 .	40
b. 1817, s. 1855, m. 1842.	Stafford . . .	727 .	1,830
Served in 51st Foot and 72nd Foot.			
Sat. for S. Salop.		4,767 .	5,920

** CORBETT, John, of Impney, Droitwich, &c.

🌳 *Club.* Reform, Gresham,	Worcester .	2,200 .	12,124
Devonshire.	Merioneth . .	1,570 .	1,750
b. 1817, m. 1856.	Salop . . .	410 .	450
		4,180 .	14,324

Sits for Droitwich.

CORK and ORRERY, Earl of, K.P., Marston House, Frome.

Coll. Eton, Ch. Ch. Oxon.	Somerset . .	3,398 .	5,094
Club. Brooks's, White's.	Co. Cork . .	20,195 .	6,943
b. 1829, s. 1856, m. 1853.	Co. Kerry . .	11,531 .	2,447
Serves as Master of the	Limerick . .	3,189 .	2,859
Buckhounds.			
Sat. for Frome.		38,313 .	17,343

** CORNEWALL, Rev. Sir George Henry, Bart., of Moccas Court, Hereford.

Coll. Rugby, Trin. Cam.	Hereford . .	6,946 .	7,662
b. 1833, s. 1868, m. 1867.	Beds . . .	368 .	442
		7,314 .	8,104

🐟. CORNEWALL, H. S. T., of Delbury. Sal.   2,917 .   3,398

CORYTON, Augustus, of Pentillie Castle, Saltash.

			acres.	*g. an. val.*
Coll. Eton.	Cornwall . .		8,585 .	8,774
Club. United Service.	Devon . . .		800 .	1,170
b. 1809, s. 1843.				
Served in 85th Foot.			9,385 .	9,944

*** COSBY, Robert Ashworth Godolphin, of Stradbally Hall, Queen's County.

Coll. Eton.	Queen's Co. .	10,110 .	7,077

Club. A. & N., J. U. Ser., Kild. St.
b. 1837, s. 1851, m. 1859. Served in Inniskilling Dragoons.

COTES, Charles Cecil, of Woodcote, Newport, Salop. ꕔ.

Coll. Eton, Ch. Ch. Oxon.	Salop . . .	3,116 .	4,264
Club. Brooks's, St. James's,	Stafford . .	2,911 .	4,255
Reform, Boodle's.	Montgomery .	443 .	341
b. 1846, s. 1874.			
		6,470 .	8,860

Sits for Shrewsbury. Is a Lord of the Treasury.

COTTENHAM, Earl of, Tandridge Court, Godstone.

b. 1874, s. 1881.	Surrey . . .	3,439 .	4,172
	Cheshire . .	1,117 .	1,502
		4,556 .	5,674

** COTTERELL, Sir Geers Henry, Bart., of Garnons, Hereford.

Coll. Harrow, Ch. Ch. Ox.	Hereford . .	5,066 .	8,020

Club. White's, Brooks's, Boodle's.
b. 1834, s. 1847, m. 1865. Sat for Herefordshire.
The acreage is somewhat understated, as several farms are returned in tenants' names.

COTESWORTH, W., of Cowdenknowes.
Roxburgh, Berwick	2,331 .	2,701

COTTER, Sir J. L., Bart., of Rockforest.
Cork	7,873 .	2,461

COTTESLOE, Lord. Bucks, Gloucester . | 2,683 . | 5,675 |

COTTON, H. H. P., of Quex. Kent, Midd. | 2,253 . | 4,816 |

** COULSON, Edward Foster, of Bellaport Hall, Market
    Drayton, &c.

		acres.		g. an. val.
Club. Union, Windham.	Salop . . .	1,885	.	2,893
b. 1804, s. 1866, m. 1853.	Merioneth . .	5,795	.	1,440
		7,680	.	4,333

Exclusive of the value of woods and mansions.

* COULTHURST, John, of Gargrave House, Leeds.

Coll. Winch., Magd. Cam.	York, N.&W.R.	4,140	.	4,783
Club. Junior Carlton.	Lancashire .	41	.	67
b. 1826, s. 1861, m. 1870.	Durham . .	100	.	100
		4,281	.	4,950

Exclusive of coal rents from Durham.

** COURTHOPE, George Campion, of Whiligh, Ticehurst,
    Sussex. $.

Coll. Eton, Ch. Ch. Ox.	Sussex . . .	3,026	.	2,956
b. 1811, s. 1835, m. 1841.	Kent . . .	630	.	1,521
		3,656	.	4,477

** COURTOWN, Earl of, Courtown House, Gorey, Co.
    Wexford.

Coll. Eton.	Wexford . .	14,426	.	8,605
Club. Carlton, Kild. St.	Carlow . . .	7,395	.	2,756
Dublin.	Cheshire . .	1,493	.	731
b. 1823, s. 1858, m. 1846.				
Served in Grenadier Guards.		23,314	.	12,092

** COVENTRY, Earl of, Croome Court, Worcester.

Coll. Eton, Ch. Ch. Oxon	Worcester . .	13,021	.	22,367
Club. Carlton, White's.	Gloucester . .	1,398	.	2,511
b. 1838, s. 1843, m. 1865.				
		14,419	.	24,878

Was Capt. Hon. Corps of Gentlemen-at-Arms.

COWAN, C., of Logan House.	Peebles, Midlo.	6,929	.	2,155
COWAN, J. H., of Boghall.	Linlw., Midlo.	2,357	.	2,982

*** COWLEY, Earl, K.G., G.C.B., Draycott Park, Chippenham.

		acres.		g. an. val.
Club. Ath., Travellers'.	Wilts . . .	3,945	.	7,523
b. 1804, s. 1847, m. 1833.	Essex . . .	1,433	.	11,542
	Cornwall . .	522	.	4,107
		5,900	.	23,172

Served as Attaché and Secretary of Legation at Vienna, the Hague, Stutgardt, Constantinople, Berne, and Frankfort, and as Ambassador to the French Court.

COWPER, Earl, K.G., Panshanger, Hertford, &c.

Coll. Harrow, Ch. Ch. Ox.	Herts . . .	10,122	.	13,540
Club. Brooks's, White's,	Beds . . .	9,105	.	13,394
Travellers', St.	Notts . . .	5,294	.	8,242
James's.	Essex . . .	3,227	.	4,543
b. 1834, s. 1856 and 1880,	Derby . . .	2,787	.	6,669
m. 1870.	Wilts . . .	2,536	.	2,794
Was Lord-Lieutenant of	Kent . . .	2,078	.	3,484
Ireland.	Northampton .	1,067	.	2,989
Served as Capt. Hon.	York, N. & W.R.	696	.	3,865
Corps of Gentlemen - at -	Leicester . .	913	.	802
Arms.	Suffolk . . .	44	.	70
		37,869	.	60,392

COWPER, Hon. Henry Frederick (res. Brocket Hall, Welwyn).

Coll. Harrow, Ch. Ch. Ox.	York, W.R. .	5,720	.	6,333

Club. White's, Brooks's, Trav.
b. 1838, s. 1880. Sits for Hertfordshire.

CRADOCK, Christopheb, of Hartforth, Richmond, Yorkshire.

b. 1825, s. 1852, m. 1855.	York, N.R. .	3,983	.	4,634
	Durham . .	430	.	597
		4,413	.	5,231

COWPER, C. F., of Unthank.	Cumberland	2,199	.	4,090
COX, R. S., of Broxwood.	Heref., Oxon .	2,418	.	3,487

** CRANBROOK, Viscount, G.C.S.I., Hemsted Park, Staplehurst.

			acres.		g. an. val.
Coll. Shrews.,	Oriel,	Kent . . .	5,177	.	6,391
Oxon.		Sussex . . .	11	.	35
Club. Carl., Ath., Ox. & Cam., St. Steph.					
b. 1814, m. 1838.			5,188	.	6,426

Served as Under Secretary for the Home Department, President
of the Poor Law Board, Home Secretary, Secretary of State for
War, and Secretary of State for India. Sat for Leominster and
Oxford University.

*** CRAUFURD, Edward Henry John, of Auchenames
House, W. Kilbride, N.B., &c.

Coll. Trinity, Cambridge.	Ayr	3,440	.	3,797
Club. Oxford and Cam.,	Renfrew . .	—	.	78
Brooks's.	Surrey . . .	—	.	75
b. 1816, s. 1867, m. 1863.				
Sat for Ayr Burghs.		3,440	.	3,950

Mr. Craufurd's interest in Renfrew is all in feus; the land in
Surrey is under one acre.

***GOODWIN-COLQUITT-CRAVEN, Charles, of Brock-
hampton Park, Andoversford.

Coll. Eton.	Gloucester .	2,905	.	3,017
Club. Carlton, Boodle's.	Denbigh . .	677	.	1,040
b. 1815, s. 1842, m. 1841.	Wilts . . .	505	.	550
Served in 5th Dragoon Guards.				
		4,087	.	4,607

Exclusive of a few acres Mr. C. still holds in Cheshire and Flint.

CRACKANTHORPE, W., of Newbiggin.			
Westmorland, Cumberland	2,265	.	2,008
CRAMSIE, J., of ——. Antrim	4,613	.	2,738
CRASTER, J., of Craster. Northumberland	2,880	.	4,417

CRAVEN, Earl of, Ashdown Park, Shrivenham, &c.

			acres.		g. an. val.
Coll. Harrow.	Berks . . .		19,225	.	21,767
Club. White's, Travellers',	Warwick . .		8,447	.	13,173
Guards'.	York, W.R. .		1,825	.	399
b. 1841, s. 1866, m. 1867.	Salop . . .		803	.	1,827
Served in Scots Fusilier	Wilts . . .		419	.	328
Guards.	Hants . . .		70	.	99
			30,789	.	37,593

*** CRAWFORD, Andrew Jones, of 22, Crosthwaite Park, Kingstown, Co. Dublin.

Coll. Castledawson, Trin. Co. Dublin.	Armagh .	5,928	.	3,848

b. 1809, s. 1844, m. 1859.

** CRAWFORD and BALCARRES, Earl of, Haigh Hall, Wigan, &c.

Coll. Eton, Trin. Cam.	Aberdeen . .	9,855		6,16c
Club. Carlton, Ath.	Lancashire . .	1,931	.	31,763
b. 1847, s. 1880, m. 1869.	Carmarthen .	1,670	.	1,200
Sat for Wigan.	Westmoreland	24	.	129
		13,480	.	39,252

SHARMAN-CRAWFORD, John, of Crawfordsburn, Belfast.

Coll. Trinity, Dublin.	Down . . .	5,748	.	5,943
Club. Reform, Ulster, Roy. Irish.	Meath . . .	1	.	47
b. 1809, s. 1861.		5,749	.	5,990

** CRAWLEY, John Sambrook, of Stockwood, Luton.

Coll. Trin. Cam.	Bedford . .	8,305	.	7,000
Club. Oxford & Cambridge.	Herts . . .	50	.	56
b. 1823, s. 1852, m. 1852.				
		8,355	.	7,056

** BAKER - CRESSWELL, Oswin Cumming, of Cresswell, Morpeth.

Coll. Eton, Ch. Ch. Oxon.	Northumberland 15,251	.	16,263

Club. Army & Navy.
b. 1844, s. 1879, m. 1872. Served in 3rd Hussars.

CREAGH, C., of Dangan.	Clare . . .	6,004	.	2,724

CREWE. LORD, Crewe Hall, Nantwich.

		acres.	g. an. val.
Club. Travellers'.	Cheshire . .	10,148	. 18,809
b. 1812, s. 1835.	Stafford . .	5,479	. 8,036
	Durham . .	4,093	. 1,957
	Northumberland	2,467	. 4,915
	Wilts . . .	907	. 2,171
		23,094	. 35,888

CREWE, SIR JOHN HARPUR, BART., of Calke Abbey, Ashby-de-la-Zouch. 🐍.

Coll. Rugby, Trin. Cam.	Derby . . .	12,923	. 24,204
b. 1824, s. 1844, m. 1845.	Stafford . . .	14,256	. 10,384
	Leicester . .	877	. 1,778
		28,056	. 36,366

*** CREYKE, RALPH, of Rawcliffe Hall, Selby, &c.

Coll. Eton, Trin. Cam.	York, E. & W. R.	5,273	. 10,425
Club. Brooks's, Devonsh.,	Sussex . . .	1	. 296
St. James's.			
b. 1849, s. 1858. Sits for York.		5,274	. 10,721

Exclusive of ground rents in Yorkshire.
The town of Goole is chiefly being built on this estate.

*** CROFTON, LORD, Mote Park, Roscommon.

Club. Carlton, Sackville St.	Roscommon .	11,053	. 7,332
b. 1834, s. 1869.			

CROFTON, SIR MORGAN GEORGE, BART., of Mohill Castle, Co. Leitrim.

Coll. Eton.	Leitrim . . .	9,590	. 5,387
Club. Arlington, Ral., Jun.	Longford . .	1,608	. 606
Nav. & Mil.	Roscommon .	271	. 229
b. 1850, s. 1867.			
		11,469	. 6,222

CRESSWELL, C., of Pinckney. Wilts, Sal. .	2,693	. 3,007
CROFT, H., of Stillington Hall. York . .	2,636	. 4,108
CROFTON, H. M. EARBERY, of Inchinappa.		
Cork, Wicklow, Roscommon	6,239	. 2,867
CROFTS, H. P., of Sompting. Sussex . .	2,400	. 2,534
CROKE, J., of Studley Priory. Oxon., Bucks	2,191	. 2,559

CROKER, Henry Stanley Monck, of Ballynagarde, Limerick.

		acres.	g. an. val.
b. 1846, s. 1869.	Limerick . .	3,328 .	3,647

** CROMBIE, Alexander, of Thornton Castle, Laurencekirk, N.B.

Coll. Durham G. S.	Kincardine .	2,755 .	3,537
Club. Univ. Ed., Scottish.	Aberdeen .	659 .	671
b. 1836, s. 1877, m. 1870.			
		3,414 .	4,208

CROMIE, Mrs., of Cromore, Portstewart.

s. 1875, m. 1855.	Londonderry .	3,315 .	4,306
	Co. Antrim .	3,756 .	2,912
		7,071 .	7,218

** CROSBIE, James, of Ballyheigue Castle, Tralee.

Coll. Trin. Cam.	Co. Kerry . .	13,422 .	3,793
Club. Union, Kild. St. Dub. b. 1832, s. 1849, m. 1860.			

*** TALBOT-CROSBIE, William, of Ardfert Abbey, Co. Kerry.

Coll. Trin. Cam.	Co. Kerry . .	10,039 .	4,638
Club. Union, Kildare Street, Dublin.			
b. 1816, s. 1818, m. 1st 1839, 2nd 1853, 3rd 1868.			

*** CROSSLEY, Sir Savile Brinton, Bart., of Somerleyton Hall, Lowestoft.

Coll. Eton, Ball. Oxon.	Suffolk . . .	3,163 .	5,086
b. 1857, s. 1872.	Norfolk . . .	131 .	238
		3,294 .	5,324

CROKE, J., of Studley Priory.	Oxon, Bucks	2,191 .	2,559
DELACHEROIS-CROMMELIN, S. A. H., of Carrowdore.	Antrim, Down, Tyrone	8,862 .	2,915
CROWE, Thomas, of Dromore.	Clare . .	6,121 .	2,599
CROWE, W. F., of Cahircalla.	Clare . .	3,126 .	2,022

*** CRUTCHLEY, Lieut.-Gen. Charles, of Sunninghill Park, Berks.

			acres.		g. an. val.
Coll. Eton.	Berks . . .		2,292	.	3,781
Club. Trav., U. Ser.	Northampton .		1,331	.	1,784
b. 1810, s. 1876, m. 1851.	Surrey . . .		15	.	30
	Oxford . . .		42	.	48

Is Hon. Col. of the 23rd Foot.   3,680 . 5,643

** CUBBITT, Right Hon. George, of Denbies, Dorking.

Coll. Trin. Cam.	Devon . . .	2,200	.	2,000
Club. Carlton, Jun. Carl.	Surrey . . .	3,989	.	5,509
b. 1828, s. 1855, m. 1853.	Sussex . . .	600	.	1,000

                                         6,789 . 8,509

Served as Second Church Estates Commissioner. Sits for W. Surrey.

GORDON-CUMMING, Sir William Gordon, Bart., of Altyre, Forres, N.B., &c.

Coll. Eton.	Elgin . . .	36,387	.	13,685
Club. Marl., White's, Turf.	Nairn . . .	2,112	.	155
b. 1848, s. 1866.				

Serves in Scots Fusilier Guards.   38,499 . 13,840

CUNINGHAME, John Charles, of Craigends, Paisley, &c.

Coll. Harrow, Trin. Cam.	Wigtown . .	8,306	.	6,671
Club. Carlton.	Renfrew . .	3,136	.	7,477
b. 1851, s. 1866.	Inverness . .	22,506	.	2,466

                                         33,948 . 16,614

Exclusive of 2,508*l.* in mineral rents.

CULLEY, G., of Fowberry Tower. Nhmbld.	2,935	.	3,441
CULLEY, M. T., of Coupland. Nhmbld. .	2,783	.	3,114
MILNER-GIBSON-CULLUM, G. G., of Hardwick. Suff., Beds, Hunts, York .	2,472	.	4,963
CUMINE, J., of Rattray. Aber., Banff . .	2,397	.	2,087
CUMMING, Adm., of Foston. Dby., Hants	2,678	.	6,347

* MONTGOMERY-CUNINGHAME, Sir William James, Bart., V.C., Glenmoor, Maybole, N.B., &c.

			acres.	g. an. val.
Club. Carlton, Ar. & Navy.	Ayr		3,209	3,177
b. 1834, s. 1870, m. 1869.	Lanark . .		161	152
Served in Rifle Brigade.				
Sat for Ayr Burghs.			3,370	3,329

Exclusive of some fluctuating mine rents.

** CUNINGHAME, John William Herbert, of Lainshaw, Ayr, N.B.

Coll. Eton, Ch. Ch. Oxon.	Ayrshire . .		4,677	7,410
Club. Arthur's. b. 1834, s. 1864, m. 1867.				
Served in 2nd Life Guards.				

With 740*l.* in addition for minerals.

*** CUNINGHAME, Richard Dunning Barré, of Duchrae (res. Hensol Castle), Castle Douglas, N.B.

Coll. Eton,	Kirkcudbright		2,886	1,983
Club. Arthur's, Boodle's,	Peebles . . .		4,193	2,717
St. James's. b. 1836, s. 1864.				
Served in 2nd Life Guards.			7,079	4,700

GUN-CUNINGHAME, Cornwallis Robert Ducarel, of Mount Kennedy, Co. Wicklow.

b. 1846, s. 1880.	Co. Wicklow .		10,479	5,809

*** SMITH-CUNINGHAME, William Cathcart, of Caprington Castle, Kilmarnock, N.B.

Coll. Edin., Haileybury.	Lanark . . .		2,500	1,842
Club. Carlton.	Ayrshire . .		5,156	5,946
b. 1814, s. 1857, m. 1847.				
Was in Bengal Civil Service.			7,656	7,788

Exclusive of 4,869*l.* for minerals.

PICKERSGILL-CUNLIFFE, Mrs., of Coulsdon. Surrey, York . . . . 2,963 . 3,813

CUNLIFFE, Sir Robert A., Bart., of Acton.
Denbigh, Carmarthen . . . . 2,025 . 4,150

CURE, George Edward Capel, of Blake Hall, Ongar.

		acres.	g. an. val.
b. 1852, s. 1878.	Essex . . .	3,449	. 4,190
Serves in the 20th Foot.	Suffolk . . .	99	. 160
	Gloucester .	12	. 30
		3,560	. 4,380

** CURTEIS, Edward Barrett Hodges, of Leasam, Rye, &c.

		acres.	g. an. val.
Coll. Univ. Oxon.	Sussex . . .	1,992	. 4,100
Club. Conservative.	Lincoln . .	1,482	. 1,937
b. 1839, s. 1879.	Kent . . .	12	. 18
		3,486	. 6,055

Served in the 96th Foot and 9th Lancers.

CURWEN, Henry Fraser, of Workington Hall, Cumberland, &c.

		acres.	g. an. val.
b. 1834, s. 1875, m. 1863.	Cumberland .	6,011	. 9,351
Served in 56th Foot.	Lancashire .	1,079	. 569
	Westmoreland	38	. 134
		7,128	. 10,054

CURZON, Nathaniel Charles, of Lockington Hall, Derby.

		acres.	g. an. val.
Coll. Rugby, Bras. Oxon.	Leicester . .	4,753	. 9,663
Club. Arthur's, Devonshire.	Derby . . .	544	. 1,461
b. 1829, s. 1864, m. 1853.	Stafford . . .	365	. 649
		5,662	. 11,773

CUST, Ernest Richard Charles, of Arthingworth, Northampton.

		acres.	g. an. val.
Coll. Ch. Ch. Oxon.	Northampton .	226	. 626
Club. National.	Notts . . .	1,993	. 2,341
b. 1850, s. 1875.	Lincoln . .	14,868	. 22,546
	Lancashire .	33	. 180
	Rutland . .	2	. 3
		17,122	. 25,696

CURTEIS, H. M., of Windmill Hill. Sussex.	2,747	. 3,252
*** CUSACK, Sir R. S., of Furry Park. Dub. Mea.	2,394	. 2,466
CUSACK, T. A., of Carraboola. Longford .	4,980	. 2,812

* DACRE, Lord, The Hoo, Welwyn.

				acres.	*g. an. val.*
Coll. Ch. Ch. Oxon	Herts . . .			6,658 .	9,527
Club. Bood., Whi., Bro.	Essex . . .			3,600 .	3,559
b. 1808, s. 1853, m. 1837.	Cambridge .			2,081 .	2,323
Sat. for Herts.	Suffolk . . .			978 .	1,223
				13,317 .	16,632

** DALGLEISH, John James, of Westgrange, Culross, &c., N.B.

Coll. Ed. Acad., Mer-	Argyll . . .	55,000 .	5,962
chistoun, Ed.	Perth . . .	2,400 .	1,483
Un.			
Club. New, Cons., Edin.		57,400 .	7,445
b. 1836, s. 1870.			

*** DALGLEISH, Lawrence, of Pitfirrane, Dunfermline, N.B.,&c.

Coll. Edin. Univ.	Fife	4,563 .	4,795
Club. Univ., Con., Edin.	b. 1839, s. 1878, m. 1878.		

** DALHOUSIE, Earl of, K.T., Panmure House, Muirdrum, N.B., &c.

Coll. Balliol, Oxon.	Forfarshire .	136,602 .	55,601
Club. J. U. Ser., White's.	Midlothian .	1,419 .	3,002
b. 1847, s. 1880, m. 1877.			
		138,021 .	58,603

Serves as Commander R.N., Ext. Eq. to the Duke of Edinburgh, and Lord in Waiting. Exclusive of 250*l.* mine rental. Sat for Liverpool.

** DALISON, Maximilian Hammond, of Hamptons, Tonbridge, &c.

Coll. Eton, Merton, Oxon.	Lincoln . . .	3,800 .	3,334
b. 1820, s. 1870, m. 1845.	Kent	1,562 .	3,450
		5,362 .	6,784

CUSTANCE, Sir H. F., of Weston.	Norfolk	2,913 .	3,866
CUTHBERT, T., of Garrettstown.	Cork .	3,906 .	2,865
CUTTS, John, of L. Bardfield.	Essex . .	2,737 .	4,094
HUGHES-D'AETH, Narborough, of Knowlton Court. Kent		2,144 .	2,868

DALRYMPLE, Sir Hew, Bart., of Luchie House, North
Berwick, N.B.

		acres.		*g. an. val.*
Club. U. Ser., J. U. Ser.	Haddington .	3,039	.	8,856

b. 1814, s. 1835, m. 1852.   Commanded 71st Foot.

* DALTON, John, of Sleningford Park, Ripon, &c.

Coll. Eton.	Lincoln. . .	4,900	.	6,624
Club. Boodle's, Turf, Gds.	York, N.R. .	700	.	1,413
b. 1848, s. 1871, m. 1871.				
Served in 4th Dragoon Guards.		5,600	.	8,037

** BLAKE-DALY, John Archer, of Raford, Athenry.

Coll. Oscott.	Co. Galway .	11,709	.	3,621
Club. Kild. St., Dublin. b. 1835, s. 1868, m. 1864.				

DAWSON-DAMER, Captain Lionel Seymour William, of
Came House, Dorchester.

Coll. Eton.	Dorset . . .	2,295	.	2,718
Club. White's, Carlton,	Queen's Co. .	1,548	.	1,015
Guards, Garrick.				
b. 1832, s. 1856, m. 1855.		3,843	.	3,733

Served in Scots Fusilier Guards.   Sat for Portarlington.

DANIEL, Thomas Carew, of Stoodleigh Court, Tiverton.

Club. Windham, A. and N.	Devon . . .	5,751	.	4,249

b. 1848, s. 1872, m. 1875.   Served in 2nd Life Guards.

** DARBY, Jonathan Charles, of Leap Cas., Roscrea, King's Co.

Coll. Linc., Oxon.	King's Co. .	4,637	.	2,780
b. 1855, s. 1880.	Worcester . .	270	.	290
		4,907	.	3,070

DALRYMPLE (late), James, of Langlee.

Berwick, Roxburgh	2,936	.	3,446
DALWAY, M. R., of Bella Hill. Antrim .	2,477	.	2,098

*** HALL-DARE, ROBERT WESTLEY, of Newtownbarry House,
Co. Wexford.

		acres.		g. an. val.
b. 1866, s. 1876.	Co. Wexford .	5,239	.	2,894
	Co. Carlow .	5,627	.	1,757
	Essex . . .	1,470	.	3,096
		12,336	.	7,747

DARLEY, HENRY BREWSTER, of Aldby Park, York, &c.

Coll. Chart., Trin. Cam.　York, N. & E. R.　4,787　.　6,134
Club. Arthur's, Carlton.　b. 1809, s. 1846, m. 1832.

*** DARNLEY, EARL OF, Cobham Hall, Gravesend, &c.

Coll. Eton, Ch. Ch.	Kent . . .	9,309	.	20,001
Oxon.	Co. Meath . .	25,463	.	17,349
Club. Carlton, Jun. Carlton,				
Falconry, Sackville		34,772	.	37,350
St., Dublin. b. 1827, s. 1835, m. 1850.				

*** DARROCH, DUNCAN, of Gourock House, Greenock,
N.B., &c.

Coll. Harrow, Trin. Cam.	Ross . . .	30,000	.	1,085
Club. Athenæum, O. & C.	Renfrew . .	4,248	.	4,728
b. 1837, s. 1864, m. 1864.				
Exc. of quarries to the an. val. of 250*l*.		34,248	.	5,813

*** DARTMOUTH, EARL OF, Patshull Hall, Wolverhampton, &c.

Coll. Eton, Ch. Ch. Ox.	York, W.R. .	8,024	.	20,520
Club. Carlton, Trav., St.	Stafford . .	7,316	.	16,356
Stephen's.	Bucks . . .	2,195	.	4,700
b. 1823, s. 1853, m. 1846.	Salop . . .	1,096	.	2,711
	Sussex . . .	454	.	550
	Kent . . .	391	.	10,470
	Middlesex . .	42	.	3,350
Sat for South Staffordshire.		19,518	.	58,657

D'ARCY, H., of New Forest.　Gal., Mayo, Clare 11,434　.　2,780

🐚. DARELL, REV. SIR W. L., BART., of
Fretherne.　Glou., Ches., Derby, Cork .　2,890　.　3,868

*** DARTREY, EARL OF, K.P., Dartrey House, Cootehill, Co.
Monaghan.

		acres.	*g. an. val.*
Coll. Eton, ——, Oxon.	Co. Monaghan	17,732 .	13,724
Club. Trav., Brooks's.	Waterford . .	8,918 .	4,090
b. 1817, s. 1827, m. 1841.	Armagh. . .	1,665 .	2,098
	Louth . . .	1,792 .	1,702
	Devon . . .	5 .	85

Served as Lord in Waiting.   30,112 . 21,699
The Devon land is returned as the DOWAGER LADY CREMORNE'S.

DASHWOOD, CHARLES EDMOND, of Wherstead Park, Ipswich.
b. 1857, s. 1863.   Suffolk . . .   3,218 .   4,056

** DASHWOOD, SIR HENRY WILLIAM, BART., of Kirtlington
Park, Oxford.

Coll. Harrow, C. C. C. Ox.	Oxford . . .	7,515 .	12,081
Club. Travellers'.	Lancashire .	115 .	426
b. 1816, s. 1861, m. 1845.			
		7,630 .	12,507

DASHWOOD, LADY, of The Park, West Wycombe.

b. 1801, s. 1862, m. 1823.	Bucks . . .	4,888 .	6,866
	Oxford . . .	144 .	153
		5,032 .	7,019

** D'AUMALE, H.R.H. THE DUC, Woodnorton, Evesham.
Coll. College d'Henri IV.   Worcester . .   4,604 .   7,407
b. 1822, m. 1844.
    Served as Gen. of Div. in the Fr. Army, and Gov. Gen. of Algeria.

* DAVENPORT, REV. GEORGE HORATIO, of Foxley Hall,
Hereford.

Coll. Oriel, Oxon.	Hereford . .	4,413 .	5,911
Club. Carlton.	Stafford . . .	343 .	780
b. 1832, s. 1862, m. 1866.			
		4,756 .	6,691

DAVENPORT, HENRY, of Maer Hall, Newcastle-under-Lyme.
Coll. Harrow, Ch. Ch. Ox.   Stafford . . .   4,077 .   6,954
Club. Jun. Carl., Windham.
b. 1840, s. 1869.
    A portion of this estate, rented at 82*l.* per annum, is left blank
as to extent.

* BROMLEY-DAVENPORT, William, Capesthorne, Chelford, &c. ♠.

			acres.	g. an. val.
Coll. Harrow, Ch. Ch.	Cheshire	. .	10,166 .	17,372
Oxon.	Warwick	. .	2,711 .	4,671
Club. White's, Carlton,	Stafford	. .	2,697 .	4,283
Travellers'.	Bucks	. . .	73 .	550
b. 1821, s. 1862, m. 1858.				
Sits for North Warwick.			15,647 .	26,876

** DAVIDSON, Duncan Henry Caithness Reay, of Tulloch Castle, Dingwall, N.B.

Club. Junior Carlton.   Ross. . . . 36,130 . 6,093
b. 1836, s. 1881, m. 1860.
This family have in the female line held the barony of Tulloch since 1300.

DAVIDSON, Mrs., of Ridley Hall, Bardon Mill.

           Northumberland 4,640 . 3,085

*** FERGUSON-DAVIE, Sir Henry Robert, Bart., of Creedy Park, Crediton, &c.

Club. Brooks's, Uni. Ser.	Devon . . .	9,970 .	7,850
b. 1798, m. 1823.	Somerset . .	3,250 .	3,020
	Carmarthen .	3,323 .	2,808
Served as General in the			
Army, and in 73rd Foot.		16,543 .	13,678

Sat for Haddington Burghs.
His eldest son, Lt.-Col. F.-Davie, holds the Welsh property.

DAVIES, Arthur Picton Saunders, of Pentre, Boneath, South Wales.

Coll. Eton.	Carmarthen .	4,175 .	3,407
b. 1862, s. 1873.	Cardigan . .	2,930 .	1,760
	Pembroke . .	1,012 .	524
		8,117 .	5,691

DAVIDSON, H. G., of Cantray.   Inver., Nairn   9,591 . 2,844

DAVIES, Ven. Archdeacon, of Court-y-gollen.   Brecon, Monmouth . . . . 2,813 . 2,876

*** DAVIES, ROBERT, of Bodlowdeb, Bangor.

		acres.		g. an. val.
b. 1812.	Anglesea . .	3,926	.	3,978
	Carnarvon . .	6	.	120
	Co. Dublin .	918	.	790
		4,850	.	4,888

** KEVILL-DAVIES, REV. WILLIAM TREVELYAN, of Croft Castle, Kingsland, Hereford.

Club. National.   Herefordshire .   5,000 . 7,800
b. 1826, s. 1847, m. 1845.

** DAVY, JOHN WILLIAM, of Kilverstone Hall, Thetford, &c.

Coll. Eton, Ex. Oxon.	Norfolk . .	4,294	.	3,380
b. 1836, s. 1876, m. 1862.	Suffolk . . .	20	.	21
		4,314	.	3,401

Inclusive of 100 acres which belong to the DOWAGER MRS. DAVY, for life.

** HARRIES-CAMPBELL-DAVYS, WILLIAM DAVYS, of Neuaddfawr, Llandovery.

Coll. Trinity, Oxon.	Brecon . .	1,948	.	897
b. 1812, s. 1832, m. 1847.	Carmarthen .	4,035	.	2,124
	Argyll . . .	2,285	.	1,918
		8,268	.	4,939

The Scottish estate belongs to his eldest son.

** DAWNAY, HON. PAYAN, of Beningborough Hall, York.

Coll. Eton, Ch. Ch. Ox.   York, N.R. .   8,500 . 10,000
Club. Oxford & Cambridge.
b. 1815.

*** DAVIES, RICHARD, of Treborth. Angl., Carnarvon, Dublin	2,379	.	2,750
DAVIES, T. H., of Clareston. Pembroke .	2,802	.	3,059
DAVIS, JOHN, of Rathpeacon. Cork. . .	3,167	.	2,059
DAVIS, MISS H., of ——. Glo., Heref., Sal.	2,259	.	4,190
DAWKINS, LT.-COL., of Over Norton. Oxon	2,512	.	4,010

** DAWSON, Edward Finch, of Launde Abbey, Leicester.

			acres.		g. an. val.
Coll.	Eton.	Leicester . .	3,376	.	5,102
Club.	Army and Navy.	b. 1836, s. 1859, m. 1862.			

Served in Inniskilling Dragoons in the Crimea.

*** MASSY-DAWSON, George Staunton King, of Ballyna-
courty, Tipperary.

Club.	N. and M., Union,	Co. Tipperary	19,093	.	6,331
	Kildare St., Dublin.	Limerick . .	165	.	197
b. 1816, s. 1850, m. 1st 1854, 2nd 1869.					
Served in 14th Light Dragoons.			19,258	.	6,528

** DAWSON (Trustees of late Col.), of Moyola Park, Castle
Dawson.

Coll.	Harrow, Ch. Ch. Oxon.	Londonderry .	2,618	.	1,835
d. 1877.		Co. Cavan .	1,116	.	440
		Co. Dublin .	1	.	1,319
			3,735	.	3,594

** DEAKIN, James, of Werrington Park, Launceston.

b. 1873, s. 1881.	Lancashire .	100	.	16,000
	Cornwall . .	2,200	.	5,000
	Devon . . .	2,000	.	2,250
	Cheshire . .	157	.	2,000
		4,457	.	25,250

DEASE, Gerald, of Orangefield, Co. Cavan, &c.

b. 1854, s. 1874.	Co. Cavan . .	4,647	.	2,829
Serves in 7th Foot.	Co. Westmeath	2,315	.	1,698
		6,962	.	4,527

O'REILLY-DEASE, Matthew, of Dee Farm, Dunleer, Co.
Louth, &c.

Coll.	Paris University.	Co. Louth . .	1,894	.	1,902
Club.	Reform.	Co. Cavan . .	1,417	.	892
b. 1819, s. 1819.		Co. Mayo . .	2,366	.	53
Sat for Co. Louth.		Limerick . .	446	.	501
		Co. Dublin .	181	.	334
		Co. Meath .	184	.	109
			6,488	.	3,791

* PRESCOTT-DECIE, Richard, of Bockelton Court, Tenbury.

		acres.	*g. an. val.*
Coll. Woolwich.	Worcester . .	2,169 .	2,259
Club. Jun. United Service.	Hereford . .	1,112 .	1,323
b. 1838, m. 1860.	Salop . . .	6 .	71
Served in Royal Engineers.			
		3,287 .	3,653

Mrs. P.-Decie's mother owns a large part of this property.

DECIES, Lord, Bolam House, Morpeth, &c.

Club. Carlton, Guards, Jun.	Co. Meath .	979 .	889
United Service.	Northumberland	6,394 .	6,767
b. 1811, s. 1855, m. 1860.	Westmoreland	20 .	177
Served in Grenadier Guards.			
		7,393 .	7,833

DE CLIFFORD, Lord (residence) Kirkby Mallory, Hinckley.

b. 1855, s. 1877, m. 1879.	Co. Mayo . .	11,594 .	5,156
	Co. Galway .	1,406 .	535
		13,000 .	5,691

The Galway estate stands in Dow. Lady de Clifford's name.

** DEEDES, William, of Sandling Park, Hythe.

Coll. Harrow.	Kent . . .	4,904 .	5,539
Club. Carl., Gun, A. & N.			
b. 1834, s. 1862, m. 1861.			
Served in R. Br. in Crimea and Ind. Mutiny.			
Sat for E. Kent.			

*** DE FREYNE, Lord, French Park, Roscommon, &c.

Coll. Downside, Beau-	Roscommon .	34,400 .	13,584
mont.	Sligo . . .	4,059 .	1,488
b. 1855, s. 1868, m. 1877.	Galway . . .	328 .	159
	Mayo . . .	1 .	—
		38,788 .	15,231

The rent of the one acre in Co. Mayo does not amount to 1*l.*

DEANE, W. A., of Webbery. Suff., Devon .	2,737 .	2,845
DE BILLE, Mrs., of Slaghtfreedan. Tyrone .	12,680 .	2,503
DE BOISI, Count. Tipp., Kilk., Lim., Clare	5,767 .	2,910
DE BURGHO, Lady, of Island House. Limerick, Wexford	4,216 .	2,498

** DE HOGHTON, Sir Charles, Bart., of Walton Hall, Preston, &c. ♨.

	acres.	g. an. val.
b. 1823, s. 1876, m. 1863. Lancashire .	4,700	13,397

Served in 73rd Foot.

This estate is in the hands of Trustees of the late Sir Henry de Hoghton, and Sir Charles is only part owner.   Ground rents are not included.

*** DELAMERE, Lord, Vale Royal, Northwich. ♨.

Coll. Eton, Ch. Ch. Cheshire . .	6,794	11,631
Oxon.		

Club. Carlton.   b. 1811, s. 1855, m. 1st 1848, 2nd 1860.

Served in 1st Life Guards.   Sat for Denbigh and Montgomery.

Inclusive of 1,444*l.* for saltworks.

** DELAP, Rev. Robert, of Monellan, Killygordon, Co. Donegal.

Coll. Win., Trin. Dublin.	Co. Donegal .	5,923	2,031
Club. Carlton, Kildare St.,	Bucks . . .	2,241	3,516
Dub., R. St. Geo.	Beds	1,807	2,938
Yacht Club.	Northampton .	329	508
b. 1802, m. 1834.			
		10,300	8,993

** DE LA POER, Edmond (Count), of Gurteen la Poer, Kilsheelan, Waterford.

Club. Reform, Brooks's, St.	Waterford . .	13,448	4,963
George's, Kild. St.	Tipperary . .	12	8
b. 1841, s. 1851, m. 1881.			
		13,460	4,971

Sat for Co. Waterford ; was Chamberlain to Pope Pius IX.

This family claims the De la Poer and Curraghmore Peerage.

** DE LA WARR, Earl, Buckhurst Park, Tonbridge Wells. ♨.

Coll. Balliol, Oxon.	Sussex . . .	17,185	10,827
Club. Carlton, White's.	Cambridge . .	3,240	6,454
b. 1817, s. 1870 and 1873,	Oxford . . .	2,941	4,325
m. 1867.			
		23,366	21,606

The Kentish property (Knole) passed to his Lordship's younger brother on his succeeding to the De la Warr Peerage.

DELACOUR, James, of Sunny Hill. Cork .	5,379	2,246

*** PHILLIPPS DE L'ISLE, Ambrose Charles, of Garendon
    Park, Loughborough, &c.

		acres.	g. an. val.
Coll. Oscott.	Leicester . .	7,358 .	15,334

b. 1834, s. 1878, m. 1st 1861, 2nd 1880.

DE L'ISLE and DUDLEY, Lord, Penshurst Place, Tonbridge,
    &c.

Coll. Eton.	Kent . . .	4,356 .	5,748
Club. Carlton, White's,	York, N.R. .	4,896 .	4,484
Boodle's.			
b. 1828, s. 1851, m. 1850.		9,252 .	10,232

Served in Royal Horse Guards.

** DELMÉ, Henry Peter, of Cams Hall, Fareham.

| *Coll.* Eton. | Hampshire . | 6,258 . | 6,986 |

Club. Berkeley, Han. Sq.   b. 1793, s. 1815, m. 1826.
    Served in 88th Foot in Peninsular and American (1813) wars.

DE MAULEY, Lord, Langford House, Lechlade, &c.

Coll. Eton.	Somerset . .	2,457 .	7,433
Club. Travellers', Brooks's,	Oxford . . .	1,255 .	1,901
Ath., White's.			
b. 1815, s. 1855, m. 1838.		3,712 .	9,334

Sat for Poole and for Dungarvan.   "All wrong"—Ld. de M.

*** DENBIGH, Earl of, Newnham Paddox, Lutterworth, &c.

Coll. Eton, Trin. Cam.	Leicester . .	370 .	1,100
Club. Carlton, Travellers',	Flint	2,848 .	5,240
St. George's.			
b. 1823, s. 1865, m. 1st 1846, 2nd 1857.		3,218 .	6,340

*** DENISON, William Evelyn, of Ossington Hall, Newark.

Coll. Eton, Woolwich.	Notts . . .	3,674 .	6,103
Club. J. U. S., Carl., St.	Lincoln . .	2,635 .	4,067
Steph.			
b. 1843, s. 1873.		6,309 .	10,170

Served in R. H. Art.   Sat for Nottingham.

DE MONTMORENCY, Rev. W., of Castle			
Morres. Kilkenny		4,845 .	2,849
DE MORELLA, Countess, of Wentworth.			
Surrey, Merioneth		2,424 .	3,169

*** DENNY, Sir Edward, Bart., of Tralee (res. 31, The
     Grove, West Brompton, S.W.)   *acres.   gr. an. val.*
Coll. Exeter, Oxon.   Kerry . . .   21,479   .   9,685
b. 1796, s. 1831.

** DENT, John Coucher, of Sudeley Castle, Winchcombe.
Coll. Eton, Magd. Oxon.   Gloucester . .   3,111   .   4,332
Club. Conservative.   Worcester . .   236   .   339
b. 1819, s. 1855, m. 1847.   ─────────────────
                                               3,347   .   4,671

** DENT, John Dent, of Ribston Hall, Wetherby, &c.
Coll. Eton, Trin. Cam.   York,E.&W.R.   6,324   . 10,962
Club. Brooks's, O. & C.   Lincoln . .   2,130   .   3,608
b. 1826, s. 1875, m. 1855.   ─────────────────
     Sat for Scarborough and Knaresborough.   8,454   . 14,570

** DERBY, Earl of, Knowsley, Prescot, &c.   ⚓.
🌳 *Coll.* Eton, Rugby, Trin. Lancashire . 57,000   . 156,735
         Cam.   Cheshire . .   9,500   .   6,460
Club. Travellers'.   Flint. . . .   92   .   78
                              Kent   . . .   950   . unstated
                              Surrey . . .   1,400   .   do.
b. 1826, s. 1869, m. 1870.   ─────────────────
                                              68,942   . 163,273
     Served as Under Secretary for Foreign Affairs, Secretary for
Colonies, Secretary of State for India, and Secretary for Foreign
Affairs.   Sat for King's Lynn.
     Exclusive of 900 acres leased for buildings, and returned in the
tenants' names.

** DERING, Sir Edward Cholmeley, Bart., of Surrenden
      Dering, Pluckley.   ⚓.
Coll. Ch. Ch. Oxon.   Kent   . . .   7,280   . 12,000
Club. Carl., Trav., Oxf. and Cam.   b. 1807, s. 1811, m. 1832.
     Sat for Wexford, Romney, and for East Kent.

** DERING, George Edward, of Lockleys, Welwyn, &c.
Coll. Rugby.   Herts . . .   535   .   1,045
b. 1831, s. 1859.   Durham . .   1,020   .   759
                              Co. Galway .   11,206   .   4,502
                                              ─────────────────
     Mr. Dering claims the ⚓ mark.   12,761   .   6,306

* DENT, W., of Crosby Ravensworth. Westd.   2,900   .   2,000

DE ROBECK, BARON, of Gowran Grange, Naas, Co. Kildare.

		acres.	g. an. val.
Coll. Sandhurst.	Dublin . . .	1,660 .	2,098
Club. Army & Navy, Kild.	Kildare . . .	1,838 .	1,358
St., Dublin.	Wicklow . .	2,038 .	1,654
b. 1823, s. 1858, m. 1856.			
Served in 8th Foot.		5,536 .	5,110

** DE ROS, LORD, Old Court, Strangford, Co. Down.

Coll. Eton.	Co. Down . .	2,952 .	3,866
Club. Carlton.	Meath . . .	1,271 .	1,148
b. 1827, s. 1874, m. 1853.			
		4,223 .	5,014

Served in 1st Life Guards and as Lord in Waiting, and Equerry to the Prince Consort and to the Queen.

*** DERWENT, LORD, Hackness, Scarborough.

Coll. Eton.   York, N.R. . 12,764 . 10,026
Club. Brooks's, Tra., Dev. b. 1829, m. 1850.
Served in 2nd Life Guards. Sat for Scarborough.

** DE SALIS, COUNT JOHN, of Hillingdon Place, Uxbridge, &c.

Coll. Eton.	Limerick . .	4,026 .	3,349
b. 1864, s. 1871.	Armagh . .	3,663 .	5,392
	Middlesex . .	388 .	1,040
		8,077 .	9,781

** DESART, EARL OF, Desart Court, Kilkenny.

Coll. Eton.	Kilkenny . .	8,000 .	5,778
Club. Carl., White's, Beac.	Tipperary . .	932 .	500
b. 1845, s. 1865, m. 1st 1871, 2nd 1881.		8,932 .	6,278

Served in Grenadier Guards.

** DE TABLEY, LORD, Tabley, Knutsford.

Coll. Eton, Ch. Ch. Oxon. Cheshire . . 6,195 . 14,647
Club. Travellers', St. James's.
b. 1811, s. 1827, m. 1st 1832, 2nd 1871.
Served as Lord in Waiting and as Treasurer of the Household.

DE RODES, W. HATFIELD, of Barlborough.
          Derby, York . . . . 2,293 . 3,922

** DE TRAFFORD, Sir Humphrey, Bart., of Trafford Park, Manchester. ♨.

			acres.		g. an. val.
Coll. Oscott.	Lancashire	.	7,300	.	30,750
Club. Carlton.	Cheshire .	.	2,500	.	5,760

b. 1808, s. 1852, m. 1855.

Served in Royal Dragoons.   9,800 . 36,510

Exclusive of large parts of the Chat and other "Mosses."

DE VESCI, Viscount, Abbeyleix House, Queen's Co.

Coll. Eton.	Dublin .	.	.	420	. 31,713
Club. Guards, White's, Trav.	Queen's Co.	.		15,069	. 9,410
b. 1844, s. 1875, m. 1872.	Cork	.	.	818	. 3,445
	Kent	.	.	375	. 646

Serves in Coldstream Guards.   16,682 . 45,214

*** DE VIRTE, Baroness, of Benholme Castle, Kincardine, N.B., &c. (res. Ripafratta, Pisa, Italy).

s. 1869, m. 1849.	Kincardine	.	740	.	1,096
	Devonshire	.	2,705	.	2,587

    3,445 . 3,683

*** DEVON, Earl of, Powderham Castle, Exeter, &c. ♨.

Coll. Westm., Ch. Ch.	Devon .	.	.	20,049	. 30,995
Oxon.	Co. Limerick	.		33,026	. 14,525
Club. Carlton, Athenæum.					
b. 1807, s. 1859, m. 1830.				53,075	. 45,520

Served as Poor Law Inspector, Secretary Poor Law Board, Chancellor Duchy Lancaster, President of Poor Law Board. Sat for South Devon.

D'ESTERRE, H. V., of Castle Henry.
Clare, Limerick . . . . 3,147 . 2,108

DE VERE, Sir Stephen, Bart., of Curragh
Chase. Limerick . . . . 4,166 . 2,123

DEVONSHIRE, Duke of, K.G., F.R.S., Chatsworth, Bakewell.
&c. 🪙.

		acres.	g. an. val.
Coll. Eton, Trin. Cam.	Derbyshire .	89,462	89,557
Club. Ath., Ox. and Cam.,	York, W.R. .	19,239	16,718
Jun. Ox. and Cam.	Lancashire .	12,681	12,494
b. 1808, s. 1858, m. 1829.	Sussex . .	11,062	14,881
	Somerset . .	3,014	4,918
	Lincoln . .	1,392	2,657
	Cumberland .	983	1,925
	Middlesex . .	524	3,079
	Notts . . .	125	130
	Stafford . . .	26	40
	Cheshire . .	28	21
	Co. Cork . .	32,550	19,326
	Co. Waterford	27,483	15,000
	Co. Tipperary	3	4
		198,572	180,750

Sat for Cambridge University, for Malton, and for North
Derbyshire.

Included in the above is a Derbyshire rental of 6,257*l.* standing
in Lord Hartington's name.

DE WINTON, Walter, of Maesllwych Castle, Hay.

b. 1868, s. 1878.	Radnor . .	4,955	6,193
	Glamorgan .	2,458	6,333
	Brecon . .	2,485	3,115
	Hereford . .	2	1
		9,900	15,642

·** TENNYSON-D'EYNCOURT, Admiral Edwin Clayton,
🌲   C.B., of Bayons Manor, Market Rasen, &c.

Coll. Westm., Roy. Nav. C.	Lincoln . .	3,504	6,200

Club. Uni. Ser., Travellers'. b. 1813, s. 1871, m. 1859.
Served in Royal Navy.

CLIFTON-DICCONSON, William Charles, of Wrightington
Hall, Wigan. 🪙.

b. 1822, s. 1881, m. 1881.	Lancashire .	4,380	9,983

DEW, Tomkyns, of Whitney. Hereford .	2,549	4,178

DICKINSON, Francis Henry, of Kingweston, Somerton.

		acres.		*g. an. val.*
Coll. West., Trin. Cam.	Somerset . .	4,279	.	5,843

Club. Ath., U. Uni.   b. 1813, s. 1837, m. 1835.
Sat for West Somerset.

** DICKSON, Alexander, M.D., of Hartree, Peebles, N.B., &c.

Coll. Edin. Univ.	Peebles. . .	2,237	.	2,598
Club. Western Glas.,New Ed.	Lanark . . .	1,416	.	1,323
b. 1836, s. 1866.				
		3,653	.	3,921

Regius Professor of Botany, University of Glasgow.

** DICKSON, Archibald, of Hassendeanburn, Coldstream, N.B.

b. 1840, s. 1876.	Roxburgh . .	4,139	.	3,531
	Berwick . .	1,367	.	2,237
		5,506	.	5,768

DICKSON, Major-Gen., of Croon Castle, Limerick, &c.

Club. Army and Navy.	Berks . . .	1,294	.	1,687
b. 1828, s. 1870.	Limerick . .	8,559	.	2,924
	Tipperary . .	513	.	374
Served in 16th Lancers.		10,366	.	4,985

** WINGFIELD-DIGBY, George Digby, of Sherborne Castle.
Dorset.

Coll. Westm., Ch. Ch. Ox.	Dorset . . .	21,230	.	36,106
Club. Jun. United Ser.	Somerset . .	5,125	.	8,512
b. 1797, s. 1856, m. 1824.	Warwick . .	528	.	1,474
		26,883	.	46,092

HUME-DICK, W. W. Fitz-W., of Hume-wood. Wicklow	4,770	.	2,534
DICKSON, S. F., of Creaves. Limerick . .	2,540	.	2,076
DICKSON, W. R., of Chisholme. Rox., Slk.	4,656	.	2,614
♟. DIGBY (late K. H.), of Lauderstown. Kildare, Sligo, Westmeath, Wicklow .	3,580	.	2,382

*** DIGBY, Lord, Minterne House, Cerne, &c. ✠.

		acres.	g. an. val.
Coll. Harrow.	Dorset . . .	1,886 .	2,291
Club. Trav., Carl., Jun. Carl.,	Warwick . .	124 .	228
Jun. Uni. Ser.	King's Co .	29,722 .	12,745
b. 1809, s. 1856, m. 1837.	Queen's Co. .	938 .	542
Served in 9th Lancers.	Co. Mayo . .	6,835 .	162

39,505 . 15,968

The Mayo estate belongs to the Hon. E. H. T. Digby.

** DIGBY, John Wingfield, of Coleshill Park, Birmingham.

		acres.	g. an. val.
Coll. Merton, Oxon.	Warwick . .	8,904 .	15,080
Club. Arthur's, Jun. Uni.	Worcester . .	182 .	369
Service.			
b. 1830, s. 1878, m. 1858.		9,086 .	15,449

** DILLON, Sir John Fox, Bart., of Lismullen, Navan, Co. Meath.   (Baron of the Holy Roman Empire.)

Coll. Magd. Cambridge.   Co. Meath . .   3,209 .   3,106
Club. Kildare Street, Dublin.   b. 1843, s. 1875, m. 1879.

DILLON, Viscount, Dytchley Park, Charlbury.

b. 1812, s. 1879, m. 1843.	Oxfordshire .	5,444 .	6,989
	Co. Mayo . .	83,749 .	19,231
	Roscommon .	5,435 .	2,477
	Westmeath .	136 .	65
Served in the Home Office.			

94,764 . 28,762

DIXIE, Sir Alexander Beaumont Churchill, Bart., of Bosworth Park, Hinckley.

Coll. Harrow.	Leicester . .	5,379 .	10,405
Club. Raleigh.	Notts . . .	523 .	666
b. 1851, s. 1872, m. 1875.	Derby . . .	31 .	44

5,933 . 11,115

FETHERSTON-DILKE, W. G., of Maxtoke.
Warwick . . . .   2,731 .   3,845
DIMSDALE, Baron, of Essenden.   Herts,
Essex, Devon . . . .   2,382 .   3,641

** DOBBS, Conway Richard, of Castle Dobbs, Carrickfergus.

			acres.	*g. an. val.*
Club.	Sackville St. Dub.	Antrim . . .	5,060	5,065
b. 1796, s. 1840, m. 1st 1826,	Kildare . .	7,971	2,424
2nd 1875.				
			13,031	7,489

Served in Royal Navy (Commander). Sat for Carrickfergus.

*** MARRIOTT-DODINGTON, Thomas, of Horsington House, Wincanton.

			acres	*g. an. val.*
Coll.	Trin. Cam.	Surrey . . .	1	530
b. 1839, s. 1876, m. 1865.		Somerset . .	3,286	6,284
		Dorset . . .	66	170
			3,353	6,984

DODSON, Rt. Hon. John George, of Conyboro', Lewes, &c.

Coll.	Eton, Ch. Ch. Oxon.	Sussex . . .	2,916	3,167
Club.	Ref., Brooks's, U.	York, W.R. .	181	300
	Uni., Devonshire.			
b. 1825, s. 1858, m. 1856.			3,097	3,467

Served as Financial Secretary to the Treasury, and Deputy Speaker House of Commons. Sat for East Sussex and Chester. Sits for Scarborough. Is Pres. of the Local G.B.

*** DODSWORTH, Sir Charles Edward Smith, Bart., of Thornton Watlass, Bedale.

Coll.	Eton.	York,N.&W.R.	4,042	5,464
b. 1853, s. 1858.	Excl. of mineral rents.			

DIXON, Miss, of Holton Park. Lincoln .	2,275	2,308
DIXON, Will. Smith, of Govanhill. Lank., Renfrew, Linlithgow, Ayr	2,843	10,868
DOBBIN, Col., of Annagh. Arm., Cav. .	3,461	2,704
DOBBS, C. E., of Glenariff. Ant., Kild. . .	7,648	2,446
DOBEDE, of Exning. Suff., Cambs. . . .	2,485	3,622
DOD, Mrs., of Llannerch. Denb., Flint., Ches.	2,245	3,663

** DOMVILLE, Sir Charles Compton William, Bart., of
    Santry House, Dublin, &c.   *acres.*   *g. an. val.*
Coll. Sandhurst.   Co. Dublin . 6,262 . 17,374
Club. Brooks's, Boodle's, Jun. Uni. Ser., Sackville Street.
b. 1822, s. 1857, m. 1861. Served in 13th Light Dragoons.

Sir C. Domvile's acreage is much larger, as eleven of his
biggest tenants are returned as owners of their holdings.

DOMVILE, William Compton, of Thornhill, Co. Wicklow, &c.

Club. Carlton.	Dublin . . .	1,513	. 1,819
b. 1825, m. 1854.	Mayo . . .	6,040	. 2,056
	Queen's Co. .	1,512	. 999
	Wicklow . .	1	. 2
		9,066	. 4,876

*** DONEGALL, Marquis of, K.P., G.C.H., C.B., The Castle,
        Belfast, &c. $. (Kt. Com. Legion Honour.)

Coll. Eton, Ch. Ch. Oxon.	Donegal . .	8,155	. 6,829
Club. Brooks's, White's,	Antrim . . .	14,617	. 32,320
Boodle's, Uni. Serv.	Londonderry .	193	. 563
b. 1797, s. 1844, m. 1st 1822,	Down . . .	31	. 1,937
2nd 1862.		22,996	. 41,649

Served in 7th Hussars and as Aide-de-Camp to the Queen,
Vice-Chamberlain of the Household, and Captain Yeoman of the
Guard. Sat for Carrickfergus, for Belfast, and for Co. Antrim.

The above rental partly arises from nearly 140,000 acres, chiefly
in Donegal, let on leases for ever.

** DONERAILE, Viscount, Doneraile Court, Co. Cork.

Coll. Eton, Ch. Ch. Oxon.	Co. Cork . .	16,400	. 8,500
Club. Arthur's, White's,	Waterford . .	12,300	. 6,500
Carlton.			
b. 1818, s. 1854, m. 1851.		28,700	. 15,000

DOHERTY, R., of Redcastle. Donegal . . 6,363 . 2,040
DOLLING, R. W. Ratcliffe, of Magheralin,
    Londonderry, Down, Armagh . . . . 3,950 . 2,434
DOMVILLE, Sir J. Graham, Bart., of
    Palermo. Kent, Herts, Lincoln . . . 2,682 . 3,067

DONINGTON, Lord.

The agent writes "that in the Government return Lord Donington's possessions are much mixed up with those of Lord Loudoun"———whom see———no other correction has, however, reached me.

DONOUGHMORE, Earl of, K.C.M.G., Knocklofty, Clonmel.

		acres.	g. an. val.
Coll. Eton, Balliol, Oxon.	Tipperary . .	4,711 .	4,763
Club. Carlton, St. James's,	Waterford . .	2,878 .	2,136
Garrick.	Co. Cork . .	1,972 .	1,508
b. 1848, s. 1866, m. 1874.	Wexford . .	1,307 .	1,163
	Kilkenny . .	486 .	216
	Monaghan . .	373 .	318
	Dublin . . .	143 .	245
	Louth . . .	80 .	75
		11,950 .	10,424

Served as British Commissioner to E. Roumelia under the Berlin Treaty.

** COTTRELL-DORMER, Charles Walter, of Rousham Hall, Oxford, &c.

Coll. Eton.	Oxford . .	2,341 .	2,547
b. 1860, s. 1880.	Westmoreland	2,956 .	1,862
Serves in 13th Hussars.	York, W.R. .	907 .	1,459
	York, E.R. .	1,649 .	2,454
		7,853 .	8,322

The Westmoreland and W.R. estates belong to his mother; the E.R. one to his grandmother.

*** DORMER, Lord, Grove Park, Warwick, &c.

Coll. Oscott.	Warwick . .	2,246 .	3,950
Club. Trav., Pratt's.	Bucks . . .	1,189 .	2,070
b. 1830, s. 1871, m. 1st 1866, 2nd 1871.		3,435 .	6,020

Served in Royal Horse Guards, Grenadier Guards, and 74th Highlanders, in the Crimea and Indian Mutiny.

DONOVAN, R., of Ballymore.	Wex., Tip. .	4,268 .	2,488
DORCHESTER, Lord.	Tyr., Meath, Hants	14,521 .	2,955

AKERS-DOUGLAS, Aretas, of Chilstone Park, Maidstone, &c.

			acres.	g. an. val.
Coll. Eton, Univ. Oxon.	Kent	. .	3,753 .	4,937
Club. Union, Carlton.	Dumfries	. .	6,629 .	6,013
b. 1851, s. 1856, m. 1875.	Midlothian	. .	3,106 .	1,388
	Lanark	. .	2,190 .	752

Exclusive of a mineral rent of 2,909*l.*
Sits for E. Kent.   15,678 . 13,090

*** SCOTT-DOUGLAS, Sir George Henry, Bart., of Springwood Park, Kelso, N.B.

Club. Carlton, Army and   Roxburgh . .   5,568 .   6,771
       Navy.   b. 1825, s. 1836, m. 1851.
Served in 34th Foot.   Sat for Roxburghshire.

** MALCOLM-DOUGLAS, Miss, of Cavers, Hawick, N.B.

s. 1878.   Roxburgh . .   9,840 .   7,937

BLACKER-DOUGLAS, St. John Thomas, of Grace Hall, Lurgan, &c.

Club. Carlton, Kild. St.,	Down	. . .	2,791 .	3,293
Dublin.	Kerry	. . .	8,159 .	2,298
	Armagh	. .	266 .	385
b. 1822, s. 1849 and 1880, m. 1855.				
			11,216 .	5,976

** ROBINSON-DOUGLAS, William Douglas, of Orchardton, Castle Douglas, N.B., &c.

Coll. Ch. Ch. Oxon.   Kirkcudbright   5,320 .   3,430
Club. National.   b. 1851, s. 1878, m. 1879.

HERIOT-MAITLAND-DOUGALL, Adml., of Scotscraig. Fife	2,625 .	2,891
DOUGLAS, Sir J., G.C.B., of Glenfinart. Arg.	15,597 .	2,589
DOUGLAS, Hon. Mrs., of Strathendry. Fife	2,080 .	2,687
JOHNSTONE-DOUGLAS, A. H., of Lockerbie House. Dumfries	2,336 .	3,345
DOWNIE, Miss (the late), of Appin. Arg., Fife	37,345 .	2,764

DOWDESWELL, William, of Pull Court, Tewkesbury.

		acres.		*g. an. val.*
Coll. West., Ch. Ch. Oxon.	Worcester . .	3,960	.	7,529

Club. Athenæum. b. 1804, s. 1851, m. 1839.

Sat for Tewkesbury.

Inclusive of a rental of 1,832*l.* returned as belonging to his eldest son.

DOWNE, Dowager Viscountess, Baldersby Park, Thirsk, &c.

b. 1825, s. 1857, m. 1st 1843,	York, N., E., &	22,237	.	26,843
2nd 1863.	W.R.			

DOWNE, Viscount, Danby Lodge, Yarm. $.

Coll. Eton, Ch. Ch. Oxon.	York, N., E., &	15,515	.	19,257
Club. Carlton, White's.	W.R.			
b. 1844, s. 1857, m. 1869.	Essex . . .	3	.	5

Serves in 2nd Life Guards. 15,518 . 19,262

** DOWNSHIRE, Marquis of, Hillsborough Castle, Co. Down.

b. 1871, s. 1874.	Berks . . .	5,287	.	4,853
	Suffolk . . .	281	.	316
	Co. Down . .	78,051	.	73,378
	Wicklow . .	15,766	.	5,018
	King's Co. . .	13,679	.	7,261
	Antrim . . .	5,787	.	4,925
	Kildare . . .	1,338	.	940

120,189 . 96,691

DOYNE, Charles Mervyn, of Wells, Gorey, Co. Wexford.

Coll. Magd. Cam.	Wexford . .	7,134	.	4,692
Club. Carlton, St. James's,	Carlow . . .	3,203	.	2,561
Boodle's, Kild. St., Dublin.	Kildare . . .	518	.	299
b. 1839, s. 1870, m. 1867.		10,855	.	7,552

FULLER-ELLIOT-DRAKE, Sir Francis George Augustus, Bart., of Nutwell Court, Exeter, &c.

Club. Carlton.	Devon . . .	7,573	.	8,844
b. 1837, s. 1870, m. 1861.	Surrey . . .	92	.	249

Served in Royal Horse Guards. 7,665 . 9,093

** TYRWHITT-DRAKE, Thomas, of Shardeloes, Amersham.

		acres.	g. an. val.
b. 1817, s. 1852, m. 1843.	Lincoln . . .	8,502	. 11,205
	Bucks . . .	5,767	. 7,483
The last pty. belongs to	Cheshire . .	3,834	. 5,516
" Mr. Drake and another "	Oxford . . .	360	. 482
		18,463	. 24,686

SAWBRIDGE-ERLE-DRAX, John Samuel Wanley, of Holnest Park, Sherborne, &c.

		acres.	g. an. val.
Club. Windham, Carlton.	Dorset . . .	15,069	. 11,631
b. 1800, s. *jur. uxo.* 1828,	Kent . . .	3,173	. 3,292
m. 1827.	Lincolnshire .	1,610	. 2,449
Sat for Wareham.	Wilts. . . .	1,902	. 2,093
	Somerset . .	883	. 1,344
	York, N.R. .	623	. 1,034
Of this total, Miss Drax is	Surrey . . .	327	. 1,322
retd. as owner of 8,953 acres.			
		23,587	. 23,165

DREWE, Major-General, of the Grange, Honiton. ⚓.

Club. Army and Navy.   Devon . . .   3,684 .   4,756
b. 1830, s. 1874, m. 1858.
Served in 23rd Foot at Alma, Inkerman, and Sebastopol.

** DROGHEDA, Marquis of, K.P., Moore Abbey, Monastrevan, Co. Kildare.

		acres.	g. an. val.
Coll. Eton.	Kildare . . .	16,609	. 8,951
Club. Carlton, Travellers'.	Queen's Co. .	2,688	. 1,515
White's, Royal Irish.			
b. 1825, s. 1837, m. 1847.		19,297	. 10,466

Lord D. does not include here anything on perpetuity leases.

DRUMMOND, Hon. Arthur Hay, of Cromlix Cottage, Dunblane, &c., N.B.

Club. Carlton, Marlb.   Perthshire . .   7,683 . 5,239
b. 1833, m. 1855.
Served as Captain Royal Navy.

DROUGHT, T. A., of Lettybrook. King's Co.   3,594 . 2,014

DRUMMOND, Edgar Atheling, of Cadlands, Southampton.

			acres.		*g. an. val.*
Club. Carlton, Travellers'.	Bucks	. . .	562	.	672
b. 1825, s. 1865, m. 1858.	Hants	. . .	5,175	.	5,842
Served in Royal Navy.			5,737	.	6,514

760*l.* of this total is returned as belonging to his mother, Lady Elizabeth F. Drummond.

** WILLIAMS-DRUMMOND, Sir James Hamlyn, Bart., of Edwinsford, Llandilo, S. Wales, &c.

Coll. Eton.	Carmarthen	.	9,281	.	6,357
Club. Guards, Whi., Pratt's.	Midlothian	.	482	.	1,234
b. 1857, s. 1866.					
Serves in Grenadier Guards.			9,763	.	7,591

** DRUMMOND, Robert, of Palace Gate, Kensington.

Coll. Eton.	Co. Kerry	. .	29,780	.	3,065
Club. Travellers'.					
b. 1822, s. 1858, m. 1854.					

DUBERLY, William, of Gaynes Hall, St. Neot's.

Coll. Eton.	Huntingdon	.	3,712	.	5,320
Club. Guards, Brooks's,	Bedford	. .	345	.	366
Beaconsfield.	Cambridge	. .	647	.	983
b. 1841, s. 1864, m. 1874.					
Served in Grenadier Guards.			4,704	.	6,669

** DU CANE, Sir Charles, K.C.M.G., of Braxted Park, Witham.

Coll. Chart. Ex. Oxon. Essex . . . 5,409 . 7,044
Club. Carlton, Conservative, Travellers', Boodle's, Marlb.
b. 1825, s. 1850, m. 1863.
Served as Lord of the Admiralty and Governor of Tasmania. Sat for Maldon and for N. Essex. Is Chairman of H.M. Board of Customs.

** DRYDEN, Sir E. H. Leigh, Bart., of
Canons Ashby. Northamptonshire. . 2,615 . 3,500

** DUCIE, EARL OF, Tortworth Court, Falfield, Gloucestershire, &c.

			acres.		*g. an. val.*
Coll.	Eton.	Gloucester	.	5,193	.	8,419
Club.	Ath., Brooks's, Trav.	Oxford . . .	8,798	.	13,430
b. 1827, s. 1853, m. 1849.	Lancashire	.	1	.	122
Served as Capt. Yeoman					
of the Guard. Sat for Stroud.		13,992	.	21,971

*** DUCKETT, WILLIAM, of Duckett's Grove, Carlow, &c.

Coll.	Eton, Ch. Ch. Oxon.	Carlow . . .	4,923	.	4,208
Club.	Cons., Kild. Street,	Co. Wicklow .	1,156	.	1,000
	Dublin, R. St. Geo.	Co. Dublin .	16	.	200
	Yacht Club.	Kildare . .	499	.	380
b. 1822, s. 1866, m. 1868.	Wexford . .	48	.	60
		Queen's Co. .	5,004	.	3,854
			11,646	.	9,702

*** DUCKWORTH, REV. WILLIAM ARTHUR, of Orchardleigh Park, Frome, &c.

Coll.	Eton, Trin. Cam.	Somerset . .	2,174	.	4,086
Club.	Athen., Uni. Univ.	Lancashire. .	1,332	.	4,995
b. 1829, s. 1876, m. 1859.					
			3,506	.	9,081

The Lancashire rental includes 3,374*l.* of chief rents.

DUDLEY, EARL OF, Witley Court, Stourport.

Coll.	Eton, Ch. Ch. and	Roxburgh . .	1,086	.	2,825
	Trin. Oxon.	Worcester . .	14,698	.	48,545
Club.	Carlton, White's, St.	Stafford . .	4,730	.	68,460
	James's.	Merioneth . .	4,472	.	3,114
b. 1817, s. 1835, m. 1st 1851,	Salop . . .	568	.	232
	2nd 1865.				
			25,554	.	123,176

*** DUFF, GARDEN ALEXANDER, of Hatton Castle, Turiff, N.B.

Coll.	Har., Trin. Cam.	Aberdeen . .	11,576	.	9,661
Club.	Hanover Square.				
b. 1853, s. 1866, m. 1878.					

STERRIT-DUFF, MRS., of Corsindae. Aber.   4,481   .   2,171

GORDON-DUFF, Lachlan Duff, of Drummuir Castle, Keith, N.B., &c.

		acres.	*g. an. val.*
Club. United Service.	Banff . . .	13,053 .	7,418
b. 1817, s. 1855, m. 1847.	Aberdeen . .	4,328 .	2,356
Served in 20th Foot.	Elgin . . .	557 .	673
Sat for Banffshire.			
		17,938 .	10,447

The bulk of the Elgin property is returned as belonging to his eldest son, T. D. G.-Duff.

** DUFF, Robert William, of Fetteresso Castle, Stonehaven, N.B., &c.

		acres.	*g. an. val.*
Club. Brooks's, Army and	Kincardine .	8,922 .	4,536
Navy.	Banff . . .	2,671 .	2,416
b. 1835, s. 1861, m. 1871.	Aberdeen . .	1,588 .	2,851
Served in the Royal Navy.			
Sits for Banffshire.		13,181 .	9,803

DUFFERIN, Earl of, K.P., K.C.B., G.C.M.G., Clandeboye, Belfast.

Coll. Eton, Ch. Ch. Oxon.	Co. Down . .	18,238 .	21,043

Club. Trav., Ath., Royal Irish. b. 1826, s. 1841, m. 1862.

Served as Governor-General of Canada, Lord in Waiting, Commissioner in Syria, Under Secretary for India and for War, and Ch. D. Lancaster; was Amb. to Russia; is Amb. to Turkey.

*** DUGDALE, William Stratford, of Merevale Hall, Atherstone.

		acres.	*g. an. val.*
Coll. Balliol, Oxon.	Warwick . .	5,689 .	10,418
Club. Carlton, Ox. & Cam.	Stafford . .	5 .	15
b. 1828, s. 1871, m. 1871.			
		5,694 .	10,433

DUFFIELD, C.P., of Marcham. Berks .	2,521 .	3,037
DUGDALE, Henry, of Crathorne. York	2,038 .	2,352
DUGDALE (late), J., of Ivy Bank. Lan.,York	4,086 .	2,151
DUGDALE, Jas. Broughton, of Wroxall Abbey. Warwickshire, Lancashire . .	2,046 .	3,137

DUKE, Sir James Bart., of Laughton Lodge, Hurst Green.

			acres.	*g. an. val.*
Coll. Eton.	Sussex . .		4,275 .	4,172

b. 1865, s. 1873.

*** DUNALLEY, Lord, Kilboy, Nenagh.

Coll. Trin. Cam.	Tipperary . .	21,081 .	7,162

b. 1807, s. 1854, m. 1841.

** DUFF-DUNBAR, Garden, of Hempriggs Castle, Wick, N.B., &c.

Club. E. I. Uni. Ser.	Caithness . .	26,880 .	11,045

b. 18—, s. 1875, m. 1876.
  Served in 79th Highlanders during Indian Mutiny.

* DUNBAR, John George Henry William, of Woburn, Donaghadee, &c.

Coll. Eton.	Donegal . .	5,247 .	1,522
Club. White's, Boodle's,	Tyrone . .	1,513 .	1,391
Carlton, Marlb.,	Co. Down . .	787 .	1,244
Turf.	Armagh . .	508 .	558
b. 1848, s. 1875.	Londonderry .	275 .	217
	Antrim . . .	20 .	797
	Suffolk . . .	822 .	1,020
	Norfolk . . .	617 .	1,074

  Serves in 1st Life Guards.   9,789 .   7,823

*** DUNBAR, Sir William, Bart., of Mochrum, Kilcowan, N.B.

Coll. Edin. Univ.	Wigtown . .	3,680 .	3,483
Club. Brks.'s, New Ed.	Perth . . .	8 .	120

b. 1812, s. 1841, m. 1842.
                                              3,688 .   3,603

  Served as Jun. Ld. of the Treasury, Keeper P. Seal to the Pr. of Wales; is Comptroller Gen. of the Exchequer, and Keeper of Gt. Seal to the Pr. of Wales for Scotland. Sat for Wigtown Burghs.

DUNCAN, James, of Benmore. Argyll .	12,260 .	2,483
DUNCAN, J. F., of Upper Merrion Street, Dublin, Limerick, Sligo	2,348 .	2,542

** DUNCOMBE, Hon. Arthur, of Kilnwick Percy, Pocklington, &c. *acres.* *g. an. val.*

Club. Uni. Ser., Carlton, York,N.&E.R. 8,302 . 12,653
    Cons. b. 1806, s. 1863, m. 1st 1836, 2nd 1877.
    Served in Royal Navy (Adm.), Lord of the Admiralty, and
Groom in Waiting. Sat for Retford and for E. R. York.

DUNCOMBE, Walter Henry Octavius, of Waresley Park, St.
Neot's, &c.

Club. White's.	Huntingdon .	3,407 .	3,777
b. 1846, s. 1879.	Cambridge .	2,416 .	3,278
	York, N.R. .	2,154 .	2,018
	Bedford . .	1 .	2
Serves in 1st Life Guards.			
		7,978 .	9,075

DUNCOMBE, Sir Philip Duncombe Pauncefort, Bart.,
of Brickhill Manor, Bletchley.

Coll. Eton, Ch. Ch. Oxon.	Bucks . . .	3,361 .	6,068
Club. Carlton, Conser.	Lincoln . . .	1,643 .	2,802
b. 1818, m. 1844.	Stafford . .	1,034 .	1,295
		6,038 .	10,165

*** DUNDAS, Robert, of Arniston, Gorebridge, N.B.

Coll. Ch. Ch. Oxon.	Midlothian .	10,184 .	9,549
Club. Carlton, Travellers'.	Fife	195 .	248
b. 1823, s. 1838, m. 1845.	Co. Clare . .	134 .	84
		10,513 .	9,881

Exclusive of minerals, value 4,799*l.*, and of 300*l.* ground rents
in Co. Limerick. His mother, Mrs. Dundas-Calderwood-
Durham, has in Midlothian 666 acres, rental 1,738*l.*

* DUNDAS,Sir S.J.,Bart.,of Dunira. Perth.	5,729 .	2,725
DUNDAS (late), J., of Ochtertyre. Perth, Radnor, Surrey	4,632 .	2,242
DUNDAS (late), James, of Dundas. Linlithgow	2,094 .	4,783

*** MURRAY-DUNLOP, Mrs., of Corsock, Dalbeattie, N.B.

		acres.	g. an. val.
s. 1851, m. 1844.	Kirkcudbright	12,774	. 5,213

** DUNMORE, Earl of, Dunmore, Stirling, N.B., &c.

		acres.	g. an. val.
Coll. Eton.	Inverness . .	74,000	. 2,339
Club. Guards, Carlton, Turf.	Stirling . .	4,620	. 8,072
b. 1841, s. 1845, m. 1866.			
		78,620	. 10,411

Served in Scots Fusilier Guards and as Lord in Waiting.
Without shooting rents and exclusive of 4,000*l.* for minerals.

DUNNE, the Misses (three), of Brittas, Clonaslie, Q. Co., &c.

		acres.	g. an. val.
b. 187–, 187–, 187–, s. 1878.	Queen's Co. .	9,215	. 2,833
	Roscommon .	1,544	. 777
	Co. Dublin .	583	. 725
		11,342	. 4,335

DUNRAVEN, Earl of, K.P., Adare Manor, Limerick, &c.

		acres.	g. an. val.
Coll. Ch. Ch. Oxon.	Glamorgan .	23,751	. 23,974
Club. White's, Guards,	Gloucester .	537	. 471
Windham, Garrick.	Limerick . .	14,298	. 10,814
b. 1841, s. 1871, m. 1869.	Co. Kerry . .	1,005	. 123
	Co. Clare . .	164	. 96
Served in 1st Life Guards.		39,755	. 35,478

The Gloucester property and land in Glamorgan, rented at 40*l.*, are retd. as belonging to the Dowager Lady Dunraven (Lady Hylton).

DUNSANDLE and CLANCONAL, Lord, Dunsandle, Galway.

		acres.	g. an. val.
Club. Carlton, Kildare St.	Co. Galway .	33,543	. 11,860
b. 1810, s. 1847, m. 1864.	Tipperary .	3,514	. 5,333
Served in 11th Light Dragoons.		37,057	. 17,193

---

	acres.	g. an. val.
DUNLOP, Hon. Mrs., of Monasterboice.		
Louth, Cavan	3,265	. 2,301
DUNN, George, of——. Northumberland .	2,653	. 3,138

*** DUNSANY, LORD, Dunsany Castle, Navan.

		acres.	*g. an. val.*
Club. Carlton, Travellers',	Co. Meath . .	4,379 .	7,219
United Service.	Kilkenny . .	2,320 .	855
b. 1808, s. 1852, m. 1846.	Co. Cavan . .	31 .	26
Served in Royal Navy	Radnor . .	1,670 .	1,580
(Vice-Admiral ret.)			
		8,400 .	9,680

** DU PRÉ, CALEDON GEORGE, of Wilton Park, Beaconsfield.

Coll. Eton, Ch. Ch. Ox. Bucks . . . 6,876 . 10,500
Club. Carl., Cons., Trav., J. U. Ser.
b. 1803, s. 1870, m. 1833.
Served in 1st Life Guards. Sat for Bucks.

* DURHAM, EARL OF, Lambton Castle, Durham. ⚓.

Coll. Eton.	Durham . .	14,664 .	63,929
	Northumberland	15,807 .	7,742
b. 1855, s. 1879.			
Served in Coldstream Guards.		30,471 .	71,671

*** DUTTON, HON. JOHN THOMAS, of Hinton House, Alresford.

Coll. Har., Ch. Ch. Ox. Hants . . . 5,124 . 6,970
b. 1810, s. 1862, m. 1836.
             All woods not included.

*** DUTTON, HON. RALPH HENEAGE, of Timsbury Manor, Romsey.

Coll. Trinity, Cambridge.	Hants . . .	3,470 .	4,436
Club. Athenæum, Carlton.	Somerset . .	1,280 .	1,597
b. 1821, s. 1864, m. 1848.			
Sat for S. Hants and for Cirencester.		4,750 .	6,033

DUPPA, GEORGE, of Hollingbourne. Kent	2,417 .	2,217
DURANT, R., of Sharpham. Devon, Herts	2,404 .	4,553
DURRANT, SIR W. R. ESTRIDGE, BART., of		
Scottow. Norfolk	2,835 .	4,904

DYKE, Rt. Hon. Sir William Hart, Bart., of Lullingstone
Castle, Dartford.

			acres.	g. an. val.
Coll.	Har., Ch. Ch. Oxon.	Kent . . .	7,951 .	10,175
Club.	Carl., Whi., Beac.	Sussex . . .	688 .	647
b. 1837, s. 1875, m. 1870.		Herts . . .	223 .	648
Served as Secretary to the		Surrey . . .	3 .	4
Treasury.				
Sat for W. Kent ; sits for Mid Kent.			8,865 .	11,474

** BALLANTINE - DYKES, Lamplugh   Frecheville,   of
Dovenby Hall, Cockermouth.   S.

Coll.	Har., Ch. Ch. Oxon.	Cumberland .	4,762 .	5,566
Club.	Union, Oxford and Cambridge.			
b. 1854, s. 1866, m. 1879.				

** DYMOKE, Mrs. (Vicomtesse d'Aumale), of Scrivelsby,
Horncastle.

s. 1875, m. 1st 1873,	Lincolnshire .	3,605 .	4,955
2nd 1878.			

** DYNEVOR, Lord, Dynevor Castle, Llandilo, &c.

Coll.	Christ Church, Oxon.	Carmarthen .	7,208 .	7,253
Club.	Carlton, Jun. Carlton.	Glamorgan .	3,299 .	5,000
b. 1836, s. 1878, m. 1869.		Oxford . . .	176 .	209
		Wilts . . .	25 .	50
		Gloucester . .	20 .	50
			10,728 .	12,562

*** DYOTT, Richard, of Freeford Hall, Lichfield.

Coll.	Westm., Trin. Cam.	Stafford . .	2,630 .	5,274
Club.	Carlton.	Leicester . .	467 .	1,005
b. 1808, s. 1847, m. 1849.		Co. Antrim .	1,717 .	1,558
Served in 53rd Foot.		Worcester . .	613 .	607
Sat for Lichfield.				
			5,427 .	8,444

DYSART, Earl of, Buckminster Park, Grantham.

b. 1859, s. 1878.	Lincoln . .	18,025 .	29,077
	Leicester . .	8,420 .	11,631
	Surrey . . .	723 .	3,768
	Rutland . .	22 .	24
		27,190 .	44,500

A large part of the Surrey est. has been alienated (1878–9).

EARDLEY, (the late) Sir EARDLEY GIDEON CULLING, BART., of
    Belvedere, Kent.

		acres.	g. an. val.
	Herts . . .	887	1,192
d. 1875.	Northampton .	2,729	4,840
	Kent . . .	103	592
	Lincoln . . .	251	472
		3,970	7,096

** EARLE, WILLIAM HENRY, of Andover, Hants.

Club. A. & N., Uni. Ser.   Hants . . .   3,000 . 3,000
b. 1830.
    Served in 17th Foot in the Crimea.

*** CLAYTON-EAST, Sir GILBERT AUGUSTUS, BART., of Hall
    Place, Maidenhead, &c.

Coll. Eton, Mag. Cam.   Berks . . .   3,223 . 5,869
Club. Union, St. Stephen's.
b. 1846, s. 1866, m. 1867.

ECCLES, JOHN STUART, of Ecclesville, Fintona, Co. Tyrone.

Club. Kildare St., St. Geo.   Tyrone . . .   9,227 . 5,074
          Yacht Club.
b. 1847, s. 1869, m. 1871.

EDEN, JOHN, of Beamish Park, Chester-le-Street.

Club. Carlton, Uni. Ser.   Durham . .   4,278 . 6,885
b. 179–, s. 1843.

EDEN, Sir WILLIAM, BART., of Windlestone Hall, Bishop's
    Auckland.

Club. J. Carl., Boodle's.	Durham . .	6,096 . 10,191
b. 1849, s. 1873.	York, W.R. .	1,832 . 3,036
Served in 8th Hussars.		
		7,928 . 13,227

EAST, JOSHUA, of Longstock. Hants . .   2,079 . 2,007
♣. EBURY, LORD. Herts, Middlesex . . 2,723 . 5,803
EDGE, J. T., of Strelly Hall. Notts . . 2,758 . 5,098

** EDMONSTONE, Sir William, Bart., C.B., of Colzium, Kilsyth, N.B., &c.

Club. Carlton, Uni. Ser.   Stirling . . .   9,778 . 7,677
b. 1810, s. 1871, m. 1841.

		acres.	*g. an. val.*
Stirling . . .		9,778	7,677

Served in Royal Navy (Vice-Admiral).   Sat for Stirlingshire.

Exclusive of minerals, returned at 8,451*l.* per annum.

** EDWARDS, Francis William Lloyd, of Nanhoron, Pwllheli.

		acres.	*g. an. val.*
Club. Jun. Carlton.	Carnarvon . .	6,769	4,906
b. 1845, s. 1875, m. 1869.	Anglesey . .	1,339	1,200
	Denbigh . .	855	719
	Bedford . .	46	90
		9,009	6,915

EFFINGHAM, Earl of, Tusmore House, Bicester, &c. ♊.

		acres.	*g. an. val.*
Coll. Harrow.	Oxford . . .	3,376	3,856
Club. Travellers'.	York, W.R. . .	1,445	3,013
b. 1806, s. 1845, m. 1832.	Northampton .	910	1,073
Sat for Shaftesbury.			
		5,731	7,942

EGERTON OF TATTON, Lord, Tatton Park, Knutsford. ♊.

		acres.	*g. an. val.*
Coll. Eton, Ch. Ch. Oxon.	Cheshire . .	8,876	18,636
Club. Carlton, Travellers'.	Lancashire. .	1,870	11,995
b. 1806, s. 1856, m. 1830.	Derby . . .	424	1,529
	Durham . .	389	330
Sat for Lymington and for N. Cheshire.		11,559	32,490

GREY-EGERTON, Sir Philip le Belward, Bart., of Oulton Park, Tarporley. ♊.

		acres.	*g. an. val.*
Coll. Eton.	Cheshire . .	8,840	14,676

Club. Turf, Army & Navy.   b. 1833, s. 1881, m. 1861.
Served in R. Brig. and Coldstream Guards.

EDGEWORTH, Antonio Eroles, of Edge-
worthstown.   Longford . . . . . .   3,255 . 2,536

EGGINTON, Mrs., of Bere Regis, Wareham, &c.

		acres.	g. an. val.
m. 1st 1853, 2nd 1871.	Dorset . . .	5,301 .	4,766
	Wilts . . .	2,706 .	3,574
		8,007 .	8,340

EGLINTON and WINTON, Earl of, Eglinton Castle, Irvine, N.B., &c.

Coll. Eton.	Ayrshire . .	23,631 .	37,029
Club. Carlton.	Lanark . . .	5,866 .	4,097
b. 1841, s. 1861, m. 1862.	Bute . . .	671 .	184
		30,168 .	41,310

Exclusive of minerals, worth 9,520*l.* per annum.

*** EGMONT, Earl of, Nork House, Epsom, &c. **S**.

Coll. Radley, Univ. Oxon.	Sussex . . .	14,021 .	12,000
Club. Carl., White's, Bood.,	Surrey . . .	3,466 .	5,088
Marl.,Wind., St. Ste.	Bucks . . .	585 .	1,226
b. 1845, s. 1874, m. 1869.	Lincoln . .	134 .	386
	Co. Cork . .	16,766 .	16,810
Sat for Midhurst.		34,972 .	35,510

ELDON, Earl of, Shirley House, Croydon, &c.

Coll. Eton, Ch. Ch. Oxon.	Durham . .	11,841 .	12,897
Club. Carlton, Jun. Carlton,	Dorset . . .	6,869 .	8,192
Travellers', Arthur's.	Gloucester . .	6,664 .	6,034
b. 1845, s. 1854, m. 1869.	Surrey . . .	387 .	1,334
		25,761 .	28,457

*** ELIBANK, Lord, Darn Hall, Eddleston, N.B., &c.

Club. Nav. & Mil., New Ed.	Haddington .	1,863 .	5,442
b. 1840, s. 1871, m. 1868.	Peebles . .	2,660 .	2,295
	Selkirk . . .	1,168 .	385
	Perth . . .	999 .	1,976
Served in Royal Navy (Commander).		6,690 .	10,098

ELD, F. F., of Seighford. Staff. . . .	2,418 .	4,276

ELGIN and KINCARDINE, Earl of.

Fife, Perth	2,895 .	5,240

ELIOTT, Sir William Francis Augustus, Bart., of Stobs
　　Castle, Hawick, N.B., &c.　　　　　　*acres.　　g. an. val.*
Coll.　Eton.　　　　　　　Roxburgh . . 19,345 . 11,509
b. 1827, s. 1864, m. 1st 1846, 2nd 1879.
　　Served in 93rd Highlanders.
　　2,575*l.* of these rents are credited to "Trustees of late Sir
W. F. Eliott."

ELLESMERE, Earl of, Worsley Hall, Manchester.　♒.
Coll.　Eton, Trin. Cam.　　Lancashire　. 10,080 . 55,421
Club.　Carlton, Travellers'.　Cheshire . . 　303 . 11,130
b. 1847, s. 1862, m. 1868.　　Northampton . 2,839 . 4,600
　　　　　　　　　　　　　Stafford . . . unstated . 139

　　　　　　　　　　　　　　　　　　13,222 . 71,290
　　About 61,000*l.* of this is credited in the return to the Bridgwater
Trustees.

** ELLICE, Mrs., of Glenquoich, Inverness, &c.
m. 1st 1836, 2nd 1867,　　Inverness . . 99,545 . 6,721
　　s. 1880.　　　　　　　Renfrew　. . 　14 . 50

　　　　　　　　　　　　　　　　　　99,559 . 6,771
** ELLIOT, Robert Henry, of Clifton Park, Kelso, N.B., &c.
Coll.　Cheltenham.　　　Roxburgh . . 5,258 . 5,580
b. 1837, s. 1873, m. 1868.　Co. Meath . . 3,025 . 3,397
The Hon. Mrs. Elliot s. in　King's Co.　. 2,496 . 2,171
　　1879 to the Irish estates.　Co. Dublin　. 1,238 . 2,088

　　　　　　　　　　　　　　　　　　12,017 . 13,236
*** CARR ELLISON, Ralph, of Dunston Hill, Gateshead, &c.
　🌳　*Coll.*　Harrow, Ch. Ch.　Northumberland 8,176 . 3,803
　　　　　　Oxon.　　　　Durham . . 1,959 . 8,334
b. 1805, s. 1817 and 1870, m. 1830.
　　　　　　　　　　　　　　　　　　10,135 . 12,137

ELLAMES, J. P., of Westhorpe.　Bucks　. 2,087 . 3,347
ELLIOT, Sir W., K.C.S.I., of Wolfelee.
　　Roxburgh . . . . 3,030 . 2,284
ELLIOT, W. C., of Harwood.　Roxburgh . 4,900 . 2,379
ELLISON (late), Mrs., of Sudbrooke.　Lin. 2,215 . 3,022

** DALRYMPLE-HORN-ELPHINSTONE, Sir James, Bart.,
of Logie Elphinstone, Pitcaple, N.B.

acres.   g. an. val.

Club. Carl., St. Ste., Trav.   Aberdeen . .   5,524 .   5,107
b. 1805, s. 1848, m. 1836.   Was a Lord of the Treasury.
Sat for Portsmouth.

MARWOOD-ELTON, Sir Edward, Bart., of Widworthy Court,
Honiton.

Coll. Eton, Bras. Oxon.   Devon . . .   3,740 .   4,207
Club. Brooks's, Reform.   Somerset . .   405 .   711
b. 1801.

                                             4,145   4,918

The Somerset property, except 4 acres, is returned as owned
by Sir E. M.-E. and others.

** ELWES, Arthur Henry Stuart, of Congham House,
King's Lynn.

Coll. Royal Naval.   Norfolk . .   3,313 .   3,074
Club. Nav. & Mil.   b. 1858, s. 1881.
Serves in the R. Navy.

ELWES, John Henry, of Colesbourne House, Cheltenham.

Coll. Ch. Ch. Oxon.   Gloucester . .   3,874 .   2,905
Club. Oxford and Cam.,   Essex . . .   675 .   1,161
Arthur's.   ─────────────
b. 1815, s. 1850, m. 1841.   4,549 .   4,066

** ELWES, Robert Hervey Monro, of Stoke College, Clare,
Suffolk.

Coll. Radley,Corpus,Oxon.   Suffolk . . .   2,578 .   2,894
Club. Reform, B.F. Arts.   Essex . . .   863 .   1,332
b. 1853, s. 1869, m. 1875.   ─────────────
                                       3,441 .   4,226

** CARY-ELWES, Valentine Dudley Henry, of Billing Hall,
Northampton, &c.

Club. Army & Navy, Carl.,   Lincoln . .   9,171 .   14,621
Junior Carlton.   Northampton .   1,027 .   2,462
b. 1832, s. 1866, m. 1st 1856, 2nd 1865.   ─────────────
                                       10,198 .   17,083
Served in 12th Lancers in Kaffir war of 1851–53.

ELTON, Sir A. H., Bt., of Clevedon Ct. Som.   2,411 .   8,206

** ELY, Marquis of, Ely Lodge, Enniskillen, &c.

			acres.		g. an. val.
Coll. Harrow.	Fermanagh	.	34,879	.	13,983
Club. Garrick, Pratt's, Kil. St.	Wexford	. .	14,023	.	9,168
b. 1849, s. 1857, m. 1875.	Kent	. . .	90	.	600
			48,992	.	23,751

*** EMERSON, James, of Easby Hall, Northallerton, &c.

b. 1824, s. 1843, m. 1846.	York, N.R.	.	6,611	.	7,616

** EMPSON, Robert Cornelius, of Ousefleet Grange, Goole, &c.

Coll. Shrewsbury. b. 1818, s. 1866, m. 1842.	York, W.R.	.	4,049	.	8,264

ENNIS, Sir John James, Bart., of Ballinahown, Athlone.

Coll. Christ Church, Oxon.	Westmeath	. .	8,774	.	4,912
Club. Reform.	Meath	. . .	1,573	.	1,817
b. 1842, s. 1878.	Dublin	. . .	326	.	499
Sits for Athlone.	Roscommon	.	262	.	175
			10,935	.	7,403

* ENNISKILLEN, Earl of, Florence Court, Enniskillen.

Coll. Har., Ch. Ch. Oxon.	Fermanagh	.	29,635	.	18,795
Club. Carlton, Athenæum, National, Sackv. St.	Wilts	. . .	569	.	495
b. 1807, s. 1840, m. 1st 1844, 2nd 1865. Sat for Fermanagh.			30,204	.	19,290

** ENYS, Francis Gilbert, of Enys, Penryn.

Coll. Harrow, Trin. Cam.	Cornwall	. .	3,600	.	5,200
Club. O. & C., Windham. b. 1836, s. 1872.					

EMLY, Lord. Limerick, Clare	. . . .	2,710	.	2,638
EMPSON, J. W., of Yokefleet. York	. .	2,059	.	3,479

** ERNE, EARL OF, K.P., Crom. Castle, Newtown Butler.

		acres.	g. an. val.
Coll. ——, Oxon.	Fermanagh .	31,389 .	17,039
Club. Carlton, Sackville St.,	Donegal . .	4,826 .	4,324
Dublin.	Mayo . . .	2,184 .	1,122
b. 1802, s. 1842, m. 1837.	Sligo . . .	1,966 .	1,365
		40,365 .	23,850

ERRINGTON, SIR JOHN, BART., of Puddington College, Neston, Cheshire, &c.

Club. White's, Turf.	Chester . . .	3,147 .	4,894
b. 1810, s. 1875, m. 1841.	Northumberland	10,563 .	8,487
		13,710 .	13,381

** ERROLL, EARL OF, Slains Castle, Cruden, Aberdeen, N.B.

Coll. Eton.	Aberdeen . .	4,249 .	4,268
Club. Brooks's.	Northumberland	4,015 .	5,331
b. 1823, s. 1846 and 1855, m. 1848.			
Served in Rifle Brigade in the Crimea.		8,264 .	9,599

** KENNEDY-ERSKINE, AUGUSTUS JOHN WILLIAM HENRY, of Dun House, Montrose, N.B., &c.

b. 1866, s. 1870.	Forfar . . .	1,727 .	3,654
	Carmarthen .	1,332 .	377
	Brecon . . .	474 .	77
The Welsh property belongs to Mr. E.'s mother.		3,533 .	4,108

** ERSKINE, HENRY DAVID, of Cardross, Stirling, N.B.

Coll. Harrow.	Perth . . .	6,245 .	4,020
Club. Guards.	Stirling . . .	40 .	60
b. 1838, s. 1844, m. 1861.		6,285 .	4,080

Served in Scots Fusilier Guards, and as Groom of the Robes, and Deputy Serjeant-at Arms in the House of Commons.

ERRINGTON, W. V., of High Warden. Nbld.   3,323 . 2,158

ERRINGTON, GEORGE, of Cassino. Tipperary, Kildare, Dublin, York . . . . . 2,960 . 2,043

ERSKINE, Henry William, of Pittodrie, Pitcaple, Aberdeen, N.B.

		acres.		g. an. val.
b. 1858, s. 1870.	Aberdeen . .	3,270	.	4,250

ERSKINE, Sir Thomas, Bart., of Cambo House, St. Andrews, N.B.

Club. Carlton, Boodle's.	Fife	2,937	.	6,727
b. 1824, s. 1841, m. 1847.	Carnarvon . .	586	.	570

Served in 71st Foot.

		3,523	.	7,297

** ESDAILE, Charles Edward Jeffries, of Cothelstone House, Taunton.

Coll. Univ. Oxon.   Somerset . .   3,000 . 4,166
Club. Carlton.
b. 1845, s. 1881, m. 1874.

ESMONDE, Sir Thomas Henry Grattan, Bart., of Bally-nastragh, Gorey, Co. Wexford.

b. 1862, s. 1876.	Waterford . .	701	.	506
	Kilkenny . .	629	.	357
	Tipperary . .	717	.	335
	King's Co.. .	389	.	160
	Wicklow . .	2,088	.	425
	Wexford . .	3,533	.	2,780
		8,057	.	4,563

Sir Thomas shares with two others in Co. Longford a rental of 264*l.*

*** ESSEX, Earl of, of Cashiobury Park, Watford.

Coll. Eton.	Herts . . .	5,545	.	7,805
Club. Travellers'.	Essex . . .	3,090	.	3,945
b. 1803, s. 1839,	Warwick . .	690	.	1,267
m. 1st 1825,	Roscommon .	2,906	.	2,672
2nd 1863.	Co. Meath .	1,303	.	2,443
	Co. Dublin .	658	.	743
	Co. Wicklow .	678	.	61
		14,870	.	18,936

Exclusive of 180 acres of English woodland—county not specified.

** BUCKNALL-ESTCOURT, Rev. Edmund Hiley, of Estcourt, Tetbury, &c. ♖.

			acres.		*g. an. val.*
Coll.	Harrow, Balliol and	Gloucester . .	1,746	.	2,750
	Merton, Oxon.	Wilts . . .	3,629	.	5,624
b. 1803, s. 1876, m. 1830.		Derby . . .	410	.	601
		Middlesex . .	9	.	13
			5,794	.	8,988

** SOTHERON-ESTCOURT, George Thomas John, of Darrington Hall, Pontefract, &c. ♖.

Coll.	Harrow, Balliol,	York,E.&W.R.	5,757	.	8,164
	Oxon.	Wilts . . .	unstated	.	1,100
Club.	Carlton, Turf, St. James's.				
b. 1839, s. 1876, m. 1863.			5,757	.	9,264

Sits for N. Wilts.

In this case the son's property is not totalled with that of the father; for whom, *see* preceding notice.

** DAVIES-EVANS, Herbert, of High Mead, Llanbythan.

Club.	Junior Carlton.	Carnarvon . .	2,808	.	1,863
b. 1842, s. 1869, m. 1869.		Carmarthen .	1,966	.	1,170
		Pembroke . .	20	.	10

Served in 10th Hussars and in the
Royal Navy.   4,794 . 3,043

This family have held the Llanbythan estate in the male line since 1555, and in the female much longer.

** EVANS, Owen, of Broom Hall, Pwllheli, Carnarvon, N. Wales.

b.1816,s.1869,m.1846.   Carnarvon . .   5,560 . 5,150

** EVANS, Thomas William, of Allestree Hall, Derby.

Coll.	Trin. Cam.	Derbyshire .	6,799	.	10,757
Club.	Brooks's, Athenæum,	Stafford . . .	1,327	.	1,964
	Devonshire, Reform.				
b. 1821, s. 1856, m. 1846.			8,126	.	12,721

Sits for S. Derbyshire.

EUSTACE, Mrs., of Robertstown. Cork, Kildare, King's Co., Westmeath . . .	3,938	.	2,236
** EVANS, Ed. Bickerton, of Whitbourne Court. Hereford, Worcester	2,586	.	4,000

** EVELYN, Francis Lyndon, of Corton, Presteign.

			acres.		*g. an. va'.*
b. 1859, s. 1869.	Hereford	. .	4,601	.	5,257
	Radnor .	. .	479	.	709
			5,080	.	5,966

** EVERED, Robert Guy, of Otterhampton, Bridgwater, &c.

Coll. West, Corp. C. Ox.   Somerset . .   3,142 . 3,916
b. 1806, s. 1848 and 1867, m. 1829.

** EVERSFIELD, Charles Gilbert, of Denne Park, Horsham.

Coll. Eton, Ch. Ch. Oxon.   Sussex . . .   3,124 . 4,756
b. 1822, s. 1825, m. 1849.

*** ORR-EWING, Archibald, Ballikinrain, Killearn, N.B., &c.

Coll. Glasgow University.	Stirling . . .	5,840	.	3,065
Club. Carlton, New Ed.,	Dumbarton .	201	.	4,320
Western Glasgow.				
b. 1819, m. 1847.		6,041	.	7,385
Sits for Dumbartonshire.				

*** EWING, Mrs., of Strathleven, Dumbarton, N.B.

s. 1853, m. 1836.   Dumbarton . 9,180 . 3,623

*** EXETER, Marquis of, Burghley House, Stamford.

Coll. Eton, St. John's,	Northampton .	15,625	.	21,027
Cam.	Rutland . .	8,998	.	16,388
Club. Carlton, Jun. Carl.,	Lincoln . . .	3,095	.	10,768
United Ser., Cons.	Leicester . .	553	.	861
b. 1825, s. 1867, m. 1848.				
Served as Aide-de-Camp to the Queen,		28,271	.	49,044

Capt. of Hon. Corps of Gentlemen at
Arms, is Hereditary Grand Almoner.
Sat for S. Lincoln and for N. Northamptonshire.

*** EVELYN, W. J., of Wotton.	Sur., Sus. .	3,601	.	2,971
EVERARD, N. T., of Randalstown.	Meath	2,311	.	2,188
EVERETT, Henry, of Biddesden.	Wilts,			
Leicester, Hants		2,448	.	3,279
EVERSLEY, Viscount.	Hants	2,388	.	3,008
EVERY, Sir H. F., Bart., of Egginton.	Der.	2,231	.	4,930

EYRE, CHARLES, of Welford Park, Newbury.

			acres.		*g. an. val.*
Coll. Harrow, Ch. Ch. Ox.	Berks	. . .	5,737	.	7,121
Club. Athenæum.	Herts	. . .	409	.	592
b. 1806, s. 1831, m. 1st 1835, 2nd 1858.					
			6,146	.	7,713

EYRE, THOMAS JOSEPH, of Uppercourt, Freshford, Co. Kilkenny.

Club. Reform.	Kilkenny	. .	1,909	.	2,165
b. 1821, m. 1861.	Co. Galway	.	1,752	.	890
	Tipperary	. .	762	.	555
	Co. Louth	. .	696	.	797
	Waterford	. .	164	.	264
	Surrey	. . .	1	.	138
			5,284	.	4,809

EYTON, THOMAS SLANEY, of Eyton, Wellington, Salop, &c. ⚓.

Coll. St. John's, Cam.	Salop	. . .	3,749	.	6,427
b. 1843, s. 1880, m. 1866.	York, N.R.	.	295	.	377
			4,044	.	6,804

*** RUTTLEDGE-FAIR, MRS., of Cornfield, Hollymount, Co. Mayo.

m. 1851.	Mayo	. . .	2,765	.	2,574
	Galway	. . .	2,799	.	503
			5,564	.	3,077

FAIRHOLME, GEORGE KNIGHT ERSKINE, of Old Melrose, N.B. (res. Bregenz, Austria).

b. 1822, s. 1868, m. 1857.	Midlothian	.	6,200	.	2,020
	Roxburgh	. .	1,300	.	1,700
			7,500	.	3,720

EXMOUTH, VCT., Canonteign.	Devon . .	2,864	.	2,755
EYRE, G. E., of Warens.	Hants, Wilts . .	2,539	.	3,541
⚓. EYSTON, C. J., of East Hendred.	Berks	2,857	.	3,488
⚓. FAIRFAX, T. F., of Newton Kyme.	York	2,803	.	4,900

*** FALKLAND, Viscount, G.C.H., Scutterskelfe, Yarm. ♠.

Club. Boodle's.

		acres.		g. an. val.
York, N.R. . .	3,011	.	4,464

b. 1803, s. 1809, m. 1st 1830, 2nd 1859.

Served as Governor of Bombay and of Nova Scotia, Lord in Waiting, Lord of the Bedchamber, and Captain of the Yeomen of the Guard.

FALMOUTH, Viscount, Mereworth Castle, Maidstone, &c. ♠.

Club. White's, Arthur's, Turf.

	acres.		g. an. val.
Cornwall . .	25,910	.	35,953
Kent . . .	4,696	.	6,951
	30,606	.	42,904

b. 1819, s. 1852, m. 1845.

An additional rental of 126*l.* in Cornwall is given under the heading " Lord F. and another." Lady F. is owner of 4,258 acres in Kent, out of the total 4,696.

FANE, Edmond Douglas Veitch, of Boyton House, Heytesbury.

Coll. Merton, Oxon.

Wilts . . .	3,864	.	3,007

Club. Carlton.   b. 1837, s. 1872, m. 1875.

Served as Sec. of Legation at Brussels and Copenhagen.

*** FANE, John Augustus, of Wormsley, Tetsworth. ♠.

b. 1830, s. 1875, m. 1860.

	acres.		g. an. val.
Essex . . .	2,594	.	4,195
Oxford . . .	1,622	.	1,662
Bucks . . .	540	.	490
Dorset . . .	532	.	870
	5,288	.	7,217

Served in 46th Foot in the Crimea.

*** FANE, Neville Hamlyn Batson, of Clovelly Court, Bideford, &c.

Coll. Mag. Cam.
b. 1858, s. 1868.

	acres.		g. an. val.
Devon . . .	5,500	.	3,700
Lincoln . . .	407	.	663
Hants . . .	4,300	.	3,200
	10,207	.	7,563

FARMER, William Robert Gamul, of Nonsuch Park, Cheam.

		acres.	g. an. val.
Coll. Eton.	Suffolk . . .	2,160 .	3,213
Club. Carlton, Guards.	Surrey . . .	2,148 .	1,973
b. 1838, s. 1860, m. 1861.	Montgomery .	3,673 .	1,171
	Cambridge .	827 .	1,115
	Huntingdon .	687 .	905

Served in Grenadier Guards.   9,495 . 8,377

*** FARNHAM, Lord, Farnham, Cavan.

 Coll. Trin. Dublin. Co. Cavan . 25,920 . 18,250
 Club. Sackville St.
b. 1803, s. 1868, m. 1st 1839, 2nd 1864.
Sat for Co. Cavan.

* FARQUHARSON, Henry Richard, of Tarrant Gunville, Blandford.

Coll. Jesus, Cam. Dorset . . . 5,476 . 3,680
Club. St. Stephen's.
b. 1847, s. 1871, m. 1878.

** FARQUHARSON, James John, of Langton House, Blandford.

Coll. Eton, Ch. Ch. Oxon. Dorset . . . 6,063 . 7,300
b. 1806, s. 1871, m. 1837.

FARQUHARSON, James Ross, of Invercauld, Ballater, N.B.

Club. Guards.	Aberdeen . .	87,745 .	9,567
b. 1834, s. 1862, m. 1864.	Perth . . .	20,056 .	1,508
	Ayr	1,760 .	1,899

Served in Scots Fusilier Guards.   109,561 . 12,974

Col. F. holds the Ayrshire land in conjunction with Hon. J. Manners Yorke.

** FARQUHARSON, Robert, of Finzean, Aboyne, N.B.

Coll. Edin. University. Aberdeen . . 16,809 . 6,166
Club. J. U. Ser., Reform.
b. 1835, s. 1876. Served in Coldstream Guards.
Sits for W. Aberdeenshire.

** FARQUHARSON, ROBERT FRANCIS OGILVIE, of Haughton
    House, Alford, N.B.   *acres.*   *g. an. val.*
Club. Scottish.   Aberdeen . .   4,500 .   3,733
b. 1823, s. 1854, m. 1857.

** FARRELL, JOHN ARTHUR, of Moynalty, Kells, Co. Meath.
Coll. Oscott.   Co. Meath . .   4,790 .   5,000
Club. Arthur's, St. George's, Kildare Street, Dublin.
b. 1825, s. 1870, m. 1860.

*** FARRER, REV. MATTHEW THOS., of Ingleboro', Lancaster.
Coll. Westm., Trin. Cam.   York, W.R. . 11,512 .   9,403
b. 1816, s. 1879, m. 1st 1843, 2nd 1848.

FAULKNER, WILLIAM, of Kempsford, Evesham.
                Gloucester . .   3,071 .   4,465

*** FAWKES, AYSCOUGH, of Farnley Hall, Otley, &c.
    b. 1831, s. 1871, m. 1866. York . . . 11,850 . 12,460

** FELLOWES, EDWARD, of Ramsey Abbey, Huntingdon, &c.
   Coll. Charterhouse.   Huntingdon . 15,629 . 22,128
   Club. Carl., Uni. Serv. Norfolk . .   4,083 .   3,609
b. 1809, s. 1837, m. 1845.   Cambridge .   309 .   466
  Served in 15th Hussars.
  Sat for Hunts.   20,021 . 26,203

FELLOWES, ROBERT, of Shottesham Park, Norwich.
Coll. Eton, Trin. Cam.   Norfolk . .   7,758 . 11,078
Club. Carlton.   Huntingdon .   1 .   2
b. 1817, s. 1869, m. 1845.
                     7,759 . 11,080

FARQUHARSON, MAJ.-GEN., of Breda. Aber. 2,688 .   6,299
FARRER, G., of Brayfield. Buc., Bed., Den. 2,966 .   4,724
FARRER, W. D. M. C., of Gurthalocha. Tipp. 8,297 .   2,962
FAWCETT, J. of N. Bailey. Nhmbld., Dur. 2,738 .   3,603
FERGUSON-FAWSITT, JOHN DANIEL, of
    Walkington. York . . . . . . 2,192 .   3,428

*** FENWICK, THOMAS, of Burrow Hall, Kirkby-Lonsdale.

			acres.	*g. an. val.*
Coll.	Eton, Ch. Ch. Oxon.	Lancashire .	3,165 .	4,380
Club.	Reform, N. Univ.	York, W.R. .	809 .	398
b. 1842, m. 1875.		Westmoreland	83 .	160

4,057 .	4,938

MR. FENWICK'S mother is owner of this estate for life.

** FERGUSON, GEORGE ARTHUR, of Pitfour, Mintlaw, N.B.

Club.	Carlton, Travellers'.	Aberdeen . .	12,305 .	10,492
b. 1835, s. 1867, m. 1861.		Banff . . .	10,845 .	9,446
Served in Gren. Guards in the Crimea.				

23,150 .	19,938

MUNRO-FERGUSON, RONALD CRAWFURD, of Raith House, Kirkcaldy, N.B., &c.

b. 1860, s. 1868.	Ross . . .	15,022 .	3,904
	Fife	7,135 .	12,337
	Elgin . . .	3,349 .	2,494

Exclusive of 1,582*l.* for minerals.	25,506 .	18,735

** FERGUSON, WILLIAM, F.R.S., of Kinmundy House, Mintlaw, N.B.

Coll.	Aberdeen.	Aberdeen . .	4,068 .	3,900
Club.	Univ. Ed., R. Nor. Ab.	b. 1823, s. 1862, m. 1856.		

FEILDEN, GEN. C. M. G., of Witton Pk. Lan.	2,611 .	7,314
FAY, JOHN, of Moyne Hall. Cavan . . .	4,179 .	2,566
FENTON, JOSEPH, of Bamford Hall. Lan.	2,936 .	2,961
FENWICK, J. C. J., of Longframlington. Northumberland, Durham	2,111 .	5,195
OLIPHANT-FERGUSON, G. H. H., of Broadfield. Cumberland	2,027 .	3,021
FERGUSON, JOHN, of ——. Donegal . .	3,769 .	2,225

** FERGUSSON, Right Hon. Sir James, Bart., K.C.M.G., of
Kilkerran, Maybole, N.B.   *acres.*   *g. an. val.*
Coll. Rugby, Uni. Oxon.   Ayr . . . .   22,630 . 13,334
Club. Carlton, White's, Marlborough, Junior Carlton, Guards.
b. 1832, s. 1849, m. 1st 1859, 2nd 1873.
    Served in Grenadier Guards in the Crimea (wounded at Inker-
man), Under Secretary for India, Under Secretary for Home
Department, Governor of South Australia and of New Zealand.
Is Governor of Bombay.   Sat for Ayr.
    Exclusive of 204*l.* for mines.

** FERGUSSON, Robert Cutlar, of Craigdarroch, Moniave,
N.B., &c.

Club. Guards.	Kirkcudbright	1,539	.	1,707
b. 1855, s. 1859.	Dumfries . .	2,264	.	1,755
Serves in Scots Guards.				
		3,803	.	3,462

FERMOY, Lord, Trabolgan, Whitegate, Co. Cork, &c.

Club. Garrick, Kild. Street.	Co. Cork . .	15,543	.	6,572
b. 1850, s. 1874, m. 1877.	Waterford . .	774	.	429
	Co. Limerick .	4,997	.	4,070
		21,314	.	11,071

The property in Co. Limerick is Lady Fermoy's.

FERRALL, John Nolan, of Loughboy, Ballyhaunis, Co. Mayo.

Coll. Trin. Dub.	Roscommon .	869	.	374
Club. Uni. Service, Dublin.	Co. Mayo . .	9,731	.	3,072
		10,600	.	3,446

*** TAAFE-FERRALL, Henry Edward, of Moylurg, Boyle,
Co. Roscommon.

Coll. Downside, Bath.   Roscommon .   5,140 .   3,453
Club. Uni. Ser., Dublin.   b. 1832, s. 1853, m. 1855.

JOHNSON-FERGUSON, Mrs., of Auchin-
    heath. Lanark . . . .   3,861 .   2,053

BUSFIELD-FERRAND, William, of St. Ives, Bingley.

			acres.		*g. an. val.*
Club. Carlton.	York, W.R.	.	3,906	.	7,698

b. 1809, m. 1st 1831, 2nd 1847.
   Sat for Knaresborough and for Devonport.

** FERRERS, Earl, Chartley Castle, Stafford, &c.   𝕾.

Coll. Trin. Cam.	Stafford	. .	6,862	.	10,011
Club. Carlton, Beaconsfield.	Leicester	. .	1,801	.	2,693
b. 1847, s. 1859.	Derby	. . .	2	.	3
			8,665	.	12,707

FETHERSTON, Rev. Sir George Ralph, Bart., of Ardagh
   House, Longford (res. Chapmanslade, Westbury).

b. 1852, s. 1869.	Longford	. .	8,711	.	5,606

*** FETHERSTONEHAUGH, Miss, of Up Park, Petersfield.

s. 1874.	Sussex	. . .	5,983	.	5,558

FEVERSHAM, Earl of, Duncombe Park, Helmsley, &c.

Coll. Eton, St. John's, Ox.	York, N.R.	.	39,312	.	34,328

Club. Jun. Carlton, Carlton, Travellers'.
   b. 1829, s. 1867, m. 1851.   Sat for E. Retford and N. Riding.
   Duncombe Park was burnt down about New Year, 1879.

FFOLKES, Sir William Hovell Browne, Bart., of Hillington
   Hall, King's Lynn, &c.

Coll. Harrow, Trin. Cam.	Norfolk	. .	8,111	.	10,139

Club. Brooks's, Boodle's.   b. 1847, s. 1860, m. 1875.
   Sits for King's Lynn.

FETHERSTONHAUGH, Cecil H. Digby, of Bracklyn. Westmeath	4,711	.	2,583
FETHERSTONHAUGH, R. Steele, of Rockview. Meath, Westmeath . . .	3,148	.	2,862
FETHERSTONHAUGH, William, of Glanmore. Mayo, Westmeath . . .	10,277	.	2,381
** FFARINGTON, Miss, of Worden. Lanc.	2,604	.	6,023
FFOULKES, J. Jocelyn, of Eriviatt. Denb., Flint, Merioneth	3,050	.	2,257

FFOLLIOT, John, of Hollybrook, Boyle, Co. Sligo.

			acres.		g. an. val.
Club. Kildare Street, Dub.	Sligo	. . .	4,168	.	1,948
b. 1824, s. 1868, m. 1856.	Donegal	. .	1,783	.	845
	Leitrim .	. .	1,473	.	349
			7,424	.	3,142

*** FIELDEN, John, of Grimston Park, Tadcaster, &c.

b. 1822, m. 1857.	York, W.R.	.	2,974	.	6,272
	Lancashire	.	405	.	2,728
			3,379	.	9,000

*** FIFE, Earl of, K.T., Duff House, Banff, &c.

Coll. Eton.	Aberdeen	. .	135,829	.	16,240
Club. Brooks's, White's,	Banff	. . .	72,432	.	36,379
City Lib.	Elgin	. . .	40,959	.	18,693
b. 1849, s. 1879.	Elgin	. . .	unstated .		1,251
Sat for Elgin and Nairn.					
Is Capt. Hon. Corps of Gentlemen at Arms.			249,220	.	72,563

** FILMER, Sir Edmund, Bart., of East Sutton Park, Staplehurst. ⚓.

Club. Carlton, Guards,	Kent	. . .	6,596	.	9,221
Army and Navy.	Berks	. . .	5	.	150
b. 1835, s. 1857, m. 1858.	Essex	. . .	7	.	24
Served in Grenadier Guards.					
Sat for W. Kent; sits for Mid Kent.			6,608	.	9,395

The Berks property belongs to the Dowager Lady F.

** WYNNE-FINCH, Charles Arthur, of Voelas, Denbigh, &c.

Club. Guards, Arthur's,	Denbigh	. .	8,025	.	3,908
Travellers'.	Carnarvon	. .	5,565	.	3,778
b. 1841, s. 1874.	York, N.R.	.	1,116	.	1,816
Served in Scots Fusilier	Leicester	. .	404	.	674
Guards.	Rutland	. .	34	.	177
	Middlesex .	.	14	.	419
			15,158	.	10,772

FFYTCHE. J. L., of Thorpe. Lincoln, Derby, Bucks, Rutland			2,909	.	5,499
FIELDEN, J., of Beachamwell. Norfolk .			4,341	.	2,523

FINCH, GEORGE HENRY, of Burley-on-the-Hill, Oakham.

			acres.		*g. an. val.*
Coll. New, Oxon.	Rutland	. .	9,183	.	15,098
Club. Carlton.	Essex	. . .	4,318	.	7,650
b. 1835, s. 1870, m. 1st 1861,	Bucks	. . .	3,657	.	5,565
2nd 1871.	Northampton	.	174	.	130
Sits for Rutlandshire.			17,332	.	28,443

FINGALL, EARL OF, Killeen Castle, Co. Meath.

Club. Hibernian, Uni. Ser.	Meath	. . .	9,589	.	8,680
b. 1859, s. 1881.	Berks	. . .	5	.	47
			9,594	.	8,727

** FITZGERALD, SIR AUGUSTINE, BART., of Carrigoran, Ennis, Co. Clare.

Coll. Winch., Addiscombe.	Co. Clare	. .	14,915	.	8,000
Club. Uni. Ser., U. S. Dub.	Cornwall	. .	1,436	.	1,600
b. 1809, s. 1865, m. 1st 1832, 2nd 1881.					
Served in Bengal Horse Artillery.			16,351	.	9,600

** FITZGERALD, CHARLES LIONEL, of Turlough Park, Castlebar, Co. Mayo.

Coll. Harrow, Ch. Ch. Ox.	Co. Mayo	. .	8,339	.	3,779

Club. Kild. St., Dublin, Carlton, Hanover Square.
b. 1833, s. 1854, m. 1st 1859, 2nd 1873.

*** FITZGERALD, DESMOND JOHN EDMUND (Knight of Glin), of Glin Castle, Limerick.

b. 1840, s. 1866, m. 1861.	Limerick	. .	5,697	.	3,825

DALTON-FITZGERALD, SIR GERALD RICHARD, BART., of Castle Ishen, Cork, &c.

Club. Marlb., Army and	Lancashire	. .	3,159	.	6,356
Navy.	Essex	. . .	1,414	.	1,584
b. 1832, s. 1867, m. 1861.	Co. Cork	. .	3,244	.	1,804
	Tipperary	. .	33	.	37
Served in Royal Navy.			7,850	.	9,781

FINLAY, A. S., of Castle Toward. Argyll.	6,758	.	2,867
FINLAY, K., of Dunlossit. Argyll . . .	17,676	.	2,882

FITZGERALD, Lord Maurice (*jure uxoris*), of Johnstown
Castle, Wexford.

		acres.		g. an. val.
b. 1852, m. 1880.	Wexford . .	15,216	.	8,840

Served in the Royal Navy.

*** PURCELL-FITZGERALD, Mrs., of Boulge Hall, Wood-
bridge, &c.

m. 1843, s. 1879.	Waterford . .	2,277	.	2,244
	Lancashire . .	575	.	7,000
	Suffolk . . .	675	.	931
	Sussex . . .	48	.	350
		3,575	.	10,525

*** FITZGERALD, Sir Maurice, Bart. (Knight of Kerry),
of Glanleam, Valentia, &c.

Coll. Harrow.	Co. Kerry . .	5,372	.	2,207
Club. Trav., Marlborough.	Co. Carlow. .	2,694	.	1,643
b. 1844, s. 1880.		8,066	.	3,850

Serves in R. Brig. and as Equerry to H.R.H.
the Duke of Connaught.

FITZGERALD, Mrs., of Shalstone House, Buckingham, &c.

s. 1848, m. 1832.	Hants . . .	3,716	.	3,206
	Bucks . . .	1,651	.	2,142
	Wilts . . .	108	.	238
		5,475	.	5,586

This includes 148 acres in Bucks and 517 in Hants, held by
her son, R. P. Fitzgerald, R.N., and Mrs. R. Fitzgerald.

** PENROSE-FITZGERALD, Robert Uniacke, of Corkbeg
Island, Whitegate, Co. Cork.

Coll. West., T. Hall, Cam.	Co. Cork . .	5,307	.	4,450
Club. Carlton, St. James's,	Queen's Co. .	764	.	415
Kildare St.				
b. 1839, s. 1857, m. 1867.		6,071	.	4,865

FITZGERALD, F. L., of Graney. Kildare	4,381	.	2,774

| FITZGERALD, Rev. Richard, of Coole-
noule. Queen's County, Fermanagh .	3,676	.	2,184

WILSON-FITZGERALD, William Henry, of Adelphi, Corrofin, Co. Clare.

		acres.		g. an. val.
Coll. Rugby, Univ. Oxon.	Co. Clare . .	9,164	.	3,473

Club. New University. b. 1842, s. 1872.

FITZ-GIBBON, Lady Louisa Isabella Georgina, of Mount Shannon, Lisnagry, Limerick.

b. 1827, s. 1873, m. 1847.	Limerick . .	10,316	.	6,694
	Tipperary . .	3,178	.	1,426
		13,494	.	8,120

FITZ-HARDINGE, Lord, Berkeley Castle, Gloucester.

Coll. Rugby.	Gloucester . .	18,264	.	31,836
Club. Turf.	Dorset . . .	1,471	.	1,483
b. 1826, s. 1867, m. 1857.	Middlesex . .	539	.	398

Served in Royal Horse Guards.

Sat for Cheltenham.   20,274 . 33,717

Lady Fitzhardinge has out of the Middlesex property a rental of 188*l.*

** FITZHERBERT, Basil Thomas, of Swynnerton Park, Stone, &c. ⚫.

Club. Travellers'.	Stafford . . .	5,567	.	5,788
b. 1836, s. 1863, m. 1858.	Derby . . .	845	.	1,836
		6,412	.	7,624

** FITZ-HERBERT, Richard Ruxton, of Black Castle Navan, &c.

Coll. Chel., Trin. Dub.	Co. Meath . .	2,011	.	3,500
b. 1841, s. 1879, m. 1865.	Monaghan . .	2,387	.	1,877
		4,398	.	5,377

FITZ-HERBERT, Sir William, Bart., of Tissington Hall, Ashbourne, &c. ⚫.

Coll. Charterhouse.	Notts . . .	5,846	.	7,244
b. 1808, s. 1858, m. 1836.	Derby . . .	2,914	.	5,488
	Kent . . .	418	.	1,458
	Stafford . . .	7	.	9
		9,185	.	14,199

FITZHUGH, THOMAS LLOYD, of Plâs Power, Wrexham.

			acres.	g. an. val.
Coll. Harrow.	Denbigh	. .	3,336	. 5,486
Club. Arthur's, Travellers',	Salop	. . .	363	. 344
Guards.	Flint .	. . .	26	. 87
b. 1819, s. 1856, m. 1847.				
Served in Grenadier Guards.			3,725	. 5,917

* FITZWILLIAM, EARL, K.G., Wentworth House, Rotherham, &c. ♠.

			acres.	g. an. val.
Coll. Trinity, Cambridge.	York, N., E., and			
Club. Bro., Trav., Sac. St.	W.R. . . .		22,192	. 87,406
b. 1815, s. 1857, m. 1838.	Northampton .		881	. 1,664
Sat for Malton and for	Cambridge. .		522	. 1,004
Co. Wicklow.	Derby . .		308	. 667
Ld. F., writing to *The*	Huntingdon .		75	. 178
Times, calls his Irish pro-	Lincoln . . .		17	. 28
perty 93 acres less than	Co. Wicklow .		89,891	. 46,444
here stated — the rental	Kildare . . .		1,532	. 1,255
2,646*l.* more. The Nptn.	Wexford . .		325	. 155
pty. is returned as LADY				
MILTON'S.			115,743	. 138,801

FITZWILLIAM, GEORGE CHARLES, of Milton Park, Peterborough. ♠.

		acres.	g. an. val.
b. 1866, s. 1874.	Huntingdon .	5,202	. 7,055
	Northampton .	18,116	. 32,492
		23,318	. 39,547

** WILLIS-FLEMING, JOHN EDWARD ARTHUR, of Stoneham Park, Southampton, &c.

		acres.	g. an. val.
b. 1871, s. 1872.	Hants . . .	11,610	. 16,000

** FLETCHER, JAMES, of Rosehaugh, Avoch, N.B.

			acres.	g. an. val.
Club. Union, Jun. Carl.,	Ross	. . .	11,095	. 9,270
New Edin.	Forfar .	. .	2,317	. 4,547
b. 1810, s. 1856, m. 1852.	Cromarty . .		880	. 122
	Lancaster . .		6	. 239
			14,298	. 14,178

FITZSIMMONS, G., of Dunsona. Antrim . 2,144 . 2,244

** FLETCHER, JOHN, of Salton Hall, Haddington, N.B.

			acres.	g. an. val.
Coll. Trin. Cam.	Haddington .		3,928 .	6,456

Club. Carlton, Boodle's.
b. 1827, s. 1879, m. 1866.

FLETCHER, PHILLIPS LLOYD, of Nerquis Hall, Mold.

b. 1822, s. 1868.	Flint . . .	1,744 .	2,012
	Merioneth . .	2,133 .	1,196
		3,877 .	3,208

** FLOOD, WILLIAM HANFORD, of Farmley, Kilkenny, &c.

Coll. Trinity, Cambridge.	Kilkenny . .	4,789 .	5,000
b. 1810, s. 1840, m. 1848.	Worcester . .	1,577 .	2,364
		6,366 .	7,364

*** FLUDYER, REV. SIR JOHN HENRY, BART., of Ayston House, Uppingham.

Coll. St. John's, Cam.	Rutland . .	2,638 .	3,968
Club. Junior Carlton.	Monmouth .	1,774 .	1,906
b. 1803, s. 1876, m. 1832.	Berks . . .	312 .	331
	Wilts . . .	102 .	732
	Leicester . .	9 .	6
	Lincoln . . .	6 .	8
		4,841 .	6,951

One acre in Rutland is owned by Sir J. FLUDYER's eldest son. The greater part of the property in that county will be found returned as possessed by a mythical " Rev. J. H. Hudyer."

FLANAGAN, RT. HON. S. W., of Drumdoe. Sligo, Roscommon, Clare	4,442 .	2,049
HESKETH - FLEETWOOD, SIR PETER LOUIS, BART., of Plaistow. Lancashire.	2,069 .	4,322
FLETCHER, MRS., of Bersted Lodge. Sussex, Lincoln	2,392 .	4,004
FLOOD, W., of Paulstown. Kilkenny . .	3,852 .	2,345

** FOLEY, The Lady Emily, Stoke Edith Park, Hereford.

			acres.		g. an. val.
b. 1805, s. 1846,	Hereford	. .	5,561	.	8,207
m. 1832.	Worcester	. .	1,700	.	5,000
	Stafford	. .	944	.	1,452
			8,205	.	14,659

** HODGETTS-FOLEY, Henry John Wentworth, of Prestwood, Stourbridge.

Coll. Eton, Ch. Ch. Oxon.	Stafford	. .	4,182	.	6,550
Club. Travellers'.	Worcester	. .	50	.	140
b. 1828, s. 1861, m. 1854.					
Sat for South Staffordshire.			4,232	.	6,690

*** FOLJAMBE, Francis John Savile, of Osberton Hall, Worksop, &c.

Coll. Eton, Ch. Ch. Oxon.	Notts	. . .	9,289	.	11,462
Club. Brooks's, Boodle's.	York,N.&W.R.		5,206	.	8,619
b. 1830, s. 1869, m. 1856.	Lincoln	. .	3	.	59
Sits for East Retford.			14,498	.	20,140

FORBES, Sir Charles John, Bart., of Newe, Strathdon, N.B., &c.

Club. Carlton.	Aberdeen	. .	29,238	.	5,992
b. 1843, s. 1877, m. 1864.					

** FORBES, Duncan, of Culloden, Inverness, &c.

b. 1851, s. 1879.	Ross	. . .	6,393	.	3,814
	Inverness	. .	3,644	.	3,903
	Nairn	. . .	2,011	.	650
			12,048	.	8,367

FORBES, Lord, Castle Forbes, Whitehouse, N.B.

Coll. Oriel, Oxon.	Aberdeen	. .	13,621	.	5,675
Club. Athenæum, Carlton.	b. 1829, s. 1868.				

FOORD, Rev. R. H. F., of Foxholes.   York   2,919   .   2,789

*** FORBES, Mrs., of The House of Haddo, Huntly, N.B.

		acres.	g. an. val.
m. 1825, s. 1879.	Aberdeen . .	161 .	178
	Banff . . .	5,400 .	4,615
		5,561 .	4,793

FORBES, Sir William Stuart, Bart. (of Pitsligo), of Fettercairn, Laurencekirk, N.B., &c.

b. 1835, s. 1866, m. 1865. Kincardine . 5,007 . 4,056

** FORBES, Sir William, Bart., of Cragievar Castle, Aberdeen, N.B., &c.

Coll. Eton. Aberdeen . . 9,347 . 8,539
Club. Carlton, Eton and Harrow, Hanover Square.
b. 1836, s. 1846, m. 1st 1858, 2nd 1862.
　　Served in Coldstream Guards in the Crimea.

*** FORBES, William, of Callendar House, Falkirk, N.B.

Coll.	Ch. Ch. Oxon.	Stirling . . .	13,041 .	14,312
Club.	Carlton, Boodle's,	Kirkcudbright	40,445 .	8,821
	New Ed., Kild.	Dumfries . .	2,416 .	960
	St. Dublin.	Ayr	603 .	1,319
b. 1833, s. 1855, m. 1st 1859,		Dumbarton .	199 .	30
2nd 1868.				
Exclusive of 6,540*l.* for minerals.			56,704 .	25,442

FORBES, William Nathaniel, of Dunnottar, Stonehaven, N.B., &c.

Club. Jun. Carlton.	Kincardine .	6,528 .	5,493
b. 1826, s. 1851, m. 1st 18—,	Aberdeen . .	1,300 .	163
2nd 18—.			
		7,828 .	5,656

*** FORDE, Col. William Brownlow, of Seaforde, Co. Down.

Club. Carl., Jun. Uni. Ser. Co. Down . . 20,106 . 15,990
b. 1823, s. 1856, m. 1855.
　　Served in 67th Foot. Sat for Co. Down.

OGILVIE-FORBES, G., of Boyndlie. Aber. 3,325 . 2,040
FORBES, W., of Medwyn. Peebles . . . 2,600 . 2,022

*** FORDYCE, ALEXANDER DINGWALL, of Brucklay Castle, Aberdeen, N.B.

		acres.	g. an. val.
b. 1873, s. 1875.	Aberdeen . .	20,903 .	12,967
	Kincardine .	46 .	1,091
		20,949 .	14,058

FORESTER, GEN. LORD, Willey Park, Broseley. 🐍

Club. Carlton, White's.	Salop . . .	14,891 .	21,046
b. 1807, s. 1874, m. 1862.	Stafford . .	724 .	1,535
		15,615 .	22,581

Served in R.H.G., was Gr. of the Bedchamber to Geo. IV. and Wm. IV., and Comp. of the Household. Sat for Wenlock.

FORTEATH, MRS., of Bunny Park, Nottingham.

	Notts . . .	3,923 .	5,949

*** FORTESCUE, CYRIL DUDLEY, of Boconnoc, Lostwithiel, &c. 🐍

Coll. Eton, Ch. Ch. Oxon.	Cornwall . .	20,148 .	14,703
Club. St. James's, Guards, White's.	Bucks . . .	2,837 .	3,390
b. 1847, s. 1877.		22,985 .	18,093

Serves in Coldstream Guards.

Part of the Bucks property has been sold since correction.

** FORTESCUE, EARL, Castle Hill, South Molton. 🐍

Coll. Harrow, Trin. Cam.	Devon . . .	20,171 .	17,245
Club. Ath., Brooks's, Trav.	Lincoln . .	5,116 .	5,874
b. 1818, s. 1861, m. 1847.	Gloucester . .	1,071 .	2,099
Served as Commissioner in	Cornwall . .	571 .	470
Lunacy, Lord of the	Waterford . .	3,958 .	2,985
Treasury, and Chairman			
of Metropolitan Com-		30,887 .	28,673
missioners of Sewers.			

Sat for Plymouth and for Marylebone.

BLAKE-FORSTER, F., of Ashfield. Gal., 4,901 . 2,768
Clare

HAIRE-FORSTER, REV. A. N., of Ballynure. 2,093 . 2,024
Monaghan.

FORTESCUE, JOHN CHARLES WILLIAM, of Stephenstown, Dundalk.

		acres.	*g. an. val.*
Coll. Woolwich.	Co. Louth . .	5,262 .	5,070

Club. Army and Navy.
b. 1822, s. 1845, m. 1857.
   Served in Royal Artillery.

*** FOSTER, REV. SIR CAVENDISH HERVEY, BART., of Glyde Court, Louth (res. Thoydon Garnon, Epping).

Coll. Eton, Magd. Cam.	Co. Louth . .	3,442 .	3,263
b. 1817, s. 1857, m. 1844.	Essex . . .	64 .	100
		3,506 .	3,363

   Exclusive of 650*l.* tithes, but inclusive of 578*l.* out of the Irish rental standing in his eldest son's name.

** FOSTER, WILLIAM, of Hornby Castle, Lancaster, &c.

Club. Reform.	Lancashire .	10,841 .	8,000
b. 1821, s. 1878,	York, W.R. .	1,884 .	1,098
m. 1st 1848, 2nd 1867.		12,725 .	9,098

FOSTER, WILLIAM ORME, of Apley Park, Bridgnorth, &c.

Club. Athen., Brooks's.	Salop . . .	8,547 .	17,850
b. 1814, s. 1853, m. 1843.	Worcester . .	1,917 .	4,266
	Stafford . .	874 .	1,624
	Wexford . .	9,724 .	4,686
Sat for South Staffordshire.		21,062 .	28,426

FORSYTH, J. N. M., of Quinish. Argyll .	13,600 .	2,129
FOSTER, A. B., of Warmwell. Dorset. .	2,712 .	2,386
FOSTER, E. B., of Anstey. Cam., Suff., Hunts	2,079 .	5,261
FOSTER, F. J., of Castlering. Louth . .	3,005 .	2,830
FOSTER, J. W., of Lawkland Hall. York .	3,642 .	2,001

*** SCRYMSOURE - FOTHRINGHAM, Walter Thomas James, of Fothringham, Forfar, N.B., &c.

		acres.	g. an. val.
b. 1862, s. 1864 and 1875.	Forfar . . .	12,529	. 13,399

FOUNTAINE, Algernon Charles (*jure uxoris*), of Narford Hall, Brandon.

b. 1841, m. 1876.	Norfolk . .	6,318	. 6,859

** FOWLER, John, of Braemore, Loch Broom, N.B., &c.

Club.	Jun. Carl., Cons.,	Ross. . . .	39,530	. 4,000
	St. Stephen's,	Inverness . .	7,618	. 760
	Whitehall	York, W.R. .	61	. 990
b. 1817, m. 1850.		Lincoln . .	39	. 136
			47,248	. 5,886

** FOWLER, Robert, of Rahinston, Enfield, Co. Meath.

Coll.	Trinity, Dublin.	Co. Meath . .	8,026	. 6,884
Club.	Sackville Street, Dublin.	b. 1824, s. 1868, m. 1856.		

** LANE-FOX, George, of Bramham Park, Tadcaster, &c.

Coll.	Eton, Ch. Ch. Oxon.	York, W.R. .	15,000	. 17,000
Club.	Carlton, Boodle's.	Leitrim . . .	18,850	. 6,000
b. 1816, s. 1848, m. 1837.		Waterford . .	5,219	. 3,000
			39,069	. 26,000

** FOX, John Wilson, of Statham Lodge, Warrington, &c.

Coll.	Eton, Bras. Oxon.	Cheshire . .	2,052	. 6,060
Club.	Ox. and Cam., Army	Lincoln . . .	1,556	. 2,018
	and Navy, Road.	Lancashire .	51	. 271
b. 1825, s. 1843, m. 1863 and 1876.			3,659	. 8,349

Served in 12th Lancers in the Kaffir war of 1851–52.

FOULIS, Sir J. L., Bart., of Colinton. Midl.	2,804	. 2,163
FOWLE, W. H., of Durrington. Wilts, Hants	2,448	. 2,433
FOXCROFT, E. T. D., of Hinton. Somt., York	2,474	. 3,162

FOX, WILLIAM HENRY, of Bradwell Grove, Burford.

			acres.		g. an. val.
Coll.	Trinity, Cambridge.	Oxford . . .	4,554	.	5,645
Club.	New Univ., Garrick.	York, W.R. .	800	.	5,624
b. 1843.					
			5,354	.	11,269

The Yorkshire estate belongs to his father, SAMUEL FOX.

** FRAMPTON, REV. WILLIAM CHARLTON, of Moreton House, Dorchester. ⚓.

			acres.		g. an. val.
Coll.	Trinity, Cambridge.	Dorset . . .	8,998	.	6,047
b. 1811, s. 1879.					

FRANK, FREDERICK BACON, of Campsall, Doncaster, &c.

			acres.		g. an. val.
Coll.	Trinity, Cambridge.	York, W.R. .	2,232	.	2,931
Club.	Travellers', Dev.	Norfolk . .	1,777	.	2,830
b. 1827, s. 1834, m. 1854.					
			4,009	.	5,761

FRANKFORT DE MONTMORENCY, VISCOUNT (res. Theydon Bower, Epping, Essex).

		acres.		g. an. val.
b. 1806, s. 1822, m. 1835.	Kilkenny . .	4,610	.	2,158
Served in 10th Hussars.	Clare . . .	1,653	.	618
	Cavan . . .	1,054	.	536
	Carlow . . .	636	.	493
LADY FRANKFORT has the Clare property.		7,953	.	3,805

** FRASER, FREDERICK MACKENZIE, of Castle Fraser, Aberdeen, N.B., &c.

			acres.		g. an. val.
Coll.	Rugby.	Aberdeen . .	4,247	.	3,697
Club.	Trav., Carl., U. Serv.				
b. 1831, s. 1871, m. 1st 1871, 2nd 1879.					

		acres.		g. an. val.
WILSON-FRANCE, R. J. B., of Rawcliffe Hall. Lancashire		2,198	.	3,446
FRANKS (late), J. H., Trustees of. Leic. .		2,724	.	5,085
FRASER, A. T. F., of Abertarff. Inverness.		20,063	.	2,247
FRASER, JOHN, of Balnain. Inverness . .		10,306	.	2,208

ALLAN-FRASER, PATRICK, of Hospitalfield, Arbroath, N.B., &c.

		acres.		g: an. val.
b. 1810, s. 1873, m. 1843.	Perth . . .	2,722	.	1,537
	Forfar . . .	1,045	.	1,890
	Warwick . .	257	.	633
		4,024	.	4,060

FRASER, WILLIAM, of Kilmuir, Isle of Skye, N.B.

Club. Uni. Serv., Edin. Inverness . . 46,142 6,250
b. 1827, s. 1843.

** HUSSEY-FREKE, AMBROSE DENIS, of Hannington Hall, Highworth, Wilts, &c.

Coll. Eton, Ch. Ch. Oxon. Wilts . . . 3,911 . 5,925
Club. Carlton. b. 1836, s. 1849, m. 1862.

FRENCH, MRS., of Lough Erritt, Frenchpark, Co. Roscommon.

s. 1873, m. 1839.	Roscommon .	12,270	.	3,472
	Co. Sligo . .	1,224	.	427
	Co. Cork . .	79	.	39
		13,573	.	3,938

** FRENCH, ROBERT, of Monivea Castle, Galway.

Coll. Rugby. Co. Galway . 10,121 . 3,703
Club. Travellers', Turf. b. 1833, s. 1876, m. 1863.
Served as Secretary to the Embassy at Vienna.

FRENCH, SAVAGE, of Cuskinny, Queenstown, Co. Cork.

Coll. Westm.,Ch.Ch.Oxon. Co. Cork . . 8,159 . 4,553
b. 1840, s. 1878, m. 1869.

FRASER, MRS., of Bunchrew. Inver., Sur.	2,723	.	2,801
FREDERICK (reps. of late SIR R.). Lincoln	2,328	.	2,877
** WILLIAMS-FREEMAN,W.P.,of Clapton.			
Hunts, Northamptonshire	2,610	.	3,275
FRENCH, C., of Cloonyquin. Roscommon	3,701	.	2,933

** FRERE, GEORGE EDWARD, F.R.S., of Roydon Hall, Diss.

		acres.	*g. an. val.*
Coll. Charterh.,Edin.Univ.	Suffolk . . .	2,574 .	3,638
Club. Athenæum.	Norfolk . . .	1,070 .	1,501
b. 1807, s. 1846, m. 1840.	Essex . . .	841 .	958
	Northumberland	27 .	106
		4,512 .	6,203

*** FREWEN, EDWARD, of Brickwall House, Northiam, Sussex, &c.

Coll. St. John's, Cam.	Sussex . . .	3,590 .	5,400
Club. Cons., Carlton.	Leicester . .	4,218 .	7,869
b. 1850, s. 1870, m. 1873.	Kent. . . .	29 .	56
	Rutland . .	55 .	106
		7,892 .	13,431

* PAGE-FRYER, MRS., of Battlesden, Bedford, &c.

s. 1874.	Bedford. . .	2,214 .	3,000
The rents are but a rough	Oxon . . .	1,898 .	2,000
apportmnt. by the compiler	Kent . . .	982 .	unstated
of MRS. FRYER's share of SIR	Middlesex . .	40 .	50
E. PAGE-TURNER's estates,			
on the basis of the Govt. ret.		5,134 .	5,050

FULLERTON, ALEXANDER GEORGE, of Ballintoy Castle, Co. Antrim, &c.

Coll. Eton.	Co. Antrim .	5,611 .	2,919
b. 1808, m. 1833.	Gloucester . .	1,243 .	2,158
Served in R. H. Gds.	Sussex . . .	7 .	81
Was Attaché in Paris.			
" Hopelessly wrong "—A. G. F.		6,861 .	5,158

** FULLERTON, REV. CHAS. GARTH, of Thrybergh, Rother-ham, &c.

b. 1838, s. 1881, m. 1862.	York, W.R. .	3,331 .	13,000

FRYER, J. R., of Chatteris. Cambs., Hunts,			
Norfolk		2,100 .	3,426
FRYER, W. R., of Lytchett Minster. Dorset		2,260 .	2,863

GABBETT, Rev. Joseph, of Ardvullen, Killmallock, Co. Limerick.

		acres.	g. an. val.
Coll. Trinity, Dublin.	Limerick . .	3,533 .	3,191
Club. County, Limerick.	Tipperary . .	40 .	51
b. 1807, s. 1846, m. 1839.			
		3,573 .	3,242

ROKEWODE-GAGE, Lady, of Hengrave Hall, Bury St. Edmund's.

b. 1818, s. 1872, m. 1842.	Suffolk . . .	6,210 .	7,669

*** GAGE, Viscount, Firle Place, Lewes. ⚓.

Coll. Eton, Ch. Ch. Oxon.	Sussex . . .	12,352 .	13,337
Club. Marlborough. b. 1854, s. 1877.			

GAINSBOROUGH, Earl of, Exton Park, Oakham, &c.

Coll. Oscott.	Rutland . .	15,076 .	23,716
Club. J. U. Serv., Boodle's,	Gloucester . .	3,170 .	4,851
St. George's.	Leicester . .	159 .	168
	Warwick . .	68 .	150
	Lincoln . . .	89 .	99
	Northampton .	6 .	7
b. 1850, s. 1881, m. 1st 1876, 2nd 1880.			
Served in 10th Hussars.		18,568 .	28,991

*** GALLOWAY, Earl of, Galloway House, Garlieston, N.B., &c.

Coll. Har., Ch. Ch. Oxon.	Wigtown . .	23,203 .	24,864
Club. Carlton, Travellers'.	Kirkcudbright	55,981 .	7,333
b. 1835, s. 1873, m. 1872.			
		79,184 .	32,197

Served in R.H.G., and as Lord High Commissioner to the Assembly of Established Kirk of Scotland. Sat for Wigtownshire.

⚓ FULFORD, F D., of Fulford. Devon .	2,987 .	2,289
⚓ FURSDON, Rev. E., of Cadbury. Devon	2,826 .	3,272
GALBRAITH, J. S., of Clanabogan. Tyrone, Longford	6,080 .	2,859

GALWAY, Viscount, Serlby Hall, Bawtry.

			acres.		g. an. val.
Coll.	Eton, Ch. Ch. Oxon.	Cornwall . .	162	.	199
Club.	Boodle's, Carlton,	Notts . . .	4,081	.	5,969
	Jun. Carl., Trav.	York,E.&W.R.	2,765	.	4,389

b. 1844, s. 1876, m. 1879.
Sits for N. Notts.   7,008 · 10,557

Ld. G. & " another " are retd. as joint owners of 45 a. more.

*** GAMMELL, Major Andrew, of Drumtochty Castle, Aberdeen, N.B.

Club.	Carlton, Uni. Service.	Aberdeen . .	3,946	.	3,396
b. 18—.		Kincardine .	6,523	.	2,224
Served in 43rd Foot.		Perth . . .	1,262	.	2,074
		Forfar . . .	369	.	348

            12,100 . 8,042

** GAPE, James John, of St. Michael's Manor, St. Alban's.

b. 1826, s. 1874, m. 1851.	Cambridge .	1,750	.	1,629
	Herts . . .	1,360	.	1,435
	Lincoln . . .	136	.	135

            3,246 . 3,199

** GARD, Mrs. Mary Eliza, of Rougemont, Exeter, &c.

s. 1868, m. 1829.   Devon . . .   3,243 · 4,546

*** GARDNER, John Dunn, of Chatteris House, Cambridge.

Coll.	Westminster.	Cambridge .	3,676	.	8,750
Club.	Carlton.	Huntingdon .	16	.	34

b. 1811, s. 1839, m. 1st 1847,
               2nd 1853.   3,692 . 8,784
Sat for Bodmin.

GAMMELL, J., of Ardiffery.	Aberdeen .	2,193	.	2,168
GARDNER, Rev. J., of Pilling.	Lanc., York	2,181	.	2,853
GARDNER, R., of Sansaw.	Salop . . ,	2,964	.	4,444

** GREENHILL-GARDYNE, Col. Charles, of Glenforsa, Isle
of Mull, N.B., &c.

			acres.		*g. an. val.*
Coll. Edinburgh.	Argyll . . .		20,000	.	2,011
Club. Guards.	Forfar . . .		4,078	.	4,273
b. 1831, s. 1867, m. 1858.					
Served in Cdstm. Gds. & 92nd Foot.			24,078	.	6,284

** GARLAND, Edgar Walter, of 15, Queen's Gate, S.W.

Coll. Eton, New, Oxon.	Essex . . .		2,306	.	3,990
b. 1814, s. 1845, m. 1844.	Lincoln. . . .		1,904	.	3,500
	Surrey . . .		35	.	510
			4,245	.	8,000

** GARNETT, Henry, of Wyreside, Lancaster.

b. 1814, s. 1852, m. 1839. Lancashire	.	3,511	.	3,178

GARNETT, William, of Bleasdale Tower, Garstang, &c.

Coll. Eton, Ch. Ch. Oxon. Lancashire	.	4,703	.	5,476
Club. Uni. Univ. b. 1851, s. 1873, m. 1876.				

** GARNETT, William Stawell, of Williamstown House,
Kells, Co. Meath.

Coll. King Edw., Birm. Co. Meath	.	3,014	.	3,184
Club. Sackv. St., F. B., Dub. b. 1838, s. 1856, m. 1859.				

** CARPENTER-GARNIER, John, of Rooksbury Park, Fareham, &c.

Coll. Har.,Ch.Ch.Ox.	Hants . . .		2,401	.	2,862
Club. Carl.,St.James's.	Devon . . .		2,500	.	3,095
b. 1839, s. 1842 and 1864, m. 1868.					
Sits for South Devon.			4,901	.	5,957

DRAKE-GARRARD, C. B., of Lamer. Herts		2,543	.	3,185
GARRATT, J., of Bishop's Court. Devon		2,049	.	4,178
GARTH, T. C., of Haines Hill. Berks .		2,581	.	4,082

** GARVAGH, Lord, Garvagh Lodge, Co. Derry, &c.

		acres.	g. an. val.
Coll. Ch. Ch. Oxon.	Londonderry .	8,427 .	4,459
Club. Carlton, White's, Sal.	Co. Cavan . .	5,803 .	2,804
b. 1852, s. 1871, m. 1877.	Co. Down . .	1,176 .	1,462

15,406 . 8,725

CHARLOTTE, Dow. LADY G., owns most of this property.

TRENCH-GASCOIGNE, FREDERICK CHARLES, of Parlington Park, Aberford, York, &c.

Club. Jun. Uni. Ser.	York, W.R. .	5,685 .	9,611
b. 1814, m. 1850.	Argyll . .	5,591 .	1,013
	Limerick . .	7,766 .	5,548
	Westmeath .	313 .	167

Served in 66th Foot. 19,355 . 16,339

*** GASKELL, CHARLES GEORGE MILNES, of The Abbey, Wenlock, &c.

Coll. Eton, Trin. Cam.	York . . .	1,640 .	3,190
Club. Brooks's, Trav., St.	Salop . . .	1,144 .	3,100
James's.	Lancashire .	1,609 .	4,442
b. 1842, s. 1873, m. 1876.			

4,393 . 10,732

** GAUSSEN, ROBERT GEORGE, of Brookman's Park, Hatfield.

Club. Gds., Carlton.	Herts . .	3,566 .	4,246

b. 1843, s. 1880, m. 1870.
Served in Gren. Guards.

** CHANDOS-POLE-GELL, HENRY, of Hopton Hall, Wirksworth.

Club. Jun. Carl., Boodle's.	Derbyshire .	3,744 .	4,467

b. 1829, s. 1863, m. 1st 1851, 2nd 1869.

GASKELL, H. L., of Kiddington. Oxon., Lanc.	2,832 .	4,722
GATTY, C. H., of Felbridge. Surr., Suss.	2,171 .	2,046
GAY, J., of Thurning. Norfolk	2,282 .	3,174
GEARY, SIR F., BART., of Oxon Hoath. Kent	2,843 .	5,077
GEORGE, MISS, of Cherrington. Gloucester	2,411 .	2,842

GERARD, LORD, Garswood, Walton-le-Willows. ♨.

			acres.	g. an. val.
Coll.	Oscott.	Lancashire .	6,192 .	42,487
Club.	Boodle's, White's.	Lincolnshire .	915 .	1,184
b. 1808, s. 1854, m. 1849.				
			7,107 .	43,671

Served in the Carabineers, and as A.D.C. to the Queen.

GERRARD, THOMAS, of Boyne Hill, Navan.

Coll.	Winchester.	Co. Meath .	4,748 .	5,034
Club.	Kild. St., Sackville St., Dublin. b. 1834, s. 1836.			

** GERVAIS, FRANCIS JOHN, of Cecil, Augher, Co. Tyrone.

Coll.	Cheam, Trin. Dub.	Tyrone . . .	7,727 .	5,034
Club.	F. B. Dublin.	Monaghan . .	252 .	256
b. 1819, s. 1849, m. 1852.				
			7,979 .	5,290

** GIBBS, HENRY HUCKS, of Aldenham Park, Elstree.

Coll.	Rugby, Ex. Oxon.	Herts . . .	2,088 .	3,940
Club.	Carl., J.Carl., Ath.	Oxford . . .	1,260 .	2,167
b. 1819, m. 1845.		Berks . . .	57 .	70
			3,405 .	6,177

CAREW-GIBSON, GEORGE CAREW, of Sandgate, Pulborough.

Coll.	Eton, Pemb. Oxon.	Sussex . . .	3,772 .	2,648
b. 1843, s. 1860, m. 1866.		Surrey . . .	794 .	436
		Worcester . .	2 .	5
			4,568 .	3,089

SAMUEL-GIBBON, J., of Trecastle. Glam.	2,475 .	2,069
GIBBONS, SIR J., BART., of Stanwell. Midd. York, Berks, Staffs.	2,675 .	3,710
GIBBS, A., of Tyntesfield. Somt., Dev., Glou.	2,873 .	4,951
GIBSON, H., of Ongar. Essex	2,648 .	2,897
GIBSON, J., of Whelprigg. Westm., Lanc., York	2,728 .	2,207
GIBSON, W., of Rockforest. Tipperary .	5,214 .	2,245

** GIBSON, GEORGE STACEY, of Hill Ho., Saffron Walden.

				acres.		*g. an. val.*
Coll. Tottenham Sch.						
b. 1818, s. 1877, m. 1845.	Essex	.	.	3,103	.	2,955
	York	.	.	177	.	350
	Cambs	.	.	20	.	95

Exc. of 2,000*l.* for house-ppty.   3,300 . 3,400

** GIFFARD, WALTER THOMAS COURTENAY, of Chillington Hall, Wolverhampton. ♠.

b. 1839, s. 1877, m. 1879.	Stafford	.	.	7,164		10,959
	Salop	.	.	34	.	68
	Flint	.	.	684	.	630

       7,882 . 11,657

* GILBERT, CAREW DAVIES, of Trellissick, Truro, &c.

Coll. Eton, Trin. Cam.	Sussex	.	.	3,526	.	5,734
Club. Boodle's, Arthur's.	Cornwall	.	.	2,895	.	3,000
b. 1852, s. 1854, m. 1881.						

       6,421 . 8,734

The Sussex property is entered under his mother's (HON. MRS. GILBERT'S) name, while really the Cornish estate only, which is here a little overstated, belongs to her.

*** GILLESPIE, DAVID, of Mountquhanie, Cupar-Fife, N.B.

Coll. Edin., Ch. Ch. Oxon.	Fife	.	.	.	3,443	.	4,896
b. 1814, s. 1827, m. 1840.							

*** GILMOUR, ALLAN, of Eaglesham House, Glasgow, N.B.

Coll. Glasgow Univ.	Renfrew	.	.	16,931	.	12,765
Club. Western, Glasgow.						
b. 1820, s. 1849 and 1858, m. 1850.						

*** GILSTRAP, WILLIAM, of Fornham Park, Bury St. Edmund's.

b. 1816, m. 1847.	Suffolk	.	.	.	4,880	.	5,720

GIFFORD, T., of Busta.	Zetland	.	.	.	30,960	.	2,875
GILLANDERS, G. F., of Highfield.	Ross	.	10,000	.	2,255		
GILMOUR, A., of Lundin.	Fife	.	.	.	2,728	.	5,243

** GIST, Samuel, of Warmington Grange, Stanway, Winchcomb.

		acres.	g. an. val.
b. 1832, s. 1845.	Gloucester . .	2,180	3,273
	Oxford . . .	1,009	2,242
	Warwick . .	720	1,205
	Northampton .	106	165
	Worcester . .	5	8
		4,020	6,893

The present value of this property is about 8,000*l.*

* GLADSTONE, Right Hon. William Ewart, of Hawarden Castle, Flint.

Coll. Eton, Ch. Ch. Oxon.	Flint . . .	6,908	17,565
Club. Uni. University.	Lancashire .	10	608
b. 1809, s. 1875, m. 1839.			
		6,918	18,173

Served as L. Treas., U. Sec. for Colonies, M. Mint, V. P. B. of Trade, Col. Sec., Ch. Exc., Prime Minister, and in same office coupled with the Chship. of the Exc., which offices he again holds Sat for Newark, Ox. Univ., S. Lancashire, and Greenwich. Sits for Midlothian. His eld. son owns much of these properties.

** GLADSTONE, Sir Thomas, Bart., of Fasque, Fettercairn, N.B., &c.

Coll. Eton, Ch. Ch. Oxon.	Kincardine .	45,062	9,174
Club. Carlton, Travellers'. b. 1804, s. 1851, m. 1835.			

Sat for Queenboro, Portarlington, Leicester, and Ipswich.

** GLASGOW, Earl of, Crauford Priory, Fife, N.B., &c.

Coll. Ch. Ch. Oxon.	Ayrshire . .	25,613	15,785
Club. Carlton.	Fife	5,625	9,024
b. 1825, s. 1869, m. 1856.	Renfrew . .	4,579	7,441
Sat for Bute.	Bute . . .	1,833	1,979
	Dumbarton .	175	359
		37,825	34,588

Exclusive of 6,500*l.* for mine rents.

GIPPS, G. B., of Howletts.   Kent . . . .   2,910 . 2,743

---

* BASKERVYLE-GLEGG, John, of Withington Hall, Chelford.

		acres.	g. an. val.
b. 1877, s. 1877.	Cheshire . .	3,702 .	7,293

*** GLYN, Sir Richard George, Bart., of Gaunt's House, Wimborne.

Coll. Merton, Oxon.	Dorset . . .	9,620 .	12,676
Club. Brooks's, Boodle's,	Wilts . . .	67 .	90
Army and Navy.	Somerset . .	83 .	127
b. 1831, s. 1863, m. 1868.			
Served in Royal Dragoons in the Crimea.		9,770 .	12,893

* GODDARD, Ambrose Lethbridge, of the Lawn, Swindon.

Coll. Har., St. John, Cam.	Wilts . . .	3,821 .	8,162
Club. Carlton. b. 1819, s. 1854, m. 1847.			
Sat for Cricklade.			

GODFREY, Sir John Fermor, Bart., of Kilcoleman Abbey, Milltown, Co. Kerry.

b. 1828, s. 1873, m. 1856.	Kerry . . .	5,986 .	3,218
Served in 2nd Drag. Gds.	Co. Cork . .	106 .	85
		6,092 .	3,303

** GODMAN, Joseph, of Park Hatch, Godalming, &c.

Coll. Eton, Em. Cam.	Sussex . . .	2,540 .	5,334
Club. Arthur's.	Surrey . . .	2,460 .	1,949
b. 1831, s. 1874, m. 1857.			
		5,000 .	7,283

** GOFF, Joseph Granville Stuart, of Hale Park, Salisbury, &c.

Coll. Eton.	Hants . .	1,448 .	1,835
Club. Naval and Military.	Wilts . . .	1,400 .	1,200
b. 1851, s. 1872.	King's Co. .	791 .	361
Serves in 43rd Foot.			
		3,639 .	3,396

GLASCOTT, W. M., of Alderton, Wexf., Kilk.	3,290 .	2,341
ROBERTSON-GLASGOW, R. B., of Montgreenan. Ayr	2,645	2,408

GOFF, Thomas Clarence Edwards, of Oakport (res. Carriglea, Kingstown, Co. Dublin).   *acres.   g. an. val.*
b. 1867, s. 1876.   Co. Roscommon   5,429 .   3,738
                              Co. Sligo . .   808 .   392

                                                 6,237 .   4,130

GOING, Benjamin Freud, of Ballyphillip, Killenaule.
b. 1851, s. 1878, m. 1879.   Tipperary . .   6,398 .   3,434

** GOLDSMID, Sir Julian, Bart., of Somerhill, Tonbridge, &c.
   Coll. Univ. London.   Kent   . . .   6,530 .   8,000
   Club. Ath., Brooks's, Gloucester . .   4,770 .   4,700
          St. Jas., Ref.   Hants . . .   1,800 .   1,600
b. 1838, s. 1866 & 1878,   Berks   . . .   980 .   1,280
   m. 1868.   Sussex . . .   193 .   20,000
Sat for Honiton and Rochester.

                                                14,273 .   35,580

GOOCH, Sir Alfred Sherlock, Bt., of Benacre, Wangford.
Coll. Eton.   Suffolk . . .   7,186 .   7,490
b. 1851, s. 1881, m. 1880.

*** GOOLD, Mrs., of Dromadda, Glin, Co. Limerick.
s. 1877.   Limerick . .   10,966 .   3,090

** GORDON, Alexander Henry, of Fyvie, Aberdn., N.B., &c.
b. 1813, s. 1879, m. 1842.   Aberdeen . .   11,700 .   9,061
                             Kincardine .   1,354 .   1,050
Served in the Indian Navy.

                                                13,054 .   10,111

GOLDNEY, Sir G., Bt., of Beechfield.
   Wilts . . . .   2,735 .   6,263
GOODACRE, John, of Lutterworth. Leic.,
   Warwick, Nottingham, Sussex   . . .   2,197 .   4,478
GOODBODY, Jonathan, of Castletown.
   King's Co., Westmeath . . . . . .   3,560 .   2,000
GOODBODY, Marcus, of Inchmore. King's
   Co., Westmeath . . . .   3,191 .   2,103
GOODLAKE,T. L., of Wadney. Berks, Glo.   2,632 .   4,377

*** GORDON, Carlos Pedro, of Kildrummy Castle, Mossat,
   N.B., &c.   *acres.*   *g. an. val.*
b. 1814, s. 1866, m. 1838.   Aberdeen . . 12,973 .   6,873
   Was V.-Consul at Xerez.

** GORDON, George John Robert, of Ellon Castle, Ellon,
   N.B.
   Coll. Edin. University. Aberdeen . .   6,000 .   5,178
Club. New Edinburgh.
b. 1812, s. 1873, m. 1871.
   Was Minister Plenipotentiary to Wurtemburg and Hanover.

** WOLRIGE-GORDON, Henry, of Esslemont, Ellon, N.B.
Coll. Marl., Exeter, Oxon. Aberdeen . .   4,962 .   4,502
Club. New Edin., St. Ste-
       phen's, Carlton.
b. 1831, m. 1856.

*** GORDON, James Wilkinson, of Cairness, Lonmay, N.B.
b. 1824, s. 1841, m. 1857.   Aberdeen . .   4,100 .   3,476

FELLOWES-GORDON, Mrs., of Knockespock, Aberdeen, N.B.
s. 1878, m. 1857.   Aberdeen . .   6,709 .   3,438

** BELLAMY-GORDON, Hon. Mrs., of Kenmure Castle, New
   Galloway, N.B.
b. 1797, s. 1847, m. 1815.   Kirkcudbright 14,093 .   4,229
   This estate has been held by this family since 1297.

GORDON, Miss, of Kemble House, Cirencester.
s. 1864.   Wilts . . .   2,912 .   4,001
                            Gloucester . .   3,710 .   3,837
                            Dorset . . .   9 .   15
                                            ───────   ───────
                                             6,631 .   7,853

* GORDON, A. H., of Avochie.   Banff .   3,021 .   2,200
GORDON, A. M., of Newton.   Aberdeen .   3,369 .   2,989
** CONWAY-GORDON, Col., of Lynwood
   Ho. Linc., Cumb. . . . .   2,476 .   2,778
GORDON, Henry, of Manar.   Aberdeen .   2,260 .   2,114

GORDON, ROBERT FRANCIS, of Florida Manor, Killinchy, Co. Down.

			acres.	*g. an. val.*
Coll. Trinity, Dublin.	Down . . .	4,768	.	5,597
Club. Carlton, Sack. St.	Tyrone . . .	8,806	.	1,489
b. 1791, s. 1837, m. 1825.				
		13,574	.	7,086

KNOX-GORE, SIR CHARLES JAMES, BART., of Belleek Manor, Ballina.

Coll. Eton, Trinity, Dublin.	Co. Mayo . .	22,023	.	8,294
Club. Kildare Street, Dub.	Co. Sligo . .	8,569	.	2,788
b. 1831, s. 1873.				
Served in 66th Foot.		30,592	.	11,082

** GORE, LIEUT.-COL. EDWARD ARTHUR, of Derrymore, O'Callaghan's Mills, Co. Clare.

Coll. Eton. Co. Clare . . 8,561 . 4,722
Club. A. & N., Wind., U. Ser., Sackv. St., and R. St. G. Y. C.
b. 1839, s. 1848.
Commands 6th Inniskilling Dragoons ; was in 3rd Hussars.

GORING, SIR CHARLES, BART., of Highden, Steyning. **S.**

Club. Army and Navy.	Sussex . . .	3,956	.	3,835
b. 1828, s. 1859, m. 1st 1850,	York, W.R. .	466	.	954
2nd 1857.				
Served in 12th Lancers.		4,422	.	4,789

GORING, REV. JOHN, of Wiston Manor, Steyning. **S.**

Coll. Ch. Ch. Oxon. Sussex . . . 14,139 . 13,705
Club. Carlton. b. 1824, s. 1849, m. 1861.

*** GORMANSTON, VISC., Gormanston Castle, Balbriggan, &c.

Club. Carlton, A. & N.	Co. Meath .	9,657	.	8,048
	Co. Dublin .	1,300	.	1,316
b. 1837, s. 1876, m. 1861.				
		10,957	.	9,364

Served in 60th Rifles in Ind. Mut., and as Com. Ed. in Ireland.

* GORDON, LADY M., of Northcourt, Hants	2,345	.	3,419
GORDON, MRS. CATHERINE. Peebles . .	4,827	.	2,049
GLENDONWYN-GORDON, SIR R., BART., of Letterfourie. Banff, Dumf., Kirk .	2,331	.	2,719

GOSFORD, Earl of, K.P., Gosford Castle, Market Hill, Co. Armagh.

			acres.		*g. an. val.*
Coll.	Harrow.				
Club.	Brooks's, White's,	Armagh . .	12,177	.	13,705
	Militia and Yeo-	Co. Cavan . .	6,417	.	4,229
	manry, Travellers',				
	St. James's.		18,594	.	17,934

b. 1841, s. 1864, m. 1876.

*** GOSLING, Robert, of Hassobury, Bishop Stortford.

Club.	Arth. J. Carlton.	Essex . . .	4,962	.	6,033
b. 1831, s. 1869, m. 1st	Herts . . .	185	.	400
1856, 2nd 1861.				
			5,147	.	6,433

* GOUGH, Richard Douglas, of Yniscedwin, Swansea.

Coll.	Har., Exeter, Oxon.	Glamorgan . .	3,234	.	1,813
Club.	United University.	Brecon . . .	2,155	.	1,223
b. 1800, s. 1835, m. 1840.				
			5,389	.	3,036

** GOUGH, Viscount, Lough Cutra Castle, Gort., Co. Galway, &c.

Coll.	Trin., Dublin.	Co. Galway .	9,003	.	4,235
Club.	Carlt., Ath., Kild. St.	Queen's Co. .	1,045	.	783
b. 1816, s. 1869, m. 1st 1840,	Tipperary . .	893	.	723
2nd 1846.	Dublin . . .	72	.	378
	Kildare . . .	2,695	.	1,784
Served in Grenadier Guards.		13,708	.	7,903

** LEVESON-GOWER, Granville William Gresham, of Titsey Place, Limpsfield. 🌳.

Coll.	Eton, Ch. Ch. Oxon.	Surrey . . .	6,930	.	5,234
Club.	Brooks's, Travellers'.	Kent . . .	183	.	266
b. 1838, s. 1860, m. 1861.				
Sat for Reigate.		7,113	.	5,500

Inclusive of waste lands.

GOUGH, G., of Birdhill.	Limerick . . .	2,398	.	2,539
🌳. LEVESON-GOWER, J., of Bill Hill.				
	Berks	2,041	.	2,867

** GRÆME, Patrick James Frederick, of Inchbrakie, Crieff, N.B., &c.

				acres.		g. an. val.
Coll. Harrow, Trin. Cam.	Perth	.	.	5,088	.	3,211

Club. Naval and Military. b. 1849, s. 1854.
Served in 79th Highlanders.

*** GRAFTON, Duke of, C.B., Euston Hall, Thetford, &c.

			acres.		g. an. val.
Coll. Harrow.	Suffolk . . .	11,127	.	11,180	
Club. Travellers', White's.	Northampton .	14,507	. }	28,104	
b. 1819, s. 1863, m. 1858.	Bucks . . .	139	. }		
Was Attaché at Naples.					
Sat for Thetford.		25,773	.	39,284	

GRAHAM, Sir Frederick Ulrick, Bart., of Netherby. Carlisle.

Club. Travellers', Carlton.	Dumfries . .	33	.	40
b. 1820, s. 1861, m. 1852.	Cumberland .	25,270	.	26,696
	York, W.R. .	105	.	85
Served in 1st Life Guards.				
Was Attaché at Vienna.		25,408	.	26,821

*** GRAHAM-BARNS-GRAHAM, Allan, of Lymekilns, E. Kilbride, &c., N.B.

Club. Western, Glasgow,	Renfrew . .	1,686	.	2,690
Uni. Edin.	Lanark . . .	1,098	.	4,500
b. 1835, s. 1875, m. 1868.	Ayr	609	.	1,172
	Stirling . . .	851	.	557
Mine rents not included.				
		4,244	.	8,919

GRAHAM, Reginald John, of Edmond Castle, Carlisle.

Coll. Harrow, Trin. Cam.	Cumberland .	3,984	.	2,246
Club. Oxf. & Cam.	Northumberland	3,270	.	3,832
b. 1822, s. 1879, m. 1856.	Sussex . . .	11	.	562
		7,265	.	6,640

GRADWELL, P., of Carlanstown. Mea., Wm.	4,014	.	2,217
MAXTONE-GRAHAM, Jas., of Cultoquhey.			
Perth	2 519	.	3,117

** GRAHAM, Col. William, of Mossknowe, Ecclefechan, N.B.

		acres.	g. an. val.
Coll. Magd. Oxon.	Dumfries . .	4,319 .	4,993

Club. Uni. Ser., New Edin.   b. 1797, s. 1832, m. 1830.
Served in 12th, 16th, and 17th Lancers.

** GRANARD, Earl of, K.P., Castle Forbes, Longford.

Coll. Eton.	Longford . .	14,978 .	6,636
Club. J. U. Ser., Boodle's,	Leitrim . . .	4,266 .	1,576
Kild. St., Dublin.	Wexford . .	2,050 .	1,628

b. 1833, s. 1837, m. 1st 1858, 2nd 1873.

Was Attaché at Dresden.   21,294 . 9,840

** GRANT, Sir Archibald, Bart., of Monymusk, Aberdeen, N.B.

Coll. Eton.	Aberdeen . .	14,881 .	7,698

Club. Army and Navy, Uni. Eton and Harrow.
b. 1823, s. 1863.   Served in 4th Light Dragoons.

MACPHERSON-GRANT, Sir George, Bart., of Ballindalloch
Castle, Elgin, N.B., &c.

Coll. Harrow, Ch. Ch. Ox.	Banff . . .	14,223 .	3,616
Club. Brooks's.	Elgin . . .	7,848 .	2,476
b. 1839, s. 1850, m. 1861.	Inverness . .	103,372 .	5,454

           125,443 . 11,546

An "undetermined moor" in Elgin is shared by Sir G. M.-Grant with Mr. Grant of Wester Elchies.

** GRANT, Henry Alexander, of Wester Elchies, Craigellachie, N.B.

b. 1827, s. 1877, m. 1873.	Elgin . . .	20,462 .	5,382
	Banff . . .	4,212 .	1,285

           24,674 . 6,667

GRAHAM, R. C., of Skipness. Argyll, Ayr.	15,002 .	2,026
GRAHAME, Fras. Barclay, of Morphie.		
Kincardine, Wigtown, Midlothian . .	2,701 .	3,230
GRANT, C. T. C., of Kilgraston. Perth .	2,346 .	3,545
GRANT, Sir J., of Rothiemurchus. Inv. .	24,457 .	2,290
GRANT, R., of Druminner. Aberdeen .	4,197 .	2,901

*** GRANT, IAN ROBERT JAMES MURRAY, of Glenmoriston,
    Inverness, N.B., &c.

		acres.	g. an. val.
Coll. Eton.	Inverness . .	73,494 .	4,954
b. 1860, s. 1868.	Elgin . . .	4,063 .	2,400
	Nairn . . .	10 .	10
		77,567 .	7,364

MACPHERSON-GRANT (late), THOMAS, of Craigo, Montrose,
    N.B.

b. 1815, s. 1856, d. 1881.	Inverness . .	36 .	10
	Forfar . . .	4,713 .	7,082
		4,749 .	7,092

GRANTLEY, LORD, Kettlethorpe Hall, Wakefield, &c. ⚕.

Coll. Harrow.	York, W.R. .	7,376 .	10,246
Club. Carlton, White's,	Surrey . . .	2,199 .	3,556
Wanderers'.	Westmoreland	1,146 .	352
b. 1855, s. 1877, m. 1879.			
		10,721 .	14,154

The Surrey estate belongs to the DOWAGER LADY GRANTLEY.

BELLEW-GRATTAN, SIR HENRY CHRISTOPHER, BART., of
    Mount Bellew, Galway.

b. 1860, s. 1867.	Co. Galway .	10,516 .	5,355
	Queen's Co. .	10,593 .	5,923
	Roscommon .	1,895 .	696
		23,004 .	11,974

His mother, Mrs. BELLEW-GRATTAN, is retd. as owner of the
Q. Co. property.   SIR HENRY is, however, the only son.

** GRAY, HAROLD WILLIAM STANNUS, of Graymount, Belfast.

b. 1867, s. 1879.	Antrim . . .	7,100 .	6,000

GORDON-GRAY, MRS., of Carsegray, Forfar, N.B.

s. 187–, m. 18 —.	Forfar . . .	3,260 .	4,849

GRANT, S., of Alford. Lin., Suff., Norf. . 2,079 . 2,686

** LLOYD-GREAME, Rev. YARBURGH GAMALIEL, of Sewerby
House, Bridlington.

		acres.	g. an. val.
Coll. Rugby, Trin. Cam.	York E. and		
b. 1813, s. 1867, m. 1839.	N.R. .	7,000 .	7,756

** GREEN, EDWARD, of Ken Hill, King's Lynn.

Club. Carlton.	Norfolk . .	3,000 .	4,950
b. 1831, m. 1859.	York . . .	4 .	12
Sat for Wakefield.			
		3,004 .	4,962

** GREENWOOD, FREDERICK BARNARDISTON, of Swarcliffe
Hall, Ripley, Yorkshire.

Coll. Eton, Ch. Ch. Ox.	York, W.R. .	6,077 .	9,275
Club. Brooks's. b. 1854, s. 1874.			

** GREER, JAMES, of Mullaghmore, Omagh, Co. Tyrone.

Coll. Trin. Dublin.	Tyrone . . .	6,905 .	3,113
Club. Univ. Dublin.			
b. 1817, s. 1872, m. 1865.			

* GREG, THOMAS RICHARD, of Ballymenoch, Belfast.

Club. Carl., Bood., Turf,	Antrim . . .	3,546 .	4,683
White's, Portland,	Co. Down . .	492 .	813
Ulster.			
b. 1805, s. 1830, m. 1838.		4,038 .	5,496

GREGOR, FRANCIS GLANVILLE, of Trewarthenick, Grampound.

Club. Carlton.	Cornwall . .	4,206 .	4,626
b. 1816, s. 1865.			

GREENE, LT.-COL., of Whittington Hall. Lan.	2,517 .	4,602
GREG, R. P., of Coles Pk. Ches., Her., Lanc. .	2,324 .	5,996
GREGORY, RT. HON. SIR W., K.C.M.G., of Coole Park. Galway	4,893 .	2,378
GREGSON, L. A., of Murton. Dur., York .	2,873 .	4,098
GREHAN, G., of Clonmeen. Cork . . .	2,319 .	2,716
GREIG, T., of Glencarse. Perth, Renfrew .	4,460 .	2,244

*** SHERWIN-GREGORY, Mrs., of Harlaxton Manor, Grantham, &c.

		acres.		g. an. val.
s. 1869, m. 1829.	Lincoln . .	3,670	.	6,142
	Notts . . .	2,664	.	8,515
	Leicester . .	582	.	967
		6,916	.	15,624

*** WELBY-GREGORY, Sir William Earle, Bart., of Den-
ton Hall, Grantham, &c. 🅂.

Coll. Eton, Ch. Ch. Ox.	Lincoln . . .	12,292	.	20,680
Club. Carlton, St. Stephen's.	Leicester . .	1,953	.	2,532
b. 1829, s. 1875, m. 1863.	Notts . . .	2,659	.	3,918
Sat for Grantham, sits for S. Lincoln.				
		16,904	.	27,130

* GRENFELL, William Henry, of Taplow Ct., Maidenhead.

Coll. Harrow, Ball. Ox.

Club. White's, Reform.	Berks . . .	2,505	.	4,775
b. 1855, s. 1867.	Bucks . . .	690	.	2,449
Sits for Salisbury.		3,195	.	7,224

NEVILLE-GRENVILLE, Ralph, of Butleigh Court, Glaston-
bury.

Coll. Eton, Magd. Cam.	Somerset . .	3,434	.	5,770

Club. Carlton. b. 1817, s. 1854, m. 1845.
Was L. of the Treasury. Sat for Windsor, E. & Mid. Som.

GRESLEY, Sir Robert, Bart., of Drakelowe, Burton-on-
Trent. 🅂.

Coll. Eton.	Derby . . .	3,241	.	7,943
b. 1866, s. 1868.	Leicester . .	506	.	568
		3,747	.	8,511

*** GREVILLE, Algernon William Bellingham, of Granard
(res. 45, Sussex Gardens). 🅂.

Coll. Eton.	Longford . .	8,821	.	7,906

Club. Reform, Garrick.
b. 1815, s. 1866, m. 1st 1844, 2nd 1847, 3rd 1863.
Served in Rifle Brigade.

** GREVILLE, LORD, Clonyn Castle, Delvin, Co. Westmeath, &c. ⚓.

		acres.		g. an. val.
Club. Reform, Travellers',	Westmeath .	9,783	.	11,575
United Service.	Roscommon .	3,990	.	1,992
b. 1821, m. 1840.	Cavan . . .	1,970	.	1,182
Served in 1st Life Guards.	Longford . .	1,236	.	955
Sat for Co. Longford.	Cork . . .	451	.	409
	Kent . . .	1,178	.	2,081

18,608 . 18,194

** GREY, EARL, K.G., G.C.M.G., Howick House, Lesbury. ⚓.
Coll. Trinity, Cambridge.   Northumberland 17,599 . 23,724
Club. Travellers', Athenæum.   b. 1802, s. 1845, m. 1832.
Served as Under Secretary for the Colonies, Secretary for the Home Department, Secretary at War, and Colonial Secretary. Sat for Winchelsea, Higham Ferrers, Northumberland, and Sunderland.

*** GRIERSON, SIR ALEXANDER DAVIDSON, BART., of Rock Hall, Dumfries, N.B., &c.

b. 1858, s. 1879.	Dumfries . .	3,700	.	3,450
	Hants . . .	13	.	96

3,713 . 3,546

** GRIFFITH, HUGH THOMAS DAVIES, of Caerhun, Carnarvon.

s. 1879.	Montgomery .	1,461	.	1,527
	Flint . . .	1,066	.	1,479
	Carnarvon . .	1,572	.	2,116
	Denbigh . .	243	.	191

4,342 . 5,313

⚓. GREY, RT. HON. SIR GEORGE, BART., G.C.B., of Falloden. Northumberland	2,913	.	4,089
BACON-GREY, H., of Styford. Northumb.	2,386	.	2,977
GRIFFIN, M. H., of Pell Wall. Salop, Staff.	2,796	.	4,739
WALDIE-GRIFFITH, SIR G. R., BART., of Hendersyde. Anglesea, Rox., Berwick	2,413	.	3,522
GRIFFITH, W., of Garn. Den., Mer., Fl.	3,231	.	2,624

WYNNE-GRIFFITH (late), John Griffith, of Llanfair Hall, Carnarvon.

		acres.		g. an. val.
b. 18—, m. 18—, d. 187-.	Carnarvon . .	3,338	.	2,716
	Merioneth . .	823	.	303
		4,161	.	3,019

** GRIMSTON, Mrs., of Kilnwick, Hull, &c. $.

m. 1856, s. 1879.	York, E.R. .	3,432	.	5,108

GROGAN, Sir Edward, Bart., of Moyvore, Co. Westmeath, &c.

Coll. Winch., Trin. Dub.	Westmeath	.	1,950	.	1,318
Club. Carlton, Kildare St.	King's Co.	.	3,207	.	1,853
b. 1802, m. 1867.	Wexford	. .	1,333	.	255
Sat for Dublin City.					
			6,490	.	3,426

GROGAN, William, of Slaney Park, Baltinglass, Co. Wicklow.

Coll. Trinity, Dublin.	Westmeath	.	1,596	.	1,042
Club. Kildare St., Dublin.	Wicklow	. .	3,761	.	2,106
b. 1814, s. 1854, m. 1862.					
			5,357	.	3,148

** GROSVENOR, Rt. Hon. Lord Richard de Aquila, of Stalbridge Park, Blandford. $.

Coll. Westm., Trin. Cam.   Dorset . . .   4,762 . 9,944
Club. Whi., Trav., Bro., St. Jas., Ref.
b. 1837, m. 1st 1874, 2nd 1879. Served as V.-Ch. Hhd. ; is Sec. Tr. Sits for Flintshire.

GROVE, Miss, of Zeals House, Mere, Bath.

s. 1859.	Wilts . . .	3,188	.	4,295
	Dorset . .	1,119	.	1,796
		4,307	.	6,091

GRIMSTON, J. R., of Neswick. York .	2,504	.	3,985
GRIMWOOD, J. G., of Woodham Mortimer.			
Essex	2,506	.	3,653

** GROVE, Sir Thomas Fraser, Bart., of Ferne House, Salisbury.

			acres.	g. an. val.
Club. Brooks's, A. & N.	Wilts	. .	7,248 .	6,603
b. 1823, s. 1858, m. 1848.	Somerset	. .	181 .	308
Served in 6th Dragoons.	Cornwall	. .	226 .	200
Sat for South Wilts.				
			7,655 .	7,111

This family have held Ferne since 1563, and other Wilts property since 1440.

** GRYLLS, Col. Shadwell Morley, of Lewarne, Liskeard.

Coll. Woolwich.	Cornwall	. .	5,500 .	3,879
Club. Army and Navy, St. Stephen's.				
b. 1831, s. 1863, m. 1863.				

Served in Royal Artillery in Crimea and Indian Army.

GUILFORD, Earl of, Waldershare Park, Dover, &c.

Coll. Eton.	Kent	. . .	8,065 .	9,912
Club. Gds., Carl., White's.	Suffolk	. . .	2,864 .	3,704
b. 1851, s. 1861, m. 1874.				
Served in Royal Horse Guards.			10,929 .	13,616

** GULSTON, Alan James, of Dirleton, Llandilo, &c.

b. 1813, s. 1840, m. 1841.	Carmarthen	.	7,154 .	10,976
Served in 47th Foot.				

*** GUN, Wilson, of Rattoo, Tralee.

Coll. Trinity, Dublin.	Co. Kerry	. .	12,272 .	4,134
Club. Union.	Limerick	. .	20 .	11
b. 1809, s. 1837, m. 1839.				
			12,292 .	4,145

** GUNNING, Rev. Sir Henry John, Bart., of Horton House, Northampton.

Coll. Charterho., Ball. Oxon.	Northampton	.	3,853 .	5,499
Club. Union.	Bucks	. . .	159 .	252
b. 1797, s. 1862, m. 1st 1827,	Lancashire	. .	97 .	255
2nd 1879.	Co. Longford	.	2,033 .	1,035
	Roscommon	.	704 .	402
			6,846 .	7,443

GUILLAMORE, Viscount. Lim., Cork . 4,846 . 2,381

*** GURDON, ROBERT THORNHAGH, of Letton, Shipdham.

			acres.		g. an. val.
Coll. Eton, Trin. Cam.	Norfolk . . .		4,842	.	6,250
Club. Brooks's, U. Univ.	Suffolk . . .		1,221	.	1,732
b. 1829, s. 1881, m. 1st 1862,	Northumberland		4,971	.	834
2nd 1874.					
Sits for S. Norfolk.			11,034	.	8,816

*** GURNEY, JOHN, of Sprowston Hall, Norwich. $.

			acres.		g. an. val.
Coll. Har., Trin. Cam.	Norfolk . .		2,594	.	4,084
Club. New Univ.	Essex . . .		120	.	550
b. 1845, m. 1871.	Forfar . . .		9,000	.	1,595
			11,714	.	6,229

* GURNEY, JOHN HENRY, of Keswick Hall, Norwich. $.

			acres.		g. an. val.
Club. Windham.	Norfolk . .		8,498	.	8,136
b. 1819, m. 1846.	Essex . . .		204	.	827
	Herts . . .		1	.	2
Sat for King Lynn.			8,703	.	8,965

Held as trustee under wills of late HUDSON G. and R. H. GURNEY.

** GUTHRIE, ARBUTHNOT CHARLES, of Duart, I. of Mull, N.B.

			acres.		g. an. val.
Club. Ath., Un., R.T.Y.C.	Argyll . . .		23,012	.	3,217
b. 1825, s. 1865, m. 1860.					

** GUTHRIE, JOHN, of Guthrie Castle, Arbroath, N.B., &c.

			acres.		g. an. val.
Coll. Harrow.	Forfar . . .		3,231	.	5,026
b. 1856, s. 1877. Serves in 26th Foot.					

GWYN, HOWEL, of Duffryn House, Neath.

			acres.		g. an. val.
Coll. Trin. Oxon.	Glamorgan . .		4,609	.	7,285
Club. Carl., Ox. and Cam.	Brecon . . .		2,016	.	1,580
b. 1806, s. 1830, m. 1851.	Carmarthen .		1,496	.	7,285
Sat for Falmouth and for Brecon.			8,121	.	16,150

GUISE, SIR W. V., BART., of Elmore. Glo.	2,087	.	4,002
GUNDRY, MRS., of The Hyde. Dor., Som.	2,950	.	2,547
GURDON, P., of Assington. Suffolk . . .	2,841	.	3,626
GUTHRIE, C. S., of Scotscalder. Caith. .	13,934	.	2,631

GWYNNE, ALBAN, of Monachty, Ciliau-Aeron, Cardigan.

		acres.	g. an. val.
b. 1849, s. 1865, m. 1878.	Cardigan . .	3,794 .	3,678

*** HADDINGTON, EARL OF, of Arderne Hall, Tarporley, &c.

Coll. Ch. Ch. Oxon.	Cheshire . .	6,256 .	12,172
Club. Carlton, White's.	Berwick . .	14,279 .	15,099
b. 1827, s. 1870, m. 1854.	Roxburgh . .	4,708 .	5,079
	Haddington .	8,302 .	13,678
	Lanark . . .	501 .	588
		34,046 .	46,616

HAGGERSTON, SIR JOHN DE MARIE, BART., of Ellingham, Alnwick.

b. 1852, s. 1858.   Northumberland 14,285 .   8,623

*** HAIG, JAMES RICHARD, of Blairhill, Stirling, N.B., &c.

Coll. Rugby, Trin. Cam.	Kinross . .	1,690 .	2,644
Club. Union, Gar., R.V.Y.C.,	Perth . . .	1,557 .	1,692
Cons., Edin.	Sussex . . .	816 .	1,403
b. 1831, s. 1865, m. 1857.	York, E.R. .	479 .	510
	Kent	2 .	4
		4,544 .	6,253

*** HAIGH, GEORGE HENRY, of Grainsby Hall, Great Grimsby.

Coll. Trinity, Cam.   Lincoln . .   5,232 .   11,352
Club. Union.   b. 1829, s. 1853, m. 1859.

** HALDON, LORD, Manor House, Torquay, &c.

Coll. Eton.   Devon . . .   10,109 . 109,275
Club. Carl., J.Carl.,White's,   Three-fourths of Torquay and St.
   J. U. Ser.   Mary Church stands on this property.
b. 1818, s. 1860, m. 1845.   The rental represents both what is
                   paid to Lord H. as ground rents and
   Sat for S. Dev. & E. Dev.   the whole value of the built-over
                   property payable to others during
                   the term of the building leases.

GUTHRIE, D. C., of Cragie.   Inv., Forfar .   6,478 .   2,775
HACKETT, COL., of Moor Park.   Tippe-
   rary, King's Co. . . . .   3,700 .   2,378

** HALE, CHARLES CHOLMELEY, of King's Walden Park, Hitchin.

			acres.	g. an. val.
Coll. Eton.	Herts	. .	6,905	. 10,130
Club. Boodle's, Carlton,	Beds.	. . .	1,094	. 1,660
Army and Navy.				

b. 1830, s. 1852, m. 1st 1852, 2nd 1870.	7,999	.	11,790

Served in Rifle Brigade in Canada and at the Cape.

** BLAGDEN-HALE, ROBERT, of Alderley, Wotton-under-Edge.

Coll. Winch., Corp. Oxon.	Gloucester	.	3,120	.	4,350

Club. Bood., O. & C., Carl., Garr.

b. 1807, s. 1855, m. 1832. Sat for W. Gloucestershire.

** HALFORD, SIR HENRY ST. JOHN, BART., of Wistow Hall, Leicester.

Coll. Eton, Merton, Oxon.	Leicester	. .	3,053	.	6,000

Club. Carlton. b. 1828, s. 1868, m. 1853.

** HALIFAX, VISCOUNT, G.C.B., Hickleton Hall, Doncaster, &c.

Coll. Eton, Oriel, Oxon.	York, E, and			
Club. Ath., Brooks's, Trav.	W.R.	. .	10,142	. 12,169

b. 1800, s. 1846, m. 1829.

Served as Sec. Treas., Sec. Adm., Ch. Exc., Pres. B. of Cont., First L. Adm., Sec. St. India, and L. P. Seal. Sat for Grimsby, Wareham, Halifax, and Ripon.

CRAGIE-HALKETT, JOHN CORNELIUS, of Cramond, Edinburgh, N.B.

b. 1830, s. 1877, m. 1854.	Lanark . . .	2,249	.	1,357
Served in 45th Foot.	Midlothian . .	637	.	2,520
	Linlithgow . .	226	.	161
		3,112	.	4,038

HALL, SIR BASIL FRANCIS, BART., of Dunglass, Dunbar, N.B.

b. 1828, s. 1876, m. 1877.	Berwick . .	7,948	.	8,029
	Haddington .	887	.	2,158
		8,835	.	10,187

HAINES, J. P., of Bagendon.	Gloucester .	2,263	.	2,925
HALES, MISS, of Hales Place.	Kent . .	2,980	.	3,843
HALL, A. W., of Barton Abbey.	Oxon. .	2,470	.	4,228

* HALL, ERNEST RICHARD BRADLEY, of Bishop Burton, Beverley.

		acres.	*g. an. val.*
b. 1865, s. 1874.	York, E.R. .	4,798 .	9,232

*** HALL, MRS., of Whatton Manor, Nottingham.

m. 1840, s. 1879.	Notts . . .	2,663 .	5,241
	Leicester . .	556 .	916
	Lincoln . .	20 .	40
		3,239 .	6,197

HALL, RICHARD, of Inismore Hall, Lisbellew, Co. Fermanagh.

Coll. Trinity, Dublin.	Fermanagh .	6,540 .	2,407
b. 1809, m. 1840.	Louth . . .	724 .	684
	Roscommon .	465 .	335
	Tipperary . .	369 .	279
	Leitrim . . .	588 .	225
	Wicklow . .	272 .	169
		8,958 .	4,099

All these estates, except the first and third, are returned as belonging to "representatives of ROBT. HALL," his father.

** HALL, WILLIAM HENRY, of Six-Mile Bottom, &c., Cambridge.

Coll. Rugby, Ball. Oxon.	Cambs. . . .	5,956 .	7,612
Club. Reform.	Oxford . . .	1,330 .	2,811
b. 1837, s. 1872 and 1880,	Bucks . . .	1,016 .	1,941
m. 1st 1868, 2nd 1875.			
		8,302 .	12,364

*** HALL, WILLIAM JAMES, of Narrow Water, Warrenpoint.

Coll. R.M.A.Woolwich.	Co. Down . .	3,648 .	4,358
Club. J. U. Ser.,Kild.St.	Co. Armagh .	2,656 .	3,581
	Co. Louth . .	500 .	285
b. 1835, s. 1873, m. 1st 1863, 2nd 1875.			
		6,804 .	8,224

Served in R. Artillery in Crimea and Ind. Mutiny.

HALL, J. M., of Tangy. Argyll	7,450 .	2,500
HALL, L. K., of Hollybush. Stafford . .	2,166 .	3,754
HALL, W. T. T., of Syndale. Kent . .	2,315 .	9,931

HALLIDAY, MAJ.-GEN., or Carnmoney (res. 23, Hanover
   Square, W.)   *acres.*   *g. an. val.*
Club. Uni. Ser., A. & N.   Co. Antrim   .   3,228   .   3,054
b. 1809, s. 1870.   Commanded 36th Foot.

   This pty. is returned under " HALLIDAY, A. H., reps. of."

** HALLIDAY, WILLIAM HALLIDAY, of Glenthorne, Lyn-
   mouth, &c.

Coll. Winc., Ball. Oxon.	Devon . . .	1,571	1,355
Club. Oxford and Cam.	Kent . . .	1,127	1,520
b. 1828, s. 1834, m 1860.	Somerset . .	511	329
		3,209	3,204

** HALSEY, THOMAS FREDERICK, of Gaddesden Place, Hemel
   Hempstead.

Coll. Eton, Ch. Ch. Oxon.	Herts . . .	2,100	3,381
Club. Carlton, Uni. Univ.	Dorset . . .	1,325	1,715
b. 1839, s. 1869, m. 1865.	Kent . . .	438	700
Sits for Herts.	Bucks . . .	48	43
		3,911	5,839

** HAMBRO (BARON), CHARLES JOSEPH THEOPHILUS, of Milton
   Abbey, Blandford.

Coll. Trin. Cam.   Dorset . . .   9,622 . 12,000
Club. Carl., J. Carl., Whi., Bood., Arth., Garr.
b. 1834, s. 1877, m. 1857.
   Sat for Weymouth.

HUGHES-HALLETT, REV. JAS., of Higham.
   Kent, Essex . . . .   2,017 . 2,858
HALLOWES, REV. BRABAZON, of Glapwell.
   Derby, Notts, Suffolk . . . . . .   2,852 . 3,367
HALSEY, H. W. R. WESTGARTH, of Henley
   Park.   Surrey, Somerset . . . . .   2,697 . 3,808
HOLDEN-HAMBROUGH, O. W., of Pipe-
   well.   Northampton, Middlesex   2,135 . 4,190

*** COLE-HAMILTON, Major Arthur William, of Beltrim, Newtown-Stewart.

			acres.		g. an. val.
Coll.	Trin. Dub., St. Mary Hall, Oxon.	Co. Tyrone .	16,811	.	4,890

Club. Kild. St., Dublin. b. 1806, s. 1823, m. 1831.

HAMILTON, Dacre Mervyn, of Cornacassa, Co. Monaghan.

Club. Sackville St., Dub.	Monaghan . .	7,315	.	4,168
b. 1837, s. 1877, m. 1873.	Longford . .	532	.	419
		7,847	.	4,587

** HAMILTON and BRANDON, Duke of, Hamilton Palace, Glasgow, N.B., &c.

Coll.	Ch. Ch. Oxon.	Bute	102,210	.	18,702
Club.	Carl., Turf, Gun, Garrick.	Lanark . . .	45,731	.	38,441
		Linlithgow .	3,694	.	7,445
b. 1845, s. 1863, m. 1873.		Stirling . . .	810	.	911
		Suffolk . . .	4,939	.	8,017
		Berks . . .	2	.	120
			157,386	.	73,636

Serves as Hered. Keeper of Holyrood Palace.
Exclusive of a mineral rent of 67,006*l.*

HAMILTON, Gawin William Rowan, of Killyleagh, Belfast.

Coll.	Chel., Univ. Oxon.	Co. Down . .	1,118	.	2,238
Club.	Naval & Mil.	Kildare . .	2,040	.	1,477
b. 1844, s. 1860 and 1879,		Queen's Co. .	572	.	411
m. 1876.		Dublin . . .	145	.	397
			3,875	.	4,523

Served in 7th Drag. G.

HAMILTON, Hugh, of Pinmore, Girvan, N.B.

Coll.	Eton.	Ayrshire . .	8,441	.	3,833

Club. Army and Navy. b. 1828, s. 1836, m. 1st 1853, 2nd 1869.
Served in K. D. G. " Very incorrect," correction refused.

HAMILTON, Sir Chas. J. Jas., Bart., of Iping. Sussex, Pembroke			2,969	.	2,785
HAMILTON, John, of Sundrum. Ayr .			2,944	.	3,280

HAMILTON, Ion Trant, of Abbotstown House, Dublin, &c.

		acres.	g. an. val.
Coll. Trin. Cam.	Dublin . . .	3,647 .	6,788
Club. Carl.,Arthur's,White's,	Queen's Co. .	2,245 .	1,025
Sack. St., Dublin.	Co. Down . .	751 .	823
b. 1839, s. 1863, m. 1877.	Co. Meath . .	246 .	233
Sits for Co. Dublin.			
		6,889 .	8,869

*** BUCHANAN-BAILLIE-HAMILTON, John, of Cambus-more, Callander, N.B., &c.

Club. Jun. Carlton.	Perth . . .	12,172 .	3,207
b. 1837, m. 1869.			

HAMILTON, Lady, of Plâs Llanstephan, Carmarthen, &c.

s. 1876, m. 1834.	Pembroke . .	2,214 .	2,053
	Carmarthen .	855 .	313
	Cardigan . .	145 .	127
	Co. Tyrone .	1,283 .	812
		4,497 .	3,305

** NISBET-HAMILTON, The Lady Mary, Biel, Prestonkirk, N.B., &c.

s. 1854, m. 1828.	Lincoln . . .	9,032 .	12,800
	Haddington .	16,664 .	26,000
		25,696 .	38,800

BUCHANAN-HAMILTON, John, of Leny. Perth, Stirling, Dumbarton	4,032 .	2,479
HAMILTON, John, of St. Ernans. Donegal.	17,955 .	2,740
HAMILTON, J. G. C., of Dalzell. Lank.	2,460 .	14,959
HAMILTON, John Wallace Ferrier, of Cairnhill. Linlithgow, Ayr	2,256 .	3,540
HAMILTON, M., of Craighlaw. Wig.,Kirk.	6,542 .	2,761
HAMILTON, P. B., of Wilton. Monm. .	2,545 .	2,046
McNEILL-HAMILTON, W. H., of Raploch. Lanark	2,282 .	2,759

** HAMOND, Anthony, of Westacre, Brandon.

			acres.		gr. an. val.
Coll. Eton, Trin. Cam.	Norfolk	. .	10,139	.	9,917

Club. Boodle's. b. 1834, s. 1869, m. 1874.

** HAMPTON, Lord, Westwood Park, Droitwich, &c.

Coll. Eton, Ch. Ch. Oxon.	Worcester	. .	4,867	.	8,210
Club. Carlton.	Norfolk	. .	383	.	416
b. 1826, s. 1880, m. 1849.	Pembroke	. .	250	.	211
			5,500	.	8,837

HANBURY, John Capel, of Pontypool Park, Monmouth.

b. 1853, s. 1861.	Monmouth	.	10,210	.	20,660
	Glamorgan	.	763	.	7,127
			10,973	.	27,787

*** HANBURY, Osgood, of Holfield Grange, Coggeshall, &c.

Club. Windham.	Essex	. .	3,791	.	5,469
b. 1826, s. 1858, m. 1st 1854,	Suffolk	. .	232	.	434
2nd 1866.			4,023	.	5,903

HANDCOCK, Gerald Carlile Stratford, of Carantrila Park, Dunmore, Co. Galway.

Coll. Wellington.	Co. Galway.	.	7,865	.	3,459

b. 1858, s. 1871. Serves in 19th Foot.

HAMLYN, S. C., of Leawood. Devon	.	4,285	.	2,693
** HAMMOND, W. O., of St. Alban's. Buc., Kent		2,900	.	4,099
HAMOND, W. Parker, of Pampisford. Cambridge, Surrey, Essex		2,557	.	4,081
** HANBURY, R., of Poles. Herts, Ess., Wilts.		2,351	.	4,280
DAVENPORT-HANDLEY, J. W. H., of Clipsham. Rutland, Notts, Lincoln	.	2,539	.	5,489

HANKEY, Mrs., of Balcombe Place, Hayward's Heath.

		acres.		g. an. val.
s. 1881, m. 1825.	Sussex . . .	2,462	.	2,361
	Rutland . .	1,388	.	1,581
		3,850	.	3,942

** HANMER, Sir Wyndham Edward, Bart., of Bettisfield Park, Whitchurch, Salop, &c.

Club. Conservative.	Flint	7,318	.	10,970
b. 1810, s. 1881, m. 1842,	Denbigh . .	2,593	.	2,095
and 1877.	Bucks . . .	879	.	1,088
	Bedford . . .	869	.	667
	Salop . . .	1	.	3

Served in Royal Horse Guards Blue.　11,660 . 14,823

The Flint and Salop estates only are corrected.

*** HARBERTON, Viscount (residence Lyston Court, Ross, Co. Hereford).

Coll. Trin. Cam.　　Co. Kildare . 5,223 . 3,799
Club. Uni. University.　b. 1836, s. 1862, m. 1861.

** HARCOURT, Edward William, of Nuneham Park, Abingdon, &c.

Coll. Ch. Ch. Oxon.	Middlesex .	2	.	1,500
Club. Carlton, Travellers'.	Oxon . . .	7,520	.	10,000
b. 1825, s. 1871, m. 1849.	Berks . . .	681	.	1,000
	Sussex . . .	3	.	500

Sits for Oxfordshire.　　　　　8,206 . 13,000

HANKEY, Lady E., Knockeevon. Tip.,
　Kent . . . . 3,902 . 2,859
RAINSFORD-HANNAY, F., of Kirkdale.
　Kirk. . . . . 3,938 . 2,185
*** ⚓ VERNON-HARCOURT, Egerton,
　of Buxted Park. Sussex, Hants . . . 2,759 . 3,425

HARDWICKE, EARL OF, Wimpole Hall, Royston, &c.

			acres.	g. an. val.
Coll. Harrow, Trin. Cam.	Cambridge .	18,978	.	26,349
Club. Carl., Trav., White's.	Hants . . .	112	.	629
b. 1836, s. 1873, m. 1863.	Huntingdon .	221	.	76
	Suffolk . . .	66	.	61
	Herts . . .	5	.	6
Served 7th & 11th Huss., as Com. Hhold. and M. Buckhds. Sat for Cambs.		19,382	.	27,121

** HARDY, CHARLES STEWART, of Chilham Castle, Canterbury.

Coll. Eton, Ch. Ch. Oxon. Kent . . . 3,300 . 4,500
Club. Junior Carlton. b. 1842, s. 1867, m. 1865.
 Served in 37th Foot.

*** HARE, HUMPHREY JOHN, of Docking Hall, King's Lynn.

 Coll. Charterho., Wadh. Norfolk . . 3,778 . 3,758
 Oxon.
b. 1811, s. 1856, m. 1833.

*** HARE, SIR GEORGE RALPH LEIGH, BART., of Stow Hall, Downham Market.
 Norfolk . . 11,310 . 12,044
b. 1866, s. 1880.

HAREWOOD, EARL OF, Harewood House, Leeds.

Coll. Eton, Ch. Ch. Oxon.	York, N. and			
Club. Carlton, Travellers'.	W.R. . .	29,078	.	36,798
b. 1824, s. 1857, m. 1st	Bucks . . .	542	.	1,320
1845, 2nd 1858.				
		29,620	.	38,118

HARDY, SIR J., BART., of Dunstall. Staffs., Warwick	2,338	.	5,618
** COZENS-HARDY, W. HARDY, of Lether-ingsett Hall. Norfolk	2,929	.	3,764
HARE, COL., of Calder. Linl., Midl. . .	2,484	.	4,271
HARE, J. P., of Durrow. Tipperary, Cork .	4,010	.	2,742
HARE, HON. R., of St. Michaels, Co. Lim. .	3,687	.	2,524
HARE, T. W., of Berthddu. York, Montg.	4,076	.	2,455
HARENC (late), HENRY BENJAMIN. Kerry.	5,979	.	2,121

** HARFORD, John Charles, of Blaise Castle, Bristol, &c.

		acres.	g. an. val.
Coll. Harrow.	Cardigan . .	6,156 .	4,444
b. 1860, s. 1875.	Gloucester .	1,060 .	2,857
	Carmarthen .	345 .	360
		7,561 .	7,661

HARLECH, Lord, Derrycarne, Dromod, Co. Leitrim, &c.

Coll. Eton.	Carnarvon . .	8,570 .	2,769
Club. Carlton, Uni. Ser.,	Merioneth . .	6,354 .	2,810
Sackville Street.	Salop . . .	3,600 .	5,365
b. 1819, s. 1876, m. 1850.	Montgomery .	2,934 .	2,824
Served in 13th Light	Denbigh . .	711 .	518
Dragoons.	Berks . . .	24 .	283
Sat for Co. Sligo and for	Sligo . . .	21,019 .	5,933
Co. Leitrim.	Leitrim . .	9,634 .	3,759
	Westmeath .	2,794 .	1,434
	Mayo . . .	2,546 .	606
	Roscommon .	172 .	99
		58,358 .	26,400

HARLEY, Robert William Daker, of Brampton Bryan, Presteign. 💰.

Coll. Westm., Mag. Cam.	Hereford . .	9,901 .	11,203
Club. Carl., Jun. Carlton.	Salop . . .	204 .	252
b. 1846, s. 1872, m. 1878.	Radnor . . .	116 .	77
		10,221 .	11,532

** KING-HARMAN, Edward Robert, of Rockingham, Boyle, Co. Longford, &c.

Coll. Eton.	Longford . .	28,779 .	14,683
Club. Carl., B. F. Arts, Eton	Roscommon .	29,242 .	18,441
and Har., Kild. St.	Sligo . . .	12,629 .	5,344
and U.S. Dublin.	Westmeath .	1,239 .	851
b. 1838, s. 1875, m. 1861.	Queen's Co. .	1,024 .	786
Served in 60th Rifles in the Indian Mutiny.			
Sat for Sligo.		72,913 .	40,105

HARGREAVES, J. D., of Silwood.   Berks,
York, Waterford . . . . 2,427 . 2,918
HARGREAVES (late), J., of Burnley. Lanc. 2,194 . 5,657

** HARRIES, GEORGE HARRIES, of Rickestone, Milford Haven, &c.

		acres.	g. an. val.
Coll. Eliz. Guernsey, Pemb. Cam.	Pembroke . .	5,173 .	5,036

b. 1818, s. 1869, m. 1855.

Value somewhat overstated.

HARRINGTON, EARL OF, Elvaston Castle, Derby. 🐍.

		acres.	g. an. val.
Coll. Queen's Col. Belfast, Ch. Ch. Oxon.	Derby . . .	4,569 .	12,576
	Cheshire . .	8,138 .	11,096
Club. White's.	Durham . .	196 .	807
b. 1844, s. 1881, m. 1869.	Northampton .	38 .	40
	Leicester . .	3 .	9
		12,944 .	24,528

Out of this total ELIZABETH LADY HARRINGTON has the Durham property and 329*l.* in Derby, while LADY PHILLIPPA STANHOPE owns Gawsworth Old Hall, in Cheshire.

HARRIS, JOHN MORGAN JENKINS, of Treferig House, Pontypridd.

		acres.	g. an. val.
b. 1855, s. 1879.	Brecon . . .	3,996 .	2,719
	Carmarthen .	3,691 .	950
	Glamorgan . .	462 .	286
		8,149 .	3,955

*** HARRIS, LORD, Belmont, Faversham.

🌳 *Coll.* Eton, Ch. Ch. Oxon. Kent . . . 4,609 . 7,201
Club. Carlton, Boodle's. b. 1851, s. 1872, m. 1874.

** SLATER-HARRISON, EDWARD, of Shelswell Park, Bicester.

Coll. Eton. Oxford . . . 4,716 . 5,000
Club. Carlton, Arthur's. b. 1832, s. 1874, m. 1865.

HARRISON, JOHN, of Snelston Park, Ashbourne.

Coll. Eton, Ch. Ch. Oxon. Derbyshire . 5,004 . 8,311
Club. Carlton. b. 1819, s. 1871.

HARRIS, C. E., of Tylney.	Hants, York .	2,761 .	4,156
HARRIS, W. O., of Wooton.	Northampton	2,335 .	4,797
HARRISON, B. D., of Scalehow. Lanc., Wmd., Bucks		2,329 .	2,1ᶜ

HARRISON, Richard Davison, of Holywood House, Belfast.

		acres.	g. an. val.
b. 1854, s. 1873.	Co. Down . .	3,653 .	3,921

*** HULTON-HARROP, William Edward Montagu, of Lythwood Hall, Shrewsbury, &c. ♨.

Coll. Magd. Cam.	Salop . . .	3,394 .	2,900
Club. Bood., N. Univ.	Lancashire .	144 .	3,600
b. 1848, s. 1866, m. 1878.	Flint . . .	334 .	175
	York . . .	74 .	110
		3,946 .	6,785

HARROWBY, Earl of, K.G., Sandon Hall, Stafford, &c.

Coll. Ch. Ch. Oxon.	Stafford . .	4,940 .	7,461
Club. Travellers'.	Lincoln . .	4,253 .	6,849
b. 1798, s. 1847, m. 1823.	Gloucester . .	3,207 .	5,714
	Warwick . .	225 .	267
Was Sec. Ind. B., Ch. Dy. Lanc., and			
L. P. Seal. Sat for Tiverton & Liverpool.		12,625 .	20,291

HARTLEY (late), W. H. H., of Bucklebury Ho., Reading, &c.

d. 1881.	Berks . . .	4,952 .	5,325
	Gloucester . .	2,772 .	4,672
		7,724 .	9,997

** HARTOPP, Edward Bourchier, of Dalby Hall, Melton Mowbray, &c.

Coll. Eton, Ch. Ch. Oxon.	Leicester . .	5,423 .	8,186
Club. Ox. and Cam., Trav.,	Co. Kerry . .	24,222 .	2,408
Carlton.	Limerick · .	4,545 .	3,251
b. 1809, s. 1813, m. 1834.			
Sat for North Leicester.		34,190 .	13,845

Value a little under-estimated.

HARRISON, J. S., of Brandesburton. York	2,006 .	2,424
HARRISON, Mrs., of Olivers.　Essex, Suff.	2,985 .	3,880
HARRISON, R. J., of Caerhowel.　Montg.	2,059 .	2,435
HART, G. V., of Kilderry.　Doneg., Lderry.	7,032 .	2,845

LEE-HARVEY, Henry, of Castle Semple, Lochwinnock, N.B.

		acres.		g. an. val.
b. 1823, s. 1872, m. 1855.	Renfrew . .	6,500	.	5,561

*** HARVEY, John, of Carnousie, Turriff, N.B.

Club. Conservative.	Banff . . .	3,424	.	3,296
b. 1841, s. 1867, m. 1873.				

** HARVEY, John Edmund Audley, of Ickwellbury, Biggles-wade, &c.

b. 1851, s. 1879, m. 1873.	Beds . . .	2,137	.	3,804
	York . . .	1,168	.	963
	Notts . . .	1,057	.	880
	Lincoln . .	134	.	83
Serves in 42nd Foot. Was in Ashanti War.		4,496	.	5,730

HARVEY, Robert, of Fairfield House, Cheltenham.

b. 1837, s. 1881.	Co. Donegal .	25,593	.	3,398
	Gloucester . .	15	.	199
		25,608	.	3,597

HARVEY, Sir Robert Bateson, Bart., of Langley Park, Slough.

Coll. Eton, Ch. Ch. Oxon.	Co. Antrim .	7,485	.	4,389
Club. Carlton.	Somerset . .	1,394	.	1,428
b. 1825, s. 1863, m. 1st 1855,	Bucks . . .	2,013	.	3,028
2nd 1874.	Dorset . . .	195	.	267
Sits for Bucks.	Berks . . .	1	.	142
		11,088	.	9,254

The Antrim property is returned as belonging to " Robert Harvey," of " Langley Park."

HARTLEY, Leonard. York, Westmoreland	2,594	.	4,019
HARTLEY, R. W., of Beech Pk. Kild., Mea.	2,044	.	2,182
CRADOCK-HARTOPP, Sir J. W. Bart., of Four Oaks. Leicester, Warwick, Rutland	2,181	.	4,110
HARVEY, E. H., of Mintiaghs. Donegal .	12,212	.	2,309
HARVEY, G. M., of Malin Hall, Donegal .	12,212	.	2,727

** HASELL, John Edward, of Dalemain, Penrith.

			acres.	g. an. val.
Coll.	Harrow, Oriel, Oxon.	Cumberland .	1,434	. 1,977
Club.	New University.	Westmoreland	3,407	. 1,561
b. 1839, s. 1872, m. 1877.				
			4,841	. 3,538

HASTINGS, Lord, Melton Constable, Dereham, &c. 🦂.

			acres.	g. an. val.
Coll.	Eton, Trin. Cam.	Norfolk . . .	12,737	. 17,483
Club.	St. James's, Carlton,	Northumberland	6,716	. 26,920
	White's, Turf, Marl.	Kent . . .	105	. 49
b. 1857, s. 1872, m. 1880.				
			19,558	. 44,452

** HATFEILD, Thomas Godfrey, of Thorp Arch Hall, Tadcaster.

Coll.	Rugby, Trin. Cam.	York, W.R.	. 3,011	. 4,766
Club.	Union. b. 1837, s. 1863, m. 1872.			

HATHERTON, Lord, Teddesley Park, Penkridge.

Coll.	Eton.	Staffordshire .	14,901	. 23,196
Club.	Travellers', Brooks's. b. 1815, s. 1863, m. 1841.			
Sat for Walsall and South Staffordshire.				

** HATHORN, Col. John Fletcher, of Castle Wigg, Whithorn, N.B.

Coll.	Harrow.	Wigtown . .	3,582	. 5,169
Club.	Carlton. b. 1839, s. 1842, m. 1875.			
Serves in Coldstream Guards.				

** FINCH-HATTON, Hon. Murray Edward Gordon, of Haverholme Priory, Sleaford. 🦂.

			acres.	g. an. val.
Coll.	Hertford and Balliol,	Lincoln . . .	3,710	. 4,788
	Oxon.	Notts . . .	741	. 2,288
Club.	Carlton, White's.			
b. 1851, s. 1858, m. 1875.			4,451	. 7,076

HASLER, W. W., of Aldingbourne.	Sussex	2,722	. 3,150
🦂 FINCH-HATTON, Edward H.	Cambs.	2,063	. 3,763

HAWARDEN, Viscount, Dundrum, Cashel.

		acres.	g. an. val.
Coll. Eton.	Tipperary . .	15,272 .	8,781

Club. Carlton, White's, United Service, Kildare Street.
b. 1817, s. 1856, m. 1845.
   Served in 2nd Life Guards and as a Lord in Waiting.

* HAWKE, Frances, Lady, Womersley Park, Pontefract.

s. 1869, m. 1848.	York, W.R. .	6,187 .	8,007

** HAWKINS, Christopher Henry Thomas, of Trewithen, Probus, Cornwall.

Coll. Trin. Cam.	Cornwall . .	12,119 .	14,049

Club. Uni. Univ., Athenæum.   b. 1820, s. 1829, m. 1868.

*** HAWKSHAW, Sir John, F.R.S., of Hollycombe, Liphook.

Coll. Leeds Grammar	Sussex . . .	3,989 .	2,908
School.	Dorset . . .	112 .	331
Club. Athenæum.	Hants . . .	65 .	70
b. 1811, m. 1835.			
		4,166 .	3,309

HAWLEY, Sir Henry James, Bart., of Leybourne Grange, Maidstone.

b. 1815, s. 1875, m. 18—,	Lincoln . . .	4,638 .	5,702
2nd 1877.	Kent . . .	1,521 .	3,188
	Northampton .	1,366 .	3,103
	Middlesex . .	28 .	218
		7,553 .	12,211

** LEITH-HAY, Col. Alexander Sebastian, C.B., Leith Hall, Kenethmount, Aberdeen, N.B.

Club. J. U. Ser., Arth.,	Aberdeen . .	12,546 .	7,916
New Ed.			

b. 1819, s. 1862, m. 1861.
   Commanded 93rd Highlanders in Crimea and Indian Mutiny.

** HAY, James Gordon, of Seaton, Aberdeen.

Coll. Eton.	Aberdeen . .	3,342 .	5,960

Club. Carl., Nor. Abn.
b. 1815, s. 1862, m. 1878.

** HAY, SIR ROBERT, BART., of King's Meadows, Haystoune,
　　Peebles, N.B.

		acres.		*g. an. val.*
Club. Carl., Salisbury.	Peebles . .	9,155	.	4,408
b. 1825, s. 1867, m. 1853.	Selkirk . . .	600	.	106

		9,755	.	4,514

** HAY, WILLIAM JAMES, of The Castle, Dunse, Berwick, N.B.

Club. E.I.U. Ser., New Ed.	Berwickshire .	5,812	.	10,093
b. 1827, s. 1876, m. 1865.				

　　Was in Bengal C. S.

HAYES, SIR SAMUEL HERCULES, BART., of Drumboe Castle,
　　Stranorlar.

Coll. Harrow.	Donegal . .	22,825	.	6,356
Club. Carlton, White's, Arthur's.				
b. 1840, s. 1860, m. 1878.				

　　Served in 2nd Life Guards.

*** FRANCE-HAYHURST, REV. THOMAS, of Bostock Hall,
　　Middlewich.

Coll. Trin. Cam.	Cheshire . .	10,855	.	24,591
b. 1803, s. 1869, m. 1st 1830, 2nd 1836.				

　　Included above is a rental of 2,775*l.* owned by his eldest son.

*** HEADFORT, MARQUIS OF, Headfort House, Kells, Co.
　　Meath, &c.

Club. Carlton, White's,	Co. Cavan . .	14,251	.	9,011
Trav., SackvilleSt.,	Co. Meath . .	7,544	.	10,361
Kild. St., Dublin.	Westmoreland .	12,851	.	13,686
b. 1822, s. 1870, m. 1st 1842,	York, W.R. . .	4,534	.	2,305
2nd 1875.	Lancashire . .	3,393	.	4,198
Sat for Westmoreland.	Cumberland .	3	.	3
	Glamorgan .	178	.	42

		42,754	.	39,606

　　LORD BECTIVE (who has not corrected his share) is owner of the
English estates.

PATERSON-BALFOUR-HAY, EDM. DE				
HAYA, of Leys. Perth, Fife	2,917	.	7,871
HAY, R. J. A., of Nunraw. Linlithgow .	2,593	.	3,939

*** HEADLEY, Lord, Aghadoe House, Killarney, &c.

			acres.		g. an. val.
Coll.	Harrow, Univ. Oxon.	Co. Kerry .	12,769	.	5,600
Club.	Carlton, Beaconsfd.	Yorkshire . .	2,235	.	5,120
b. 1845, s. 1877, m. 1867.		Essex . . .	1,038	.	2,668
			16,042	.	13,388

** HEATH, Robert, of Biddulph Grange, Congleton, &c.

Club. Cons., Carlton.	Staffs. . . .	2,982	.	4,200
b. 1816, m. 1843.	Cheshire . .	338	.	600
Sat for Stoke-on-Trent.		3,320	.	4,800

HEATHCOTE, John Moyer, of Connington Castle, Stilton.

Coll. Eton, St. John's, Cam.   Huntingdon .   7,144 . 11,386
Club. Brooks's, Arthur's.
b. 1800, s. 1838, m. 1833.   Sat for Huntingdonshire.

** HEATHCOTE, Sir William Perceval, Bart., of Hursley Park, Winchester.

Coll. Winc., Eton.   Hampshire . 14,189 . 14,154
Club. St. George's. b. 1826, s. 1881, m. 1849.
Served in 7th Hussars.

** UNWIN-HEATHCOTE, Unwin, of Shephalbury, Stevenage.

b. 1818, s. 1862, m. 1848.	Herts . . .	2,700	.	3,723
	Derby . . .	200	.	382
	Notts . . .	143	.	230
		3,043	.	4,335

HAYWARD, F., of Hestley. Suffolk, Norf.	2,479	.	4,031
🌰. HAZLERIGG, Sir A. G., Bart., of Noseley. Leicester	2,162	.	3,837
HEADLAM, M., of Gilmonby. York, Dur., Wmd., Rut.	2,326	.	2,050
HEARD, R., of Palacetown. Cork, Tipp.	10,851	.	2,784
HEATH, A. B., of Faccombe. Hants . .	3,231	.	2,358
*EDWARDS - HEATHCOTE, Justinian H., of Apedale. Stafford	2,800	.	12,541

HEDDLE, JOHN GEORGE MOODIE, of Melsetter House, Kirkwall, N.B., &c.

		acres.	*g. an. val.*
Coll. Edin. Univ.	Orkney . . .	50,410 .	3,527

Club. Scottish. b. 1844, s. 1869, m. 1870.

*** HELY, GORGES, of Foulk's Court, Johnstown, Co. Kilkenny.

b. 1840, s. 1863, m. 1864. Kilkenny . . 6,461 . 4,426

** HELYAR, HORACE AUGUSTUS, of Coker Court, Yeovil.

Coll. Trin. Cam.	Somerset . .	3,349 .	4,964
Club. St. James's, Union.	Devon . . .	375 .	563

b. 1853, s. 1880, m. 1877.
Was in the Diplomatic Service. 3,724 . 5,527

HEMMING, RICHARD, of Bentley Manor, Bromsgrove, &c.

b. 1818, m. 1846.	Perth . . .	10,000 .	155
	Worcester . .	2,486 .	4,862
	Warwick . .	2,275 .	3,352

14,761 . 8,369

*** WALKER-HENEAGE, MAJOR CLEMENT, V.C., of Compton Basset, Calne.

Coll. Eton, Ch. Ch. Oxon.	Wilts . . .	6,513 .	9,518

Club. Uni. Ser., Travellers'.
b. 1833, s. 1875, m. 1865.
Served in the 8th Hussars in the Crimea and India.

HENEAGE, EDWARD, of Hainton Hall, Wragby. ⚓.

Coll. Eton.	Lincoln . .	10,761 .	15,527

Club. Trav., Brooks's, Turf.
b. 1840, s. 1864, m. 1864.
Served in 1st L. G. Sat for Lincoln. Sits for Gt. Grimsby.

HEATHCOTE, R., of Lobthorpe. Linc. .	2,911 .	3,535
HEATHCOTE, REV. T., of Lenton. Linc.	2,022 .	3,741
HEMSWORTH, H. W., of Shropham. Norf.	2,868 .	3,798
HENDERSON, D., of Abbotrule. Roxburgh	2,340 .	2,503
CLAYHILLS-HENDERSON, GEORGE D., of Invergowrie. Perth, Forfar	2,138 .	4,026
HENDERSON, R., of Nuthurst, Sus., Sur., Renf.	2,787 .	2,817

** HENLEY, Lord, Watford Court, Rugby.

			acres.	g. an. val.
Coll.	Eton, Ch. Ch. Oxon.	Northampton .	1,764 .	4,116
Club.	Brooks's.	Dorset . . .	3,602 .	4,400
b. 1825, s. 1841, m. 1st 1846,				
	2nd 1870.		5,366 .	8,516
Sat for Northampton.				

* HENNIKER, Lord, Thornham Hall, Eye, &c.

			acres.	g. an. val.
Coll.	Eton, Trin. Cam.	Suffolk . . .	10,910 .	15,158
Club.	Carl., White's, Marl.,	Norfolk . .	122 .	177
	St. James's.	York, E.R. .	5 .	18
b. 1842, s. 1870, m. 1864.		Co. Wicklow .	3 .	4
			11,040 .	15,357

Sat for E. Suffolk. Was Ld. in Waiting.

*** HENRY, Frederick Hugh, of Lodge Park, Straffan.

			acres.	g. an. val.
Coll.	Rugby.	Galway . . .	1,075 .	408
Club.	Royal Irish, Ulster,	Antrim . . .	2,289 .	2,407
	Belfast, Kild. St. Dub.	Kildare . . .	440 .	533
b. 1815, s. 1856, m. 1860.		Dublin . . .	379 .	507
		Meath . . .	323 .	450
			4,506 .	4,305

Served in 35th Foot.

Exclusive of the acreage of lands leased in perpetuity, and of a rent of 961*l.* in Co. Mayo arising from lands thus leased.

		acres.	g. an. val.
HENDRICK, T., of Kerdiffstown. Kildare		3,088 .	2,535
HENLEY, Right Hon. J. Warner, of Waterperry. Oxon, Bucks.		2,624 .	3,354
HENN, Thomas Rice, of Paradise. Clare .		7,664 .	2,765
HENNING, Gen., of Frome Whitfield. Dor., Som.		2,775 .	4,012
HENRY, Charles J., of ———. Tipperary		3,870 .	2,052
HENRY, E. C., of Cas. Townsend. Lderry.		3,171 .	2,058
HENRY, Hon. Mrs., of Redpath. Bw., Rox.		4,746 .	2,531
** HENRY, H., of Firmount. Galway, Kildare		6,656 .	2,442

*** HERBERT, Lieut.-Col. George Edward, of Glan Hafren, Newtown, N. Wales, &c.

		acres.		*g. an. val.*
Club.- Uni. Ser., E. I. U. Ser.	York, N.E. and			
b. 1809, s. 1876, m. 1869.	W.R. . .	1,514	.	2,608
	Montgomery .	4,031	.	2,640
Served in 9th Bengal Light Cavalry.				
Present at occupation of Lahore.		5,545	.	5,248

HERBERT, Henry Arthur, of Muckross Abbey, Killarney.

		acres.		*g. an. val.*
Club. Brooks's, Travellers'.	Co. Kerry . .	47,238	.	10,547
Guards, Army and Navy.				
b. 1840, s. 1866, m. 1866.				
Served in Coldstream Guards. Sat for Co. Kerry.				

HERBERT, John Arthur Edward, of Llanarth Court, Raglan.

Club. Brooks's, St. George's.	Monmouth	.	4,641	. 24,355
b. 1818, s. 1848, m. 1846.				
Was in Diplomatic Service.				

HERBERT, William, of Clytha House, Usk.

Coll. Stonyhurst.	Monmouth	.	4,542	. 10,623
Club. Arthur's, St. George's.				
b. 1798, s. 1805, m. 1833.				

** HERON, William Cowan, of Maryfield, Holywood.

Coll. Belfast Academy.	Co. Down . .	3,529	.	3,652
Club. Union, Belfast. b. 1819.				

HEPBURN (late), J. S., of Coquhalzie. Perth	7,238	.	2,433
BUCHAN-HEPBURN, Sir T., Bart., of Smeaton. Haddington	2,772	.	8,512
HEPBURN (late), W. R., of Rickarton, Kinc.	5,400	.	2,624
DOPPING-HEPENSTAL, Ralph A., of Derrycassan. Longford, Wicklow . .	3,269	.	2,034
HERBERT, Hon. R. C., of Orleton. Sal., Mgy.	2,737	.	4,916
HEREFORD, R., of Sufton Court. Hereford	2,153	.	3,686
HEREFORD, Viscount. Bre., Rad., Hfd.	2,100	.	2,241

*** PERRY-HERRICK, Mrs., of Beaumanor Park, Loughborough.

		acres.	g. an. val.
s. 1876, m. 1862.	Leicester . .	6,560 .	12,295
	Monmouth . .	4,094 .	5,543
	Hereford . .	3,041 .	4,447
	Radnor . . .	52 .	40
		13,747 .	22,325

HERRIES, Lord, Carlaverock Castle, Dumfries, N.B.

Coll. Stonyhurst.	Dumfries . .	5,814 .	6,257
Club. Athenæum, Boodle's,	Kirkcudbright .	3,423 .	885
St. George's.	York, E.R . .	6,858 .	8,205
b. 1837, s. 1876, m. 1875.	Lincoln . . .	2,800 .	3,805
		18,895 .	19,152

HERRIES, Mrs., of Frimley Park, Farnborough.

s. 1871, m. 1858.	York, W.R. .	2,965 .	6,819
	Surrey . . .	246 .	541
		3,211 .	7,360

HERTFORD, Marquis of, G.C.B., Ragley Hall, Alcester. ♣.

Coll. Harrow.	Warwick . .	10,281 .	15,344
Club. Uni. Ser., Carlton.	Worcester . .	217 .	468
b. 1812, s. 1870, m. 1839.	Co. Antrim .	998 .	1,560
Served as Equerry to the	Co. Down . .	793 .	1,020
Queen, and as Lord			
Chamberlain, and in		12,289 .	18,392
Scots Fusilier Guards.			

HESKETH, Edward Fleetwood, of Meols Hall, Southport.
♣.

Coll. Chelt., New, Oxon.	Lancashire . .	4,128 .	24,909
Club. Jun. Uni. Ser.			
b. 1834, s. 1876.			

The extraordinary rental in comparison with acreage is accounted for by the fact that Southport, a flourishing watering-
place, has sprung up on this estate and on Mr. Weld-Blundell's,
the ground landlords being credited (erroneously) with the whole
gross annual value.

FERMOR-HESKETH, Sir Thomas George, Bart., of Rufford
    Hall, Ormskirk, &c. ♠.

		acres.	*g. an. val.*
Club. Carlton, Jun. Carlton.	Lancashire . .	9,394 .	19,598
b. 1849, s. 1876, m. 1880.	Northampton .	5,784 .	11,975
Served in Rifle Brigade.	York, N.R. . .	15 .	60
		15,193 .	31,633

* BAMFORD-HESKETH, Robert, of Gwrych Castle, Aber-
    gele. ♠.

Coll. Harrow.	Denbigh . .	3,086 .	3,654
b. 1826, s. 1861, m. 1851.	Cheshire . .	768 .	1,912
Served in 2nd Life Guards.	Derby . . .	440 .	326
	†Carnarvon . .	201 .	171
	Flint	137 .	179
	†Lancashire . .	26 .	500
		4,658 .	6,742

    † These rentals much understated.

HEYGATE, Sir Frederick William, Bart., of Bellarena,
    Londonderry.

Coll. Eton, Trin. Cam.	Londonderry .	5,507 .	2,585
Club. Carlton, Cons.	Donegal . .	3,338 .	1,702
b. 1822, s. 1844, m. 1851.			
Sat for Co. Derry.		8,845 .	4,287

** MOUNSEY-HEYSHAM, George William, of Castletown,
    Carlisle.

Coll. Trin. Cam.	Cumberland .	3,381 .	4,810
Club. Oxford & Cam. b. 1831, s. 1881, m. 1861.			

*** HEYTESBURY, Lord, Heytesbury House, Bath.

Coll. Eton, St. John's, Cam.	Wilts . . .	7,025 .	8,835
Club. Carlton, Travellers'.	Hants . . .	4,805 .	5,036
b. 1809, s. 1860, m. 1833.	Co. Wicklow .	1,473 .	1,594
Sat for the Isle of Wight.			
		13,303 .	15,465

HICKSON, P. O'Hara, of Fermoyle. Kerry 13,443 . 2,533

*** HEYWOOD, Mrs., of Cloverley Hall, Whitchurch, Salop, &c.

		acres.	g. an. val.
m. 1836, s. 1877.	Salop . . .	3,364 .	4,555
	Lancashire . .	685 .	2,493
		4,049 .	7,048

HILDYARD, John Richard Westgarth, of Hutton Bonville Hall, Northallerton, &c.

Coll. Trin. Cam. Durham . . . 3,200 . 3,524
Club. O. & C., Brooks's. b. 1813, m. 1860.

THOROTON-HILDYARD, Thomas Blackborne, of Flintham Hall, Newark.

Coll. Eton, Ch. Ch. Oxon.	Notts . . .	2,134 .	3,721
Club. Carlton.	York, E.R. .	2,128 .	2,929
b. 1821, s. 1830, m. 1842.			
Sits for S. Notts.		4,262 .	6,650

HILL, Rev. John Richard, of Thornton Dale, Pickering.

Coll. University, Oxon. York, N.R. . 7,632 . 4,457
b. 1811, s. 1855, m. 1842.

** HILL, Viscount, Hawkstone, Shrewsbury. 🜨

Club. Carlton, White's, Salop . . . 16,554 . 21,000
Gun.
b. 1833, s. 1875, m. 1st 1855,
2nd 1875. Sat for N. Salop.

** HIPPISLEY, Henry, of Lamborne Place, Lambourn.

Club. Conservative.	Berks . . .	2,013 .	1,959
b. 1808, m. 1st 1839,	Oxon . . .	2,065 .	3,405
2nd 1851.			
		4,078 .	5,364

HIGGINS, W. F., of Turvey House. Bedfordshire, Northampton, Bucks . . .	2,946 .	4,401
HILLAS, R., of Seaview. Sligo, Dublin .	7,771 .	2,714
HILLS, Robert, of Colne Park. Essex .	2,156 .	2,874
HINDE, Mrs., of Over Silton. York, Lanc.	2,072 .	2,274

** HIPPISLEY, JOHN, F.R.S., of Ston-Easton Park, Bath.

			acres.		g. an. val.
Coll. Rugby, Oriel, Oxon.	Somerset	. .	4,216	.	7,845

Club. Athenæum.
b. 1804, s. 1843, m. 1st 1831,
                2nd 1843.

** HOARE, SIR HENRY AINSLIE, BART., of Stourhead House, Bath.

Coll. Eton, St. John's, Cam.	Wilts	. . .	5,996	.	6,059
Club. Turf, Brooks's, Trav.	Somerset	. .	5,310	.	6,577
b. 1824, s. 1857, m. 1845.	Dorset	. . .	2,681	.	3,452

Sat for Windsor and Chelsea.   13,987 . 16,088

HOARE, HENRY HUGH ARTHUR, of Wavendon House, Woburn.

b. 1865, s. 1873.	Devon	. . .	1,715	.	2,206
	Bucks	. . .	1,317	.	2,362
	Bedford	. .	216	.	381
	Essex	. . .	10	.	15

                                          3,258 . 4,964

HOARE, PETER MERRIK, of Kelsey Manor, Beckenham, &c.

Club. Carlton, Boodle's.	Devon	. . .	1,524	.	2,991
b. 1843, s. 1877, m. 1st 1865,	Lancashire	. .	1,550	.	1,852
2nd 1881.	Kent	. . .	201	.	2,301

Sat for Southampton.

                                          3,275 . 7,144

** HODSON, SIR GEORGE FREDERICK JOHN, BART., of Holy-
    brooke House, Bray, &c.

Coll. Trinity, Dublin.	Bucks	. . .	26		unstated
Club. Athenæum.	Co. Cavan	. .	4,349	.	2,269
b. 1806, s. 1831, m. 1852.	Wicklow	. .	1,211	.	1,186
	Meath	. . .	729	.	635
	Westmeath	.	502	.	337

                                          6,817 . 4,427

HODGSON, J., of Gilston Park.   Herts, Ess.   2,091 . 3,248

*** McGAREL-HOGG, Sir James Machnaghten, Bart., of Magheramorne, Larne, Co. Antrim.

		acres.	g. an. val.
Coll. Eton, Ch. Ch. Oxon.	Antrim . . .	3,541 .	4,083

Club. Carlton, Travellers', St. Stephen's.
b. 1823, s. 1876, m. 1857.

Served in 1st Life Guards, is Chairman of the Metropolitan Board of Works. Sat for Bath ; sits for Truro.

** HOLDEN, Rev. Atkinson Alexander, of Nuttall Temple, Nottingham.

Coll. Ch. Ch. Oxon.	Notts . . .	3,641 .	7,204

b. 1808, s. 1872, m. 1841.

* GWYNNE-HOLFORD, James Price William, of Buckland, Brecknock.

Club. Carlton.	Glamorgan .	1,165 .	11,401
b. 1833, s. 1881.	Brecon . . .	7,741 .	5,000
	Carmarthen .	3,820 .	1,340
Served in 16th Lancers. Sat for Brecknock.		12,726 .	17,741

The rental partly arises from minerals.

** HOLFORD, Robert Stayner, of Weston Birt, Tetbury.

Coll. Harrow, Oriel, Oxon.	Gloucester .	9,332 .	12,531
Club. Carlton, Ath., Burl.	Wilts . . .	2,929 .	3,842
Fine Arts.	Kent . . .	2,335 .	3,772
b. 1808, s. 1839, m. 1854.	Hants . . .	1,723 .	1,132
Sat for E. Gloucestershire.		16,319 .	21,277

HOLLAND, The Lady, Holland House, Kensington, &c.

b. 1812, s. 1859, m. 1833.	Wilts . . .	5,514 .	6,695
	Surrey . . .	277 .	762
		5,791 .	7,457

The schedule of Lady Holland's property would be greatly altered were the return inclusive of the Metropolis.

HOG, T. A., of Newliston.	Linl., Fife, Midlo.	2,560 .	5,427
HOLBECH, Acdn., of Farnborough.	War., Ox.	2,958 .	5,767
HOLDEN, E. C. S., of Aston Hall.	Dby., Leic.	2,628 .	4,806
HOLDEN, Rev. J. S., of Lackford.	Suffolk	2,327 .	2,157

** HOLLOND, Rev. Edmund, of Benhall Lodge, Saxmundham.

		acres.	g. an. val.
Coll. Queen's, Cambridge.	Suffolk . . .	2,349 .	4,146
Club. National.	Norfolk . . .	1,038 .	1,319
b. 1804, s. 1845, m. 1st 1839, 2nd 1852.	Dorset . . .	856 .	606
		4,243 .	6,071

** HOLMESDALE, Visc. (L. Amherst), Linton Park, Maidstone.

Coll. Eton.	Kent . . .	16,209 .	28,731
Club. Gds., Carlton, St.	Stafford . .	874 .	1,034
Stephen's, Trav.	Sussex . . .	970 .	979
b. 1836, m. 1862.			
Served in Coldstream Guards.		18,053 .	30,744
Sat for W. Kent and Mid Kent.			

Lord H. masses the whole acreage and rental, so it is here entered as in the return for the two small properties, and the balance put to Kent.

** MILNE-HOME, David, of Paxton Ho., Berwick, N.B.

Coll. Chel., Tr. Cam. & Ed. U. Berwick . . 9,144 . 16,500
Club. Carl., J. Carl., New Ed.
b. 1838, s. 1876, m. 1867.
Sits for Berwick. Serves in R. H. Gds.

** HOME, Earl of, The Hirsel, Coldstream, N.B., &c.

Coll. Eton.	Lanark . . .	61,943 .	24,770
Club. Carl., Trav., White's.	Roxburgh . .	25,380 .	7,995
b. 1834, s. 1881, m. 1870.	Berwick . . .	10,422 .	12,881
	Forfar . . .	5,209 .	7,356
	Renfrew . .	1,325 .	3,063
	Ayr	2,271 .	567
		106,550 .	56,632

Ex. of minerals, val. 5,916*l.*

HOLLAND, E. T. (purchaser from), of Dumbleton. Gloucester	2,145 .	3,947
HOLLEY, J. H., of Oaklands. Devon, Norfolk	2,236 .	2,028
HOLMES, G. J., of Brooke Hall. Norfolk .	2,932 .	4,121
BINNING-HOME, G. H. M., of Ardgaty. Stirling, Perth, Roxburgh	3,512 .	2,559

** HONE, MRS., of St. Dolough's Park, Dublin.

		acres.		*g. an. val.*
m. 1839, s. 1880.	Dublin . . .	1,058	.	1,446
	Co. Meath . .	1,618	.	939
	Tipperary . .	1,687	.	455
	King's Co. . .	226	.	137
	Cavan . . .	200	.	130
		4,789	.	3,107

*** HONYWOOD, MRS., of Mark's Hall, Coggeshall.

		acres.		*g. an. val.*
s. 1859, m. 1847.	Essex . . .	6,898	.	8,474
	Kent . . .	561	.	681
		7,459	.	9,155

HONYWOOD, SIR JOHN WILLIAM, BART., of Evington Place, Ashford.

b. 1857, s. 1878, m. 1877.	Kent . . .	5,601	.	5,875

*** FULLERTON-ACLAND-HOOD, SIR ALEXANDER BATE-MAN PERIAM, BART., of St. Audries, Bridgwater, &c.

Coll. Rugby.	Somerset . .	11,337	.	17,431

Club. Carlton.

b. 1819, s. 1851, m. 1849.
   Served in Royal Horse Guards Blue.   Sat for W. Somerset.

** BERESFORD-HOPE, ALEXANDER JAMES BERESFORD, of Bedgebury Park, Cranbrook, Kent.

Coll. Harrow, Trinity,	Kent . . .	4,321	.	3,586
Cambridge.	Derby . . .	709	.	831
Club. Carl., Ath., U. Un.,	Stafford . . .	552	.	817
Ox. & C., N. Un.	Sussex . . .	146	.	175
b. 1820, s. 1854, m. 1842.		5,728	.	5,409

   Sat for Maidstone and Stoke-on-Trent.
   Sits for Cambridge University.

HOMFRAY, J. R., of Penllyne. Gla., Mnmth.	2,663	.	9,326
HONYWOOD, W., of Chilton. Berks,Wil. Suf.	2,546	.	3,568
HOOD (late), HENRY, of Pepper Hall. York	2,234	.	3,048
HOOD, S. F., of Nettleham. Lincoln . .	2,515	.	3,205
HOOD, VISCOUNT. War., Nhnts., Bucks .	2,600	.	5,311

*** HOPE, Henry Walter, of Luffness, Drem, N.B.

			acres.		g. an. val.
Coll. Eton.	Haddington	.	3,201	.	6,379
Club. Carlton.	Fife		2,509	.	4,856
b. 1839, s. 1863.					
Served in Grenadier Guards.			5,710	.	11,235

HOPE, Mrs., of Deepdene, Dorking, &c.

s. 1861, m. 1841.	Surrey . . .		3,931	.	4,799
	Gloucester . .		4,893	.	5,338
	Warwick . .		1,249	.	1,668
	Co. Monaghan		11,700	.	10,333
			21,773	.	22,138

*** HOPE, Thomas Arthur, of Stanton, Bebington, Birkenhead.

b. 1817, m. 1839.	Co. Tyrone	.	14,006	.	2,385
	Cheshire . .		2,220	.	5,291
	Flint . . .		447	.	700
	Lancashire . .		18	.	488
			16,691	.	8,864

** HOPETOUN, Earl of, Hopetoun House, S. Queensferry, N.B., &c.

Coll. Eton.	Linlithgow . .		11,870	.	19,018
Club. Carlton, White's.	Lanark . . .		19,180	.	3,246
b. 1860, s. 1873.	Haddington	.	7,967	.	15,369
	Dumfries . .		2,549	.	634
	Fife		941	.	1,717
			42,507	.	39,984

Exc. of minerals to the ann. val. of 3,974*l.*

HOPE, G., of Bordlands. Pee., Bwk., Lanark	3,438	.	2,000
HOPKINS, R. J., of Tidmarsh. Berks . .	2,670	.	3,894
HOPKINSON, Rev. W., of Great Gidding. Huntingdon, Lincoln, Nhnts., Cam., Rut.	2,044	.	2,854

** HOPTON, JOHN, of Canon ffrome Court, Ledbury, &c.

				acres.		g. an. val.
Coll.	Rugby,	Brase.	Hereford . .	3,600	.	4,500
	Oxon.		Gloucester . .	850	.	1,700
Club.	Junior Carlton.		Worcester . .	1,082	.	1,500

b. 1810, s. 1870, m. 1843.
Served in 3rd Dragoon Guards.   5,532 . 7,700

** HORNBY, EDMUND GEOFFRY STANLEY, of Dalton Hall, Burton, Westmoreland.

Coll.	Eton,Trin.Hall,Cam.	Lancashire . .	3,736	.	4,380
Club.	Jun. Carlton,U.Univ.	Westmoreland	206	.	252

                                                    3,942 . 4,632

HORNBY, EDWARD OWEN, of The Hook, Fareham.

Coll. St. John's, Cam.   Hants . . .   3,109 .   3,217
Club. Union, Uni. Univ., Ox. and Cam., Oriental.
b. 1811, s. 1872, m. 1849.

** HORNER, JOHN FRANCIS FORTESCUE, of Mells Park, Frome

Coll. Eton, Ball. Oxon.   Somerset . . . 6,786 . 10,184
Club. Brooks's, Arthur's, Uni. Univ.
b. 1842, s. 1874.

*** HORNYOLD, JOHN VINCENT, of Blackmore Park, Upton-on-Severn, &c.

Coll.	Oscott.	Worcester . .	3,572	.	8,150
Club.	Brooks's, St. Geo.,	Hereford . .	10	.	4
	St. James's.				

b. 1818, s. 1859, m. 1846.   3,582 . 8,154
    This is exclusive of leaseholds in Malvern and Malvern Wells.

HORNBY, ADMIRAL SIR G. T. PHIPPS, K.C.B.,
    of Lordington.   Sussex . . . . . .   4,479 .   2,776
HORNE, E. W., of Stirkoke.   Caithness .   7,117 .   2,476

** WILMOT-HORTON, Rev. Sir George Lewis, Bart., of
    Osmaston Hall, Derby, &c.

		acres.		g. an. val.
Coll. Eton, Trin. Cam.	Derby . . .	3,710	.	7,900
Club. Travellers'.	Stafford . . .	750	.	1,350
b. 1825, s. 1880, m. 1849.	Northampton .	731	.	1,291
	Cheshire . .	621	.	1,114
	Leicester . .	224	.	400
		6,036	.	12,055

** HOTHAM, Lord, Dalton Hall, Beverley, &c. ⚓.

Coll. Tunbridge Wells.	York, N.&E.R.	20,352	.	26,126

Club. Carlton, York County.
b. 1838, s. 1872.   Served in Royal Navy, in the Russian War
        Not inclusive of purchases since 1874.

*** HOTHFIELD, Lord, of Hothfield Place, Ashford, &c.

Coll. Eton, Ch. Ch. Oxon.	Westmoreland	17,093	.	13,830
Club. Brooks's, Garrick.	Kent . . .	10,144	.	16,108
b. 1844, s. 1871, m. 1872.	York, W.R. .	11,953	.	15,919
	Cumberland .	86	.	130
		39,276	.	45,987

HOUBLON, John Archer, of Hallingbury, Bishop Stortford, &c

Club. Carlton, Uni. Ser.,	Essex . . .	7,127	.	9,035
Burl. Fine Arts.	Lincoln . . .	6,939	.	8,805
b. 1805, s. 1831, m. 1st 1829,	Herts . . .	1,449	.	1,647
2nd 1848.		15,515	.	19,487

** HOUGHTON, Lord, Fryston Hall, Ferrybridge, &c.

Coll. Trin. Cam. (Hon.	York, W.R. .	5,429	.	8,542
Fellow).	Lincoln . .	1,357	.	2,024
Club. Ath., Boodle's, Trav.	Notts . . .	780	.	1,169
b. 1809, s. 1858, m. 1851.	Stafford . .	3	.	8
	Derby . . .	30	.	44
Sat for Pontefract.		7,599	.	11,787

HORSFALL, W. (reps. of). Montgomery.		2,381	.	2,289

HORT, Sir John Josiah, Bart., of Hortland.
    Kildare, Queen's Co., Cavan, Fermanagh   3,956 . 2,234

** HOULDSWORTH, James, of Coltness, Wishaw, N.B.

		acres.		g. an. val.
Club. Windham, Devon-	Lanark . .	3,717	.	11,498
shire.	Argyll . . .	2,430	.	725
b. 1825, s. 1868, m. 1858.	Notts . . .	65	.	156
		6,212	.	12,379

Exclusive of 21,239*l.* mineral rental in Lanark.

*** BLAKISTON-HOUSTON, John, of Orangefield, Belfast.

Club. Carlton, Ulster, Bel-	Co. Down . .	5,999	.	6,686
fast, Kildare Street,	Antrim . . .	28	.	181
Dublin.	Armagh . . .	1,086	.	1,342
b. 1829, s. 1857, m. 1859.	Dublin . . .	111	.	300
		7,224	.	8,509

HOWARD, Lady Audrey, of 3, Queen Anne Street, W.

m. 1873, s. 1880.	Norfolk . .	4,044	.	4,402

** HOWARD, Henry Charles, of Greystoke Castle, Penrith. ♋.

Coll. Harrow, Trin. Cam.	Cumberland .	15,225	.	8,700
Club. Boodle's, Arthur's.	Westmoreland	2,100	.	450
b. 1850, s. 1875, m. 1878.	Surrey . . .	215	.	99
		17,540	.	9,249

His mother owns the Surrey property.

* HOWARD of GLOSSOP, Lord, Glossop Hall, Manchester, &c. ♋.

Coll. Trin. Cam.	Derby . . .	9,108	.	12,293
Club. Brooks's, Trav.	Cheshire . .	3	.	unstated
b. 1818, m. 1st 1851,	Inverness . .	8,800	.	809
2nd 1863.		17,911	.	13,102

Served as V.-Ch. of the Hhold. & Dep. E. Marshal. Sat for Horsham and for Arundel. The figures in Derby are understated.

HOUSTOUN, J. F., of Clerkington. Hadd.   5,148 . 2,267

HOWARD, PHILIP HENRY, of Corby Castle, Carlisle. **S.**

		acres.		*g. an. val.*
Coll. Stonyhurst.	Cumberland .	1,056	.	2,175
Club. Brooks's, Athenæum.	Salop . . .	3,917	.	2,806
b. 1801, s. 1842, m. 1843.	Durham . .	1,437	.	1,728
	Warwick . .	725	.	1,157
	Gloucester . .	162	.	297
Sat for Carlisle.		7,297	.	8,163

HOWARD, ROBERT, of Broughton Hall, Wrexham.

Coll. St. John's, Cam.	Derby . . .	2,344	.	3,213
Club. Reform, Hanov. Sq.	Flint . . .	1,170	.	2,132
b. 1828, m. 1852.	Cheshire . .	688	.	3,744
	Denbigh . .	1	.	4
		4,203	.	9,093

HOWE, EARL, C.B., Gopsal Hall, Atherstone, &c.

b. 1822, s. 1876, m. 1858.	Notts . . .	11,600	.	3,975
Served in Gren. Guards, also	Leicester . .	9,755	.	18,024
in Kaffir War, and at the	Bucks . . .	4,956	.	5,526
siege of Delhi. Is a	Suffolk . . .	4,695	.	6,076
Major-General in the	Essex . . .	1,492	.	2,067
Army, and Hon. Col.	Warwick . .	643	.	603
17th Foot.	Derby . . .	264	.	399
	Cheshire . .	182	.	273
	Worcester . .	47	.	12
	Kent . . .	22	.	37
	Flint . . .	13	.	40
		33,669	.	37,032

*** HOWTH, EARL OF, Howth Castle, Dublin.

Coll. Eton.	Dublin . . .	7,377	.	16,498
Club. Travellers', Arthur's.	Co. Meath . .	2,061	.	2,438
b. 1827, s. 1874.				
Served in 7th Hussars.		9,438	.	18,936
Sat for Galway.				

HOWARD, FITZALAN, of Long Sutton. Cambridge, Lincoln, Norfolk, Essex . . .	2,620	.	4,356
HOWAT, ROBERT K., of Mabie. Kirk .	2,566	.	2,139
HOWELL, FRANCIS, of Ethie. Cornwall .	2,705	.	3,546

HUDDART, George Augustus, of Brynkir, Tremadoc.

			acres.		g. an. val.
Club. Con., Carlton, Union.		Carnarvon . .	7,555	.	3,674
b. 1808, m. 1841.		Merioneth . .	237	.	173
			7,792	.	3,847

*** HUGHES, Hugh Robert, of Kinmel Park, Abergele, &c.

Coll. Rugby, Ch. Ch.		Denbigh . .	13,287	.	19,229
Oxon.		Flint . . .	2,061	.	2,582
Club. Carlton, White's.		Carnarvon . .	875	.	1,286
b. 1827, s. 1852, m. 1853.					
			16,223	.	23,097

HUGHES, John Williams Gwynne, of Tregib, Llandilo.

b. 18—, s. 1880, m. 1880.	Carmarthen .	6,797	.	3,990

*** HUGHES, William Bulkeley, of Plâs Côch, Llanfair-pwll. Anglesea.

Coll. Harrow.	Anglesea . .	5,404	.	5,002
Club. Union.				

b. 1797, s. 1836, m. 1st 1825,
            2nd 1866. Sat for Carnarvon.

** HULSE, Sir Edward, Bart., of Breamore House, Salisbury.

Coll. Eton, Ch. Ch. Oxon,	Hants . . .	4,518	.	7,424
Fellow of All	Essex . . .	1,499	.	4,707
Souls, Oxon.	Dorset . . .	270	.	222
Club. Carlton, Ox. and	Wilts . . .	12	.	17
Cam., Athenæum	Co. Tipperary	653	.	1,342
b. 1809, s. 1854, m. 1854.				
		6,952	.	13,712

HUBBARD, Right Hon. J. G., of Adding-ton. Bucks, Bedfordshire, Kent . .	2,576	.	4,887
💲 HUDDLESTON, F., of Sawston. Cambs.	2,368	.	3,333
DONALDSON - HUDSON, Charles, of Cheswardine. Salop, Stafford, Cumb. .	2,404	.	3,911
HUGHES, W. G., of Glancothy. Carn., Carm.	2,022	.	3,551
HUGHES, Mrs. S., of Offley Place. Herts·	2,070	.	2,884

*** HULTON, William Wilbraham Blethyn, of Hulton Park, Bolton. ♨.

		acres.	g. an. val.
Coll. Rugby, Trin. Cam.			
Club. J. Carl., Arthur's.	Lancashire . .	3,304 .	6,989

b. 1844, s. 1879, m. 1st 1867, 2nd 1879.

HUMBLE, Sir John Nugent, Bart., of Cloncoskoran Castle, Dungarvan, Co. Waterford.

Coll. Ch. Ch. Oxon.	Waterford . .	6,435 .	3,918
Club. Union.	Tipperary . .	189 .	207

b. 1818, s. 1834, m. 1846.

	6,624 .	4,125

*** HUMPHRYS, John Winter, of Ballyhaise House, Cavan.

Coll. Rugby.	Co. Cavan . .	5,146 .	4,010
Club. New, Cheltenham.	Westmeath .	3,164 .	1,719
b. 1829, s. 1877, m. 1854.	Wexford . .	1,398 .	517

	9,708 .	6,246

HOLDICH-HUNGERFORD, Henry Vane Forester, of Dingley Park, Market Harborough, &c.

Coll. Harrow.	Northampton .	5,286 .	8,850
Club. Boodle's, Pratt's.	Leicester . .	97 .	192

b. 1852, s. 1872, m. 1875.

	5,383 .	9,042

** FITZCLARENCE-HUNLOKE, Hon. Mrs., of Wingerworth Hall, Chesterfield.

s. 1865, m. 1856.	Derby . . .	6,006 .	8,463

** HUNT, Rowland, of Boreatton Park, Shrewsbury, &c.

Coll. Eton, Magd. Cam.	Salop . . .	3,569 .	6,102
b. 1858, s. 1878.	Leicester . .	350 .	944

	3,919 .	7,046

*** HUNTER, Alexander Chambers, of Tillery, Aberdeen, N.B., &c.

Club. Beacfd., Han. Sq., U.	Aberdeen . .	3,687 .	3,146
Edin. R. Nor. Aberdeen.			

b. 1838, s. 1866, m. 1871. Served in Bombay Staff Corps.

HUNTER, Miss, of Hafton, Dunoon, N.B.

		acres.	g. an. val.
s. 1880.	Argyll . . .	5,740 .	4,569

Inclusive of 1,000*l.* per annum for Dunoon Pier.

** HUNTER, Richard, of Thurston, Dunbar, N.B.

Club. Junior Carlton.	Haddington .	6,492 .	5,713
b. 1851, s. 1879.	Berwick . .	1,220 .	1,280
		7,712 .	6,993

HUNTINGDON, Earl of, Clashmore House, Waterford, &c.

Coll. Ch. Ch. Oxon.	Waterford . .	6,450 .	3,966
Club. St. James's, Carlton,	King's Co. .	3,379 .	1,919
Falconry, Trav.,	Galway . . .	3,694 .	880
Kildare Street.			
b. 1841, s. 1875, m. 1867.		13,523 .	6,765

Vt. Hastings is returned as owner of the estate in K. Co.

HUNTINGFIELD, Lord, Heveningham Hall, Yoxford.

Coll. Eton.	Suffolk . . .	16,869 .	22,177
Club. Carlton, Turf, Gun.			
b. 1818, s. 1844, m. 1839.			

The Dowager Lady H. has out of this total 5,157 acres, rented at 7,252*l.*

HUNTLY, Marquis of, Aboyne Castle, Aberdeen, &c.

Coll. Eton, Trin. Cam.	Aberdeen . .	80,000 .	11,215
Club. White's, City Lib.	Huntingdon .	5,711 .	8,645
b. 1847, s. 1863, m. 1869.			
		85,711 .	19,860

Was a L. in waiting and Capt. H.C. of Gentlemen-at-Arms.

HUNTER, James, of Glen App.	Ayr . .	8,580 .	2,705
HUNTER, John, of ———.	Down . . .	2,419 .	2,803
HUNTER, P., of Auchterarder.	Perth, Sal.	2,238 .	3,596
HURRELL, H., of Madingley.	Cambridge.	2,209 .	3,500

HURST, ROBERT HENRY, of Horsham Park, Sussex, &c.

			acres.		*g. an. val.*
Coll.	West., Trin. Cam.	Sussex . . .	2,976	.	4,504
Club.	Ox. and Cam., Ref.	Gloucester .	1,357	.	1,594

b. 1817, s. 1857 and 1875, m. 1859.
Sat for Horsham.

	4,333	.	6,098

** HURT, ALBERT FREDERICK, of Alderwasley, Derby.

Club.	Jun. Carlton, Army	Stafford . . .	740	.	1,085
	and Navy.	Derby . . .	4,799	.	6,376

b. 1835, s. 1861, m. 1862.
Served in R.N. in Black Sea and   5,539 . 7,461
Sea of Azoff during Russian War.

* HUSSEY, EDWARD, of Scotney Castle, Lamberhurst, &c.

Coll.	Ch. Ch. Oxon.	Kent . . .	3,001	.	4,105
Club.	Travellers'.	Sussex . . .	2,153	.	2,558
b. 1802, s. 1817, m. 1853.		Surrey . . .	1	.	unstated

The last property is in Southwark,
and therefore very valuable.   5,155 . 6,663

STRONG-HUSSEY, ANTHONY, of Westown, Balbriggan, Dub.

b. 1850, s. 1880.

	Co. Meath . .	4,100	.	2,659
	Co. Dublin .	600	.	661

	4,700	.	3,320

HUSSEY-HUSSEY, RICHARD, of Upwood, Huntingdon.

Coll. Ch. Ch. Oxon.   Huntingdon . 3,135 . 4,042
Club. Oxford and Cambridge.   b. 1815, s. 1842.

*** HUSSEY, SAMUEL MURRAY, of Edenburn, Gortatlea, Co. Kerry.

Club. Union.   Co. Kerry . . 7,087 . 3,900
b. 1824, m. 1853.

HUSTLER, W. T., of Acklam.   York, Durh. 2,599 . 3,689

** HUTCHINS, Samuel Newburgh, of Ardnagashel, Bantry.

		acres.		g. an. val.
Coll. Trinity, Dublin.	Co. Cork . .	8,775	.	6,099
b. 1834, s. 1880, m. 1873.	Westmeath .	363	.	342
	Co. Cavan . .	897	.	184
	Co. Dublin .	——	.	42
		10,035	.	6,667

HUTCHINSON, Timothy, of Egglestone Hall, Darlington.

b. 1819, m. 1842.	Durham . .	4,297	.	3,695
	York, N.R. .	2,019	.	1,881
		6,316	.	5,576

*** HUTCHISON, Graham, of Balmaghie House, Castle-Douglas, N.B.

Coll. Glasgow Univ.	Dumbarton .	2	.	250
Club. Cons. and Western,	Kirkcudbright	3,113	.	2,826
Glasgow.				
b. 1848, s. 1859, m. 1873.		3,115	.	3,076

** HUTTON, George Morland, of Gate Burton Hall, Gainsborough.

Club. Trav., Bood., A. & N. Lincoln . . . 3,431 . 4,800
b. 1834, s. 1877, m. 1870. Served in 46th Foot in the Crimea.

HUTTON, John Timothy d'Arcy, of Aldburgh Hall, Masham, &c.

b. 1847, s. 1874, m. 1868.   York, N.R. . 12,048 . 8,683
Served in 1st Royal Dragoons.
His mother has 7,620*l.* out of these rents.

HYDE, John, of Creg, Fermoy, Co. Cork.
b. 1803, s. 1832.   Co. Cork . . 8,919 . 3,524

HUTCHINSON, Thomas Lecky, of Ballymoney. Ant., Lond.	3,547	.	2,032
FORD-HUTCHINSON, W., of Stranocum. Ant.	2,730	.	2,219
HUTTON, J., of Solberghe. York, Durham	2,947	.	5,706

** HYLTON, Lord, Merstham House, Redhill, &c.

				acres.		g. an. val.
Coll.	Eton, Oriel, Oxon.	Surrey	. .	4,445	.	5,155
Club.	Carlton, White's, Ath.,	Somerset	. .	4,293	.	8,204
	Boodle's, Turf.	Hants	. .	1,320	.	3,713
b. 1829, s. 1876, m. 1st 1858,						
	2nd 1879.			10,058	.	17,072

Sat for Wells. Served in 4th L. Drs. at Balaclava, and in Cm. Gds.

ILCHESTER, Earl of, Redlynch, Bruton, &c.

				acres.		g. an. val.
Coll.	Eton, Ch. Ch. Oxon.	Dorset	. . .	15,981	.	18,515
Club.	St. Jas., Gun, Trav.,	Somerset	. .	13,169	.	19,992
	Salisbury.	Wilts	. . .	2,133	.	2,521
b. 1847, s. 1865, m. 1872.		Devon	. . .	1,566	.	2,424
Served as Capt H. C. of						
Gentlemen-at-Arms.				32,849	.	43,452

INCHIQUIN, Lord, Dromoland, Newmarket-on-Fergus, Co. Clare.

Coll.	Trin. Cambridge.	Clare	. . .	20,321	.	11,681
Club.	Carl., St. Jas., Kild. St.					
b. 1839, s. 1872, m. 1st 1862, 2nd 1874.						

INGILBY, Sir Henry Day, Bart., of The Castle, Ripley.

Coll.	Magd. Oxon.	York, W.R.	.	10,609	.	11,149
Club.	Bood., Ox. and Cam.	Lincoln	. .	1,271	.	2,389
b. 1826, s. 1870, m. 1862.						
				11,880	.	13,538

MEYNELL-INGRAM, Hon. Mrs., of Hoarcross, Burton-on-Trent, &c.

b. 1840, s. 1871, m. 1863.	York, N.R. and				
	W.R.	. .	12,176	.	32,560
	Stafford	. .	8,800	.	8,604
	Lincoln	. .	4,204	.	4,292
	Salop	. . .	25	.	35
			25,205	.	45,491

SELWIN-IBBETSON, Sir Henry John, Bart., of Down Hall. Essex, York. . . 2,098 . 3,090

* INNES, ALEXANDER, of Raemoir House, Banchory, N.B.

		acres.	g. an. val.
Coll. Trin. Cam.	Kincardine .	6,998 .	5,738

b. 1812, s. 1863, m. 1842.

*** MITCHELL-INNES, ALEXANDER, of Ayton Castle, Berwick, N.B., &c.

Club. Carl., Jun. Uni. Ser.,	Berwick . .	5,780 .	10,949
New & Cons. Edin.	Haddington .	527 .	2,415

b. 1811, s. 1860, m. 1st 1840, 2nd 1852.

Served in 47th Foot.		6,307 .	13,364

** INNES, ARTHUR CHARLES, of Dromantine, Newry, Co. Down.

Coll. Eton.	Down . . .	3,237 .	4,522
Club. Carl., Jun. Carl., Sack. St.			

b. 1834, s. 1835, m. 1858.   Sat for Newry.

** INNES, LIEUT.-COL. THOMAS, of Learney House, Torphins, N.B.

Club. Jun. Nav. & Mil.	Aberdeen . .	6,923 .	3,264

b. 1814, s. 1863, m. 1839.

ROSE-INNES, THOMAS GILZEAN, of Netherdale, Turriff, &c.

b. 1831, s. 1856, m. 1853.	Banff . . .	3,771 .	2,690
	Aberdeen . .	3,744 .	2,448
	Inverness . .	2,291 .	285
		9,806 .	5,423

*** INSOLE, JAMES HARVEY, of Ely Court, Llandaff, &c.

Coll. Melksham Sch.	Somerset . .	7,201 .	5,077
Club. Pall Mall.	Glamorgan .	1,107 .	4,100

b. 1821, s. 1851, m. 1834.

		8,308 .	9,177

* ILDERTON, Rev. T., of Ilderton, Nhmbd. 4,000 . 2,500

INGLIS, MAJ.-GEN., C.B., of Hildersham.
　　Cambridge, Essex . . . . 2,295 . 2,585

** IREMONGER, William Henry, of Wherwell Priory, Andover.

		acres.	*g. an. val.*
Coll. Eton.	Hants . . .	5,103 .	4,156

Club. Army and Navy.
b. 1845, s. 1862, m. 1st 1871, 2nd 1873.
Served in 32nd Foot.

** IRVINE, Alexander Forbes, of Drum Castle, Drumoak, N.B.

Coll. Aber. Uni., Edi. Uni.   Aberdeen . .   7,689 .   5,209
b. 1818, s. 1861, m. 1848.   This family has held Drum since 1326.

*** IRVINE, Edward Tottenham, of St. Aidans, Ferns, Co. Wexford.

Coll. Eton.   Co. Wexford   5,000 .   3,543
Club. Army and Navy, Kildare Street, Dublin.
b. 1832, s. 1834, m. 1861.   Served in 16th Lancers.

MERVYN-D'ARCY-IRVINE (late), Henry Huntley, of Castle Irvine, Irvinestown, Co. Fermanagh, &c.

d. 1881.	Fermanagh .	6,187 .	5,547
	Co. Tyrone .	3 .	0
		6,190 .	5,547

The Tyrone rental does not reach 1*l.*

*** IRVINE, John Gerard, of Killadeas, Enniskillen, &c.

Club. Sackville St., Dub.	Fermanagh .	11,602 .	5,556
b. 1824, s. 1860, m. 1860.	Tyrone . . .	2,033 .	719
	Monaghan . .	9 .	18
	Louth . . .	470 .	513
		14,114 .	6,806

*** IRVING, John, of Burnfoot House, Ecclefechan, N.B.

Coll. Charterhouse, Paris   Dumfries . .   4,997 .   4,102
        University, Bonn.
Club. Carlton, Arthur's, Windham.   b. 1805, s. 1822, m. 1851.

IRBY, Mrs., of Boyland.   Norfolk . . .   2,460 .   3,919
DOUGLAS-IRVINE, Walter, of Grange-
    muir.   Fife, Surrey . . . .   2,746 .   5,674

** ISHAM, Sir Charles Edmund, Bart., of Lamport Hall, Northampton. 🐍.

		acres.		*g. an. val.*
Coll. Rugby, Bras. Oxon.	Northampton .	3,112	.	5,699
b. 1819, s. 1846, m. 1847.	Leicester . .	1,118	.	1,674
		4,230	.	7,373

** JACKSON, Sir Henry Mather, Bart., of Llantilio, Monmouth.

Coll. Harrow, Trin. Oxon.	Monmouth .	3,137	.	4,200
Club. Oxford and Cambridge.				
b. 1855, s. 1881.				

** JAMES, Sir Walter Charles, Bart., of Betteshanger Park, Sandwich.

Coll. Westm., Ch. Ch. Ox.	Northumberland	3,968	.	2,224
Club. Travellers', Carlton.	Kent . . .	2,319	.	4,725
	Durham . .	330	.	6,000
b. 1816, s. 1829, m. 1841.				
Sat for Hull.		6,617	.	12,949

The return gives Sir W. a rental of 25,000*l.* in Durham, made up of the total values of property where he is only ground landlord.

JAMESON, John James, of St. Marnock's, Malahide, Co. Dublin.

Coll. Trinity, Dublin.	Meath . . .	4,092	.	3,741
Club. University, Dub.	Mayo . . .	7,012	.	106
	Dublin . . .	514	.	321
	Roscommon .	257	.	177
		11,875	.	4,345

IRWIN, B., of Streamstown.	Sligo, Donegal	5,738	.	2,614
IRWIN, R., of Rathmoyle.	Roscommon .	3,628	.	2,300
IRWIN, T. A., of Lynehow.	Cumberland.	2,215	.	2,470
** IVES, Gen., of Moyns.	Ess., Nfk., Suf., Berw.	2,501	.	4,174
JACKSON, W. E. R., of Ahanesk.	Cork, Wat.	4,543	.	2,067
JACSON, C. R., of Barton.	Lancashire .	2,541	.	3,838
JAMES, D. W., of Ightham Court.	Kent .	2,332	.	2,791

** JARDINE, Sir Alexander, Bart. (of Applegirth), of
Jardine Hall, Lockerbie, N.B.   *acres.*   *g. an. val.*

Coll. Edin., Woolwich.   Dumfries . .   5,538 .   5,818
Club. New, Edinburgh.
b. 1829, s. 1874, m. 1861.

*** JARDINE (late), Andrew, of Lanrick Castle, Doune,
N.B., &c.

d. 1881.   Dumfries . .   9,131 .   8,239
                                 Perth . . .   2,823 .   2,879
                                                _____
                                                11,954 .   11,118

*** JARDINE, Robert, of Castlemilk, Lockerbie, N.B.

   Coll. Edinburgh.   Dumfries . .   8,668 .   11,232
   Club. Brooks's, Ref.   Roxburgh . .   1,098 .   1,150
b. 1826, m. 1867.   Devon . . .   355 .   1,000
                                                _____
Sat for Ashburton ; sits for Dumfries.   10,121 .   13,382

*** JARVIS, George Eden, of Doddington Hall, Lincoln.

Coll. Eton.   Lincoln. . .   2,529 .   2,800
Club. Carlton, Boodle's.   Warwick . .   1,230 .   1,410
b. 1840, s. 1873, m. 1863.   Notts . . .   958 .   1,584
                               Kent . . .   3 .   30
                                                _____
                                                4,720 .   5,824
          Served in Queen's Bays and 18th Hussars.

** DUNNINGTON-JEFFERSON, Joseph John, of Thicket
Priory, York.

Coll. Eton, Trin. Cam.   York,E.&W.R.   7,811 .   12,003
b. 1845, s. 1880, m. 1870.

** JAQUES, R. M., of Easby Abbey. York.   2,548 .   5,259
JARDINE, J., of Dryfeholm. Roxb., Dumf.   5,684 .   2,510
JARRATT, George James, of Bury. York.   2,241 .   2,525

** JENKINS, Maj.-Gen., of Cruckton, Shrewsbury, &c.

		acres.	g. an. val.
Club. United Service.	Salop . . .	2,797 .	4,932
	Warwick . .	711 .	1,142
b. 1821, s. 1877 and 1879, m. 1847.		3,508 .	6,074

Commanded 19th Hussars, present at Aliwal, Chillianwallah, &c.

** BLANDY-JENKINS, John, of Kingston Bagpuize, Abingdon.

Coll. Eton.	Berkshire . .	1,142 .	2,203
Club. Conservative.	Glamorgan .	6,102 .	3,030
b. 1839, s. 1844, m. 1861.		7,244 .	5,233

All the Glamorgan property is down in Mrs. B. Jenkins's name except 18 acres.

JENKINSON, Sir George Samuel, Bart., of Eastwood Park, Gloucester.

Coll. Winchester.	Gloucester . .	3,047 .	4,300
Club. Carlton, A. & N.	Wilts . . .	577 .	1,217
b. 1817, s. 1855, m. 1845.		3,624 .	5,517

Served in 8th Hussars. Sat for North Wilts.

** JENNER, Robert Francis Lascelles, of Wenvoe Castle, Cardiff.

Coll. Eton, Trin. Hall, Cam.	Glamorgan .	5,381 .	5,200

Club. Army and Navy, Carlton.
b. 1826, s. 1860, m. 1873. Served in 41st Foot and 7th Foot.

** JERNINGHAM, Hubert Edward Henry, of Longridge Towers, Berwick-on-Tweed. ⚓.

Coll. Paris University	Northumberland	3,572 .	9,086

Club. Ath., St. Jas., Ref., Brooks's.
b. 1842, m. 1874.
  Was Attaché at Vienna. Sits for Berwick-on-Tweed.

** JERSEY, EARL OF, Middleton Park, Bicester. ♣.

		acres.	g. an. val.
Coll. Eton, Balliol, Oxon.	Glamorgan .	10,000	18,000
Club. Carlton, St. Stephen's,	Oxford . . .	5,735	7,000
Junior Carlton.	Middlesex . .	1,993	7,117
b. 1845, s. 1859, m. 1872.	Kent . . .	568	950
Was Lord in Waiting.	Warwick . .	1,093	1,532
		19,389	34,599

** PARKER-JERVIS, HON. EDWARD SWYNFEN, of Aston Hall, Sutton Coldfield, Birmingham.

Coll. Bath, Ch. Ch. Ox.	Stafford . .	8,020	14,751
Club. Carlton.	Warwick . .	164	173
b. 1815, s. 1844 and 1856, m. 1838.			
		8,184	14,924

** ELLIS-JERVOISE, FRANCIS JERVOISE, of Herriard Park, Basingstoke, &c.

Coll. Chart., Merton, Oxon.	Hants . . .	6,183	5,140
Club. Conservative.	Wilts . .	3,663	4,917
b. 1809, s. 1847, m. 1st 1838,			
2nd 1842.		9,846	10,057

** CLARKE JERVOISE, SIR ARTHUR, BART., of Idsworth Park, Horndean, Hants.

b. 1856, s. 1881.	Hants . . .	7,877	4,798
	Sussex . . .	1,055	615
Served in Coldstream Guards.		8,932	5,413

* JODRELL, REV. SIR EDWARD REPPS, BART., of Sall Park, Reepham, &c.

Coll. Eton, Queen's, Ox.	Norfolk . .	4,100	4,462
Club. Hanover Sq., Eton	Oxford . . .	1,436	1,589
and Harrow.	Derby . . .	436	684
b. 1825, s. 1861, m. 1852.			
		5,972	6,735

JODRELL, E., of Bayfield Hall.	Norfolk .	2,407	3,081

* JODRELL, Thomas Jodrell Phillips, of Yeardsley, Stockport, &c.

		acres.		*g. an. val.*
Coll. Trin. Cam.	Cheshire . .	3,130	.	2,733
Club. Athenæum.	Derbyshire . .	575	.	606
b. 1807, s. 1868.				
		3,705	.	3,339

** JOHNSON, John George, of Winkleigh Court, Torrington.

Coll. Eton, Bras. Oxon.   Devon . . .   8,251 .   5,183
Club. Carlton, Arthur's, Garrick, Windham.
b. 1829, s. 1869, m. 1856.   Sat for Exeter.

** JOHNSON, Sir John Henry, Kt., of St Osyth Priory, Colchester.

Coll. Heidelberg.   Essex . . .   3,940 .   4,500
Club. Jun. Athenæum, R.T.Y.C., R.V.Y.C.
b. 1826, s. 1868, m. 1868.

JOHNSTON, Gen., of Carnsalloch, Dumfries, N.B., &c.

Club. Uni. Ser., Army and	Dumfries . .	2,409	.	2,821
Navy, Travellers'.	Kirkcudbright	765	.	688
b. 1807, s. 1849.				
Served in 84th Foot, commanded 66th Foot.		3,174	.	3,509

*** JOHNSTON, William, of Kinlough House, Kinlough, Co. Leitrim.

Coll. Armagh, Trin. Dub.	Leitrim . .	14,395	.	4,379
b. 1814, s. 1838, m. 1856.	Donegal . .	498	.	362
	Fermanagh .	723	.	314
	Sligo . . .	332	.	305
		15,948	.	5,360

JOHNSON, A. C., of Wytham-on-the-Hill. Linc.	2,547	.	3,809
JOHNSON, J. W. D., of Sarre. Linc., Kent	2,896	.	4,379
JOHNSON, Lady, of Belfast. Ant., Rosc.	4,521	.	2,380
JOHNSON (late), Mrs., of Llanerchydol. Montg.	2,696	.	5,284
JOHNSTON, R. E., of Glencore. Ferm. .	7,157	.	2,885

JOHNSTONE, Sir Frederick John William, Bart., of
   Westerhall, Langholm, N.B., &c.   *acres.*   *g. an. val.*

			acres		g. an. val.
Coll. Eton, Ch. Ch. Oxon.	Dumfries	. .	17,064	.	6,834
Club. Carlton, Turf, Gar.,	Dorset .	. .	200	.	2,716
Travellers'.					
b. 1841, s. 1841. Sits for Weymouth.			17,264	.	9,550

JOHNSTONE, George, of Lathrisk, Falkland, N.B., &c.

Fife .	. .	10.005	.	14,017
Perth	. .	3,631	.	1,409
Midlothian .	.	1,500	.	739
		15,136	.	16,165

** BUTLER-JOHNSTONE, Henry Alexander, of Culcairn,
   Evanton, N.B.

Coll. Eton, Ch. Ch. Oxon.	Ross . . .	24,350	.	3,294
Club. Carlton, Athenæum.				

b. 1837, s. 1879, m. 1877. Sat for Canterbury.

JOHNSTONE, James, of Alva, Stirling, N.B., &c.

Coll. Rugby, Edinburgh.	Selkirk . . .	8,614	.	2,505
Club. Athenæum.	Stirling. . .	5,340	.	4,004
b. 1801, s. 1830, m. 1st 1846,	Clackmannan .	1,587	.	721
2nd 1862.				
Sat for Clackmannanshire.		15,541	.	7,230

** HOPE-JOHNSTONE, John James, of Raehills, Annandale,
   Lockerbie, N.B.

Coll. Eton,	Dumfries . .	64,079	.	27,884
Club. Carl., White's, Gds.,	Lanark . . .	1,287	.	352
Cons., Uni. Ser.				
b. 1843, s. 1876.		65,366	.	28,236

Served in Gren. Guards and Rifle Brigade.   Sat for Dumfriesshire.

JOICEY, Edward, of Newton Hall, Stocksfield-on-Tyne, &c.

b. 186–, s. 1881.	Durham . .	5,816	.	5,508
	Northumberland	2,038	.	2,055
		7,854	.	7,563

JOHNSTONE, J., of Halleaths. Dumf.,
   Surr. . . . . 2,135 . 3,044

*** JONES, Frederick Arthur Gerwyn, of Pantglas, Carmarthen, &c.

			acres.		g. an. val.
Coll. Harrow, Merton,	Carmarthen	.	8,280	.	5,384
Oxon.	Brecon .	. .	148	.	50
Club. Eton.& Har., J. Carl.	Cardigan	. .	308	.	25
b. 1857, s. 1878.	Radnor	. .	96	.	65
			8,832	.	5,524

JONES, John, of Donington, Albrighton, &c.

b. 1805, m. 1826.	Salop . . .	1,918	.	2,939
	Montgomery .	1,160	.	105
	Stafford . .	blank	.	868
		3,078	.	3,912

** JONES, John Carstairs, of Gelli-Gynan, Mold, &c.

Coll. R.M.C. Sandhurst.	Denbigh . .	2,328	.	1,955
Club. Army and Navy.	Flint . . .	699	.	2,053
b. 1827, s. 1864 and 1878, m. 1856.				
Served in 2nd Dragoon Guards.		3,027	.	4,008

JONES, John Joseph, of Abberley Hall, Stourport.

Club. Cons., Jun. Carl.	Worcester . .	3,519	.	4,860
b. 18—.				

HAMILTON-JONES, Kenrick John Charles, of Moneyglass House, Co. Antrim, &c.

b. 1860, s. 1881.	Down . . .	690	.	762
	Antrim . . .	2,212	.	2,306
	Armagh . .	3,027	.	1,897
	Fermanagh .	3,690	.	1,428
	Tyrone . . .	268	.	184
		9,887	.	6,577

JOLLIFFE (late), Charles. Cumberland	2,383	.	3,206
JOLY, J. R., of Hollywood, K. Co., Cl., Me.	4,229	.	2,110
JONES, F. L., of Garthllwyd. Salop, Montg.	2,081	.	2,268
JONES, John, of The Grove Salop. . .	2,212	.	2,545

** JONES, MISS, of Hayle Place, Maidstone, &c.

		acres.	g. an. val.
s. 1811.	Co. Leitrim .	9,839 .	4,213
	Kent . . .	65 .	489
		9,904 .	4,702

JONES, MORGAN, of Llanmilo, St. Clears, Carmarthen.

Coll. Harrow, Uni. Oxon.	Carmarthen .	11,031 .	5,867
Club. Union, Uni. Univ.	Cardigan . .	418 .	416
b. 1829, s. 1843, m. 1st 1852,	Pembroke . .	622 .	329
2nd 1858,			
3rd 1875.		12,071 .	6,612

** JONES, SIR WILLOUGHBY, BART., of Cranmer Hall, Fakenham.

Coll. Eton, Trin. Cam.	Norfolk . . .	3,627 .	5,353
Club. Athenæum, Brooks's.			
b. 1820, s. 1845, m. 1856.			
Sat for Cheltenham.			

** KAVANAGH, ARTHUR MCMURROUGH, of Borris House, Carlow.

Club. Carlton, Royal Yacht.	Carlow . . .	16,051 .	7,905
b. 1831, s. 1854, m. 1855.	Kilkenny . .	7,341 .	5,032
Sat for Co. Wexford and	Wexford . .	5,013 .	2,201
Co. Carlow.	Westmeath .	620 .	470
		29,025 .	15,608

JONES, JOHN HAWTREY, of Mullinabro. Wexford, Kilkenny, Wicklow, Waterford	2,738 .	2,251
JONES, MISS, of Derry Ormond. Cardigan	4,782 .	2,570
JONES, MISS, of Llansantffraid. Denbigh .	3,239 .	2,892
JONES, R. E., of Cefn Bryntalch. Mont. .	2,055 .	3,059
JONES, W., of Glandenys. Card. Carm.	4,141 .	2,048
ATKINSON-JOWETT, JAMES, of Clock House. York	2,930 .	6,078

*** LISTER-KAY, John Cunliffe, of Fairfield Hall, Adding-
    ham, &c.   *acres.*   *g. an. val.*
    b. 1810, s. 1853, m. 1846.   Kent . . .   5,276 .   5,980
                                 York . . .   1,623 .   3,810
                                 Argyll . . . 8,120 .   851
                                                ─────────────────
                                                15,019 . 10,641

*** KEANE, Admiral Hon. George Disney, C.B. (*jur. uxo.*),
    of Mere Hall, Knutsford.
    b. 1817, m. 1881.   Cheshire . . . 4,706 .   9,850
    Served in Kaffir War, 1851–2.

** KEANE, Sir Richard Francis, Bart., of Cappoquin House,
   Waterford.
Coll. Harrow.   Co. Waterford   8,909 .   3,237
Club. Union, Kild. St. Dublin.
b. 1845, s. 1881, m. 1872.

** CUTHBERT-KEARNEY, Thomas, of Garrettstown, Kinsale.
Coll. Chelt., Jesus, Cam.   Co. Cork . .   3,906 .   2,865
Club. New University.   Co. Kerry . .   3,407 .   685
b. 1843, s. 1854.   ─────────────────
                                              7,313 .   3,550

** POWYS-KECK, Harry Leycester, of Stoughton Grange,
   Leicester.
Coll. Brasenose, Oxon.   Leicester . . 6,529 . 12,156
Club. National, Carlton.
b. 1841, s. 1863. Acreage somewhat overstated.

* RUCK-KEENE, Edmund, of Swyncombe, Henley-on-Thames.
  Club. A. & N., Arthur's,   Oxford . . .   2,819 .   2,111
  b. 1822, s. 1880, m. 1864.   Cambridge . .   1,917 .   2,307
                               Suffolk . . . 1,327 .   1,488
                               Essex   . . .   183 .   170
  Served in 2nd Dragoon Guards.   ─────────────────
                                              6,246 .   6,076

───

AYLWARD-KEARNEY, J., of Shankhill.
    Kilkenny, Carlow . . . .   3,811 .   2,751
KEARNEY, J., of Culmolyn. Mea., Wmea.   2,511 .   2,429
KEATS, T. G., of Porthill. Devon . . .   2,664 .   3,030

** KEKEWICH, Trehawke, of Peamore, Exeter.

		acres.	g. an. val.
Coll. Harrow, Ch. Ch. Ox.	Cornwall	2,603 .	3,350
Club. Uni. University.	Devon . . .	2,131 .	2,592
b. 1823, s. 1873, m. 1st 1849,			
2nd 1881.		4,734 .	5,942

*** KELLY, John Joseph Roche, of Rockstown Castle, Limerick.

		acres.	g. an. val.
b. 1835, s. 1875, m. 1st 1865,	Limerick . .	2,190 .	4,500
2nd 1875.	Galway . . .	1,610 .	264
	Co. Mayo . .	3,405 .	84
		7,205 .	4,848

** KEMMIS, Thomas, of Shaen, Maryborough.

Coll. Eton.	Queen's Co. .	5,800 .	3,325
Club. Kildare St. Dub.	b. 1837, s. 1844, m. 1858.		

*** KEMMIS, William, of Ballinacor, Rathdrum, Co. Wicklow.

Coll. Trinity, Dublin.	Wicklow . .	8,041 .	1,436
b. 1836, s. 1881, m. 1862.	Queen's Co. .	4,706 .	2,483
Serves in R. Artillery.			
		12,747 .	3,919

** KENMARE, Earl of, K.P., Killarney House, Co. Kerry.

Club. White's, Brooks's,	Co. Kerry . .	91,080 .	25,252
Travellers'.	Co. Cork . .	22,700 .	3,497
b. 1825, s. 1871, m. 1858.	Limerick . .	4,826 .	5,724
Served as Compt. of the			
Household, V.-Chamber-		118,606 .	34,473
lain, Lord in Waiting, and			
is L. Chamberlain. Sat for Co. Kerry.			

The value is much understated.

KEIR, P. S., of Kindrogan. Perth . . .	10,000 .	2,445
FOORD-KELCEY, G., of Smeeth. Kent .	2,565 .	2,081
⚥ KELLY, R., of Kelly. Devon, Cornwall	2,858 .	3,686
KEMBLE, Mrs., of Cowbridge Ho. Wilts,		
Som.	2,219 .	3,752
KEMP, Sir K. H., Bart., of Gissing. Norf.	2,133 .	3,163

** KENNAWAY, SIR JOHN HENRY, BART., of Estcot, Ottery
St. Mary. *acres.* *g. an. val.*

Coll. Harrow, Ball. Oxon. Devon . . . 4,045 . 5,038
Club. Carl., Ath. b. 1837, s. 1873, m. 1866. Sits for E. Devon.

** KENNEDY, FRANCIS THOMAS ROMILLY, of Dalquharran
Castle, Maybole, N.B., &c.

b. 1842, s. 1879, m. 1868. Ayr . . . . 4,141 . 5,990
Exclusive of 900*l.* for mines.

*** KENNEDY, SIR JOHN CHARLES, BART., of Johnstown
Kennedy, Rathcoole, Co. Dublin, &c.

Coll. Eton, Trin. Cam.	Waterford . .	6,680 .	2,596
b. 1856, s. 1880, m. 1879.	Co. Dublin .	1,447 .	1,183
		8,127 .	3,779

KENSINGTON, LORD, St. Bride's, Haverfordwest.

Coll. Eton.	Pembroke . .	6,537 .	4,974
Club. Brooks's, Guards,	Radnor . . .	394 .	162
Reform,Travellers'.	Cardigan . .	203 .	140
b. 1835, s. 1872, m. 1867.	Carmarthen .	337 .	103
		7,471 .	5,379

Served in Coldm. Gds., and as Groom in
Waiting. Is Compt. Household. Sits for Haverfordwest.

* KENYON, LORD, Gredington Hall, Whitchurch, Salop.

Coll. Eton.	Flint . . .	4,552 .	6,041
b. 1864, s. 1869.	Denbigh . .	3,026 .	4,367
	Lancashire . .	237 .	1,769
	Salop . . .	126 .	120
		7,941 .	12,297

KENDALL, N., of Pelyn. Cornwall . 2,276 . 2,341

KENNEDY, J. L., of Knocknalling. Kirk.,
Lanc. . . . . 2,646 . 2,039

*** KEPPEL, Rev. William Arnold Walpole, of Lexham
Hall, Swaffham, &c.

			acres.	g. an. val.
Coll. Westm., Trin. Cam.	Norfolk	. .	2,855 .	3,407
b. 1804, s. 1859, m. 1830.	Lancashire	.	300 .	2,159
			3,155 .	5,566

** MURRAY-KER, Andre Allen, of Newbliss House, Co.
Monaghan.

Coll. Fein. I., Tr. Dub.   Monaghan .   3,605 . 3,265
Club. Sackville Street.   b. 1818, s. 1827, m. 1854.

* KER, Richard William Blackwood, of Montalto, Bally-
nahinch, &c.

Club. Naval and Military.   Down . . . 20,544 . 22,196
b. 1850, s. 1879, m. 1876.   Served in 1st Dragoons (Royals).

** KERRISON, Sir Edward Clarence, Bart., of Oakley
Park, Scole, &c.

Coll. Eton, Ch. Ch. Oxon.	Suffolk . .	9,955 .	16,691
Club. Carlton, Travellers'.	Norfolk . .	1,906 .	1,917
b. 1821, s. 1853, m. 1844.			
Sat for Eye and for East Suffolk.		11,861 .	18,608

KESTEVEN, Lord, Casewick House, Stamford.

Coll. Eton, Magd. Cam.	Lincoln . .	4,209 .	7,771
Club. Carlton.	Northampton .	2,082 .	3,085
b. 1851, s. 1874.			
		6,291 .	10,856

KETTLEWELL, Charles Thomas, of Dumbleton, Evesham.

Coll. Jesus, Cam.	Gloucester . .	2,145 .	3,947
Club. Salisbury.	Northumberland	1,925 .	2,143
b. 1859, m. 1880.	York, W.R. .	113 .	184
		4,183 .	6,274

KETTON, Robert William, of Felbrigg Park, Norwich.

Coll. Eton, Merton, Oxon.   Norfolk . . . 4,442 . 4,209
b. 1856, s. 1872.

SCOTT-KERR, W., of Sunlaws.   Roxburgh   2,662 . 3,154

** KILMAINE, Lord, Gaulston Park. Killucan, Co. Westmeath. &c.

		acres.		g. an. val.
Coll. Trin. Dublin.	Co. Mayo . .	11,564	.	5,363
Club. Carlton, Travellers',	Westmeath .	2,122	.	1,560
Kild. St. Dublin.	Roscommon .	979	.	576
b. 1843, s. 1873, m. 1877.				
		14,665	.	7,499

** KILMOREY, Earl of, Shavington Hall, Market Drayton, &c.

		acres.		g. an. val.
Coll. Eton, Ch. Ch. Oxon.	Cheshire . .	5,453	.	8,632
Club. Carl., White's, Marl.,	Salop . . .	2,921	.	3,595
Turf, Garrick.	Middlesex . .	43	.	840
b. 1842, s. 1880, m. 1881.	Flint. . . .	32	.	44
	Co. Down . .	40,902	.	17,591
	Co. Armagh .	3,061	.	3,320
Sat for Newry.		52,412	.	34,022

** KIMBERLEY, Earl of, Kimberley Hall, Wymondham. ⚓.

		acres.		g. an. val.
Coll. Eton, Ch. Ch. Oxon.	Norfolk. . .	10,805	.	15,195
Club. Brooks's, Travellers',	Cornwall . .	342	.	9,805
Devonshire, Athen.				
b. 1826, s. 1846, m. 1847.		11,147	.	25,000

Served for Un. Sec. For. Aff. (twice), Envoy to St. Petersburg, Un. Sec. for Colonies, Un. Sec. for India, L. Lieut. of Ireland, Ld. P. Seal, and Sec. Colonies. Again holds that Office.

The Cornish rental is overstated, as it partly arises from lands built over, the whole gross rateable value being entered in Lord Kimberley's name.

KING, Sir Gilbert, Bart., of Charlestown, Drumsna, Co. Roscommon.

		acres.		g. an. val.
b. 1812, s. 1825, m. 1833.	Sligo . . .	4,328	.	2,133
	Roscommon .	1,858	.	1,280
	Co. Leitrim .	480	.	315
		6,666	.	3,728

		acres.		g. an. val.
KILGOUR, William, of Tulloch. Aberdeen		2,740	.	2,018
KING, E. R., of Chadshunt. Warwick . .		2,994	.	3,837
KING, F., of Fryern. Sussex, Dorset, Wilts		2,666	.	2,771

*** KING, JOHN GILBERT, of Ballylin, Ferbane, King's Co.

		acres.	g. an. val.
Coll. Trin. Dublin.	King's Co. .	10,242 .	4,673
Club. Carl., Sackville St.	Roscommon .	954 .	844
b. 1822, s. 1857.			
Sat for King's County.		11,196 .	5,517

KING, MRS., of Ashby-de-la-Launde, Sleaford.

s. 1875, m. 1866.	Lincolnshire .	5,128 .	7,485

** KING, HON. PETER JOHN LOCKE, of Brooklands, Weybridge.

Coll. Harrow, Trin. Cam.	Surrey . . .	3,520 .	5,882
Club. Athen., Devonshire.	Sussex . . .	523 .	223
b. 1811, s. 1833, m. 1836.	Devon . . .	588 .	493
Sat for E. Surrey.		4,631 .	6,598

*** KINGSALE, ADELAIDE, LADY. Lea Cas., Kidderminster.

m. 1855, s. 1877.	Cork . . .	3,473 .	2,180
	Worcester . .	1,019 .	2,046
		4,492 .	4,226

*** KINGSCOTE, COL., C.B., of Kingscote, Wotton-un.-Edge. 💰.

Club. Brooks's, White's.   Gloucester. .   3,956 .   4,529
b. 1830, s. 1861, m. 1st 1851,
           2nd 1856.
   Served in Scots Fus. Gds., A.-D.-C. to LORD RAGLAN through Crimean War, was G. in Waiting. Sits for W. Gloucester.

*** KINGSCOTE, HON. MRS., of Ciamaltha, Newport, Co. Tipperary.

m. 1833, s. 1879.	Co. Tipperary .	9,912 .	4,240

KINGSMILL, WILLIAM HOWLEY, of Sydmonton Court, Newbury.

Coll. Harrow, Ch.Ch.Oxon.   Hants . . .   5,361 .   4,630
Club. Conservative.   b. 1838, s. 1865, m. 1871.

KING, F. J., of Staunton Park.	Hereford .	2,084 .	3,043

** KINGSTON, Anna, Countess of, Mitchelstown Castle, Cork.

		acres.	g. an. val.
Club. (Mr. Webber's) Kild.	Co. Cork . .	24,421 .	17,845
Street, Dublin.	Limerick . .	250 .	106
s. 1867, m. 1st 1860,			
2nd 1873.		24,671 .	17,951

Her second husband, Mr. William Downes Webber, of Kellyville, has—

s. 1867, m. 1873.	Leitrim . . .	350 .	200
	Kildare .	200 .	135
	Queen's Co. .	504 .	345
	Co. Sligo . .	2,756 .	1,019
		28,481 .	19,650

KINGSTON, Earl of, Kilronan Castle, Carrick-on-Shannon.

Coll. Rugby.	Roscommon .	17,726 .	7,620
Club. Carlton, White's,	Co. Sligo . .	1,783 .	1,075
Kildare St.,Dublin.	Co. Leitrim .	1,554 .	141
b. 1848, s. 1871 and 1878,	Co. Dublin .	196 .	191
m. 1872.	Westmeath .	48 .	37
		21,307 .	9,064

*** KINLOCH, Alexander John, of Park, Aberdeen, N.B., &c.

Coll. Edin., H. S. & Un.	Aberdeen . .	1,681 .	1,118
Club. R. Northern, Aber.	Kincardine .	4,532 .	2,995
b. 1818, s. 1838, m. 1841.			
		6,213 .	4,113

** KINLOCH, Sir John George Smyth, Bart., of Kinloch, Meigle, N.B., &c.

Coll. Chelt., Trin. Cam.	Perth . . .	2,854 .	5,487
Club. Devonshire, New Ed.	Forfar . . .	1,251 .	232
b. 1849, s. 1881, m. 1878.			
		4,105 .	5,719

KINLOCH, Sir A., Bart., of Gilmerton.		
Had.	2,846 .	7,673

** KINLOCH, George W. A. (Trustees for), of Balharry, Alyth, N.B.

		acres.	*g. an. val.*
Coll. Cheltenham, Jesus, Cambridge.	Forfar . . .	5,097 .	1,097
	Perth . . .	2,262 .	5,009
b. 1853.			
		7,359 .	6,106

** GRANT-KINLOCH, Col., of Logie, Kirriemuir, N.B., &c.

Coll. Sandh., St. And.	Banff . . .	5,894 .	2,864
Club. Carlton, White's.	Forfar . . .	2,800 .	3,800
b. 1807, s. 1824, m. 1st 1837, 2nd 1872.		8,694 .	6,664

Served in 2nd L. Guards and 68th Foot, and as Ins.-Gen. of Foreign Legions. The Banff estate is Mrs. Kinloch's.

KINNAIRD, Lord, Rossie Priory, Inchture, N.B.

Coll. Eton.	Perth . . .	11,704 .	16,246
Club. Athenæum.	Kent . . .	114 .	757
b. 1814, s. 1878, m. 1843.			
Sat for Perth, was in Diplom. Service.		11,818 .	17,003

** KINNOUL, Earl of, Dupplin Castle, Perth, N.B., &c.

Coll. R.M.C. Sandhurst.	Perth . . .	12,657 .	15,413
Club. Carl., Marlb., Sal.			
b. 1827, s. 1866, m. 1848. Served in 1st Life Guards.			

*** KINTORE, Earl of, Keith Hall, Inverurie, N.B., &c.

Coll. Eton, Trin. Cam.	Kincardine .	8,325 .	12,536
Club. Carlton, Marlb.	Aberdeen . .	17,021 .	16,959
b. 1852, s. 1880, m. 1873.	Forfar . . .	87 .	56
		25,433 .	29,551

** KIRK, William Millar, of Ransfort Park, Gorey, Co. Wexford.

Club. Devonshire, Liberal, Dublin.	Queen's Co. .	4,062 .	2,733
	Wexford . .	1,519 .	1,463
b. 1827, m. 1853.	Monaghan .	720 .	550
	Co. Armagh .	214 .	924
		6,515 .	5,670

KIRBY, Mrs., of Maesyneuadd-Talsarnau, Harlech.

		acres.	*g. an. val.*
s. 1849, m. 1824.	Merioneth . .	13,409	3,944
	Denbigh . .	2,474	908
	Flint . . .	129	128
	Carnarvon . .	10	8
		16,022	4,988

** KIRKLINTON, George Graham, of Kirklinton, Carlisle.

Coll. Eton, Ch. Ch. Ox. Cumberland . 3,000 . 3,270
Club. Windham, N. Univ. b. 1853, s. 1868.

** MAITLAND-KIRWAN, Mrs., of Gelston Castle, Castle Douglas, N.B.

s. 1862, m. 1842. Kirkcudbright 5,080 . 5,000

KNATCHBULL, Sir Wyndham, Bart., of Merstham Hatch, Ashford. ♣.

Club. Carlton, Jun. Carlton. Kent . . . 4,638 . 7,224
b. 1844, s. 1871. Sat for E. Kent.
    An additional 483 acres rented at 930*l.* are returned as belonging to the Dowager Lady Knatchbull.

*** ROUSE-BOUGHTON-KNIGHT, Andrew Johnes, of Downton Castle. ♣.

Coll. Eton, Trin. Cam.	Hereford . .	10,348	11,786
Club. United University.	Salop . . .	170	256
b. 1826, s. 1856, m. 1858.			
		10,518	12,042

** KNIGHT, Frederick Winn, C.B., of Simonsbath, Exmoor, &c.

Coll. Charterhouse.	Devon . . .	5,721	1,555
Club. Carl., St. Stephen's.	Worcester . .	207	1,270
b. 1812, s. 1850, m. 1850.	Somerset . .	16,103	7,027
		22,031	9,852

Served as Sec. P. L. Board. Sits for W. Worcestershire.

KIRKPATRICK, Alex. R., of Donacomper.		
Kildare, Wicklow	3,641	2,006
KIRWAN, Miss, of Castle Hacket. Galway	8,774	2,924
♣ ** KNATCHBULL, Wyndham, of Babbington. Somerset	2,513	3,719

** KNIGHT, Montagu George, of Chawton House, Alton.

			acres.	g. an. val.
Coll.	Eton, Mag. Oxon.	Hants . . .	5,044 .	4,291
Club.	Junior Carlton. b. 1844, s. 1879, m. 1870.			

KNIGHTLEY, Sir Rainald, Bart., of Fawsley, Daventry. ⚓

Club.	Carlton, White's,	Northampton .	8,041 .	13,182
	Turf, Boodle's.			
b. 1819, s. 1864, m. 1869. Sits for S. Northamptonshire.				

KNOX, Charles Howe Cuff, of Creagh, Ballinrobe, Co. Mayo.

Coll.	Harrow, Ch. Ch. Ox.	Mayo . . .	24,374 .	8,850
b. 1840, s. 1867, m. 1869.	Donegal . .	446 .	722
Served in 8th Hussars.				
			24,820 .	9,572

*** KYNASTON, Rev. Walter Charles Edward, of Hardwicke Hall, Ellesmere.

Coll.	Trin. Dublin.	Salop . . .	3,518 .	5,212
Club.	Junior Carlton.	Montgomery .	966 .	1,178
b. 1830, s. 1868, m. 1860.				
			4,484 .	6,390

** MONEY-KYRLE, Lt.-Col., of Homme Ho., Dymock, Gloucester.

Coll.	Winchester.	Hereford . .	2,701 .	4,107
b. 1812, s. 1868, m. 1st 1842,	Wilts . . .	1,383 .	1,833
	2nd 1865.			
Served in 32nd Foot in Canadian Rebellion.		4,084 .	5,940

KNIGHT, H., of Cloakham. Devon, Dorset	2,986 .	4,522
KNOX, A. G., of Rappa. Mayo, Galway .	10,722 .	2,788
KNOX, G., of Prehen. Lnderry., Donegal .	4,528 .	2,673
KNOX, U. A., of Mt. Falcon. Mayo, Sligo	5,589 .	2,246
SNEYD-KYNNERSLEY, T. C., of Loxley.		
Stafford	2,230 .	3,785
LADE, Mrs., of Nash Court. Kent . . .	2,407	6,059

LAHIFF, James Daniel, of Cloon, Gort, Co. Galway.

			acres.	g. an. val.
Coll.	Trinity, Dublin.	Co. Galway .	10,799 .	3,853
b. 18—		Co. Clare . .	128 .	143
			10,927 .	3,996

*** LAMBARDE, Multon, of Beechmont, Sevenoaks.

Coll.	Westm., Sandhurst.	Kent . . .	3,453 .	4,485
Club.	Union. b. 1821, s. 1866, m. 1848. Served in 37th Foot.			

* LAMINGTON, Lord, Lamington, Biggar, N.B.

Coll.	Eton, Trin. Cam.	Lanark . . .	10,833 .	5,539
Club.	Carlton, Boodle's.	Haddington .	1,750 .	4,244
b. 1816, s. 1872, m. 1844.	Hants . . .	125 .	680
Sat for Bridport, Lanarkshire, Honiton,				
and I. of Wight.		12,708 .	10,463

Exclusive of 1,388*l.* for minerals.

** LAMONT, John Henry, of Ardlamont, Greenock, N.B.

b. 1854, s. 1862.	Argyll . .	12,000	3,327
Serves in 9th Lancers.			

LANDOR, Walter Savage, of Llanthony Abbey, Abergavenny. &c.

b. 1822, s. 1864.	Monmouth .	2,829 .	2,355
	Warwick . .	687 .	1,286
		3,516 .	3,641

LANESBOROUGH, Earl of, Lanesborough, Belturbet, Co. Cavan.

Coll.	Rugby.	Co. Cavan . .	7,946 .	6,240
Club.	Carl., Kildare Street,	Fermanagh .	6,606 .	5,339
	Sackville Street.	Leicester . .	1,845 .	5,840
b. 1839, s. 1866, m. 1864.				
Served in Royal Navy (Commander).		16,397 .	17,419

POWER-LALOR, G., of Long Orchard.

Tipperary	7,311 .	2,841

LALOR, T., of Cregg.   Tipperary, Waterford   3,400 .   2,813

LAMB, Sir A., Bt., of Beauport.   Suss., Leic.   2,638 .   3,546

LANGDALE, CHARLES, of Celbridge Abbey, Co. Meath, &c.

			acres.		*g. an. val.*
Club. St. George's.	Surrey	. .	10	.	60
b. 1822, s. 1868, m. 1852.	York, E.R.	.	3,891	.	3,892
	Monaghan	. .	1,390	.	1,090
	Kildare	. . .	519	.	624
	Co. Meath	. .	486	.	460
			6,296	.	6,126

LANGFORD, LORD, Summerhill House, Co. Meath.

Coll. Eton.	Limerick	. .	3,855	.	3,634
Club. Carlton, Gds., Kild.	Dublin	. . .	3,659	.	3,472
St. & Sack.St., Dub.	Meath	. . .	2,231	.	2,175
b. 1848, s. 1854.					
Served in Grenadier Guards.			9,745	.	9,281

LANGHAM, SIR JAMES HAY, BART., of Cottesbrooke Park, Northampton.

Coll. Eton, Ch. Ch. Oxon.	Northampton	.	9,118	.	14,362
b. 1802, s. 1833, m. 1828.	Oxford	. . .	532	.	505
	Huntingdon	.	19	.	16
			9,669	.	14,883

*** GORE-LANGTON, WILLIAM STEPHEN, of Newton Park, Bristol.

Coll. Eton, Ch. Ch. Oxon	Somerset	. .	6,660	.	14,175
Club. Carlton, J. Carl.	Gloucester	. .	1,523	.	2,058
b. 1847, s. 1873, m. 1870.					
Sits for Mid Somerset.			8,183	.	16,233

LAMONT, J., of Knockdow. Arg., Stir., Ren.	6,775	.	2,427
LANE, H. C., of Middleton. Sussex . .	2,556	.	2,313
₷ LANE, J. H. B., of K. Bromley. Sta., Berks	2,707	.	4,736
LANGDALE, S. Durh., Nbland. . . .	2,010	.	2,416
LANGDON, J. C., of Parrocks Lodge. Som. Dor., Dev.	2,252	.	3,347
LANGTON, B. R., of Langton. Lincoln .	2,661	.	4,211

*** LANSDOWNE, Marquis of, Bowood Park, Calne, &c.

		acres.	g. an. val.
Coll. Eton, Ball. Oxon.	Wilts . . .	11,145 .	20,824
Club. Brooks's, Ref., Turf.,	Hants . . .	4 .	48
White's, Travellers'.	Co. Kerry ⌐ .	94,983 .	9,553
b. 1845, s. 1866, m. 1869.	Co. Meath . .	12,995 .	10,790
Served as Lord of the	Queen's Co. .	8,980 .	5,310
Treasury, Under Secretary	Dublin . . .	2,132 .	3,182
for War, and Under Sec. for	Limerick . .	1,642 .	2,965
India.	King's Co. .	617 .	542
	Perth . . .	9,070 .	8,025
	Kinross . .	1,348 .	786

142,916 . 62,025

The Dow. Lady L. owns the Scotch properties.

*** LASLETT, William, of Abberton Hall, Pershore.

b. 1801, m. 1842.	Worcester . .	2,521 .	4,717
Sat for Worcester.	Gloucester .	2,893 .	3,606
	Hereford . .	2,771 .	3,316

8,185 . 11,639

* LATHOM, Earl of, Lathom House, Ormskirk. 🐍.

Coll. Eton, Ch. Ch. Oxon.　Lancashire . . 　7,213 . 　21,869
Club. Carlton, White's, Trav., Marl., Turf.
b. 1837, s. 1853, m. 1860.
　Served as L. in Waiting and Capt. Yeo of the Guard.
　　Acreage understated, rental somewhat overstated.

** LA TOUCHE, John, of Harristown, Newbridge, Co. Kildare.

Coll. Ch. Ch. Oxon.	Kildare . . .	11,282 .	7,951
Club. Brooks's, Kildare St.	Leitrim . . .	3,323 .	1,360
b. 1814, s. 1844, m. 1843.	Dublin . . .	706 .	849

15,311 . 10,160

** LA TOUCHE, William Robert, of Bellevue, Delgany, Co. Wicklow.

Coll. Harrow, Exeter, Ox.	Leitrim . . .	8,234	3,981
Club. Union, Kildare St.	Wicklow . .	1,798 .	2,964
Dublin.	Tipperary . .	1,347 .	612
b. 1810, s. 1856, m. 1867.			

11,379 . 7,557

LAUDERDALE, Earl of, Thirlestane Castle, Lauder, N.B.

		acres.	g. an. val.
Club. Conservative.	Berwick . .	24,681	16,096
b. 1822, s. 1878.	Roxburgh . .	756	740
	Haddington .	75	482
		25,512	17,318

*** LAWRENCE, Mrs., of Sevenhampton Manor, Andoversford.

s. 1878.	Gloucester . .	3,447	4,145

** LAWSON, Rev. Edward, of Longhirst, Morpeth.

Coll. Trin. Cam.　　Northumberland 3,000 . 6,480
Club. Oxford and Cambridge.
b. 1824, s. 1859, m. 1853.

*** LEVY-LAWSON, Edward, of Hall Barn Park, Beaconsfield.

Coll. London University.　Bucks . . . 3,207 . 3,802
Club. Devonshire.
b. 1833.

** LAWSON, Sir Wilfred, Bart., of Brayton, Carlisle. 🦢.

Club. Reform.	Cumberland .	7,730	11,384
b. 1829, s. 1867, m. 1860.	Durham . .	564	3,368
Sits for Carlisle.		8,294	14,752

* LAYCOCK, Joseph Frederick, of Low Gosforth, Newcastle-on-Tyne, &c.

b. 1867, s. 1881.	Northumberland	4,227	4,374
	Nottingham .	1,316	2,049
	Durham . .	367	444
		5,910	6,867

LAWDER. Rev. M., of Lawderdale.

Cav., Leit., Rosc.	5,299	2,470
LAWRENCE, Mrs., of Middleton, Carm., Gla.	2,547	2,281
LAWRIE, W. K., of Woodhall. Kirk. . .	6,569	2,276
LAWSON, Sir J., Bt., of Brough Hall. York	2,672	4,305

** LEADER, William Nicholas, of Dromagh Castle, Kanturk,
    Co. Cork, &c.   *acres.*   *g. an. val.*

Coll. Harr., Trin. Cam.	Co. Cork . .	13,554	.	5,832

Club. Jun. Carlton, Kild. St.
b. 1853, s. 1861 and 1880, m. 1881.   Served in Scots Greys.

** LEATHER, John Towlerton, of Middleton Hall, Bed-
    ford, &c.

Club. Cons., Carlton.	Northumberland	7,472	.	8,675
b. 1804, s. 1849, m. 1st 1832,	York, W.R. .	321	.	1,392
2nd 1852.	Hants . . .	13	.	153
	Derbyshire .	169	.	371
		7,975	.	10,591

LECHE, John Hurleston, of Carden Park, Chester. ☕.

Coll. Eton, Coblentz.	Cheshire . .	3,840	.	6,023

b. 1827, s. 1848, m. 1st 1850, 2nd 1855.

** LECHMERE, Sir Edmund Anthony Harley, Bart., of The
    Rhydd, Upton-on-Severn, &c. ☕.

Coll. Chart., Ch. Ch. Oxon.	Worcester . .	3,765	.	7,856
Club. Carlton.	York, N.R. .	1,902	.	3,605
b. 1826, s. 1856, m. 1858.	Gloucester . .	85	.	147
		5,752	.	11,608

    Sits for S. Worcestershire; sat for Tewkesbury.

LECONFIELD, Lord, Petworth House, Sussex, &c.

Coll. Eton, Ch. Ch. Oxon.	Sussex . . .	30,221	.	29,688
Club. Carlton, White's.	York . . .	24,733	.	31,019
b. 1830, s. 1869, m. 1867.	Cumberland .	11,147	.	6,742
Served in 1st Life Guards.	Co. Clare . .	37,292	.	15,699
	Limerick . .	6,269	.	4,820
	Tipperary . .	273	.	144
Sat for W. Sussex.		109,935	.	88,112

☕ LAWTON, W. J. P., of Lawton.   Che.,
    Staff. . . . . 2,556 . 7,492

LEATHES, H. M., of Herringfleet.   Suff., Nfk. 2,125 . 2,888

*** VAUGHAN-LEE, Vaughan Hanning, of Dillington Park,
    Ilminster, &c.

		acres.	*g. an. val.*
Coll. Eton.	Glamorgan .	9,222 .	12,757
Club. Carlton, Army and	Somerset . .	2,935 .	7,606
Navy, Gun.	Brecon . . .	3,021 .	1,630
b. 1836, s. 1868 and 1874,			
m. 1861.		15,178 .	21,993

    Served in 21st Foot. Sat for W. Somerset. Inclusive of 8,400*l.* for minerals.

** LEEDS, Duke of, Gogmagog Hills, Cambridge, &c.

Club. Arthur's, Jun. Uni.	York, N.&W.R.	14,772 .	21,470
Ser., Travellers'.	Cornwall . .	5,911 .	4,776
b. 1828, s. 1872, m. 1861.	Bucks . . .	3,117 .	5,821
	Cambridge .	436 .	664
	Middlesex . .	1 .	650
		24,237 .	33,381

    The Duke shares with "another" 217 of the Yorkshire acres here included.

*** LE FLEMING, Stanley Hughes, of Rydal Hall, Amble-
    side. $

Coll. Repton, Trin. Cam.	Westmoreland	3,617 .	2,313
Club. Pall Mall.	Cumberland .	1,175 .	1,120
b. 1855, s. 1877.	Lancashire .	650 .	519
		5,442 .	3,952

** LEGARD, Sir Charles, Bart., of Ganton Hall, York.

Coll. Eton.	York, N.&E.R.	6,407 .	7,751

Club. Carlton, White's, Turf, Boodle's.
b. 1846, s. 1866, m. 1878. Served in 43rd Foot. Sat for Scarboro'.

LEE, Edward Dyke, of Hartwell.	Bucks .	2,086 .	5,495
LEEKE, R. M., of Longford.	Salop, Flint	2,268 .	4,084
LEFROY, A., of Carrickglass.	Long., Kilk.	4,539 .	2,904

** LEGGE, Rev. Augustus George, of Mareland, Farnham, &c.

		acres.		g. an. val.
Coll. Ch. Ch. Oxon.	Hants . . .	3,356	.	3,769
b. 1835, s. 1879, m. 1864.	Sussex . . .	667	.	513
		4,023	.	4,282

WALLACE-LEGGE, William, of Malone House, Belfast.

b. 1841, s. 1868.	Co. Antrim .	8,565	.	4,844

LEGH, Charles Richard Banastre, of Adlington Hall, Macclesfield.

b. 1821, s. 1829, m. 1840.	Cheshire . .	5,829	.	11,324

** LEGH, Henry Martin, of High Legh, Knutsford. 🐌.

Club. Gds., Arths., White's.	Cheshire . .	2,798	.	6,223
b. 1839, s. 1877.	Lancashire . .	579	.	variable
Served in Grenadier Guards.				
		3,377	.	6,223

The Lancashire rental is given in the return as 953*l.*

** LEGH, William John, of Lyme Park, Stockport, &c.

Coll. Rugby.	Cheshire . .	7,100	.	13,000
Club. Carl., Bood., A. & N.,	Lancashire . .	6,700	.	32,000
White's, Trav.				
b. 1829, s. 1857, m. 1856.		13,800	.	45,000
Served in 21st Foot in the Crimea.				
Sat for S. Lancashire, sits for E. Cheshire.				

*** LEICESTER, Earl of, K.G., Holkham Park, Wells, Norfolk.

Coll. Eton, Winchester.	Norfolk . . .	44,090	.	59,578
Club. Brooks's.				
b. 1822, s. 1842, m. 1st 1843, 2nd 1875.				
Serves as Keeper of the Privy Seal to the Prince of Wales.				

PENNINGTON-LEGH, J., of Norbury Booths.	Cheshire, Sussex, Hants . .	2,979	.	5,588
LE HUNTE, G., of Artramont. Wex., Pem.		3,834	.	2,675

** WARD-BOUGHTON-LEIGH, Edward Allesley Bough-
ton, of Brownsover Hall, Rugby, &c. 🜍.

		acres.		g. an. val.
Coll. Ch. Ch. Oxon.	Warwick . .	3,100	.	6,500
Club. Carlton.	Northampton .	1,300	.	2,500
b. 1822, s. 1868, m. 1867.				
		4,400	.	9,000

** LEIGH, Egerton, of Joddrell Hall, Holmes Chapel,
Cheshire, &c. 🜍.

Coll. Eton.	Cheshire . .	3,946	.	8,391
Club. Jun. Uni. Service.				
b. 1843, s. 1876, m. 1874. Served in 1st Royal Dragoons.				

** LEIGH, Francis Augustine, of Rosegarland, Co. Wexford.

Coll. Eton, Ch. Ch. Oxon.	Co. Wexford .	8,280	.	4,052
Club. Kildare Street, Dublin.				
b. 1822, s. 1839, m. 1857. Served in 10th Hussars.				

LEIGH, Lord, Stoneleigh Abbey, Warwick, &c. 🜍.

Coll. Harrow, Trin. Cam.	Warwick . .	14,891	.	23,043
Club. Brooks's, Travellers'.	Stafford . . .	2,350	.	2,820
b. 1824, s. 1850, m. 1848.	Gloucester . .	2,232	.	3,218
	Cheshire . .	1,198	.	2,381
	Leicester . .	294	.	551
		20,965	.	32,013

"Lady Leigh" is returned for 87 acres in Monmouth, the
address given "Pontypool." This is one of the cases where the
parochial authorities have invented a title, the real owner being
Mrs. Leigh, the mother of Mr. Capel Hanbury, of Pontypool.

LEIGH, Mrs., of Luton Hoo, Luton, &c.

s. 1875, m. 1st 1843,	Bedford . .	4,265	.	6,035
2nd 1872.	Lancashire . .	704	.	4,707
	Cheshire . .	715	.	1,062
	Herts . . .	823	.	1,141
		6,507	.	12,945

** LEIGH, Roger, of Barham Court, Maidstone.

			acres.	g. an. val.
Coll. Ch. Ch. Oxon, Trin.	Kent	. .	2,270 .	5,703
Cam.	Lancashire	.	2,337 .	25,000
Club. Travellers'.				
b. 1840, s. 1867, m. 1861.			4,607 .	30,703

Sits for Rochester. " Largely inclusive of mine rents."

** LEIGH, William, of Woodchester Park, Stonehouse.

Coll. Oscott.	Gloucester . .	3,847 .	4,600

b. 1829, s. 1873, m. 1859.

LEIGHTON, Sir Baldwyn, Bart., of Loton Park, Shrewsbury.

Coll. Eton, Ch. Ch. Oxon.	Shropshire . .	4,085 .	5,406
Club. Carlton, St. James's,	Montgomery .	11 .	15
Athenæum.			
b. 1836, s. 1871, m. 1864.		4,096 .	5,421

Sits for S. Salop.

*** LEINSTER, Duke of, Carton, Maynooth, Co. Kildare.

Coll. Ch. Ch. Oxon.	Kildare . . .	71,977 .	54,741
b. 1819, s. 1874, m. 1847.	Co. Meath . .	1,123 .	1,136
Serves on Com. of Education			
in Ireland. Sat for Co. Kil-		73,100 .	55,877
dare.			

*** LEITH, Alexander, of Glenkindie, Aberdeen, N.B., &c.

Coll. Trin. Cam.	Aberdeen . .	8,566 .	4,504

Club. Junior Carlton, St. Stephen's, Windham, New Edin.
b. 1817, s. 1859, m. 1843. Serves in the R. Sc. Archers.

His mother, Lady Leith, has in the same county 474 acres, rented at 683*l*.

* LEITRIM, Earl of, 44, Grosvenor Street, W.

Club. Carlton.	Donegal . .	54,352 .	9,406
b. 1847, s. 1878, m. 1873.	Leitrim . . .	2,500 .	1,600
Served in R. Navy.		56,852 .	11,006

FORBES-LEITH, Rev. W., of Whitehaugh.

Aberdeen	3,864 .	2,852

** LENNARD, Sir John Farnaby, Bart., of Wickham Court,
    West Wickham.

		acres.		g. an. val·
Coll. R.M.A., Woolwich.	Kent . . .	3,002	.	4,900
Club. Carlton, Uni. Ser.	Surrey . . .	1,097	.	1,000
b. 1816, s. 1861, m. 1st 1847,	Lincoln . .	771	.	1,736
2nd 1852.				
		4,870	.	7,636

    Served in Royal Artillery and on board ship during blockade of
North Coast of Spain (Carlist War).

BARRETT-LENNARD, Sir Thomas, Bart., of Belhus, Rom-
    ford, &c.

		acres.		g. an. val·
Coll. Peterhouse, Cam.	Essex . . .	3,691	.	5,529
Club. Brooks's, Uni. Univ.	Norfolk . .	2,124	.	1,474
b. 1826, s. 1857, m. 1853.	Suffolk . . .	570	.	741
	Co. Monaghan	7,920	.	10,908
	Co. Fermanagh	107	.	127
		14,412	.	18,779

    Lady Lennard has a rental of 20*l.* included here.

** LENNOX, Lord Alexander Francis Charles Gordon, of
    21, Pont St., S.W.

		acres.		g. an. val·
Club. Carlton, White's.				
b. 1825, s. (*jur. uxor.*), 1878,	Lancashire .	4,695	.	4,670
m. 1863.	York . . .	604	.	214
Sat for Shoreham. Served in R.H. Gds.				
Not inclusive of coal rents.		5,299	.	4,884

    See "Abingdon" and "O'Hagan."

** HANBURY-KINCAID-LENNOX, Hon. Charles Spencer
    Bateman, of Lennox Castle, Lennoxtown, N.B.

		acres.		g. an. val·
Coll. Eton, Brase., and All-	Stirling . . .	7,606	.	8,313
Souls, Oxon.	Dumbarton .	80	.	140
Club. Arthur's, Carlton, Turf.				
b. 1827, s. 1861 (*jur. uxor.*), m. 1861.		7,686	.	8,453

    Served in 2nd L.G. Sat for Herefordshire and Leominster.
        Exclusive of a mineral rent of 610*l.* in Stirling.

		acres		g. an. val·
* LELY, W. G., of Arnoldfield.	Linc., Staffs.	2,400	.	4,000
LENDRUM, J., of Magheracross.	Tyr., Fer.	3,989	.	2,582

*** MACALPINE-LENY, WILLIAM, of Dalswinton, Dumfries, N.B., &c.

			acres.		g. an. val.
Coll.	Eton, Ch. Ch. Oxon.	Dumfries . .	5,724	.	4,282
Club.	Carl., A. & N., New Ed.	Kirkcudbright	1,219	.	167
b. 1839, s. 1867, m. 1869.					
	Served in 15th Hussars.		6,943	.	4,449

LESLIE, CHARLES STEPHEN, of Slindon House, Arundel, &c.

		acres.		g. an. val.
b. 1832, s. 1870, m. 1853.	Aberdeen . .	8,940	.	7,388
	Derby . . .	4,878	.	6,909
	Sussex . . .	4,350	.	3,707
	Gloucester .	822	.	818
		18,990	.	18,822

** LESLIE, J. EDMUND DOUGLAS, of Leslie Hill, Ballymoney.

		acres.		g. an. val.
b. 1828, s. 1881.	Antrim . . .	7,428	.	5,449

** LESLIE, SIR JOHN, BART., of Glasslough, Co. Monaghan.

			acres.		g. an. val.
Coll.	Harrow, Ch. Ch. Ox.	Monaghan .	13,674	.	11,540
Club.	White's, Trav., Carl.,	Donegal . .	28,827	.	3,473
	Ath., Sack. St.	Tyrone . . .	1,103	.	913
b. 1822, s. 1831, m. 1856.		Fermanagh .	877	.	653
	Served in 1st Life Guards.				
	Sat for Co. Monaghan.		44,481	.	16,579

*** CRAWFORD-LESLIE, MRS., of Rothie., Aberdeen, N.B.

		acres.		g. an. val.
s. 1877, m. 1845.	Aberdeen . .	7,164	.	5,237

LESLIE, MRS., of Ballibay House, Ballibay.

		acres.		g. an. val.
s. 1838, m. 1st 1827, 2nd 1844.	Co. Monaghan	5,556	.	5,134

LEONARD, J., of Macetown. Dub., Kild., Mea. . . . . 2,101 . 2,184

LESLIE, J., of Ballyward. Donegal, Down . 3,051 . 2,141

** LESLIE, Mrs., of Warthill, Aberdeen, &c., N.B.

		acres.		g. an. val.
s. 1880, m. 1848.	Aberdeen . .	4,164	.	4,560

This family have held Warthill in direct male line since 1518.

** L'ESTRANGE, Hamon, of Hunstanton Hall, King's Lynn.

Coll. Eton, Ch. Ch. Oxon.	Norfolk . . .	7,803	.	12,413
Club. St. James's, Ox. and Cam., Brooks's.				
b. 1840, s. 1862, m. 1866.				

Was in H.M. Diplomatic Service as Secretary.

LETHBRIDGE, Sir Wroth Acland, Bart., of Sandhill Park, Taunton, &c.

Coll. Rugby.	Somerset . .	3,420	.	6,515
Club. Army & Navy, Gun.	Dorset . . .	249	.	261
b. 1831, s. 1873, m. 1861.	Cambridge . .	54	.	148
Served in Rifle Brigade.	Devon . . .	84	.	83
		3,807	.	7,007

LEVEN & MELVILLE, Earl of, Glenferness, Dunphail, N.B.

Coll. Eton, Trin. Cam.	Nairn . . .	7,805	.	1,317
Club. Carlton, Pall Mall.	Fife	1,019	.	1,761
b. 1817, s. 1876.				
		8,824	.	3,078

** LEVETT, Col. Theophilus John, of Wichnor Park, Burton.

Club. Carlton.	Stafford . . .	2,700	.	4,500
b. 1829, s. 1853, m. 1855.	Warwick . .	500	.	1,000
Served in 1st Life Guards.				
Sits for Lichfield.		3,200	.	5,500

LEVINGE, Sir Richard George Augustus, Bart., of Knock drin Castle, Mullingar, Co. Westmeath.

Club. Army and Navy.	Co. Westmeath	5,017	.	3,373
b. 1811, s. 1848, m. 1st 1849,	Huntingdon .	1	.	4
2nd 1870.				
Served in 5th Drn. Guards & 43rd Foot.		5,018	.	3,377
Sat for Westmeath.				

LESLIE (late), W., of Nethermuir.	Aberd.	2,299	.	2,960

** LEWIS, Charles Edward, of St. Pierre, Chepstow.

		acres.	*g. an. val.*
Coll. Rugby.	Monmouth .	4,504 .	6,059
Club. Boodle's, Jun. Carl.			
b. 1830, s. 1872, m. 1858.			

LEWIS, Charles William Mansel, of Stradley, Llanelly.

Coll. Eton, Ball. Oxon.	Carmarthen .	3,161 .	4,276
Club. Uni. Univ., Jun. Ath.			
b. 1845, s. 1872, m. 1875.			

** LEWIS, Rev. Sir Gilbert Frankland, Bart., of Harpton
      Court, Kington.

Coll. Eton, Mag. Cam.	Radnor . .	10,000 .	7,000
Club. Athenæum.	Hereford . .	6 .	5
b. 1808, s. 1863, m. 1843.			
		10,006 .	7,005

** LEWIS, John Delaware, of Membland Hall, Ivybridge, &c.

Coll. Eton, Trin. Cam.	Devon . . .	1,923 .	2,216
Club. Reform, Union, Gar.,	Hants . . .	2,649 .	1,711
Devonshire.			
b. 1828, m. 1868. Sat for Devonport.		4,572 .	3,927

Mr. L. has since 1876 sold in Devon and bought in Hants.

LEWIS (Daughters of the late W. W.), of Newhouse, Cardiff.

s. 1871.	Glamorgan .	3,429 .	5,489
	Monmouth .	120 .	31
		3,549 .	5,520

LEWES, W. P., of Llysnewydd. Carm., Card.	3,188 .	2,267
LEWIS, H., of Greenmeadow. Glamorgan.	2,882 .	2,208
LEWIS, Henry Owen, of Inniskeen. Monaghan, Meath, Longford, Dublin . . .	3,773 .	2,863
LEWIS, J. L., of Henllan. Carm., Pem. .	2,603 .	2,434
LEWIS, Mrs. M. A., of Lanaeron. Cardigan	4,397 .	2,591

** LEYCESTER, RAFE OSWALD, of Toft Hall, Knutsford.

			acres.	g. an. val.
Coll.	Eton, Ch. Ch.	Cheshire . .	3,825 .	7,040
	Oxon.	Carnarvon . .	132 .	260
Club.	Arthur's.	Lancashire. .	13 .	2,700
b. 1844, s. 1851, m. 1867.				
			3,970 .	10,000

LEYLAND, THOMAS, of Haggerstone Castle, Beal.

Club.	Jun. Uni. Ser.	Northumberlnd.	17,644 .	16,198
b. 1812, m. 1840.		Lancashire .	3,426 .	36,781
			21,070 .	52,979

Served in 15th Hussars and 2nd Life Guards.

MR. LEYLAND has but a rental of 1,821*l.* in Lancashire ; the rest of the property in that county is owned by MRS. NAYLOR LEYLAND, his eldest son's wife.

LICHFIELD, EARL OF, Shugborough Park, Stafford.

Club.	White's, Travellers',	Stafford . .	21,433 .	41,560
	Brooks's.	Suffolk . . .	97 .	482
b. 1825, s. 1854, m. 1855.				
			21,530 .	42,042

Was in the Foreign Office.   Sat for Lichfield.   " Figures absurd and unaccountable."—LD. L.

LIDDELL, GEORGE WILLIAM, of Sutton House, Hull.

b. 1867, s. 1873.	York,N.&E.R.	4,616 .	2,896
	Westmoreland	147 .	124
		4,763 .	3,020

LILFORD, LORD, Lilford Hall, Oundle, &c.

Coll.	Harrow, Ch. Ch. Ox.	Northampton .	7,998 .	11,618
Club.	Carl., Trav., Garrick,	Lancashire .	7,552 .	14,776
	Oriental.	Huntingdon .	4 .	4
b. 1833, s. 1861, m. 1859.				
			15,554 .	26,398

HAMPTON-LEWIS, THOMAS L., of Bodior.

Anglesea, Denbigh, York	2,454 .	2,141
* LEY, J. H. F., of Trehill. Devon . . .	2,996 .	4,500
LIDDELL, C., of Peasemarsh. Suss., Kent	2,523 .	3,315

** LIMERICK, Earl of, Dromore Castle, Limerick.

		acres.	g. an. val.
Club. Carlton, Arthur's.	Limerick . .	4,083 .	13,680
b. 1840, s. 1866, m. 1862,	Co. Clare . .	1,550 .	769
2nd 1877.	Co. Cork . .	76 .	537
		5,709 .	14,986

Served in Rifle Brigade.
Inclusive of the rental of nearly 3,000 acres let on long leases and returned in the lessees' names.

LINDOW, Jonas, of Eben Hall, Egremont, &c.

Coll. Queen's, Oxon.   Cumberland .   4,032 .   4,280
b. 1847, s. 1878.

BURNS-LINDOW, Jonas Lindow, of Irton House, White-haven.

Club. Conservative.   Cumberland .   5,934 .   6,790
b. 1837, m. 1867.

LINDSAY, Sir Coutts, Bart., of Balcarres, Colinsburgh, Fife, N.B.

Club. Travellers', Garrick,	Fife	4,672 .	9,619
Guards.	Hereford . .	616 .	830
b. 1824, s. 1837, m. 1864.		5,288 .	10,449

Served in Grenadier Guards.   5,288 .   10,449
Lady Lindsay has 596*l.* of the Hereford property.

** LOYD-LINDSAY, Sir Robert James, K.C.B., V.C., of Lockinge House, Wantage, &c.

Coll. Eton.   Berks . . .   20,528 .   26,492
Club. Gds., Trav., Carl., Farmers', Ath., J. Cons., U. Serv.
b. 1832, m. 1858.
Served in Scots Guards, as A.D.C. to Gen. Simpson in the Crimea, is Ex. Eq. to H.R.H. the Prince of Wales. Was Financial Secretary for War. Sits for Berks.

LIMERICK, John, of Union Hall. Cork	8,181 .	2,260
SANDYS-LINDESAY, J. E., of Loughry.		
Tyr.	2,821 .	2,645
LINDSAY, Earl of. Fife	2,205 .	5,548

*** LINDSEY, EARL OF, Uffington House, Stamford. 🐍.

			acres.		g. an. val.
Coll.	Eton.	Lincoln . . .	4,790	.	9,286
Club.	Carlton.				

b. 1815, s. 1877, m. 1854.　Served in Grenadier Guards.

** LINDSEY, JOHN (of Gortavale), E. Woodhay, Newbury.

Club.	Army and Navy.	Tyrone . . .	3,749	.	2,931
	Jun. United Ser.	Hants . . .	114	.	304

b. 1813, s. 18—, m. 1849.

Served in 2nd Life Guards.　　　　3,863 . 3,235

** LINDSEY, MISS, of Hollymount House, Ballinrobe, Co.
🌳　　Mayo.

s. 1874.　　　　　　　Co. Mayo . . 5,376 . 4,154

CANN-LIPPINCOTT, ROBERT, of Over Court, Almondsbury,
　　　Bristol.

Coll.	Eton, Ch. Ch. Oxon.	Gloucester . .	3,554	.	6,877

b. 1810, s. 1831, m. 1832, 2nd 1854.

*** LISBURNE, EARL OF, Crosswood, Aberystwith, &c.

Coll.	Eton, Ch. Ch. Oxon.	Cardigan . .	42,720	.	13,616
Club.	Carl., Conservative.	Carmarthen .	40	.	40
	Arthur's, Boodle's.	Middlesex .	1	.	20

b. 1836, s. 1873, m. 1st 1858,
　　　　　　2nd 1878.　　　　42,761 . 13,676

*** LISGAR, THE LADY, and TURVILLE, SIR FRANCIS
　　　CHARLES FORTESCUE, K.C.M.B., Lisgar Ho., Baillie-
　　　borough, Co. Cavan, &c.

Club.	Arthur's.	Co. Cavan . .	8,924	.	7,007
Lady L. s. 1876, m. 1st 1835,		Oxford . . .	1,498	.	2,457
	2nd 1878.	Leicester . .	699	.	1,509
Sir F. T. b. 1831, s. 1859,		Northampton .	292	.	485
m. 1878.					

　　　　　　　　　　　　　11,413 . 11,458
Was P. Sec. to Lord Lisgar in Ionian Is., N.S. Wales, and Canada.
LADY LISGAR's estate (Cavan) only corrected.

*** LISLE, MRS., of Acton House, Alnwick.

b. 1797, s. 1877, m. 1821.　Northumberland 9,929 . 4,684

LISMORE, Viscount, Shanbally, Clogheen, Co. Tipperary.

			acres.		*g. an. val.*
Coll.	Oriel, Oxon.	Tipperary . .	34,945	.	13,089
Club.	Travellers', White's,	Co. Cork . .	6,067	.	2,555
	Kildare Street.	Limerick . .	1,194	.	710
b. 1815, s. 1857, m. 1839.					
	Served in 17th Lancers.		42,206	.	16,354

*** CUNLIFFE-LISTER, Samuel, of Swinton Park, Bedale, &c.

Club. Devonshire.	York, N.R.	.	24,240	.	11,749
b. 1815, s. 1852, m. 1854.	Do., W.R.	.	329	.	5,504
			24,569	.	17,253

The N.R. estate only corrected.

** LISTOWEL, Earl of, K.P., Convamore, Mallow, Co. Cork.

Coll. Eton.	Kerry . . .	30,000	.	16,000
Club. White's, Brooks's.	Cork . . .	5,541	.	3,500
b. 1833, s. 1856, m. 1865.				
Served in Scots Fus. Gds. in Crimean		35,541	.	19,500

War (wounded at Alma).

*** LIVESEY, Joseph Montague, of Stourton Hall, Horncastle.

Coll. Eton.	Lincoln . . .	5,571	.	10,225
Club. Orntl., Ref., Dev.	Lancashire .	———	.	1,400
b. 1851, s. 1854, m. 1872.				
		5,571	.	11,625

LLANOVER, The Lady, Llanover, Abergavenny, &c.

s. 1867, m. 1823.	Monmouth .	6,312	.	6,652
	Glamorgan .	221	.	1,484
		6,533	.	8,136

LISTER, G. S., of Hirst Priory, Linc., Yk., Notts.	2,074 .	2,864
LISTER, M. H., of Burwell Park. Lincoln .	2,116 .	2,786
LITTLEDALE, W. F., of Whaley, Wic., Arm., Meath	4,583 .	2,287
LIVINGSTONE, H. D., of Westport, Mayo, Galway	2,228 .	2,816
LLEWELLYN, G., of Baglan. Glamorgan .	2,846 .	2,228

DILLWYN-LLEWELYN, John, of Penllergare, Swansea.

		acres.	g. an. val.
Club. Athenæum.	Glamorgan .	8,797	6,737
b. 1810, s. 1855, m. 1833.	Brecon . . .	3,587	1,848
	Carmarthen .	2,483	1,354
		14,867	9,939

** LLOYD, Arthur Philip, of Leaton Knolls, Shrewsbury.

		acres.	g. an. val.
Coll. Eton, Ch. Ch. Oxon.	Salop . . .	3,617	4,881
Club. Carlton, Arthur's.	Montgomery .	1,157	1,410
b. 1833, m. 1863.			
		4,774	6,291

** LLOYD, Guy, of Croghan House, Boyle, Co. Roscommon.

		acres.	g. an. val.
Coll. Trinity, Cambridge.	Co. Roscommon	7,302	4,238
Club. National, Sackville	Co. Leitrim .	1,262	738
Street, Dublin.			
b. 1833, s. 1860, m. 1865.		8,564	4,976

*** LLOYD, Sir Marteine Owen Mowbray, Bart., of Bron-wydd, Llandissil, &c.

		acres.	g. an. val.
Club. Arthur's.	Pembroke . .	3,738	3,049
b. 1851, s. 1877, m. 1878.	Cardigan . .	2,150	1,544
	Carmarthen .	2,030	1,944
	Glamorgan . .	28	60
		7,946	6,597

Sir Marteine as Lord of the Barony of Kemes holds certain rights over 30,000 acres in Pembroke worth 70*l.* per annum.

LLOYD, Edward Owen Vaughan, of Rhagatt, Corwen, &c.

		acres.	g. an. val.
Coll. Eton, Oxon.	Denbigh . .	3,083	2,725
Club. Beaconsfield, Jun.	Merioneth . .	1,280	792
Carlton.			
b. 1857, s. 1878.		4,363	3,517

		acres.	g. an. val.
LLOYD, C., of Brunant. Carm., Card. .		6,004	2,606
LLOYD, G. Whitelocke, of Strancally. Waterford, Cork, Limerick, York, Essex		2,942	2,441
HARRIS-LLOYD, Capt., Carmarthen . .		3,194	2,329
LLOYD, H., of Plâs-cil-y-bebyll. Glamorgan		2,887	2,263

** LLOYD, Richard Thomas, of Aston Hall, Oswestry, &c.

			acres.		*g. an. val.*
Club. Carl., White's, Grds.	Salop	. . .	3,434	.	5,658
b. 1820, s. 1866, m. 1852.	Essex	. . .	544	.	1,114
Served in Grenadier Guards.					
			3,978	.	6,772

LEWIS-LLOYD, Robert, of Nantgwillt, Rhayader.

Coll. Eton, Magd. Cam.	Cardigan	. .	3,521	.	1,393
Club. Uni. University.	Brecon .	. .	2,084	.	378
b. 1836, s. 1870, m. 1865.	Radnor .	. .	1,892	.	796
	Pembroke	. .	399	.	478
			7,896	.	3,045

** LLOYD, William, of Rockville, Drumsna, Co. Roscommon.

Coll. Chelt., St. John's,	Co. Galway	.	300	.	405
Cambridge.	Roscommon	.	7,394	.	4,438
b. 1858, s. 1870.					
			7,694	.	4,843

LOCKHART, Gen., C.B., of Camnethan, Wishaw, N.B.

b. 1820, s. 1873, m. 1861. Lanark . . . 4,422 . 5,250
  Served in 78th Foot. Was in Persian Campaign, Indian
Mutiny, Lucknow, Bareilly, &c.

MACDONALD-LOCKHART, Sir Simon, Bart., of Lee Castle,
  Lanark, N.B., &c.

Coll. Eton.	Lanark .	. .	31,566	.	21,050
Club. Carlton, St. James's.	Edinburgh .	.	700	.	1,327
b. 1849, s. 1870.	Selkirk .	. .	8	.	10

Serves in 1st Life Guards.   32,274 . 22,387
  Exclusive of 869*l.* for minerals in Lanarkshire.

LLOYD, L. L., of Glangwilly. Carmarthen 3,840 . 2,249
LLOYD, T. E., of Coedmore. Card.,
  Carm., Pem. . . . . 4,872 . 2,674

****** ELLIOTT - LOCKHART, William, of Borthwickbrae, Hawick, N.B., &c.

			acres.	*g. an. val.*
Coll. Harrow.	Lanark . . .		2,280 .	2,554
Club. Jun. United Service.	Roxburgh . .		1,884 .	1,046
b. 1833, s. 1878, m. 1866.	Selkirk . . .		2,978 .	1,042
			7,142 .	4,642

Served in 26th and 74th Foot.

Mr. Lockhart has land in Lanark rented at 250*l.* in common with "others."

** LODER, Robert, of Whittlebury Park, Towcester, &c.

		acres.	*g. an. val.*
Coll. Emmanuel, Cam.	Northampton .	4,687 .	6,413
Club. Carlton.	Bucks . . .	2,154 .	2,445
b. 1823, s. 1871, m. 1847.	Sussex . . .	1,700 .	568
	Wilts . . .	1,700 .	2,101
Sits for Shoreham.		10,241 .	11,527

* EVANS-LOMBE, Henry, of Bylaugh Park, East Dereham, &c.

Coll. Corpus, Cam.	Norfolk . . .	13,832 .	17,789

Club. Carlton.   b. 1819, s. 1878, m. 1849.

LONDESBOROUGH, Lord, Londesborough Lodge, Scarborough, &c. ⚓.

Coll. Eton.	York, N.E. and		
Club. Brooks's, Turf, Trav.,	W.R. . .	52,655 .	67,876
Garrick.			

b. 1834, s. 1860, m. 1863.   Sat for Beverley and for Scarborough.

LOFFT, R. E., of Troston Hall. Suffolk .	2,919 .	3,421
LOMAX, J., of Clayton Hall. Lancashire .	2,988 .	6,291
LOMAX, T. O., of Bodfach. Mont., Lanc.	2,825 .	2,922

LONDONDERRY, Marquis of, K.P., Seaham Hall, Sunderland, &c.

			acres.	g. an. val.
Coll.	Eton, Ball. Oxon.	Durham . .	12,823 .	56,825
Club.	Carl., Trav., White's,	Montgomery .	7,399 .	4,330
	Windham, U. Ser.,	Merioneth . .	2,685 .	1,752
	St. James's, Sack. St.	Co. Down . .	23,554 .	34,484
		Londonderry .	2,189 .	1,542
		Donegal . .	1,673 .	1,185

b. 1821, s. 1854 and 1872, m. 1846.

Served in 1st Life Guards.   50,323 . 100,118

Sat for N. Durham.

** LONG, Fortescue Walter Kellett, of Dunston Hall, Norwich.

Coll.	Ch. Ch. Oxon.	Norfolk . . .	3,555 .	5,600

b. 1843, s. 1874.

** LONG, Mrs., of Bromley Hill, Kent.

s. 1881, m. 1866.	Fife	2,338 .	2,988
	Lincoln . . .	1,104 .	1,769
	Bucks . . .	331 .	467
	Cambridge . .	120 .	203
	Kent . . .	24 .	136

     3,917 . 5,563

** LONG, Walter Hume, of Wraxall, Trowbridge.

Coll.	Harrow, Ch. Ch. Ox.	Wilts . . .	13,829 .	22,034
Club.	White's, Nat., Carl.,	Somerset . .	841 .	1,018
	Turf.	Merioneth . .	688 .	95
b. 1854, s. 1875, m. 1878.		Montgomery .	46 .	66

Sits for N. Wilts.   15,404 . 23,213

This fam. has held (in continuous m. succ.) Wraxall since 1470.

** LONG, Walter Jervis, of Preshaw Ho., Bishop's Waltham, &c.

Coll.	Oriel, Oxon.	Hants . . .	3,225 .	2,531
b. 1816, s. 1871, m. 1839.		Somerset . .	1,573 .	4,452

     4,798 . 6,983

*** LONG, William Beeston, of Hurt's Hall, Saxmundham.

			acres.	*g. an. val.*
Coll. Har., Ch. Ch. Oxon.	Suffolk .	. .	2,850 .	3,778
Club. Boodle's, St. James'.	Cambridge .	.	784 .	1,012
b. 1833, s. 1875, m. 1859.				
			3,634 .	4,790

LONGFIELD, Mountifort John Courtenay, of Cas. Mary, Cloyne.

Coll. Eton, B.N.C. Oxon.	Co. Cork .	.	10,813 .	7,885
b. 1858, s. 1864. Serves in 2nd L. Guards.				

* LONGFIELD, Richard, of Longueville, Mallow, Co. Cork.

Coll. Oswestry, St. Jo., Cam.	Co. Cork .	.	11,239 .	4,540
Club. Carl., Kild. St.	Limerick .	.	1,881 .	1,514
b. 1802, s. 1842, m. 1st 1832,				
2nd 1841.			13,120 .	6,054
Sat for Co. Cork.				

** LONGFORD, Earl of, G.C.B., Pakenham Hall, Castle Pollard, Co. Westmeath.

Coll. Winchester.	Dublin .	. .	420 .	31,713
Club. Carl., White's, Uni.	Westmeath	.	15,014 .	9,384
Ser., Sack. St.	Longford .	.	4,555 .	6,101
b. 1819, s. 1860, m. 1862.				
			19,989 .	47,198

Served as Adjutant-General in the Crimea and in India, Under Secretary of State for War, and is a General in the Army.

DAMES-LONGWORTH, Francis Travers, Q.C., of Glynwood, Athlone, &c.

Coll. Trinity, Dublin.	Roscommon	.	1,192 .	593
Club. Kildare St.	Westmeath	.	6,547 .	3,665
b. 1834, s. 187—, m. 1860.	Galway .	. .	3,271 .	1,971
	King's Co.	.	2,422 .	459
	Lancashire	.	7 .	43
			13,439 .	6,731

LONSDALE, Earl of, Lowther Castle, Penrith, &c. ♣.

			acres.	g. an. val.
Coll.	Eton.	Cumberland .	28,228	42,818
Club.	Carlton.	Westmoreland	39,229	27,141
b. 1857, s. 1881, m. 1878.		Rutland . .	493	1,251
		Lancashire .	115	123
			68,065	71,333

** LOPES, Sir Massey, Bart., of Maristow, Roborough, &c.

			acres.	g. an. val.
Coll.	Winc., Oriel, Oxon.	Devon . . .	11,977	9,320
Club.	Carlton, Conser., St. Stephen's.	Wilts . . .	126	1,348
b. 1818, s. 1854, m. 1st 1854, 2nd 1874.			12,103	10,668

Was a Lord of the Admiralty. Sat for Westbury. Sits for South Devon.

*** LOTHIAN, Marquis of, K.T., Newbattle Abbey, Dalkeith, N.B., &c.

			acres.	g. an. val.
Coll.	Eton, New, Oxon.	Norfolk . . .	8,073	9,107
Club.	Carlton, Travellers'.	Roxburgh . .	19,740	23,684
b. 1833, s. 1870, m. 1865.		Midlothian .	4,548	12,412
			32,361	45,203

Serves as Lord Privy Seal of Scotland, was in H.M. Diplomatic Service, and served on the Staff through the Persian War. Exclusive of 6,296*l.* for mines, and inclusive of 8,986*l.* in Norfolk owned by the Marchioness Dowager.

LOUDOUN, Earl of, Rowallan Castle, Kilmarnock, N.B.

			acres.	g. an. val.
Club.	Carlton, White's.	Ayr	18,638	15,286
b. 1855, s. 1873, m. 1880.		Leicester . .	10,174	17,722
		Derby . . .	2,750	5,212
		York, W.R. .	1,348	1,757
			32,910	39,977

This includes Lord Donington's property, which is hopelessly mixed up therewith in the return, but is exclusive of 2,259*l.* mine rent in Ayrshire.

LOUTH, Lord, Louth Hall, Drogheda.

			acres.		*g. an. val.*
Coll.	Eton.	Co. Louth . .	3,578	.	3,983
Club.	Jun. Uni. Ser., Wand.,	Co. Meath . .	161	.	150
	R.T.Y.C., S.G.Y.C.,	Monaghan . .	178	.	131
	Uni. Ser., Dub.	Galway . . .	4	.	2
b. 1832, s. 1849, m. 1867		Somerset . .	178	.	338
and 1877.					
Served in 24th Foot and 79th Foot.			4,099	.	4,604

LADY LOUTH owns the Meath Estate.

*** LOVAT, Lord, Beaufort Castle, Beauly, N.B.

Club.	Trav., Brooks's,	Inverness .	181,791	.	30,300
	St. George's. b. 1828, s. 1875, m. 1866.				

** LOVELACE, Earl of, East Horsley Towers, Leatherhead, Surrey, &c.

Coll.	Eton, Trin. Cam.	Surrey . . .	10,214	.	12,384
Club.	Athenæum, Brooks's.	Leicester . .	4,568	.	7,838
b. 1805, s. 1833, m. 1st 1835,		Somerset . .	3,008	.	1,561
2nd 1865.		Warwick . .	663	.	1,028
		Devon . . .	28	.	4
			18,481	.	22,815

LOW, Francis Wise, of Kilshane, Co. Tipperary.

Coll.	St. John's, Cam.	Tipperary . .	4,949	.	4,121
Club.	Kildare Street.	Co. Cork . .	182	.	146
b. 181–, s. 185–, m. 1st 1860,					
2nd 1864.			5,131	.	4,267

LOVETT, P. C., of Liscombe. Bucks . .	2,000	.	3,200
IMPEY-LOVIBOND, Col., of Riffhams.			
Essex, Kent, Gloucester	2,509	.	3,117
LOW, G. P., of Sunvale. Limerick, Cork .	3,336	.	2,181
LOWE, Col., of Gosfield, Essex	2,698	.	4,792

** DRURY-LOWE, William Drury Nathaniel, of Locko
    Park, Derby.   *acres.*   *g. an. val.*

		acres.		g. an. val.
Club. Carlton.	Derby . . .	4,680	.	10,887
b. 1828, s. 1877, m. 1876.	Denbigh . .	60	.	73

    Served in 11th Hussars & 3rd L. Dragoons 4,740 . 10,960

*** LOWNDES, George Alan, of Barrington Hall, Harlow.

Coll. Trin. Cambridge	Essex . . .	3,634	.	4,379
Club. Carlton.	Derby . . .	16	.	8
b. 1829, s. 1840, m. 1st 1856,				
2nd 1864.		3,650	.	4,387

** SELBY-LOWNDES, William, of Whaddon, Stony Strat-
    ford, &c.

Club. Carlton.   Bucks . . .   7,537 . 11,923
b. 1807, s. 1840, m. 1st 1833,
         2nd 1854.

** LOWRY, Robert William, of Pomeroy House, Co. Tyrone.

Coll. Eton, Bras. Oxon.   Co. Tyrone . 8,158 . 3,848
Club. Eton & Har., Sackville St.
b. 1816, s. 1869, m. 1852 and 1880.

    Mr. Lowry has purchased additional property since the return
(not here entered).

LOWTHER, Sir Charles Hugh, Bart., of Swillington House,
    Leeds, &c.

b. 1803, s. 1868, m. 1834.   York,N.&W.R. 6,085 . 18,572

LOWNDES, E. C., of Cas. Combe. Wilts,				
Derby	2,833	.	4,479
LOWNDES, W., of The Bury. Bucks, Herts	2,284	.	3,118
LOWRY, James Corry, of Rockdale. Tyro.	3,141	.	2,348
LOWTHER, W. G., of Shrigley. Cheshire.	2,118	.	3,547

LOYD, Lewis, of Monks Orchard, West Wickham, Surrey, &c.

			acres.	g. an. val.
Coll. Eton, Trin. Cam.	Cheshire	. .	1,755 .	3,035
Club. Carl., Ath., Oxford	Surrey .	. .	1,058 .	1,953
and Cambridge.	Kent .	. .	286 .	1,360
b. 1811, s. 1863. m. 1845.	Lancashire .	.	138 .	2,447
			3,237 .	8,795

LUCAN, Earl of, G.C.B., Laleham House, Chertsey, &c. ⚓.

Coll. Westminster.	Co. Mayo .	.	60,570 .	12,940
Club. Carlton, United Ser.	Dublin .	. .	32 .	179
b. 1800, s. 1839, m. 1829.	Surrey .	. .	159 .	319
Sat for Co. Mayo.	Middlesex .	.	984 .	2,329
	Cheshire	. .	1,191 .	1,656
			62,936 .	17,423

Served in 8th Dragoons and 1st Life Guards, commanded the Cavalry in the Crimea, was wounded at Balaclava, is a General in the Army; he served with the Russians against the Turks in the Balkan Campaign of 1829.

** LUCAS, Edward Scudamore, of Cas. Shane, Monaghan, &c.

Coll. Eton, Ch. Ch. Oxon.	Co. Monaghan		9,955 .	7,934
Club. Brooks's, Sac. St.	Hereford .	.	5,706 .	5,000
b. 1853, s. 1874.	Monmouth .	.	804 .	349
			16,465 .	13,283

Most of the English property is his mother's.

** LUCAS, Richard, of Edithweston Hall, Stamford, &c.

Club. Army and Navy.	Rutland .	.	1,631 .	2,689
b. 1820, s. 1846, m. 1847.	York,E.&W.R.		1,034 .	1,985
	Lincoln .	.	982 .	1,703
Served in 2nd Life Guards.			3,647 .	6,377

LOXDALE, J., of Castlehill. Card., Staffs.	4,915 .	2,604
LUCAS, T., of Ashstead	2,710 .	3,085
*** LUCY, Mrs. E. B., of Duxbury. Lanc., Dur.	2,672 .	4,519

LUCY, HENRY SPENCER, of Charlecote Park, Warwick.

		acres.	*g. an. val.*
Coll. Ch. Ch. Oxon.	Warwick . .	5,765 .	11,927
Club. Arthur's, Gun.	Gloucester . .	118 .	160
b. 1830, s. 1851, m. 1865.			
		5,883 .	12,087

** SANDYS-LUMSDAINE, EDWIN ROBERT JOHN, of Blanerne, Edrom, N.B., &c.

b. 1864, s. 1873.	Berwick . .	2,603 .	2,364
	Fife	428 .	1,181
		3,031 .	3,545

** LUMSDEN, HUGH GORDON, of Auchendoir, Lumsden, N.B.

Club. Raleigh, Union.	Aberdeen . .	15,499 .	6,886
b. 1850, s. 1859, m. 1874.			

** LUMSDEN, WILLIAM HARRY, of Balmedie, Abn., N.B.

Coll. Magdalen, Oxon.	Aberdeen . .	7,397 .	6,728
Club. Junior Carlton.			
b. 1852, s. 1875, m. 1877.			

LUND, JAMES, of Malsis Hall, Crosshills, Leeds, &c.

b. 1829.	Yorkshire . .	3,343 .	5,609

** LURGAN, LORD, Brownlow House, Lurgan.

Coll. Eton.	Armagh . .	15,166 .	20,424
Club. Brooks's, Gds., Whi.,	Co. Down . .	110 .	165
Bachelors', Ulster.			
b. 1858, s. 1882.		15,276 .	20,589
Served in 36th Foot. Now in Gren. Gds.			

LUDLOW (late), of Heywood Ho. Wilts, Som.	2,257 .	4,308
LUMSDEN, MRS., of Cushnie. Aberdeen	5,000 .	2,588

** LUTLEY, John Habington Barneby, of Brockhampton, Worcester. 🌣.
                                                        acres.   *g. an. val.*
Coll. Eton, Ch. Ch. Oxon.   Hereford . .   3,061 .   5,104
Club. Carlton, Junior Carlton.
b. 1840, s. 1846, m. 1864.

** LUTTRELL, George Fownes, of Dunster Castle, Somerset, &c.

Coll. Eton, Ch. Ch. Oxon.   Somerset . .   15,374 .   21,882
Club. Devonshire, Ox. and   Devon . . .   154 .   118
   Cam., Boodle's.   _____
b. 1826, s. 1867, m. 1852.   15,528 .   22,000

*** AMES-LYDE, Lionel Neville Frederick, of Thornham Cottage, King's Lynn, &c.

Coll. Eton.   Norfolk . . .   1,878 .   2,586
Club. Guards.   Herts . . .   1,732 .   2,056
b. 1850, s. 1873, m. 1873. Beds . . .   482 .   626
                            Somerset . .   60 .   90
   Served in Grenadier Guards.   _____
                                              4,152 .   5,358

LYELL, Leonard, of Kinnordy, Kirriemuir, N.B., &c.

b. 1850, s. 1875 and 1876, Forfar . . .   8,313 .   10,363
m. 1874.
   6,040*l.* of these rents are returned as owned by "Trustees of late Charles Lyell" "and others."

*** LYNCH, John Wilson, of Duras, Kinvara, Co. Galway, &c.

Coll. Ushaw, Liege.   Co. Clare . .   3,106 .   1,056
Club. J. U. S., U. Ser., Dub. Co. Galway .   5,789 .   2,255
b. 1831, s. 1864, m. 1865.   _____
                                              8,895 .   3,311

LYLE, Rev. J., of Knockintarn. Londdrry.   3,071 .   2,772

LYON, Major William, of Balentore Cas., Kirriemuir, N.B., &c.

		acres.	g. an. val.
Club. Travellers'.	Forfar . . .	6,888 .	1,427
b. 180—, m. 1860.	Sussex . . .	466 .	3,111
Served in 8th Hussars.			
Sat for Seaford.		7,354 .	4,538

LYSTER, The Lady Charlotte Barbara, Rowton Castle, Shrewsbury (res. Tunbridge Wells).

b. 1799, s. 1863, m. 1824.	Salop . . .	6,297 .	5,642

*** LYTTELTON, Lord, Hagley Hall, Stourbridge. ⚬.

Coll. Eton, Trin. Cam.	Worcester . .	5,907 .	9,170
Club. Brooks's.	Hereford . .	1,032 .	1,093
b. 1842, s. 1876, m. 1878.			
Sat for E. Worcestershire.		6,939 .	10,263

** LYTTON, Earl of, Knebworth Park, Stevenage.

Coll. Harrow, Bonn.	Hertford . .	4,863 .	5,366

Club. St. Jas., Carl., Ath., Whi., Marl., Empire.
b. 1831, s. 1873, m. 1864.
   Served as Attaché at Washington, Florence, Paris, the Hague and Vienna ; as Cons.-Gen. at Belgrade and on Special Service in Servia ; as Sec. Legation at Copenhagen, Athens, Lisbon, and Madrid ; as Sec. of Embassy at Vienna and Paris, Minister at Lisbon and Viceroy and Gov.-Gen. of India.

LYVEDEN, The Lady, Farming Woods, Thrapstone, &c.

s. 1873, m. 1823.	Northampton .	4,138 .	5,529

** MACADAM, Frederick, of Craigengillan, Dalmellington, N.B.

b. 1864, s. 1878.	Ayr	15,000 .	5,000
	Kirkcudbright	20,000 .	4,000
Exc. of 2,000*l.* for minerals.		35,000 .	9,000

LYON, J. S., of Kirkmichael.	Dumfries .	2,994 .	2,532
** LYON, T. H., of Appleton.	Ches., Lanc.	2,580 .	9,000

** MACALISTER, Keith, of Glenbarr Abbey, Greenock, N.B.

		acres,	g. an. val.
Club. Union, New Edin.	Argyll . . .	20,000 .	3,000

b. 1803, s. 1830, m. 1st 1830,
2nd 1858.

MACARTNEY, Carthenac George, of Lissanoure, Antrim.

b. 1869, s. 1874.	Antrim . . .	12,532 .	6,355
	Co. Meath . .	310 .	219
	Londonderry .	276 .	209
		13,118 .	6,783

*** McCAUSLAND, Conolly Thomas, of Drenagh, Limavady.

Coll. Eton, Ch. Ch. Oxon.	Londonderry .	12,886 .	6,257
Club. Carlton.	Roscommon .	4,799 .	2,911
b. 1828, s. 1862, m. 1867.			
Was in the Diplomatic Service.		17,685 .	9,168

*** MACCLESFIELD, Earl of, Shirburn Castle, Tetsworth, &c. $.

Coll. Eton, Ch. Ch. Oxon.	Oxford . . .	5,518 .	8,801
Club. Carlton.	Stafford . . .	5,947 .	7,872
b. 1811, s. 1850, m. 1st 1839,	Devon . . .	3,088 .	1,264
2nd 1842.			
Sat for Oxfordshire.		14,553 .	17,937

McCLINTOCK, George Perry, of Seskinore House, Omagh.

Coll. Cheltenham.	Co. Tyrone .	4,553 .	3,209
Club. United Service.			
b. 1839, m. 1860.			

McCULLOCH, Walter, of Ardwall, Gatehouse, N.B.

b. 1807, s. 1858.	Kirkcudbright	4,275 .	3,064

MACAN, R., of Drumcashel.	Arm., Louth .	2,191 .	2,256
McBRIDE, James, of Greenock.	Cork . .	4,629 .	2,602
McCLINTOCK, J. W., of Moyle.	Carlow .	3,098 .	2,741
McCREAGH, Lady, of Shoulden.	Hants .	3,600 .	2,906
McCONNEL, W., of Knockdolian.	Lanc , Ayr	3,241 .	2,348

** MACDONALD, Maj.-Gen. Alastair McIan, of Dun
    Alastair, &c., Perthshire, N.B.   *acres.*   *g. an. val.*

			acres		g. an. val.
Club. United Ser., Turf.	Perth	. . .	21,000	.	4,563

b. 1830, s. 1866.

    Served as A.D.C. to Gen. Pennefather in the Crimea
(severely wounded at Alma and Inkerman), A.D.C. to H.R.H.
the Duke of Cambridge, Ass. Adj.-Gen. Commands the
N. British District.

MORETON-MACDONALD, John Ronald, of Largie Castle,
    Tainloan, N.B.

Club. Kild. St. Dublin.	Argyll	. . .	12,775	.	4,025

b. 1873, s. 1879.

** MACDONALD, Lord, Armadale Castle, I. of Skye, N.B., &c.

Coll. Eton.	Inverness	. .	129,919	.	11,613
Club. Carl., Cons., Edin.	Bucks	. . .	2,500	.	5,000

b. 1853, s. 1874, m. 1875.

132,419	.	16,613

*** MACDONALD, William Macdonald, of St. Martin's
    Abbey, Perth, N.B., &c.

Coll. Sandhurst.	Perth	. . .	22,600	.	9,191
Club. Carlton, National,	Forfar	. . .	2,801	.	5,617
New Edin.	Aberdeen	. .	2	.	0

b. 1822, s. 1834 and 1841, m. 1849.

25,403	.	14,808

    Served in H.M. Bodyguard of Scottish Archers.

** McDOUALL, James, of Logan, Stranraer, N.B.

Coll. Eton.	Wigtown	. .	16,290	.	11,785
Club. Carlton, Jun. Carlton,	Kirkcudbright		2,600	.	1,346
New Edin.	Peebles	. . .	2,900	.	850
b. 1840, s. 1872, m. 1869.	Haddington	.	143	.	460

21,933	.	14,441

MACDONNELL, M., of Dunmore.	Gal. .	9,114	.	2,065
ARMSTRONG-MACDONNELL, Col., of				
New Hall.	Clare	6,610	.	2,947
MACDOWALL, H., of Garthland.	Renfrew	2,825	.	2,706

** MACGEOUGH, ROBERT JOHN, of Silverbridge House, Newtown Hamilton, Co. Armagh.

		acres.	g. an. val.
b. 1838, s. 1866, m. 1869.	Co. Armagh .	7,213	4,079

McINROY, MAJOR WILLIAM, of The Burn, Brechin, N.B.

Coll. Glasgow and Edin.	Kincardine .	4,988	3,182
Club. Jun. Uni. Service.	Perth . . .	632	290
b. 1804, m. 1839.	Forfar . . .	23	8
Served in the Army.		5,643	3,480

MUIR-MACKENZIE, SIR ALEXANDER, BART., of Delvine, Dunkeld, N.B., &c.

Coll. Harrow.	Perth . . .	4,241	6,419

b. 1840, s. 1855, m. 1871.   Served in 78th Highlanders.

MACKENZIE, SIR ARTHUR GEORGE RAMSAY, BART., of Coul House, Dingwall, N.B.

b. 1865, s. 1873.	Ross. . . .	43,189	5,214

*** MACKENZIE, COLIN JAMES, of Portmore, Eddleston, N.B.

Coll. Glenld., Haileybury.	Peebles . . .	9,685	4,859

Club. Carlton, New Edinburgh.
b. 1835, s. 1862, m. 1871.   Was in Bengal Civil Service.

McEVOY, E. F., of Tobertynan. Me., Lgfd., Leitrim	5,256	2,872
MACFIE, D. J., of Borthwick. Midl., Fife	2,643	2,326
MACFIE, R., of Airds. Argyll, Renfrew .	6,814	2,373
McGILLDOWNY, J., of Clare Park. Antrim	3,811	2,449
McGILLICUDDY, THE, of The Reeks. Ker.	15,518	2,175
MACHELL, J. P., of Hollow Oak. Lanc.	2,264	2,260
McINROY, W., of The Lude. Perth . .	15,880	2,460
MACK, T., of Tunstead Hall. Norfolk .	2,168	4,116

** MACKENZIE, EDWARD PHILIPPE, of Auchenskeoch, Dumfries, N.B.

		acres.	g. an. val
Coll. Harr., St. Joh. Ox.	Kirkudbright .	6,400 .	3,000
Club. Junior Carlton.	Dumfries . .	282 .	500

b. 1842, s. 1880, m. 1865.
    Served in 9th Lancers.

                                    6,682 . 3,500

MACKENZIE (of Kilcoy), SIR EVAN, BART., of Belmaduthie, Munlochy, N.B.

Coll. Eton.	Ross. . . .	24,658 .	7,257

Club. Garrick. b. 1816, s. 1845, m. 1844.

*** MACKENZIE, HUGH, of Dundonnell, Ullapool, N.B.

b. 1845, s. 1881, m. 1876.   Ross . . . 64,335 . 4,038
    MR. MACKENZIE has colonial estates as well.

*** MACKENZIE, JAMES, of Glenmuick, Ballater, N.B., &c.

		acres.	g. an. val
Coll. Aberdeen.	Aberdeen . .	29,500 .	1,300
Club. Marlborough, Turf,	Ross . . .	35,800 .	2,200
Oriental, Devons.	Forfar . . .	7,129 .	435
b. 1824, m. 1849.	Surrey . . .	300 .	600

                              72,729 . 4,535

STEWART-MACKENZIE (of Seaforth), JAMES ALEXANDER FRANCIS HUMBERSTONE, of Brahan Castle, Dingwall, N.B.

b. 1847, s. 1881, m. 1844.   Ross . . . 8,051 . 7,905
    Serves in 9th Lancers.

MACKENZIE, JOHN, of Glack, Daviot, N.B., &c.

Coll. H. Sch., Edinb.   Aberdeen . . 4,036 . 3,825
b. 1795, s. 1877, m. 1822.

** MACKENZIE, SIR KENNETH SMITH, BART., of Gairloch, Dingwall, N.B.

Club. Arthur's, Travellers'.   Ross . . . 164,680 . 9,344
b. 1832, s. 1843, m. 1860.
          Served as Attaché at Washington.

SHAW-MACKENZIE, J. ANDREW, of Newhall. Cromarty, Ross . . . . . . 7,163 . 2,639

** MACKENZIE (of Findon), MAJOR, of Mountgerald House, Dingwall, N.B.

		acres.	*g. an. val.*
Coll. Rugby.	Ross . . .	5,804 .	4,022

Club. Army and Navy. b. 1830, s. 1865, m. 1858.

　　　　Served in 79th Highlanders and 14th Foot.

** MACKENZIE, WILLIAM DALZIEL, of Fawley Court, Henley-on-Thames, &c.

Coll. Harr., Magd. Oxon.	Oxford . . .	⎫		
Club. Carlton, J. Carl.	Bucks . . .	⎬ 3,990 .	4,000
b. 1840, s. 1880, m. 1863.	Berks . . .	⎭	
	Norfolk . . .	5,700 . ⎫	
	Suffolk . . .	8,300 . ⎬ 3,500	
	Dumfries . .	1,750 .	3,800
	Inverness . .	8,000 .	350
	Lancashire . .	10 .	1,200
		27,750 .	12,850

*** MACKIE, JOHN GLADSTONE, of Auchencairn House, Castle Douglas, N.B.

Coll. Magd. Hall, Oxon.	Kirkcudbright	4,167 .	4,794

Club. R.T.Y.C. b. 1854, s. 1876.

** MACKINNON, WILLIAM ALEXANDER, of Acryse Park, Canterbury, &c.

Coll. West., St. John's,	Kent . . .	4,363 .	5,000
Cambridge.	Wilts . . .	670 .	660
Club. Union, Ox. and Cam.	Essex . . .	248 .	314
b. 1813, s. 1870, m. 1846.	Lancashire . .	465 .	500
Sat for Rye and for Lymington.		5,746 .	6,474

MACKENZIE, JOHN ORD, of Dolphinton.		
Lanark, Peebles	3,027 .	2,262
** MACKENZIE, KEITH, of Gillotts. Oxon.	2,870 .	3,800
MACKENZIE, T., of Corryvoulzie. Ross	21,229 .	2,640
MACKIE, J., of Bargaly. Kirkcudbright .	10,850 .	**2,532**

** MACKINTOSH, ALFRED DONALD (THE MACKINTOSH), of
Moy Hall, Inverness, N.B.　　　　*acres.*　*g. an. val.*

Coll. Cheltenham.	Inverness . .	124,181	. 12,816
Club. N. & M., Carl., Garr.	Glamorgan .	2,114	. 16,195

b. 1851, s. 1876, m. 1880.

Served in 71st Highlanders.　　　126,295　.　29,011

MACKINTOSH, ÆNEAS WILLIAM, of Raigmore, Inverness, N.B.

Club. Reform.　　　　Inverness . .　6,556　.　4,368
b. 1819, m. 1856.　Sat for Inverness-shire.

MACQUEEN-MACKINTOSH, MRS., of Hardington, Biggar,
N.B., &c.

s. 1879, m. 1872.	Peebles . . .	4,093	. 2,016
	Lanark . . .	1,216	. 1,089
	Argyll . . .	3	. 110

The small property is her husband's.　　5,312　.　3,215

*** McKISSACK, ROBERT, of Ardgye, Alves, N.B.

	Elgin . . .	4,165	. 3,629
	Nairn . . .	28	. 25

　　　　　　　　　　　　　　　4,193　.　3,654

MACKWORTH, SIR ARTHUR WILLIAM, BART., of Glen Uske,
Bridgend, South Wales, &c.

Club. National, J.U.S.	Monmouth .	1,861	. 2,570
b. 1842, s. 1857, m. 1865.	Glamorgan .	1,342	. 1,079

Serves in Royal Engineers.

　　　　　　　　　　　　　　　3,203　.　3,649
His mother has out of this a rental of 906*l.*

MACKINTOSH, MRS., of Havering. Ess., Nairn	2,487	. 4,523
MACLACHLAN, R., of Maclachlan. Arg. .	12,000	. 2,005
** MACLAINE, M. G., of Lochbuy. Arg.	30,000	. 2,367
MACLAREN, MRS., of Islay. Argyll . .	5,509	. 2,151
MACLEAN, A. T., of Ardgour. Argyll . .	40,000	. 2,514

** MACLEOD, Norman (The Macleod), of Dunvegan Castle, Isle of Skye, N.B.

			acres.	*g. an. val.*
Coll.	Harrow.	Inverness . .	141,679 .	8,464
Club.	Athenæum, Carlton.	b. 1812, s. 1835, m. 1837.		

Serves as Assistant-Secretary to Department of Science and Art.

** MACLEOD, Robert Bruce Æneas, of Cadboll, Cromarty, N.B., &c.

Coll.	Royal Naval.	Ross and Cro-		
Club.	Army and Navy, New Edinburgh.	marty . .	11,827 .	10,761

b. 1818, s. 1853, m. 1857.
Served in Royal Navy (Commander) in Syrian War of 1840.

McMAHON, Sir William Samuel, Bart., of Fecarry House, Mountfield, Co. Tyrone, &c.

Club. St. James's, Carlton.	Co. Tyrone .	16,326 .	3,375
b. 1839, s. 1873.	Co. Clare . .	4,671 .	1,747
Served in 2nd Life Guards and as Attaché at Stutgardt, Florence, Munich, and Constantinople.	Co. Dublin .	32 .	180
		21,029 .	5,302

** WORKMAN-MACNAGHTEN, Sir Francis Edmund, Bart., of Dundarave, Bushmills, Co. Antrim.

Club. U. Ser., Carlton.	Co. Antrim .	7,134 .	7,062
b. 1828, s. 1876, m. 1866.	Co. Armagh .	920 .	1,739
Served in 8th Hussars in Crimean Campaign.	Londonderry .	227 .	136
		8,281 .	8,937

** MACNAMARA, Arthur, of Eaton Bray, Dunstable, &c.

Club. White's.	Bedford . .	3,957 .	6,231
b. 1829, s. 1851, m. 1854.	Herts . . .	1,443 .	1,769
		5,400 .	8,000

** MACNAMARA, Henry Valentine, of Doolin, Ennis, &c.

		acres.	g. an. val.
Coll. Harrow, Trin. Cam.	Co. Clare . .	15,246 .	6,932

b. 1861, s. 1873.

*** MACNEAL, Hector, of Ugadale, Campbelton, N.B., &c.

Club. Jun. U. Ser., New	Argyll . . .	11,000 .	4,251
U. Ser. Ed.			

b. 1822, s. 1861, m. 1862.   Served in 79th Highlanders.

** McNEILE, Henry Hugh, of Parkmount, Belfast.

Coll. Trin. Cam.	Co. Antrim .	7,011 .	4,300
Club. Carlton.			

b. 1829, s. 1855, m. 1859.   Served in 5th Dragoon Guards.

** MACONCHY, George, of Rathmore (res. Corrinagh, Torquay).

Coll. Trin., Dublin.	Longford . .	10,319 .	3,137
Club. Sack. St., Han. Sq.			

b. 1818, s. 1843, m. 1st 1843, 2nd 1867.

** MACPHERSON, Charles Julian Brewster, of Belleville, Inverness, N.B.

Coll. Trin. Cam.	Inverness . .	26,773 .	3,200
b. 1855, s. 1878, m. 1880.	Roxburgh . .	145 .	152
		26,918 .	3,352

** MACPHERSON, Ewen, C.B. (Cluny Macpherson), of Cluny Castle, Kingussie, N.B.

Coll. Edinburgh.	Inverness . .	42,000 .	4,500
Club. Junior United Service, New Edinburgh.			

b. 1804, s. 1817, m. 1832.   Served in 42nd Highlanders.

McNAB, A., of Techmuiry. Abn., Cln., Stir.	2,048 .	2,960
MACNEALE, Mrs. King's Co., Q. Co. .	6,035 .	2,809
CAMPBELL-McNEILL, Miss, of Saddell. Argyll	12,805 .	2,935
McNEILL, Rt. Hon. Sir John, G.C.B., of Burnhead. Argyll, Midlothian . . .	11,266 .	2,305
MACPHERSON, Col., of Glentruim. Inv.	21,000 .	2,350
McVEAGH, F., of Drewstown. Meath .	2,270 .	2,135

*** OMMANEY-McTAGGART, Mrs., of Ardwell House, Stranraer, N.B.

		acres.	*g. an. val.*
s. 1867, m. 1839.	Wigtown . .	5,998 .	7,357

MADDEN, John, of Hilton Park, Clones, Co. Monaghan, &c.

Coll. Eton.	Monaghan .	4,644 .	3,467
Club. Jun. Carl., Sack. St.,	Co. Leitrim .	3,549 .	1,400
Kildare St., Dublin.			
b. 1836, s. 1844, m. 1864.		8,193 .	4,867

*** MADDEN, John, of Roslea, Co. Fermanagh.

Coll. Harr., Pet., Cam.	Co. Fermanagh	10,498 .	4,076
Club. Kild. St., J. Carl.	Monaghan	628 .	600
b. 1819, s. 1842, m. 1st 1847,			
2nd 1870.		11,126 .	4,676
Served in 41st Foot, in Affghan War.			

MAGAN, Miss, of Clonearl, King's Co.

s. 1880.	Westmeath .	5,604 .	3,525
	Co. Meath .	4,418 .	3,086
	Co. Kildare .	2,374 .	1,086
	King's Co. .	1,023 .	652
	Co. Dublin .	165 .	388
		13,584 .	8,737

MAGENIS, Henry Cole, of Finvoy, Ballymoney.

Coll. Woolwich.	Co. Antrim .	6,816 .	3,698
Club. Junior United Service.	Co. Down . .	2,407 .	1,983
b. 1831, s. 1852, m. 1860.			
Is a Major in R. Artillery.		9,223 .	5,681

** MAHER, Matthias Aidan, of Ballinkeele, Enniscorthy, Co. Wexford.

Club. Stephen's Green, Dub.	Co. Wexford .	4,950 .	3,392
b. 1846, s. 1860.	Kilkenny . .	1,081 .	740
	Meath . . .	528 .	345
		6,559 .	4,477

The last property belongs to his mother.

MAHER, Mrs., of Turtulla.	Tipperary .	4,452 .	2,993

*** PAKENHAM-MAHON, Henry Sandford, of Strokestown House, Co. Roscommon.

		acres.	g. an. val.
Club. Carlton.	Westmeath . .	1,143 .	964
b. 1823, s. 1863, m. 1847.	Roscommon .	26,980	14,116
Served in 8th Hussars.			
		28,123 .	15,080

** MAHON, Rev. Sir William Vesey Ross, Bart., of Castlegar, Ahascragh, Co. Galway, &c.

		acres.	g. an. val.
Coll. Trinity, Dublin.	Co. Galway .	8,619 .	3,788
Club. Kildare St., Dublin.	Roscommon .	860 .	570
b. 1813, s. 1852, m. 1853.			
		9,479 .	4,358

Exc. of the living of Rawmarsh, Yorkshire.

*** MAINWARING, Salusbury Kynaston, of Oteley Park, Ellesmere.

		acres.	g. an. val.
Coll. Eton, Ch. Ch. Oxon.	Salop . . .	3,664 .	5,346
Club. Carlton, Boodle's,	Cheshire . .	1,755 .	3,260
Travellers'.	Flint	205 .	382
b. 1844, s. 1862, m. 1869.	Denbigh . .	82 .	215
		5,706 .	9,203

* MAINWARING, Townshend, of Galltfaenan, Denbigh.

		acres.	g. an. val.
Coll. Rugby, Bras. Oxon.	Denbigh . .	10,685 .	4,327
b. 1807, m. 1837. Sat for Denbigh.			

Mr. Mainwaring states that he holds property in four other counties, but omits particulars as to extent. The return gives "Miss M., of Galltfaenan," 170 acres in Cheshire and Flint.

	acres.	g. an. val.
MAHONY, D., of Grangecow. Wic., Crk., Ker., Lim.	5,761 .	2,167
MAHONY, R. J., of Dromore. Kerry . .	26,173 .	2,636
LEE-MAINWARING, Hon. Mrs., Lin., York, Dur.	2,669 .	3,999
MAINWARING, C. H., of Whitmore. Staffs.	2,666 .	4,053

MAITLAND, Elphinstone Vans-Agnew, of Balcreggan House, Freugh, N.B.

		acres.	g. an. val.
b. 1856, s. 1881.	Wigtown . .	7,848	. 5,881

*** RAMSAY GIBSON-MAITLAND, Sir James, Bart., of Clifton Hall, Edinburgh.

Coll. St. Andrew's.	Midlothian .	4,505	. 14,246
Club. N. & M., Carl., Garr.	Stirling . . .	5,678	. 5,968
b. 1848, s. 1876, m. 1869.	Linlithgow . .	45	. 114
Served in 4th Dragoon Guards.			
		10,228	. 20,328

Exclusive of 329l. for minerals.

FULLER-MAITLAND, William, of Stanstead Hall, Bishop's Stortford, &c.

Coll. Ch. Ch. Oxon.	Essex . . .	3,128	. 4,103
Club. Reform, Brooks's,	Brecon . . .	3,841	. 1,547
Oxf. and Cam.	Berks . . .	211	. 440
b. 1844, s. 1876.	Middlesex . .	1	. 184
Sits for Brecon.	Kirkcudbright	464	. 348
		7,645	. 6,622

** TALBOT de MALAHIDE, Lord, Malahide Castle, Dublin. ⚲.

Coll. Trin. Cambridge.	Co. Dublin .	1,893	. 3,908
Club. Athenæum, Kild. St.	Co. Cavan . .	1,133	. 641
b. 1805, s. 1850, m. 1842.	Westmeath . .	547	. 396
Served as Lord in Waiting.			
Sat for Athlone.		3,573	. 4,945

The late Lady T. de M. (and presumably her son) had in Scotland 2,645 acres rented at 5,279*l.*

MAITLAND, D., of Dundrennan. Kirk. .	2,309	. 2,240
MAITLAND, Rev. J. W., of Loughton. Ess.	2,334	. 2,970
SCOTT-MAKDOUGALL, Miss, of Makerstoun. Roxburgh	2,513	. 4,763
MALCOLMSON, R., of Kilcommon. Tipp.	2,644	. 2,600

** MALCOLM, John, of Poltalloch, Lochgilphead, N.B., &c.

			acres.	g. an. val.
Coll. Harrow, Ch. Ch. Ox.	Argyll	. . .	83,279	. 19,500
Club. Carlton, Uni. Univ.,	Lincoln	. . .	1,577	. 3,822
Fine Arts.	Kent	. . .	535	. 1,267
b. 1805, s. 1857, m. 1832.	Surrey	. . .	220	. 400
			85,611	. 24,989

MALMESBURY, Earl of, G.C.B., Heron Ct., Christchurch, &c.

Coll. Eton, Oriel, Oxon.	Hants	. . .	4,155	. 4,727
Club. Carl., Jun. Carlton,	Wilts	. . .	1,079	. 1,479
Athenæum.	Dorset	. . .	212	. 98
b. 1807, s. 1841, m. 1830, 2nd 1880.				
Sat for Wilton.			5,446	. 6,304

Served as Secretary for Foreign Affairs, and as Lord Privy Seal.

** MALONE, John, of Baronstown, Ballinacargy, Mullingar.

Coll. Trinity, Dublin.	Co. Westmeath	13,715	. 10,203
b. 1817, s. 1866, m. 1st 1844,			
2nd 1868.			

MALTON, Mrs., of 16, Great Cumberland Street, Hyde Park, W.

	Co. Meath	.	2,883	. 2,215
	Co. Dublin	.	847	. 3,578
			3,730	. 5,793

** MANCHESTER, Duke of, K.P., Kimbolton Castle, St. Neots, &c.

Coll. Sandhurst.	Huntingdon	.	13,835	. 20,589
Club. Carlton, Marlb.	Cambridge	. .	1,124	. 1,849
b. 1823, s. 1855, m. 1852.	Bedford	. .	55	. 80
Served in Grenadier Guards.	Co. Armagh	.	12,298	. 17,842
Was A.D.C. to the Go-				
vernor of the Cape, and			27,312	. 40,360
Lord of the Bedchamber				
to the Prince Consort.				

Sat for Bewdley and Hunts.

$ MALET, Sir Alexander, Bart., K.C.B.,
   of Wilbury. Wilts, Hants, Leic. . . . 2,942 . 2,700

MANSFIELD, Earl of, K.T., Scone Palace, Perth, N.B., &c.

		acres.	g.	an. val.
Coll. Westminster.	Perth . .	31,197	.	23,052
Club. Carlton, Travellers'.	Dumfries . .	14,342	.	13,389
b. 1806, s. 1840, m. 1829.	Clackmannan .	1,705	.	1,751
Served as Lord High Com.	Fife	795	.	638
to the Kirk of Scotland,	Middlesex . .	539	.	730
and as a Lord of the	Derby . . .	250	.	268
Treasury.	Cheshire . .	224	.	3,110
Sat for Aldboro', Wood-	Cumberland .	22	.	30
stock, Norwich, and for				
Perthshire.		49,074	.	42,968

Exclusive of coals rented at 1,886*l.*

*** MANSFIELD, George Patrick Lattin, of Morristown
Lattin, Naas, Co. Kildare.

Coll. Oscott.	Co. Kildare .	4,542	.	3,709
Club. Kildare St., Dublin,	Waterford . .	1,097	.	708
St. George's.				
b. 1820, s. 1842, m. 1843.		5,639	.	4,417

*** MANVERS, Earl, Thoresby Park, Ollerton, &c.

Coll. Eton, Ch. Ch.	Notts . . .	26,771	.	36,788
Oxon.	Lincoln . . .	5,010	.	6,020
Club. Carl., Beac., Sal.	Derby . . .	3,729	.	5,067
b. 1825, s. 1860, m. 1852.	Wilts . . .	1,500	.	2,400
Sat for South Notts.	York, W.R. .	1,026	.	1,374
		38,036	.	51,649

The Wilts figures are only approximate—the value does not
include mines or tithe.

MANFIELD, W., of Portesham.	Dorset, Dev.	2,000	.	2,892
MANLEY, A. E., of Manley.	Staf., War., Dby.	2,150	.	3,059
MANSERGH, J. S., of Greenane.	Tipperary	2,086	.	2,406

*** MAR and KELLIE, Earl of, Alloa Park, Alloa, N.B., &c.

			acres.	g. an. val.
Coll.	Radley, Brase. Oxon.	Clackmanan .	6,163	. 8,256
Club.	Carlton, Jun. Carlton,	Fife	149	. 325
	New Edinburgh.			
b. 1839, s. 1872 and 1875.			6,312	. 8,581
m. 1863.				

Exclusive of 5,320*l.* for mines, feu duties, &c.

Some other properties are returned under " MAR," which belong to the other claimant to the earldom, the case not being decided against MR. GOODEVE ERSKINE when the materials for the return were collected.

MARJORIBANKS, SIR JOHN, BART., of Lees, Coldstream, N.B.

Coll.	Eton, Ch. Ch. Oxon.	Berwick . .	3,332	. 6,063
Club.	Carlton, Fine Arts.	Northumberland	820	. 850
b. 1830, s. 1834, m. 1858.				
			4,152	. 6,913

MARJORIBANKS, THE LADY, Ladykirk, Berwick, N.B.

s. 1873, m. 1834.	Berwick . .	6,832	. 11,754

MARKER, RICHARD, of Combe, Honiton.

Coll.	Harrow, Ch. Ch. Ox.	Devon . . .	6,527	. 6,833
Club.	St. James's.	Dorset . . .	804	. 644
b. 1835, s. 1865, m. 1865.	Somerset . .	128	. 270
		7,459	. 7,747

Including 380*l.* retd. in his mother's name.

MARLAY, CHARLES BRINSLEY, of Belvedere, Mullingar, Co. Westmeath, &c.

Coll.	Eton, Trin. Cam.	Westmeath .	9,059	. 5,766
Club.	Trav., White's, Carl.	Louth . . .	3,067	. 3,126
b. 1831, s. 1847.	Co. Cavan .	1,668	. 929
	Limerick . .	453	. 428
	King's Co. .	38	. 33
		14,285	. 10,282

MARCON, LT.-COL., of Wallington. Norfolk 2,007 . 2,616

MARGESSON, COL., of Finden. Sus., Sur. 2,401 . 3,087

MARLBOROUGH, Duke of, K.G., Blenheim Palace, Wood-stock. $

		acres.	g. an. val:
Coll. Eton, Oriel, Oxon.	Oxford . . .	21,944 .	34,341
Club. Ath., Carlton.	Wilts . . .	1,534 .	2,106
b. 1822, s. 1857, m. 1843.	Berks . . .	33 .	110
Served as Lord Steward			
of the Household, Pres.		23,511 .	36,557
Privy Council, and Lord			

Lieutenant of Ireland. Sat for Woodstock.

SMITH-MARRIOTT, Sir William Henry, Bart., of Down House, Blandford.

Coll. Harrow, Ball. Oxon.	Dorset . . .	3,893 .	3,985

Club. Windham. b. 1835, s. 1864, m. 1868.

** MARSHALL, George Hibbert, of Patterdale Hall, Penrith, &c.

Coll. Rugby.	Cumberland .	4,010 .	2,547
Club. Arthur's, Garrick.	Westmoreland	719 .	1,002
b. 1832, s. 1881.			
		4,729 .	3,549

MARSHALL, Maj.-Gen., C.M.G., of Broadwater, Godalming.

Club. Army and Navy.	Sussex . . .	102 .	70
b. 1829, m. 1861.	Surrey . . .	3,012 .	5,634
Served in 2nd L. Gds.,	Kent . . .	1,092 .	920
Commanded Cav. Brig. in			
Zulu War, was A.D.C. to		4,206 .	5,624
the Duke of Cambridge.			

MARRIOTT, C., of Cotesbach. Leicester .	2,074 .	3,289
MARSHALL, R. D., of Cookridge. Cum., Yk.	3,473 .	2,010
MARSHALL, R. J., of Callinafercy. Kerry	5,955 .	2,403
MARSHALL, W., of Treworgy. Cornwall .	3,085 .	2,639
MARSHALL, W. K., of Baronne Court, Tipperary, Armagh, King's Co., Tyrone .	3,913 .	2,227
MARSHAM, C. R., of Stratton Strawless. Nfk.	2,212 .	2,606
MARSHAM, C. J. B., of Caversfield. Buc., Ox., Fife.	2,211 .	3,619

WYKEHAM-MARTIN, CORNWALLIS PHILIP, of Leeds Castle,
    Maidstone, &c. ⚓.

		acres.	g. an. val.
Coll. Eton, Merton, Oxon.	Kent . . .	3,239 .	5,190
b. 1855, s. 1878, m. 1876.	Warwick . .	2,347 .	3,484
	Hants . . .	1,412 .	1,862
	Northampton .	545 .	1,198
	Worcester . .	197 .	236
	Oxford . . .	106 .	192

Much of this belongs to his mother.   7,846 . 12,162

*** MARTIN, EDWARD DOWNES, of Shrigley, Killyleagh, Co.
    Down.

b. 1868, s. 1876.	Tyrone . . .	1,999 .	1,866
	Tipperary . .	1,790 .	2,190
	Co. Down . .	50 .	100

    3,839 . 4,156

** WOOD-MARTIN, WILLIAM GREGORY, of Woodville, Sligo.

Club. J. U. S., A. & N.	Co. Sligo . .	5,857 .	3,981
b. 1847, s. 1874, m. 1873.	Co. Galway .	1,205 .	663
Served in 44th Foot.			

    7,062 . 4,644

A large part of these estates belongs to his mother.

** MARTON, GEORGE BLUCHER HENEAGE, of Capernwray,
    Burton-in-Kendal.

Coll. Trin. Cam.	Lancashire .	4,000 .	5,760
Club. Carlton, Arthur's, St.	York, W.R. .	693 .	594
James's.			
b. 1839, s. 1866, m. 1867.		4,693 .	6,354

MARTIN, A., of Evershot.	Dorset, Devon	2,065 .	3,166
MARTIN, RT. HON. SIR S.	Londonderry	2,166 .	2,422
MARTIN, W. A. H., of Upper Hall.			
Hereford, Worcester, Gloucester . .		2,377 .	3,799

** STORY-MASKELYNE, Mervyn Herbert Nevil, F.R.S., of Basset Down House, Swindon, &c.

		acres.	g. an. val.
Coll. Wadham, Oxon.	Brecon . .	3,658 .	1,014
Club. Athenæum.	Wilts . . .	1,487 .	3,172
b. 1823, s. 1879, m. 1858.	Gloucester . .	279 .	1,631
Kept the minerals at B. Museum.			
Sits for Cricklade.		5,424 .	5,817

*** MASON, Robert Harvey Humfrey, of Necton, Swaffham.

Coll. Eton, Trin. Cam.	Norfolk . . .	4,050 .	6,500
Club. New University.			
b. 1843, s. 1878, m. 1873.			

MASSEREENE and FERRARD, Viscount, K.P., Oriel Temple, Co. Louth, &c.

Club. Carlton, Travellers',	Co. Antrim .	11,777 .	8,649
Gun, Sackville St.	Co. Louth . .	7,193 .	5,234
Dublin.	Co. Meath . .	2,045 .	1,122
b. 1842, s. 1863, m. 1870.	Monaghan . .	9 .	8
		21,024 .	15,013

** BOLTON-MASSY, John, of Clareville, Blackrock, &c.

Coll. Trinity, Dublin.	Limerick . .	2,259 .	2,150
Club. Kildare St., Limerick	Co. Dublin .	908 .	1,124
County.			
b. 1818, s. 1871.		3,167 .	3,274

MASSY, Haworth Peel (*jur. ux.*), of Blaendyffryn, Carmarthen.

Coll. Eton.	Cardigan . .	5,417 .	2,429
b. 1842, m. 1873.	Carmarthen .	1,459 .	802
Served in 22nd Foot.		6,876 .	3,231

MARTYN, E. J., of Tullyra.	Galway . .	4,932 .	2,424
MARWOOD, G., of Little Busby.	York .	2,938 .	3,636
MASON, G. W., of Morton Hall.	Notts .	2,463 .	3,383

MASSY, Lady, of Doonas House, Clonlara, Co. Clare.

		acres.	*g. an. val.*
s. 1870, m. 1818.	Co. Clare . .	4,623 .	3,173

*** MASSY, Lord, The Hermitage, Castle Connell, &c.

Club. Carl., Kild. St. Dub.	Limerick . .	8,432 .	5,441
b. 1835, s. 1874, m. 1863.	Leitrim . . .	24,571 .	6,660
		33,003 .	12,101

MASSY, William Hugh Massy Hutchinson, of Mount Massy, Macroom, Co. Cork.

b. 1828, s. 1852, m. 1868.	Co. Cork . .	13,363 .	3,105

*** MASTER, Thomas William Chester, of The Abbey, Cirencester, &c.

Coll. Harrow, Ch. Ch. Ox.	Gloucester .	7,190 .	13,722

Club. Carlton, Junior Carlton.
b. 1815, s. 1868, m. 1840.   Sat for Cirencester.

** MATHESON, Sir Alexander, Bart, of Ardross, Alness, N.B., &c.

Coll. Edinburgh.	Ross . . .	220,433 .	23,223
Club. Reform, Brooks's.	Inverness . .	230 .	3,238
b. 1805, m. 1st 1840,			
2nd 1853.		220,663 .	26,461

Sat for Inverness ; sits for Ross and Cromarty shires.

*** MATHESON, Lady, of Lews Cas. Stornoway, N.B.

m. 1843, s. 1878.	Ross . . .	406,070 .	17,676
	Sutherland .	18,490 .	2,670
		424,560 .	20,346

MATCHAM, W. E., of Newhouse.   Wil., Sus   2,814 .   2,185

MATHIAS, LEWIS, of Lamphey Court, Pembroke.

		acres.	g. an. val.
Coll. Brasenose, Oxon.	Pembroke . .	4,562 .	4,113

b. 1813, s. 1851, m. 1845.

MAULE, HON. MRS., of Maulesden, Brechin, N.B.

s. 1859, m. 1844.   Forfar . . .   6,992 .   3,639

** HERON-MAXWELL, SIR JOHN, BART., of Springkell, Ecclefechan, N.B.

Coll. Royal Naval.   Dumfries . .   13,391 .   8,758
Club. Carlton, United Service.
b. 1808, s. 1844, m. 1833.
    Served in Royal Navy (Captain) and in the Coast Guard.

*** CONSTABLE-MAXWELL, ALFRED PETER, of Terregles, Dumfries, N.B.

Coll. Stonyhurst.   Kirkcudbright   12,396 .   14,430
Club. J. U. S., N. and M., Ral., Cons.
b. 1841, s. 1873.
        Served in 92nd Highlanders.

** MAXWELL, SIR HERBERT EUSTACE, BART., of Monreith, Whauphill, N.B.

Coll. Eton, Ch, Ch. Oxon.   Wigtown . .   16,877 .   15,569
Club. Carlton, Junior Carlton.
b. 1845, s. 1877, m. 1869.   Sits for Wigtownshire.
        This property has been in this family since 1481.

MATURIN, DANIEL BAIRD. Tyrone . .	4,900 .	2,471
*** MAUNSELL, G. W., of Merrion Sq. Dub., Kild., Lim., Meath, Wmeath., Wex. .	3,438 .	2,710
** MAUNSELL, J., of Oakly. Kild., Lim.	2,428 .	2,424
MAUNSELL, JOHN, of Edenmore. Limerick	5,011 .	2,559
MAXWELL, G., of Glenlee. Kirk. . . .	15,090 .	2,736
MAXWELL, MRS., of St. Clerans. Galway .	4,156 .	2,240
MAXWELL, SIR W., BART., of Cardoness. Kirkcudbright, Dumfries	6,385 .	2,248

** HERON-MAXWELL, John Maxwell, of Kirrouchtree, &c.,
  Newton Stewart, N.B.   *acres.*   *g. an. val.*

Club. Jun. Uni. Service.   Kirkcudbright   12,300 . 3,452
b. 1836, s. 1870, m. 1868.
     Served in 1st Royals. Sits for Kirkcudbright.

** PERCEVAL-MAXWELL, Robert, of Groomsport House,
  Bangor, Co. Down, &c.

		acres.		*g. an. val.*
Coll. Brasenose, Oxon.	Co. Down . .	8,469	.	8,944
Club. Carlton, Union, Sack.	Tipperary . .	2,353	.	1,491
St. Dublin.	Co. Meath . .	911	.	1,040
b. 1813, m. 1839.	Co. Cork . .	695	.	657
		12,428	.	12,132

*** MAXWELL (late), Rev. Robert Walter, of Birdstown,
  Londonderry.

b. 1811, s. 1870, d. 1879.	Donegal . .	4,516	.	2,123
	Co. Tyrone .	1,261	.	682
	Londonderry .	3,570	.	1,451
		9,347	.	4,256

*** MAXWELL, Wellwood Herries, of Munches, Dalbeattie.

Coll. Edin., Exeter, Ox.   Kirkcudbright   4,597 . 4,728
Club. New Edin.
b. 1817, s. 1858, m. 1844.   Sat for Kirkcudbrightshire.

** STIRLING-MAXWELL, Sir William (late), Bart., of Keir,
  Dunblane, N.B., &c.

b. 1818, s. 1865, m. 1865,	Perth . . .	8,863	.	5,731
d. 1878.	Lanark . . .	5,691	.	8,741
	Renfrew . .	4,773	.	13,012
	Stirling . . .	1,487	.	2,370
		20,814	.	29,854

Exclusive of 4,389*l.* for quarries and minerals.

These estates are to be divided between the present Baronet
and his younger brother (both minors).

MAYO, EARL OF, Palmerstown House, Straffan, Co. Kildare.

		acres.	g. an. val.
Coll. Eton.	Kildare . .	4,915	5,247
Club. Guards, Carlton,	Co. Meath .	2,360	2,192
Garrick, Marlb.	Co. Mayo . .	559	251
b. 1851, s. 1872.			
		7,834	7,690

Served in 10th Hussars and Gr. Gds.

MEADE (Trustees of), HON. ROBERT HENRY.

	Co. Down . .	13,492	13,719

MEATH, EARL OF, Kilruddery Castle, Bray, Co. Wicklow.

Coll. Eton.	Co. Wicklow .	14,717	6,011
Club. Travellers'.	Co. Dublin .	36	1,934
b. 1803, s. 1851, m. 1837.	Hereford . .	695	1,453
Sat for Co. Dublin.			
		15,448	9,398

*** MEDLYCOTT, SIR WILLIAM COLES, BART., of Ven House, Milborne Port.

Coll. Trin. Oxon.	Somerset . .	3,556	7,445
Club. Oxford and Cam.	Dorset . . .	247	280
b. 1806, s. 1835, m. 1830.	Wilts . . .	6	5
		3,809	7,730

*** MELDON, JAMES DILLON, of 24, Merrion Square, Dublin.

Coll. Stonyhurst, Trin. Dub.	Galway . . .	4,933	4,843
b. 1803, m. 1832.	Mayo . . .	886	500
	Kildare . . .	158	300
	Wexford . .	1,700	2,100
		7,677	7,743

*** WHYTE-MELVILLE, JOHN (of Bennochy), of Mount Melville, St. Andrew's, N.B., &c.

Coll. Trin. Cam.	Fife . . .	2,940	6,150
Club. White's.	Norfolk . .	556	1,006
b. 1797, s. 1818, m. 1819.			
Served in 9th Lancers.		3,496	7,156

The English property is the late LADY CATH. W.-M.'s.

** MENZIES, Sir Robert, Bart., of Menzies, Aberfeldy, N.B., &c.

		acres.	*g. an. val.*
Coll. Univ. Oxon.	Perth . . .	98,284 .	11,467

b. 1817, s. 1844, m. 1846.

*** MENZIES, Robert Stewart, of Hallyburton, Coupar Angus, &c., N.B.

Coll. Harr., Ch. Ch. Oxon.	Forfar . . .	5,349 .	7,200
b. 1856, s. 1880.	Perth . . .	361 .	201
		5,710 .	7,401

** STEUART-MENZIES, William George, of Meggernie Castle, Glenlyon, N.B., &c.

Coll. Harrow.	Perth . . .	33,000 .	3,824

b. 1858, s. 1870.

*** MEREDYTH, Sir Henry, Bart., of Norelands, Thomas-town, Co. Kilkenny.

Coll. Trin. Cam.	Kilkenny . .	3,217 .	3,512
Club. Brooks's, Uni. Univ.,	Co. Down . .	3,071 .	3,216
Kildare St. Dub.	Co. Kildare .	128 .	141
b. 1800, s. 1859, m. 1828.		6,416 .	6,869

METCALFE, James, of Ings House, Hawes.

b. 1839, s. 1873.	York, N.R. .	4,620 .	3,640

DEMPSTER-METCALFE, Lady, of Dunnichen, Forfar, N.B.

s. 1875, m. 1856.	Forfar . . .	3,970 .	4,867

METHUEN, Lord, Corsham House, Chippenham.

Club. Brooks's, Uni. Ser.,	Wilts . . .	5,542 .	10,208
White's, Boodle's.			

b. 1818, s. 1849, m. 1844.
Served in 71st Foot, and as A.D.C. to the Queen, is a Lord in Waiting.

MENZIES, Hon. Mrs., of Chesthill.	Perth	16,117 .	2,723
METCALFE, F. M., of Julians.	Herts, Nfk., Cam., Linc.	2,305 .	3,077

MEUX, Sir Henry, Bart., of Theobalds, Cheshunt.

			acres.	*g. an. val.*
Coll. Eton, Ch. Ch. Oxon.	Wilts	. . .	11,895	16,194
b. 1817, s. 1841, m. 1856.	Herts	. . .	2,702	6,017
Sat for Herts.	Middlesex .	.	501	1,005
	Beds	. . .	11	16
	Kent	. . .	1	275
			15,110	23,507

MEXBOROUGH, Earl of, Methley Park, Leeds. ⚓.

Coll. Eton, Trin. Cam.	York, W.R.	.	6,969	31,309
Club. Carl., Trav., White's.	Herts	. . .	1,769	1,854
b. 1810, s. 1860, m. 1st 1842,	Notts	. . .	527	1,157
2nd, 1861.	Kent	. . .	269	245
Sat for Gatton and for Pontefract.			9,534	34,565

The Kentish property belongs to Lady M.

** TAPPS-JERVIS-MEYRICK, Sir George Eliott Meyrick, Bart., of Hinton Admiral, Christchurch, &c.

Coll. Ch. Ch. Oxon.	Anglesea	. .	16,918	13,283
Club. Cons., Jun. Carl.	Hants	. . .	4,286	3,358
b. 1827, s. 1842 and 1876, m. 1849.				
			21,204	16,641

CHARLTON-MEYRICK, Sir Thomas, Bart., of Bush, Pembroke, &c.

Coll. Eton.	Pembroke .	.	4,253	21,737
Club. Boodle's, Windham.	Salop	. . .	3,911	8,368
b. 1836, s. 1856, m. 1860.				
Sat for Pembroke.			8,164	30,105

MICKLETHWAIT, Henry Sharborne Nathaniel, of Iridge Place, Battle.

Coll. Royal Naval.	Norfolk	. .	5,356	5,931
Club. Union.	Sussex	. . .	2,671	4,089
b. 1814, s. 1877.	Suffolk .	. .	1,839	2,089
Served in Royal Navy	Co. Westmeath		713	500
(Commander).				
			10,579	12,609

Part of this estate stands in the name of "Wincklethwaite"

MIDDELTON, William, of Stockeld Park, Wetherby, &c.

		acres.	g. an. val.
Coll. Stonyhurst.	York, W.R. .	4,338 .	5,817

b. 1815, s. 1866.

MIDDLETON, Sir Arthur Edward, Bart., of Belsay Castle, Newcastle-on-Tyne. ♣.

Coll. Rugby, Trin. Cam.   Northumberland 9,079 .   9,712
Club. Brooks's, Travellers'.
b. 1838, s. 1867, m. 1871.   Sat for Durham.
   He re-assumed the name of Middleton in lieu of Monck in 1876.

** BROKE-MIDDLETON, Sir George Nathaniel, Bart., C.B., of Shrublands Park, Needham Market, &c. ♣.

Coll. Charterhouse.   Suffolk . . .   9,500 .   9,000
Club. Carlton, United Service, St. James's.
b. 1812, s. 1855, m. 1853.
   Served in Royal Navy at siege of St. Jean d'Acre, at Navarino, Sebastopol, and the taking of Bomarsund ; is a Vice-Admiral and Knight of the Medjidie.

*** MIDDLETON, Lord, Wollaton Hall, Nottingham, &c. ♣.

Coll. Eton.	Ross . . .	63,000 .	1,957
Club. Carl., Boodle's,	York,N.&E.R.	14,045 .	15,606
Jun. Carl., Gds.'	Notts . . .	15,015 .	26,157
b. 1844, s. 1877, m. 1869.	Lincoln . .	3,809 .	5,077
Served in Scots Fus. Guards.	Warwick . .	3,641 .	5,173
	Stafford . .	50 .	4
	Derby . . .	16 .	40
		99,576 .	54,014

** MIDLETON, Viscount, Peper Harrow, Godalming, &c.

Coll. Eton, Balliol, Ox.	Surrey . . .	3,105 .	2,734
Club. Carl.,Athenæum.	Co. Cork . .	6,475 .	8,018
b. 1830, s. 1870, m. 1853.			
Sat for Mid Surrey.		9,580 .	10,752

MICHELL, J., of Forcett. York, Dur., Kinc.   2,868 .   **3,663**

**' MIERS, HENRY NATHANIEL, of Ynispenllwch, Swansea.

		acres.	*g. an. val.*
Club. Wanderers'.	Glamorgan .	4,961 .	3,723

b. 1848, s. 1869, m. 1870.

He is sole owner of but 1,300 acres ; the authorities who furnished the return have calculated MR. M.'s share of some 10,000 a. which he holds in common with other members of his family.

MILBANK, SIR FREDERICK ACCLOM, BART., of Thorp Perrow, Bedale, &c.

Coll. Harrow.	Durham . .	3,734 .	17,279
Club. Brooks's, Boodle's,	York, N.R. .	1,696 .	1,815
Devonshire, Turf.			
b. 1820, m. 1844.		5,430 .	19,094

Served in 79th Highlanders.   Sits for N. Riding.

** MILBANK, MARK WILLIAM VANE, of Barningham, Barnard Castle.

b. 1819, s. 1881, m. 1845.	York, N.R. .	9,026 .	8,500

** MILDMAY, SIR HENRY BOUVERIE PAULET ST. JOHN, BART., of Dogmersfield Park, Winchfield, Hants.

Club. White's, Trav.,	Hants . . .	7,562 .	8,956
Brooks's.	Essex . . .	3,321 .	6,075
b. 1810, s. 1848, m. 1851.			
Served in 2nd Dragoon Guards.		10,883 .	15,031

MILES, MARTHA FRANCES, of Elston House, Devizes.

	Wilts . . .	4,627 .	4,146

MILES, PHILIP NAPIER, of Kings-Weston House, Bristol.

b. 1865, s. 1881.	Gloucester . .	3,207 .	9,092

MILDMAY, H. B., of Shoreham Pl.	Kent	2,564 .	3,563
** MILDMAY, H. G., of Hazelgrove.	Som.	2,500 .	5,000

MILES, Sir Philip John William, Bt., of Leigh Ct., Bristol.

			acres.		gr. an. val.
Coll. Eton, Trinity, Cam.	Somerset . .		4,929	.	6,442
Club. Army and Navy, Carl.	Co. Kerry . .		555	.	426
b. 1825, s. 1878, m. 1848.					
Served in 17th Lancers.			5,484	.	6,868
Sits for E. Somerset.					

BARKER-MILL, Lady, of Mottisfont, King's Somborne, Romsey.

s. 1860, m. 1828.	Hants . . .	5,040	.	5,751

MILLER, Sir Charles John Hubert, Bt., of Froyle, Alton.

Coll. Eton.	Hants . . .	4,008	.	4,667
b. 1858, s. 1868. Serves in Coldsm. Gds.				

*** MILLER, John, of Leithen Lodge, Innerleithen, N.B., &c.

Coll. Ayr Acad., Edin.	Peebles . . .	13,000	.	3,117
b. 1805, m. 1834.	Kincardine .	2,750	.	3,523
Sat for Edinburgh.		15,750	.	6,640

** MILLER, Thomas Horrocks, of Singleton, Poulton-le-Fylde.

Coll. Harrow.	Lancashire . .	3,223	.	5,856
Club. R.T.Y.C. b. 1846, s. 1865, m. 1869.				

MILLER, Sir William Frederick, Bart., of Barskimming, Mauchline, N.B.

b. 1868, s. 1875.	Ayrshire . .	4,453	.	3,823

MILLS, John, of Bisterne, Ringwood.

Coll. Ch. Ch. Oxon.	Hants . . .	4,144	.	4,512
Club. Carlton.	Warwick . .	172	.	355
b. 1836, s. 1871, m. 1868.		4,316	.	4,867

MILLS, Sir Charles H., Bart., of Hillingdon Court. Middlesex, Yorkshire . . 2,710 . 6,118

MILLS, Rev. H., of Pillerton. Warwick . 2,630 . 3,992

MILLS, T. R., of Saxham. Suffolk . . . 2,460 . 3,102

** MILLS, Joseph Trueman, of Clermont, Watton, &c.

		acres.	g. an. val.
Club. Reform.	Norfolk . . .	8,000 .	8,258
b. 1836, s. 1879, m. 1858.	Herts . . .	3,000 .	4,993
	Kent . . .	1,000 .	2,727
	Leicester . .	1,800 .	2,013
		13,800 .	17,991

These rents have been (for a time) much lowered.

*** MILNER, Sir Frederick George, Bart., of Nun Appleton, Tadcaster.

Coll. Eton, Ch. Ch. Oxon.	York, W.R. .	5,491 .	8,977
Club. Brooks's, Turf, St. James's. b. 1849, s. 1880, m. 1880.			

MILWARD, Mrs., of Thurgarton Priory, Southwell.

m. 1840, s. 1879.	Nottingham .	3,816 .	6,911

** MINTO, Earl of, K.T., Minto House, Hawick, N.B., &c.

Coll. Eton, Trin. Cam.	Roxburgh . .	8,663 .	6,888
Club. Brooks's, Travellers'.	Forfar . . .	3,446 .	3,308
b. 1814, s. 1859, m. 1844.	Fife	2,930 .	2,596
Served as Chairman Board of Lunacy for Scotland.	Selkirk . . .	1,032 .	264
		16,071 .	13,056

Sat for Hythe, Greenock, and Clackmannan.
Exclusive of minerals rented at 2,804*l.*

MILLTOWN, Earl of, Q. Co., K. Co., Wic., Dub., Tip.	5,042 .	2,597
MILNE, John, of Muchalls. Kincardine .	2,196 .	3,303
MILNE, J. D., of Ardmiddle. Aberdeen .	3,668 .	2,493
MINET (late), of Baldwyns. Kent, Dorset, Som.	2,681 .	3,995
S. MITFORD, H. R., of Exbury Park. Hants	2,120 .	2,019

** MIREHOUSE, Richard Walter Byrd, of Angle, Pembroke.

		acres.	g. an. val.
Coll. Eton, Univ. Oxon.	Pembroke . .	3,456	3,401
Club. Boodle's, Jun. Army.	Stafford . .	408	3,236
and Navy.	Cheshire . .	220	386
b. 1849, s. 1864, m. 1881.	Salop . . .	117	100
		4,201	7,123

Mr. M. is eld. son of Col. Levett, of Milford, who owns all the three smaller properties—these are uncorrected.

** OSBALDESTON-MITFORD, Colonel, of Mitford, Morpeth, &c. ⚓.

Club. Army and Navy.	Northumberland	4,620	4,330
b. 1809, s. 1870, m. 1844.	York, E.R. .	8,052	10,023
Served in 18th Foot and			
2nd W. I. Regt.		12,672	14,353

Inclusive of 518*l.* in Mrs. Mitford's name.

** MOIR, Alastair Erskine Graham, of Leckie, Stirling, N.B.

b. 1863, s. 1864.	Stirling . . .	3,450	3,520
	Perth . . .	304	380
		3,754	3,900

MOLESWORTH, Lady, of Pencarrow, Bodmin, &c.

s. 1855, m. 1st 182–,	Cornwall . .	8,064	6,747
2nd 1844.	Devon . . .	8,967	4,240
	Huntingdon .	3	10
		17,034	10,997

⚓. MITFORD, W. T., of Pitshill. Sussex. .	2,071	2,524
MOLISON, Francis, of Errol. Perth. . .	2,135	7,038
MOLONY, W. M., of Kiltanon. Clare . .	10,095	2,596

---

* MOLYNEUX, Rev. Sir John Charles, Bart., of Castle Dillon, Co. Armagh.

		acres.		g. an. val.
Coll. Christ's, Cam.	Co. Armagh .	6,009	.	4,598
b. 1843, s. 1879, m. 1873.	Co. Kildare .	2,226	.	1,530
	Limerick . .	1,378	.	1,002
	Queen's Co. .	6,726	.	952
	Co. Dublin .	221	.	[1,918]
		16,560	.	10,000

The return gives a total acreage of 12,693, and a rental of 8,082*l.* ; it, however, ignores the Dublin estate. The late Sir Capel Molyneux claimed a total rental of over 10,000*l.*, but did not specify the proportion to each county, the first four being entered as in the return, and Co. Dublin being vaguely credited with the balance.

*** MONCK, Viscount, G.C.M.G., Charleville, Bray.

Coll. Trinity, Dublin.	Kilkenny . .	5,544	.	3,509
Club. Bro. Ath. Arthur's.	Co. Wicklow .	2,478	.	1,648
b. 1819, s. 1849, m. 1844.	Wexford . .	5,717	.	2,941
Was Com. Ch. Temporali-	Co. Dublin .	193	.	2,237
ties for Irel., Gov. of	Co. Westmeath	212	.	131
Canada, L. of the Treas.,				
and L. P. Seal to the P. of		14,144	.	10,466
Wales. Sat for Ports-				
mouth.				

* MONCKTON, Edward Philip, of Fineshade, Wansford.

Coll. Trin. Cam.	Northampton .	928	.	1,275
Club. Junior Carlton.	Rutland . .	2,183	.	4,060
b. 1840, s. 1878, m. 1866.				
		3,111	.	5,335

** MONCKTON, Francis, of Somerford Hall, Brewood, Stafford.

Coll. Eton, Ch. Ch. Oxon.	Stafford . .	6,050	.	11,900

Club. Carlton, Junior Carlton, Boodle's.
b. 1844, s. 1858.   Sits for West Staffordshire.

MORE-MOLYNEUX, W., of Loseley. Surrey	2,406	.	3,249

MONCREIFFE, Sir Robert Drummond, Bart., of Moncreiffe
House, Bridge of Earn, N.B.

		acres.		*g. an. val.*
Coll. Harrow.	Perth . . .	4,743	.	7,247

Club. Marlb., Guards.
b. 1856, s. 1879, m. 1880. Served in Scots Gds.

** MONSON, Lord, Gatton Park, Reigate, &c. 🦢.

Coll. Ch. Ch. Oxon.	Lincoln . . .	8,100	.	16,000
Club. Brooks's, Ral.,	Surrey . . .	2,034	.	5,800
Dev., Grafton.				
		10,134	.	21,800

b. 1829, s. 1862, m. 1869.
Was Treas. Hhd.
Sat for Reigate.

*** MONTAGU, Andrew, of Ingmunthorpe, Wetherby, &c.

Club. Union, Carlton.	York, W.R. .	20,700	.	35,234
b. 180–, s. 1847.	Nottingham .	3,254	.	12,200
	Cornwall . .	2,657	.	3,495
	Northumberland	648	.	2,100
	Devon . . .	6	.	5
		27,265	.	53,034

MONTEAGLE, Lord, Mount Trenchard, Limerick.

Coll. Harrow, Trin. Cam.	Limerick . .	6,445	.	5,046
Club. N. Uni., Reform.	Co. Kerry . .	2,310	.	1,091
b. 1849, s. 1866, m. 1875.				
		8,755	.	6,137

** MONTEITH, Robert, of Carstairs House, Lanark, N.B.

Coll. Trin. Cam.	Lanark . . .	5,608	.	12,690
Club. Oxford and Cambridge.				

b. 1812, s. 1848, m. 1844.
Serves in H.M. Bodyguard of Scottish Archers.

MONTAGU, J., of Elm. Cam., Hunts., York   2,125 .   2,954

*** GRAHAM-MONTGOMERY, Sir Graham, Bart., of Stobo
Castle, Stobo, N.B.

		acres.	g. an. val.
Coll. Ch. Ch. Oxon.	Peebles . . .	18,172 .	7,055
Club. Carl., U. S., Cons.	Kinross . . .	2,454 .	4,830
b. 1823, s. 1839, m. 1845.	Somerset . .	8 .	19
Served as L. of the Treas.			
Sat for Peebles and Selkirk.		20,634 .	11,904

The rental of fishings in Loch Leven is included, but not the
acreage of the water, viz., 3,443.

*** MONTGOMERY, Hugh, of Grey Abbey, Newtownards.

Coll. Eton,Ch.Ch.Ox. Co. Down . . 5,580 . 5,907
Club. Carlton. b. 1821, s. 1831, m. 1846.

** MONTGOMERY, Hugh de Fellenberg, of Blessingbourne,
Fivemiletown, Co. Tyrone.

Coll. Ch. Ch. Oxon.	Co. Fermanagh	7,996 .	2,441
Club. United University.	Co. Tyrone .	4,552 .	2,484
b. 1844, s. 1844, m. 1870.			
		12,548 .	4,925

MONTGOMERY, Robert George, of Convoy House, Raphoe.

b. 1814, s. 1846. Donegal . . 8,861 . 3,640

MOLYNEUX-MONTGOMERIE,Cecil T., of Garboldisham. Norfolk	2,588 .	2,798
MONTGOMERY, A.,of Potters Walls. Ant.	3,736 .	2,511
MONTGOMERY, A. S., of Ballykeel. Mea., Wmea.	4,378 .	2,751
LYONS-MONTGOMERY, Hugh, of Belavel. Leitrim	10,179 .	2,791
MONTGOMERY, Sir Robert, K.C.B., of Newpark. Londonderry, Donegal . .	3,540 .	2,032

** MONTGOMERY, ROBERT JAMES, of Benvarden, Ballymoney.

		acres.	g. an. val.
Coll. Magd. Cambridge.	Co. Antrim .	7,797	. 4,164
Club. Army and Navy,	Londonderry .	736	. 1,040
Carlton.	Dublin . . .	19	. 253
b. 1828, s. 1876, m. 1864.	Donegal . .	227	. 242
		8,779	. 5,699

Served in 5th Drn. Gds. in Crimea.

*** MONTROSE, DUKE OF, K.T., Buchanan Castle, Glasgow, N.B.

		acres.	g. an. val.
Coll. Eton.	Stirling . . .	68,565	. 16,681
Club. Gds., Carl., Garr.,	Perth . . .	32,294	. 6,131
New Ed., Stir-	Dumbarton .	2,588	. 2,060
ling County.			
b. 1852, s. 1874, m. 1876.		103,447	. 24,872

Served in Coldstream Guards and 5th Lancers.
Exclusive of 20*l.* for a quarry.

** MOORE, ARTHUR JOHN, of Mooresfort, Co. Tipperary.

Club. St. George's.	Co. Tipperary	10,199	. 5,400
b. 1851, s. 1869, m. 1877.	Sits for Clonmel.		

MOORE, GEORGE AUGUSTUS, of Moorehall, Ballyglass, Co. Mayo.

Club. Union.	Co. Mayo . .	12,371	. 3,524
b. 1852, s. 1870.	Co. Galway .	41	. 24
	Roscommon .	110	. 72
		12,522	. 3,620

MONYPENNY, J. R. B., of Hadlow. Fife, Kent, Sus.	2,379	. 6,611
MONTGOMERY-MOORE, A., of Garvey. Tyr.	2,686	. 2,110
MOORE, REV. E., of Theobalds. Kent, Buc.	2,260	2,145

MOORE, GEORGE JOHN, of Appleby Hall, Atherstone.

			acres.	*g. an. val.*
Coll. Eton, Ch. Ch. Oxon.	Leicester	. .	2,468	. 4,431
Club. Boodle's, Carlton,	Derby	. . .	1,310	. 2,731
Jun. Carlton.	Lincoln	. . .	1,223	. 1,272
b. 1842, s. 1871, m. 1874.	Northampton	.	723	. 1,497
	Warwick	. .	272	. 493

	5,996	. 10,424

** GUNNING-MOORE, JOHN BYERS, of Loymount, Cookstown.

Coll. Peterhouse, Cam.   Tyrone . . .   4,798 .   4,600
Club. New Univ., Ulster, Belfast.   b. 1840, s. 1875, m. 1869.
  1,300 acres of this estate belong to MR. G. MOORE's father.

** CARRICK-MOORE, JOHN, of Corsewall, Stranraer, N.B., &c.

Coll. West., Queen's, Cam.	Surrey	. . .	166	. 225
Club. Athenæum.	Wigtown	. .	3,362	. 2,920
b. 1805, s. 1860, m. 1835.	Kirkcudbright		3,515	. 2,132
	Ayr	. . . .	2,079	. 1,726

	9,122	. 7,003

MOORE, STEWART JAMES, of Ballydivity, Dervock, Co. Antrim.

b. 1847, s. 1870, m. 1872.   Co. Antrim .   8,242 .   3,334
  Served in 11th Hussars.

MORANT, JOHN, of Brokenhurst Park, Lymington.

Coll. Ch. Ch. Oxon.   Hants . . .   5,596 .   8,266
Club. Boodle's.
b. 1825, s. 1857, m. 1st 1855, 2nd 1866.

MONTGOMERY-MOORE, F. ACHESON, of
      Aughnacloy. Tyrone . . . . . .   2,746 . 2,671
MOORE, REV. G. B., of Tunstall. Kent .   2,254 . 3,997
MOORE, S., of Barne. Tip., Cork, Wat. .   2,141 . 2,184
MOORE, W. M., of Grimeshill. Wmld., York. 2,031 . 2,121

** HOME-DRUMMOND-MORAY, Charles Stirling, of Blair Drummond, Stirling, N.B., &c.

		acres.	g. an. val.
Club. Carlton.	Perth . . .	38,797	29,720
b. 1816, s. 1864 and 1876,	Berwick . .	1,494	1,586
m. 1845.	Stirling . . .	377	708
Served in 15th Hussars and 2nd Life Guards.		40,668	32,014

The Abercairny estate has been in this family since 1300.

* MORAY, Earl of, Doune Lodge, Perth, N.B., &c.

		acres.	g. an. val.
Club. Travellers'.	Perth . . .	40,553	10,800
b. 1814, s. 1872 and 1878.	Elgin . . .	21,669	9,420
Inc. of 3,000*l.* for salmon	Fife	7,463	8,735
fisheries, but exc. of 2,350*l.*	Inverness . .	7,035	5,171
for mines.	Kircudbright .	339	345
Only the late LADY GRAY'S	Midlothian .	238	1,405
estates are corrected.	Nairn . . .	315	202
In LADY GRAY'S name :			
	Perth . . .	2,478	7,873
	Forfar . . .	1,539	2,912
		81,629	46,863

** MORDAUNT, Sir Charles, Bart., of Walton Hall, Warwick.

		acres.	g. an. val.
Coll. Eton, Ch. Ch. Oxon.	Somerset . .	4,123	8,057
Club. Arthur's, Carlton.	Warwick . .	3,325	4,735
b. 1836, s. 1845, m. 1866, 2nd 1878.			
Sat for S. Warwickshire.		7,448	12,792

*** MORE, Robert Jasper, of Linley Hall, Bishop's Castle, &c.

		acres.	g. an. val.
Coll. Shrew., Ball. Ox.	Salop . . .	5,593	4,680
Club. Brooks's, Oxf. and	Montgomery .	298	220
Cam., Devonshire.	Hereford . .	198	120
b. 1836, s. 1869, m. 1871.			
Sat for S. Salop.		6,089	5,020

Exclusive of about 3,200*l.* for rental of lead mines. Mr. More points out that while lead mines are equally rateable with coal and iron mines, the Parliamentary Return ignores them, but that the Local Government Board has promised him to amend this should a second edition of the Return be issued.

** PALMER-MOREWOOD, Charles Rowland, of Alfreton.

			acres.	g. an. val.
Coll. St. John's, Oxon.	Derby . .		4,400 .	6,000
Club. Junior Carlton, Wind.	Warwick . .		1,700 .	3,500
b. 1843, s. 1873, m. 1873.				
			6,100 .	9,500

Inclusive of 200 acres held by Mr. P. Morewood in common with "others," but exclusive of mine rents.

*** MORISON, Mrs., of Bognie, Huntly, N.B.

s. 1879, m. 1836.	Aberdeen . .	8,440 .	5,886

*** MORISON, Mrs. of Mountblairy, Turriff, N.B.

s. 1874, m. 1836.	Banff . . .	4,064 .	3,066
	Aberdeen . .	1,792 .	1,268
		5,856 .	4,334

** MORLEY, Dowager Countess of, Whiteway, Chudleigh.

s. 1877, m. 1834, 2nd 1842.	Co. Cavan . .	10,540 .	2,734
	Devon . . .	1,924 .	2,465
		12,464 .	5,199

** MORLEY, Earl of, Saltram House, Plympton.

Coll. Eton, Ball. Oxon.   Devon . . .   4,238 . 8,209
Club. Brooks's, Travellers'.   b. 1843, s. 1864, m. 1876.
Was L. in Waiting, is U. Sec. for War.

MORRELL, George Herbert *(jur. ux.)*, of Headington, Oxon.

Coll. Rugby, Exeter, Oxon.	Oxford . . .	2,795 .	9,370
Club. New University.	Berks . . .	820 .	785
b. 1845, m. 1874.			
		3,615 .	10,155

MORELAND, W., of Raheen. Cork, Lim.	2,406 .	3,249
BROWN-MORISON, J. Brown, of Murie.		
Perth, Kinross	2,082 .	4,167
MORLAND, W.C., of Lamberhurst, Kent, Sus.	2,781 .	4,947

MORRIS, CHARLES JOHN, of Berth Lloyd, Montgomery, &c.

		acres.		g. an. val.
Coll. Eton, Ch. Ch. Oxon.	Montgomery .	3,923	.	2,501
b. 1831, s. 1866 and 1878,	Stafford . .	2,051	.	3,127
m. 1862.	Salop . . .	992	.	2,184
		6,966	.	7,812

MORRIS (late), RICHARD, of Dunkettle, Cork.

d. 1880.	Co. Cork . .	6,494	.	3,292

*** MORRISON, ALFRED, of Fonthill House, Hindon, Wilts.

Coll. Edin., Trin. Cam.	Wilts . . .	7,704	.	6,195
Club. Brooks's, Reform.	Dorset . . .	480	.	376
b. 1821, m. 1866.				
		8,184	.	6,571

*** MORRISON, CHARLES, of Basildon Park, Reading, &c.

Club. Reform.	Argyll . . .	67,000	.	16,439
b. 1817, s. 1857.	Berks . . .	6,987	.	12,206
	Suffolk . . .	811	.	1,513
	Oxon . . .	531	.	724
	Essex . . .	403	.	552
		75,732	.	31,434

** MORRISON, GEORGE, of Hampworth Lodge, Salisbury.

Coll. Eton, Ball. Oxon.	Bucks . . .	3,070	.	5,308
Club. Brooks's, Travellers',	Wilts . . .	2,647	.	1,356
New Univ.	Oxford . . .	516	.	806
b. 1839.				
		6,233	.	7,470

Inc. of 500 acres which, since the return, he has purchased from the Eccl. Coms. in Wilts., and vaguely est. at 10*s.* per acre.

MORRIS, SIR J. A., BART., of Sketty.	Glam.	2,064	.	3,478
MORRIS, T. C., of Bryn Merddyn.	Carm.	2,642	.	2,172
** MORRIS, S., of Wretham.	Norfolk . .	6,556	.	2,000
MORRIS, WILLIAM, of Cwm.	Carmarthen .	2,810	.	2,994
MORRISON, FRANK, of Hole Park.	Kent .	2,913	.	3,754

*** MORRISON, Walter, of Malham Tarn, Leeds.

			acres.		g. an. val.
Coll. Eton, Ball. Oxon,	York, W.R.	.	13,705	.	4,371
Club. Reform, Uni. Univ.	Hereford .	.	148	.	140
b. 1836.					
Sat for Plymouth.			13,853	.	4,511

** MORRITT, Robert Ambrose, of Rokeby, Barnard Castle.

		acres.		g. an. val.
Club. Carl., A. & N., New	York,N.&W.R.	7,200	.	8,400
Edin.	Durham . . .	1	.	3
b. 1816, s. 1874, m. 1872.	Westmoreland	58	.	124
Served in 77th Foot				
		7,259	.	8,527

*** MORTON, Earl of, Dalmahoy, Midcalder, &c., N.B.

			acres.		g. an. val.
Club. Trav., Carlton.	Midlothian	.	10,411	.	14,763
b. 1818, s. 1858, m. 1st 1844,	Argyll .	.	49,814	.	1,870
2nd 1853.	Berwick	.	2,551	.	1,050
Served in 11th Hussars.	Linlithgow	.	91	.	75
	Fife . .	.	1,644	.	3,450
	Leicester	.	650	.	1,080
			65,161	.	22,288

Inc. 8,812*l.* of L. Aberdour's.

* MORTON, Henry Thomas (res. Biddick Hall, Durham).

		acres.		g. an. val.
Club. Ref., Wind., Dev.	Northumberland	6,336	.	3,006

** MOSLEY, Sir Tonman, Bt., of Rolleston, Burton-on-Trent.

			acres.		g. an. val.
Coll. Magd.Cambridge.	Stafford .	.	3,446	.	7,000
Club. Army and Navy.	Derby .	.	50	.	100
b. 1813, s. 1871, m. 1847.	Bucks .	.	207	.	400
Served in Inniskilling Dragoons.					
			3,703	.	7,500

MORTLOCK, E. J., of Abington.	Cambridge	2,827	.	4,196
MOSELEY, Walter, of Buildwas.	Salop .	2,260	.	2,690

** MOSTYN, Sir Pyers William, Bart., of Talacre, Rhyl.

		acres.	g. an. val.
b. 1846, s. 1882, m. 1880.	Flint . . .	4,184 .	9,000

LLOYD-MOSTYN, Llewelyn Nevill Vaughan, of Gloddaeth, Llandudno.

b. 1856, m. 1879.	Flint . . .	5,462 .	10,474
	Carnarvon . .	2,025 .	4,053
	Denbigh . .	292 .	225
		7,779 .	14,752

** MOTT, John Thomas, of Barningham Hall, Norwich.

Coll. Harrow, Ch. Ch. Oxon. Norfolk . . .   5,331   5,863
Club. Hanover Square.
b. 1809, m. 1833. Inclusive of 6 acres in his eldest son's name.

** MOUNT, William George, of Wasing Place, Reading.

Coll. Eton, Ball. Oxon.	Berks . . .	4,191 .	5,153
Club. Oxf. and Cam.	Hants . . .	6 .	10
b. 1824, s. 1869, m. 1862.			
		4,197 .	5,163

* MOUNTCASHELL, Earl of, Moore Park, Kilworth, Cork.

Coll. Trin. Cam.	Co. Cork . .	5,961 .	3,606
Club. National.	Tipperary . .	383 .	119
b. 1792, s. 1822, m. 1819.	Ditto . . .	6,000 .	unstated
		12,344 .	3,725

The second entry for Tipperary is all down in the Gov. return in the tenants' names. Lord M. does not mention the rental.

** MOUNT-EDGCUMBE, Earl of, Mount Edgcumbe, Devonport, &c. ≋.

Coll. Harrow, Ch. Ch. Oxon.	Cornwall . .	13,288 .	17,680
Club. Carlton, Travellers',	Devon . . .	4,935 .	6,501
White's, Marl., Turf.			
b. 1832, s. 1861, m. 1858.		18,223 .	24,181

Served as Equerry, Lord of the Bedchamber, Extra Lord of the Bedchamber to the Prince of Wales, and Lord Chamberlain. Sat for Plymouth.

MOSTYN of Llewesog, Denb., Flint, Mer., Oxon., Carn.	4,153 .	2,791

** MOUNTGARRET, Viscount, Ballyconra, Kilkenny.

		acres.	g. an. val.
Coll. Worc., Oxon.	Kilkenny . .	14,073 .	8,503
Club. Carlton, Ox. & Cam.	Co. Wexford .	505 .	303
b. 1816, s. 1846, m. 1844.	York, W.R. .	120 .	800
		14,698 .	9,606

** MOUNT-TEMPLE, Lord, Broadlands, Romsey, &c.

		acres.	g. an. val.
Coll. Eton.	Hants . . .	6,135 .	7,609
Club. Reform, Athenæum,	York, W.R. .	1,249 .	1,862
Trav., Brooks's.	Herts . . .	23 .	11
b. 1811, s. 1865, m. 1st 1843,	Co. Dublin. .	738 .	6,788
2nd 1848.			
		8,145 .	16,270

Served in Royal Horse Guards, and as Lord of the Treasury, of the Admiralty, Under Secretary for the Home Department, President Board of Health, Vice-President of Council of Education and Vice-President of the Board of Trade, and First Commissioner of the Board of Works. Sat for Hertford and S. Hants.

MOUTRAY, Rev. John James, of Favor Royal, Aughnacloy.

		acres.	g. an. val.
Coll. Trinity, Dublin.	Co. Tyrone .	6,554 .	4,771
b. 1802, s. 1836.	Co. Monaghan	48 .	34
		6,602 .	4,805

Inc. 9*l.* in his eldest son's name.

*** MULHOLLAND, John, of Ballywalter Pk., Greyabbey, &c.

		acres.	g. an. val.
Club. Carlton, Sack. St.	Co. Down . .	13,506 .	17,625
	Tyrone . . .	1,182 .	1,799
b. 1819, s. 1866, m. 1851.			
Sits for Downpatrick.		14,688 .	19,424

MASSINGBERD-MUNDY, Charles John Henry, of South Ormsby Hall, Alford.

		acres.	g. an. val.
Coll. Eton, Ch. Ch. Oxon.	Lincoln . . .	3,358 .	4,784
Club. Carlton. b. 1808, s. 1863, m. 1838.			

MOWBRAY, G., of Grangewood, Lei., Nbld., Dy. 3,010 . 2,166

* MUNDY, Sir Robert Miller, K.C.M.G. (*jur. ux.*), of
    Littlecote, Hungerford.   *acres.*   *g. an. val.*

			acres		g. an. val.
Coll. Woolwich.	Wilts	. .	5,574	.	6,452
Club. United Service.	Somerset	. .	1,517	.	2,089
b. 1813, s. 1881, m. 1841.	Berks	. .	238	.	448
Served in R.A., as L.-Gov.	Hants	. .	66	.	275
of Grenada, and of Br.					
Honduras.			7,395	.	9,264

        The last estate only belongs to him.

MUNRO, Sir Charles, Bart., of Foulis Castle, Dingwall, N.B.

Coll. Edinburgh.   Ross   . .   4,458   .   3,780
b. 1795, s. 1848, m. 1st 1817, 2nd 1853.
    Served in 45th Foot, at Badajoz, C. Rodrigo, Salamanca,
Vittoria, Orthes, and Toulouse.

        This property is returned as his eldest son's.

** MUNRO, Sir Thomas, Bart., of Lindertis, Kirriemuir, N.B.

  Coll. Eton,Ch.Ch.Ox.   Forfar   . . .   5,702   .   6,580
  Club. White's, Travellers', Carlton.
b. 1819, s. 1827.   Served in 10th Hussars.

** MURE, William, of Caldwell, Beith by Glasgow, N.B.

b. 1870, s. 1880.	Renfrew	. .	3,624	.	4,387
	Ayr	. . .	1,400	.	1,861
			5,024	.	6,248

    Exclusive of 997*l.* for minerals and quarries.

MULCOCK, H. J., of Ropley. Hants . .	2,572	.	2,439
§ MUNCASTER, L. Cum., Lanc., Wmld.	5,811	.	2,629
MUNDY, A. E. M., of Shipley. Notts, Dby.	2,879	.	6,810
MUNDY, F. N., of Markeaton. Derby. .	2,765	.	7,749
MUNTZ, G. F., of Umberslade. War., Wor.	2,562	.	4,212
MURLAND, Samuel, of Woodlawn. Down	2,237	.	3,220

MURPHY, Patrick Edward, of Ballinacloon, Mullingar, Co.
Westmeath.

		acres.	*g. an. val.*
b. 18—.	Westmeath .	9,693 .	6,020

MURPHY, William, of Mount Merrion, Stillorgan, Co. Dublin.

Club. Reform.	Roscommon .	5,422 .	3,779
b. 1833, m. 1856.	Co. Meath . .	2,660 .	2,665
	Co. Dublin .	29 .	279
		8,111 .	6,723

*** MURRAY, Lt.-Col. John, of Polmaise Castle, Stirling, N.B.

Club. Carl., Marl., Gds.	Stirling . . .	6,813 .	9,047

b. 1831, s. 1862, m. 1st 1859, 2nd 1877.
  Served in Grenadier Guards in the Crimea.
  Exclusive of 846*l.* for coals and minerals.

** MURRAY, Sir Patrick Keith, Bart., of Ochtertyre,
Crieff, N.B.

Coll. Trin. Cam.	Perth . . .	17,876 .	11,051

Club. New, Edinburgh.
b. 1835, s. 1861, m. 1st 1870, 2nd 1876.
  Served in Grenadier Guards.

MURRAY, William Hugh Eric, of Geanies, Tain, N.B.

b. 1858, s. 1876.	Ross . . .	5,303 .	4,400

*** MUSGRAVE, Sir Richard George, Bart., of Edenhall,
Penrith.

b. 1872, s. 1881.	Cumberland .	10,543 .	9,780
Exclusive of mine rents.	Westmoreland	3,121 .	2,440
	Durham. . .	1,785 .	2,796
		15,449 .	15,016

MURPHY, John. Rosc., Dub., Lim., Cork	6,515 .	2,477
MURPHY, J., of Castletown. Lou.,Arm.,Wic.	3,110 .	2,916
SCOTT-MURRAY, C., of Hambleden. Buc.	2,528 .	4,231
MURRAY, J. W., of Cringletie. Peeb., Lnk.	5,838 .	2,950
MURRAY, Lady J., of Otterburn. Nhmbd.	5,049 .	2,037
MURRAY, Sir John, Bart., of Philiphaugh. Selkirk, Roxburgh	2,799 .	3,035

** MUSGRAVE, Sir Richard John, Bart., of Tourin, Cappo-
quin, Co. Waterford, &c. 🍂.   *acres.*   *g. an. val.*

Coll. Eton.   Waterford . .   8,282 .   5,245
Club. Windham, Kildare St., Co. Kilkenny   124 .   181
          Dublin.   ⎯⎯⎯⎯⎯⎯⎯⎯⎯⎯⎯
b. 1850, s. 1874.   8,406 .   5,426

** WYKEHAM-MUSGRAVE, Wenman Aubrey, of Barnsley
Park, Cirencester, &c.

Coll. Eton, Ch. Ch. Oxon.   Gloucester . .   4,399 .   4,729
Club. Junior Carlton.   Oxon . . .   5,386 .   8,170
b. 1838, s. 1879, m. 1870.   Bucks . . .   4,590 .   7,100
                               Durham . .   1,464 .   1,812
                               Kent . . .   460 .   2,000
                               Cumberland .   196 .   280
                                              ⎯⎯⎯⎯⎯⎯⎯⎯⎯⎯⎯
                                               16,495 . 24,091

MUSKERRY, Lord, Springfield Castle, Drumcolloher, Limerick.

b. 1854, s. 1868, m. 1872.   Wexford . .   10,324 .   7,575
    Serves in Royal Navy.   Limerick . .   3,161 .   1,976
                               Tipperary . .   742 .   394
                               Co. Carlow .   419 .   324
                               Waterford . .   351 .   222
                               Kilkenny . .   252 .   228
                               Co. Cork . .   28 .   17
                                              ⎯⎯⎯⎯⎯⎯⎯⎯⎯⎯⎯
                                               15,277 . 10,736

Only 2,995*l.* of these rents are his Lordship's, the rest being
held by his mother, the Hon. Mrs. Deane-Morgan, who also
holds 541 acres in common with Lady Granard.

MUSSENDEN, Mrs., of Larchfield, Hillsborough, Co. Down.

m. 1866.   Co. Down . .   3,098 .   3,520

MUSGRAVE, Jas. & John, of Drumglass.
    Donegal . . . . 23,693 .   2,659

*** MUSTERS, JOHN CHAWORTH, of Annesley Pk., Nottingham.

			acres.	*g. an. val.*
Coll.	Eton, Ch. Ch. Ox.	Notts . . .	8,211 .	13,787
Club.	Carlton, Boodle's.			

b. 1838, s. 1849, m. 1859.

** MYNORS, ROBERT BASKERVILLE, of Evancoyd, Kington.

Coll.	Eton, Ch. Ch. Oxon.	Radnor . .	7,000 .	5,760
Club.	Oxford and Cam.	Hereford . .	1,041 .	1,430

b. 1819, s. 1866, m. 1852.

	8,041 .	7,193

* NAESMYTH, SIR JAMES, BT. (of Posso), Dalwick, Stobo, N.B.

Club.	National.	Peebles . .	15,485 .	3,557

b. 1827, s. 1876, m. 1850. Served in Bengal C.S.

** NAIRNE, WILLIAM, of Dunsinane, Balbeggie, Perth, N.B.

Coll.	Trin. Cambridge.	Perth . . .	3,330 .	3,529
Club.	New Edinburgh.	b. 1852, s. 1866.		

*** ELLIS-NANNEY, HUGH JOHN, of Gwynfryn, Criccieth, &c.

Coll.	Eton, Brase. Oxon.	Carnarvon . .	7,587 .	4,575
Club.	Junior Carlton.	Merioneth . .	4,150 .	1,142
b. 1845, s. 1870, m. 1875.		Montgomery .	335 .	97

	12,072 .	5,814

Some of these lands are given in the return to a " MR. VANNEY."

** NAPER, JAMES LENNOX, of Loughcrew, Oldcastle, Co. Meath.

Coll.	Eton, Ch. Ch. Oxon.	Co. Meath .	18,863 .	15,581
Club.	Travellers', Carlton.	Westmeath .	176 .	77

b. 1825, s. 1868, m. 1877.

	19,039 .	15,658

MYTTON, D. H., of Garth. Mgy., Heref. .	2,678 .	4,574
CHICHESTER-NAGLE, JOSEPH, of Calverleigh. Devon, Cork	3,495 .	2,784

*** NAYLOR, John, of Leighton Hall, Welshpool, &c.

			acres.		g. an. val.
Coll. Eton, Trin. Cam.	Montgomery .		11,257	.	12,687
b.1813, s. 1872, m.1846.	Salop . . .		467	.	153

Value of woods not included. 11,724 . 12,840

*** NAYLOR, Richard Christopher, of Hooton Hall, Chester, &c

Coll. Eton.	Cheshire . .		3,128	.	7,300
Club. Carlton, Arthur's.	Northampton .		5,174	.	10,239
b. 1814, m. 1st 1854,	Lancashire .		331	.	2,662
2nd 1856.					
			8,633	.	20,201

*** NEAVE, Sir Thomas Lewis Hughes, Bart., of Dagnam, Romford, &c.

b. 1874, s. 1877.	Anglesea . .		5,739	.	4,300
	Essex . . .		3,796	.	5,956
	Somerset . .		240	.	85
	Surrey . . .		9	.	35
	Kent . . .		176	.	223
			9,960	.	10,599

** NEELD, Sir John, Bart., of Grittleton, Chippenham, &c.

Coll. Harr., Tr. Cam.	Wilts . . .		13,112	.	18,658
Club. Carl., Bood., Con.	Middlesex . .		668	.	2,056
b. 1805, s. 1856, m. 1845.	Herts . . .		27	.	38
Was Gent. of the Privy	Gloucester . .		5	.	9
Chamber. Sat for Crick-					
lade and for Chippenham.			13,812	.	20,761

NAPIER and ETTRICK, Lord, K.T. Selkirk, Midlothian	6,991	.	2,316
NAPPER (late), J., of Ifold. Suss., Sur. .	3,880	.	2,861
NATION, W. H. C., of Rockbeare. Dev., Somerset	2,743	.	5,466
NEAL, William, of Kingsdon. Somerset .	2,170	.	3,650

*** NELSON, Earl, Trafalgar, Salisbury.

			acres.	g. an. val.
Coll. Eton, Trin. Cam.	Wilts	. . .	7,196 .	5,800
Club. Carlton. b. 1823, s. 1835, m. 1845.				

*** NESBITT, Alexander, of Lismore, Crossdoney, Co. Cavan.

Club. Athenæum.	Co. Cavan . .	9,735 .	5,981
b. 1817, s. 1856, m. 1856.	King's Co. . .	1,482 .	276
	Sussex . . .	280 .	187
		11,497 .	6,444

DOWNING-NESBITT, Miss, of Leixlip Ho., Kildare.

s. 1874.	Roscommon .	3,641 .	1,627
	Londonderry .	5,638 .	2,221
	King's Co. .	2,555 .	1,642
	Co. Antrim .	321 .	294
	Co. Kildare .	36 .	90
		12,191 .	5,874

Miss Nesbitt has in common with Count Susi 620 acres in Limerick, rented at 673*l.*

NEVILE, George, of Stubton, Newark.

b. 1822, m. 1846.	Lincoln . .	2,574 .	3,949
	Notts . . .	1,012 .	1,628
	York, W.R. .	15 .	9
		3,601 .	5,586

** NEVILE, Ralph Henry Christopher, of Wellingore Hall, Grantham, &c.

Coll. Trin. Cam.	Lincoln . . .	6,486 .	9,625
Club. St. James's.	Northampton	44 .	83
b. 1850, s. 1861, m. 1871.	Notts . . .	1 .	9
		6,531 .	9,717

3,900 acres more belong to his mother for life.

NETTERVILLE, Vis., Tip., Gal., Meath. . 3,332 . 2,153

** NEWALL, John Lightfoot, of Forest Hall, Ongar.

		acres.	g. an. val.
Club. Reform.	Essex . .	3,723 .	6,500
b. 1826, m. 1849.			

NEWBOROUGH, Lord, Glynnllivon Park, Carnarvon.

Coll. Rugby, Ch. Ch. Ox.	Carnarvon . .	22,063 .	16,234
Club. Athenæum.	Denbigh . .	3,822 .	2,448
b. 1803, s. 1832, m. 1834.	Anglesea . .	1,745 .	1,141
	Merioneth . .	1,170 .	2,903
		28,800 .	22,726

NEWCASTLE, Duke of, Clumber Park, Ollerton, &c. 🐍.

Coll. Eton.	Notts . . .	34,467 .	73,098
b. 1864, s. 1879.	Derby . . .	827 .	1,124
	York, W.R. .	237 .	307
	Lincoln . .	16 .	18
		35,547 .	74,547

** NEWCOME, Mrs., of Feltwell Hall, Brandon.

s. 1871, m. 1846.	Norfolk. . .	5 034 .	3,49c

The rental is net; the greater half of this estate belongs to her son, F. D'A. W. C. Newcome, of Hockwold Hall.

** NEWCOMEN, Arthur Henry Turner, of Kirkleatham Hall, Redcar.

Club. Junior Carlton, Turf.	York, N.W. .	4,545 .	5,431
b. 1844, s. 1865, m. 1863.			

NEWDEGATE, Charles Newdigate, of Arbury, Nuneaton, &c.

Coll. Eton, King's, Lon.,	Warwick . .	5,318 .	8,318
& Ch. Ch. Oxon.	Middlesex . .	1,491 .	2,524
Club. Arth., Carl., Trav.,			
Nat., Whi., Boodle's.		6,809 .	10,842
b. 1816, s. 1832. Sits for N. Warwickshire.			

NEVILE, G., of Thorney Hall.	Nottingham	2,373 .	2,263
NEVILL, E. A., of Dangstein.	Hants, Nfk. .	2,915 .	3,261

** NEWDIGATE, Lieut.-Col., of West Hallam, Derby.

			acres.		g. an. val.
Coll. Roy. Mil. Sandhurst.	Derby	. .	2,062	.	5,385
Club. Carlton, Uni. Ser.	Warwick	. .	1,262	.	1,719
b. 1822, s. 1862, m.1st 1859,	Stafford	. .	856	.	1,143
2nd 1870.					
Served in Coldstream Guards.			4,180	.	8,247

Incl. of 153 ac. of Crown leaseholds ; the rental is overstated.

*** NEWMAN, John Adam Richard, of Dromore, Mallow.

Coll. Eton,Magd.Cam.	Co. Cork	. .	5,872	.	3,513
Club. Carl., Kild. St.					

b. 1844, s. 1859, m. 1870.
              Inclusive of about 400*l.* of head rents.

NEWMAN, Sir Lydston, Bart., of Mamhead, Exeter.

Club. Army and Navy.	Devon	. . .	5,290	.	6,587

b. 1823, s. 1854, m. 1860.   Served in 7th Hussars in the Crimea.

** NEWTON, Andrew Willoughby, of Killymeel, Dungannon.

Coll. Upp. Trin. Dublin.	Co. Donegal	.	10,486	.	2,151
Club. St. Ste., U. Dublin.	Co. Leitrim	.	1,126	.	397
b. 1849, s. 1877, m. 1872.	Co. Tyrone	.	496	.	583
			12,108	.	3,131

** NEWTON, George Onslow, of Croxton Park, St. Neots.

Coll. Eton, Trin. Cam.	Cambridge	. .	2,794	.	3,371
Club. Arthur's, Boodle's.	Huntingdon	.	3,209	.	3,711
b. 1830, s. 1851, m. 1st 1852,					
2nd 1858, 3rd 1878.			6,003	.	7,082

NEWTON, John Gubbins, of Bridestowe.

s. 1872.	Devon	. . .	6,490	.	4,143

NEWENHAM, Rev. E., of Coolmore. Cork	2,740	.	3,643
HARDING-NEWMAM, of Nelmes, Ess., Dev.	2,236	.	3,571

*** NEWTON, PHILIP JOCELYN, of Dunleckney, Bagenalstown.

		acres.	g. an. val.
Coll. Eton, Ch. Ch. Oxon.	Co. Carlow .	5,134 .	4,026

Club. Kildare St. Dublin.
b. 1818, s. 1853, m. 1st 1841, 2nd 1851.

** NEWTON, THOMAS HENRY GOODWIN, of Barrell's Park, Henley-in-Arden, &c.

Coll. St. John's, Cam.	Argyll . . .	25,000 .	1,821
Club. National.	Warwick . .	973 .	2,042
b. 1836, s. 1862, m. 1st 1861,	Worcester . .	387 .	446
2nd 1865.		26,360 .	4,309

The Scotch estate (Glencreepesdale) is shared by MR. NEWTON with his brother, the REV. HORACE NEWTON.

** NICOLL, GEORGE WHITLOCK, of The Ham, Cowbridge.

Club. Athenæum.	Glamorgan . .	1,375 .	1,859
b. 1816, s. 1871, m. 1853.	Monmouth . .	1,956 .	1,884
		3,331 .	3,743

NICHOLL, JOHN COLE, of Merthyr Mawr, Bridgend.

Coll. Eton, Ch. Ch. Oxon.	Glamorgan . .	4,894 .	6,565

Club. Ath., J. U. S.
b. 1823, s. 1853, m. 1860. Served in R. Brig.

*** NICHOLSON, CHR. ARMYTAGE, of Balrath Burry, Kells.

Coll. Trinity, Cambridge.	Meath . . .	7,693 .	6,277

Club. Trav., Prince's, M. C. C., Sack. St. b. 1825, s. 1872, m. 1858.

* NICOL, WILLIAM EDWARD, of Ballogie, Aberdeen, N.B.

Club. R. Nortnern, Aber.	Aberdeen . .	6,200 .	1,950
b. 1846, s. 1872, m. 1873.	Kincardine .	2,350 .	3,402
		8,550 .	5,352

The Kincardine estate (uncorrected) belongs to his mother.

NEWTON, F. W., of Barton. Som., Linc.	2,664 .	3,615
HAY-NEWTON, W. D. O., of Newton. Had.	2,857 .	2,818
NIBLETT, J. D. T., of Haresfield. Glou.	2,003 .	3,512

*** NICOLSON, James Badenach, of Glenbervie House,
 Drumlithie, Fordoun, N.B.   *acres.* *g. an. val.*
b. 1832, s. 1878, m. 1864. Kincardine . 9,642 . 4,646

NIGHTINGALE, Miss F., of Lea Hurst, Matlock, &c.

s. 1874 and 1880.	Wilts. . . .	533 .	573
Highly distinguished for	Derby . . .	1,381 .	2,216
her services to the sick and	Hants . . .	2,413 .	1,502
wounded in the Crimean			
War.			
		4,327 .	4,291

NORBURY, Earl of, Cabra Honse, Dublin, &c.

Coll. Harrow.	Co. Tipperary .	7,798 .	3,050
b. 1862, s. 1873.	Co. Clare . .	2,453 .	782
	Co. Mayo . .	1,024 .	264
	Co. Sligo . .	1,006 .	313
		12,281 .	4,409

*** NORTHCLIFFE, Rev. Charles Best, of Langton House,
 Malton, &c.

Coll. Univ. Durham.
s. 1833 and 1881. York, E.R. . 3,528 . 4,550

*** NORFOLK, Duke of, Arundel Castle, Sussex, &c. ♿.

Club. St. James's., Trav.,	York, W.R. .	19,440 .	39,897
St. George's.	Sussex . . .	21,446 .	27,557
b. 1847, s. 1860, m. 1877.	Norfolk. . .	4,460 .	5,095
Is Hereditary Earl Mar-	Surrey . . .	3,172 .	2,247
shal of England.	Derby . . .	1,274 .	493
	Suffolk . .	47 .	194
	Stafford. . .	25 .	74
	Notts . . .	2 .	39
		49,866 .	75,596

Not inclusive of the value of mines or of shooting.

NICHOLSON, W., of Basing Park. Hants 3,014 . 2,323

** NORMAN, Rev. Charles Frederick, of Mistley Place, Manningtree.

			acres.		g. an. val.
Coll.	K. Coll. Sch., St.	Essex . . .	2,186	.	4,930
	Cath. Cam.	Suffolk . . .	1,079	.	1,375
Club.	United University.	Somerset . .	1	.	85
b. 1829, s. 1862, m. 1854.					
			3,266	.	6,390

This includes some 200 acres of salt marshes in Suffolk, which are omitted in the return.

NORMANBY, Marquis of, G.C.M.G., Mulgrave Castle, Whitby.

Club. Travellers', Brooks's.	York, N.R.	.	6,834	.	7,037
b. 1819, s. 1863, m. 1844.					

Served in S. F. Gds., was Compt. of the Hhold., T. of the Hhold., Gov. of Nova Scotia, a L. in Waiting, Capt. of the Gent.-at-Arms, Gov. of Queensland and of New Zealand. Is Gov. of Victoria. Sat for Scarborough.

*** NORMANTON, Earl of, Somerley, Ringwood.

Coll. Wstm., Trin. Cam.	Lincoln . .	7,020	.	14,900
Club. White's, Trav.,	Wilts . . .	10,060	.	10,819
Brooks's, St. Jam.,	Hants . . .	9,468	.	7,290
Marlborough.	Northampton .	1,065	.	2,030
b. 1818, s. 1868, m. 1856.	Dorset . . .	1,153	.	840
Sat for Wilton.	Co. Tipperary	7,625	.	6,868
	Co. Kilkenny .	5,567	.	4,643
	Co. Limerick .	1,003	.	890
		42,961	.	48,280

NORMAN, G. W., of Bromley. Kent, Suss., Hants	2,849	.	4,704
LEE-NORMAN, L., of Corbollis. Lou., Mea.	2,155	.	2,261
NORMAN, Thomas, of Glengollan. Donegal	5,411	.	2,333

NORTH, Col., and NORTH, Baroness, Wroxton Abbey,
 Banbury, &c.   *acres.*   *g. an. val.*

Coll.	Sandhurst.	Oxford . .	3,620	.	6,940
Club.	Carl., White's, Trav.,	Northampton .	2,246	.	4,576
	U. Ser., Marlb.	Warwick . .	697	.	1,453

b. 1804, m. 1835.

              6,563 . 12,969

   Served in 18th Foot. Sits for Oxfordshire.

 Col. N. is returned as owner of all these lands but 1,257 acres
in Oxfordshire ; for other estates see North, Hon. W. H. J., his
son.

** NORTH, North, of Thurland Castle, Kirkby Lonsdale (res.
 Dinard, France).

Club. Jun. United Service.   Lancashire   .   3,471   .   3,045
b. 1824, s. 1865, m. 1856.   Served in Indian Army.

NORTH, Hon. William Henry John, of Kirtling Tower, Newmarket.

Coll.	Eton, Ch. Ch. Oxon.	Cambridge	.	3,130	.	4,243
Club.	Carlton, White's,	Essex . .	446	.	909
	Boodle's.	Warwick . .	25	.	94

b. 1836, m. 1858.
 Served in 1st Life Guards.   3,601 . 5,246

NORTHAMPTON, Marquis of, Castle Ashby, Northampton,
 &c. ♣.

Coll. Royal Naval.	Northampton .	9,649	.	13,114
Club. Travellers'.	Warwick . .	4,985	.	8,288
b. 1818, s. 1877, m. 1844.	Bucks . . .	3	.	3
Served in Royal Navy in	Argyll . . .	8,000	.	1,221
Chinese War ; a Vice-	Kinross . . .	864	.	1,244
Admiral.				

           23,501 . 23,870

NORTH, Charles, of Rougham.   Norfolk   .   2,580   .   3,547

*** NORTHBROOK, Earl of, G.C.S.I., Stratton Park, Micheldever Station.

		acres.	*g. an. val.*
Coll. Ch. Ch. Oxon.	Hants . . .	9,236 .	10,974
Club. Brooks's, Travellers'.	Kent . . .	823 .	1,736
b. 1826, s. 1866, m. 1848.			
		10,059 .	12,710

Served as L. of the Adm., U. Sec. State for War, U. Sec. for India, U. Sec. Home Dept., Sec. to the Adm., U. Sec. for War, and Gov.-Gen. of India, is First L. of the Admiralty.   Sat for Falmouth.

** NORTHCOTE, Rt. Hon. Sir Stafford Henry, Bart., G.C.B., of Pynes, Exeter.

Coll. Eton, Ball. Oxon.	Devon . . .	5,663 .	6,000
Club. Carlton, Athenæum.	b. 1818, s. 1851, m. 1843.		

Served as Legal Sec. to B. of Tr., Finl. Sec. to the Treas., P. B. of Trade, Sec. S. for India, and Ch. of the Exchequer. Sat for Dudley and for Stamford.   Sits for N. Devon.

NORTHESK, Earl of, Ethie House, Arbroath, N.B., &c.

Club. Guards, Carl., St. Jas.	Forfar . . .	4,844 .	7,761
b. 1843, s. 1878, m. 1865.	Hants . . .	2,843 .	1,822
Served in Scots Guards.	Stafford . . .	48 .	175
		7,735 .	9,758

*** NORTHUMBERLAND, Dowager Duchess of, Stanwick Park, Darlington.

b. 1820, s. 1865, m. 1842.	York, N.R. .	5,683 .	8,320

NORTHUMBERLAND, Duke of, Alnwick Castle, Northumberland.

Coll. Eton, St. John's, Cam.	Northumber-		
Club. Uni. Ser., Travellers'.	land . .	181,616 .	161,874
b. 1810, s. 1867, m. 1845.	Surrey . . .	3,765 .	6,697
Served in Gren. Gds., was	Middlesex . .	882 .	7,226
L. of the Adm., V.-P. of B.	Durham . .	134 .	251
of Trade, and L. P. Seal.			
		186,397 .	176,048

Sat for Beeralston and N. Northumberland.

NORTHEY, Rev. E. W., of Woodcote.

Surrey, Wilts	2,905 .	4,835

---

* NORTHWICK, Lord, Northwick Pk., Moreton in-Marsh, &c.

			acres.		*g. an. val.*
Coll.　Harrow, Ch. Ch. Ox.	Worcester	. .	4,215	.	6,317
Club.　Carlton, Ath., O. &	Salop	. .	2,095	.	3,166
C., Uni. Service.	Rutland	. .	1,885	.	3,233
b. 1811, s. 1859, m. 1869.	Middlesex	. .	1,260	.	2,713
Served in 1st Life Guards.	Gloucester	. .	346	.	490
Sat for Evesham and for	Wilts	. .	88	.	1,789
E. Worcestershire.	Hereford	. .	6	.	17
			9,895	.	17,725

*** NORTON, Daniel, of Northwood Park, Ruislip, &c.

b. 1806, m. 1st 1831,	Kent	. .	5,207	.	6,547
2nd 1870.	Middlesex	. .	250	.	999
	Herts	. .	58	.	70
	Hants	. .	2	.	150
			5,517	.	7,766

*** LOWNDES-STONE-NORTON, Capt. and Mrs., of Brightwell Park, Tetsworth, &c.

Coll.　Sandhurst.	Oxford	. .	2,761	.	4,324
Club.　Guards, Carlton.	Surrey	. .	1,346	.	1,125
b. 1839, s. 1862 and 1877,	Devon	. .	368	.	720
m. 1862.			4,475	.	6,169

Served in Gren. Gds. and 2nd Life Gds.

** NORTON, Lord, K.C.M.G., Hams Hall, Birmingham, &c.

Coll.　Ch. Ch. Oxon.	Warwick	. .	2,814	.	7,125
Club.　Carlton.	Stafford	. .	1,352	.	7,550
b. 1814, m. 1842.	Rutland	. .	349	.	1,550
			4,515	.	16,225

Served as Pres. B. of Health, V.-P. of the Council of Education, U. Sec. Colonies, and Pres. B. of Trade.

Sat for N. Staffordshire.　The first two rentals are understated.

NUGENT, Colonel Andrew, of Portaferry, Co. Down.

		acres.		g. an. val.
Coll. Eton, Trin. Cam.	Co. Down . .	4,638	.	7,675
Club. Ar. & Na., Uni. Ser.	Westmeath .	2,137	.	1,670
b. 1834, s. 1857.				
Served in Scots Greys.		6,775	.	9,345

*** NUGENT, Lady, of Ballinlough, Delvin, Co. Westmeath.

s. 1859, m. 1842.	Westmeath	.	4,697	.	4,540
	Co. Meath	.	684	.	508
			5,381	.	5,048

NUGENT, Sir Walter George, Bt., of Donore, Walterstown.

Coll. Ushaw.	Westmeath	.	7,218	.	4,637
Club. Ral., Steph. Green.	Co. Longford.		737	.	475
b. 1828, s. 1874, m. 1860.			7,955	.	5,112

Served in 33rd Foot in the Crimea.

NUNN, Edward Westby, of St. Margaret's, Co. Wexford.

Coll. Eton, Christ's, Cam.	Co. Wexford .	5,008	.	4,441
Club. Conservative.	Co. Carlow .	91	.	130
b. 1818, s. 1852.				
		5,099	.	4,571

OAKELEY, William Edward, of Tan-y-Bwlch, Harlech.

Coll. Eton, Corpus, Oxon. Merioneth . . 7,169 . 15,603
Club. Arth., Bood., Marl. b. 1828, m. 1860.
    Inclusive of 304*l.* in Hon. Mrs. Oakeley's name.

NOTLEY, Mrs., of Combe Sydenham.		
Somerset, Devon, Dorset	2,809 .	3,491
NUGENT, Sir G. E., Bt., of W. Harling. Nfk.	4,350 .	2,342
NUGENT, J. J., of Clonlost. Wmea., Cork	3,420 .	2,466
OAKELEY, J., of Oakeley. Sal., Here., Mgy.	2,736 .	3,054

O'BEIRNE, Hugh, of Jamestown Lodge, Drumsna, Co. Leitrim.

b. 1800, m. 1822.

		acres.		g. an. val.
Leitrim	. .	7,662	.	3,329
Roscommon	.	248	.	92
		7,910	.	3,421

*** O'BRIEN, Edward William, of Cahirmoyle, Ardagh.

Coll. St. Col., Tr. Dub. Co. Limerick . 4,997 . 5,316
Club. Athenæum. b. 1837, s. 1864, m. 1863, 2nd 1880.
Inclusive of the rent of lands leased in perpetuity.

O'BRIEN, Horace Stafford, of Blatherwycke Pk., Wansford, &c.

Club. Kildare St.
b. 1842, s. 1880, m. 1869.
Served in 2nd Dragoons.

		acres.		g. an. val.
Rutland	. .	562	.	978
Northampton	.	1,955	.	2,454
Co. Clare	. .	11,630	.	6,231
Limerick	. .	5,263	.	1,277
Tipperary	. .	7,984	.	6,532
		27,394	.	17,472

*** O'CALLAGHAN, Charles George, of Ballinahinch, Tulla.

Coll. Shr., Trin. Ox. Co. Clare . . 8,735 . 3,745
Club. A. & N., Kild. St.
b. 1821, s. 1829, m. 1856. Served in 1st Drag. Gds.

O'CONNELL, Sir Maurice James, Bt., of Lakeview, Killarney.

Club. Garrick. Co. Kerry . . 18,752 . 3,050
b. 1822, s. 1872, m. 1855.

OAKES, J. H. P., of Nowton Court. Suffolk .	2,840	.	4,317
O'BRIEN, J., of Ballinalacken. Clare, Lim.	5,611	.	2,022
O'BYRNE, J., of Corville. Tip., Louth .	3,905	.	2,752
O'BYRNE, W. R., of Cabinteely. Dub., Wic.	2,658	.	2,679

O'CONNELL, Mrs., of Longfield, Cashel, &c.

		acres.		g. an. val.
s. 1875, m. 1865.	Tipperary . .	2,215	.	2,306
	Co. Clare . .	4,740	.	1,293
	Co. Cork . .	1,102	.	1,085
		8,057	.	4,684

O'CONNOR, William, of Rockfield House, Blackrock, &c.

b. 1850, s. 1873, m. 1874.	Tipperary . .	6,178	.	6,212
	Co. Dublin .	78	.	1,378
	Limerick . .	837	.	493
		7,093	.	8,083

*** O'CONOR-DON, The, of Belenagare, French-park.

Coll. Downside, Bath.	Roscommon .	11,466	.	4,948
Club. Ref., Ath., St. Geo.	Co. Sligo . .	1,184	.	487
b. 1838, s. 1847, m. 1868, 2nd 1879.				
Sat for Co. Roscommon.		12,650	.	5,435

ODELL, Herbert Francis Edward, of Carriglea, Dungarvan.

b. 1875, s. 1879.	Waterford . .	3,192	.	3,227

MORE O'FERRALL, Ambrose Richard, of Balyna House, Enfield, Co. Kildare.

Club. Windham, Kildare	Hereford . .	1,677	.	1,955
St. Dub.	Co. Kildare .	3,213	.	2,305
b. 1846, s. 1880, m. 1872.	Co. Carlow .	1,106	.	446
	Co. Longford .	449	.	302
	Co. Meath .	380	.	329
	Co. Dublin .	11	.	165
		6,836	.	5,502

O'CONNOR, P., of Cairnsfoot. Sligo, Rosc.	5,151	.	2,708
O'CONOR, A. M., of Elphin Pal. Rosc. .	6,927	.	2,915
O'CONOR, D. M., of Clonalis. Rosc., Sligo	2,776	.	2,030
O'DONELL, Sir G. Glendining, Bart., of Newport House. Mayo	7,488	.	2,232
O'FARRELL, C., of Dalyston. Galway . .	5,131	.	2,493

** MORE-O'FERRALL, Dominick, Kildangan Castle, Monas-
   terevan, Co. Kildare.

		acres.	*g. an. val.*
Club. Raleigh.	Co. Meath . .	3,307 .	3,200
b. 1854, s. 1875.	Co. Mayo . .	4,086 .	1,337
	Co. Kildare .	1,354 .	715
		8,747 .	5,252

OGILBY, Claud William Leslie, of Altnachree, Donemanagh.

b. 1851, s. 1873, m. 1875.	Tyrone . . .	7,050 .	3,511
Served in 31st Foot.			

OGILBY, Robert Alexander, of Ardnargle, N.-Limavady.

b. 1850, s. 1872.	Londonderry .	9,735	3,805
Serves in 4th Foot.			

*** OGILVIE, Thomas Elliot, of Chesters, Jedburgh, N.B.

Coll. Haileybury.	Roxburgh . .	1,761 .	2,198
b. 1821, s. 1876.	Haddington .	1,269 .	825
Served in Bengal Civil Service.			
		3,030 .	3,023

The smaller estate is his mother's.

** OGILVIE, Donald (of Clova), of Balnaboth, Kurriemuir, N.B.

Coll. Haileybury.	Forfar . .	21,893 .	3,515
Club. Junior Carlton.			
b. 1824, s. 1863, m. 1867.	Served in Bengal Civil Service.		

WEDDERBURN-OGILVY, Col., of Ruthven, Meigle, N.B.

Club. United Service	Forfar . . .	6,336 .	5,734
b. 1814, s. 1853, m. 1856.	Served in 2nd Life Guards.		

*** OGLANDER, Lady, of Parnham, Beaminster, &c.

s. 1874, m. 1845.	Hants . . .	3,824 .	4,460
	Dorset . . .	3,117 .	4,256
	Somerset . .	572 .	1,250
The Dorset woods are here left out			
		7,513 .	9,966

OGILVY, John, of Inshewan. Forfar . . 2,716 . 2,244

* OGLE, John Saville, of Kirkley Hall, Newcastle-on-Tyne.

			acres.		g. an. val.
Coll. Eton.	Northumberland	7,408	.	7,895
Club. St. James's, Travellers', Brooks's.				

b. 1836, s. 1869.

* O'HAGAN, Lord, K.P., Woodlands, Clonsilla, Co. Dublin.

Club. Ath.,Ref.,Univ.Dub.,	Lancashire	.	4,695	.	4,670
Stephen's Green,	Yorkshire	. .	604	.	214
Dublin.					

b. 1812, s. (*jur.uxor.*) 1878,m.1836,2nd 1871. 5,299 . 4,884
    Served as Queen's Serjeant, Sol.-Gen. and Att.-Gen. for Ireland,
Judge of Court of C. Pleas, Lord Chan. of Ireland, Com. of
National Edn. and of Char. Donations. Sat for Tralee.
    Lady O'Hagan's share of the Towneley estates was calculated
by Lord Norreys.

** O'HARA, Charles William, of Cooper's Hill, Ballymote, &c.

Coll. Trinity, Dublin.	Co. Sligo	. .	21,070	.	8,324
Club. Carlton. b. 1817, s. 1850, m. 1858. Sat for Co. Sligo.					

** OKEOVER, Haughton Charles, of Okeover Hall, Ash-
        bourne. ₰.

Coll. Eton, Ch. Ch. Oxon.	Stafford	. .	2,939	.	4,500
Club. Arthur's.	Derby	. . .	988	.	1,700
b. 1825, s. 1836, m. 1859.					
			3,927	.	6,200

* KINGTON-OLIPHANT, Thomas Laurence, of Charlton
        House, Wimbledon, &c.

Coll. Eton, Balliol, Oxon.	Perth	. . .	4,940	.	4,354
Club. National.	Surrey	. . .	2	.	400
b 1831, s. 1867, m. 1856.			4,942	.	4,754

O'GRADY, The, of Killballyowen. Lim., Kil.	2,101	.	2,360
O'KEEFE, Mrs.,of Ballinacourty. Waterford	4,837	.	2,483
O'KELLY, P. de P., of Barrettstown. Kild., Wexford	3,512	.	2,505
O'LEARY, J. M'C., of Coomlagane, Cork .	5,896	.	2,034
OLIPHANT, L. J., of Condie. Perth, Kin.	3,877	.	2,922

OLIVER, Silver Charles, of Inchera, Glounthane, Co. Cork.

			acres.	*g. an. val.*
Coll. Trinity, Dublin.	Co. Cork	. .	6,738	. 2,150
b. 18—	Limerick	. .	2,156	. 824
	Tipperary	. .	849	. 393
	Waterford	. .	187	. 182
	Kilkenny	. .	189	. 91
			10,119	. 3,640

** O'NEILL, Rev. Lord, Shane's Castle, Co. Antrim.

Coll. Trinity, Dublin.   Co. Antrim . 65,919 . 44,000
Club. Carlton, Kildare Street, Dublin.
b. 1813, s. 1855, m. 1st 1839, 2nd 1858.

*** SAVILL-ONLEY, Onley, of Stisted Hall, Braintree.

			acres.	*g. an. val.*
Coll. Chart.,Pem.Cam.	Essex	. . .	3,054	. 4,519
Club. Carl., Uni. Univ.	Norfolk	. . .	6	. 30
b. 1795, s. 1843, m. 1st 1818,	Suffolk	. . .	2	. 68
2nd 1851.				
			3,062	. 4,617

ONSLOW, Andrew George, of Oxenhall, Newent.

			acres.	*g. an. val.*
b. 1830, s. 1879, m. 1861.	Gloucester	. .	3,862	. 5,447
Served in 97th Foot.	Hereford	. .	31	. 27
			3,893	. 5,474

*** HUGHES-ONSLOW, Arthur, of Balkissock, Ballantrae, N.B., &c.
Coll. Eton.   Ayr . . . . 14,827 . 4,293
b. 1862, s. 1870.

---

	acres.	*g. an. val.*
OLIVER, R. S., of Boltonbridge. Kerry, Kilkenny, Waterford	5,120	. 2,443
OLIVER, R., of Blakelaw, Roxburgh . .	2,002	. 2,369
** O'NEILL, Hon. R. T., of Derrynoid. Londonderry, Tyrone	5,648	. 2,242
ONSLOW, G. J., of Risby. York, Lincoln .	2,303	. 3,475

*** ONSLOW, Earl of, Clandon Park, Guildford, &c. 🐍.

		acres.	g. an. val.
Coll. Eton, Exeter, Ox.	Norfolk . . .	217 .	380
Club. Carlton, White's.	Surrey . . .	11,761 .	8,761
b. 1853, s. 1870, m. 1875.	Essex . . .	1,510 .	1,731
Was a Lord in Waiting.			
		13,488 .	10,872

*** ONSLOW, Sir William Wallace Roderic, Bart., of Hengar House, Bodmin, &c.

Coll. Marlborough.	Cornwall . .	5,419 .	2,197
Club. Naval and Military.	Wilts . . .	1,638 .	1,037
b. 1845, s. 1876, m. 1873.			
		7,057 .	3,234

Served in 12th Foot in New Zealand (medal).

** ORANMORE and BROWNE, Lord, Castle Macgarret, Claremorris, Co. Mayo, &c.

Coll. Harrow, Trin. Cam.	Ayrshire . .	2,720 .	3,600
Club. Carlton, National.	Co. Mayo . .	4,243 .	4,860
b. 1819, s. 1860, m. 1859.			
		6,963 .	8,460

Exclusive of 1,534*l.* for minerals in Ayrshire. The Scotch property is Lady Oranmore's.

*** BLACKETT-ORD, Mrs., of Whitfield Hall, Langley Mills.

s. 1855, m. 1842.	Northumberland	15,868 .	14,076

** CAMPBELL-ORDE, Sir John William Powlett, Bart., of Kilmory, Lochgilphead, N.B., &c.

Coll. Eton.	Inverness . .	81,099 .	4,975
Club. Carl., A. & N., New	Argyll . . .	4,646 .	1,398
Ed. b. 1827, s. 1879, m. 1862.			
Served in 42nd Highlanders.		85,745 .	6,373

** ORDE, William, of Nunnykirk, Morpeth.

Coll. Eton, Univ. Oxon.	Northumberland	13,666 .	7,903
Club. Eton and Harrow.			
b. 1854, s. 1875.			

*** O'REILLY, JOSEPH RICHARD, of Sans Souci, Booterstown.

		acres.	*g. an. val.*
Coll. Oscott, Trin. Dub.	Longford . .	2,464 .	1,277
Club. Road, U.S. Dub.	Westmeath .	835 .	601
b. 1843, s. 1870, m. 1873.	Meath . . .	704 .	656
	Co. Dublin .	31 .	914
		4,034 .	3,448

ORFORD, EARL OF, Wolterton Park, Aylsham, &c. S.

Coll. Eton, Trin. Cam.	Norfolk	12,341 .	15,313

Club. Carlton, White's, Travellers', St. George's, Turf.
b. 1813, s. 1858, m. 1841. Sat for E. Norfolk.

** ORKNEY, EARL OF, K.C.M.G., Glanmore, Templemore.

Club. Carl., Army & Navy.	Co. Tipperary .	7,877 .	4,113
b. 1827, s. 1877, m. 1872.	Queen's Co. .	1,438 .	367
Served in Scots F. Gds.	Co. Kerry . .	1,642 .	550
and with 71st Foot in the	Buckingham .	1 .	1
Crimea (Knt. of the Medjidie).		10,958 .	5,031

ORMATHWAITE, LORD, Newcastle Court, Radnor, &c.

Coll. Eton, Trin. Cam.	Radnor . . .	12,428 .	8,126
Club. Carl., White's, Marl.	Cumberland .	2,090 .	1,209
b. 1827, s. 1881, m. 1858.	Berks . . .	627 .	990
Sat for Leominster and	Hereford . .	3 .	15
Radnorshire.	Co. Kerry . .	8,907 .	2,619
	Co. Cork . .	2,206 .	1,708
		26,261 .	14,667

ORMONDE, MARQUIS OF, The Castle, Kilkenny.

Coll. Harrow.	Co. Tipperary	15,765 .	7,240
Club. Carlton, Travellers', Roy. Irish, Sack. St.	Co. Kilkenny .	11,960 .	8,191
b. 1844, s. 1854, m. 1876. Served in 1st Life Guards.		27,725 .	15,431

O'REILLY, J., of Beltrasna. Cavan, Meath.		4,589 .	2,836
ORLEBAR, R., of Hinwick. Beds, Dev., Nptn.		2,669	4,446

ORMROD, Mrs., of Wyersdale Park, Garstang.

		acres.	g. an. val.
s. 1875, m. 1838.	Lancashire .	5,290 .	7,195
	York, W.R. .	16 .	23
		5,306 .	7,218

*** ORR, James, of Harviestoun Castle, Dollar, N.B.

Coll. Glasgow Univ.	Clackmannan .	4,726 .	3,912
b. 1812, s. 1874.	Lanark . . .	140 .	44
	Perth . . .	335 .	350
		5,201 .	4,306

*** OSBORN, Sir George Robert, Bart., of Chicksands Priory, Biggleswade, &c.

Coll. Westm., Ch. Ch. Ox.   Bedford   .   .   3,049   .   4,695
Club. Travellers'. b. 1813, s. 1848, m. 1st 1835, 2nd 1871.
    Served in 85th Foot.

* BERNAL-OSBORNE, daughters of the late (2), Ralph, of Newtown Anner, Clonmel.

s. 1881, m. 1874 and 1874.	Co. Tipperary .	942 .	870
	Waterford . .	12,242 .	4,983
		13,184 .	5,853

OSBORNE, Lord William Godolphin, of Tulliallan Castle, Kincardine, Alloa, N.B.

Club. White's, Marl.	Kincardine .	3,030 .	3,470
b. 1804, m. 1st 1843,	Perth . . .	4,006 .	5,239
2nd 1870.	Stirling . . .	42 .	100
Served in 26th Foot, 16th Lancers and 10th Hussars, was Mil. Sec. to the Governor-General of India.		7,078 .	8,809

ORME, R., of Enniscrone.   Sligo, Mayo   .   4,499   .   2,186
ORME, R. W., of Owenmore.   Sligo, Mayo   .   11,771   .   2,002

** O'SHEE, NICHOLAS RICHARD POWER, of Gardenmorris, Kill, Co. Waterford.

		acres.	g. an. val.
Club. Garrick.	Waterford . .	4,995 .	2,941
b. 1821, s. 1859, m. 1865.	Co. Kilkenny .	2,496 .	2,721
		7,491 .	5,662

** OSMASTON, JOHN, of Osmaston Manor, Derby.

		acres.	g. an. val.
Coll. Rugby.	Nottingham .	3,615 .	6,207
b. 1831, s. 1873, m. 1st 1853,	Derby . . .	2,678 .	5,844
2nd 1861.	Leicester . .	344 .	560
		6,637 .	12,611

*** OSSINGTON, VISCOUNTESS, 40, Upper Brook-st. W.

		acres.	g. an. val.
b. 1806, s. 1879, m. 1827.	Ayrshire . .	8,247 .	16,978

Exc. of 2,975*l.* for minerals.

*** OSWALD, RICHARD ALEXANDER, of Auchincruive, Ayr, N.B., &c.

		acres.	g. an. val.
Coll. Harrow.	Ayr	11,564 .	24,011
Club. Carl., St. Jam., J. U.	Kirkcudbright	24,556 .	17,863
Ser., Bood., Turf.			
b. 1841, s. 1871, m. 1868.		36,120 .	41,874
Served in 29th Foot.	Inclusive of mines.		

OVERSTONE, LORD, Overstone Park, Northampton.

		acres.	g. an. val.
Coll. Eton. Trin. Cam.	Northampton .	15,045 .	30,679
Club. Uni. Univ., Brooks's,	Warwick . .	4,460 .	7,654
Reform, Athen.	Bucks . . .	5,072 .	8,849
b. 1796, s. 1859, m. 1829.	Cambridge .	2,402 .	4,135
Sat for Hythe.	Huntingdon .	1,712 .	2,946
	Leicester . .	1,276 .	2,064
LORD O. states that this list	Oxon . . .	501 .	997
"is so fearfully incorrect, that	Berks . . .	284 .	474
it is impossible to correct it."	Middlesex . .	24 .	201
It is, however, given exactly	Bedford . .	50 .	83
as in the blue book of 1876.	Carmarthen .	23 .	16
		30,849 .	58,098

*** HUMPHREYS-OWEN, Arthur Charles, of Glansevern, Garthmyll, Montgomery.

		acres.	g. an. val.
Coll. Harrow, Trin. Cam.	Montgomery .	4,482 .	4,368

Club. Athenæum, Ox. and Cam., Savile.
). 1836, s. 1876, m. 1874.

OXENDEN, Sir Henry Chudleigh, Bart., of Broome Park, Canterbury. 🐚.

Coll. Eton, St. John's, Cam.	Kent . . .	5,266 .	5,370

Club. Uni. University.
b. 1795, s. 1838, m. 1st 1830,
                2nd 1848.

* PACKE, Hussey, of Prestwold Hall, Loughborough, &c.

Coll. Eton, Trin. Cam.	Leicester . .	3,309 .	5,139
Club. Arth., Brooks's.	Lincoln . . .	2,925 .	6,668

b. 1846, s. 1874, m. 1872.

		6,234 .	11,807

PAGET, Richard Horner, of Cranmore Hall, Shepton Mallet.

Coll. Sandhurst.	Somerset . .	3,443 .	5,577
Club. Carlton, Ar. and Na.	Stafford . .	134 .	1,424
b. 1832, s. 1866, m. 1866.	Stafford . .	left blank .	805

Served in 66th Foot.

		3,577 .	7,806

Sat for E. Somerset ; sits for Mid Somerset.
A considerable part of the estate in Somerset will be found entered under the name of Payett, R. H.

MOSTYN-OWEN, A., of Woodhouse. Salop	2,174 .	3,459
OWEN, M. W., of Cwmgloyne. Pem., Carm.	4,166 .	2,357
BULKELEY-OWEN, Rev. T. M. B., of Tedsmore. Salop, Montgomery . . .	2,534 .	3,617
OWEN, W. S., of Withybush. Pembroke .	2,332 .	3,253
OWENS, James, of Holestone. Antrim .	3,774 .	2,972
PADWICK, Mrs., of Horsham Manor. Sus.	2,884 .	3,166
** PAGET, H. F., of Elford. Staffordshire	2,400 .	3,500

PAGET, Thomas Tertius, of Humberstone, Leicester, &c.

Club. Reform, Brooks's,		acres.		g. an. val.
Devonshire.	Leicester . .	3,950	.	8,948
b. 1807, m. 1850.	Northampton .	832	.	1,936
Sits for S. Leicestershire.		4,782	.	10,884

PAKENHAM, Rev. Arthur Hercules, of Langford Lodge, Crumlin, Co. Antrim.

Coll. Caius, Cambridge.	Co. Antrim .	14,629	.	15,601
Club. Carlton.　b. 1824, s. 1854.				

** PALLISER, John, C.M.G., of Comragh, Kilmacthomas, &c.

Club. National, Kild.	Waterford . .	9,825	.	4,000
Street, Dublin.	Tipperary . .	3,561	.	2,588
b. 1817, s. 1862.	Kilkenny . .	460	.	212
		13,846	.	6,800

Served on the International Boundary Commission ; surveyed the line between Lake Superior and the Pacific ; discovered a new pass (available for a railroad) through the Rocky Mountains.

** PALMER, Sir Geoffrey, Bt., of Carlton Pk., Rockingham. ♟

Coll. Eton, Ch. Ch. Oxon.	Leicester . .	1,692	.	2,970
Club. Travellers', Ox. and	Northampton .	2,428	.	4,559
Cam., Uni. Univ.				
b. 1809, s. 1865.		4,120	.	7,529

GOLDING-PALMER, Rev. Henry, of Holme Park, Reading.

Coll. Trin. Cam.	Berks . . .	3,818	.	6,159
Club. United University.	Oxon . . .	1,208	.	1,819
b. 1816, s. 1880, m. 1857.		5,026	.	7,978

PAKENHAM, Hon. E. M., of Cookesboro'. Wm.		4,557	.	2,882
PALEY, John, of Lancliffe.　York, Suffolk		2,007	.	2,351
PALMER, C. C., of Rahan.　Kildare . .		2,342	.	2,048
PALMER, C. M., of Grinkle Park.　York		2,664	.	2,804

PALMER, Sir Roger William Henry, Bart., of Keenagh, Crossmolina, Co. Mayo, &c.

		acres.	g. an. val.
Coll. Eton.	Co. Mayo . .	80,990	14,625
Club. Carlton, Boodle's,	Co. Sligo . .	9,570	1,229
Garrick, Arthur's.	Co. Dublin .	3,991	4,706
b. 1832, s. 1869.	Cambridge . .	3,329	4,338
Served in 2nd Life Guards,	Denbigh . .	1,011	1,357
and 11th Hussars in the	Flint . . .	45	114
Crimea. Is a Lieut.-	Dorset . . .	11	34
General. Sat for Co.	Berks . . .	7	258
Mayo.			
		98,954	26,661

*** PAPILLON, Thomas, of Crowhurst Park, Battle.

Coll. Winch, Ch. Ch.	Sussex . . .	3,680	3,570
Oxon.	Essex . . .	1,278	2,250
b. 1803, s. 1838, m. 1825.	Kent. . . .	17	17
		4,975.	5,837

The Essex estate belongs to his eldest son.

** TOWNLEY-PARKER, Thomas T., of Cuerden Hall, Preston.

Club. Junior Carlton.	Lancashire . .	7,335	13,069
	York, W.R. .	711	58
b. 1822, s. 1879, m. 1846.			
		8,046	13,127

PARKER, Edward, of Brownsholme, Clitheroe, &c.

b. 1846, s. 1879.	York, W. & E.R.	2,177	1,908
	Lancashire . .	929	1,538
		3,106	3,446

PALMER, F., of Withcote. Leicester . .	2,677	4,378
PALMER, G., of Reading. Sur., Berks, Hants, Ox.	2,001	2,446
** PARES, E. H., of Hopwell. Leic., Dby.	2.974	6,305
PARFITT, Monsignor, of Mitford. Wil., Som.	2,576	5,252
PARK, John, of Ollerton Hall. Lancashire.	2,559	5,020

** PARKER, Sir William, Bart., of Melford Hall, Long Melford.

			acres.	*g. an. val.*
Club. Jun. Uni. Ser.	Middlesex . .		—— .	160
b. 1826, s. 1856, m. 1855.	Suffolk . . .		3,482 .	4,720
Served in 44th Foot and on the Staff.				
The value is considerably understated . .			3,482 .	4,880

*** JONES-PARRY, Thomas Love Duncombe, of Madryn, Pwllheli.

Coll. Rugby, Uni. Oxon. Carnarvon . . 10,025 . 5,750
Club. Jun. U. Ser., Reform. b. 1832, s. 1853.
Sat for Carnarvonshire.

PATTISON, Mrs. Pringle, of the Haining, Selkirk, N.B.

s. 1868, m. 1849.	Selkirk . . .	4,800 .	3,307
	Roxburgh . .	2,527 .	1,410
		7,327 .	4,717

PARKER, Admiral, of Delamore. Devon.	2,442 .	2,400
PARKER, A., of Castlelough. Tip., Cork, Cla.	4,509 .	2,705
PARKER, W., of Hanthorpe. Linc., Leic.	2,163 .	4,306
PARKER, Col., of Clopton. Suff., Nptn., Ox.	2,049 .	3,330
* PARKINSON, R. J. H., of Ravendale. Linc.	2,500 .	3,000(?)
PARNELL, Hon. H., of Anneville. Wmeath.	2,900 .	2,070
JONES-PARRY, Mrs., of Aberdunant. Carnarvon, Anglesea	4,699 .	2,626
PARRY, T. G., of Highnam. Gloucester .	2,270 .	4,335
PARTRIDGE, H. T., of Hockham. Norfolk	2,741 .	2,999
PATERSON, G. F., of Castle Huntly. Perth	2,227 .	6,168
PATERSON, W., of Montgomerie. Ayr .	2,552 .	3,127

*** PAWSON, William John, of Shawdon, Whittingham, &c.

	acres.		g. an. val.
Club. J. Carl., R.Y.S. Northumberland	6,938	.	5,405

b. 1817, s. 1854, m. 1843.

** PEASE, Mrs. Gurney, of Southend, Darlington, &c.

s. 1873, m. 1871.	Hereford . .	3,923	.	4,730
	York . . .	800	.	1,077
	Durham . .	26	.	306
		4,749	.	6,113

The York estate is held in trust for her son.

*** PECKOVER, Algernon, of Harecroft House, Wisbeach.

b. 1803, s. 18— and 1877,	Norfolk . .	1,216	.	2,578
m. 1828.	Cambridge .	1,487	.	2,736
	Suffolk . . .	409	.	603
	York, W.R. .	279	.	750
		3,391	.	6,667

In this case, correspondence with the owner has disclosed a curious instance, and one which the compiler has reason to believe by no means a solitary one, of a farm being sometimes entered in the return in the tenant's name instead of the owner's. In this case the farm was rented at 504*l.*

COCHRAN-PATRICK, Robert William, of Ladyland. Ayr, Renfrew	3,118	.	2,415
PATRICK, W. R., of Trearne. Ayr . . .	2,506	.	5,245
PATTON (late) of Glenalmond. Perth . .	11,796	.	2,646
*** PAULET, Mrs., of Duxbury. Lanc., Durham	2,672	.	4,519
PEACHEY, W., of Ebernoe. Sussex, Glou.	2,760	.	2,435
PEARETH, Mrs., of Usworth. Durham, Northampton, Warwick	2,311	.	4,113
* PEASE, J.W.,of HuttonLowcross. Yk.,Corn.	2,500		2,075

** PEEL, EDMUND, of Bryn-y-Pys, Ruabon, N. Wales, &c.

			acres.		g. an. val.
Coll.	Eton, Ch. Ch. Oxon.	Flint . . .	2,897	.	5,574
Club.	Carlton, Arthur's.	Norfolk . .	2,689	.	4,083
b. 1826, s. 1872, m. 1st 1855,		Denbigh . .	1,555	.	3,171
2nd 1866.		Montgomery .	1,325	.	2,442
			8,466	.	15,270

** PEEL, JONATHAN, of Knowlmere, Clitheroe, &c.

			acres.		g. an. val.
Coll.	St. John's Cam.	Lancashire .	600	.	4,866
Club.	Ox. and Cam.	Yorkshire . .	2,419	.	2,220
b. 1806, s. 1839, m. 1st 1833,					
2nd 1838.			3,019	.	7,086

PEEL, RIGHT HON. SIR ROBERT, BART., G.C.B., of Drayton Manor, Tamworth.

			acres.		g. an. val.
Coll.	Harrow, Ch. Ch. Oxford.	Stafford . .	6,453	.	17,044
		Warwick . .	3,075	.	6,871
Club.	Brooks's, Boodle's, Carl., Turf, Sack. St. Dublin.	Lancashire .	395	.	617
b. 1822, s. 1850, m. 1856.			9,923	.	24,532

Served as Attaché at Madrid, Chargé d'Affaires in Switzerland, Lord of the Admiralty, Secretary to Special Mission to St. Petersburg, and Chief Secretary for Ireland. Sat for Tamworth.

** PEEL, WILLIAM, of Taliaris Park, Llandilo.

		acres.		g. an. val.
b. 1803, s. 1838, m. 1836.	Carmarthen .	3,197	.	3,113

BROOKE-PECHELL, SIR G. S., BART., of Paglesham. Essex, Hants, Dublin . . 2,469 . 3,107

PEEL, A. W., of Sandy Lodge. Beds, Herts 2,226 . 3,020

PEEL, W. C., of Trenant. Cornwall, Glou., Lanc. . . . . 2,415 . 2,468

PEEL, X. DE C. R., of Denant. Pem., Carm. 2,460 . 2,159

** BERESFORD-PEIRSE, Sir Henry Monson de la Poer, Bart., of The Hall, Bedale. *acres. g. an. val.*

Coll. Eton, Trin. Cam.   York, N.R. . 6,199 . 7,500
Club. Brooks's, Carlton. b. 1850, s. 1873, m. 1873.

*** THURSBY-PELHAM, James Arthur Harvey, of Cound Hall, Shrewsbury.

b. 1869, s. 1878.   Salop . . . 6,053 . 5,931

** CHILDE-PEMBERTON, Charles Orlando, Millichope Park, Church Stretton. 🍎.

Coll. Harrow, Ch. Ch. Ox. Salop . . . 3,364 . 4,696
Club. Oxford and Cambridge. b. 1812, s. 1848, m. 1849.

** PEMBERTON, Edward Leigh, of Torry Hill, Sittingbourne.

Coll. Eton, St. John's, Oxon. Kent . . . 6,280 . 6,708
Club. Arthur's, Carlton.
b. 1822, s. 1877, m. 1849.   Sits for E. Kent.

*** PEMBERTON, Richard Laurence, of Hathorn Towers, Seaham, &c.

Coll. Eton, Pemb. Oxon.   Durham . . 4,340 . 8,866
Club. Carlton, Windham, Athenæum.
b. 1831, s. 1843, m. 1st 1854,
            2nd 1867.
Exclusive of certain mining royalties in Durham and S. Wales. This family have held lands in Durham since the time of Henry IV.

** PEMBROKE, Earl of, Wilton House, Salisbury.

		acres	val
Coll. Eton.	Wilts . . .	42,244	40,500
Club. Carlton.	Westmoreland	31	57
b. 1850, s. 1861 and 1862,	Co. Dublin .	2,301	35,586
m. 1874.	Co. Wicklow .	230	1,577
Served as Under Secretary for War.			
		44,806	77,720

The Westmoreland property is Lady Pembroke's. English estates alone corrected.

PELLY, Sir Harold, Bart., of Upton.
    Huntingdon, Essex, Cambridge . . . 2,780 . 3,925

** PENDARVES, William Cole, of Pendarves, Redruth.

			acres.	*g. an. val.*
Coll. Eton, Ch. Ch. Oxon.	Cornwall . .	3,065	.	4,223
Club. Arthur's.	Somerset . .	519	.	1,107
b. 1841, s. 1872.				
The last estate belongs to his mother.		3,584	.	5,330

*** PENNEFATHER, Edward, Q.C., of Rathsalla, Dunlavin, Co. Wicklow, &c.

Coll. Balliol, Oxon.	Co. Wicklow .	2,136	.	1,759
Club. Kildare St. Dublin.	Sussex . . .	1,242	.	1,330
b. 1809, s. 1847, m. 1841.	Kent . . .	38	.	100
		3,416	.	3,189

PENNYMAN, James Stovin, of Ormesby Hall, Middlesborough.

Coll. Durham Univ.	York, N.R. .	2,223	.	2,915
Club. Junior Carlton.	Durham . .	940	.	886
b. 1830, s. 1870, m. 1855.				
		3,163	.	3,801

PENRHYN, Lord, Penrhyn Castle, Bangor, &c.

Club. Arthur's, Uni. Ser.,	Carnarvon .	41,348	.	62,622
White's, Guards,	Northampton .	5,377	.	7,409
Carl., Travellers',	Denbigh . .	2,625	.	750
Boodle's.	Kent . . .	121	.	67
b. 1800, m. 1st 1833,	Bucks . . .	77	.	170
2nd 1846.				
Served in Scots Fusilier Guards.		49,548	.	71,018

Sat for Carnarvonshire. Inclusive of land bought from Sir C. Mordaunt in 1877.

** PENRICE, Thomas, of Kilvrough House, Swansea.

Coll. Eton.	Glamorgan .	5,411	.	5,250
b. 1820, s. 1846, m. 1852.				

PEMBERTON, H., of Trumpington. Cam.,
Carm. . . . . 2,747 . 6,474

STALLARD-PENOYRE, Thomas James,
of The Moor. Hereford . . . . . 2,035 . 2,680

*** PENRUDDOCKE, Charles, of Compton Park, Salisbury, &c.

		acres.	g. an. val.
Coll. Eton, Ch. Ch. Ox.	Wilts . . .	3,208 .	4,478
b. 1828, s. 1849, m. 1853.	Somerset . .	580 .	912
		3,788 .	5,390

** PEPLOE, Major, of Garnstone Castle, Hereford, &c.

		acres.	g. an. val.
Coll. Rugby, Trin. Cam.	Hereford . .	5,200 .	6,800
Club. Carl., A. & N., Gun,	York, E.R. .	648 .	2,225
Hurlingham, N. & M.		5,848 .	9,025

b. 1829, s. 1869, m. 1860.
  Served in 4th Dragoon Guards.   Sat for Herefordshire.

** PERCEVAL, Alexander, of Temple House, Ballymote.

		acres.	g. an. val.
Coll. Eton.	Co. Sligo . .	7,821 .	4,612
Club. E. & H., Boodle's.			

b. 1859, s. 1866, m. 1881.

HEBER-PERCY, Algernon Charles, of Hodnet, M. Drayton, &c

		acres.	g. an. val.
Coll. Eton, St. John's, Cam.	Salop . . .	2,791 .	5,576
Club. Carlton.	York, N. E.		
b. 1812, m. 1839.	and W. R. .	3,983 .	7,527
Served in Rifle Brigade.	Lincoln . .	673 .	1,421
		7,447 .	14,524

*** PERSSE, Burton Robert Parsons, of Moyode Castle, Athenry, Co. Galway.

		acres.	g. an. val.
Club. Falconry, Kildare St.	Co. Galway .	6,838 .	6,166
Dublin.	King's Co. . .	966 .	278
b. 1828, s. 1859, m. 1852.	Kilkenny . .	1,124 .	1,003
	Roscommon .	1,597 .	322
		10,525 .	7,769

PERROTT, J. W., of Monkstown.	Cork .	2,262 .	2,161
PERRY, E. H., of Belleek Castle.	Mayo .	5,108 .	2,082
PERRY, Samuel, of Woodroof.	Tipperary	2,768 .	2,873

PERSSE, Dudley, of Roxborough, Loughrea, Co. Galway.

		acres.		g. an. val.
Club. Army and Navy.	Co. Galway .	12,785	.	5,537
b. 1829, s. 1878.	Roscommon .	800	.	465
Served in 7th Fusiliers.				
		13,585	.	6,002

** PETRE, Henry, of Dunkenhalgh, Accrington.

Coll. Stonyhurst.   Lancashire . .   5,754 . 10,995
Club. White's, Marlborough, Travellers', Turf.
b. 1821, s. 1852, m. 1846.

** PETRE, Lord, Thorndon Hall, Brentwood.

Club. Trav., Athenæum,   Essex . . . 19,085 . 22,595
    St. George's.   b. 1817, s. 1850, m. 1843.

PEYTON, Sir Thomas, Bart., of Swifts House, Bicester, &c.

Coll. Addiscombe.	Oxford . . .	1,977	.	2,626
Club. Civil and Uni. Ser.,	Cambridge .	1,375	.	3,266
b. 1817. s. 1872, m. 1852.	Huntingdon .	606	.	901
Served in Madras S. C., and				
D. Q. M. Gen., is Maj.-		3,958	.	6,793
Gen. Madras Army retd.				

** PHELPS, John Vandeleur, of The Lodge, Broadford.

b. 1866, s. 1881.   Co. Clare . .   7,291 . 3,110

** PHIBBS, William, of Seafield, Sligo.

Coll. Trinity, Dublin.	Co. Sligo . .	10,507	.	5,713
b. 1802, s. 1839, m. 1840.	Roscommon .	834	.	342
Served in 11th Light Dragoons.				
		11,341	.	6,055

PETERS (late), of Penwarne. Cornw. . .	2,302	.	2,813
PETRE, E. H., of Whitley. Lanc., Warwick	2,902	.	4,689
PETRE, J. B., of Westwick. Norfolk . .	2,384	.	3,395
PETTIWARD, R. J., of Finborough. Suffolk	2,475	.	3,625
PHELIPS, C., of Briggins Pk. Herts, Ess.	2,925	.	4,840
PHELIPS, W., of Montacute. Somerset .	2,926	.	5,238

** PHILIPPS, Charles Edward Gregg, of Picton Castle, Haverfordwest.

		acres.	g. an. val.
Coll. Cheltenham.	Pembroke . .	19,745 .	21,151
Club. J. Carl., Beac.	Carmarthen .	3,339 .	2,664
b. 1840, s. 1876, m. 1868.	York . . .	21 .	1,391
		23,105 .	25,206

The Yorkshire land belongs to Mr. Fisher, whose eldest son is Mr. C. E. G. Philipps.

LLOYD-PHILIPPS, John Allen, of Dale Castle, Milford, &c.

b. 1824, s. 1879, m. 1845.	Pembroke . .	3,206 .	2,259
Served in 82nd Foot.	Cardigan . .	2,682 .	1,561
	Carmarthen .	1,849 .	977
		7,737 .	4,797

PHILIPS, Sir George Richard, Bart., of Weston House, Chipping Norton.

Coll. Eton, Trin. Cam.	Warwick . .	5,396 .	8,902
Club. Athenæum, Reform,	Worcester . .	600 .	708
Brooks's.	Gloucester .	649 .	961
b. 1789, s. 1847, m. 1819.	Oxford . . .	48 .	84
Sat for Steyning, Kidder-			
minster, and Poole.		6,693 .	10,655

** PHILIPS, Robert Needham, of Snitterfield, Stratford, &c.

Coll. Rugby, Man. N. C.	Warwick . .	3,388 .	5,813
Club. Ath., Bro., Ref., Dev.	Lancashire .	508 .	2,467
b. 1815, m. 1st 1845;	Kent . . .	152 .	255
2nd 1852.			
Sits for Bury.		4,048 .	8,535

LLOYD-PHILIPPS, Frederick Lewis, of			
Penty Park. Pembroke, Carmarthen .	2,824 .	2,09
ALLEN-PHILIPPS (late), of St. Brides. Pem.	3,651 .	2,971

PHILLIPS, JOHN FREDERICK LORT, of Lawrenny, Pembroke.

		acres.	*g. an. val.*
Club. Junior Carlton.	Pembroke .	6,522 .	5,709
b. 1854, s. 1866.			

*** PIGOTT-SMYTH-PIGOTT, JOHN HUGH WADHAM, of Brockley Court, Bristol, &c.

Coll. Lubeck Univ.   Somerset . .   6,000 .   12,000
Club. R.Y.S., R.T.Y.C., R.H.Y.C., R.V.Y.C., R.D.Y.C., R.W.Y.C.
b. 1819, s. 1854, m. 1857.

** PIGOTT, ROBERT HENRY ARMAND, of Capard, Rosenallis, Queen's Co.

b. 1830, m. 1st 1861,	Queen's Co. .	4,932 .	1,073
2nd 1875.	Limerick . .	3,477 .	2,590
		8,409 .	3,663

PILKINGTON, SIR LIONEL MILBORNE SWINNERTON, BART., of Chevet Park, Wakefield, &c. ⚓.

Coll. Charterhouse.	York, W.R. .	4,808 .	5,639
Club. Carlton, Arthur's,	Stafford . .	2,195 .	6,079
Boodle's.	Monmouth .	1,457 .	1,382
b. 1835, s. 1855, m. 1857.	Hereford . .	149 .	188
	Kent . . .	135 .	309
		8,744 .	13,597

** MANSEL-PLEYDELL, JOHN CLAVELL, of Whatcombe House, Blandford, &c. ⚓.

Coll. St. John's, Cam.   Dorset . . .   8,699 .   7,435
Club. Boodle's, Athenæum.
b. 1817, s. 1863, m. 1st 1844, 2nd 1849.
    Is entitled to the ⚓ mark as a younger branch of the MAUNSELLS of Thorpe-Malsor.

PHIPPS, R. L. H., of Leighton. Wilts, Som.   2,129 .   5,338

*** PLOWDEN, WILLIAM FRANCIS, of Plowden, Lydbury-North, Salop, &c. 🐟.

		acres.	g. an. val.
Coll. Beaumont, Stony-	Salop . . .	5,196 .	5,140
hurst.	Northampton .	738 .	1,824
Club. St. Geo., Raleigh.			
b. 1856, s. 1870, m. 1874.		5,934 .	6,964

*** SCOTT-PLUMMER, CHARLES HENRY, of Sunderland Hall, Selkirk, N.B., &c.

Coll. Eton.	Roxburgh . .	1,748 .	2,115
b. 1859, s. 1880.	Selkirk . . .	1,735 .	1,520
Serves in 86th Foot.			
		3,483 .	3,635

*** PLUNKET, MOST REV. LORD (Bishop of Meath), Old Connaught House, Bray.

Coll. Chel., Trin. Dub.	Co. Monaghan	2,324 .	1,680
Club. National, Kild. St.	Co. Cork . .	1,057 .	859
and Univ. Dublin.	Co. Dublin .	186 .	715
b. 1828, s. 1871, m. 1863.			
		3,567 .	3,254

*** POCHIN, WILLIAM ANN, of Edmondthorpe Hall, Oakham.

Coll. Trin. Cam.	Leicester . .	5,865 .	10,748
Club. Oxford and Cam.	Lincoln . .	1,539 .	2,849
b. 1820, s. 1831, m. 1841.	Rutland . .	387 .	685
		7,791 .	14,282

PINNEY, COL., of Somerton. Som., Dors. .	2,630 .	3,556
PLACE, E. G., of Loch Dochart. Perth, York	10,982 .	2,071
PLAISTOWE, J., of Lee. Bucks, Norfolk .	2,382 .	3,437
PLUMPTRE, C. J., of Fredville. Kent . .	2,420 .	3,660
POCHIN, R. G., of Braunstone. Leicester .	2,252 .	4,462

CHANDOS-POLE, Reginald Walkelyne, of Radbourne Hall,
Derby, &c. ⚓.

					acres.		*g. an. val.*
Coll.	Eton.	Derby	.	.	4,540	.	9,004
Club.	Guards, Boodle's.	Stafford	.	.	225	.	281
b. 1853, s. 1873.		York, W.R.	.		12	.	15
Served in Grenadier Guards.							
					4,777	.	9,300

** POLE, Sir William Edmund, Bt., of Shute, Axminster. ⚓.

Coll.	Winch., Ch. Ch. Ox.	Devon	.	.	5,846	.	7,416
Club.	Oxford and Cam.	Berks	.	.	unstated	.	370
b. 1816, s. 1874, m. 1841.							
					5,846	.	7,786

** POLLEN, Sir Richard Hungerford, Bart., of Rodbourne,
Chippenham, &c.

b. 1878, s. 1881.	Hants	.	.	3,036	.	3,319
	Wilts	.	.	1,466	.	2,125
				4,502	.	5,444

CRAWFURD-POLLOK, Sir Hew, Bart., of Pollok Castle,
Newton Mearns, Glasgow, N.B.

b. 1843, s. 1867, m. 1871.	Renfrew	.	.	3,145	.	3,941
Served in the United States Cavalry.						

Lady C. Pollok has a rental of 602*l.* out of this estate.

POLLOK, John Broom, Glasgow, N.B., &c.

Coll.	Magd. Cam.	Co. Galway	.	29,366	.	12,727
b. 1850, s. 1881, m. 1873.		Co. Dublin	.	211	.	586
		Renfrew	.	3,761	.	4,055
		Argyll	.	.	5,046	.	800
		Ayr .	.	.	702	.	268
		Lanark .	.	50	.	100
				39,136	.	18,536

Exclusive of 338*l.* for quarries and mines in Scotland.

VAN NOTTEN-POLE, Sir P., Bart., of Todenham. Gloucester, Warwick	.	.	2,823	.	4,452
WELLER-POLEY, J. G., of Boxted. Suff.		2,312	.	.	2,508
WELLER-POLEY, Mrs., of Wicken. Suff.		2,749	.		3,286

*** POLTIMORE, Lord, Court Hall, North Molton. 💲.

		acres.	g. an. val.
Coll. Har.,Ch.Ch.Ox.	Devon . . .	19,883 .	21,800

Club. Bro., Marl., Bood.
b. 1837, s. 1858, m. 1858.
  Was Treas. of the Household.   Excl. of profits of woods.

*** POLWARTH, Lord, Mertoun Ho., St. Boswell's, N.B., &c.

Club. Carlton.	Berwick. . .	4,714 .	7,118
b. 1838, s. 1867, m. 1863.	Roxburgh . .	4,102 .	5,798
	Haddington .	1,848 .	2,327
		10,664 .	15,243

** TALBOT-PONSONBY, Charles William, of Inchiquin, Youghal.

Club. Naval and Military.	Co. Cork . .	10,367 .	6,768

b. 1843, s. 1866, m. 1868.   Served in Royal Navy.

** PONSONBY, Chambre Brabazon, of Kilcooley, Thurles.

b. 1839, s. 1877, m. 1873.	Tipperary . .	6,184 .	3,500
Served in 10th Hussars.	Limerick . .	3,426 .	4,426
	Kilkenny . .	1,260 .	650
	Dublin . . .	unstated .	250
		10,870 .	8,826

* LEYBORNE-POPHAM, Francis William, of Hunstrete, Bristol, &c.

Coll. Eton.	Somerset . .	1,103 .	1,979
b. 1862, s. 1880.	Wilts . . .	2,000 .	2,000
	Surrey . . .	238 .	1,774
		3,341 .	5,753

** PORTAL, Melville, of Laverstoke House, Overton, Hants.

Coll. Harrow, Ch. Ch. Ox.	Hants . . .	10,966 .	10,922

Club. Carlton.   b. 1819, s. 1848, m. 1855.   Sat for N. Hants.

PONSFORD, John, of Ford.	Devon . .	2,441 .	2,385

PORTARLINGTON, Earl of, K.P., Emo Park, Queen's Co.

		acres.	g. an. val.
Club. Carlton.	Queen's Co. .	11,149 .	6,050
b. 1822, s. 1845, m. 1847.	Tyrone . . .	4,756 .	2,169
	Tipperary . .	2,897 .	2,214
	King's Co. . .	1,126 .	364
		19,928 .	10,797

*** PORTEOUS, David Scott, of Lauriston Castle, Montrose, N.B.

Coll. Harrow, Bras. Oxon.	Kincardine .	3,437 .	5,534

Club. Naval and Military.   b. 1852, s. 1872, m. 1875.
            Served in 2nd Dragoons (Scots Greys).

PORTER, Henry Richard Mansel, of Birlingham House, Pershore, &c.

Coll. Harrow, Sandhurst.	Worcester . .	2,158 .	4,117
Club. Naval and Military.	Essex . . .	932 .	1,282
b. 1857, s. 1879, m. 1881.			
Served in 1st Roy. Drs.		3,090 .	5,399

* PORTER, John Grey Vesey, of Belleisle, Enniskillen.

s. 1818, m. 1863.	Co. Fermanagh	11,880 .	5,762
	Co. Longford .	5,024 .	2,581
	Co. Tyrone .	4,756 .	2,169
		21,660 .	10,512

The bulk of these estates is given in the return to "Reps. of Rev. J. G. Porter," his father.   Mr. Porter only avows his ownership of 5,160 acres in Fermanagh, and a half-share in 28 small farms with his sister.

POOLE, Rev. W., of Hentland.   Hereford   2,041 . 3,686

*** PORTLAND, Duke of, Welbeck Abbey, Worksop, &c.

		acres.	g. an. val.
Club. Carlton, White's,	Notts . . .	43,036 .	35,752
Guards.	Northumberland	12,337 .	10,477
b. 1857, s. 1879.	Derby . . .	8,074 .	9,643
Served in Coldstream	Lincoln . . .	903 .	1,366
Guards.	Norfolk . . .	591 .	986
	Worcester . .	9 .	30
	Bucks . . .	5 .	25
	Ayr	17,244 .	19,671
	Caithness . .	101,000 .	10,400

Exclusive of 19,570*l.* for mines.	183,199 .	88,350

PORTMAN, Viscount, Bryanston, Blandford, &c.

Coll. Eton, Ch. Ch. Oxon.	Somerset . .	24,339 .	35,557
Club. United University.	Dorset . . .	7,798 .	9,478
b. 1799, s. 1823, m. 1827.	Devon . . .	1,754 .	937
Served as Councillor to the			
Prince of Wales and Lord		33,891 .	45,972
Warden of the Stannaries.	Sat for Dorset and for Marylebone.

*** PORTSMOUTH, Earl of, Hurstborne Park, Whitchurch, Hants, &c. **ς.**

Coll. Rugby, Trin. Cam.	Hants . . .	17,460 .	14,731
Club. Brooks's, Boodle's.	Devon . . .	16,414 .	11,399
b. 1825, s. 1854, m. 1855.	Somerset . .	646 .	321
	Co. Wexford .	12,464 .	9,820

	46,984 .	36,271

*** POULETT, Earl, Hinton House, Crewkerne, &c. **ς.**

Coll. R.Mil.Sandhurst.	Somerset . .	22,123 .	21,885
Club. Arthur's, Army	Hants . . .	6 .	113
and Navy,Turf.			
b. 1827, s. 1864, m. 1st 1849.		22,129 .	21,998
2nd 1871.			

Served in 22nd Foot, at the storming of Boree Heights and destruction of 5 villages, with General Boileau's force in Afghanistan in 1854 (medal); also in 2nd and 54th Foot.

POSTLE, J. S., of Smallburgh. Norfolk .	2,185 .	3,685

** POWELL, George Ernest John, of Nanteos, Aberystwith.

		acres.		g. an. val.
Coll. Eton, Bras. Oxon.	Cardigan . .	21,933	.	9,024
b. 1842, s. 1878, m. 1881.	Brecon . . .	11,704	.	556
	Montgomery .	37	.	17
		33,674	.	9,597

POWELL, Thomas Harcourt, of Drinkstone Park, Bury St. Edmund's.

		acres.		g. an. val.
Coll. Eton.	Pembroke . .	3,083	.	3,393
Club. Guards, Garrick.	Suffolk . . .	1,105	.	1,611
b. 1819, s. 1855.	Essex . . .	403	.	610
Served in Scots Fus. Gds.	Wilts	49	.	37
		4,640	.	5,651

POWER, Sir John Talbot, Bart., of Edermine House, Enniscorthy, Co. Wexford.

Club. Ref., Badminton.	Wexford . .	10,205	.	7,427
b. 1845, s. 1877, m. 1876.	Co. Dublin .	6	.	52
Sat for Co. Wexford.				
		10,211	.	7,479

POWER, Joseph O'Neil, of Newton House, Tramore, Co. Waterford.

b. 18—, m. 1869,	Co. Tipperary	7	.	66
2nd 1881.	Co. Waterford	4,524	.	4,007
	Co. Kilkenny	3,788	.	2,857
		8,319	.	6,930

POTTS, Henry, of Glanrafon. Denbigh, Flint, Cheshire	2,954	.	3,268
POWELL, A. P. E., of Hurdcott. Wilts, Som.	2,585	.	3,124
POWELL, W., of Maesgwynne. Carm., Pem.	3,479	.	2,716
POWER, K., of Hill. Heref., Glo., Monm.	2,074	.	8,258

POWER, PATRICK JOSEPH MAHON, of Faithlegg House, Waterford.

		acres.	g. an. val.
Club. Kildare St. Dublin.	Waterford . .	4,699 .	3,268
b. 1820, s. 1873, m. 1859.	Wexford . .	1,658 .	1,284
		6,357 .	4,552

*** POWER, SIR RICHARD CRAMPTON, BART., of Kilfane, Thomastown, Co. Kilkenny.

		acres.	g. an. val.
Coll. Trin. Cam.	Kilkenny . .	2,811 .	2,132
Club. Boodle's, Kildare	Tipperary . .	5,357 .	2,573
Street, Dublin.	Wicklow . .	367 .	379
b. 1843, s. 1873, m. 1869.	Waterford . .	267 .	665
	Beds . . .	1,445 .	2,177
		10,247 .	7,926

*** POWERSCOURT, VISCOUNT, K.P., Powerscourt, Enniskerry, Co. Wicklow.

		acres.	g. an. val.
Coll. Eton.	Co. Wicklow .	40,986 .	9,781
Club. White's, Brooks's,	Co. Wexford .	11,641 .	5,426
Marl., Fine Arts.	Co. Dublin .	631 .	1,178
b. 1836, s. 1844, m. 1864.			
Served in 1st Life Guards.		53,258 .	16,385

** POWIS, EARL OF, Powis Castle, Welshpool, &c. ⚓.

		acres.	g. an. val.
Coll. Eton, St. John's, Cam.	Montgomery .	33,545 .	28,000
Club. Carlton, Ox. and	Salop . . .	26,986 .	29,000
Cam., Travellers',	Radnor . . .	19 .	22
White's.	Denbigh . .	9 .	2
b. 1818, s. 1848.			
Sat for N. Salop.		60,559 .	57,024

POYNDER (late), of Hillmarton Manor, Calne, &c.

		acres.	g. an. val.
See " DICKSON " among	Wilts . . .	5,913 .	11,688
" Addenda."	Kent . . .	41 .	1,495
	Suffolk . . .	337 .	426
	Middlesex . .	263 .	912
	Essex . . .	289 .	316
	Hants . . .	65 .	91
		6,908 .	14,928

POWYS, HON. L. W. H., of Bewsey. Lanc. 2,896 5,881

* PRATT, EDWARD ROGER MURRAY, of Ryston Hall, Downham
Market.   *acres.*   *g. an. val.*

Coll. Eton, Trin. Cam.   Norfolk . . 3,518 . 5,819
Club. St. James's, Brooks's. b. 1847, s. 1867, m. 1881.

PRATT, MERVYN, of Cabra Castle, Kingscourt, Co. Cavan, &c.

Coll. Trin. Dub., S. Mary   Co. Mayo . . 17,955 . 3,393
         Hall, Oxon.   Co. Cavan . .   8,095 . 5,285
Club. Sackville St. Dublin. Co. Meath . .   1,014 .   793
b. 1807, s. 1863, m. 1834.
                                             ─────────────────
                                              27,064 . 9,471

** PRESCOTT, SIR GEORGE RENDLESHAM, BART., of Isenhurst,
Hawkhurst, &c.

Coll. Eton.   Sussex . . . 2,121 . 2,100
Club. Jun. Carlton, Marl.   Kent . . .   1,113 . 1,860
b. 1846, s. 1850, m. 1872.   Flint . . .   511 .   812
Served in 2nd Life Guards.   Bucks . . .   105 .   220
                               Oxford . . .   83 .   169
                               Middlesex . .   33 .   80
                               Herts . . .   112 .   224
                                             ─────────────────
                                               4,078 . 5,465
         His mother has the Kentish and Oxford estates.

** PRESTON, SIR JACOB HENRY, BART., of Beeston Hall,
Norwich.
  Coll. Westm., Trin.   Norfolk . . 4,800 . 7,000
          Cambridge.
  Club. Oxford and Cambridge. b. 1812, s. 1823, m. 1846.

PRESTON, JOHN JOSEPH, of Bellinter, Navan, Co. Meath.

Coll. Trinity, Dublin.   Co. Meath . 7,415 . 6,839
Club. Kildare St. Dublin.   b. 1815, s. 1839, m. 1842.

PRESTON, MRS., of Lee, Chulmleigh.
s. 18—, m. 18—.   Devon . . . 11,280 . 6,243

MACKWORTH-PRAED, HERBERT B., of
Ousden. Suffolk, Cambridgeshire. . . 2,198 . 3,055

** PRESTON, Thomas Henry, of Moreby Hall, York.

		acres.	g. an. val.
Coll. Eton.	York, E. & W.R.	5,348	7,325
Club. Carlton, Arthur's.			

b. 1817, m. 1847.   Served in 7th Hussars.

** PRICE, James Charles, of Saintfield House, Co. Down, &c.

Club. Ulster, Belfast.	Co. Down . .	6,807	7,641

b. 1807, s. 1855, m. 1840.

*** GREEN-PRICE, Sir Richard, Bart., of Norton Manor, Presteign.

Coll. Worcester Sch.	Radnor . .	8,774	7,638

Club. Union.   b. 1803, s. 1861, m. 1st 1837,
2nd 1844.

Sat for Radnor Dist.   Sits for Radnorshire.

** PRICE, Richard John Lloyd, of Rhiwlas, Bala, &c.

Coll. Eton, Ch. Ch. Oxon.	Merioneth . .	40,500	10,600
Club. Carlton, Boodle's,	Denbigh . .	164	177
White's, Jun. Carl.,	Carnarvon . .	600	314
V.Y.C., Kennel.			
b. 1842, s. 1864, m. 1869.		41,264	11,091

*** PRINGLE, James Thomas, of Torwoodlee, Galashiels, N.B.

Coll. Royal Naval.	Selkirk . . .	5,401	2,723
Club. Han. Sq., U.S.	Roxburgh . .	2,500	1,357
and Cons. Ed.,			
Union, Brighton.		7,901	4,080

b. 1832, s. 1859, m. 1869.
Served in Royal Navy in Burmese War of 1852, and in the Baltic during Russian War.

PRICE, Gen., of Mongewell. Oxon, Kent	2,711	3,229
PRICE, W., of Cas. Piggin. Pem., Carm., Card.	3,904	2,543
PRICKARD, Mrs., of Dderw. Rad., Bre.	4,083	2,040
PRIDEAUX (late), Lady, of Netherton. Devon, Essex, Herts	2,261	3,154

PRINGLE (late), LADY E., Langton House, Dunse, N.B.

d. 188–.		*acres.*		*g. an. val.*
	Berwick . .	8,121	.	8,500
	Hants . . .	12	.	285
		8,133	.	8,785

** PRIOR, MRS., of Kirklington, Ripon, &c.

b. 1814, m. 1836, s. 1881.	York . . .	4,800	.	5,000
	Co. Kilkenny .	22,232	.	11,745
		27,032	.	16,745

PRITCHARD, JOHN, of Stanmore, Broseley.

b. 1797, s. 1861, m. 1847. Salop . . . 3,254 . 5,123
Sat for Bridgenorth.

** WEGG-PROSSER, FRANCIS RICHARD, of Belmont, Hereford.

Coll. Eton, Ball. Oxon. Hereford . . 3,734 . 6,200
Club. Carlton, St. George's.
b. 1824, s. 1849, m. 1850. Sat for Herefordshire.

BRUCE-PRYCE, ALLAN CAMERON, of Duffryn, Cardiff.

Coll. Exeter, Oxon. Glamorgan . 3,398 . 3,544
Club. Athen., New University.
b. 1836, m. 1st 1858, 2nd 1873.

PRYOR, ARTHUR, of Hylands, Chelmsford.

Coll. Eton. Essex . . . 3,255 . 4,975
Club. Carlton. b. 1816, m. 1841.

** PRYSE, SIR PRYSE, BART., of Gogerddan, Aberystwith.

Coll. Eton.	Cardigan . .	28,684	.	10,634
Club. J. U. S., Bro.,A. & N.	Montgomery .	3,351	.	473
b. 1838, s. 1855, m. 1859.	Pembroke . .	322	.	217
Served in Royal Horse Guards.		32,357	.	11,324

PROBYN, E., of Huntley Manor.	Gloucester	2,743	.	4,130
PROCTOR, E. B., of Aberhafesp.	Montg.	2,737	.	2,454
PRYCE, R. D., of Cyfronydd.	Mont., Mer.	2,113	.	3,422

** PUGH, DAVID, of Manoravon, Llandilo, &c.

		acres.	g. an. val.
Coll. Rugby, Ball. Oxon.	Carmarthen .	7,292 .	4,773
Club. Oxford and Cam.	Cardigan . .	884 .	500

b. 1806, s. 1827.

Sat for Carmarthenshire. 8,176 . 5,273

PULLEINE, MRS., of Clifton Castle, Bedale.

s. 1879, m. 1841.	York, N. & E.R.	2,818 .	3,881
	Northumberland	753 .	524
	Durham . .	470 .	319

4,041 . 4,724

** GILES-PULLER, ARTHUR GILES, of Youngsbury, Ware.

Coll. Eton, Trin. Cam.	Herts . . .	2,888 .	4,480
Club. Athenæum, Arthur's.	Essex . . .	1,077 .	1,575

b. 1833, s. 1864.

3,965 . 6,055

PONSONBY-PURDON, GEORGE FREDERICK ROBERT, of Tinerana, Killaloe, Co. Clare.

b. 1840, s. 1864, m. 1867.	Co. Clare . .	6,298 .	2,564
Serves in Royal Navy.	King's Co. . .	2,504 .	1,817

8,802 . 4,381

** BAGWELL-PUREFOY, COL., of Greenfield, Tipperary.

Coll. Harrow. Tipperary . . 8,063 . 3,069
Club. Union, Kild. St. Dublin. b. 1819, s. 1846, m. 1st 1854,
2nd 1861.

Served in 4th Hussars and 3rd Dragoon Guards.

BOUVERIE-PUSEY, SIDNEY EDWARD, of Pusey, Farringdon.

Coll. Ch. Ch. Oxford. Berks . . . 5,022 . 7,082
Club. Brooks's. b. 1839, s. 1855, m. 1871.

PUGH, L. P., of Abermaed. Cardigan . . 6,894 . 2,369
PULTENEY, K., of Northerwood. Hants,
Sus. . . . . 2,039 . 2,066

** PUTLAND, the three sisters of the late George, of Bray Head House, Co. Wicklow. s. 1876.

These ladies have all married quite recently (1879).

	acres.	g. an. val.
Kilkenny .	3,229 .	949
Co. Cork . .	4,521 .	3,138
Queen's Co. .	1,174 .	890
Co. Wicklow .	295 .	696
Tipperary . .	484 .	654
	9,703 .	6,327

** PUXLEY, Henry Lavallin, of Llangan, St. Clears, &c.
Coll. Eton, Bras. Oxon.
Club. Jun. Carl., Kild. St.
b. 1833, s. 1860, m. 1st. 1857, 2nd 1875.

	acres.	g. an. val.
Co. Cork . .	9,518 .	3,527
Carmarthen .	6,522 .	4,969
Pembroke . .	333 .	380
	16,373 .	8,876

The Lavallin estate (Co. Cork) has been in the hands of the family since King John's time.

*** PYE, Henry John, of Clifton Hall, Tamworth, &c.
Coll. Magdalene, Cam.
Club. Oxford and Cam.
b. 1802, s. 1833, m. 1825.

	acres.	g. an. val.
Stafford . . .	3,240 .	5,556
Middlesex . .	11 .	70
	3,251 .	5,626

** PYM, Francis, of The Hasells, Sandy, Beds, &c.
Coll. Ch. Ch. Oxford.
Club. Arthur's, Boodle's.
b. 1849, s. 1860.
Served in 1st Life Guards.

	acres.	g. an. val.
Bedford . . .	1,497 .	4,500
Huntingdon .	1,500 .	2,060
Herts . . .	631 .	1,020
Cambridge . .	2 .	7
	3,630 .	7,587

QUEEN, Her Majesty The
b. 1819, s. 1837, m. 1840.

	acres.	g. an. val.
Aberdeen . .	25,350 .	2,392
Hants . . .	1,963 .	3,100
Surrey . . .	128 .	69
	27,441 .	5,561

This list only gives the strictly private estates of the Queen, though there may have been some mixing in the return of Crown property, as such, with Her Majesty's freeholds. The Crown property in Berks, representing the Windsor estate, is given as 10,203 acres, of the annual value of 22,434*l.* The Surrey estate is returned under "Executors of the late Prince Consort."

The Queen purchased Claremont in 1882.

QUEENSBERRY, MARQUIS OF, Kinmount, Annan, N.B.

			acres.		*g. an. val.*
Coll. Eton, Magd. Cam.	Dumfries . .		13,243	.	13,384

Club. Boodle's, Turf.   b. 1844, s. 1858, m. 1866.

*** QUICKE, JOHN, of Newton St. Cyres, Exeter.

		acres.		*g. an. val.*
Coll. Eton, Trin. Cam.	Devon . . .	3,663	.	5,502
Club. Arthur's.	Cornwall . .	150	.	100
b. 1816, s. 1859, m. 1847.	Somerset . .	10	.	59
		3,823	.	5,661

QUIN, LORD GEORGE, Quinsborough, Sixmilebridge, Clare.

Club. Travellers'.	Co. Clare . .	2,850	.	2,018
b. 1792, m. 1st 1814,	Tipperary . .	3,078	.	753
2nd 1847.	Limerick . .	889	.	538
		6,817	.	3,309

** DELME-RADCLIFFE, MRS., of Hitchin Priory, Herts.

s. 1875, m. 1831.	Herts . . .	2,900	.	4,600
	Beds . . .	926	.	1,290
		3,826	.	5,890

RADCLIFFE, SIR JOSEPH PERCIVAL PICKFORD, BART., of Rudding Park, Wetherby, &c.

Coll. Cath. Hall, Camb.	York, W.R. .	2,872	.	7,271
Club. St. George's.	Lancashire .	457	.	1,291
b. 1824, s. 1872, m. 1854.	Stafford . .	22	.	127
	Monmouth .	92	.	92
		3,443	.	8,781

** RADNOR, EARL OF, Longford Castle, Salisbury, &c.

Coll. Har., Ch. Ch.	Wilts . . .	17,000	.	23,000
Oxon.	Berks . . .	4,334	.	7,500
Club. Carl., Boodle's.	Kent . . .	3,266	.	11,200
b. 1815, s. 1869, m. 1840.	Gloucester . .	270	.	1,200
		24,870	.	42,900

LD. R.'s Metropolitan pty. is not included.

QUIN, W., of Loughloher. Tipperary . .		2,581	.	2,295
💲 RADCLYFFE, CHARLES JAMES, of Foxdenton. Dorset, Lancashire, York . .		2,811	.	2,361

*** RAMSAY, Sir Alexander Entwistle, Bart., of Balmain, N.B. (res. Green Lane, Wavertree, Liverpool).

			acres.	*g. an. val.*
Coll. St. Andrew's.	Kincardine	.	4,028	. 3,760

b. 1837, s. 1875, m. 1863, 2nd 1880.

*** RAMSAY, Sir Jas. Henry, Bart., of Bamff, Alyth, N.B.

Coll. Rugby, Ch. Ch.	Perth	.	.	12,845	. 3,745
Oxon.	Forfar	.	.	1,027	. 1,225
Club. Oxford and Cam.					
b. 1832, s. 1871, m. 1st 1861,				13,872	. 4,970
2nd 1873.					

"This estate has been held in male line by charter since 1232."

*** RAMSAY, John, of Kildalton, Greenock, N.B.

Coll. Glasgow University.	Argyll	. .	54,250	. 9,242

Club. Windham, Athenæum.
b. 1814, m. 1st 1857, 2nd 1871.
　Served on the Sco. B. of Ed., and as Com. und. End. Inst. Act. Sat for Stirling ; sits for Falkirk.

** RAMSAY, Col. John, of Straloch, Aberdeen, N.B., &c.

Coll. Eton, Trin. Cam.	Aberdeen	. .	3,056	. 2,716
Club. Carlton, Jun. Carl.,	Banff	. . .	2,088	. 1,888
New Edinburgh.				
b. 1831, s. 1832, m. 1858.			5,144	. 4,604

** WARDLAW-RAMSAY, Robert Balfour, of Whitehill, Edinburgh, N.B., &c.

Coll. Ed., Haileybury.	Clackmannan .		4,147	. 2,429
Club. Carlton.	Midlothian . .		2,963	. 3,822
b. 1815, s. 1837, m. 1842.	Fife		368	. 1,245
Served in Bengal C. S.	Peebles . . .		22	. 10
			7,500	. 7,506

Exclusive of 2,312*l.* for mines.

RAILTON, H., of Snittlegarth.	Cumberland	2,504	.	2,434
RAMSHAY (late), J., of Milton Hall.	Cumb.	2,403	.	2,583

** RAMSDEN, Sir John William, Bart., of Byram, Ferry-
Bridge, &c.

			acres.	g. an. val.
Coll. Eton, Trin. Cam.	Lincoln . . .		800 .	1,400
Club. Brooks's, Athenæum,	York, W.R. .	11,248 .	168,420
Travellers'.	Inverness . .	138,000 .	11,474

b. 1831, s. 1839, m. 1865.

Served as Under Secretary for War.   150,048 . 181,294

Sat for Taunton, Hythe, the W.R., and Monmouth. Sits for
E. Div. of W.R.

Inclusive of a rental of 1,819*l.* belonging to Hon. Mrs.
Ramsden, his mother. This is one of the cases specially noted
in the return, where (in Yorkshire) the gross estimated rental
forms no criterion of the income received by the landlord.

RANELAGH, Viscount, K.C.B., Mulgrave Ho., Fulham, S.W.

Club. Carlton.	Norfolk . . .	3,043 .	5,691

b. 1812, m. 1820.   Served in 1st Life Guards.

RANFURLY, Earl of, Dungannon Park, Co. Tyrone.

Coll. Harr., Trin. Cam.	Co. Tyrone .	9,647 .	10,958
Club. Carl., White's, Ral.	Fermanagh . .	506 .	279

b. 1856, s. 1875, m. 1880.

		10,153 .	11,237

*** RANKIN, Patrick, of Otter House, Kilfinan, Argyll, N.B.

b. 1844, s. 1873.	Lanark . . .	4,365 .	3,196
Exc. of 2,972*l.* for mines,	Argyll . . .	4,200 .	1,552
the real inc. of which was	Stirling . . .	956 .	719
(1877) much higher.			

		9,521 .	5,467

** RASHLEIGH, Jonathan, of Menabilly, Par, Cornwall, &c.

Coll. Har., Ball. Ox.	Cornwall . .	30,156 .	9,000
b. 1820, s. 1871, m. 1st 1843,	Devon . . .	242 .	750
2nd 1869.	Co. Mayo . .	5,475 .	883
The Cornish acreage in-	Co. Sligo . .	1,023 .	658
cludes waste, the rental in			
Cornwall is always increas-		36,896 .	11,291
ing as lives drop.			

RANKIN, J., of Bryngwyn.   Heref., Ches.   2,959 . 5,130

** RATHDONNELL, Lord, Drumcar, Dunleer, Co. Louth, &c.

		acres.		*g. an. val.*
Coll. Eton.	Carlow . . .	8,058	.	6,408
Club. Carlton, Naval	Louth . . .	3,000	.	2,500
and Military,	Fermanagh .	2,600	.	2,600
Raleigh, Kil-	Monaghan . .	1,006	.	1,120
dare Street,	Tyrone . . .	2,886	.	886
Dublin.	Meath . . .	1,215	.	736
b. 1848, s. 1866 and 1879,	Dublin . . .	600	.	810
m. 1874.	Kildare . . .	558	.	340

Served in Scots Greys.

19,923 . 15,400

** CLERK-RATTRAY, Lieut.-Gen., C.B., of Craighall-Rattray, Blairgowrie, N.B.

Coll. Rugby.   Perth . . . 3,370 . 3,700
Club. Carlton, Uni. Ser.   b. 1832, s. 1851.
Served in 90th Regt. in Crimea and Indian Mutiny.

RAVENSWORTH, Earl of, Eslington Park, Alnwick, &c.

Coll. Eton, Ch. Ch. Oxon.   Northumberland 7,458 .. 11,924
Club. Carlton.   Durham . . 6,393 . 27,240
b. 1821, s. 1878, m. 1852.
Sat for S. Northumberland.   13,851 . 39,164

** RAWSON, Miss, of Nidd Hall, Ripley.

s. 1844.	Yorkshire . .	7,604	.	10,388
	Hereford . .	1,307	.	1,091
	Lancashire .	160	.	566

9,071 . 12,045

*** RAWSTORNE, Lawrence, of Penwortham Priory, Preston.

Coll. Eton, Ch. Ch.   Lancashire . 4,369 . 10,666
     Oxon.
Club. Jun. Carlton, St. James's.   b. 1842, s. 1850, m. 1871.

RAWLINSON, W., of Duddon.   Lanc., Cum. 3,527 . 2,321

* RAYER, William Carew, of Holcombe Court, Wellington, Somerset.

		acres.	g. an. val.
Coll. Eton, Ch. Ch. Oxon.	Devon . . .	2,445 .	3,624
b. 1820, s. 1866, m. 1869.	Glamorgan .	1,512 .	2,231
	Somerset . .	50 .	45
Rental understated.			
		4,007 .	5,900

** RAYLEIGH, Lord, F.R.S., Terling Place, Witham.

Coll. Harrow, Trin.	Essex . . .	8,632 .	12,800
Cam. (senior wrangler, 1865).			

Club. Ath., New Uni. b. 1842, s. 1873, m. 1871.

** PRITCHARD-RAYNER, George, of Trescawen, Llangefni.

Club. Junior Uni. Ser.	Anglesea . .	2,741 .	2,263
b. 1843, s. 1881, m. 1871.	Cambridge .	1,126 .	2,414
Served in 5th Drag. Guards.			
		3,867 .	4,677

CREWE-READ, Offley Malcolm, of Plâs Dinam, Llandinam, N. Wales.

Club. Uni. Ser., Brooks's.	Montgomery .	3,518 .	2,619
b. 1821, s. 1862, m. 1848.	Flint . . .	424 .	608
Served as Capt. R. Navy.			
		3,942 .	3,227

READE, Sir Chandos Stanhope Hoskyns, Bart., of Carreglwyd, Anglesea.

b. 1851, s. 1868, m. 1880.	Anglesea . .	3,764 .	3,273
Was in Madras C. Service.			

*** REAY, Lord (*jur. uxo.*), Stow, Carolside, Earlston, N.B.

Club. Ath., Trav., St. James's.	Midlothian .	7,930 .	6,857
b. 1839, s. (to the title) 1876,	Selkirk . .	3,133 .	1,663
m. 1877.	Berwick . .	2,282 .	2,560
Was Gentleman of the	Roxburgh . .	1,976 .	1,390
Chamber to the King of the			
Netherlands.		15,321 .	12,470

READE, Joseph, of Shipton Court. Oxon . 2,018 . 2,826

*** GURDON-REBOW, Hector John, of Wyvenhoe Park, Colchester.

			acres.		g. an. val.
Coll. Eton, Trin. Cam.	Essex . . .	2,475	.	4,621
Club. Brooks's.	Suffolk . . .	1,072	.	1,688
b. 1846, s. 1870, m. 1873.	Surrey . . .	662	.	580
Served in 2nd Life Guards.				
		4,209	.	6,889

REDESDALE, Earl of, Birdhope Craig, Redesdale, Northumberland, &c. ♨.

Coll. Eton, New, Oxon.	Northumberland	17,204	.	3,381
Club. Carlton, Boodle's,	Gloucester .	4,368	.	5,743
White's, St. Ste.	Warwick . .	2,184	.	2,877
b. 1805, s. 1830.	Oxford . . .	2,132	.	2,664
Serves as Chairman of	Worcester . .	282	.	485
Committees in the House	Wilts . . .	327	.	315
of Lords.				
		26,497	.	15,465

** REDINGTON, Christopher Talbot, of Kilcornan, Oranmore, Co. Galway.

Coll. Oscott, Ch. Ch. Oxon.	Co. Galway .	9,454	.	4,281
Club. Kildare St. Dublin.	Wexford . .	2,956	.	1,491
b. 1847, s. 1862.				
		12,410	.	5,772

REEVE, Colonel John, of Leadenham House, Grantham.

Club. Carl., Guards, U. Ser.	Lincoln . .	5,216	.	9,207
b. 1822, s. 1864, m. 1st 1857, 2nd 1863.				
Served in Grenadier Guards.				

** RENDLESHAM, Lord, Rendlesham Hall, Woodbridge.

Coll. Eton, Ch. Ch. Oxon.	Suffolk . . .	19,869	.	19,275
Club. Carlton.	Herts . . .	3,969	.	5,500
b. 1840, s. 1852, m. 1861.	Ayr	190	.	249
Sits for E. Suffolk.				
		24,028	.	25,024

REEVES, E. H., of Cas. Kevin.   Cork, Lim.   2,910   .   2,182

*** BIRCH-REYNARDSON, CHARLES SAMUEL THOMAS, of Holywell, Stamford.

			acres.		*g. an. val.*
Coll. Eton, Tr. Cam.	Lincoln	. .	6,004	.	8,950
Club. Carl., Boodle's.	Rutland	. .	40	.	49
b. 1810, s. 1854, m. 1st 1836, 2nd 1867.			6,044	.	8,999

** RIBBLESDALE, LORD, Gisburne Park, Skipton.

		acres.		*g. an. val.*
Coll. Harrow.	York, W.R. .	4,667	.	6,859
Club. Pr.,Whi.,Bood.,Turf.	Lancashire . .	52	.	121
b. 1854, s. 1876, m. 1877.				
Serves in Rifle Brigade, was in 64th Foot.		4,719	.	6,980

Is a Lord in Waiting.

RICHARDS, ARTHUR WILLIAM MORDAUNT, of Ardamine, Gorey, Co. Wexford.

b. 1860, s. 1879.	Co. Wexford .	2,995	.	2,367
	Co. Dublin .	378	.	2,102
Serves in the Scots Greys.				
		3,373	.	4,469

** RICHARDSON, JOHN GRUBB, of Moyallon, Gilford, Down.

Ballitore School.	Armagh . .	6,092	.	6,800
b. 1813, m. 1844 and 1853.	Down . . .	286	.	725
		6,378	.	7,525

CAMPBELL-RENTON, C., of Lamberton. Ber.	2,487	.	2,699
REYNARD, E. H., of Sunderlandwick. York	2,604	.	3,473
REYNOLDS, E., of Paxton. Hunts, Beds	2,246	.	3,424
RICARDO, H. G., of Gatcombe. Glo., Heref.	2,266	.	3,005
RICARDO, MRS., of Bromsberrow. Worcester, Gloucester, Hereford, Warwick .	2,841	.	4,112
RICE, ADM., C.B., of Dane Court. Kent .	2,864	.	3,788
RICHARDS, MRS., of Cerrig Llwydion. Denbigh, Merioneth	6,472	.	2,888

RICHARDSON (late), of Somerset, Coleraine, Co. Derry.

		acres.	*g. an. val.*
d. 1875.	Londonderry .	18,159 .	7,424

RICHMOND AND GORDON, DUKE OF, K.G., Goodwood, Chichester, &c.

Coll. Westm., Ch. Ch. Ox.	Banff . . .	159,952 .	23,841
Club. Carl., White's, Trav.,	Aberdeen . .	69,660 .	24,747
St. Stephen's.	Inverness . .	27,409 .	1,182
b. 1818, s. 1860, m. 1843.	Elgin . . .	12,271 .	10,618
Served in Royal Horse Gds.	Sussex . . .	17,117 .	19,283
Was Pres. of P. L. B., Pres.	York, N.R. .	2 .	12
of the B. of Trade, and			
L. Pres. of the Council.		286,411 .	79,683
Sat for W. Sussex.			

** RIDDELL, FRANCIS HENRY, of Cheeseburn Grange, Newcastle-on-Tyne.

Coll. Ushaw.	Northumberland	2,740 .	3,200
Club. Brooks's.	York, N.R. .	710 .	1,100
b. 1813, s. 1871, m. 1862.	Westmoreland	310 .	310
		3,760 .	4,610

** RIDDELL, JOHN GIFFARD, of Felton Park, Acklington, &c.

Coll. Oscott.   Northumberland 14,011 . 12,319
b. 1830, s. 1870, m. 1st 1854, 2nd 1866.

RIDDELL, SIR THOMAS MILLES, BT., of Strontian, Bonaw, N.B.

Club. A. and N., New Ed.   Argyll . . . 54,418 . 3,672
b. 1822, s. 1861, m. 1851.
  Served in 7th Dragoon Guards in the Kaffir War.

*** RIDLEY, SIR MATTHEW WHITE, BART., of Blagdon, Morpeth.

Coll. Harrow, Ball. Oxon.   Northumberland 10,152 . 12,189
Club. Carlton.   b. 1842, s. 1877, m. 1873.
  Was U. Sec. Home Dep. Sits for N. Nmbld. Exc. of mines and house rents.

RICHARDSON, REV. J., of Sandy.	Beds	2,091 .	2,722
RICHARDSON, MRS. M., of Sneaton.	York	2,183 .	2,040

*** RIDLEY, Thomas, of Park End, Hexham.

		acres.		*g. an. val.*
Coll. Shrewsbury.	Northumberland	10,427	.	5,753
Club. Windham. b. 1817, s. 1865.				

*** RIPON, Marquis of, K.G., G.C.S.I., Studley Royal, Ripon, &c.

Club. Brooks's, Ref., Ath.,	York, N. & W.R.	14,668	.	20,842
Trav., Uni. Ser.	Lincoln . .	7,102	.	8,284
b. 1827, s. 1859, m. 1851.				
		21,770	.	29,126

Served as Sec. St. for War, Sec. St. for India, and Lord Pres. of the Council. Was Pres. of Joint High Com. at Washington on the "Alabama" Claims. Is Viceroy of India. Sat for Hull, Huddersfield, and the N. Riding.

** FOX-PITT-RIVERS, Maj.-Gen., F.R.S., of Rushmore, Salisbury.

	Dorset . . .	24,942	.	33,682
	Wilts . . .	2,762	.	1,714
b. 1827, s. 1880, m. 1853.				
		27,704	.	35,396

Served in Grenadier Guards. Present at Alma and Sebastopol.

** RIVIS, Thomas Edward, of Newstead House, Malton.

b. 1846, s. 1879, m. 1877.	York, N. & E.R.	8,300	.	12,702
Served in 13th Hussars.				

ROBARTES, Lord, Lanrhydock, Bodmin.

Coll. Harrow, Ch. Ch. Ox.,	Cornwall . .	22,234	.	30,730
Club. Ath., Brooks's, Wind., N. Univ.				
b. 1844, s. 1882, m. 1878. Sat for E. Cornwall.				

RISLEY, H., of Deddington, Oxf., Mon., Npton. . . . . 2,084 . 3,666

RITCHIE, W., of Middleton. Midlothian . 2,652 . 3,137

*** CROMPTON-ROBERTS, Charles Henry, of Drybridge,
Monmouth.

			acres.	g. an. val.
Coll. Cheltenham.	Monmouth	.	2,865	. 3,878
Club. Jun. Carlton.	Worcester .	.	156	. 800
b. 1832, m. 1862.				
Sat for Sandwich.			3,021	. 4,678

*** ROBERTSON, David Souter, of Murlingden, Brechin, N.B.

			acres.	g. an. val.
Coll. Edinburgh Univ.	Lanark . .	.	4,170	. 2,366
Club. Cons., Uni. Ser., Edin.	Forfar . .	.	689	. 1,403
b. 1802, s. 1869, m. 1st 1835,	Linlithgow	.	100	. 95
2nd 1847.	Stirling . .	.	200	. 510
			5,159	. 4,374

Exclusive of 1,200*l.* for mines (fluctuating).

ROBERTSON, George Coke, of Widmerpool, Nottingham, &c.

			acres.	g. an. val.
Coll. Eton.	Notts . .	.	2,690	. 3,015
Club. A. & N., N. & M.	Lincoln .	.	1,288	. 1,849
b. 1839, s. 1870, m. 1873.				
Served in 17th Lancers.			3,978	. 4,864

*** RICHARDSON-ROBERTSON, General Robert, C.B., of
Tulliebelton, Perth, N.B., &c.

			acres.	g. an. val.
Club. Carlton, Uni. Ser.	Perth . .	.	4,462	. 4,240

b. 1809, s. 1850, m. 1st 1850, 2nd 1869.
Served in 3rd and 7th D. Gds. in Kaffir War and Boers' Rebellion.

ROBINSON, Christopher William, of Dullingham House,
Newmarket.

			acres.	g. an. val.
b. 1836, s. 1857 and 1875,	Cambridge .	.	2,396	. 3,170
m. 1870.	Suffolk . .	.	1,670	. 2,068
			4,066	. 5,238

ROBERTS, T. W., of Glassenbury.	Kent	.	2,628	.	2,270
ROBERTSON, C., of Kindeace.	Ross .	.	16,800	.	2,056
ROBERTSON, H., of Palé.	Mer., Den.. Sal.		2,850	.	2,376
ROBERTSON, J. C. D., of Washingley.	Hunts		2,128		2,740

ROBINSON, Mrs., of Vowchurch, Hereford.

		acres.	g. an. val.
Hereford . .		3,282 .	3,717

ROCH, William Francis, of Butter Hill, Haverfordwest.

Coll. Ch. Ch. Oxford. Pembroke . . 5,665 . 5,103
Club. Windham.
b. 1849, s. 1858, m. 1874. Served in Royal Navy.
2,008 acres stand in Mr. R.'s name; the rest are in his mother's.

ROCHE, Sir David Vandeleur, Bart., of Carrass, Croom.

Club. Kild. St., J. U. Ser. Co. Limerick . 3,951 . 3,457
b. 1833, s. 1865, m. 1st 1867, 2nd 1872.

** ROCHE, Thomas Redington, of Ryehill, Monivea, Galway.

Coll. Oscott, Munich Univ.	Co. Galway. .	3,217 .	1,178
Club. St. George's, Kildare	Kilkenny . .	1,572 .	1,943
Street, Dublin.	Limerick . .	1,116 .	559
b. 1837, s. 1864, m. 1858.	Co. Mayo . .	88 .	54
		5,993 .	3,734

*** ROCHFORT, Horace William Noel, of Clogrenane, Carlow.

Coll. Eton, Trin. Cam.	Co. Carlow .	1,623 .	1,231
Club. Carlton.	Co. Dublin .	972 .	1,397
b. 1809, s. 1844, m. 1st 1837, 2nd 1845.	Queen's Co. .	797 .	474
		3,392 .	3,102

RODD, Francis Rashleigh, of Trebartha Hall, Launceston.

b. 1839, s. 1880. Cornwall . . 7,912 . 6,823

ROBINSON, Sir F., Bt., of Cranford. Nptn.	2,087 .	4,737
ROBINSON, Henry, of Leyburn. York .	2,175 .	2,487
ROBINSON, Sir J., Bt., of Rokeby. Louth	2,941 .	2,733
ROCHE, F., of Rochemount. Carm., Bre., Cork	3,731 .	2,082

** RODDAM, RODDAM JOHN, of Roddam Hall, Alnwick.

			acres.		g. an. val.
Coll. Clare, Cam.	Northumberland		5,256	.	3,589
Club. Military. b. 1857, s. 1881, m. 1879.					

** RODEN, EARL OF, Hyde Hall, Sawbridgeworth, &c. 🐍

Coll. Harrow.	Co. Louth . .	4,151	.	7,944
Club. U. Ser., Carl.	Co. Down . .	8,903	.	3,264
b. 1823, s. 1880, m. 1851.	Essex . . .	1,134	.	1,171
	Herts . . .	408	.	698

Served in Scots F. Guards in the Crimea.

		14,596	.	13,077

RODNEY, LORD, Berrington, Leominster.

Club. Carlton, Guards.	Hereford . .	4,444	.	5,943
b. 1857, s. 1864.	Sussex . . .	1,744	.	1,361
Serves in 1st Life Guards.	Hants . . .	81	.	236
Was in 4th Foot.				

		6,269	.	7,540

The Hants property belongs to the DOWAGER LADY RODNEY; of the Sussex estate 555 acres are shared with MAJOR PIPON.

** ROGERS, CHARLES COLTMAN, of Stanage Park, Knighton, &c.

Club. Brooks's, N. Univ.	Radnor . .	3,217	.	2,749
Coll. Eton, Bras. Oxon.	Salop . . .	1,721	.	1,402
b. 1854, s. 1878.	Hereford . .	750	.	757

		5,688	.	4,908

*** ROGERS, JOHN PEVERELL, of Penrose, Helston.

Coll. Eton, Wellington.	Cornwall . .	6,214	.	5,812
Club. Jun. Uni. Ser.				

b. 1846, s. 1880, m. 1880. Serves in R. Artillery.

ROE, R., of Lorne Park. Tipperary, Limerick	5,186	.	2,581
ROGERS, J., of Holt Hall. Nfk., Linc., Herts	2,148	.	3,043
ROGERS, J. T., of Riverhill. Kt., Berks, Ess.	2,086	.	3,610

** COXWELL-ROGERS, Richard Rogers, of Dowdeswell
    Court, Andoversford, &c.   *acres.*   *g. an. val.*

Coll. Trin. Dub., Pem. Ox. Gloucester .   4,379 .   5,364
b. 1803, s. 1848, m. 1848.
  This family have held most of these lands continuously since
Henry VII.

** ROGERSON, James Alex., of Gillesbie, Lockerbie, N.B.

Club. Conserv., New Edin. Dumfries . .   9,284 .   4,098
b. 1842, s. 1872, m. 1863.   Served in 61st Foot.

ROKEBY, Lord, G.C.B., Hazelwood, Watford, &c.

Club. Uni. Ser., Guards.	York, N.R. .	2,835	.	4,021
b. 1798, s. 1847, m. 1826.	Northumberland	1,622	.	4,137
Served in Scots Fus. Gds.	Herts . .	348	.	911
and 77th Foot. A General	Cambridge .	55	.	102
in the Army, commanded	Kent . . .	3	.	9
a division in the Crimea;				
was at Quatre Bras and		4,863	.	9,180
Waterloo.				

*** ROLLE, Hon. Mark George Kerr, of Stephenstone, Tor-
    rington. ♣.

Coll. Eton.   Devon .   .   55,592 .   47,170
Club. Boodle's, Carl., Trav.
b. 1835, m. 1860.

** ROLLO. Lord, Duncrub Castle, Perth, N.B., &c.

Coll. Trin. Cam.	Perth . . .	10,148	.	8,418
Club. Athen., Uni. Univ.,	Dumfries . .	7,220	.	3,044
Brooks's.				
b. 1835, s. 1852, m. 1857.		17,368	.	11,462

*** ROLLS, John Allan, of The Hendre, Monmouth.

Coll. Eton, Ch. Ch. Oxon. Monmouth .   4,082 .   3,710
Club. Carlton, Arthur's, Junior Carlton.
b. 1837, s. 1870, m. 1868.   Sits for Monmouthshire.

NEVILLE-ROLFE, E., of Heacham.   Norf 2,787 .   3,843

ROLT, JOHN WILLIAM, of Ozleworth Park, Wootton-under-Edge.

		acres.		*g. an. val.*
b. 1860, s. 1876.	Gloucester .	3,095	.	3,406

** ROMNEY, EARL OF, The Mote, Maidstone.

Coll. Eton, Ch. Ch. Ox.	Kent . . .	4,023	.	12,000
Club. Carl., Gar., Whi.	Norfolk . .	900		750
b. 1841, s. 1874, m. 1863.				
		4,923	.	12,750

ROSEBERY, EARL OF, Dalmeny Park, Queensferry, N.B., &c.

Coll. Eton, Ch. Ch. Oxon.	Midlothian .	18,540	.	13,323
Club. White's, Turf., Ref.,	Linlithgow .	5,680	.	8,902
Garrick, Brooks's,	Norfolk . .	2,051	.	3,488
St. James's.	Bucks . .	5,473	.	9,219
b. 1847, s. 1868, m. 1878.	Herts . . .	495	.	979
Served as Com. on Scot-	Kent . . .	169	.	287
tish Endowments. Is Un.	Suffolk . . .	3	.	281
Sec. H. Dep., and Mem. of				
Sco. Com. of Council on Edn.		32,411	.	36,479

Exclusive of 2,616*l.* for mines.
The four last estates belong to the COUNTESS.

** ROSS, SIR CHARLES WILLIAM FREDERIC AUGUSTUS, BART., of
Balnagown Castle, Tain, N.B., &c.

Coll. Eton, Ch. Ch. Oxon.	Ross . . .	300,000	.	14,000
b. 1812, s. 1814, m. 1st 1841,	Sutherland .	55,000	.	1,764
2nd 1865.	Lanark . . .	1,500	.	1,500
		356,500	.	17,264

The return only gives SIR CHARLES 110,000 acres in Ross.

ROMILY, LORD (part shared with " others ").			
Glamorgan, Radnor	2,771	.	3,535
ROSE, MISS, of Mullaghmore. Monaghan .	3,942	.	2,187
ROSE, HUGH LAW, of Tarlogie. Ross . .	3,039	.	2,029
ROSE, JAMES, of Kilravock. Nairn . . .	4,395	.	2,345

** ROSS, COL., of Cromarty House, Cromarty, N.B.

			acres.		g. an. val.
Coll. Edin. Ac., Glas. Univ.	Cromarty . .	7,437	.	5,348
Club. Army and Navy, New	Ross	1,646	.	1,340
Edin., R.C.Y.C.				
b. 1825, s. 1852, m. 1849.		9,083	.	6,688

Served in 92nd Highlanders.

ROSSE, EARL OF, F.R.S., Birr Castle, Parsonstown, K. Co., &c.

			acres.		g. an. val.
Coll. Trinity, Dublin.	King's Co. . .	22,513	.	8,964
Club. Carlton, Athenæum.	Tipperary . .	2,633	.	1,496
b. 1840, s. 1867, m. 1870.	York, W.R. .	1,340	.	5,089
		26,486	.	15,549

The Yorkshire estate stands in the name of the COUNTESS DOWAGER.

ROSSLYN, EARL OF, Dysart House, Kirkcaldy, N.B.

			acres.		g. an. val.
Coll. Eton, Merton, Oxon.	Fife	3,211	.	8,449
Club. Carlton, White's,	Midlothian .	99	.	737
Beac., Han. Sq.				
b. 1833, s. 1866, m. 1866.		3,310	.	9,186

Served as Lord High Commissioner to the General Assembly of the Kirk of Scotland. Exclusive of 1,224*l.* for mines.

** ROSSMORE, LORD, Rossmore Park, Co. Monaghan.

Coll. Rugby.	Monaghan . .	14,839	.	13,427
Club. Carlton, Turf, Marlb., Boodle's, Garrick.				

b. 1853, s. 1874. Served in 1st Life Guards and 9th Lancers.

ROTHERAM, EDWARD, of Crossdrum, Oldcastle, Co. Meath.

Club. R. Dub. Yacht.	Co. Meath . .	5,308	.	5,036
b. 1810, m. 1835.	Co. Cavan . .	1,290	.	940
		6,598	.	5,976

ROTHES, COUNTESS OF, Leslie House, Fife, N.B.

s. 1859, m. 1861.	Fife	3,562	.	7,347

LEITH-ROSS, JOHN, of Arnage.	Aberdeen	2,050	.	2,063
ROSS, MRS., of Shandwick.	Ross . . .	2,869	.	2,721

ROTHSCHILD, Sɪʀ Nᴀᴛʜᴀɴɪᴇʟ Mᴇʏᴇʀ, Bᴛ., of Tring Pk., &c.

		acres.	g. an. val.
Coll. Trinity, Cambridge.	Bucks . . .	9,959	17,216
Club. Marl., Brooks's, City	Herts . . .	2,939	5,413
Lib., St. James's.	Northampton .	1,772	2,817
b. 1840, s. 1879, m. 1867.	Middlesex . .	620	3,356
Sits for Aylesbury.	Beds. . . .	88	99
		15,378	28,901

ROTHWELL, Tʜᴏᴍᴀs, of Rockfield House, Kells, Co. Meath.

Coll. Magd. Oxon.	Co. Meath . .	3,161	3,407
Club. Conser., Kildare St.	Tipperary . .	365	310
b. 1834, s. 1853, m. 1866.			
		3,526	3,717

*** ROUND, Jᴀᴍᴇs, of Birch Wood, Colchester.

Coll. Eton, Ch. Ch. Ox.	Essex . . .	5,266	6,851
Club. Carl., U. Un., Far.	Middlesex . .	152	770
b. 1842, s. 1867, m. 1870.			
Sits for E. Essex.		5,418	7,621

This includes the Birch Hall estate in the possession for life of Mʀs. Cʜᴀʀʟᴇs Gʀᴀʏ Rᴏᴜɴᴅ, his aunt.

* ROUNDELL, Rɪᴄʜᴀʀᴅ Fᴏᴜʟɪs, of Gledstone, Skipton.

b. 1872, s. 1881.   York, W.R. .   7,451 . 8,695

** ROUS, Tʜᴇ Mɪssᴇs, of Courtyrala, Cardiff, &c.

s. 1876.	Glamorgan .	1,210	1,114
	Pembroke . .	1,164	1,058
	Monmouth .	977	1,728
		3,351	3,900

*** ROWAN, Rᴇv. Rᴏʙᴇʀᴛ Wɪʟsᴏɴ, of Mount Davys, Bally-mena, Co. Antrim.

Coll. Fngn. In., Tr. Dub.   Co. Antrim . 3,423 . 3,299
b. 1810, s. 1855, m. 1834.

ROW, W. N., of Cove.   Devon, Somerset .   2,164 . 2,765

ROWE, EBEN HENRY, of Ballycross, Bridgtown, Co. Wexford.

		acres.	*g. an. val.*
Coll. Trinity, Dublin.	Co. Wexford .	8,002 .	5,245
b. 1851, s. 1876.			

ROWLEY, SIR CHARLES ROBERT, BART., of Tendring Hall, Stoke-by-Nayland, Colchester.

Club. Travellers'.	Suffolk . . .	7,324 .	9,907
b. 1800, s. 1857, m. 1830.	Essex . . .	1,292 .	1,701
Served in Gren. Guards.			
		8,616 .	11,608

** ROWLEY, GEORGE FYDELL, of Priory Hill, St. Neots, &c.

Coll. Eton.	Huntingdon .	1,629 .	3,905
b. 1851, s. 1878.	Lincoln . . .	1,406 .	3,378
	Rutland . . .	522 .	1,148
	Cambridge . .	18 .	23
		3,575 .	8,454

ROXBURGHE, DUKE OF, Floors Castle, Kelso, N.B., &c.

Coll. Eton, Ch. Ch. Ox.	Roxburgh . .	50,459 .	43,820
Club. Brooks's, White's.	Berwick . .	6,096 .	816
b. 1839, s. 1879, m. 1874.	Haddington .	3,863 .	6,281
Serves in Queen's Body-			
guard of Scottish Archers.		60,418 .	50,917
Sat for Roxburghshire.			

** RUSHBROOKE, MISS, of Elmers, Surbiton, &c.

	Surrey . . .	2,390 .	2,402
	Co. Cork . .	1,261 .	9,864
		3,651 .	12,266

ROWCLIFFE, C., of Milverton. Som., Dev.	2,593 .	2,839
RUDGE, E. C., of Evesham. Wor., War., Northampton	2,234 .	6,037
RUFFORD, F. T., of Bellbroughton. Worc.	2,113 .	4,665
RUSH, G. A., of Elsenham. Nptn., Ess., Herts, Suff.	2,979 .	4,877

RUSHOUT, Sir Charles Hamilton Rushout, Bart., of Seizincote, Stow-on-the-Wold.

		acres.	g. an. val.
b. 1868, s. 1879.	Gloucester . .	3,681 .	4,658
	Worcester . .	312 .	206
		3,993 .	4,864

** RUSSELL, Earl, Ardsalla, Navan, Co. Meath. 🐍

Coll. Winchester.	Co. Meath . .	3,167 .	3,763
b. 1865, s. 1878.	Co. Louth . .	1,017 .	764
		4,184 .	4,527

** RUSSELL, James George Ferguson, of Aden House, 🌳 Mintlaw, N.B., &c. (res. Br. Legn., Copenhagen).

Club. Arthur's, St. James's.	Aberdeen . .	12,000 .	8,000
b. 1836, s. 1875, m. 1858.			

Is in the Diplomatic Service.

*** WATTS-RUSSELL, Mrs., of Biggin Grange, Oundle.

s. 1879, m. 1835.	Northampton .	5,349 .	8,840

*** OLIVER - RUTHERFURD, William Alexander, of Edgerston, Jedburgh, N.B.

Coll. Trin. Cam.	Roxburgh . .	7,723 .	3,706
b. 1818, s. 1879, m. 1st 1861,	Cumberland .	756 .	560
2nd 1872.			
		8,479 .	4,266

RUSSELL, Sir C., Bt., of Swallowfield. Berks	2,381 .	3,224
FRANKLAND - RUSSELL (late), Lady. York	2,531 .	3,585
RUSSELL, W. D., of Newton House. York	2,257 .	3,959

** RUTHVEN, Lord, Harperstown House, Taghmon, Co. Wexford.

		acres.		g. an. val.
Club. Carlton, White's.	Co. Wexford .	2,200	.	2,100
b. 1838, s. 1864, m. 1869.	Perth . . .	2,519	.	4,083
Served in Rifle Brigade in	Haddington .	2,875	.	4,662
the Crimea and India.	Lanark . . .	30	.	136
		7,624	.	10,981

The Irish property has been held for 700 years.
The return gives the two last properties to Lady Ruthven.
Exclusive of mines worth about 2,000*l.* per annum.

*** RUTLAND, Duke of, K.G., Belvoir Castle, Grantham, &c. ♣.

Coll. Eton, Trin. Cam.	Leicester . .	30,188	.	46,241
Club. Carlton, White's,	Derby . . .	27,069	.	31,710
St. Stephen's.	Cambridge . .	6,585	.	9,505
b. 1815, s. 1857.	Lincoln . . .	2,837	.	4,757
Served as Lord of the	Suffolk . . .	1,591	.	2,214
Bedchamber to the late	Notts . . .	1,103	.	1,811
Prince Consort.	Rutland . .	764	.	1,248
Sat for Stamford and				
for N. Leicestershire.		70,137	.	97,486

** RUTSON, John, of Newby Wiske, Thirsk.

Coll. Trin. Cam.	York, N.R. .	5,351	.	8,885
Club. United University, Devonshire.				
b. 1829, s. 1867.				

RUTZEN, Baron de, of Slebech Park, Haverfordwest.

Coll. Eton, Magd. Cam.	Pembroke . .	5,573	.	4,216
Club. Junior Carlton. b. 1825, s. 1860.				

*** RYLAND, Miss, of Barford, Birmingham.

	Warwick . .	3,132	.	6,262
	Worcester . .	265	.	943
		3,397	.	7,205

RUTTLEDGE, D., of Barbersft. Gal., Mayo	6,388	.	2,491
RUXTON, William, of Ardee House. Louth	2,262	.	2,279
RYE, R. T., of Ryecourt. Cork	3,422	.	2,383

** SACKVILLE, Lord, Knole, Sevenoaks, &c. 🐍.

			acres.	gr. an. val.
Club. Trav., Carlton.	Gloucester . .		2,391	. 4,250
b. 1820, s. 1876, m. 1st 1847,	Sussex . . .		4,080	. 3,400
2nd 1873.	Kent . . .		1,960	. 3,450
Served in Gren. Guards,	Herts . . .		120	. 150

Served in Gren. Guards, and as Groom in Waiting; is Extra Lord in Waiting.

8,551 . 11,250

STOPFORD-SACKVILLE, Mrs., of Drayton Ho., Thrapstone.

s. 1872, m. 1837.   Northampton .   4,667   .   8,723

St. ALBANS, Duke of, Redbourne Hall, Brigg, &c.

Coll. Eton, Trin. Cam.	Lincoln . . .	5,255	. 6,466
Club. Brooks's, White's.	Notts. . . .	3,743	. 4,489
b. 1840, s. 1849, m. 1st 1867,			
2nd 1874.		8,998	. 10,955

Is Her. G. Falconer and Reg. Ct. of Chan.   Was Capt. Y. of the Gd.

** St. AUBYN, Sir John, Bt., of St. Michael's Mt., Marazion.

Coll. Eton, Trin. Cam.	Cornwall . .	5,134	. 3,949
Club. Brooks's, Trav.,	Devon . . .	1,421	. 91,263
Ox. & C., Boodle's.			

6,555 . 95,212

b. 1829, s. 1872, m. 1856.   Sits for W. Cornwall.

This is a case specially referred to where, in Devon, through including in the ground landlord's name the whole rents, the nominal is greatly in excess of the real income.

** MOLESWORTH-St. AUBYN, Rev. St. Aubyn Hender, of Clowance, Camborne.

Coll. Ch. Ch. Oxon.   Cornwall . .   6,299   .   8,796
Club. Ox. and Cam.   b. 1833, s. 1868, m. 1862.

*** ST. CLAIR, Madame, of Duxbury.

Lancashire, Durham   2,672   .   4,519

ST. JOHN, E. J., of Slinfold.   Berks, Sussex   2,245   .   **2,144**

St. GEORGE (late ?), Arthur, of Tyrone House, Galway.

		acres.	*g. an. val.*
b. 1813, s. 1877.	Galway . . .	15,777 .	4,453

MANSERGH-St. GEORGE, Richard James, of Headford Cas.

Coll. Eton.	Galway . . .	7,495 .	4,460

Club. Kildare St. Dublin. b. 1838, s. 1858, m. 1860.
Served in 3rd Light Dragoons.

*** St. GERMANS, Earl of, Port Eliot, St. Germans.

Club. St. James's, Marl.,	Cornwall . .	5,961 .	8,098
Trav.	Wilts . . .	2,975 .	4,950
b. 1835, s. 1881, m. 1881.	Gloucester . .	2,711 .	4,143
Served in R.N., is in the F.O.	Kent . . .	1,144	unstated.
		12,791 .	17,191

*** St. JOHN of BLETSOE, Lord, Melchbourne, Bedford. ☙

Club. Carlton.	Bedford . .	7,853 .	11,082
b. 1840, s. 1874, m. 1868.	Huntingdon .	585 .	818
		8,438 .	11,900

** St. LEGER, Colonel John, of Park Hill, Rotherham.

Club. Carl., Trav.,	York, W.R. .	1,676 .	2,199
Jun. Uni. Ser.	Notts . . .	3 .	3
b. 1823, s. 1862, m. 1858.	Co. Limerick .	3,500 .	2,850
Served in 53rd and 85th Foot,			
in the Sutlej Campaign.		5,179 .	5,052

* St. LEONARDS, Lord, 33, Elvaston Place, S.W.

Club. Carlton.	Kent . . .	1,304 .	821
b. 1847, s. 1875, m. 1876.	Cambridge .	1,067 .	1,252
	Hants . . .	1,273 .	1,083
	Berks . . .	774 .	1,159
	Surrey . . .	84 .	803
	Sussex . . .	67 .	10
		4,569 .	5,128

These lands all stand in the late Lord's name ; Lord St. L.'s relatives hold about one-third.

St. QUINTIN, William Herbert, of Scampston Hall, York, &c.

		acres.	g. an. val.
Coll. Eton, Ch. Ch. Oxon.	York, E.R. .	7,033 .	10,244
b. 1851, s. 1876.			

St. VINCENT, Viscount.

		acres.	g. an. val.
Coll. Harrow.	Lincoln . .	2,444 .	2,265
Club. Army and Navy.	York, E.R. .	2,041 .	3,760
b. 1850, s. 1879.	Notts . . .	6 .	11
	Stafford . . .	1 .	3
Served in 8th Huss. in Zulu War.			
Is in 16th Lancers.		4,492 .	6,039

SALISBURY, Marquis of, K.G., Hatfield House, Herts, &c.

		acres.	g. an. val.
Coll. Eton, Ch. Ch. and	Herts . . .	13,389 .	18,372
All Souls, Oxon.	Dorset . . .	3,118 .	2,922
Club. Carl., Ath., J. Carl.	Lancashire .	1,796 .	7,999
b. 1830, s. 1868, m. 1857.	Essex . . .	758 .	2,632
Served as Sec. St. for India,	Middlesex . .	960 .	1,219
Special Amb. to the Con-	Bedford . .	89 .	134
stantinople Conference, and	Norfolk . .	80 .	123
Sec. St. for F. Affairs.	Wilts . . .	12 .	12
Sat for Stamford.			
		20,202 .	33,413

SALTOUN, Lord, Philorth House, Fraserburgh.

Coll. R.M.C. Sandhurst.   Aberdeen . . 10,762 . 11,929
Club. Carlton, Army and Navy, United Service.
b. 1820, s. 1853, m. 1849.   Served in 28th Foot.
    Inc. of 700 ac. in the name of "Trustees of late Lord S."

SALVIN, Marmaduke Charles, of Burn Hall, Durham. ⚲.

		acres.	g. an. val.
Coll. Ushaw.	Durham . .	2,080 .	15,224
b. 1812, m. 1845.	Hereford . .	1,726 .	2,103
		3,806 .	17,327

890 ac. in Dur. and half the rental is in his eld. son's name.

SALTMARSHE, P., of Saltmarshe. York .	2,776 .	4,337
⚲ SALVIN, H. T. T., of Croxdale. Durham	2,340 .	2,638

** SALWEY, ALFRED, of Hay Park, Ludlow, &c. 🐚.

			acres.	g. an. val.
Coll.	Downing, Cam.	Hereford . .	3,064 .	3,136
Club.	Conservative.	Salop . . .	129 .	481
b. 1841, s. 1871, m. 1862.				
			3,193 .	3,617

*** SANDBACH, HENRY ROBERTSON, of Halfodunos, Abergele.

			acres.	g. an. val.
Coll.	Glasgow University.	Denbigh . .	4,514 .	4,112
Club.	Athenæum.	Carnarvon . .	464 .	100
b. 1807, s. 1851, m. 1st 1832,				
	2nd 1855.		4,978 .	4,212

SANDES, MRS., of Oak Park, Tralee.

s. 1879, m. 1857.	Kerry . . .	11,172 .	3,297

WILLS-SANDFORD, THOMAS GEORGE, of Castlerea House, Co. Roscommon.

Coll.	Har., Ch. Ch. Oxon.	Roscommon .	24,410 .	10,194
Club.	Carlton, Kildare St. Dublin. b. 1817, s. 1859, m. 1842.			

SANDWICH, EARL OF, Hinchingbrook House, Huntingdon.

			acres.	g. an. val.
Coll.	Trin. Cam.	Co. Limerick .	2,844 .	3,082
Club.	Carl., U. S., Trav.	Dorset . .	5,286 .	5,693
b. 1811, s. 1818, m. 1st 1838,	Huntingdon .	3,219 .	7,522
2nd 1865.	Cornwall . .	28 .	126
		11,377 .	16,423

Was Capt. Gen.-at-Arms and M. of the Buckhounds.

*** SANDYS, MYLES, of Graythwaite Hall, Ulverstone.

	Coll.	Shrewsbury.	Middlesex . .	1 .	945
	Club.	J. U. Ser., E. I. U.	Lancashire .	3,304 .	3,050
		Ser., N. and M.			
b. 1837, s. 1871.				3,305 .	3,995

Served in 73rd Foot and 7th Foot in the Indian Mutiny.
This family has held this estate since the time of RICHARD II.

SANDES, T. W., of Sallowglen.	Kerry . .	7,147 .	2,783

** SANFORD, WILLIAM AYSHFORD, of Nynehead Court, Wellington, Somerset.   *acres.*   *g. an. val.*

Coll. Eton, Trin. Cam.   Somerset . .   5,057 .   8,170
Club. Brooks's.
b. 1818, s. 1871, m. 1st 1857, 2nd 1874.

Served as Colonial Secretary of West Australia. Nearly half this estate is in Devon, but, being situate in a Union embracing parishes in both counties, is returned as entirely in Somerset. Mr. S. has properties in the Metropolitan area—unreturned. This family have held half these estates in male succession since Richard II. ; the other, since James I.

SAUNDERSON, EDWARD JAS., of Cas. Saunderson, Belturbet.

Club. Brooks's, Kildare St.   Co. Cavan .   12,362 .   7,370
b. 1837, m. 1865.   Sat for Co. Cavan.

SAURIN, MARK ANTHONY, of Orielton, Pembroke, &c.

Coll.   Trinity, Dublin.   Pembroke . .   5,752 .   5,851
Club. Union.   Carmarthen .   140 .   73
b. 1815, m. 1844.   _____

                                           5,892 .   5,924

Inclusive of 1,986*l.* standing in his son CAPT. SAURIN's name.

** SAVILE, AUGUSTUS WILLIAM, of Rufford Abbey, Ollerton.

b. 182-, s. 1881.   Notts . . .   17,820 .   17,213
                         York, W.R. .   16,000 .   35,000
Is Ass. Master of the Ceremonies.   _____

                                         33,820 .   52,213

SANDYS, LORD.   Worcester . . . . .   2,585 .   6,668
SARTORIS, E., of Warnford.   Carm., Corn.,
    Hants . . . .   2,230 .   4,988
*** SAUNDERS, C. M., of Wennington.
    Lanc., York . . . .   6,256 .   2,340
SAUNDERS, R. J. P., of Saunders Gr.   Wick.   3,143 .   2,059
SAUNDERS, W. F. D., of Glanrhydeo.   Carm.   2,836 .   2,285
SAUNDERSON, L., of Dromkeen.   Cav. .   4,160 .   2,664

GRAVES-SAWLE, Sir Charles Brune, Bart., of Penrice, St. Austell, &c.   *acres.*   *g. an. val.*

Coll. Eton, Clare, Cam.	Cornwall . .	3,050	.	11,417
Club. Reform, Uni. Ser.	Devon . . .	341	.	1,502
b. 1816, s. 1865, m. 1846.				
Sat for Bodmin.		3,391	.	12,919

    Inclusive of 96*l.* in Devon in Lady Sawle's name.

** SAWYER, Maj.-Gen., of Heywood Lodge, Maidenhead.

Coll. Westminster.	Oxford . . .	2,515	.	3,794
Club. A. &. N., Uni. Ser.	Berks . . .	747	.	1,289
b. 1813, s. 1876, m. 1840.				
Served in 6th Dragoons in the Crimea		3,262	.	5,083
and Indian Mutiny.				

SAYE and SELE, Rev. Lord, Broughton Castle, Banbury.

Coll. Winch. New, Oxon.	Oxford . . .	1,623	.	3,870
Club. Brooks's.	Huntingdon .	2,461	.	3,164
b. 1799, s. 1847, m. 1st 1827,	Lincoln . . .	2,743	.	5,456
2nd 1857.	Worcester . .	28	.	31
		6,855	.	12,521

** SCARBROUGH, Earl of, Sandbeck Park, Rotherham, &c. $.

Coll. Eton.	Lincoln . .	11,270	.	15,248
Club. White's, Boodle's.	York, W.R. .	8,640	.	10,335
b. 1813, s. 1856, m. 1846.	Durham . .	1,788	.	6,014
Served in 7th Hussars.		21,698	.	31,597

SCARISBRICK, Charles, of 5, Palace Gate, W.

Club. Junior Carlton.	Lancashire .	3,505	.	34,811
b. 1839, s. 1860, m. 1860.				

SCARISBRICK, William (res. Frankfort, Prussia).

b. 183–, s. 1860.	Lancashire .	3,133	.	33,960

SAYER, John, of Pett.   Kent, Gloucester .   2,075   .   2,712

*** SCARSDALE, Rev. Lord, Kedleston, Derby. **S.**

			acres.		*g. an. val.*
Coll. Rugby, Merton, Ox.	Derby . . .		9,606	.	17,296
Club. Carlton, Arthur's.	Leicester . .		323	.	563
b. 1831, s. 1856, m. 1856.					
			9,929	.	17,859

SCHREIBER, Mrs., of Henhurst, Woodchurch, Staplehurst.
s. 1863, m. 1823.　　　　Kent . . . 　3,234 . 　3,072

SCHROETER, Frederick A., of Mottingham, Eltham, Kent.

		Sussex . . .	2,559	.	2,186
		Essex . . .	1,252	.	1,803
		Kent . . .	232	.	194
			4,043	.	4,183

*** SCOTT, Sir Edward Henry, Bart, of Amhuinnsuidh, Harris, N.B., &c.

Club. Carl., Conservative.	Inverness . .	59,125	.	3,271
b. 1842, s. 1880, m. 1865.	Kent . . .	798	.	2,481
		59,923	.	5,752

SCOTT, Hercules, of Brotherton House, Fordoun, N.B.
Coll. Harrow, Haileybury.　Kincardine　.　3,912 . 　5,388
Club. E. India Uni. Ser.　b. 1823, m. 1857.
　Served in Bengal Civil Service.

*** SCOTT, John Charles Addyes, of Ratlinghope, Shrews-
bury, &c.

Coll. University, London.	Salop . . .	5,340	.	4,021
b. 1830, s. 1856 and 1874,	Stafford . . .	383	.	1,261
m. 1863.				
		5,723	.	5,282

　　　　Some of the pty. in Salop is his mother's.

SCARLETT, J. W., of Achamore.　Argyll . 　3,679 . 　2,288
** SCLATER, Mrs., of Ampney. Glou.　.　2,034 . 　3,000
SCOTT, Sir A. D. B., Bart., of Great Barr.
　　Staffordshire, Warwick, Worcester . . .　2,105 . 　3,951
SCOTT, G. A. J., of Rotherfield.　Hants, Kent　3,164 ·　2,933

SCOTT, JOHN HENRY FRANCIS KINNAIRD, of Gala House, Galashiels, N.B., &c.

		acres.		g. an. val.
b. 1859, s. 1877.	Selkirk . . .	3,600	.	3,396
	Aberdeen . .	190	.	150
		3,790	.	3,546

MONTAGU-DOUGLAS-SCOTT, LORD HENRY JOHN, of Beaulieu, Southampton.

Coll. Eton.	Hants . . .	8,922	.	7,341
Club. Carlton, St. Stephen's.	Peebles . .	24	.	45
b. 1832, m. 1865.				
Sat for Selkirk. Sits for S. Hants.		8,946	.	7,386

SCOTT, MRS., of Betton l'Estrange, Shrewsbury, &c.

s. 1875, m. 1840.	Salop . . .	1,304	.	4,831
	Merioneth . .	2,140	.	1,132
		3,444	.	5,963

*** SCOURFIELD, SIR OWEN HENRY PHILLIPPS, BART., of Williamston, Haverfordwest, &c.

Coll. Harrow, Ch. Ch. Ox.	Pembroke . .	11,243	.	8,722
Club. U. U., Carl., Bood.	Carmarthen .	2,196	.	1,365
b. 1847, s. 1876, m. 1877.				
		13,439	.	10,087

SCRATTON, DANIEL ROBERT, of Ogwell, Newton Abbot, &c.

b. 1819, m. 1844.	Devon . . .	2,639	.	3,808
	Essex . . .	2,117	.	1,286
		4,756	.	5,094

SCOTT, J. C., of Kildysart. Clare . . .	6,431	.	2,953
CORSE-SCOTT, MRS., of Sinton. Sel., Rox.	2,531	.	2,301
SCOTT (late), MRS., of Stourbridge. Salop, Worcester, Warwick, Staffordshire, Herts	2,629	.	5,076
MACMILLAN-SCOTT, W., of Wauchope. Roxburgh, Selkirk	4,993	.	2,864
SCOTT, W. E., of Willsboro. Lderry., Ant.	3,555	.	2,741
SCOTT, SIR W., BT., of Ancrum. Rox., For.	2,516	.	4,753

** SCROPE, SIMON THOMAS, of Danby-upon-Yore, Bedale, &c. ♠.

		acres.	g. an. val.
Coll. Stonyhurst.	Lincoln . . .	2,600 .	3,800
b. 1822, s. 1872, m. 1855.	York, N.R. .	2,462 .	1,850
		5,062 .	5,650

SCUTT, REV. T. S. (the late), of Bognor, Sussex.

Sussex . . .	3,914 .	3,110

*** SEAFIELD, EARL OF, Cas. Grant, Grantown, N.B., &c.

		acres.	g. an. val.
Coll. Eton.	Inverness . .	160,224 .	19,895
b. 1851, s. 1881, m. 1850.	Elgin . . .	96,760 .	23,154
Served in 1st Life Guards.	Banff . . .	48,946 .	35,178
		305,930 .	78,227

Inc. of 195*l.* belonging to LOUISA COUNTESS of S.

SEBRIGHT, SIR JOHN GAGE SAUNDERS, BART., of Besford Court, Pershore, &c. ♠.

		acres.	g. an. val.
Coll. Ch. Ch. Oxon.	Herts . . .	3,886 .	6,155
Club. St. James's, Windham,	Worcester . .	2,929 .	6,288
Brooks's, Verulam.	Surrey . . .	1 .	736
b. 1843, s. 1864, m. 1865.	Beds . . .	394 .	388
		7,210 .	13,567

** SEELY, CHARLES, of Brooke House, Isle of Wight, &c.

		acres.	g. an. val.
Coll. Lincoln School.	Hants . . .	9,264 .	10,725
Club. Reform.	Derby . . .	286 .	2,741
b. 1803, m. 1831.	Surrey . . .	170 .	1,200
Sits for Lincoln.			
His eld. son has lately bt. land in Notts.		9,720 .	14,666

PIKE-SCRIVENER, MRS., of Sibton. Suff.	2,039 .	2,850
SCULLY, J., of Shanballymore. Tipperary	2,662 .	2,763
SCULLY, RODOLPH. Tip., Lim.	2,757 .	2,136
* SCULLY, V., of Mantlehill House. Tipp.	2,500 (?) .	2,500(?)
SCURFIELD, G., of Hurworth. Dur., York	2,157 .	4,793
SEATON, LD. Dev., Carl., K. Co., Kild. .	5,890 .	2,341

** SEFTON, EARL OF, Croxteth Hall, Liverpool. 🦢.

		acres.		*g. an. val.*
Coll. Eton.	Lancashire .	20,250	.	43,000

Club. Trav., Brooks's, St. Jas., Gds., Whi., U. S., Bood.
b. 1835, s. 1855, m. 1866.
Served in Grenadier Guards in the Crimea.
This does not include building land in and close to Liverpool,
the value of which is increasing.

** SELBY, WALTER CHARLES, of Biddlestone, Rothbury. 🦢.

Coll. Cat. Uni., Kensn.	Northumberland 30,000	.	10,550

Club. Arthur's.
b. 1858, s. 1868, m. 1881.

** SELKIRK, EARL OF, St. Mary's Isle, Kirkcudbright.

Coll. Eton, Ch. Ch. Oxon.	Kirkcudbright	20,823	.	19,749
Club. Ath.,U.S.,Carl.,Trav.	Linlithgow	1,441	.	1,724

b. 1809, s. 1820, m. 1878.

22,264	.	21,473

Is Keeper of the G. Seal of Scotland.   Exc. of 20*l.* for mines.

*** SERGISON, WARDEN, of Cuckfield Pk., Hayward's Heath.

Coll. Ch. Ch. Oxon.	Sussex . . .	4,850	.	5,500

Club. Jun. Uni. Ser. b. 1835, s. 1868, m. 1867.
Served in 4th Hussars.

* CHESMENT-SEVERN, JOHN PERCY, of Penybont, Radnor.

Coll. Eton, Ch. Ch. Oxon.	Radnor . . .	8,471	.	3,155
Club. Ox. & C., Carlton.	Montgomery .	65	.	55

b. 1814, s. 1875.

8,536	.	3,210

The acreage is mere guesswork, never having been surveyed, it
may be 1,000 acres from the truth, or even more.

** SEVERNE, JOHN EDMUND, of Thenford, Banbury, &c.

Coll. Brasenose, Oxon.	Salop . . .	3,542	.	3,754
Club. Carlton, A. & N.	Northampton .	1,103	.	2,544
b. 1826, s. 1855, m. 1858.	Montgomery .	515	.	339
Served in 16th Lancers,	Leicester . .	199	.	321
and 10th Hussars.	Warwick . .	187	.	336

Sat for Ludlow ; sits for S. Salop.

5,546	.	7,294

His mother has the last two properties.

SERGEANTSON, G. J., of Hanlith. York .	2,012	.	2,197

*** CLAY-KER-SEYMER, Harry Ernest, of Hanford, Blandford, &c.

			acres.		g. an. val.
Club. Trav., Turf, White's,	Berwick	. .	4,681	.	5,570
St. James's, Arth.	Dorset .	. .	2,285	.	2,995

b. 1832, m. 1864.

Served as Sec. to the Embassy at Paris.	6,966	.	8,565

All this property stands in Mrs. Seymer's name.

*** SEYMOUR, Alfred, of Norton Hall, Northampton, &c. ⚓.

Coll. Eton, Ch.Ch.Ox.	Wilts	. .	3,406	.	3,635
Club. Trav., Brooks's,	Northampton	.	2,238	.	5,086
Burl.,FineArts,	Salop .	. .	2,940	.	3,013
Turf,Cosmop.	Somerset	. .	1,776	.	4,148

b. 1824, s. 1877, m. 1866.

Sat for Totnes and for Salisbury.	10,360	.	15,882

** LUCAS-SHADWELL, William, of Fairlight Hall, Hastings.

Coll. Pembroke, Cam.	Sussex .	. .	3,689	.	4,230

Club. New University.   b. 1852, s. 1875, m. 1878.

*** SHAFTESBURY, Earl of, K.G., St. Giles', Cranbourne.

Coll. Harrow, Ch. Ch. Ox.	Dorset .	. .	17,317	.	12,536
Club. Athenæum.	Hants .	. .	3,250	.	2,080
b. 1801, s. 1851, m. 1830.	Wilts	. .	1,218	.	1,467

	21,785	.	16,083

Served as Com. B. of Control, a L. of the Adm., and as Ecc. Com.
Sat for Woodstock, Dorchester, Dorset, and Bath.
Incl. of copyholds the t. val. would reach 16,440*l*.

DUNCOMBE-SHAFTO, Robert, of Whitworth Park, Durham.

Club. Brooks's.	Durham	. .	4,154	.	10,497
b. 1806, s. 1848, m. 1838.	Berks .	. .	6	.	12

Sat for N. Durham.	4,160	.	10,509

SHAFTO, William Henry, of Bavington Hall, Newcastle.

b. 1834, s. 1876, m. 1856.	Northumberland	4,640	.	3,425

SFORZA, The Duchess. Leicester, Stafford . | 2,159 | . | 3,272

** SHAKERLEY, Sir Charles Watkin, Bart., C.B., of Somerford Park, Congleton.

		acres.	g. an. val.
Club. Boodle's, Garrick.	Cheshire . .	5,978 .	11,109

b. 1833, s. 1857, m. 1858.

SHANNON, Earl of, Castle Martyr, Co. Cork.

Coll. Eton.	Co. Cork . .	11,232 .	12,319

Club. Trav., Carl. b. 1833, s. 1868, m. 1st 1859,
2nd 1868.

Served as Attaché at Frankfort and Vienna.

SHARP, Adam, of Clyth (res. Rothes, Moray, N.B.)

	Caithness . .	12,850 .	3,531
	Elgin . . .	1 .	99
		12,851 .	3,630

Exclusive of 50*l.* for quarries.

SHAW, John Ralph, of Arrowe Park, Woodchurch, Cheshire.

Coll. Ch. Ch. Oxon.	Ross. . . .	8,300 .	645
Club. Conservative.	Cheshire . .	879 .	1,629
b. 1811, m. 1837.	Lancashire .	1 .	2,263
		9,180 .	4,537

*** SHEEPSHANKS, Rev. Thomas, of Arthington, Otley, &c.

Coll. U.Lon.,Tr.Cam.	York, W.R. .	7,002 .	9,152

Club. National. b. 1817, s. 1872, m. 1849.

** SHEFFIELD, Earl of, Sheffield Park, Uckfield.

Coll. Eton.	Sussex . .	4,537 .	3,585
Club. Carlton, Travellers'.	York, W.R.	731 .	947
b. 1832, s. 1876.	Co. Meath . .	1,085 .	1,031
Served as Attaché at Copen-	Co. Louth . .	115 .	71
hagen and Constantinople.			
Sat for E. Sussex.		6,468 .	5,634

SHEFFIELD, Sir Robert, Bart., of Normanby Park, Brigg.

		acres.	g. an. val.
Coll. Corpus, Oxon.	Lincoln . .	9,370 .	13,480

Club. Carlton, Boodle's.　b. 1823, s. 1862, m. 1866.

Served in Royal Horse Guards.

Sir Robert and "another" have jointly in the same county 150 acres, rented at 191*l.*

** SHELLEY, Edward, of Avington House, Winchester.　$.

Club. Army and Navy,	Hants . . .	5,342 .	4,735
Scientific.	Sussex . . .	285 .	366

b. 1827, s. 1866, m. 1866.

Served in 16th Lancers.		5,627 .	5,101

** SHELLEY, Sir John, Bart., of Shobrooke Park, Crediton.

Coll. Marl., Univ. Ox.	Devon . . .	6,500 .	7,300

Club. N. Univ., Bachelors', J. Carl.

b. 1848, s. (to Shobrooke) 1880.

SHELLEY, Lady, of Maresfield Park, Uckfield.

s. 1867, m. 1832.	Sussex . . .	3,865 .	3,685
	Lancashire . .	1,187 .	2,338
		5,052 .	6,023

SHEPHERD, James, of Aldie, Cruden, N.B.

b. 1837.	Aberdeen . .	4,923 .	3,576

Out of this total "Trustees of the late James Shepherd, of Aldie," have a rental of 2,422*l.*

SHEPHERD, Mrs., of Kirkby Moorside.

	York, N.R. .	3,791 .	4,421

SHEPPARD, Rev. Henry Alexander Graham, of Rednock, Stirling, N.B., &c.

Coll. Trin. Cam.	Surrey . . .	32 .	88
b. 1835.	Fife	654 .	1,663
	Stirling . . .	2,775 .	2,949
		3,461 .	4,700

$. SHELDON, H. J., of Brailes.　War. . | 2,370 . | 4,231

BOND-SHELTON, Captain, of The Argory.

Armagh, Tyrone, Westmeath	2,451 .	2,404

SHEPPARD, John George, of Campsey Ashe, Wickham Mt.

			acres.		*g. an. val.*
Coll.	Harrow, Trin. Cam.	Suffolk . . .	7,041	.	7,949

Club. Carlton, National. b. 1824, s. 1830, m. 1846.

SHERBORNE, Lord, Sherborne Park, Northleach, &c.

Coll.	Eton.	Hants . . .	150	.	100
Club.	White's, Salisbury.	Gloucester . .	15,773	.	21,345

b. 1804, s. 1862, m. 1st 1826, 2nd 1857.

The Hants pty. is Lady Sherborne's. 15,923 . 21,445

*** SHERBROOKE, Henry, of Oxton, Southwell.

Coll.	Eton,Trin.Hall,Cam.	Notts . . .	4,462	.	6,242

Club. Boodle's. b. 1810, s. 1847, m. 1840.

SHERIDAN, Richard Brinsley, of Frampton Court, Dorchester.

Club.	White's,Brooks's,Tr.,	Dorset . . .	11,468	.	12,765

R.Y,S. Cowes. b. 1809, s. 1817, m. 1835.

Sat for Shaftesbury and for Dorchester.

*** SHIFFNER, Rev. Sir George Croxton, Bart., of Coombe Place, Lewes. 🌿.

Coll.	Har., Ch. Ch. Oxon.	Sussex . . .	3,993	.	4,419
Club.	Junior Carlton.	Lancashire . .	364	.	891

b. 1819, s. 1863, m. 1854.

4,357 . 5,310

* SHIFFNER, Mrs., of Copgrove, Boroughbridge.

s. 1877, m. 1841.	York . . .	5,565	.	8,351

A part (unstated) of the Sussex . . . 86 . 218
Yorkshire property belongs
to Capt. Scarlett, of Achamore.

5,651 . 8,569

SHERIFFE, Mrs., of Henstead. Suffolk . 2,133 . 2,715

*** SHIRLEY, EVELYN PHILIP, of Ettington Park, Stratford-on-Avon, &c. ♋.

			acres.		*g. an. val.*
Coll. Eton, Magd. Oxon.	Co. Monaghan		26,386	.	20,744
Club. National.	Warwick . .		1,769	.	2,221
b. 1812, s. 1856, m. 1842.	Worcester . .		605	.	779
			28,760	.	23,744

Sat for Co. Monaghan and for S. Warwick.

** SHREWSBURY AND TALBOT, EARL OF, Ingestre Hall, Stafford, &c. ♋.

			acres.		*g. an. val.*
Coll. Eton.	Stafford . .		18,954	.	29,898
Club. Carlton.	Chester . . .		9,500	.	20,000
b. 1860, s. 1877.	Worcester . .		3,608	.	6,010
Is Hereditary Lord High	Salop . . .		2,186	.	4,140
Steward of Ireland.	Derby . . .		1,359	.	1,935
	Glamorgan .		81	.	124
	Northampton .		20	.	250
	Berks . . .		19	.	19
	Oxford . . .		2	.	6
			35,729	.	62,382

Inc. of a rental of 20*l.* in the COUNTESS DOWAGER'S name, but exc. of the val. of the minerals under 2,000 acres in Glamorgan.

SHUCKBURGH, SIR GEORGE THOMAS FRANCIS, BART., of Shuckburgh Park, Daventry. ♋.

			acres.		*g. an. val.*
Club. Union, Arthur's.	Warwick . .		3,368	.	6,103
b. 1827, s. 1876.	Northampton .		134	.	187
Served in Scots Fusilier					
Guards in the Crimea.			3,502	.	6,290

** SHUTTLEWORTH, JOSEPH, of Old Warden Pk., Biggleswade, &c.

			acres.		*g. an. val.*
Club. Reform.					
b. 1819, m. 1st 1842,	Bedford . .		3,000	.	6,633
2nd 1861.	Lincoln . . .		800	.	1,290
			3,800	.	7,923

♋. SHIRLEY (late), SIR H.   Monaghan .   4,197   .   2,829

* KAY-SHUTTLEWORTH, Sir Ughtred James, Bart., of Gawthorpe Hall, Burnley, &c.

			acres.		*g. an. val.*
Coll.	Harrow, London,	Lancashire .	3,171	.	4,853
	University.	Westmoreland	961	.	423
Club.	Ath., Ref., Dev.	York, W.R. .	10	.	20

b. 1844, s. 1877, m. 1871. 4,142 . 5,296

Sat for Hastings. Sir Ughtred claims the ⚶ mark.

** SIBTHORP, Coningsby Charles, of Canwick, Lincoln, &c.

Coll.	Eton, Magd. Oxon.	Lincoln . . .	6,000	.	8,000
Club.	Oxford and Cam.,	Herts . . .	1,700	.	2,300
	Oriental.				

b. 1846, s. 1861, m. 1876. 7,700 . 10,300

** SIDMOUTH, Viscount, Up Ottery Manor, Honiton, &c.

Club.	Carlton, Army and	Devon . . .	4,500	.	4,900
	Navy.	Stafford . . .	1,000	.	2,490
b. 1824, s. 1864, m. 1848.		Berks . . .	281	.	652
Served in Royal Navy.		Oxford . . .	124	.	178
Sat for Devizes.					

5,905 . 8,220

** SILVERTOP, Henry Charles, of Minsteracres, Newcastle.

Club.	Brooks's, St. George's.	Northumberland	3,594	.	2,841
b. 1826, s. 1849, m. 1st 1852,		Durham . .	628	.	631
2nd 1862.					

4,222 . 3,472

SHORT, J. H., of Edlington. Lincoln. . .	2,252	.	3,296
SHULDHAM, E. A., of Dunmanway. Cork	13,039	.	2,231
SHULDHAM, John, of Moigh. Longford .	2,571	.	3,681
SHULDHAM, Miss, of Marlesford. Suffolk	2,099	.	2,977
SHUTTLEWORTH, J., of Hathersage. Dby.	2,303	.	2,006
SIDEBOTTOM, J. Nowell, of Acres Bank. Gloucester, Cheshire, Derby, Lancashire	2,600	.	11,182
SILLIFANT, A. O., of Coombe. Devon .	2,920	.	2,729

SIMEON, Sir John Stephen Barrington, Bart., of Swainston,
Isle of Wight.   *acres.*   *g. an. val.*

Club. N. & M., Brooks's,   Hants . . .   8,724 .   8,056
Bachelors.

b. 1850, s. 1870, m. 1872.   Served in Rifle Brigade.

Sir John shares with "others" an additional 12 acres.

*** BRIDGEMAN-SIMPSON, Mrs., of Babworth Hall, Retford.

s. 1873, m. 1830.   Notts . . .   5,593 .   7,810

* SINCLAIR, Sir John George Tollemache, Bart., of Thurso
Castle, N.B.

Club. Trav., New, Edin.   Caithness . .   78,053 . 12,833
b. 1824, s. 1868, m. 1853, div. 1878.
Served in Scots Fus. Gds.   Sits for Caithness.   Was Page of
Honour to the Queen.

Exclusive of quarries rented at 1,378*l.*

** SINCLAIR, Lord, Herdmanston, Haddington, N.B., &c.

Coll. Sandhurst.	Roxburgh . .	2,251	. 1,300
Club. Carlton, U. Ser.	Berwick . .	1,550	. 3,900
b. 1830, s. 1880, m. 1870.	Haddington .	545	. 1,400
		4,346	. 6,600

Served in 57th Foot in the Crimea (Alma and Inkermann) and
during the Indian Mutiny and N. Zealand War.

SINCLAIR, Mrs., of Forss, Thurso, N.B.

s. 1876, m. 1828.   Caithness . . 12,700 .   5,117
With 492*l.* for quarries.

SIMPSON (late), A., of Colyhill.   Aber., Fife 2,854 .   2,809
SIMPSON, R., of Cobairdy.   Aberdeen, Banff 2,394 .   2,055

** THOMSON-SINCLAIR, William Sinclair, of Dunbeath
    Castle, Caithness, N.B.   *acres.*   *g. an. val.*

Club. New, Edin.   Caithness . .   57,757 ·   6,377
b. 1844, s. 1876, m. 1872.
                    With 27*l.* for quarries.

** SINCLAIR, Sir Robert Charles, Bart., of Stevenson,
    Haddington, N.B., &c.

Club. Arthur's, Uni. Ser.,   Caithness . . 18,874 ·   5,285
        New, Edin.   Haddington .   473   ·   1,041
b. 1820, s. 1863, m. 1st 1851,   ———————————————
                2nd 1876.   19,347 ·   6,326
            Served in 38th Foot.

*** DULEEP-SINGH, H.H. The Maharajah, Elveden Hall,
    Thetford.

Club. Marlborough, Carl.,   Suffolk . . .   17,210 ·   4,755
        Garrick, Oriental.   b. 1838, s. 1839, m. 1864.

** SINGLETON, Henry Corbet, of Aclare, Ardee, Meath.

Club. Kildare St., Dublin.   Co. Meath .   5,857 ·   4,731
b. 1837, s. 1872.   Served in 30th Foot (Major).

** SINGLETON, Henry Sydenham, of Mell, Co. Louth, &c.

Club. Travellers', Sackville Co. Cavan   .   6,609 ·   3,633
        Street, Dublin.   Co. Louth . .   1,487 ·   2,350
b. 1819, m. 1864.   Co. Meath   .   765   ·   591
                             Hants . . .   18   ·   141
                                               ———————————————
                                                8,879 ·   6,715

* CRAWFORD-SINGLETON, Thomas, of Fort Singleton,
    Emyvale, Co. Monaghan, &c.

Coll. Trinity, Dublin.   Co. Monaghan   4,489 ·   1,378
b. 1807, s. 1843.   Co. Fermanagh   3,216 ·   1,971
    Served in the Army.   Co. Cavan . .   766 ·   187
                            Co. Tyrone   .   399 ·   292
                            Co. Dublin   .   258 ·   433
                                            ———————————————
                                             9,128 ·   4,261

SINCLAIR, Sir J., Bt., of Barrock. Caith.   6,900 ·   2,354

SITWELL, Sir Geo. Reresby, Bt., of Renishaw, Chesterfield.

			acres.	g. an. val.
Coll. Eton, Ch. Ch. Oxon.	Derby . . .	3,506	.	10,136
b. 1860, s. 1862.	York, W.R. .	1,544	.	2,471
	Warwick . .	532	.	719
		5,582	.	13,326

Exc. of 349*l.* in his mother's name.

*** SITWELL, Robert Sacheverell, of Stainsby, Derby.

b. 1796, s. 1874, m. 1821.	Derby . . .	3,669	.	5,674
Served in 29th Foot at	Warwick . .	418	.	623
Waterloo.		4,087	.	6,297

HURT-SITWELL, Willoughby, of Ferney Hall, Craven Arms.

Club. Arthur's.	Salop . . .	3,402	.	3,011
b. 1827, s. 1835, m. 1st 1853,	Hereford . .	67	.	66
2nd 1858.		3,469	.	3,077

*** GORDON-CUMING-SKENE, John, of Parkhill, Aberdeen, N.B., &c.

Coll. Eton, Trin. Cam.	Aberdeen . .	8,992	.	7,238
b. 1827, s. 1837, m. 1st 1856, 2nd 1860.				

** SKENE, William Baillie, of Pitlour, Strathmiglo, N.B.

Coll. Harrow, Corpus and	Fife	2,878	.	4,219
All Souls, Oxon.	Kinross. . .	537	.	483
Club. U. U., Arth., Ath.				
b. 1838, s. 1866, m. 1874.		3,415	.	4,702

** SKIPWORTH, George Borman, of Moortown Ho., Lincoln.

b. 1820, s. 1860, m. 1846.	Lincoln . . .	5,300	.	8,000

SITWELL, W. H., of Barmoor.	Nmbld.	.	3,766	.	2,855
SKENE, Miss, of Rubislaw.	Aberdeen . .	3,849	.	2,950
SKERRETT, P. R., of Athgoe.	Dub., Galw.	4,702	.	2,229

** SLIGO, Marquis of, Westport House, Co. Mayo.

			acres.		*g. an. val.*

   Coll. Eton, Cam.   Co. Mayo . . 114,881 . 19,000
   Club. Trav., Ath., Cosm.
b. 1820, s. 1845, m. 1st 1847, 2nd 1858, 3rd 1878.
     Exclusive of fee farms, both as to area and rental.

SLINGSBY, Thomas, of Scriven Park, Knaresborough, &c.

Club. White's, Carlton.   York . . . 6,407 . 10,485
b. 1829, s. 1869, m. 1860. Served in R. H. Gds.
   Inc. 3,373*l.* held jointly with Mrs. Slingsby.

** SMALL, James, of Dirnanean, Pitlochrie, N.B., &c.

Club. New, Edinburgh.   Forfar . . . 11,261 . 2,110
b. 1835, s. 1859, m. 1867.   Perth . . . 9,193 . 3,043

                                  20,454 . 5,153

BOWYER-SMIJTH, Sir William, Bart., of Hill Hall, Epping.

Coll. Eton, Trin. Cam.   Essex . . . 2,819 . 3,597
Club. Carlton.   Norfolk . . . 4,418 . 5,503
b. 1814, s. 1850, m. 1839.
   Sat for S. Essex.   7,237 . 9,100

** SMITH, Abel, of Woodhall Park, Ware.

   Coll. Har., Trin. Cam.   Herts . . . 11,212 . 14,617
   Club. Carlton, Travellers'. b. 1829, s. 1859, m. 1853.
   Sits for Herts.

DUFF-ASSHETON-SMITH, George William, of Vaynol, Bangor, &c.

Club. Carlton, Jun. Carl.   Carnarvon . . 33,752 . 42,255
b. 1848, s. 1859.   Anglesea . . 730 . 767

                                  34,482 . 43,022

KENYON-SLANEY, W., of Hatton. Sal. . 2,809 . 4,860
SLATER, S., of North Carlton. Lincoln . 2,223 . 3,394

SMITH, HENRY, of Horbling, Folkingham.

		acres.	g, an. val.
Club. Conservative.	Lincoln . . .	3,639 .	7,253
b. 1820, m. 1846.			

** SMITH, RT. HON. WILLIAM HENRY, of Greenlands, Henley-on-Thames, &c.

		acres.	g, an. val.
Club. Carlton, National,	Suffolk . . .	5,150 .	8,000
Ath., St. Steph.	Bucks . . .	1,100 .	1,770
b. 1825, s. 1865, m. 1858.	Berks . . .	527 .	715
		6,777 .	10,485

Was Sec. of the Treas. and First L. Adm. Sits for Westminster.

*** MORE-SMYTH, HON. CHARLES WILLIAM, of Ballynatray, Youghal.

		acres.	g, an. val.
Coll. Eton.	Cork . . .	unstated .	311
Club. R. C. Yacht, Han. Sq.,	Co. Waterford	7,208 .	3,697
Eton and Harrow.	Co. Limerick .	272 .	407
b. 1826, m. 1848.			
		7,480 .	4,415

** SMYTH, JOHN, of Masonbrook, Loughrea, Co. Galway.

		acres.	g, an. val.
Coll. Ushaw.	Co. Galway .	9,670 .	5,049
b. 1835, s. 1868, m. 1863. Served in 15th Foot.			

		acres.	g, an. val.
SMITH-SLIGO, A. V., of Inzievar. Fife, Perth, Midlothian, Lanark		2,938 .	6,806
SMITH, SIR C. C., BART., of Suttons. Essex		2,485 .	3,931
SMITH, JAMES, of Olrig. Caithness . .		2,734 .	2,274
SMITH, JOHN L., ——. Tipperary . . .		4,534 .	2,120
SMITH, W. C., of Shortgrove. Essex, Cambs.		2,904 .	4,744
SMITHWICK, E., of Kilcreene. Kilkenny		2,022 .	2,240

SMYTH, Sir John Henry Greville, Bart., of Ashton Court,
  Bristol.   *acres.*   *g. an. val.*
Coll. Eton, Ch. Ch. Oxon.   Somerset . .   13,542 .   27,087
Club. Windham.   Gloucester . .   1,432 .   3,299
b. 1836, s. 1852.
                                              ─────────────────
                                              14,974 .   30,386
  Exclusive of a rental of 5,079*l.* arising from 3,252 acres in
Gloucester shared with "another."

** SMYTH, Hon. Leicester, C.B., of Drumcree, Killucan.

Coll. Eton.   Co. Westmeath   4,431 .   3,188
Club. Uni. Ser., A. & N.,   Leicester . .   1 .   7
    Trav., Kild. St.   ─────────────────
b. 1829, m. 1866.   4,432 .   3,195
  Served in the R. Brig. in Kaffir War and in the Crimea.   Was
Ass. Mil. Sec. to Lord Raglan and Dep. Q.-M.-G. in Ireland.   Is
L.-Gen. in the Army.

** SMYTH, Ralph, of Gaybrook, Mullingar, Co. Westmeath.

Coll. Tonbridge School.   Co. Westmeath   6,287 .   4,711
Club. A. & N., Arthur's,   Co. Antrim .   5,592 .   2,641
    Kild. St.   ─────────────────
b. 1831, s. 1878, m. 1861.   11,879 .   7,352
  Served in 17th Foot in the Crimea (Sebastopol and Kinburn).

** SMYTH, Thomas James, of Ballynegall, Mullingar.

Coll. Trinity, Dublin.   Co. Westmeath   9,778 .   6,886
Club. J. U. Ser., Kild. St. Co. Meath . .   150 .   111
b. 1833, s. 1856, m. 1864.   King's Co. .   343 .   453
                              Kildare . . .   785 .   318
                                              ─────────────────
                                             11,056 .   7,768

*** SMYTH, William Henry, of Elkington Hall, Louth.

Coll. Harrow, Caius, Cam.   Lincoln . . .   4,100 .   6,946
b. 1821, s. 1873, m. 1849.
    This family has held this estate since A.D. 1284.

───

* SMYTH, Rev. C., of L. Houghton. Nptn.   2,900(?) . 5,000(?)

SMYTH, E. R. S., of Mount Henry.   King's
    Co., Longford, Monaghan, Queen's Co.   4,446 .   2,369

SMYTH, P., of Headborough.   Waterford,
    Cork . . . . ,   3,241 .   2,617

SMYTHE, Sir Charles Frederick, Bart., of Acton Burnell, Shrewsbury, &c.

		acres.		*g. an. val:*
Coll. St. Gregory's, Down-	Salop . . .	5,313	.	5,499
side.	Warwick . .	3,501	.	5,054
Club. Brooks's,St.George's.	Durham . .	70	.	47
b. 1819, s. 1856, m. 1855.				
		8,884	.	10,600

*** SMYTHE, William, of Methven Castle, Perth, N.B.

Coll. Westm., Ch. Ch. Ox.	Perth . . .	5,128	.	6,642
Club. Athenæum, New, Ed.	Peebles . . .	24	.	11
b. 1803, s. 1847, m. 1st 1838.				
2nd 1849.		5,152	.	6,653
Served as Sec. to the Board of Supervision.				

* SNEYD, Rev. Walter, of Keele, Newcastle, Staffs. 🛡.

Coll. Westm., Ch. Ch. Ox.	Stafford . .	9,232	.	18,329
Club. Travellers'. b. 1809, s. 1870, m. 1856.				

SOMERS, Earl, Eastnor Castle, Ledbury, &c.

Coll. Ch. Ch. Oxon.	Worcester . .	6,265	.	9,311
Club. Trav., Gar., Ath.,	Hereford . .	6,668	.	7,338
Carl., St. James's.	Gloucester . .	121	.	197
b. 1819, s. 1852, m. 1850.	Kent . . .	13	.	3
Served as Lord in Waiting.				
Sat for Reigate.		13,067	.	16,849

* SOMERSET, Duke of, K.G., Bulstrode Park, Gerrard's Cross, &c. 🛡.

Coll. Eton, Ch. Ch. Oxon.	Devon . . .	8,138	.	14,465
Club. Athenæum, Trav.	Somerset . .	6,553	.	7,858
b. 1804, s. 1855, m. 1830.	Wilts . . .	5,824	.	7,859
Served as Lord of the	Lincoln . .	2,865	.	4,476
Treasury, Sec. Board of	Bucks . . .	1,640	.	2,284
Control, Un. Sec. Home	Cambridge .	289	.	516
Dep., Ch. Com. of Woods	Norfolk . .	32	.	60
and Forests, Ch. Com. of	Dorset . . .	46	.	59
Works, and First Lord of the				
Admiralty. Sat for Totnes.		25,387	.	37,577

SMYTHE, W. B., of Barbavilla. Gal., Mea.	5,035	.	2,320
SOLLY, W., of Sergehill. Herts, Kent, War.	2,279	.	3,448

** SOMERVELL, James, of Sorn Castle, Mauchline, N.B.

		acres.		*g. an. val.*
b. 1845, s. 1881.	Ayr	6,245	.	3,775
	Lanark . . .	218	.	799
		6,463	.	4,574

Exclusive of 12*l.* for minerals.

** SONDES, Earl, Lees Court, Faversham, &c.

Coll. Eton.
Club. Carl., Trav., Whi.
b. 1824, s. 1874, m. 1859.
Served in R. H. Gds.   Sat for E. Kent.

	Kent . . .	14,157	.	23,000
	Norfolk . . .	4,939	.	7,000
		19,096	.	30,000

*** SOUTHESK, Earl of, K.T., Kinnaird Castle, Brechin, N.B.

Coll. Sandhurst.
Club. Brooks's, Travellers'.
b. 1827, s. 1849, m. 1st 1849, 2nd 1860.
Served in Grenadier Guards and 92nd Foot.

	Forfar . . .	22,699	.	21,917

The attainder against this peerage was reversed in 1855, with restoration to the original precedence of 1633.

SOUTHWELL, Visct., Castle Mattress, Limerick.

b. 1872, s. 1878.	Co. Limerick .	4,032	.	3,190
	Co. Leitrim .	4,017	.	1,419
	Co. Cavan .	2,252	.	1,432
	Donegal . .	1,147	.	1,201
	Co. Kerry . .	329	.	28
	Monmouth .	4	.	6
		11,781	.	7,276

SOWERBY, George, of Putteridge Park, Luton, &c.

b. 1832, s. 1868, m. 1863.	Herts . . .	2,804	.	4,098
	Bedford . .	1,809	.	1,829
	Cumberland .	1,289	.	1,611
	York, N.R. .	99	.	229
		6,001	.	7,767

*** SPALDING, Augustus Frederick Montagu, of The
    Holme, New Galloway, N.B., &c.   *acres.*   *g. an. val.*

Club. Carlton, Garrick.   Kirkcudbright   3,785 · 4,400
b. 1838, s. 1869.   Served in the Admiralty Office.

*** SPARKE, Edward Bowyer, of Gunthorpe, E. Dereham.

Coll. Eton, Trin. Cam.	Norfolk	. .	3,775	·	6,805
Club. Carl., Uni. Univ.	Cambridge	.	1,562	·	2,678
b. 1832, s. 1870, m. 1872.	Somerset	. .	110	·	234

                                 5,447 · 9,717

    The Norfolk return utterly ignores the Sparkes of Gunthorpe,
having credited the Rev. E. B. Sparke of Feltwell with the whole
of both estates, and distributed the Cambridgeshire property under
the somewhat varied spellings of "Spark," "Sparke," and
"Sparks," all of whom are put into Holy Orders.

*** SPARROW, Arthur, of Preen Manor, Shrewsbury.

Club. St. Stephen's.	Salop	. .	3,027	·	3,362
	Stafford	. .	290	·	1,534
b. 1826, s. 1867, m. 1851.					

                                 3,317 · 4,896

** SPARROW, William Arthur, of Albrighton, Shrewsbury.

b. 1847, s. 1881, m. 1873.	Salop	. .	2,226	·	2,424
	Stafford	. .	310	·	5,418
	Worcester	. .	499	·	650
	Monmouth	.	849	·	643
	Hereford	. .	483	·	656

                                 4,367 · 9,791

SPEIR, Robert Thomas Napier, of Culdees, Perth, N.B., &c.

Coll. Eton, Ch. Ch. Oxon.	Perth	. . .	1,619	·	1,971
Club. St. James's.	Renfrew	. .	1,575	·	3,908
b. 1841, s. 1853 and 1874,					
m. 1868.			3,194	·	5,879

              Exclusive of 2,735*l.* for minerals.

SPAIGHT, W., of Derry Castle.   Tipp., Clare   5,849 · 2,497
SPARLING, W., of Petton.   Salop, York .   2,680 · 3,452

*** SPEIRS, Alexander Archibald, of Elderslie, Paisley, N.B., &c.

b. 1869, s. 1869.

		acres.	*g. an. val.*
Renfrew	. .	11,287	17,134
Lanark	. . .	206	640
		11,493	17,774

Exclusive of 70*l.* for quarries.

*** SPENCER, Earl, K.G., Althorp Park, Northampton. $.

Coll. Harrow, Trin. Cam.
Club. Reform, Brooks's.
b. 1835, s. 1857, m. 1858.
Was G. of the Stole to the late P. Consort and the P. of Wales., and L. Pres. of the Council. Is Lord Lieutenant of Ireland.
Sat for S. Northamptonshire.

Warwick	. .	3,392	5,743
Northampton	.	16,800	29,060
Norfolk	. .	2,533	2,280
Herts	. . .	3,017	5,600
Bucks	. . .	771	1,615
Leicester	. .	670	1,270
Surrey	. . .	2	1,196
		27,185 *.	46,764

** SPITTY, Thomas Jenner, of Billericay, Brentwood.

Coll. Peterhouse, Cam.
b. 1812, s. 1858, m. 1863.

Essex	. . .	3,029	3,656

DOUGLAS - MONTAGU - SCOTT - SPOTTISWOODE, Lady John, Spottiswoode, Lauder, &c.

s. 1870, m. 1836.

Berwick	. .	11,412	5,425

SPROT, Mark, of Riddell, Selkirk.

Coll. Trin. Cam.
Club. National, New Edin.
b. 1802, s. 1817, m. 1829.

Roxburgh	. .	3,278	3,426
Lanark	. . .	103	177
Selkirk	. . .	1	3
		3,382	3,606

HOME-SPEIRS, Sir G., Bt. Stir., Ayr, Sur.	7,270	2,744
SPEKE, William, of Jordans. Somerset .	2,536	4,570
SPENCER, W. F., of Spring Gr. Wor., War.	2,309	3,318
SPERLING, H. J., of Dynes Hall. Essex, Suff.	2,999	4,323
SPICER, J., of Spye Pk. Wilts, Sur. . .	2,078	3,298
SPLATT, W. F., of Flete. Devon	2,486	3,931

STACKPOOLE, Mrs., of Ballyalla, Ennis, Co. Clare.

		acres.	g. an. val.
s. 1879, m. 186–.	Co. Clare . .	7,441	3,609

STAFFORD, Lord, Costessy Park, Norwich, &c. **S.**

Club. Athenæum, Brooks's.	Salop . . .	5,345	13,842
b. 1802, s. 1851, m. 1st 1829,	Norfolk . . .	2,995	3,766
2nd 1859.	Stafford . . .	1,710	4,680
Sat for Pontefract.			
		10,050	22,288

STAIR, Earl of, K.T., Oxenfoord Castle, Dalkeith, N.B., &c.

Coll. Harrow.	Wigtown . .	82,666	43,509
Club. Brooks's, Gds., U. S.	Ayr	19,758	13,703
b. 1819, s. 1864, m. 1846.	Midlothian .	13,827	10,512
Served in Scots Gds. and	Haddington .	88	110
as L. H. Com. to the Ass.	Hants . . .	31	71
of the Kirk of Scotland.			
Sat for Wigtown.		116,370	67,905
Exclusive of 1,122*l.* for mines.			

The Ayrshire estate stands in the Countess's name ; small parts of the other estates are shared with "Trustees of the late Earl."

STAMFORD and WARRINGTON, Earl of, Enville Hall, Stourbridge, &c. **S.**

Coll. Eton, Trin. Cam.	Leicester . .	9,012	12,876
Club. Athenæum, Carlton,	Cheshire . .	8,612	16,000
Cons., Travellers',	Stafford . . .	7,339	11,367
Boodle's.	Lancashire . .	5,231	17,465
b. 1827, s. 1845, m. 1st 1848,	Salop . . .	606	508
2nd 1855.	Worcester . .	68	130
	York, W.R. .	93	46
	Warwick . .	1	1
		30,962	58,393

SPURWAY, of Springrove.	Dev., Som. .	2,610	2,947
STACKPOOLE, R., of Edenvale.	Clare .	7,771	2,950

** STANCOMB, WILLIAM, of Blount's Court, Devizes.

		acres.		g. an. val.
b. 181–, m. 1841.	Wilts . . .	1,660	.	3,000
	Pembroke . .	1,468	.	1,000
		3,128	.	4,000

STANDISH, CHARLES HENRY LIONEL WIDDRINGTON, of Standish Hall, Wigan. ♯.

Club. Brooks's.	Lancashire . .	3,080	.	6,962
b. 1822, s. 1863, m. 1846.				

STANDISH, ROWLAND EDMOND WALTER PERY, of Scaleby Castle, Carlisle (res. Farley Hill, Reading).

b. 1820, s. 1845, m. 1850.	Cumberland .	3,422	.	3,611
Served in 6th Foot.	Essex . . .	127	.	255
		3,549	.	3,866

** FANE-BENETT-STANFORD, VERE, of Preston Place, Brighton, &c.

Coll. Marlborough.	Sussex . . .	1,800	.	14,200
Club. Army and Navy, Turf,	Wilts . . .	5,026	.	9,876
Orleans, St. Steph.,	Surrey . . .	170	.	730
Carlton, Boodle's.	Middlesex . .	1	.	500
b. 1839, s. 1856, m. 1867.				
		6,997	.	25,306

Served in 43rd Foot and on Commander-in-Chief's Staff in the Indian Mutiny. Sat for Shaftesbury. This family has held property in Wilts since Edward I.

** STANHOPE, EARL, Chevening, Sevenoaks. ♯.

Coll. Harrow.	Kent . . .	4,343	.	3,891
Club. Carlton, Trav.	Devon . . .	5,186	.	3,101
St. Stephen's.	Derby . . .	2,583	.	4,900
b. 1838, s. 1875, m. 1869.	Queen's Co. .	2,129	.	2,000
Served in G. Gds., and as				
L. of the Trea., is First C. Est. Com.		14,241	.	13,892
Sat for E. Suffolk.				

** SCUDAMORE-STANHOPE, Sir Henry Edwyn Chandos, Bart., of Holm Lacy, Hereford. 🝔.

			acres.	g. an. val.
Coll. Balliol, Oxon.	Hereford	. .	5,039	. 6,224
Club. Travellers', Brooks's,	Herts	. . .	152	. 256
b. 1821, s. 1874, m. 1851.				
			5,191	. 6,480

*** STANHOPE, James Banks, of Revesby Abbey, Boston.

Coll. Wmr.,Ch.Ch.Ox.	Lincoln	. . .	7,847	. 13,015
Club. Carlton, Boodle's, Gun, Arthur's, Travellers'.				
b. 1821, s. 1825. Sat for N. Lincoln.				

** SPENCER-STANHOPE, Walter Thomas William, of Cannon Hall, Barnsley, &c.

Coll. Eton,Ch.Ch.Ox.	York, W.R.	.	11,357	. 11,070
Club. Carlton, Travellers', St. Stephen's.				
b. 1827, s. 1873, m. 1856. Sat for the S.W. Riding.				

*** STANIER, Francis, of Peplow Hall, Market Drayton, &c.

Coll. Heidelberg.	Salop	. . .	4,499	. 5,430
Club. Jun. Carl.,Wind.	Stafford	. .	350	. 1,012
b. 1838, s. 1856, m. 1860.				
			4,849	. 6,442

** STANLEY, Edward James (of Crosshall), of Quantock Lo., Bridgwater. 🝔.

Coll. Ch. Ch. Oxon.	Lancashire	. .	1,384	. 2,922
Club. Travellers', White's.	Somerset	. .	5,772	. 5,338
b. 1826, s. 1870, m. 1872.				
Sits for W. Somerset.			7,156	. 8,260

The Somerset property belongs to Hon. Mrs. Stanley, his wife. "Crosshall" is now a mere farmhouse near Ormskirk, but this family have always been "Stanleys of Crosshall."

STANLEY of ALDERLEY, Lord, Alderley Park, Chelford, Crewe. 🝔.

Coll. Eton, Trin. Cam.	Cheshire	. .	5,011	. 12,082
Club. Travellers'.	Anglesea	. .	5,960	. 4,238
b. 1827, s. 1869, m. 1862.				
			10,971	. 16,320

Was Att. at Constantinople and Sec. of L. at Athens.

*** STANLEY, Mrs., of Landshipping (res. Brussels).

		acres.	*g. an. val.*
b. 1803.	Pembroke . .	4,787 .	4,540

* SLOANE-STANLEY, Hans, of Paultons, Romsey.

Coll. Eton.   Hants . . .   5,150 .   3,604
Club. A. & N. b. 1840, s. 1879, m. 1866.
   Served in 16th Lancers.

*** STANLEY, Hon. William Owen, of Penrhos, Holyhead.
🐚.

Coll. Eton, and Germany.   Anglesea . .   5,808 .   5,086
Club. Travellers'. b. 1802, m. 1832.
   Served in Gren. Gds. Sat for Anglesea, Chester, and Beaumaris.

** STAPLES, Sir Nathaniel Alexander, Bart., of Lissane,
   Cookstown, Co. Tyrone.

Coll. Addiscombe.	Co. Tyrone .	3,078 .	2,036
Club. Scientific.	Co. Dublin .	1,457 .	1,416
b. 1817, s. 1865, m. 1846.	Londonderry .	990 .	566
Served in Bengal Artillery.			
		5,525 .	4,018

*** STAPLES, Robert, of Dunmore, Durrow, Queen's Co.

Coll. Trinity, Cambridge.	Londonderry .	4,003 .	1,729
Club. Carlton, St. James',	Queen's Co. .	1,924 .	1,187
Sac. St.	Co. Mayo . .	1,385 .	865
b. 1823, s. 1863, m. 1846.			
		7,312 .	3,781

STAPYLTON, Henry Miles, of Myton Hall, Helperby.

Coll. Sandhurst.   York, N.R. .   5,119 .   8,280
Club. A. & N., U. Ser., Ref.
b. 1831, s. 1864, m. 1865. Served in 2nd Dragoon Guards.

SLOANE-STANLEY, F., of Tedworth.
    Wil., Hants . . . . 3,580 . 2,666
STAPLETON, Sir F. G., Bart., of Greys.
    Oxon, Dorset, Kent . . . . . . 2,078 . 4,198

*** STARKIE, LE GENDRE NICHOLAS, of Huntroyde, Burnley, &c. 🏊.

			acres.	g. an. val.
Coll. Upp. Trin., Cam.	Lancashire	.	8,355 .	19,423
Club. O. & C., Carl., Uni.	York, W.R.	.	209 .	121
Ser., Bood., Gar.				

b. 1828, s. 1865, m. 1867. Sat for Clitheroe. 8,564 . 19,544
Exclusive of mines.

** ALCOCK-STAWELL, COL., of Kilbrittain Cas., Co. Cork.

Club. United Service, Jun.	Co. Cork . .	11,336 .	6,452
United Service.	Co. Limerick	318 .	300

b. 1808, m. 1845.
Served in Royal Welsh Fusiliers. 11,654 . 6,752

** STEERE, LEE, of Jayes, Dorking.

Coll. Harrow, Trin. Oxon.	Surrey . . .	3,771 .	3,215
Club. Carlton.	Sussex . . .	1,296 .	626

b. 1803, s. 1832, m. 1826.
Sat for W. Surrey. 5,067 . 3,841
   Though unnoticed in MR. SHIRLEY'S work, this family claims to have held Jayes without any break since the Conquest.

COWELL-STEPNEY, SIR ARTHUR KEPPEL, BART., of Llanelly, Carmarthen.

Coll. Eton.	Carmarthen .	9,841 .	7,047
Club. Travellers', Brooks's,	Berks . . .	6 .	153
Reform, St. James's.			

b. 1834, s. 1877, m. 1875. 9,847 . 7,200
   Served in the F. O. Sat for Carmarthen.

STEUART, ANDREW, of Auchlunkart House, Keith, N.B.

Coll. Trinity, Cambridge.	Banff . . .	6,329 .	4,440
s. 1822, m. 1847.	Elgin . . .	483 .	122
Sat for Cambridge.			

6,812 . 4,562

STAVELEY, the MISSES, of Sleningford. Yk.	2,385 .	3,097
STAVELY, J., of Croydon Pk., Dub., Lim.	4,207 .	2,522
STEELE, RT. HON. SIR T. M., K.C.B. Perth	2,895 .	2,911

** SETON-STEUART, Sir Henry James, Bart., of Touch
House, Stirling, &c., N.B. *acres.* *g. an. val.*

| *Club.* J. Carl., New Ed., | Stirling . . . | 4,801 | . | 2,500 |
| and Cons. | Lanark . . . | 2,673 | . | 1,879 |

b. 1812, s. 1838, m. 1852.

| | | 7,474 | · | 4,379 |

Is Her. Armour-Bearer and Squire of the Royal Body in Scotland.
Exclusive of 1,300*l.* for mines.

STEWART, Alexander John Robert, of Ards, Letterkenny.

Coll. Trinity, Cambridge.	Co. Donegal .	39,306	.	9,135
Club. Carl., Trav., Kild. St.,	Co. Down . .	5,002	.	6,520
Sackville St.				

b. 1827, s. 1850, m. 1851.

| | 44,308 | . | 15,655 |

*** STEWART, Sir Archibald Douglas, Bart. (of Grandtully), of Murtly Castle, Murtly, N.B.

Club. National. Perth . . . 33,274 . 18,040
b. 1817, s. 1871, m. 1875. Grandtully has been held since 1417.

STEWART, Sir Augustus Abraham James, Bart., of Fort
Stewart, Ramelton, Co. Donegal.

b. 1832, s. 1879. Donegal . . 7,547 . 4,486

** MURRAY-STEWART, Horatio Granville, of Cally,
Gatehouse, N.B.

Coll. Harrow, Ch. Ch. Ox.	Co. Donegal .	50,818	.	6,500
Club. Carlton, Jun. Carlton.	Kirkcudbright	45,867	.	14,615
b. 1834, s. 1845, m. 1858.	Wigtown . .	1,584	.	1,707

Rental somewhat understated. 98,269 . 22,822

LYNE-STEPHENS, Mrs., of Lynford. Norf.	6,878	.	2,736
MOORE-STEVENS, J., of Winscott. Dev.	4,186	.	2,556
STEVENS, Rev. T., of Bradfield. Berks .	2,263	.	2,879
STEWART, A. B., of Balnakeilly. Perth .	3,535	.	2,113
STEWART, C. D., of Brin. Inv., Suth. .	7,330	.	2,080
STEWART, M.J., of Southwick. Kirk., Wigt.	3,898	.	2,257

** STEWART, JOHN LORNE, of Brechacha, Isle of Coll, N.B.

			acres.		g. an. val.
Club.	Army and Navy, Uni.	Argyll . . .	14,247	.	4,118
	Service, Edinburgh.	Perth . . .	82	.	264

b. 1837, s. 1878.

Served in Scots Greys and 18th Hussars. 14,329 . 4,382

STEWART, SIR JOHN MARCUS, BART., of Ballygawley, Tyrone.

Coll.	Rugby.	Co. Tyrone .	27,905	.	6,409
Club.	Carlton.	Co. Galway .	629	.	343

b. 1830, s. 1854, m. 1856.

Served in the Inniskilling Dragoons in 28,534 . 6,752
the Crimea.

** SHAW-STEWART, SIR MICHAEL ROBERT, BART. (of Black-
Hall), of Ardgowan, Greenock, N.B.

Coll.	Ch. Ch. Oxon.	Renfrew . .	26,376	.	17,238
Club.	Carlton, Travellers'.	Ayr	92	.	140

b. 1826, s. 1836, m. 1852.

Served in 2nd Life Guards. 26,468 . 17,378

Sat for Renfrewshire. Exclusive of 573*l.* for quarries.

*** JOHNSTON-STEWART, ROBERT HATHORN, of Physgill,
Whithorn, N.B., &c.

Coll.	Eton.	Wigtown . .	5,552	.	8,166
Club.	J. U. S., New Ed.	Linlithgow .	2,036	.	3,810

b. 1824, s. 1842 and 1865, m. 1st 1851,

2nd 1856. 7,588 . 11,976

Served in 13th L. Dragoons.

** STIRLING, JOHN, of Kippendavie, Dunblane, N.B.

Club.	Carlton.	Perth . . .	6,111	.	5,586

b. 1811, s. 1816, m. 1839.

STEWART (late), of St. Fort.	Fife . . .	2,664	.	5,054
STEWART, ROBERT, of Ardvorlich.	Perth .	10,001	.	2,654
STIRLING, J., of Garden.	Perth, Stirling .	3,239	.	2,767
STIRLING, MISS, of Renton.	Berwick . .	2,674	.	2,987

** GRAHAM-STIRLING, MAJOR, of Strowan, Crieff, N.B.

			acres.	g. an. val.
Coll. Westminster.	Perth . . .		4,000 .	3,385

Club. J. U. S., New Ed.
b. 1811, s. 1811, m. 1st 1844, 2nd 1858.
Served in 42nd Highlanders.

** STOCKS, MAJOR MICHAEL, of Latheronwheel, Caithness, N.B.

Coll. St. John's, Cam.	Caithness . .	13,600 .	1,744
Club. Jun. Uni. Serv.	York, W.R. .	1,020 .	5,652
b. 1825, s. 1872, m. 1863.	Norfolk . .	1,840 .	1,810
Served in 1st Royal Dragoons.			
		16,460 .	9,206

** STOUGHTON, THOS. ANTHONY, of Ballyhorgan, Tralee, &c.

Club. Boodle's, Union,	Co. Kerry . .	11,710 .	2,398
Brooks's.	Co. Cork . .	1,288 .	706
b. 1818, s. 1862, m. 1862.	Gloucester . .	651 .	797
		13,649 .	3,901

** STOURTON, HENRY JOSEPH, of Holme Hall, York. ♣.

Coll. Stony., Ch. Ch. Ox.	York, E.R. .	3,151 .	3,777

Club. Junior Carlton. b. 1844, s. 1860, m. 1870.

MOWBRAY & STOURTON, LORD, Stourton, Knaresboro'. ♣.

Club. Carlton, Boodle's.	York, W.R. .	5,097 .	9,347

b. 1829, s. 1872, m. 1865.

STRACEY, SIR HENRY JOSIAS, BT., of Rackheath, Norwich.

Coll. Eton.	Norfolk . . .	4,842 .	7,774

Club. Carlton, Arthur's. b. 1803, s. 1851, m. 1835.
Served in 1st D. Gs. Sat for E. Nrfk., Gt. Yarmouth & Norwich.

STOBART, REV. H., of Mt. Bagnal.	Louth.	4,249 .	2,081
STOKES, T., of New Parks.	Leic., Warwick	2,297 .	4,112
STOKES, ADMIRAL, of Scotchwell.	Pemb. .	2,133 .	3,217
♣ STONOR, C. J., of Anderton Hall.	Lanc.	2,757 .	4,864
STORY, R., of Bingfield.	Cav., Tyr., Leit. .	4,157 .	2,431

*** STRADBROKE, Earl of, of Henham Hall, Wangford. ♠.

		acres.	g. an. val.
Coll. Westminster.	Suffolk . . .	12,203	15,434
Club. White's, Boodle's. b. 1794, s. 1827, m. 1857.			

Served in Coldstream Guards at Salamanca, Vittoria, St. Sebastian, Nivelle, and Bayonne; carried the colours of his regiment from Spain into France in 1813.

William the Conqueror gave the then Rous of Baddingham leave to hunt in the Dunwich Forest, which was swallowed up by the sea some centuries ago. Tradition fixes it several miles east of the present coast line. Inc. of 503 acres belonging to Lady S.

STRAFFORD, Earl of, F.R.S., of Wrotham Park, Barnet.

Coll. Sandhurst.	Middlesex . .	4,993	9,676
Club. Brooks's, White's,	Herts . . .	1,634	2,751
Boodle's, Trav.	Kent . . .	707	1,161
b. 1806, s. 1860, m. 1st 1829,	Bedford . . .	13	23
2nd 1848.	Co. Londonderry	7,647	2,738
		14,994	16,349

Served in R. Brig., as L. of the Treas., Tr. of the Hhold., and Sec. of the B. of Con. Sat for Milborne Port, for Chatham, and for Poole.

*** STRAKER, John, of Stagshaw Ho., Corbridge-on-Tyne.

Club. Union, Scottish.	Northumberland	10,959	11,074
b. 1815, m. 1846.	Durham . . .	1,417	1,082
		12,376	12,156

** WINGFIELD-STRATFORD, Edward John, of Addington Park, West Malling.

b. 1849, s. 1881.	Kent . . .	2,315	4,580
Served in Scots Guards.	Sligo . . .	7,876	3,441
The Wicklow rental does	Limerick . .	2,502	1,855
not include several farms	Co. Clare . .	2,213	916
on long leases returned in	Co. Mayo . .	2,361	238
the tenants' names.	Wicklow . .	201	128
	Co. Dublin .	2	180
		17,470	11,338

STRANGWAYS, H. Bull, of Shapwick.		
Somerset, Gloucester, Devon	2,134	3,315
STRATFORD, H. S., —. Nptn., Glo., Leic.	2,501	5,290

STRATHALLAN, Visct., Strathallan Cas., Auchterarder, N.B.

		acres.	g. an. val.
Coll. Charterhouse.	Perth . . .	7,208 .	7,611

Club. Carlton. b. 1810, s. 1851, m. 1833.
　Served as Lord in Waiting.

*** STRATHMORE AND KINGHORNE, Earl of, Glamis
　　　Castle, Forfar, &c.

Coll. Winc., Ch. Ch. Ox.	Forfar . . .	22,600 .	24,280
Club. Carlton, Han. Sq.	Perth . . .	270 .	355
b. 1824, s. 1865, m. 1853.	Sussex . . .	16 .	298
Served in 2nd Life Guards.	Herts . . .	1,800 .	3,569
		24,686 .	28,502

** STREATFIELD, Colonel Henry Dorrien, of Chidding-
　stone, Edenbridge.

Coll. Eton.	Kent . . .	4,500 .	5,098

Club. Carlton, White's.　b. 1825, m. 1854.
　　　　Served in 1st Life Guards.

*** STREATFIELD, Richard James, of Rossington, Bawtry, &c.

Club. Army & Navy.	Yorkshire . .	3,248 .	3,375
b. 1844, s. 1851 and 1877,	Sussex . . .	2,233 .	3,610
m. 1865.			
Served in 5th Drag. Gds.		5,481 .	6,985

** STRICKLAND, Sir Charles William, Bart., of Hildenley,
　Malton, &c.

Coll. Rugby, Trin. Cam.	York, N.E. and		
Club. Athenæum.	W.R. . .	16,000 .	17,000

b. 1819, s. 1874, m. 1st 1850, 2nd 1866.

STRODE, Mrs., of Newnham Park, Plympton.

s. 1874, m. 1858.	Devon . . .	1,957 .	2,431
	Cornwall . .	1,297 .	1,058
		3,254 .	3,489

STRATHNAIRN, Lord, G.C.B.　Herts,			
Cambridgeshire, Essex, Bucks . . .		2,918 .	3,603
STRONG, C., of Thorpe. Cam., Hunts., Nptn.		2,001 .	4,215

** STRONGE, Sir James Matthew, Bart., of Tynan Abbey,
Co. Armagh.

Club. Carlton, Kildare St.
Dublin.

b. 1811, s. 1864, m. 1836.
Served in 5th Dragoon Guards.
Sat for Co. Armagh.

	acres.	*g. an. val.*
Armagh . .	4,404 .	5,568
Tyrone . . .	8,426 .	3,854
Londonderry .	124 .	95
	12,954 .	9,517

** STUART, Dugald, of Loch Carron, Ross, N.B., &c.

b. 1817, s. 1876, m. 1876.

Ross. . . .	32,450 .	2,661
Argyll . . .	5,000 .	575
	37,450 .	3,236

Acreage (never surveyed) believed to be much under the mark.

* CONSTABLE-MAXWELL-STUART,   Hon. Henry,   of
Traquhair House, Innerleithen, &c.

Coll. Stonyhurst.
Club. Yorkshire County.
b. 1809, s. 1865, m. 1840.

Peebles . . .	10,778 .	4,840
Selkirk . . .	9,765 .	1,980
Dumfries . .	1,470 .	1,430
York, W.R. .	208 .	431
	22,221 .	8,681

Exclusive of 500 acres of wood. The two first estates are
returned as belonging to " Trustees of late Lord Traquhair."

VILLIERS-STUART, Henry, of Dromana, Waterford.

Coll. Durham Univ.
Club. Dev., Kild. St.,
Reform.
b. 1827, s. 1874, m. 1863.
Was formerly in Holy Orders.
Sits for Co. Waterford.

Waterford . .	30,882 .	11,463
Co. Kildare .	47 .	40
Co. Cork . .	24 .	70
	30,953 .	11,573

*** VILLIERS-STUART, Henry John Richard, of Castletown,
Carrick-on-Suir.

b. 1837, s. 1879, m. 1870.

Kilkenny . .	2,790 .	2,241
Cork. . . .	1,404 .	570
Tipperary . .	292 .	267
Waterford . .	95 .	55

Served in 68th Foot.

	4,581 .	3,133

** STUART, Colonel William, of Tempsford Hall, Sandy, &c.

			acres.		g. an. val.
Coll. Eton, St. John's,	Bedford. . .		1,951	.	2,800
Cam.	Leicester . .		1,439	.	2,200
Club. Carlton, Uni.	Somerset . .		740	.	1,260
Serv., National.	Herts . . .		370	.	929
b. 1825, s. 1874, m. 1859.	Huntingdon .		173	.	76
Sat for Bedford.	Bucks . . .		243	.	190
	Cambs. . . .		35	.	30
			4,951	.	7,485

** STUBBER, Robert Hamilton Stubber, of Moyne, Durrow.

Club. Kild. St. Dublin,	Queen's Co. .		7,388	.	4,061
A. & N., N. & M.					
b. 1844, s. 1863, m. 1877.					

*** STUCLEY, Sir George Stucley, Bart., of Moreton, Bideford, &c.

Coll. Eton, Ch. Ch. Oxon.	Devon . . .		16,155	.	11,809
Club. Brooks's.	Cornwall . .		3,574	.	4,300
b. 1812, s. 1858, m. 1st 1835,	Middlesex . .		78	.	568
2nd 1872.					
Served in Royal Horse Guards.			19,807	.	16,677
Sat for Barnstaple.					

** STUDD, Edward Fairfax, of Oxton, Exeter, &c.

Coll. Univ. Oxon.	Inverness . .		2,903	.	300
Club. New Univ.	Stafford . . .		310	.	2,950
b. 1856, s. 1878, m. 1877.	Devon . . .		700	.	600
	Worcester . .		210	.	470
	Warwick . .		120	.	132
			4,243	.	4,452

2,000*l.* of these rents are his mother's.

STIRLING-STUART, J., of Castlemilk. Lan.			2,137	.	3,260
HARINGTON-STUART, R. E. S., of Torrance. Lanark			2,971	.	2,949

** STYLE, Sir William Henry Marsham, Bart., of Glenmore,
Co. Donegal.   *acres.   g. an. val.*

Coll. Eton, Merton, Oxon.   Co. Donegal .   39,564 .   4,000
Club. Carlton, Sack. St.
b. 1826, s. 1868, m. 1848.

** SUDELEY, Lord, Gregynog, Newtown, Montgomery, &c.

Club. St. James's, Brooks's,	Montgomery .	17,158 . 13,539
Uni. Ser., Trav.	Gloucester .	6,620 . 9,590
b. 1840, s. 1877, m. 1868.	Salop . . .	175 . 211
Served in Royal Navy at		
Siege of Bomarsund, in		23,953 . 23,340
China, &c. Sat for Montgomery.		

** SUFFIELD, Lord, K.C.B., Gunton Park, Norwich.

Club. Brooks's, White's,   Norfolk . .   11,828 . 15,071
Turf, Marlborough.
b. 1830, s. 1853, m. 1854.   Served in 7th Hussars. Was Lord in
Waiting, and is Lord of the Bedchamber to the Prince of Wales.

SUFFOLK and BERKSHIRE, Earl of, Charlton Park,
Malmesbury.   §.

Coll. Harrow.   Wilts . . .   11,098 . 14,209
Club. White's, Turf, Athenæum, Travellers'.
b. 1833, s. 1876, m. 1868.   Sat for Malmesbury.

** SURTEES, Henry Edward, of Redworth Hall, Darlington,
&c.

Coll. Harrow.	Durham . .	7,377 . 4,142
Club. A.&N.,Carl.,J.Carl.,	Herts . . .	1,706 . 2,283
Turf.	Northumberland	313 . 457
b. 1819, s. 1863, m. 1st 1843,	Middlesex . .	60 . 220
2nd 1870.		
Served in 10th Hussars.	Sat for Herts.	9,456 . 7,102
Rent of mines and cottages not included.		

SULLIVAN, J., of Lacken.   Kilk., Tip. .   4,382 . 2,716
SUMMERS, Mrs., of Milton Ho.   Pemb. .   2,541 . 3,313
SUMNER, A. H., of Hatchlands.   Surrey .   2,311 . 2,973
SUMNER, F. J., of Glossop.   Derby . .   2,702 . 2,084

** SUTHERLAND, Duke of, K.G., Dunrobin Castle, Golspie,
  N.B., &c. ♒.

		acres.		g. an. val.
Club. White's, Marl., Roy.	Sutherland	1,176,454	.	56,937
Thames Yacht.	Ross . . .	149,999	.	12,002
b. 1828, s. 1861, m. 1849.	Salop . . .	17,495	.	40,418
	Stafford . . .	12,744	.	29,987
Sat for Sutherland.	York, N.R. .	1,853	.	2,323
		1,358,545	.	141,667

Almost all the Ross-shire estate belongs to the Duchess.

GRANT-SUTTIE, Sir George, Bart., of Preston Grange,
  Haddington, N.B.

b. 1870, s. 1878.	Haddington .	8,791	.	9,778
	Berwick . .	2,275	.	1,779
		11,066	.	11,557

Exclusive of 1,195*l.* for mines.

** SUTTON, Sir Richard Francis, Bart., of Benham Park,
  Newbury. ♒.

Coll. Eton.	Lincoln . .	4,890	.	9,000
b. 1853, s. 1878.	Notts . . .	694	.	1,500
	Berks . . .	3,756	.	5,000
		9,340	.	15,500

** SUTTON, Robert Nassau, of Scawby Hall, Brigg.

Coll. Eton.	Lincoln . .	7,263	.	9,044

Club. Arthur's, Oriental, Naval and Military.
b. 1850, s. 1872.   Serves in 8th Hussars.

SUTHERLAND, G., of Forss. Caithness	8,000	.	2,482
SUTTON, John S., of Elton. Durham, York	2,971	.	3,049
SWEETMAN, Mrs., of Lamberton. Q. C., Mea.	2,151	.	2,003
SWEETMAN, P., of Longtown. Kild., Wic.	3,021	.	2,496

*** SWINBURNE, Sir John, Bart., of Capheaton, Newcastle-
on-Tyne, &c. ♣.

		acres.	g. an. val.
Club. Trav., Uni. Ser., Ath.	Northumberland	28,902	13,131

Army and Navy, Brooks's.
b. 1831, s. 1860, m. 1863.
Served in Royal Navy (Commander), in Burmese War, China
War, and in the Baltic.

SYDNEY, Earl, G.C.B., Frognal, Foot's Cray, &c.

Coll. Eton, St. John's,	Kent . . .	2,165	4,301
Cambridge.	Gloucester . .	947	2,314
Club. Trav., Turf, White's.			
b. 1805, s. 1831, m. 1832.		3,112	6,615

Served as Groom in Waiting, Lord in Waiting, Captain of the
Yeomen of the Guard, and as Lord Chamberlain. Is Lord
Steward. Sat for Whitchurch.

SYKES, Christopher, of Brantinghamthorpe, Brough.

Coll. Trinity, Cambridge.	York, E.R.	3,032	4,541

Club. Carlton, White's, Marl., Boodle's.
b. 1831. Sat for Beverley. Sits for E. Riding.

SYKES, Sir Tatton, Bart., of Sledmere House, Malton.

Club. Carlton.	York, E.R.	34,010	35,870

b. 1826, s. 1863, m. 1874.

SYMONS, Mrs., of Mynde Park, Hereford.

s. 1868, m. 1864.	Hereford . .	6,056	5,089

** SYNNOT, Mark Seton, of Ballymoyer, Newtown-Hamilton,
Co. Armagh.

b. 1820, s. 1874, m. 1843.	Armagh . .	7,321	4,682

SYKES, Charles P., of West Ella. York .	2,736	4,301
SYNAN, E. J., of Ashbourne. Limerick .	2,808	2,368
SYNGE, A. Hamilton, Armagh	3,275	2,315
SYNGE (late), of Glanmore. Wick., Longford	5,962	2,425

** TAAFE, John, of Smarmore Castle, Ardee, Co. Louth.

		acres.	g. an. val.
Coll. Stonyhurst.	Louth . . .	1,277 .	1,415
Club. Stephen's Green,	King's Co. . .	1,769 .	777
Dublin.	Meath . . .	691 .	584
b. 1827, s. 1872, m. 1867.	Kildare . . .	587 .	460
	Galway . . .	823 .	333
		5,147 .	3,569

** TABOR, James, of Earl's Hall, Rochford.

Club. Reform.	Essex . . .	3,890 .	7,230

b. 1799, m. 1831.

All this property, except 400 acres, is entered in this return under the head of " Rewes, Jos.," of Prittlewell. The compiler was some months in discovering that there never was such a man, and the Local Government Board explain it as " a mistake of the copyist " for " Tabor, James "; if mistakes of this magnitude occur often, the value of the return would not be great.

*** TALBOT, Algernon Charles, of Aston Hall, Runcorn.

Coll. Lancing.	Cheshire . .	4,352 .	10,130

b. 1859, s. 187–.

This estate was originally 4,752 acres, but 400 acres and Aston Grange, together with half the rent roll, belong to Mr. Hervey Arthur Talbot, Mr. Talbot's uncle.

** TALBOT, Christopher Rice Mansel, of Margam Abbey, Taibach, South Wales, &c.

Coll. Harrow, Oriel, Oxon.	Glamorgan .	33,920 .	44,057

Club. Travellers'.
b. 1803, m. 1835.

Fully one-half this rental represents the profits of lessees of mines on this estate. Sits for Glamorganshire.

TALBOT de MALAHIDE. *See* " Malahide."

TAAFE, James, of Woodfield. Mayo . .	9,030 .	2,721
TALBOT, J. R. F. G., of Rhode Hill. Devon, Dorset, Westmeath	2,545 .	2,322
TALBOT, W., of Mt. Talbot. Rosc., Gal.	6,374 .	2,946

TANKERVILLE, Earl of, Chillingham Castle, Alnwick.

		acres.	g. an. val.
Coll. Har., Ch. Ch. Oxon.	Northumberland	28,930 .	31,416
Club. Carl., Whi., Trav.	Salop . . .	2,493 .	2,234
b. 1810, s. 1859, m. 1850.			
		31,423 .	33,650

Sat for Northumberland.
Was Capt. Hon. Corps of G.-at-Arms, and L. Steward.
Exclusive of 341 acres in Salop shared with C. S. Lloyd.

** TAYLEUR, John, of Buntingsdale Hall, Market Drayton.

Coll. Eton, Magd. Cam.	Salop . . .	5,917 .	9,317
Club. United University.	Stafford . . .	639 .	1,080
b. 1840, s. 1873, m. 1866.			
		6,556 .	10,397

TAYLEUR, ——, of Greenhill, Whitwick, Leicester.

	Leicester . .	1,807 .	2,125
	Devon . . .	1,654 .	2,369
		3,461 .	4,494

This estate is the subject of a Chancery suit.

** TAYLOR, Rt. Hon. Col., of Ardgillan Castle, Balbriggan, Co. Dublin, &c.

Coll. Eton.	Co. Meath .	9,000 .	6,227
Club. Carl., J. Carl., Trav.,	Co. Dublin .	805 .	1,004
White's, St. Ste.,	Co. Louth .	456 .	295
Sack. St.			
b. 1811, m. 1862. Sits for Co. Dublin.		10,261 .	7,526

Served in 6th Dragoon Guards, was a L. of the Treas., Sec. to
the Treas., and Chan. D. of Lancaster. A small property in
Galway is omitted.

* TAYLOR, James Arthur, of Strensham Court, Tewkesbury.

Coll. Winch., Trin. Cam.	Worcester . .	2,586 . .	5,782
Club. Union, Oxford and	Warwick . .	739 .	879
Cambridge.	Gloucester . .	600 .	638
b. 1817, s. 1832, m. 1843.			
Sat for E. Worcester.		3,925 .	7,299

TANNER, W. H., of Rockley. Wilts . . 2,526 . 2,116
⚲ TATTON, T., of Wythenshawe. Ches. 2,620 . 6,538

TAYLOR, Rev. Richard Edwards, of Moreton Hall, Clitheroe, &c.

Coll. Peterhouse, Cam.
Club. Oxford and Cam.
s. 1867.

		acres.	g. an. val.
Lancashire .	2,044 .	2,630
York, W.R. .	2,088 .	2,290
	4,132 .	4,920

** WATSON-TAYLOR, Simon, of Erlestoke, Westbury, &c.

Coll. Ch. Ch. Oxon.
Club. Boodle's, Carlton.
b. 1811, m. 1843. Sat for Devizes.

Wilts . . .	15,000 .	20,828

*** TAYLOR, Thomas, of Aston Rowant, Tetsworth.

Club. Reform.
b. 1810, m. 1857.

Lancashire .	4 .	6,101
Oxford . . .	7,185 .	10,257
Bucks . . .	839 .	1,207
	8,028 .	17,565

TAYLOR, Thomas, of Chipchase, Wark-on-Tyne, &c.

b. 1849, s. 1880, m. 1880.

Northumberland	10,844 .	9,582
Durham . .	404 .	3,731
	11,248 .	13,313

** TAYLOR, Thomas Edward, of Dodworth Hall, Barnsley, &c.

b. 1813, s. 1837 and 1870, m. 1837.

York, W.R. .	3,427 .	6,429
Notts . . .	1,352 .	1,905
	4,779 .	8,334

SHAWE-TAYLOR, Walter Taylor Newton, of Castle Taylor, Ardrahan, Co. Galway.

Coll. Harr., Trin. Cam.
Club. Kild. St. Dublin.
b. 1832, s. 1863, m. 1864.

Co. Galway .	7,679 .	3,046

TAYLOR, D. E., of Booth Hall. Cheshire, Lancashire, Gloucester . . . . . . 2,419 . 4,313

TAYLOR, G., of Kirktonhill. Kincardine . 2,489 . 2,505

* TAYLOR, William, of Holly Park, Adare.

			acres.	*g. an. val.*
Coll. Trin. Dublin.	Co. Limerick	.	3,239	.	3,138
b. 183–.				

Out of this Mr. Taylor's mother has 669 acres.

** TEMPEST, Sir Charles Henry, Bart., of Heaton, Lancashire, &c. (res. Ashby Lodge, Rugby).

			acres.	*g. an. val.*
Coll. Stonyhurst.	York, W.R.	.	4,216	.	5,000
Club. Arthur's.	Lincoln	. .	3,000	.	5,000
b. 1834, m. 1st 1862,	Lancashire	.	2,550	.	10,000
2nd 1874.			9,766	.	20,000

The return for Lancashire in this case ignores Sir C. Tempest's Baronetcy, a not uncommon thing in the returns for the Northern Counties. The first two estates belong to his eldest son.

VANE-TEMPEST, Lord Herbert Lionel.

b. 1862.	Co. Antrim	.	13,781	.	4,915

* HARRIS-TEMPLE, Hon. Robert Reginald Temple, of Waterston, Athlone.

Coll. Eton, Ch. Ch. Oxon. Co. Westmeath 4,863 . 3,327
Club. Travellers', St. Jas., Marlborough, Sackville St., Dublin.
b. 1830, s. 1852.

These figures are a good deal under the mark, as some of the tenants are returned as owners.

TEMPLEMORE, Lord, Preston Ho, Basingstoke, &c. ♘.

Coll. Eton, Ch. Ch. Oxon.	Hants	. .	2,543	.	2,308
Club. Carl., Trav., St. Ste.,	Wexford	. .	11,327	.	7,046
Sack. St.	Donegal	. .	10,856	.	7,055
b. 1821, s. 1837, m. 1st 1842,	Londonderry	.	1,890	.	979
2nd 1873.	Co. Down	. .	26	.	1,405
Served in 1st Life Guards.			26,642	.	18,793

TEMPEST, Miss, of Tong. York, Lanc.	2,847	.	5,255
TEMPLE, W., of Bishopstrow. Wilts .	2,310	.	2,677
TEMPLER, J. G. J., of Lindridge. Devon.	2,622	.	3,220

*** TEMPLETOWN, Viscount, K.C.B., Castle Upton, Temple-
patrick, Co. Antrim.

			acres.	g. an. val.
Coll.	Eton, Ch. Ch. Oxon.	Co. Antrim .	11,924 .	10,443
Club.	Guards, Uni. Ser.,	Monaghan .	12,845 .	8,774
	Carl., Trav., Sack.			
	Street, Dublin.		24,769 .	19,217

b. 1802, s. 1863, m. 1850.

Commanded the Coldstream Guards in the Crimea (wounded
at Inkerman), afterwards the 60th Rifles and 2nd Life Guards,
late General in Command of Southern and Western Districts. Sat
for Co. Antrim.

** TENNANT, Charles, of The Glen, Traquhair, N.B.

Club.	Brooks's, Reform.	Peebles . .	3,500 .	897
b. 1823, m. 1849.		Lanark . .	116 .	6,138
Sits for Peebles and Selkirk.				
			3,616 .	7,035

TENNANT, Robert, of Scarcroft Lodge, Leeds, &c.

Coll.	Leeds Gram. School.	Yorkshire . .	3,840 .	4,279
Club.	Carlton, Jun. Carl.	Argyll . . .	5,300 .	681
b. 1828, m. 1850.		Sutherland .	2,080 .	651
Sat for Leeds.				
			11,220 .	5,611

*** TEW, Percy (res. Heath Hall, Wakefield).

Coll.	Exeter, Oxon.	Sussex . . .	3,967 .	3,880

b. 1840, m. 1868.

*** THARP, William Montagu, of Chippenham Park, Soham.

Club.	Army and Navy.	Essex . . .	380 .	451
b. 1837, s. 1875, m. 1868.		Cambridge .	5,921 .	7,456
Served in 62nd Foot.		Suffolk . . .	4 .	128
			6,305 .	8,035

TENISON, W., of Shantony.	Monaghan .	2,696 .	2,013
TENNANT, J. R., of Kildwick.	York . .	3,726 .	2,063
TEULON, G. B., of Bandon.	Cork . . .	2,714 .	2,029

*** THELLUSSON, Charles Sabine Augustus, of Brodsworth
Hall, Doncaster.

		acres.	g. an. val.
Club. Army and Navy.	Wilts . . .	419 .	221
b. 1822, s. 1856, m. 1850.	York, N. and		
Served in 12th Lancers.	W.R. . .	7,875 .	12,714
	Northampton .	287 .	445
	Herts . . .	400 .	684
		8,981 .	14,064

** THISLETHWAYTE, Thomas, of Southwick Park, Farnham.

Coll. Eton, Ch. Ch. Oxon.	Hants . . .	8,084 .	9,929
Club. Arthur's. b. 1809, s. 1850, m. 1850.			

*** THOMAS, Miss, of Llwynmadoc, Builth, &c.

s. 1864.	Brecon . . .	9,235 .	3,417
	Radnor . . .	2,926 .	1,866
	Glamorgan .	2,095 .	4,759
		14,256 .	10,042

*** MEYSEY-THOMPSON, Sir Henry Meysey, Bart., of
Kirby Hall, York, &c.

Coll. Eton, Trin. Cam.	York, N. and		
Club. White's, Marl., Brooks's.	W.R. . .	5,623 .	10,600
b. 1845, s. 1874. Sat for Knaresborough.			

THOMPSON, Mrs., of Stobars, Kirkby-Stephen.

s. 1871, m. 1861.	Westmoreland	4,543 .	4,569

THEOBALD, Mrs., of Henley. Suf., Ess. .	2,026 .	3,553
*** THOMAS, E., of Welfield. Br., Rad., Ess.	5,472 .	2,243
THOMAS, Freeman, of Ratton. Sussex .	2,935 .	4,122
THOMAS, of Ystrad Mynach. Gla., Monm.	2,003 .	2,732
THOMAS, R. W., of Coedhelen. Carnarvon	2,320 .	4,357
GREEN-THOMPSON, A., of Bridekirk. Cum.	2,415 .	2,630
THOMPSON, S., of Muckamore. Ant., Don.	5,451 .	2,908

** ANSTRUTHER-THOMSON, JOHN, of Charleton, Colins-
    burgh, N.B., &c.

			acres.		g. an. val.
Coll. Eton.		Fife	4,034	.	7,505

Club. Boodle's, Army and Navy, New Edinburgh.
b. 1819, s. 1833, m. 1852.
    Served in 9th Lancers and 13th Light Dragoons.

THORNHILL, ARTHUR JOHN, of Diddington Hall, Buckden.

			acres.		g. an. val.
Coll. Eton, Trin. Cam.	Huntingdon .		2,372	.	3,718
Club. Jun. Carl., Boodle's,	Cambridge . .		2,060	.	2,213
Arthur's.	Bedford . . .		278	.	521
b. 1850, s. 1875.					
			4,710	.	6,452

* THORNHILL, THOMAS, of Riddlesworth Hall, East Harling,
    &c.

		acres.		g. an. val.
Coll. Eton, Trin. Cam.	Suffolk . . .	3,718	.	4,336
Club. Carl., Arthur's.	Norfolk . . .	2,545	.	1,911
b. 1837, s. 1875, m. 1863.				
Sits for W. Suffolk.		6,263	.	6,247

THORNHILL (late), William, of Stanton-in-the-Peak, Bake-
    well. ⚓.

		acres.		g. an. val.
d. 1875.	Derby . . .	5,564	.	6,779
	Kent . . .	845	.	1,228
		6,409	.	8,007

** CLARKE-THORNHILL, WILLIAM CAPEL, of Rushton Hall,
    Kettering.

		acres.		g. an. val.
Coll. Eton.	Northampton .	3,316	.	5,044
Club. Boodle's, Carlton,	York . . .	2,724	.	9,241
Arthur's, Army	Middlesex . .	350	.	689
and Navy, Gun.	Norfolk . . .	30	.	30
b. 1832, m. 1855.				
Served in 23rd Foot.		6,420	.	15,004

		acres.		g. an. val.
THOMPSON, THOMAS C., of Ashdown Park.				
Durham, Northumberland, Sussex, York		3,219	.	2,289
THOMPSON, WILLIAM, of Rathnally. Meath		2,154	.	2,225
THOMSON, M., of Balgowan. Perth . .		2,953	.	2,673
THOMSON, W., of Clooneavin. Down .		2,259	.	2,429

** THORNTON, Rev. Thomas Cooke, of Brockhall, Weedon.

			acres.		*g. an. val.*
Coll. Clare, Cambridge.	Northampton .		3,114	.	5,270
Club. United University.					

b. 1801, s. 1862.

** THOROLD, Sir John Henry, Bart., of Syston Park, Grantham. ♨.

Coll. Eton.	Lincoln .	. .	12,533	.	17,652
Club. Carlton.					

b. 1842, s. 1866, m. 1869.   Served in 17th Foot.   Sat for Grantham.

** MURRAY-THREIPLAND (late), Sir P., Bart., of Fingask, N.B.

d. 1882.	Caithness .	.	10,924	.	2,077
	Perth .	. .	2,814	.	3,019
			13,738	.	5,096

THROCKMORTON, Sir Nicholas William, Bart., of Coughton Court, Alcester, &c. ♨.

Club. Brooks's, Travellers',	Warwick .	.	7,618	.	9,918
Gun, St. James's.	Devon .	. .	6,589	.	4,706
b. 1838, s. 1862.	Worcester .	.	3,618	.	5,103
	Berks .	. .	3,008	.	4,539
	Bucks .	. .	1,552	.	2,826
			22,385	.	27,092

THORNTON, Miss, and THORNTON, Capt., of Milton Bryant. Beds, Hunts	2,197	.	2,673
THORPE, J., of Coddington. Notts, Argyll	2,573	.	2,537
THOYTS, William R. M., of Sulhampstead. Berks, Essex, Cheshire	2,719	.	4,531
THRING, T., of Alford House. Somerset.	2,325	.	3,983
THUNDER, Patrick, of Lagore. Meath, Westmeath, Dublin, Kildare	2,002	.	2,152

** THURLOW, LORD, Ashfield House, Ixworth, &c.

			acres.	g. an. val.
Club. Travellers', Brooks's.	Suffolk . . .		1,529 .	2,800
b. 1838, s. 1874, m. 1864.	Elgin . . .		10,518 .	1,650
	Stirling . . .		1,107 .	2,120
	Nairn . . .		'740 .	277
Is a Lord in Waiting.				
			13,894 .	6,847

Was Attaché at Stockholm, Paris, and Vienna, served on special missions to China and Washington, 2nd Sec. Leg. at the Hague, and Pr. Sec. to Gov.-Gen. of India. The Scottish estates belong to LADY THURLOW.

Exclusive of 258*l.* for mines.

** THWAITES, DANIEL, of Woodfold Park, Blackburn, &c.

			acres.	g. an. val.
Club. Carlton.	Lancashire .		2,177 .	21,328
b. 1817, m. 1859.	Leicester . .		2,392 .	3,500
Sat for Blackburn.			4,569 .	24,828

THYNNE, FRANCIS JOHN, of Haynes Park, Bedford, &c. ♠.

			acres.	g. an. val.
Coll. Balliol, Oxon.	Cornwall . .		10,224 .	7,451
Club. Travellers'.	Beds . . .		4,717 .	5,997
b. 1830, s. 1881, m. 1864.	Devon . . .		20 .	11
			14,961 .	13,459

*** DOUGHTY-TICHBORNE, SIR HENRY ALFRED JOSEPH, BART., of Tichborne Park, Alresford. ♠.

			acres.	g. an. val.
b. 1866, s. 1866.	Hants . . .		7,270 .	5,289
	Lincoln . . .		1,984 .	2,200
	Dorset . . .		1,092 .	556
	Bucks . . .		661 ,	671
			11,007 .	8,716

			acres.	g. an. val.
TIBBITS, J. B., of Barton Seagrave.	Nptn.		2,117 .	3,838
TICKELL, CAPTAIN THOMAS.	Kildare .		2,240 .	2,027

*** TIGHE, Frederick Edward Bunbury, of Woodstock, Kilkenny, &c. (res. The Priory, Christchurch, Hants).

		acres.	g. an. val.
Coll. Eton.	Co. Kilkenny .	11,970 .	5,332
Club. Travellers', Army and	Co. Westmeath	5,211 .	3,400
Navy.	Co. Carlow .	2,185 .	1,316
b. 1826, s. 1878, m. 1858.	Tipperary . .	1,803 .	1,426
Served in 53rd and 82nd	Wexford . .	591 .	196
Foot.	Co. Dublin .	3 .	219
		21,763 .	11,889

*** TISDALL, John, of Charlesfort, Kells, Co. Meath.

Coll. Trinity, Dublin.	Co. Meath .	3,962 .	4,130
Club. Sackville St. Dublin.	Limerick . .	493 .	343
b. 1815, s. 1836, m. 1837.	Kilkenny . .	575 .	355
		5,030 .	4,828

** WILSON-TODD, William Henry (*jure uxo.*), of Halnaby Hall, Croft, Darlington, &c.

Coll. Sandhurst.	York, E. and		
Club. Carlton, Ar. and Na.	N.R. . . .	4,440 .	5,400
b. 1828, m. 1855.	Lincoln . .	94 .	160
Served in 39th Foot.			
		4,534 .	5,560

** TOKE, John Leslie, of Godinton, Ashford (res. Heathcote, Frimley, Surrey).

Coll. Woolwich.	Kent . . .	3,171 .	4,392
Club. Jun. Uni. Ser.	Essex . . .	684 .	840
b. 1839, s. 1866, m. 1st 1864,			
2nd 1870.		3,855 .	5,232
Served in 96th and 2nd Foot.			

TIGHE, Lieut.-Colonel, of Rossanna. Wick.	3,459 .	2,538
TINDALL, J., of Kirby Misperton. York .	2,434 .	3,155

*** GRAHAM-TOLER, Hon. Otway Fortescue (res. Windsor House, Ryde), of Durrow Abbey, Tullamore.

		acres.		*g. an. val.*
Club. Arthur's.	Tipperary . .	8,789	.	5,317
b. 1824, s. 18—, m. 1846.	King's Co. .	4,524	.	2,526
Served in 8th Dragoons.	Queen's Co. .	3,076	.	1,881
	Westmeath .	142	.	187
		16,531	.	9,911

*** TOLLEMACHE of HELMINGHAM, Lord, Peckforton Castle, Tarporley, &c.

		acres.		*g. an. val.*
Club. Carlton, Arthur's.	Cheshire . .	28,651	.	33,614
b. 1805, m. 1st 1826,	Suffolk . .	7,010	.	9,568
2nd 1850.	Denbigh . .	35	.	77
Sat for S. Cheshire.	Flint . . .	30	.	86

Exclusive of tithes and of 3,200*l.* paid by Manchester for lands submerged by and surrounding the Corporation's reservoir.   35,726 . 43,345

** TOLLEMACHE, Wilbraham Spencer, of Dorfold Hall, Nantwich.

Coll. Westminster.	Cheshire . .	3,265	.	6,730

Club. National, Union. b. 1807, s. 1864, m. 1844.
Served in Rifle Brigade and Coldstream Guards.

TOMLINE, Colonel George, of Orwell Park, Woodbridge, &c.

Coll. Eton.	Suffolk . .	18,473	.	24,005
Club. Ath.,Trav.,Uni. Ser.,	Lincoln . .	8,439	.	11,534
Boodle's, White's.	Westmoreland	2	.	3

b. 1812. Figures said to be "Very wrong" by owner.   26,914 . 35,542
Sat for Sudbury, Shrewsbury, and Great Grimsby.

** TOTTENHAM, Arthur Loftus, of Glenfarne, Enniskillen.

Coll. Eton.	Co. Leitrim .	14,561	.	4,300
Club. Carl., Marl., Kild. St.	Co. Clare . .	257	.	131

b. 1838, s. 1851, m. 1859.
Sits for Co. Leitrim. Served in R. Brig.   14,818 . 4,431

TOMLINSON, W. H., of Kirby Lonsdale.
   York, Westmoreland, Lancashire . . .   2,047 . 2,873

TOTTENHAM, CHARLES, of Ballycurry, Ashford, Co. Wicklow.

		acres.		g. an. val.
Coll. Trinity, Cambridge.	Co. Wexford .	7,066	.	9,963
Club. Uni. University.	Co. Wicklow .	2,540	.	1,409
b. 1807, s. 1843, m. 1833.	Co. Sligo . .	1,631	.	912
Sat for New Ross.	Co. Carlow .	280	.	395
		11,517	.	12,679

*** TOTTENHAM, MAJOR, of Woodstock, Co. Wicklow, &c.

Coll. Eton, Ch. Ch. Ox.	Merioneth .	5,629	.	1,400
b. 1845, s. 1878, m. 1874.	Denbigh . .	2,601	.	1,322
Exclusive of mine rents.	Wexford . .	4,735	.	2,165
	Co. Wicklow .	660	.	791
		13,625	.	5,678

TOWER, CHRISTOPHER, of Huntsmore Park, Uxbridge, &c.

Coll. Harrow, Oriel, Oxon.	Essex . . .	2,481	.	4,092
Club. Boodle's.	Bucks . . .	2,034	.	4,308
b. 1804, s. 1867, m. 1836.	Bedford . .	424	.	520
Served in 7th Hussars.	Herts . . .	266	.	347
Sat for Bucks.	Middlesex . .	82	.	566
		5,287	.	9,833

The Essex and Beds properties belong to his eldest son.

** TOWNELEY, Daughters of the late JOHN (4), of Towneley, Burnley.

s. 1878.	York . . .	21,341	.	7,088
	Durham . .	2,826	.	5,236
		24,167	.	12,324

TOWNLEY, CHARLES WATSON, of Fulbourn Hall, Cambridge, &c.

Coll. Eton, Trin., Cam.	Norfolk . .	2,866	.	4,403
Club. Brooks's, Travellers'.	Cambridge .	797	.	1,112
b. 1824, s. 1855, m. 1851.	Huntingdon .	1	.	3
		3,664	.	5,518

TOOKER, W. H., of Hinton.	Hants, Som.	2,017	.	2,182

** TOWNSEND, Frederick, of Honington Hall, Shipton-on-Stour.

			acres.		g. an. val.
Coll.	Harrow, Trin. Cam.	Warwick . .	2,329	.	2,610
Club.	Arthur's.	Worcester . .	1,387	.	1,831

b. 1823, s. 1873, m. 1863.

		3,716	.	4,441

*** TOWNSHEND, Marquis, Rainham Hall, Fakenham, &c.

			acres.		g. an. val.
Coll.	Eton.	Norfolk . . .	18,343	.	20,717
Club.	Uni. Ser., Brooks's,	Herts . . .	1,565	.	1,645
	Garrick, Pall Mall,	Warwick . .	2	.	198
	Metropolitan.				

b. 1831, s. 1863, m. 1865.

		19,910	.	22,560

Was in the Foreign Office. Sat for Tamworth.
Exclusive of tithes and shooting rents, valued at about 1,000*l.*

** STEPHENS-TOWNSHEND, Maurice Fitzgerald, of Shana Court, Castle Townshend, Co. Cork, &c.

			acres.		g. an. val.
b. 1865, s. 1869.		Co. Kerry . .	8,000	.	1,892
		Co. Cork . .	12,665	.	6,794
		Gloucester . .	1,950	.	1,997

		22,615	.	10,683

TRAFFORD, Edward Southwell, of Honington Hall, Grantham (res. Wroxham, Norwich).

		acres.		g. an. val.
b. 1836, s. 1880, m. 1880.	Bucks . . .	569	.	543
	Lincoln . .	2,984	.	4,493
Part of the Cambridge-	Warwick . .	489	.	809
shire property is given	Sussex . . .	323	.	220
to "Trafford and	Cambridge .	232	.	438
Southwell" of	Norfolk . .	48	.	85
"Grantham."	York, W.R. .	33	.	79
	Kent . . .	332	.	358

		5,010	.	7,025

	acres.		g. an. val.
TOWNSEND, Rev. C. G., of Berwick Pl. Ess.	2,718	.	4,076
PAYNE-TOWNSHEND, H., of Edstaston.			
Cork, Salop, Gloucester	2,210	.	2,035
TOWNSHEND, J. H., of Myross. Cork .	6,083	.	2,139

** TRAFFORD, Edward William, of Wroxham Hall, Norwich.

			acres.	g. an. val.
Coll. Charter, Trin. Cam.	Norfolk	. .	5,624	14,567
Club. Orleans, Marlborough,	Lincoln	. .	1,331	1,915
Carlton, Turf.	Cambridge	.	155	477
b. 1809, s. 1852, m. 1st 1831,				
2nd 1840.			7,110	16,959

His eldest son owns 5,650*l.* of these rents, the total includes Mr. Trafford's share of an estate held jointly with Sir John Smith.

** TRAHERNE, John Popkin, of Coytrehen, Bridgend.

Coll. R.M.C. Sand. Glamorgan . 3,620 . 4,500
Club. Junior United Service.
b. 1826, s. 1859, m. 1852. Served in 39th Foot.

** TRAILL, James Christie, of Castle Hill, Caithness, N.B., &c.

Coll. St. John's, Oxon.	Caithness	. .	15,263	7,981
Club. United University.	Orkney .	. .	5,031	2,861
b. 1826, s. 1873, m. 1857.	Kent	. . .	170	710
			20,464	11,552

Exclusive of 1,713*l.* for quarries.

** TREDEGAR, Lord, Tredegar Park, Newport, Monmouth, &c.

Coll. Eton.	Monmouth	.	25,500	35,000
Club. Carl., Arm. and Nav.,	Glamorgan	.	6,157	10,000
Arthur's, Boodle's,	Brecon .	. .	7,300	8,000
St. Stephen's.	Kent	. . .	150	2,000
b. 1830, s. 1875.	Middlesex .	.	50	5,000
Served in 17th Lancers in the Crimea.				
Sat for Breconshire.			39,157	60,000

Exclusive of 254*l.* shared with "another."

TRANT, John, of Dovea.	Tipperary	. .	2,970	2,128
TREDENNICK, William, of Fortwilliam.				
Tyrone, Roscommon, Donegal	. . .	7,725	2,592

** SALUSBURY-TRELAWNY, Sir John, Bart., of Trelawne, Liskeard. §.

		acres.		*g. an. val.*
Coll. Westm., Trin. Cam.	Cornwall . .	8,000	.	6,000

Club. Reform.
b. 1816, s. 1856, m. 1842, 2nd 1881.
  Sat for Tavistock and E. Cornwall.

** TREMAYNE, Col. Arthur, of Carclew, Perranarworthal. §.

		acres.		*g. an. val.*
Coll. Eton, Ch. Ch. Oxon.	Cornwall . .	8,823	.	8,190

Club. Carlton, Army and Navy, Boodle's.
b. 1827, s. 1868, m. 1st 1858, 2nd 1870. Sits for Truro.
  Served in 13th Light Dragoons at Alma, Balaclava, and Sebastopol.

* TREMAYNE, John, of Heligan, St. Austell, &c. §.

		acres.		*g. an. val.*
Coll. Eton, Ch. Ch. Oxon.	Cornwall . .	5,316	.	9,137
Club. Carlton, Arthur's.	Devon . . .	5,951	.	4,860

b. 1825, s. 1851, m. 1860.

Sits for E. Cornwall.		11,267	.	13,997

  Exclusive of 41*l.* rental which Mr. Tremayne shares with "another." "Gross values altogether incorrect."—J. T.

** TRENCH, Henry Bloomfield, of Cangort, Roscrea, King's Co.

		acres.		*g. an. val.*
Club. Kildare St. Dub.	Tipperary . .	4,707	.	1,996
b. 1840, s. 1881, m. 1870.	King's Co. . .	2,113	.	1,758
	Limerick . .	1,926	.	821
	Co. Galway .	1,581	.	798
	Co. Clare . .	704	.	444
	Queen's Co. .	671	.	538
	Roscommon .	432	.	223
		12,134	.	6,578

TRELAWNY, C., of Coldrenick. Cornwall	2,524	.	3,181
TRENCH, C. O'Hara, of Clonfert. Galway	5,409	.	2,141
ASHFORDBY-TRENCHARD, J., of Nyn Park. Wilts, Herts, Gloucester, Oxon.	2,319	.	3,048
DILLON-TRENCHARD, H. L., of Lytchett. Dorset	2,895	.	3,584

** TREVELYAN, Sir Alfred Wilson, Bart., of Nettlecombe,
Taunton, &c.

		acres.		g. an. val.
b. 1802, s. 1879, m. 1835.	Northumberland	22,058	.	15,448
These figures represent	Somerset . .	6,361	.	7,309
the estate held by the	Devon . . .	565	.	1,551
late Bart. It is more than	Cornwall . .	126	.	155
probable that the first estate,				
or most of it, belongs to Sir		29,110	.	24,463
Chas. Trevelyan, Bart.				

** CELY-TREVILIAN, John Raymond, of Debden Hall,
Saffron Walden.

Coll. Winch., Sandhurst.   Essex . . .   4,337 .   4,500
Club. Naval and Military.
m. 1871.   Served in 3rd Foot (the Buffs).

Debden is now (1882) in the market.

*** TREVOR, Lord, Brynkinalt, Chirk, N. Wales.

Coll. Eton, Ball. Oxon.	Co. Down . .	11,010	.	9,142
Club. Carlton, Jun. Carl.,	Co. Antrim .	8,372	.	2,669
Boodle's, Sack. St.,	Co. Armagh .	1,219	.	1,471
Ulster, Belfast.	Salop . . .	1,743	.	1,669
b. 1819, m. 1st 1848,	Flint	954	.	1,263
2nd 1858.	Denbigh . .	396	.	1,486
Sat for Co. Down.				
		23,694	.	17,700

*** TRIMLESTON (late), Lord, Trimleston Castle, Co. Meath,
&c.

d. 1879.	Co. Meath . .	3,025	.	3,397
His only dau. m. 1868	King's Co. . .	2,496	.	2,171
R. H. Elliot of Clifton,	Co. Dublin .	1,238	.	2,088
whom see.				
		6,759	.	7,656

$ TREVELYAN, Thornton Roger, of
Netherwhitton.   Northumberland . .   2,604 .   2,601

** TROTTER, Lieut.-Col., of Mortonhall, Liberton, N.B., &c.

		acres.	g. an. val.
Coll. Harrow.	Berwick . .	6,796 .	12,737
Club. Guards.	Midlothian . .	2,515 .	7,047
b. 1844, s. 1874, m. 1866.			
Serves in Gren. Guards		9,311 .	19,784
as Capt. and Lt.-Col.			

** TROYTE, Chas. Arthur Williams, of Huntsham, Bampton.

Coll. Radley, Trin. Hall,	Devon . . .	6,627 .	7,408
Cam.	Somerset . .	180 .	260
Club. Carl., Ox. and Cam.			
b. 1842, s. 1857, m. 1864.		6,807 .	7,668

** TRYON, Colonel Thomas, of Bulwick Park, Wansford.

Coll. Eton.	Northampton .	4,706 .	8,529
Club. Army and Navy, Carlton.			
b. 1830, s. 1872, m. 1873.			
Served in 7th Foot.			

TUFNELL, John Jolliffe, of Langleys, Chelmsford.

Coll. Har., Oriel, Oxon.	Essex . . .	6,582 .	9,057
Club. Arthur's.	York, W.R. .	998 .	1,312
b. 1805, s. 1864, m. 1st 1830,	Suffolk . . .	4 .	8
2nd 1853.		7,584 .	10,377

** TURBERVILLE, Col., of Ewenny Priory, Bridgend.

Coll. Woolwich.	Glamorgan .	3,274 .	4,811
Club. U. Ser., J. U. Ser.			
b. 1827, s. 1867, m. 1857.	Served in Royal Artillery.		

TUCKER, Charles, of Coryton. Devon .	2,010 .	2,431
TUCKER, of Pavenham. Beds., Berks . .	2,733 .	4,818
TUDWAY, C. C., of Stoberry. Somerset .	2,827 .	4,511
TULL, A. R., of Crookham. Berks . . .	2,001 .	3,222

** TURBUTT, WILLIAM GLADWIN, of Ogston Hall, Alfreton.

			acres.		g. an. val.
Coll. Har., Ch. Ch.	Derby	. . .	2,974	.	4,780
Oxon.	Kent	. . .	240	.	246
Club. Windham.	Notts	. . .	9	.	74
b. 1853, s. 1872, m. 1879.					
			3,223	.	5,100

** TURNBULL, WILLIAM, of Briery Yards, Hawick, N.B., &c.

Coll. Penrith School.	Roxburgh	. .	2,482	.	2,262
b. 1806, s. 1873, m. 1833.	Selkirk	. . .	6,440	.	1,980
			8,922	.	4,242

** PAGE-TURNER (Devisees of the late), SIR E. H., BART., of Battlesden Park, Bedford.

Coll. St. Paul's Sch.	Bedford	. .	2,665	.	4,500
b. 1845, s. 1864, m. 1874.	Oxon . .⎫				
	Middlesex . ⎭		4,000	.	5,500
			6,665	.	10,000

In ultimate remainder MR. F. A. BLAYDES.

** TURNOR, CHRISTOPHER, of Stoke Rochford, Grantham.

Coll. Eton, Trin. Cam.	Lincoln	. .	20,664	.	27,513

Club. Carlton. b. 1809, s. 1829, m. 1837. Sat for S. Lincoln.

*** TURTON, EDMUND HENRY, of Upsall Castle, Thirsk, &c.

Coll. Eton.	York, N.R.	.	9,887	.	5,649

Club. Reform, Army and Navy.
b. 1825, s. 1857, m. 1856.
Served in 3rd Dragoon Gds. Including 3,909 acres of moors.

TURNBULL, J., of Abbey St. Bathans. Ber.	4,842	.	2,525
POLHILL-TURNER, F., of Howbury. Beds.	2,625	.	3,593
TURNER, JOHN, of Turner Hall. Aberdeen	2,970	.	3,087
TURNLY, R. A., of Drumnasole. Antrim .	6,503	.	2,475
** TURTON, R. B., of Kildale Hall. York	3,792	.	2,425

*** TWEEDALE, Marquis of, Yester House, Haddington,
    N.B., &c.   *acres.*   *g. an. val.*

		acres.	g. an. val.
Coll. Haileybury.	Berwick . .	18,116 .	9,572
Club. Brooks's, City Liberal.	Haddington .	20,486 .	11,485
b. 1826, s. 1878, m. 1878.	Roxburgh . .	4,505 .	4,974
	Fife	400 .	249
	Kent . . .	10 .	250
Was in the Bengal Civil Service.			
Sat for Taunton and for Haddington.		43,517 .	26,530

Exclusive of 815*l.* for mines.

*** TWEEDIE, James (of Quarter), of Rachan, Biggar, N.B., &c.

Coll. Edin. University.	Peebles . . .	13,151 .	4,691
Club. Cons., U. S., and Cons. Ed.			

b. 1831, s. 1856, m. 1863.
Served in 80th and 22nd Foot in the Burmese War (medal).

*** TWEEDMOUTH, Lord, Guisachan, Beauly, N.B., &c.

Club. Arth., Trav., Bro.	Inverness . .	19,186 .	1,429
b. 1820, m. 1848.	Berwick . .	4,060 .	7,717
Sat for Berwick-on-Tweed.			
		23,246 .	9,146

** KEMEYS-TYNTE, Col., of Halswell, Bridgwater, &c.

Coll. Eton.	Glamorgan .	9,716 .	22,949
Club. Brooks's, Trav., Uni.	Monmouth .	4,753 .	4,871
Ser., Boodle's.	Somerset . .	4,707 .	7,516
b. 1800, s. 1860, m. 1st 1821,	Leicester . .	699 .	1,757
2nd 1841.	Hereford . .	716 .	455
Sat for W. Somerset and	Brecon . . .	88 .	18
for Bridgwater.			
		20,679 .	37,566

TWISS, G., of Birdhill.	Tipperary, Cork .	3,518 .	2,078
TYLER, C., of Cottrell.	Gla., Monm. . .	2,221 .	2,594

PRATT-TYNTE, JOSEPH, of Tynte Park, Dunlavin, Co. Wicklow, &c.

Club. Kildare St. Dublin.
b. 1815, m. 1840.

	acres.	g. an. val.
Wicklow . .	2,532 .	2,186
Dublin . . .	1,047 .	1,163
Co. Cork . .	1,254 .	987
Kilkenny . .	150 .	261
Leitrim . . .	30 .	80
	5,013 .	4,677

*** TYRELL, CHARLES, of Plashwood, Haughley, Stowmarket.

Coll. Emman. Cam.
Club. Uni. Univ. b. 1805, s. 1872.

Suffolk . . .	3,462 .	4,534

Mr. TYRELL'S family have held lands in Suffolk prior to Henry VII.

** TUFNELL-TYRELL, JOHN LIONEL, of Boreham House, Chelmsford.

Coll. Harrow.
Club. Carlton, Army and Navy, Grafton.
b. 1842, s. 1877, m. 1878. Served in the Rifle Brigade.

Essex . . .	3,078 .	4,840

* TYRINGHAM, ROGER WILLIAM GIFFARD, of Tyringham, Newport-Pagnell, &c.

b. 1870, s. 1870.

Bucks . . .	4,161 .	8,394
Cornwall . .	3,509 .	6,459
Bedford . .	87 .	88
	7,757 .	14,941

TYRWHITT, SIR HENRY THOMAS, BART., of Stanley Hall, Bridgnorth, &c.

Club. Junior Carlton.
b. 1824, s. 1839, m. 1853.
Served in Rifle Brigade.

Salop . . .	4,949 .	6,903
Montgomery .	702 .	1,196
Norfolk . .	238 .	346
	5,889 .	8,445

See "TYRWHITT-WILSON" for the Berners property.

UNTHANK, C., of Intwood, Norfolk . .	2,416 .	3,644
UPTON, L., of Glyde. Louth, Herts . .	2,382 .	2,903

** FRASER-TYTLER, EDWARD GRANT, of Aldourie, Inverness, N.B., &c.

		acres.	*g. an. val.*
Club. Junior Carlton.	Elgin . . .	1,310 .	1,812
b. 1856, s. 1881, m. 1881.	Inverness . .	15,978 .	3,150
		17,288 .	4,962

** UDNY, JOHN HENRY FULLARTON, of Udny Castle, Aberdeen, N.B., &c.

Coll. Eton, Trin. H. Cam.	Aberdeen . .	9,225 .	9,041
Club. Road, Beac.			
b. 1853, s. 1861, m. 1874.			

** UPCHER, HENRY RAMEY, of Sheringham Hall, Cromer.

Coll. Harrow, Trin. Cam.	Norfolk . . .	3,748 .	2,609
b. 1810, s. 1819, m. 1838.	Bedford . .	945 .	1,586
		4,693 .	4,195

This includes 2,010 acres in Norfolk, handed over during lifetime by his father-in-law (REV. E. B. SPARKE) to MR. U.'s eldest son, MR. S., however, retaining estates in Suffolk, Norfolk, and Leicester amounting to 1,667 acres, rented at 2,887*l.*

*** UPTON, GEN. HON. ARTHUR, of Levens Hall, Milnthorpe.

Club. United Service.	Westmoreland	9,252 .	5,300
b. 1807, s. 1877, m. 1866.	Commanded 107th Foot.		

*** URQUHART, BEAUCHAMP COLCLOUGH, of Byth, Turriff, N.B., &c.

Coll. Addiscombe.	Aberdeen . .	5,837 .	6,707
Club. Oriental, Uni. Ser., Ed.			
b. 1830, s. 1861, m. 1856.	Served in the Indian Army.		

*** POLLARD-URQUHART, FRANCIS EDWARD ROMULUS, of Craigston Castle, Turriff, N.B.

Coll. R.M.A. Woolwich.	Aberdeen . .	3,998 .	3,096
Club. Junior United Ser.	Banff . . .	16 .	22
b. 1848, s. 1873.			
Serves in the Royal Horse Artillery.		4,014 .	3,118

** POLLARD-URQUHART, Walter William Dutton, of Kinturk, Castle Pollard, Co. Westmeath.

			acres.		*g. an. val.*
Coll.	S. John's, Oxon.	Co. Westmeath	5,363	.	3,955
Club.	Oxford and Cam.	Co. Meath .	558	.	637
	Arthur's, Kild. St. Dublin.	Co. Dublin .	172	.	190
b. 1847, s. 1871.			6,093	.	4,782

*** USBORNE, Thomas Masters, of Blackrock, Co. Cork.

				acres.		*g. an. val.*
Coll.	Maidstone School.	Co. Kerry . .		2,566	.	2,300
Club.	Co. Cork.	Co. Cork . .		616	.	1,324
b. 1812, s. 1851, m. 1837.		Co. Clare . .		842	.	365
		Essex . . .		130	.	1,419
				4,154	.	5,408

The English property stands in his eldest son's name.

UTHWATT, Mrs., of Maids Moreton House, Buckingham, &c.

		acres.		*g. an. val.*
s. 1877, m. 1835.	Bucks . . .	2,486	.	5,263
	Lancashire . .	1,171	.	1,159
		3,657	.	6,422

** VALENTIA, Viscount, Bletchingdon Park, Oxford. $.

			acres.		*g. an. val.*
Club.	Carl., Sack. St. Dub.,	Oxford . . .	3,207	.	5,238
	White's, Arthur's.	Northampton .	1,139	.	2,406
b. 1843, s. 1863, m. 1878.		Somerset . .	9	.	25
Served in 10th Hussars.		Co. Kildare .	2,695	.	1,215
			7,050	.	8,884

VANDELEUR, Hector Stewart, of Kilrush, Co. Clare.

			acres.		*g. an. val.*
Coll.	Eton.	Co. Clare . .	19,790	.	11,216
Club.	Kild. St. Dublin.	Limerick . .	416	.	380
b. 1836, s. 1881, m. 1867.					
Served in R. Brigade.			20,206	.	11,596

VAIZEY, John Robert, of Attwoods. Essex	2,127	.	3,469
VALPY, R., of Enborne. Berks, Som. . .	2,100	.	2,617

VANE, Sir Henry Ralph Fletcher, Bart., of Hutton-in-the-Forest, Penrith. ♜.

	acres.	g. an. val.
Coll. Ch. Ch. Oxon. Cumberland .	7,194 .	5,102

Club. Arthur's, Carlton. b. 1830, s. 1842, m. 1871.

VANSITTART, Coleraine Robert, of Shottesbrooke Park, Maidenhead, &c.

		acres.	g. an. val.
Club. Gun, Army and Navy.	Berks . . .	2,361 .	10,393
b. 1833, s. 1859.	Kent . . .	949 .	2,904
Served in 11th Hussars.			
		3,310 .	13,297

Part of this property stands in the name of his father, who died 1859.

** VAUDREY, William, of Colbury Manor, Eling, Southampton.

		acres.	g. an. val.
b. 18—, s. 18—, m. 187–.	Hants . . .	2,817 .	3,346
	Cheshire . .	297 .	343
		3,114 .	3,689

The Hampshire estate, which belongs to Mrs. Vaudrey, is "upwards of 3,000 acres, including 183 acres of foreshore."

** WILLIAMS-VAUGHAN, John, of Velinnewydd, Brecon, &c.

		acres.	g. an. val.
b. 1810, m. 1845.	Radnor . . .	2,610 .	1,616
	Brecon . . .	2,703 .	2,156
	Hereford . .	20 .	30
	Monmouth . .	17 .	12
		5,350 .	3,814

** VAUGHAN, John, of Nannau, Dolgelly, North Wales.

		acres.	g. an. val.
b. 1829, s. 1874, m. 1863.	Merioneth . .	16,443 .	4,300
	Salop . . .	145 .	220
		16,588 .	4,520

VAUGHAN, Rev. Dr., of Court Field.

	acres.	g. an. val.
Hereford, Monmouth	2,520 .	3,556

** HUTCHINSON-LLOYD-VAUGHAN, William Peisley, of
Golden Grove, Roscrea, King's Co.

		acres.		g. an. val.
Coll. St. John's, Cam.	King's Co. . .	5,867	.	2,645
Club. Sackville St. Dublin.	Tipperary . .	899	.	472
b. 1844, s. 1854, m. 1869.	Carlow . . .	980	.	951
	Westmeath . .	868	.	236
	Tyrone . . .	260	.	124
	Dublin . . .	200	.	175
		9,074	.	4,603

VAVASOUR, Sir Edward, Bart., of Hazlewood, Tadcaster. ♨.

b. 1815, s. 1847.	Yorkshire . .	4,666	.	5,434
	Stafford . .	3,814	.	4,846
		8,480	.	10,280

VENTRY, Lord, Burnham House, Dingle, Co. Kerry.

Club. Carlton, St. James's.	Co. Kerry . .	93,629	.	17,067
b. 1828, s. 1868, m. 1860.				

*** HOPE-VERE, Jas. Charles, of Blackwood, Lanark, N.B., &c.

Coll. Harrow.	Lanark . . .	6,440	.	5,676
Club. Arthur's.	Linlithgow . .	1,160	.	3,083
b. 1858, s. 1872, m. 1879.	Midlothian . .	689	.	2,575
		8,289	.	11,334

Exclusive of woodland acreage and a mine rental of 4,615*l.*

VERNER, Sir William Edward Hercules, Bart., of Church-
hill, Moy, Co. Armagh, &c.

b. 1855, s. 1873, m. 1877.	Co. Tyrone .	16,042	.	6,622
	Armagh . . .	5,436	.	4,043
	Monaghan . .	2,526	.	2,021
	Co. Wicklow .	140	.	124
	Co. Dublin .	113	.	328
		24,257	.	13,138

VAUX OF HARROWDEN, Lord. West-
meath, Kilkenny, Meath . . . . .   4,323 . 2,401

WHYTE-VENABLES, Mrs., of Redhills,
Cavan, Tyrone . . . .   3,329 . 2,297

** VERNEY, SIR HARRY, BART., of Claydon House, Winslow, Bucks.

		acres.	g. an. val.
Coll. Har., Sandhurst,	Hants . . .	650 .	736
Downing, Cam.	Derby . . .	1,140 .	1,856
Club. Travellers', Uni. Ser.	Bucks . . .	6,890 .	11,500
b. 1801, s. 1826, m. 1st 1835,	Anglesea . .	5,078 .	3,516
2nd 1858.			
		13,758 .	17,608

Served in 7th Foot and Gren. Guards; was Attaché at Stutgardt. Sat for Buckingham and for Bedford. Sits for Buckingham.

LADY VERNEY holds the two first properties; the Welsh estate belongs to his son, and is uncorrected.

** HARCOURT-VERNON, REV. EVELYN HARDOLPH, of Grove Hall, Retford.

Coll. Univ. Oxon.	Notts . . .	3,886 .	4,987
b. 1821, s. 1879, m. 1849.			

** VERNON, HARRY FOLEY, of Hanbury Hall, Droitwich.

Coll. Harrow, Magd. Oxon.	Worcester . .	7,447 .	12,828

Club. Ox. and Cam., Brooks's.
b. 1834, s. 1859, m. 1861. Sat for E. Worcestershire.

** VERNON, HENRY CHAS., of Hilton Park, Wolverhampton. 🌳

Club. Hanover Square.	Stafford . .	4,650 .	4,000
b. 1805, s. 1861, m. 1828.			

VERNON, LORD, Sudbury Hall, Derby. 🌳

Club. Travellers', White's.	Derby . . .	6,154 .	10,919
b. 1829, s. 1866, m. 1851.	Cheshire . .	2,578 .	10,983
Served in Scots Fusilier	Stafford . .	1,069 .	2,571
Guards. " Grossly wrong."—LD. V.			
		9,801 .	24,473

VERULAM, EARL OF, Gorhambury, St. Alban's.

Coll. Harrow, Ch. Ch. Ox.	Herts . . .	8,625 .	11,919
Club. Carlton.	Essex . . .	1,492 .	2,182
b. 1809, s. 1845, m. 1844.			
Served as Lord in Waiting.		10,117 .	14,101
Sat for St. Albans, Newport, and Herts.			

VERSCHOYLE, J., of Saggard. Dub., Sli.,

Don.	. 2,708 .	3,999

COLTHURST-VESEY, Col., of Lucan House, Dublin.

			acres.		*g. an. val.*
Club. Union, Kild. St. Dub.	Kildare	. .	2,778	.	1,529
b. 1826, m. 1858.	Co. Dublin	.	1,523	.	2,609
Served in 81st Foot.					
			4,301	.	4,138

** VILLIERS, Frederick Ernest (*iure uxo.*), of Closeburn, Thornhill, N.B. ♨.

Club. Brooks's, Whi., Marl.	Dumfries	. .	13,573	.	11,298
b. 1840, m. 1869.					

Serves in H.M. Body Guard of Scottish Archers.

Shared with Mrs. Villiers's sister, Viscountess Cole.

VIVIAN, Lord, Glynn, Bodmin, &c.

Club. Brooks's, Uni. Ser.,	Cornwall	. .	3,686	.	3,790
Boodle's.	Anglesea	. .	3,721	.	3,167
b. 1808, s. 1842, m. 1st 1833,	Flint	. . .	695	.	1,737
2nd 1841.	Denbigh	. .	167	.	25
Served in 7th Light Dragoons.					
Sat for Bodmin.			8,269	.	8,719

*** VINER, Henry Frederick Clare, of Newby Hall, Ripon.

Coll. Eton.	Lincoln	. .	14,443	.	18,544
Club. Travellers', Brooks's.	Yorkshire	. .	9,039	.	13,775
b. 1836, s. 1861 and 1872.	Cheshire	. .	3,223	.	5,374
The Yorkshire estate, except 496 acres,					
belongs to Lady Mary Viner.			26,705	.	37,693

VESEY, G., of Derrynabui. Galway, Mayo .	8,288	.	2,951
VICKERS, Valentine, of Offley Grove.			
Montgomery, Salop, Staffordshire . . .	2,845	.	3,823
VILLEBOIS, Henry, of Marham. Norfolk	2,370	.	2,171
VILLIERS, Hon. C. P., of Hamels Pk. Herts	2,049	.	3,025

*** HOWARD-VYSE, Howard Henry, of Stoke Place, Slough.

			acres.		g. an. val.
Coll. Eton.	Northampton	.	1,464	.	3,027
Club. White's, Turf, Jun.	Suffolk . .	.	1,171	.	1,401
Carl., Beaconsfield.	Bucks . .	.	244	.	866
b. 1858, s. 1872.	Cheshire .	.	267	.	416
	Warwick .	.	90	.	5,437
Serves in R.H. Gds.	Stafford .	.	52	.	143
			3,288	.	11,290

VYVYAN, Rev. Sir Vyell Donnithorne, Bart., of Trelo-
warren, Helstone. 🐚.

b. 1826, s. 1879, m. 1857.	Cornwall . .	9,738	.	18,147

WADDINGHAM, John, of Hafod, Aberystwith, &c.

b. 1799, m. 1837.	Cardigan . .	10,963	.	1,638
	Gloucester . .	1,969	.	2,410
Excl. of about 2,000 ac.	Montgomery .	402	.	14
of woods on the Hafod estate.				
		13,334	.	4,062

WADE, Robert Craven, of Clonebraney, Crossakiel, Co. Meath.

Club. Sackville St. Dublin.	Co. Meath . .	5,174	.	4,593
b. 1800, s. 1864.	Wicklow . .	4,055	.	3,694
	Louth . . .	367	.	284
		9,596	.	8,571

*** WAITHMAN, Robert William, of Moyne, Ballyglunin,
Co. Galway, &c.

Club. Uni. Ser. Dublin,	Co. Galway .	4,568	.	2,042
Reform.	Roscommon .	4,631	.	1,935
b. 1828, m. 1851.				
		9,199	.	3,977

This represents the Govt. valuation, the real gross rental was,
in 1879, nearly 6,000*l.*

WAKE, Sir Herewald, Bt., of Courteenhall, Northampton. 🐚.

Coll. Eton.	Northampton .	1,629	.	2,797
Club. Gun, Arthur's,	Essex . . .	1,512	.	3,013
Brooks's.				
b. 1852, s. 1865, m. 1874.		3,141	.	5,810

WADDINGTON, H., of Cavenham. Suff.,

Cam.	2,934	.	2,728

*** WAKEFIELD, WILLIAM HENRY, of Sedgwick, Kendal.

		acres.	g. an. val.
Club. Reform.	Westmoreland	6,024 .	8,335
b. 1828, s. 1866, m. 1851.	Lancashire .	993 .	1,181
	York, W.R. .	72 .	180
		7,089 .	9,696

WALDEGRAVE (late), COUNTESS, and CARLINGFORD, LORD, Dudbrooke House, Navestock, Essex, &c. ⚓.

Coll. Ch. Ch. Oxon.	Sussex . . .	2,357 .	3,552
Club. Athenæum, Brooks's,	Somerset . .	5,321 .	9,380
Reform.	Essex . . .	5,108 .	6,009
b. 1823, s. (to the English	York, E.R. .	416 .	640
property) 1879, m. 1863.	Middlesex . .	85 .	1,612
	Co. Louth . .	1,452 .	1,719
	Co. Carlow .	686 .	583
		15,425 .	23,495

Served as L. of the Treas., U. Sec. for Colonies, Ch. Sec. for Ireland, and Pres. of the B. of Trade. Is L. P. Seal. Sat for Co. Louth.

*** WALDRON, PATRICK JOHN, of Helen Park, Killenaule, &c.

Coll. Ch. Ch. Oxon.	Tipperary . .	4,060 .	3,426
Club. Jun. United Service,	Co. Mayo . .	837 .	490
Kildare St. Dublin.	Roscommon .	510 .	420
b. 1850, s. 1875.	Kilkenny . .	460 .	418
Serves in 6th Dragoons			
(Inniskillings).		5,867 .	4,754

WAKEFIELD, T. C., K. & Q. Cos. Arm., Kild.	3,527 .	2,544
WAKEFIELD, W., of Birklands. Wmld., Cum.	2,186 .	2,495
WAKEMAN, SIR OFFLEY, BART., of Rorrington. Salop, Montgomery	2,426 .	3,252
WAKEMAN, E., of Coton. Sal., Wor. . .	2,566 .	2,989
MEADE-WALDO, E., of Stonewall. Kent	2,798 .	3,837

** WALES, H.R.H., The Prince of, K.G., G.C.S.I., G.C.B., K.T., K.P., Sandringham Hall, King's Lynn, &c.

			acres.		g. an. val.
Coll.	Tr.Cam., Ch.Ch.Ox.	Aberdeen . .	6,810	.	816
Club.	Marl., Trav., U.S.,	Norfolk . .	8,079	.	8,911
	A. & N., White's,				
	Garrick.		14,889	.	9,727

b. 1841, m. 1863. Is a Field Marshal in the Army.

The Duchy of Cornwall extends over parts of seven counties, the acreage being 74,113, and the (nominal) rental 37,509*l.*, inclusive of 4,611 acres entered under the Prince's name; but it must be remembered that in the return of 1874 lead mines being unrated were unentered. The chief value of the Duchy is in its Devon and Cornwall mines, of which the very best are workings on lead.

** SUTHERLAND-WALKER, Evan Charles, of Skibo Castle, Sutherland, N.B., &c.

Club.	Windham.	York, W.R.	.	572	.	2,792
b. 1835, m. 1859.		Sutherland	.	20,000	.	3,231
		Inverness . .		6,500	.	684
				27,072	.	6,707

WALKER, Col. Geo. Gustavus, of Crawfordton, Thornhill, N.B., &c.

Coll.	Rugby, Ball. Oxon.	Inverness . .	70,940	.	3,341
Club.	Carlton.	Dumfries . .	7,146	.	3,478
b. 1831, m. 1856.		Kirkcudbright	353	.	64
Sat for Dumfrieshire.			78,439	.	6,883

WINDHAM-WALKER, Mrs., of Hanworth Hall, Cromer.

s. 1866, m. 1st 1861,	Norfolk . .	6,483	.	8,736
2nd 1868.				

WALKER, James, of Terrington.	Norfolk .	2,180	.	3,416
WALKER, J. W. M., of Hawkhills.	York .	2,301	.	2,478
CASE-WALKER, T. E., of Blythe.	Notts .	2,373	.	4,212
WALKER, W., of Bowland. Mid., Selk., Pee.,				
Rox.		3,749	.	2,034

** WALKER, Sir James, Bart., of Sand Hutton, York, &c.

			acres.		g. an. val.
Coll.	Rugby, Trin. Oxon.	York, N. & E.R.	5,819	.	9,765
Club.	United University.	Bucks . . .	795	.	1,394
b. 1803, s. 1829, m. 1st 1829,		Lancashire .	241	.	2,717
	2nd 1833.	Derby . . .	51	.	106

		6,906	.	13,982

WALKER, Thomas, of Berkswell Hall, Coventry.

b. 1817, s. 1848, m. 1840.	Warwick . .	6,117	.	9,755
	Salop . . .	1,477	.	1,904
	Stafford . .	unstated	.	199

		7,594	.	11,858

About half the Warwick property belongs to his eldest son, Mr. T. E. Walker, of Studley Castle.

** WALLACE, Sir Richard, Bart., K.C.B., of Sudbourn Hall, Wickham Market, &c.

Club.	Carl., Marlborough,	Suffolk . . .	11,224	.	11,253
	St. Stephen's, Sack-	Cambridge .	25	.	295
	ville St. Dublin.	Co. Antrim .	58,365	.	67,945
b. 1818, s. 1870, m. 1839.		Do. Down .	2,693	.	6,244
Sits for Lisburn.					

		72,307	.	85,737

** WALLER, Edmund, of Farmington Lodge, Northleach, &c.

Coll.	Brasenose, Oxon.	Gloucester .	4,104	.	4,472
Club.	Arthur's, Cons.	York, N.R. .	2,800	.	3,500
b. 1828, s. 1869, m. 1859,					
	2nd 1878.		6,904	.	7,972

The property in York is given to Edmund "Walker" in the return.

WALL, Rev. G., of Ballingarry. Tipperary .	2,437		2,042
WALL, Rev. W., of Powick. Here., Wor. .	2,387	.	4,073
WALLACE, H. R. C., of Busbie. Ayr . .	3,200	.	2,833
HOPE-WALLACE, J., of Featherstone. Nbld.	6,591	.	2,605

*** WALLER, Rev. John Thomas, of Castletown Manor, Pallaskenry, Co. Limerick.

acres. g. an. val.

Coll. Trinity, Dublin.　　Limerick . .　6,996　.　5,929
Club. Kild. Street, Dublin.
b. 1827, s. 1863, m. 1855.

*** WALROND, Sir John Walrond, Bart., of Bradfield, Collumpton. ♉.

Club. Carlton.　　　　　Devon . . .　3,645　.　6,464
b. 1818, s. 1851, m. 1845.
　　　　　　Sat for Tiverton.

Exclusive of 3,400 acres and 2,900*l.* rental returned as belonging to his eldest son's wife.

*** WALSINGHAM, Lord, Merton Hall, Thetford, &c. ♉.

Coll. Eton, Trin. Cam.	Norfolk . .	12,120	. 10,426
Club. Carlton, White's.	York, N. and		
b. 1843, s. 1870, m. 1877.	W.R. . .	5,590	. 4,416
Served as Lord in Waiting.	Suffolk . . .	1,075	. 1,336
Sat for W. Norfolk.	Huntingdon .	363	. 400
		19,148	. 16,578

The last property belongs to the Dowager Lady Walsingham.

** WALTER, John, of Bearwood, Wokingham.

Coll. Eton, Exeter, Oxon.　Berks . . .　7,054　.　9,728
Club. Reform, City.
b. 1818, s. 1847, m. 1st 1842, 2nd 1861.
　　　　Sat for Nottingham.　Sits for Berks.

WALLER, Sir E. A., Bart., of Newport. Tipp., Mayo, Limerick, Cork, Kildare .	4,328	. 2,175
WALLER, W. N., of Allenstown.　Meath .	2,687	. 2,642
WALLIS, H. A. B., of Drishane.　Cork　.	5,000	. 2,444
JOHNSON-WALSH, Sir J. Allen, Bart., of Ballykilcavan.　Queen's Co., Dublin	2,132	. 2,681

*** WALTON, James, of Dolforgan, Newtown, Mtgy., &c.

		acres.	g. an. val.
b. 18—.	Montgomery .	5,123 .	3,586
	Merioneth . .	644 .	250
	Lancashire. .	29 .	1,377
	Cheshire . .	69 .	282
	York . . .	2 .	20
	Argyll . . .	2 .	110
		5,869 .	5,625

BUTLER - CLARKE - SOUTHWELL - WANDESFORDE, Henry, of Ulcombe Place, Staplehurst, Kent, &c.

		acres.	g. an. val.
Coll. Eton.	Derby . . .	1,307 .	2,414
b. 1815, s. 1860.	Kent . . .	850 .	1,026
	Co. Clare . .	6,737 .	2,511
	Co. Limerick .	4,137 .	2,190
		13,031 .	8,141

** WARBURTON, Richard, of Garryhinch, Portarlington.

		acres.	g. an. val.
Coll. Portarlington School,	King's Co. .	5,841 .	1,814
Croydon School.	Queen's Co. .	6,285 .	5,273
Club. Kildare St. Dublin.			
b. 1846, s. 1862, m. 1867.		12,126 .	7,087

** EGERTON-WARBURTON, Rowland Eyles, of Arley Hall, Northwich. 🐚.

		acres.	g. an. val.
Coll. Eton, Corp. Ch. Ox.	Cheshire . .	7,562 .	14,834
b. 1804, s. 1813, m. 1831.			

*** WARD, Robert Edward, of Bangor Castle, Belfast.

		acres.	g. an. val.
Coll. Har., Ch. Ch. Ox.	Co. Down . .	5,830 .	8,517
Club. Travellers', Ulster, Belfast.			
b. 1819, s. 1840, m. 1857.			
Served in 10th Hussars.			

WARD, H., of Clayton-le-Dale.	Lancashire	2,226 .	3,783
WARDE, C.A. M., of Squerryes Court.	Kent	2,416 .	3,767

** WARD, WILLIAM GEORGE, of Weston Manor, Freshwater.

			acres.	*g. an. val.*
Coll.	Winchester, Ch. Ch.	Hants . . .	10,000 .	11,000
	and Balliol, Oxford.			

b. 1812, s. 1849, m. 1845.

** WARDLAW, LIEUTENANT-GENERAL, C.B., of Crebilly.

Club.	Carlton, United Ser.	Co. Antrim .	3,696 .	3,094

b. 1817, m. 1848.

Commanded the R. Drs. in the Crimea, Col. of the 7th Dr. Gds., commanded Cav. Brig. at Aldershot.

*** WARING, THOMAS, of Waringstown House, Lurgan.

Coll.	Trinity, Dublin.	Co. Down . .	3,522 ..	4,150
Club.	J. U. S., Kild. St.			

b. 1828, s. 1866, m. 1st 1858, 2nd 1874.

** WARNEFORD, REV. JOHN HENRY, of Warneford Place, Sevenhampton, Wilts.

Coll.	Worcester, Oxon.	Wilts . . .	2,410 .	4,113
Club.	Junior Carlton.	Queen's Co. .	2,394 .	1,298
b. 1818, s. 1861, m. 1851.				
			4,804 .	5,411

This family (though with one break in the direct male line) have held the Wilts property since the reign of Richard I.

** WARNER, EDWARD, of Quorndon Hall, Loughborough, &c.

b. 1804, s. 1844, m. 1848.	Nottingham .	1,084 .	1,735
Exclusive of house pro-	York, N.R. .	3,025 .	2,000
perty in Loughborough and	Leicester . .	2,014 .	5,436
certain royalties on lime.			
		6,123 .	9,171

WARNER, PATRICK, of Ardeer. Ayr . . 2,075 . 3,706

** LEE-WARNER, Henry James, of Walsingham Abbey, Fakenham.

		acres.	g. an. val.
Coll. Eton, Oriel, Oxon.	Norfolk . .	8,213 .	9,744
Club. Carlton, Athenæum.	Lincoln . .	3,700 .	6,654
b. 1809, s. 1858, m. 1846.			
		11,913 .	16,398

WARREN, Sir Augustus Riversdale, Bart., of Warren's Court, Lissarda, Co. Cork.

Club. Ath., A. and N.	Co. Cork . .	7,787 .	3,738
b. 1833, s. 1863, m. 1864.			

Served in 20th Foot in the Crimea and India.

** WARRENDER, Sir George, Bart., of Bruntsfield, Edinburgh, N.B., &c.

Coll. Eton.			
Club. 'Travellers', Carlton.	Roxburgh . .	2,260 .	1,665
b. 1825, s. 1867, m. 1854.	Haddington .	1,089 .	3,988
Served in Coldstream Gds.	Midlothian .	74 .	908
		3,423 .	6,561

** WARRY, George, of Shapwick House, Bridgwater.

Coll. Winch., Trin. Oxon.	Somerset . .	3,500 .	4,200
b. 1795, s. 1827, m. 1830.			

*** WARTER, Henry de Grey, of Longden Manor, Shrewsbury, &c.

Club. Junior Carlton.	Salop . . .	3,453 .	6,892
	Notts . . .	2,152 .	3,794
b. 1807, m. 1833, 2nd 1875.			
		5,605 .	10,686

Inc. 395 acres in Notts held under perpetual lease, but exc. of 300*l.* for coal royalties. Mr. W. has recently reduced his rents by about 1,400*l.* to meet the depression in agriculture.

---

* LEE-WARNER, R. H., of Tibberton.

Hereford . . . . under 3,000 . unstated

WARWICK AND BROOKE, EARL OF, The Castle, Warwick. ⚓.

		acres.	g. an. val.
Coll. St. John's, Oxon.	Warwick . .	8,262 .	15,623
Club. Carlton, Travellers'.	Somerset . .	1,840 .	2,713
b. 1818, s. 1853, m. 1852.			
Sat for S. Warwickshire.		10,102 .	18,336

*** WATERFORD, LOUISA, MARCHIONESS OF, Ford Castle, Cornhill, Northumberland, &c.

s. 1859, m. 1842.	Northumberland	6,556 .	11,043
	Hants . . .	475 .	930
		7,031 .	11,973

WATERFORD, MARQUIS OF, K.P., Curraghmore, Waterford.

Coll. Eton.	Co. Waterford.	39,883 .	27,707
Club. White's, Carlton, Gun,	Co. Wicklow .	26,035 .	4,620
Kild. St., Sack. St.	Co. Kilkenny .	406 .	216
b. 1844, s. 1866, m. 1st 1872,	Co. Cavan . .	305 .	161
2nd 1874.	Co. Kildare .	55 .	48
Served in 1st Life Guards.			
Sat for Co. Waterford.		66,684 .	32,752

*** WATERPARK, LORD, Doveridge Hall, Derby.

Coll. Harrow.	Co. Tipperary .	6,587 .	3,705
Club. Brooks's, Travellers',	Derby . . .	1,613 .	4,306
St. James's.	Stafford . .	91 .	308
b. 1839, s. 1863.			
Was in the Foreign Office.		8,291 .	8,319

* RICE-WATKINS, MAJOR, of Llwyn-y-brain, Llandovery.

Coll. Bath, Woolwich.	Carmarthen .	1,986 .	2,002
b. 1818, s. 1844.	Brecon . . .	6,682 .	2,895
Served in 23rd Foot.	Cardigan . .	235 .	unstated
	Pembroke . .	50 .	unstated
	Radnor . . .	13 .	unstated
		8,966 .	4,897

WATNEY, JAMES, of Haling Park.   Surrey   2,295 .   4,249

WATSON, GEORGE LEWIS, of Rockingham Castle, Northampton.

			acres.		*g. an. val.*
Coll. Eton.	Northampton .		2,222	.	3,847
Club. St. James's, Trav.	Leicester . .		2,229	.	4,090
b. 1841, s. 1852, m. 1867.	Rutland . .		95	.	227
Served in 1st Life Guards.					
			4,546	.	8,164

WATSON, JOHN, of Gelt Hall, Castlecarrock, Carlisle.

b. 18—, m. 18—.	Cumberland .	4,048	.	4,216

MRS. WATSON is retd. as owner of about half this estate.

*** WATSON, ROBERT, of North Seaton, Morpeth, &c.

Coll. Eton, Pemb. Ox.	Northumberland	4,874	.	7,374
Club. Reform.				

b. 1836, s. 1870, m. 1871.

** GIBSON-WATT, JAMES WATT, of Doldowlod, Rhayader, &c.

Coll. Rugby, Magd.	Radnor . . .	8,200	.	4,560
Cam.	Brecon . . .	2,761	.	1,440
Club. Carl.,Ox.& Cam.	Stafford . .	75	.	850
b. 1831, s. 1856, m. 1874.				
		11,036	.	6,850

** WATTS, EDW. HANSLOPE, of Hanslope, Stony Stratford.

Coll. Eton, Trin. Cam.	Bucks . . .	3,705	.	5,692
Club. Brooks's, Grafton.				

b. 1845, s. 1853, m. 1868.

** WAUCHOPE, WILLIAM JOHN, of Niddrie Marischall, Liberton, N.B.

Coll. Eton.	Roxburgh . .	3,335	.	4,478
Club. Boodle's, Jun. U. Ser.	Midlothian . .	670	.	2,594
b. 1841, s. 1874, m. 1870.				
Served in 6th (Inniskilling)		4,005	.	7,072
Dragoons and 16th Lancers.				

Exclusive of 300*l.* for mines (very fluctuating).

*** WATSON, J., of Berwick. Sal., Lanc.,			
Wor., War.	2,754	.	9,484
WATT, MISS, of Speke, Lancashire . . .	2,346	.	6,293

WAVENEY, Lord, Flixton Hall, Bungay, &c.

			acres.	g. an. val.
Club.	Brooks's, Trav., Dev.,	Suffolk . . .	10,930 .	14,168
	O. & C., U. Ser. Ref.	Norfolk . . .	1,776 .	2,417
b. 1811, s. 1869, m. 1836.		Co. Antrim .	6,546 .	6,810
Is A.D.C. to the Queen.				
Sat for Cambridge.			19,252 .	23,395

WEBB, Will. Fred., of Newstead Abbey, Nottingham, &c.

Coll.	Eton.	York, N.R. .	7,599 .	8,093
Club.	Bood., A. & N., Bro.	Notts . . .	5,859 .	3,677
b. 1829, s. 1847, m. 1857.				
Served in 17th Lancers.			13,458 .	11,770

WELD, Reginald Joseph, of Lulworth Castle, Wareham. ⚓.

Club.	St. George's.	Dorset . . .	15,478 .	13,704
b. 1842, s. 1877.		Hants . . .	47 .	150
			15,525 .	13,854

WELLINGTON, Duke of, K.G., Strathfieldsaye, Winchfield.

Coll.	Eton, Trin. Cam.	Hants . . .	15,847 .	16,873
Club.	Carlton, White's,	Herts . . .	2,246 .	3,922
	Uni. Service.	Somerset . .	529 .	617
b. 1807, s. 1852, m. 1839.		Berks . . .	494 .	750
			19,116 .	22,162

Was M. of the Horse, is a Lieut.-Gen. in the Army. Sat for Aldborough and for Norwich.
"Very incorrect."—D. of W.

WAY, B. H. W., of Denham. Buc., Midd. .	2,327 .	4,409
HARRISON-WAYNE, Mrs., of South Warnborough. Hants	2,199 .	2,070
WEALLEANS, J. D., of Flotterton. Nhmbd.	5,761 .	2,729
WEBB, T. V., of Great Gransden. Huntingdon, Cambridgeshire, Staffordshire, Suffolk .	2,601 .	3,333
SCRYMGEOUR-WEDDERBURN, H., of Birkhill. Fife, Forfar	2,051 .	6,382
⚓ WELD, John, of Leagram. Lancashire .	2,249 .	2,941
WELDON, Sir Anthony Crosdill, Bart., of Rahinderry. Queen's Co., Kildare .	2,739 .	2,206

** WELLS, WILLIAM, of Holme Wood, Stilton.

		acres.	g. an. val.
Coll. Harrow, Ball. Oxon.	Huntingdon .	6,000	8,000

Club. White's, Travellers', Brooks's. b. 1818, s. 1826, m. 1854.
Served in 1st L. Gds. Sat for Beverley and Peterborough.

*** WEMYSS AND MARCH, EARL OF, Amisfield, Haddington, N.B., &c.

Club. Carlton.	Haddington .	9,167	20,372
b. 1795, s. 1853, m. 1817.	Peebles . .	41,257	14,694
Inclusive of val. of fishings	Perth . .	3,541	7,637
and limeworks, but exclusive	Midlothian .	1,513	4,767
of 1,373*l.* for minerals.	Berwick . .	1,261	757
The English property is	Gloucester . .	4,789	6,143
uncorrected.	Worcester . .	500	598
		62,028	54,968

ERSKINE-WEMYSS, RANDOLPH GORDON, of Wemyss Castle, Kirkcaldy, N.B., &c.

b. 1858, s. 1864.	Fife	6,925	12,314

About half stands in the name of Trs. of his father. Ex. of minerals gr. an. val. 8,492*l.*

** WENLOCK, LORD, Escrick Park, York, &c. ⚓.

Coll. Eton, Trin. Cam.	York, E.R. .	20,853	21,997
Club. Brooks's, Marl.	Salop . . .	5,227	5,593
b. 1849, s. 1880, m. 1872.			
Sat for Chester.		26,080	27,590

The late LORD W. left part of the Salop est. (here included) to his second son.

WELSTEAD, of Stonely. Hunts., Sus., Nptn.	2,007	3,011
MACONOCHIE - WELWOOD, A. A., of Garvock. Fife, Midlothian	2,307	3,464

*** VERNON-WENTWORTH, FREDERICK WILLIAM THOMAS, of Wentworth Castle, Barnsley, &c. ⚲.

		acres.	g. an. val.
Coll. Ch. Ch. Oxon.	York, W.R. .	5,111 .	15,240
Club. Union.	Suffolk . . .	4,161 .	3,456
b. 1795, s. 1814, m. 1826.	Northampton .	672 .	1,229
The Scottish pty. belongs	Bucks . . .	49 .	65
to his eldest son, the shoot-	Perth . . .	12,937 .	556
ing val. omitted.			
		22,930 .	20,546

** WENTWORTH, GODFREY HAWKSWORTH, of Wooley Park, Wakefield.

b. 1827, s. 1865.	York, W.R. .	5,180 .	13,002

*** ROBERTS-WEST, JAMES, of Alscot Park, Stratford-on-Avon.

Coll. Eton, Caius, Cam.	Gloucester . .	4,153 .	5,672
Club. Ox. and Cam.,	Warwick . .	2,788 .	3,838
Arthur's.	Worcester . .	2,076 .	2,066
b. 1811, s. 1838, m. 1844.			
		9,017 .	11,576

** WEST, WILLIAM CORNWALLIS, of The Castle, Ruthin, N. Wales, &c. ⚲.

Coll. Eton.	Denbigh . .	5,457 .	9,562
Club. Devonshire, Trav.,	Hants . . .	2,210 .	2,869
St. Jas., Arthur's.	Montgomery .	160 .	732
b. 1835, s. 1868, m. 1872.	Salop . . .	34 .	81
		7,861 .	13,244

His mother owns the Hampshire estate.

** WESTBY, EDWARD PERCEVAL, of Roebuck Cas., Dundrum, &c.

Coll. Corpus Ch. Oxon.	Co. Clare . .	25,779 .	7,691
Club. Kildare St. Dublin.	Co. Dublin .	67 .	324
b. 1828, s. 1860, m. 1st 1853,			
2nd 1864.		25,846 .	8,015

WESTENRA, MRS. H.	Monaghan . . .	4,483 .	2,091

** WESTERN, Sir Thos. Chas. Callis, Bt., of Felix Hall, Witham.

			acres.	g. an. val.
Coll. Eton, Ch. Ch. Oxon.	Essex	. . .	7,875	10,838
Club. White's, Marl., St. Jas.	Suffolk	. . .	2,134	2,697
b. 1850, s. 1877.				
Served in 2nd Life Guards.			10,009	13,535

WESTMEATH, Earl of, Pallas, Tynagh, Co. Galway.

Coll. Oscott.	Co. Galway	.	14,604	4,377
Club. Kild. St., Dublin.	Roscommon	.	1,091	1,109
b. 1832, s. 1879, m. 1866.				
Served in 9th Foot.			15,695	5,486

*** WESTMINSTER, Duke of, K.G., Eaton Hall, Chester, &c.

Coll. Eton, Ball. Oxon.	Cheshire	. .	15,138	32,387
Club. Brooks's, Travellers',	Flint	. . .	3,621	4,355
Reform, White's.	Denbigh	. .	744	1,116
b. 1825, s. 1869, m. 1852.	Bucks	. . .	246	1,136
Sat for Chester. Is Master of the Horse.				
			19,749	38,994

Inclusive of house property in Chester, the acreage of which is
not stated. No notice is taken in the return of the Metropolitan
area, where the Duke owns, what is commonly supposed to be, the
most valuable London estate held by any of Her Majesty's subjects;
an uncle of the compiler tells him he shot snipe on it within a
mile of Belgrave Sq. in 1822 ; now the land is leased by the sq. ft.

* WESTMINSTER, Dowager Marchioness of, Motcombe
House, Shaftesbury.

s. 1869, m. 1819.	Dorset	. . .	8,794	21,265
	Wilts	. . .	4,112	5,693
			12,906	26,958

WESTMORLAND, Earl of, C.B., Apthorp House, Wansford. ♧.

Coll. Westminster.	Northampton	.	5,973	9,447
Club. Guards, Army and	York, W.R.	.	1,401	1,695
Navy, Turf.				
b. 1825, s. 1859, m. 1857.			7,374	11,142

Served in Coldstream Guards, went through the Punjaub and
Crimean campaigns, and was A.D.C. to Lord Raglan in the latter.
The Countess owns most of the Yorkshire estate.

MASSY-WESTROPP, JOHN THOMAS, of Attyflin, Patrickswell,
  Co. Limerick.

		acres.	*g. an. val.*
Coll. Trinity, Dublin.	Co. Clare . .	3,683 .	2,625
b. 1837, s. 1866, m. 1859.	Limerick . .	592 .	608
	Cork . . .	387 .	295
		4,662 .	3,528

** WEYLAND, JOHN, of Woodeaton, Oxford, &c.

Coll. Eton, Ch. Ch. Oxon.	Norfolk . .	4,098 .	4,878
Club. Carlton.	Oxford . . .	850 .	1,491
b. 1821, s. 1864, m. 1850.	Suffolk . . .	72 .	123
	Berks . . .	434 .	371
		5,454 .	6,863

*** WHARNCLIFFE, EARL OF, Wortley Hall, Sheffield, &c.

Coll. Eton.	York, N. and		
Club. White's, Carlton,	W.R. . .	22,544 .	34,440
Turf, Marl., Trav.	Cornwall . .	2,039 .	1,783
b. 1827, s. 1855, m. 1855.	Forfar . . .	6,926 .	10,267
Served in Gren. Guards.	Perth . . .	1,940 .	4,333
		33,449 .	50,823

** WHARTON, JOHN THOS., of Skelton, Marske-by-Sea, &c.

Coll. Char., Tr. Cam.	York, N.R. .	10,647 .	7,659
Club. O. & C., Brooks's.	b. 1809, s. 1843, m. 1854.		

** WHEELER, EDW. VINCENT, of Kyrewood, Tenbury, &c.

Coll. Rugby, Tr. Cam.	Worcester . .	3,235 .	5,208
b. 1831, s. 1853, m. 1854.	Salop . . .	372 .	750
	Hereford . .	14 .	28
		3,621 .	5,986

Incl. of 317*l.* in his mother's name.

WHALLEY, G. H., of Plâs Madoc. Denbigh,
  Montgomery, Gloucester, Radnor . . 2,554 . 3,499

WHELER, Charles Wheler, of Ledston Hall, Normanton, &c.

		acres.	g. an. val.
Coll. Eton, Ch. Ch. Oxon.	York, W.R. .	3,384 .	2,798
b. 1834, s. 1877, m. 1869.	Kent . . .	1,647 .	1,553
		5,031 .	4,351

*** WHICHCOTE, Sir Thos., Bt., of Aswarby, Folkingham. ♨.

Coll. Eton.	Lincoln . .	11,213 .	16,918
Club. White's, Arth., R.Y.S.,	Rutland . .	4 .	3
Carl.	Northampton .	1 .	2
b. 1813, s. 1829, m. 1st 1839,			
2nd 1856.		11,218 .	16,923
Served in G. Gds.			

WHITBREAD, Samuel, of Southill Park, Bedford, &c.

Coll. Rugby, Trin. Cam.	Bedford . .	13,257 .	20,399
Club. Brooks's.	Essex . . .	572 .	1,391
b. 1830, s. 1879, m. 1855.			
		13,829 .	21,790

Sits for Bedford, is Chairman of Standing Orders Committee in the House of Commons, was a Lord of the Admiralty.

WHITE, Hon. Charles W., of Cahercon, &c.

The return gives him 23,957 acres in Cos. Clare and Tippy. "Truth" in 1879 asserted that these estates are partly sold and partly on sale. The gr. an. val. was 9,548*l.* Mr. Phelps has, he informs the compiler, bought 7,141 acres of the Clare estate.

*** WHITE (late) John, of Grougar, Ayr, N.B., &c.

d. 1881.	Ayr	3,349 .	5,781
	Dumbarton .	35 .	180
	Lanark . . .	3 .	448
		3,387 .	6,409

WHELER, Sir T., Bt., ——. War., Yk., Watd.	2,578 .	3,740
BODDAM-WHETHAM, Mrs., of Kirkling-ton. Nottingham	2,900 .	4,187
WHITAKER, B. I., of Hesley. Notts, York	2,084 .	2,697

WHITE, Robert Hedges Eyre, of Glengarriffe, Cork, &c.

		acres.	*g. an. val.*
b. 1809, s. 1840, m. 1834.	Co. Cork . .	16,175 .	4,227

Served in Rifle Brigade.

** WHITE, Sir Thomas Wollaston, Bart., of Wallingwells, Worksop.

Coll. Rugby.	York, W.R. .	2,207 .	2,571
Club. United Service, Army and Navy.	Notts . . .	1,592 .	1,852
b. 1801, s. 1817, m. 1st 1824, 2nd 1827.		3,799 .	4,423

Served in 16th Lancers, 3rd Light Dragoons, and 10th Hussars.

*** WOLRYCHE-WHITMORE, Rev. Francis Henry, of Dudmaston Hall, Bridgnorth. 🏇.

Coll. Wadham, Oxon.	Salop . . .	5,117 .	6,122
Club. United University.	Worcester . .	81 .	150
b. 1820, s. 1858, m. 1845.			
		5,198 .	6,272

HAWKINS-WHITSHED, Lady, of Killincarrick, Greystones, Co. Wicklow.

s. 1871, m. 1858.	Co. Meath .	2,470 .	1,593
	Co. Dublin .	1,420 .	1,423
	Co. Wicklow .	1,142 .	1,356
	Co. Louth . .	906 .	667
		5,938 .	5,039

The Meath estate stands in her daughter's name. She m. Col. F. Burnaby in 1879.

WHITE, Miss, of Netherurd. Peeb., Lanark	6,376 .	2,255
WHITE, W. H., of Keildra. Leitrim . .	6,152 .	2,292
WHITTAKER, C., of Barming Place. Kent	2,130 .	2,932
WHITTLE, Mrs. Elizabeth. Down . .	2,711 .	3,615

WHYTE, COLONEL, of Glencar, Manor-Hamilton, &c.

			acres.	g. an. val.
Coll.	Harrow, Sandhurst.	Co. Leitrim .	10,989	4,387
Club.	Arthur's, Kildare	Co. Roscommon	1,293	934
	Street, Dublin.	Waterford . .	1,003	730
b. 1808, s. 1852, m. 1842.		Tipperary . .	629	500
		King's Co. .	208	157
			14,122	6,708

4,300*l.* of these rents belong to his eldest son's wife, MRS. WHYTE of Hatley Manor.

WICKLOW, EARL OF, Shelton Abbey, Arklow, &c.

			acres.	g. an. val.
Coll.	Rugby, Trin. Oxon.	Co. Wicklow .	22,103	10,763
Club.	Boodle's, Nav.& Mil.,	Co. Donegal .	6,440	4,818
	Kild. St.	Co. Westmeath	170	136
b. 1842, s. 1881, m. 1876, 2nd 1880.				
Served in 60th Rifles.			28,713	15,717

*** WICKSTED, GEORGE EDMUND, of Betley Hall, Crewe.

			acres.	g. an. val.
Coll.	Eton, Ch. Ch. Oxon.	Stafford . .	1,630	3,609
b. 1836, s. 1870, m. 1878.		Cheshire . .	1,536	2,598
			3,166	6,207

WIGSELL, MRS., of Sanderstead Court, Croydon, &c.

s. 1878, m. 18—.	Surrey . . .	4,196	3,532

** WILBERFORCE, REGINALD GARTON, of Lavington House, Petworth.

			acres.	g. an. val.
Club.	Junior United Ser.	Sussex . . .	3,554	3,000
b. 1838, s. 1873, m. 1867.		Berks . . .	82	100
Served in 52nd Foot in the Indian Mutiny.			3,636	3,100

* WILBRAHAM, GEORGE FORTESCUE, of Delamere House, Northwich. 💲

Coll.	Harrow, Trin. Cam.	Cheshire . .	4,321	8,426
Club.	Reform. b. 1815, s. 1852.			

Both acreage and rental (chiefly the latter) too high.

WHITWORTH, H. B., Nptn., Buc., Gla. .   2,364 .   3,365

WILDER, George, of Stanstead Park, Emsworth.

		acres.	g. an. val.
b. 1850, s. 1871, m. 1872.	Sussex . . .	3,679 .	3,364
	Hants . . .	4 .	2
		3,683 .	3,366

WILKES, John, of Wendon Lofts Hall, Saffron Walden.

Coll. St. John's, Cam.	Essex . . .	4,690 .	6,096
b. 1848, s. 1879, m. 1877.	Suffolk . . .	104 .	150
		4,794 .	6,246

** WILKINSON, Anthony, of Hulam, Castle Eden, &c.

Coll. Ch. Ch. Oxon.	Durham . .	7,940 .	5,000
Club. Arthur's, Brooks's.	Northumberland	3,250 .	800
b. 1838, s. 1851, m. 1871.			
		11,190 .	5,800

Exclusive of mine rents, which may average 7,000*l.* per annum.

*** WILKINSON, William, of Middlewood, Clitheroe, &c.

Coll. St. John's, Cam.	Lancashire . .	5 .	280
	York, W.R. .	3,765 .	4,650
b. 1827, s. 1848, m. 1858.			
		3,770 .	4,930

WILLIAMS, Francis Edward, of Malvern Hall, Solihull, &c.

b. 1804, s. 1853, m. 1838.	Worcester . .	2,931 .	6,546
	Warwick . .	2,572 .	4,779
	Hereford . .	552 .	714
	Co. Kerry . .	3,804 .	124
		9,859 .	12,163

Mr. W. is returned as joint owner of 893 acres more in Warwick with " another."

⚲ WILBRAHAM, R., of Rode Hall.	Chester	2,032 .	4,514
WILKINSON, Rev. G., of Harperley.	Dur.	2,173 .	4,549
WILLES, E., of Goodrest.	Beds, Berks, War.	2,631 .	4,255

** WILLIAMS (late) JOHN MICHAEL, of Burncoose, St. Austell, &c.

d. 1880.

		acres.		g. an. val.
Cornwall	. .	7,002	.	12,083
Devon	. . .	1,123	.	1,309
		8,125	.	13,392

This estate is unequally divided between his two sons.

WILLIAMS, MORGAN STUART, of Aberpergwm, Neath, S. Wales.

Coll. Eton, Pet., Cam.
Club. Gun, Arthur's.
b. 1846, s. 1863, m. 1873.

Glamorgan	.	3,058	.	2,817
Brecon	. . .	859	.	873
		3,917	.	3,690

*** WILLIAMS, COL. OWEN, of Temple Ho., Great Marlow, &c.

Coll. Eton.
Club. Carl., White's, Turf,
Gun, Bood., Marl.
b. 1836, s. 1875, m. 1862.
Commands R. H. Guards.
Is Silverstick in Waiting.
Sits for Marlow.

Co. Roscommon	3,062	.	963
Carnarvon . .	3,854	.	4,523
Anglesea . .	4,195	.	5,808
Bucks . . .	1,910	.	6,098
Berks , . .	438	.	1,386
Flint . . .	275	.	782
Middlesex . .	200	.	295
Denbigh . .	500	.	2,000
	14,434	.	21,855

A rather amusing instance of the "clerical" error occurs in COL. W.'s case. The return gives these estates except those in Anglesea to COL. T. PEERS WILLIAMS, his father, who died 1875; in Anglesea they are given to COL. T. WILLIAMS, of "Peers," "Menai Bridge."

BUCKLEY-WILLIAMES, PRYCE, of Pennant. Montgomery	2,282	.	2,368
WILLIAMS, E., of Herringstone. Dor., K. Co.	7,349	.	2,259
WILLIAMS, REV. GARNONS, of Abercamlais. Brecon, Hereford	2,699	.	2,827
WILLIAMS, GEORGE, of Scorrier. Cornwall	2,078	.	3,142
WILLIAMS, M. H., of Tredrea. Cornwall .	2,621	.	2,097

WILLIAMS, PENRY, of Penpont, Brecon.

		acres.		g. an. val.
Coll. Westm., Ch. Ch. Ox.	Brecon . . .	7,042	.	4,370
b. 1807, m. 1847, s. 1832.	Hereford . .	1,094	.	544
		8,136	.	4,914

** WILLIAMS, ROBERT, of Bridehead, Dorchester.

Coll. Oriel, Oxon.	Dorset . . .	4,917	.	6,400
Club. Oxford and Cam.	Surrey . . .	14	.	600
b. 1811, s. 1847, m. 1st 1847,				
2nd 1858.		4,931	.	7,000
Sat for Dorchester.				

** WILLIAMS, SIR WILLIAM GRENVILLE, BART., of Bodel-wyddan, St. Asaph.

Coll. Eton.	Denbigh . .	5,360	.	3,023
Club. Carlton, N. and M.	Flint . . .	4,011	.	5,848
b. 1844, s. 1876.				
		9,371	.	8,871
Served in 1st Life Guards and 1st Royal Dragoons.				

** WILLIAMS, SIR WILLIAM ROBERT, BART., of Heanton House, Barnstaple, &c.

Coll. Sandhurst.	Devon . . .	7,000	.	8,000
b. 1860, s. 1878, m. 1881.	Cornwall . .	1,019	.	2,171
		8,019	.	10,171

WILLIAMS, of Portmadoc. Carn., Mer. .	3,730	.	2,156
WILLIAMS, SUSAN, of Trephilip. Brecon, Glamorgan, Pembroke	2,917	.	2,780
ADDAMS-WILLIAMS, W., of Llangibby. Monmouth	2,827	.	2,981
WILLIAMSON, F., of Wavertree. Ches. .	2,069	.	3,959
WILLIAMSON, of Cardrona. Peeb., Selk.	4,696	.	2,358

** WILLIAMSON, David Robertson, of Lawers, Crieff, N.B.

			acres.	g. an. val.
Coll. Sandhurst.	Perth . . .		30,094 .	6,205

Club. New, and Cons., Ed.
b. 1830, s. 1852, m. 1853.   Served in Coldstream Guards.

WILLOUGHBY de BROKE, Lord, Compton Verney, Warwick.

Coll. Eton, Ch. Ch. Oxon.	Warwick . .	12,621 .	16,510
Club. Carlton, Gun.	Lincoln . .	2,930 .	3,558
b. 1844, s. 1862, m. 1867.	Northampton .	929 .	1,421
	Somerset . .	588 .	1,070
	Stafford . .	555 .	783
	Anglesea . .	396 .	440
	Leicester . .	126 .	133
		18,145 .	23,915

** WILLOUGHBY D'ERESBY, Baroness, Grimsthorpe, Bourne, &c.

b. 1809, s. 1871, m. 1827.	Lincoln . .	24,696 .	36,530
	Carnarvon . .	30,391 .	7,966
	Denbigh . .	296 .	555
	Perth . . .	76,837 .	28,955
		132,220 .	74,006

** WILLSON, Mildmay, of Rauceby Hall, Sleaford.

Coll. Eton.	Lincoln . .	4,532 .	7,024

Club. Guards, Junior Carlton, Arthur's
b. 1847, s. 1866.   Served in Scots Fusilier Guards.

WILLIAMSON, Rev. R., of Whickham.		
Dur.	2,079 .	2,378
WILLOUGHBY, Sir J. C., Bt., of Baldon.		
Oxon, Gloucester, Surrey, Bucks . .	2,282 .	3,926
WILSON, G., of Dunardagh. Kild., Wex.	4,346 .	2,872
WILSON, Henry S. Lee, of Crofton. York	2,015 .	3,229

*** WILLYAMS, ED. BRYDGES, of Nanskeval, St. Columb, &c.

		acres.	g. an. val.
Coll. Merton, Oxon.	Cornwall . .	4,298 .	5,145

Club. Arthur's, Brooks's, O. & C., Turf, Pratt's.
b. 1835, s. 1872, m. 1856.
  Sat for Truro and E. Cornwall. Sits for Truro.

** WILSHERE, CHARLES WILLES, of The Frythe, Welwyn.

Coll. Trinity, Cambridge.	Herts . . .	2,517 .	4,793
Club. Oxford and Cam.	Beds . . .	925 .	1,545
b. 1814, s. 1867, m. 1840.	Cambridge .	7 .	9
		3,449 .	6,347

The Frythe was purchased by this family at the dissolution of the Monasteries.

WILSON, ARTHUR MAITLAND, of Stowlangtoft, Bury St. Edm.

Coll. Eton.	Suffolk . . .	5,016 .	7,006

b. 1857, s. 1875, m. 1880.

** WILSON, CHARLES HENRY, of Warter Priory, Pocklington.

Club. Reform.	York . . .	8,500 .	8,000

b. 1833, m. 1871. Sits for Hull.

** WILSON, CHR. WYNDHAM, of Rigmaden, Kirkby Lonsdale.

b. 1844, s. 1880, m. 1st 1874,	Westmoreland	8,690 .	7,988
2nd 1879.			

** WILSON, EDWARD HUGH, of Dallam Tower, Milnthorpe.

b. 1849, s. 1879.	Westmoreland	8,730 .	10,510
	Lancashire. .	1,141 .	833
	York, W.R. .	26 .	58
		9,897 .	11,401

** WILSON, GEORGE HOLT, of Redgrave Hall, Botesdale.

Coll. Pembroke, Oxon.	Suffolk . . .	5,466 .	6,949
b. 1836, s. 1850, m. 1865.	Norfolk . .	783 .	1,048
		6,249 .	7,997

WILSON, J., of Low Nook.	Wmld., Sur. .	2,199 .	2,078
WILSON, T. J., of Stroquhan.	Dumfries .	4,198 .	2,251
** CARUS-WILSON, W. WILSON, of Casterton.	Westmld., Lancashire, York .	2,700 .	4,300

TYRWHITT-WILSON, Hon. HARRY TYRWHITT, of Keythorpe
Hall, Leicester.

			acres.		g. an. val.
Club. Carl.,Gds.,Whi.,Turf.	Leicester	. .	5,758	.	10,055
b. 1854, s. 1874.	Norfolk	. .	1,162	.	1,685
Served in Grenadier Guards.	Rutland	. .	2	.	17
Is Equerry to the Prince of Wales.					
			6,922	.	11,757

WILSON, JOHN GERALD, of Cliffe Hall, Darlington.

b. 1841, s. 1867, m. 1873.	York, N.R. . .	3,239	.	4,941
Served in 84th Foot.				

WILSON, JOSEPH, of Lisnadill, Co. Armagh, &c.

Coll. Trinity, Dublin.	Co. Armagh	.	4,049	.	4,679
Club. Sackville St. Dublin.	Co. Dublin	.	308	.	732
b. 1816, m. 1st 1850, 2nd 1853.					
			4,357	.	5,411

** WILSON, SIR MATTHEW, BART., of Eshton, Gargrave, York.

Coll. Harrow, Bras. Oxon.	York, W.R.	.	7,552	.	12,423
Club. Athenæum.	Lincoln	. .	851	.	888
b. 1802, s. 1854, m. 1826,	Lancashire	.	213	.	265
2nd 1878.					
Sat for Clitheroe. Sits			8,616	.	13,576
for the N.W. Riding.					

* MARYON-WILSON, SIR SPENCER, BART., of Charlton House,
Blackheath, &c.

Club. J. U. Ser., N. & M.	Sussex	. .	1,644	.	1,594
b. 1829, s. 1876, m. 1856.	Essex	. .	1,529	.	1,824
Served in the Royal Navy	Kent	. .	650	.	(?)
(Lieutenant).	Middlesex	. .	550	.	(?)
			4,373	.	3 418

SIR S. M.-W. omits to give his income in the two latter counties;
these two most valuable estates lie wholly within the Metropolitan
area, which is unreturned.

*** WILSON, THOMAS, of Shotley Hall, Shotley Bridge.

Coll. Ed. University.	Northumberland	3,673	.	3,837
b. 1800, m. 1868.	Cumberland .	212	.	140
	Durham . .	4	.	20
		3,889		3,997

WILTON, Earl of, Heaton Hall, Manchester, &c. 🐍.

			acres.		g. an. val.
Coll.	Eton, Ch. Ch. Ox.	Lancashire	8,013	.	27,338
Club.	Carl., White's.	York, W.R. .	775	.	2,040
b. 1833, s. 1882, m. 1858.		Stafford . .	853	.	1,173
Served in 1st Life Guards.		Somerset . .	196	.	316
Sat for Weymouth and Bath.		Leicester . .	33	.	366
		Salop . . .	1	.	1
			9,871	.	31,234

Inclusive of 138*l.* standing in his mother's name.
"These estates are now (1882) worth 65,000*l.* a year."—"Land Agent's Record."

** WIMBORNE, Lord, Canford Manor, Wimborne, &c.

			acres.		g. an. val.
Coll.	Harrow, Trin. Cam.	Ross . . .	60,000	.	1,180
Club.	St. James's, Carlton.	Dorset . . .	17,400	.	17,543
b. 1835, s. 1852, m. 1868.		Glamorgan .	5,820	.	27,979
		Brecon . . .	310	.	145
		Hants . .	9	.	9
			83,539	.	46,856

*** WINCHESTER, Marquis of, St. Mary's, Amport, Andover.
🌳 🐍.

			acres.		g. an. val.
Coll.	Eton.				
Club.	Carlton, Travellers',	Hants . .	4,797	.	4,635
	White's.				
b. 1801, s. 1843, m. 1855.		Served in 10th Hussars.			

WINCHELSEA and NOTTINGHAM, Earl of, Kirby Hall, Northampton, &c. 🐍.

			acres.		g. an. val.
Coll.	Eton, Ch. Ch. Oxon.	Northampton .	5,114	.	8,708
Club.	Carlton, Turf, Gun.	Kent . . .	6,581	.	6,527
b. 1815, s. 1858, m. 1846,		Notts . . .	741	.	2,288
	2nd 1882.	Leicester . .	355	.	574
Sat for N. Northamptonshire.		Lincoln . .	78	.	94
		Rutland . .	13	.	25
			12,882	.	18,216

** CORBETT-CORBETT-WINDER, Major, of Vaynor Park, Berriew, Montgomeryshire.

			acres.		g. an. val.
Coll.	Sandhurst.	Montgomery .	5,116	.	6,000

Club. Army and Navy. b. 1820, s. 1879, m. 1872.
Served in 52nd Foot.

*** WINDSOR, Lord, Oakly Park, Bromfield, Salop, &c.

Coll. Eton, St. John's, Cam.	Glamorgan	.	17,353	.	35,136
Club. White's, Carlton.	Salop . . .	11,204	.	14,453
b. 1857, s. 1869.	Worcester . .	8,530	.	13,574
	Flint . . .	327	.	589
	Hereford . .	40	.	26

                                      37,454 · 63,778

*** WINGFIELD, Chas. Geo., of Onslow Hall, Shrewsbury. 🙟.

Club. Carlton, St. James's,   Salop . . .   3,543 . 6,618
Junior Carlton, Army and Navy.
b. 1833, s. 1862, m. 1865.
Served in 71st Highlanders in the Crimea.

WINGFIELD, Edward Rhys, of Barrington Park, Burford.

Coll. Eton.	Bedford . .	6,229	.	8,392
Club. Junior Carlton, Naval	Glamorgan .	6,463	.	19,428
and Military.	Gloucester . .	4,333	.	5,445
b. 1849, s. 1869, m. 1871.	Oxford . . .	1,766	.	2,124
Served in 60th Rifles.				

                                      18,791 · 35,389

Mr. Wingfield is joint owner of 252 acres in Glamorgan with Miss Richards.

** WINGFIELD, John Maurice, of Tickencote Hall, Stamford, &c. 🙟.

b. 1863, s. 1880.	Rutland . .	2,905	.	4,494
	Cambridge .	245	.	413
	Leicester . .	144	.	242
	Northampton .	83	.	123
	Lincoln . .	23	.	42
	Huntingdon .	7	.	25

                                      3,407 · 5,339

* WINDHAM, W. G., of Wawne.   York . 2,500(?) . 3,000(?)

✴ WINMARLEIGH, LORD, Winmarleigh, Garstang. ⚓.

		acres.	g. an. val.
Coll. Eton, Magd. Oxon.	Lancashire .	4,200 .	7,111
Club. Carlton, Uni. Ser.,	Cheshire . .	856 .	1,262
Travellers'	Stafford. . .	282 .	479
b. 1802, s. 1827, m. 1828.			
		5,338 .	8,852

Served as A.D.C. to the QUEEN, Chairman of Committees in the House of Commons, Chancellor of the Duchy of Lancaster, and Chief Secretary for Ireland. Sat for Lancashire and for N. Lancashire. This list is exclusive of an estate at Warrington, which is being built over, and the value of it altering from day to day.

WINN, ROWLAND, of Nostell Priory, Wakefield, &c.

Coll. Trin. Cam.	Lincoln . .	5,522 .	14,029
Club. Carlton, Jun. Carlton,	York, W.R. .	2,461 .	4,558
St. Stephen's.			
b. 1820, s. 1874, m. 1854.		7,983 .	18,587

Was a Lord of the Treasury, sits for N. Lincoln.

MR. W. is given 95 acres more in York jointly with "another."

** WINNINGTON, SIR FRANCIS SALWEY, BART., of Stanford Court, Worcester. ⚓.

Coll. Eton.	Worcester . .	4,196 .	5,977
Club. Marl., St. James's.	Hereford . .	426 .	441
b. 1850, s. 1872, m. 1879.			
Served in the 66th Foot.		4,622 .	6,418

WINTER, JAMES SANDERSON, of Agher, Enfield, Co. Meath.

Club. Kildare Street and	Co. Meath. .	1,640 .	1,648
Sackv. St. Dublin.	Westmeath .	861 .	720
b. 1830, s. 1876.	Cavan . . .	940 .	560
	Kildare . .	206 .	205
		3,647 .	3,133

WINTERTON, EARL OF, Shillinglee Park, Petworth.

Coll. Eton.	Sussex . . .	3,322 .	2,042
Club. Arthur's, Carlton.	Norfolk . .	2,066 .	2,370
b. 1837, s. 1879.	Surrey . . .	372 .	471
		5,760 .	4,883

WISE (late), FRANCIS, of North Mall, Cork.

		acres.		g. an. val.
	Co. Cork . .	9,946	.	9,019
	Limerick . .	1,666	.	1,850
d. 1881.	Co. Kerry . .	9,636	.	445
		21,248	.	11,314

** WISE, HENRY CHRISTOPHER, of Woodcote, Warwick.

Coll. Oriel, Oxon.	Warwick . .	1,794	.	5,203
Club. Carlton.	Northampton .	1,467	.	2,141
b. 1806, s. 1850, m. 1st 1828,				
2nd 1863.		3,261	.	7,344

Sat for S. Warwickshire. Both totals a little overstated.

** WITHAM, REV. FATHER, of Lartington Hall, Barnard Castle.

Coll. Stonyhurst.	York, N.R. .	7,510	.	3,848
b. 1806, s. 1847.	Northumberland	6	.	17
		7,516	.	3,865

ALLAN-WODDROP, WILLIAM, of Garvald House, Dolphinton, N.B., &c.

Coll. Harrow.	Lanark . . .	3,235	.	3,113
Club. Army and Navy, New,	Peebles . .	2,225	.	760
Edinburgh.	Renfrew . .	250	.	343
b. 1829, s. 1845, m. 1856.				
Served in Scots Greys.		5,710	.	4,216

** WOLSELEY, SIR CLEMENT JAMES, BART., of Mount Wolseley, Tullow, Co. Carlow.

Club. Kildare St., Dublin.	Co. Carlow .	2,547	.	2,700
b. 1837, s. 1874, m. 1872.	Co. Wexford .	2,643	.	1,100
		5,190	.	3,800

WISDEN, T. F., of Broadwater. Sussex .	2,937	.	4,422
WITHAM, R. M., of Kirkconnell. Kirk .	2,974	.	2,739
WOLFE, R., of Forenaghts. Kildare, Limerick	2,762	.	2,351

*** WOMBWELL, Sir George Orby, Bart., of Newburgh
    Park, Easingwold. ⚲.   *acres.*   *g. an. val.*
Coll. Eton.   York, N.R. . 12,226 . 14,500
Club. Carlton, Marl., Turf, Trav.
b. 1832, s. 1855, m. 1861.
    Served in 17th Lancers at Alma and Inkerman, A.D.C. to
Lord Cardigan in the Balaclava charge.

** WOOD, Edward Herbert, of Raasay, Isle of Skye, N.B.

		acres.		*g. an. val.*
Coll. Eton, Ch. Ch. Oxon.	Inverness . .	17,551	.	2,770
Club. Windham, Raleigh.	Warwick . .	1,739	.	4,332
b. 1847, m. 1869.	Cheshire . .	631	.	1,090
	Stafford . .	331	.	1,085
All the English estates	Lancashire . .	1	.	1,015
belong to his father, Mr.	Ditto . . .	unstated	.	1,148
E. Wood, of Newbold-				
Revel, near Rugby.		20,253	.	11,440

WOOD, Mrs., of Stouthall, Swansea.

m. 1843, s. 1876.	Carmarthen .	3,859	.	2,710
	Glamorgan . .	1,321	.	7,903
	Brecon . . .	285	.	259
	Pembroke . .	221	.	178
	Cardigan . .	98	.	28
		5,784	.	11,078

*** WOOD, Thomas, of Littleton, Chertsey, &c.

Coll. Eton.	Brecon . . .	3,796	.	4,088
Club. Carlton, Guards.	York, N.R. .	1,820	.	2,870
b. 1853, s. 1872.	Middlesex . .	1,428	.	2,633
Serves in Grenadier Guards.	Surrey . . .	1,071	.	1,421
	Carmarthen .	875	.	538
	Cardigan . .	601	.	249
	Oxford . . .	305	.	460
Mr. W. has lately sold	Radnor . . .	82	.	160
a small part of the Surrey				
estate.		9,978	.	12,419

⚲ WOLLASTON, Major, of Shenton. Leic. 2,196 . 3,430
⚲ WOLSELEY, Sir Charles M., Bart., of
    Wolseley. Staffordshire . . . . 2,111 . 2,789

** WOOD, GENERAL WILLIAM MARK, of Bishop's Hall, Romford.

			acres.		g. an. val.
Coll. Eton.		Essex . . .	2,300	.	4,100
Club. Guards, Arthur's,	Glamorgan . .		1,226	.	2,900
Boodle's, Turf.	Monmouth .		1,440	.	2,200

b. 1817, s. 1854, m. 1846.

4,966 . 9,200

Served in Coldstream Guards and 60th Rifles. Was at Alma, Balaclava, and Sebastopol.

*** WOODS, EDWARD HAMILTON, of Milverton Hall, Dublin.

Coll. Chelt., Christ's, Cam.	Co. Dublin .	2,504	.	3,269
Club. Jun. Carlton, Sackville	Co. Meath .	1,433	.	1,860
Street, Dublin.				

b. 1847, s. 1879, m. 1879.

3,937 . 5,129

WOODS, HENRY, of Warnford Park, Bishop's Waltham, &c.

Club. Athenæum, Reform,	Hants . . .	3,649	.	3,474
Brooks's.	Lancashire . .	49	.	3,397

b. 1822, s. 1841, m. 1st 1854, 2nd 1864.
Sat for Wigan.

3,698 . 6,871

** WOODWARD, ROBERT, of Arley Castle, Bewdley.

b. 1801, s. 1843, m. 1839.

The Cheshire estate is	Stafford . .	3,125	.	4,805
within the Borough of Bir-	Worcester . .	805	.	2,490
kenhead.	Cheshire . .	15	.	846
	Salop . . .	1	.	16
	Lancashire .	1	.	64

3,947 . 8,221

WOOD, DANIEL (part shared), of Glossop. Hereford, Derby, York	2,276	.	3,361
WOOD, E., of Hanger Hill. Midd., Sal. .	2,678	.	5,913
WOOD, G., of Lota. Cork, Wat., Clare .	5,593	.	2,941
WOOD, J. G., of Thedden Grange. Hants	3,092	.	2,926
WOODALL, JOHN, of Scarborough. York .	2,018	.	5,905
* WOODD, B. T., of Conyngham Hall. York	2,500	.	3,100
WOODHOUSE, MISS, of Irnham. Lincoln .	2,979	.	4,172
*** WOODS, GEORGE JOHN, of——. Meath	3,139	.	2,217
*** WOODS, W., of Whitestown. Dub. .	2,192	.	2,573

*** WOODWARD, Thomas, of Hopton Court, Bewdley.

		acres.	g. an. val.
Coll. Marlborough. Salop . . .		4,024 .	3,722

b. 1836, s. 1869, m. 1864.

** WOOLCOMBE, Ven. Archdn., of Ashbury, Exbourne.

Coll. Westm., Ch. Ch. Ox.	Devon . . .	5,867 .	2,694
b. 1813, s. 1866, m. 1846.	Cornwall . .	983 .	870
		6,850 .	3,564

WORMALD, Harry Wormald, of Sawley Hall, Ripon, &c.

Coll. Shrewsbury.	York, W.R. .	4,353 .	4,971

b. 1820, s. 1871, m. 1842.

** WREY, Rev. Sir Henry Bourchier, Bart., of Tawstock
Court, Barnstaple, &c. 🦐.

b. 1797, s. 1879, m. 1st 1827,	Dorset . . .	220 .	440
2nd 1865.	Devon . . .	7,393 .	8,500
	Cornwall . .	372 .	329
		7,985 .	9,269

By the late Baronet's will the "Ilfracombe" estate is gone to
Mr. Weld, of Lulworth.

** WRIGHT, Charles Booth Elmsall, of Bolton Hall,
Clitheroe.

Coll. Eton, Trin. Cam.	York, N. and		
Club. Junior Carlton.	W.R. . .	5,200 .	6,500

b. 1848, m. 1870, s. 1850.

WORSLEY, Sir W., Bt., of Hovingham. York	2,558 .	3,225
WORTH, Rev. W. L., of Worth. Dev., Som.	2,117 .	3,126
WORTHAM, B. H., of Kneesworth. Cambridgeshire, Herts, Lincoln, Essex . .	2,306 .	4,149

WRIGHT, EDWARD CARRINGTON, of Kelvedon Hall, Brentwood.

		acres.	g. an. val.
b. 1850, s. 1865, m. 1873.	Salop . . .	2,774	2,328
	Essex . . .	882	1,251

| "Incorrect."—E. C. W. | | 3,656 | 3,579 |

WRIGHT, JAMES FREDERICK D'ARLEY, of Mottram Hall, Macclesfield.

Coll. Woolwich.	Cheshire . .	2,003	3,657
Club. Jun. United Service.	Lancashire .	1,320	1,743
b. 1827, s. 1865, m. 1857.			
Served in Royal Artillery.		3,323	5,400

** WRIGHTSON, RICHARD HEBER, of Cusworth, Doncaster, &c. (res. Warmsworth, Doncaster).

b. 1800, s. 1879, m. 1st 1832,	Yorkshire . .	4,616	7,771
2nd 1877.	Northumberland	1,158	1,636
	Durham . .	486	1,203
		6,260	10,610

Cusworth belongs for life to his elder brother's widow.

** WROTTESLEY, LORD, Wrottesley, Wolverhampton. 🦆.

🌳 *Coll.* Rugby, Ch. Ch.	Stafford . .	5,785	11,021
Oxford.			

Club. Athenæum, Travellers', Brooks's.
b. 1824, s. 1867, m. 1861. Served as Lord in Waiting.

** WROUGHTON, PHILIP, of Woolley Park, Wantage.

Coll. Har., Ch. Ch. Oxon.	Berks . . .	8,692	9,357

Club. Carlton, Boodle's.
b. 1846, s. 1862, m. 1875. Sits for Berks.

*** WYNDHAM, HON. PERCY SCAWEN, of E. Knoyle, Hindon.

Coll. Eton.	Wilts . . .	4,207	4,164

Club. Carl., White's, Gds., Trav.
b. 1835, s. 1860, m. 1860.
Served in Coldstream Guards. Sits for W. Cumberland.

| WRIGHT, EDMUND, of Halston. | Salop . . | 2,162 | 4,061 |

** WYNDHAM, Richard King, of Corhampton, Bishop's Waltham, &c.

		acres.	*g. an. val.*
b. 1815, s. 1869, m. 1839.	Hants . . .	2,980 .	2,939
	Wilts . . .	2,534 .	3,248
	Devon . . .	870 .	1,020
	Somerset . .	383 .	400
	Dorset . . .	300 .	195
		7,067 .	7,802

WYNDHAM, William, of Dinton House, Salisbury. **S.**

Coll. Harrow, Trin. Cam.	Wilts . . .	5,734 .	6,606
b. 1834, s. 1862 and 1877,	Somerset . .	11,231 .	21,015
m. 1867.	Devon . . .	6,740 .	9,794
	Surrey . . .	3 .	5
		23,708 .	37,420

WYNFORD, Lord, Wynford Eagle, Maiden Newton, Dorchester.

Club. Carlton.	Dorset . . .	2,817 .	3,347
b. 1826, s. 1869, m. 1857.	Essex . . .	403 .	392
Served in Rifle Brigade.	Kent . . .	240 .	440
		3,460 .	4,179

** WYNN, Hon. Charles Henry, of Rûg, Corwen.

Club. Carlton.	Merioneth . .	10,504 .	8,905
b. 1847, s. 1869, m. 1876.			

*** WILLIAMS-WYNN, Sir Watkin, Bart., of Wynnstay, Ruabon, &c.

Coll. Westm., Ch. Ch. Ox.	Denbigh . .	28,721 .	24,368
Club. Carl., Jun. Carlton,	Montgomery .	70,559 .	18,139
Boodle's, White's,	Merioneth . .	42,044 .	7,438
Garrick.	Salop . . .	3,856 .	4,453
b. 1820, s. 1840, m. 1852.	Flint . . .	224 .	152
Served in 1st Life Guards.	Cardigan . .	361 .	18
Sits for Denbighshire.	Cheshire . .	5 .	7
Inclusive of manorial rights.		145,770 .	54,575

WYNDHAM, G. H., of Rogate. Sus., Hants   2,991 .   5,152

** WYNNE (late), BROWNLOW, of Garthewin, Abergele.

		acres.		g. an. val.
d. 1882.	Salop . . .	unstated	.	200
	Denbigh . .	6,495	.	5,800
	Carnarvon . .	20	.	20
	Flint . . .	1	.	80
		6,516	.	6,100

** WYNNE, JOHN LLOYD, of Coed Coch, Abergele.

Club. Carlton.   Denbigh . . 9,000 . 7,000
b. 1807, s. 1862, m. 1833.

** WYNNE, OWEN, of Hazlewood, Sligo, &c.

Coll. Har., Ch. Ch. Oxon.	Co. Leitrim .	15,436	.	4,380
Club. A. & N., Jun. Carl., Sack. St.	Co. Sligo . .	12,982	.	9,711
b. 1843, s. 1865, m. 1870.		28,418	.	14,091

Served in 61st Foot.

*** WYNNE, WILL. ROBT. MAURICE, of Peniarth, Towyn.

Coll. Eton.	Merioneth . .	8,353	.	4,195
Club. Carl.,Gds.,A.&N.	Carnarvon . .	1,400	.	414
b. 1840, s. 1880.	Leicester . .	682	.	1,350
Served in Scots F. Gds.	Flint . . .	119	.	177
Sat for Merionethshire.	Salop . .	2	.	7
	Middlesex .	und. an acre	.	86
		10,556	.	6,229

** WYTHES, GEORGE, of Copt Hall, Epping, &c.

b. 1811, m. 183-.	Essex . . .	4,113	.	6,359
	Kent . . .	692	.	12,042
	Suffolk . . .	603	.	1,002
	Surrey . . .	449	.	695
		5,857	.	20,098

* WYVILL, MARMADUKE, of Constable Burton, Bedale, &c.
S.

Coll. Trin. Cam.   York,N.&W.R.   8,309 . 9,141
Club. O. & C., Trav.   b. 1815, s. 1872, m. 1845.
Sat for Richmond.

** YARBOROUGH, Earl of, Brocklesby Park, Ulceby, Lincolnshire, &c.

			acres.		*g. an. val.*
Coll. Eton, Trin. Cam.	Lincoln.	. .	56,795	.	84,000
Club. Brooks's, Marl., Bood.	Berks	. . .	98	.	649

b. 1859, s. 1875.

		56,893	.	84,649

The Berks property belongs to the Countess Dowager.

BATESON de YARBURGH, Geo. Will., of Heslington, York.

Club. Carlton.	Yorkshire	. .	9,364	.	10,010

b. 1823, s. 1875, m. 1862.

** YEO, Miss, of Fremington, Barnstaple, &c.

s. 188–.	Devon	. . .	6,470	.	6,140
	Cornwall	. .	486	.	498
	Somerset	. .	276	.	408
			7,232	.	7,046

** YORKE, John, of Bewerley Hall, Ripon.

Coll. Eton, St. John's, Cambridge.	York, W.R.	.	14,499	.	11,000

Club. Yorkshire County.
b. 1827, s. 1857, m. 1859.   Exclusive of moors.

** CARTHEW-YORSTOUN, Morden, of Irvine House, Canobie, N.B.

Club. E. India U. Ser.	Dumfries	. .	3,330	.	3,150

b. 1832, s. 1860, m. 1854.   Served in the Indian Army.

	acres		*g. an. val.*
COOKE-YARBOROUGH, George Bryan, of Campsmount. York, Lincoln . .	2,894	.	4,240
YEATMAN, Mrs., of Stock Ho. Dor., Dev.	2,400	.	3,236
YELVERTON, Hon. William H., of Whitland. Carmarthen, Pembroke . . .	2,837	.	3,040
YEOMAN, Rev. H. W., of Woodlands. York	2,736	.	2,591
YORKE, J., of Forthampton. Glo., Wor. .	2,210	.	4,093
YORKE, P. W., of Duffryn Aled. Denbigh .	3,690	.	2,605
YORKE, S., of Erddig. Denbigh, Flint .	2,341	.	4,503
YOUNG, George, of Culdaff. Donegal .	7,989	.	2,358
YOUNG, H., of Leemount. Cork, Wat. .	5,933	.	2,278

** YOUNG, JAMES, of Durris House, Aberdeen, N.B.

		acres.	g. an. val.
Coll. Edin. University.	Kincardine .	16,804 .	10,653
Club. Athenæum; Univ. Ed.			

** ZETLAND, EARL OF, Aske Hall, Richmond, &c.

Coll. Harrow, Trin. Cam.	York, N.R. .	11,614 .	21,674
Club. Brooks's, Boodle's,	Fife	5,566 .	8,339
Carl., Trav., Marl.	Stirling . . .	4,656 .	9,552
b. 1844, s. 1873, m. 1871.	Orkney . . .	29,846 .	5,617
Served in Royal Horse Gds.	Zetland . . .	13,600 .	858
Sat for Richmond.	Clackmannan .	2,726 .	3,272
	Dumbarton .	162 .	12
		68,170 .	49,324

Excl. of 7,723*l.* for mines in Scotland, and of all mines in York.

ZOUCHE, LORD, Parham Park, Pulborough, &c. ♨.

Coll. Ch. Ch. Oxon.	Sussex . . .	6,654 .	5,681
Club. Carlton, Jun. Carl.	Stafford . . .	239 .	542
b. 1851, s. 1873, m. 1875, div. 1876.			
		6,893 .	6,223

YOUNG, JAMES, of Kelly. Midlothian, Renfrew, Ayr	2,225 .	5,152
YOUNGER, W., of Auchen. Dumf., Ed. .	2,965 .	3,280

APPENDICES.

I.—A Table showing the Distribution of the Area of the United Kingdom among the Great Landowners themselves, divided into Six Classes.

Class I. No. of persons holding 100,000 acres and upwards 44

„ II. Do. do. between 50,000 and 100,000 acres 71

„ III. Do. do. between 20,000 and 50,000 acres 299

„ IV. Do. do. between 10,000 and 20,000 acres 487

„ V. Do. do. between 6,000 and 10,000 acres 617

„ VI. Do. do. between 3,000 and 6,000 acres 982

———

2,500

This table excludes holders of large areas the rental of which does not reach 3,000*l.* ; a list, however, of the more noteworthy of these exceptions is given further on. This and the following tables do not take in the Metropolitan area, the Isle of Man, or the Channel Islands, or the estate of the Hon. C. W. White.

Holders of between 2,000 and 3,000 acres, or of between 2,000*l.* and 3,000*l.* rental from estates of over 3,000 acres 1,320

This table, as well as Tables II., III., and IV., was compiled in 1879; the alterations which have since taken place in the distribution of English land would not materially alter it, or them. Some men have increased their wealth, or, in the expressive North country phrase, " kept a-scrattin of it together," while divers eminent firms of auctioneers have been kept busy dispensing the dirty acres of those more unfortunate or more lavish. In this the " merrie month of May " chaos reigns in Ireland ; in half that distracted kingdom the peasantry are now virtually owners of the soil,—paid for though it may have been, and in many cases was, with Saxon cash, the fruit of Saxon toil and industry.

I may mention that, since the Premier has taken the *détenus* of Kilmainham into his confidence, but two Irish landowners have taken the pains to correct the figures contained in the body of this work. Are they in hiding in caves or bullet-proof huts ? (they can hardly think that letters of inquiry dated from the Carlton Club are likely to contain dynamite) ; or do they consider that Irish proprietorship is so utterly illusory under the present régime that to correct is a work of supererogation ?

II.—A TABLE SHOWING THE LANDED INCOMES OF SUCH OF HER MAJESTY'S SUBJECTS AS POSSESS 3,000 ACRES RENTED AT 3,000*l.* PER ANNUM AND UPWARDS, DIVIDED INTO SIX CLASSES.

Class I. Landed incomes of 100,000*l.* and upwards ...	15
„ II. Landed incomes of between 50,000*l.* and 100,000*l.*	51
„ III. Landed incomes of between 20,000*l.* and 50,000*l.*	259
„ IV. Landed incomes of between 10,000*l.* and 20,000*l.*	541
„ V. Landed incomes of between 6,000*l.* and 10,000*l.*	702
„ VI. Landed incomes of between 3,000*l.* and 6,000*l.*	932
	2,500
Holders of 2,00*l.* rental and below 3,000*l.* or under 3,000 acres	1,320

III.—A List of some of the Holders of Exceptionally
Large Estates, the Rental of which is under
2,000*l.* per annum.

	County.	Acres.	Value.
			£
Forbes, Charles H., of Kingairloch	Argyll ...	30,000	1,873
Grierson, Andrew, of Quendale ...	Zetland...	22,006	1,131
Hill (late), Lord George A., of Ballyvar	Donegal	24,189	1,308
Macdonald, John Allan, of Glenaladale	Inverness	24,000	1,550
Macpherson of Glendale	Inverness	35,022	1,257
Nicolson, Lady, of Nicolson ...	Zetland...	24,785	1,314
Robertson, Mrs., of Struan ...	Perth ...	24,000	1,239
Smith, Thomas V., of Acharanich...	Argyll ...	22,050	1,800

IV.—A List of the Number of Great Landowners who
are Members of the following Clubs :—

Political Clubs.

Tory
{
Carlton 642
Junior Carlton 112
Conservative 65
St. Stephen's 37
}

856

Liberal
{
Brooks's 216
Reform 103
Devonshire 29
}

348

Service Clubs.

United Service	107
Junior United Service ...	72
Army and Navy... ...	120
Guards	70
Naval and Military ...	22
	391

Learned Clubs.

Athenæum	145
Oxford and Cambridge ...	79
United University ...	61
New University	16
	301

Other Clubs.

Travellers'	286
White's	169
Boodle's	145
Arthur's	119
St. James's	86
Garrick	55
Turf	54
Marlborough	52
Union	50
National	35
Windham	29
St. George's	28
Raleigh	13
	1,121

Some changes have come over clubland since 1879. The "Scottish," "Royal Irish," "Bachelors'," and "Salisbury" have, for good or evil, added themselves to the already lengthy list of clubs, while the "Junior Naval and Military" has resolved itself into a political club as the "Beaconsfield," thus adding to the disproportionate number of Great Landowners who belong to Tory clubs; which disproportion is far more affected by the numerous (and somewhat late) secessions of Whigs who cannot stomach recent Radical legislation. In Liberal circles it is rumoured that the late internecine feud at the "Reform" has numerically strengthened the "Devonshire" not a little.

V.—A LIST OF PEERS AND PEERAGES WHOSE ESTATES HAVE BEEN ADDED TO THOSE OF LARGE-ACRED PEERS IN THE PRECEDING TABLE.

None of these Peers possess the double qualification of 2,000 acres worth a minimum of 2,000l. per annum.

Those marked with 1 asterisk hold less than 50 acres; with 2, less than 500.

ALDBOROUGH, PEERAGE, reps. of.

AUCKLAND, LORD.

AVONMORE, VISCOUNT.

BEACONSFIELD, PEERAGE.

BERKELEY, EARL.**

CADOGAN, COUNTESS.**

CANNING, PEERAGE, reps. of.

CAMBRIDGE, H.R.H. DUKE OF.

CARRICK, EARL OF.

CHETWYND, VISCOUNT.

COLCHESTER, LORD.

COLERIDGE, LORD.**

BURDETT-COUTTS, BARONESS.*

CRANSTOUN, LADY.

DE BLAQUIERE, LORD.*

DENMAN, LORD.

DUNBOYNE, LORD.**

DUNDONALD, LORD.*

DUNFERMLINE, PEERAGE, reps. of.**

DUNGANNON, VISCOUNTESS.**

ELLENBOROUGH, LORD.

ELPHINSTONE, Lord.

EMLY, Lord.

FITZGERALD AND VESEY, Peerage, reps. of.**

FOLEY, Lord.**

GORT, Viscount.

GRANVILLE, Earl.

GRAVES, Lord (exactly 50 acres).

GWYDYR, Lord.

HARDINGE, Viscount.**

HAWKE, Lord.**

HOWARD DE WALDEN, Lord.*

KINGSALE, Lord.*

KINGSDOWN, Peerage, reps. of.*

LAWRENCE (late), Lord.

LE DESPENCER, Baroness.*

LIFFORD, Viscount.

LIVERPOOL, Peerage, reps. of.

LISLE, Lord.

MELVILLE, Viscount.

MILLTOWN, Earl.

MOSTYN, Lord.

MOUNTMORRES, Viscount.**

NEWBURGH, Countess of.

ONGLEY, Peerage, reps. of.*

OXFORD, Peerage, reps. of.**

PERTH, Earl of.

RADSTOCK, Lord.*

RAGLAN, Lord.**

SELBORNE, Lord.

SEMPILL, Baroness.**

SHERARD, Lord.**

SOMERVILLE, Baroness.**

TAUNTON, Peerage, reps. of.**

TENTERDEN, Lord.*

TEIGNMOUTH, Lord.

THOMOND, Peerage, reps. of.

TORPHICHEN, Lord.

TORRINGTON, Viscount.

TRURO, Lord.

WALLSCOURT, Lord.

WALDEGRAVE, Earl.**

WENSLEYDALE, Peerage, reps. of.**

WENTWORTH, Lord.**

WESTBURY, Lord.*

WOLVERTON, Lord.

The estates held by Gen. Fox-Pitt-Rivers and Mr. Menzies of Hallyburton should, with a few minor properties, be deducted from the acreage held by Peers.

VI.—TABLES SHOWING THE LANDOWNERS DIVIDED INTO EIGHT
CLASSES ACCORDING TO ACREAGE—WITH NUMBER OF OWNERS
IN EACH CLASS; AND EXTENT OF THEIR LANDS.

"Peers" include Peeresses and Peers' eldest sons.

"Great Landowners" include all estates held by commoners owning at least 3,000 acres, if the rental reaches £3,000 per annum.

"Squires" include estates of between 1,000 and 3,000 acres, and such estates as would be included in the previous class if their rental reached £3,000, averaged at 1,700 acres.

"Greater Yeomen" include estates of between 300 and 1,000 acres, averaged at 500 acres.

"Lesser Yeomen" include estates of between 100 and 300 acres, averaged at 170 acres.

"Small Proprietors" include lands of over 1 acre and under 100 acres.

"Cottagers" include all holdings of under 1 acre.

"Public Bodies" include all holdings printed in italics in the "Government Return of Landowners, 1876," and a few more that should have been so printed, being obviously Public properties.

"Peers" and "Great Landowners" are assigned to those counties in which their principal estates are situated, and are never entered in more than one county. The column recording their numbers in each county must be taken with this qualification, but the acreage of all the "Peers" or "Great Landowners" in each county is correctly given, and their aggregate number, as well as their aggregate acreage, may be learned from the summary.

ENGLISH COUNTIES.

BEDFORD.			BERKS.		
No. of Owners.	Class.	Acres.	No. of Owners.	Class.	Acres.
3	Peers	53,789	*6	Peers	48,849
14	Great Landowners	60,127	20	Great Landowners	119,604
27	Squires	45,900	40	Squires	68,000
74	Greater Yeomen ...	37,000	153	Greater Yeomen ...	76,500
195	Lesser Yeomen ...	33,150	244	Lesser Yeomen ...	41,480
1,825	Small Proprietors...	38,906	2,315	Small Proprietors...	42,376
5,302	Cottagers	824	4,172	Cottagers	1,000
244	Public Bodies ...	16,380	290	Public Bodies ...	33,940
	Waste	1,127		Waste	2,114
7,684—Total.		287,203	7,240—Total.		433,863

* Inclusive of the Queen.

	BUCKS.			CAMBRIDGE.	
No. of Owners.	Class.	Acres.	No. of Owners.	Class.	Acres.
5	Peers	87,954	1	Peers	57,783
17	Great Landowners	118,036	13	Great Landowners	70,097
29	Squires	49,300	39	Squires	*57,000
132	Greater Yeomen ...	66,000	216	Greater Yeomen ...	†99,360
357	Lesser Yeomen ...	60,690	505	Lesser Yeomen ...	85,850
2,672	Small Proprietors...	49,339	5,373	Small Proprietors...	86,793
6,420	Cottagers	1,153	6,677	Cottagers	1,193
276	Public Bodies ...	23,737	350	Public Bodies ...	63,851
	Waste	2,942		Waste	2,554
9,908—Total.		459,151	13,174—Total.		524,481

	CHESTER.			CORNWALL.	
No. of Owners.	Class.	Acres.	No. of Owners.	Class.	Acres.
13	Peers	160,655	6	Peers	85,549
27	Great Landowners	157,451	29	Great Landowners	246,216
39	Squires	66,300	48	Squires	81,600
122	Greater Yeomen ...	61,000	224	Greater Yeomen ...	112,000
309	Lesser Yeomen ...	52,530	699	Lesser Yeomen ...	118,830
5,296	Small Proprietors...	77,922	4,028	Small Proprietors...	105,295
17,691	Cottagers	4,664	8,717	Cottagers	1,186
223	Public Bodies ...	21,696	115	Public Bodies ...	8,285
	Waste	6,707		Waste	70,968
23,720—Total.		608,925	13,866—Total.		829,929

* Actual extent   † Average only 460 acres.

No. of Owners.	Class.	Acres.	No. of Owners.	Class.	Acres.
	CUMBERLAND.			**DERBY.**	
4	Peers	97,027	6	Peers	182,337
18	Great Landowners	120,418	21	Great Landowners	120,640
51	Squires	86,700	38	Squires	64,600
242	Greater Yeomen....	121,000	144	Greater Yeomen ...	72,000
943	Lesser Yeomen ...	160,310	384	Lesser Yeomen ...	65,280
4,497	Small Proprietors	120,903	6,017	Small Proprietors	95,240
9,617	Cottagers	1,957	12,874	Cottagers	1,597
141	Public Bodies ...	22,496	382	Public Bodies ...	19,262
	Waste	114,025		Waste	11,655
15,513—Total.		844,836	19,866—Total.		632,611

No. of Owners.	Class.	Acres.	No. of Owners.	Class.	Acres.
	DEVON.			**DORSET.**	
17	Peers	217,088	10	Peers	122,625
50	Great Landowners	364,566	24	Great Landowners	192,847
108	Squires	183,600	59	Squires	100,300
496	Greater Yeomen ...	248,000	131	Greater Yeomen ...	65,500
1,557	Lesser Yeomen ...	264,690	229	Lesser Yeomen ...	38,930
7,509	Small Proprietors	204,687	2,794	Small Proprietors	39,179
21,647	Cottagers	2,981	7,694	Cottagers	1,631
425	Public Bodies ...	31,372	162	Public Bodies ...	12,377
	Waste	77,868		Waste	13,751
31,809—Total.		1,594,852	11,103—Total.		587,140

No. of Owners.	DURHAM. Class.	Acres.	No. of Owners.	ESSEX. Class.	Acres.
5	Peers	129,659	5	Peers	68,328
11	Great Landowners	83,670	39	Great Landowners	202,445
33	Squires	56,100	87	Squires	147,900
141	Greater Yeomen ...	70,500	387	Greater Yeomen ...	193,500
351	Lesser Yeomen ...	59,670	953	Lesser Yeomen ...	162,010
2,376	Small Proprietors	58,566	5,476	Small Proprietors	96,172
31,205	Cottagers	4,773	14,833	Cottagers	4,033
195	Public Bodies ...	57,582	525	Public Bodies ...	76,046
	Waste	47,388		Waste	6,896
34,317—Total.		567,908	22,305—Total.		957,330

No. of Owners.	GLOUCESTER. Class.	Acres.	No. of Owners.	HEREFORD. Class.	Acres.
7	Peers	110,125	4	Peers	26,454
34	Great Landowners	165,068	26	Great Landowners	158,918
55	Squires	93,500	49	Squires	83,300
251	Greater Yeomen ...	125,500	177	Greater Yeomen ...	88,500
597	Lesser Yeomen ...	101,490	448	Lesser Yeomen ...	76,160
7,107	Small Proprietors	97,482	3,781	Small Proprietors	50,615
29,280	Cottagers	6,030	9,085	Cottagers	1,301
374	Public Bodies ...	34,446	161	Public Bodies ...	21,312
	Waste	7,429		Waste	10,073
37,705—Total.		741,070	13,731—Total.		516,633

No. of Owners.	HERTS. Class.	Acres.	No. of Owners.	HUNTINGDON. Class.	Acres.
10	Peers	82,682	6	Peers	38,214
15	Great Landowners	74,862	11	Great Landowners	61,797
39	Squires	66,300	8	Squires	13,600
138	Greater Yeomen ...	69,000	64	Greater Yeomen ..	32,000
237	Lesser Yeomen ...	40,290	179	Lesser Yeomen ...	30,430
2,184	Small Proprietors...	34,196	1,612	Small Proprietors...	27,400
9,556	Cottagers	2,339	1,816	Cottagers	399
208	Public Bodies ...	15,139	207	Public Bodies ...	21,323
	Waste	5,302		Waste	795
12,387—Total.		390,110	3,903—Total.		225,958

No. of Owners.	KENT.* Class.	Acres.	No. of Owners.	LANCASTER. Class.	Acres.
18	Peers	122,571	10	Peers	135,322
36	Great Landowners	193,741	36	Great Landowners	218,570
75	Squires	127,500	79	Squires	134,300
356	Greater Yeomen ...	178,000	257	Greater Yeomen ...	128,500
788	Lesser Yeomen ...	133,160	692	Lesser Yeomen ...	117,640
6,062	Small Proprietors...	119,790	10,845	Small Proprietors...	168,100
26,925	Cottagers	8,128	76,177	Cottagers	14,811
423	Public Bodies ...	67,717	639	Public Bodies ...	30,221
	Waste	5,302		Waste	64,305
34,683—Total.		955,909	88,735—Total.		1,011,769

* Exclusive of what lies within the Metropolitan area.

No. of Owners.	LEICESTER. Class.	Acres.	No. of Owners.	LINCOLN. Class.	Acres.
7	Peers	98,132	12	Peers	253,606
17	Great Landowners	99,398	56	Great Landowners	418,886
38	Squires	64,600	91	Squires	154,700
164	Greater Yeomen ...	82,000	497	Greater Yeomen ...	248,500
487	Lesser Yeomen ...	82,790	1,205	Lesser Yeomen ...	204,850
3,823	Small Proprietors...	71,730	14,118	Small Proprietors...	222,586
8,921	Cottagers	1,742	13,768	Cottagers	2,824
391	Public Bodies ...	18,834	750	Public Bodies ...	100,591
	Waste	298		Waste	5,762
13,848—Total.		519,524	30,497—Total.		1,612,305

No. of Owners.	MIDDLESEX.* Class.	Acres.	No. of Owners.	MONMOUTH. Class.	Acres.
5	Peers	13,789	5	Peers	61,632
4	Great Landowners	9,640	8	Great Landowners	62,417
5	Squires	8,500	14	Squires	23,800
41	Greater Yeomen ...	20,500	71	Greater Yeomen ...	35,500
168	Lesser Yeomen ...	28,560	256	Lesser Yeomen ...	43,520
2,433	Small Proprietors...	34,295	2,366	Small Proprietors...	46,963
9,006	Cottagers	6,574	4,970	Cottagers	1,082
219	Public Bodies ...	21,156	121	Public Bodies ...	14,283
	Waste	2,591		Waste	7,594
11,881—Total.		145,605	7,811—Total.		296,791

* Exclusive of London.

	NORFOLK.			NORTHAMPTON.	
No. of Owners.	Class.	Acres.	No. of Owners.	Class.	Acres.
15	Peers	194,331	13	Peers	148,236
55	Great Landowners	322,939	23	Great Landowners	132,120
113	Squires...	192,100	31	Squires	52,700
341	Greater Yeomen ...	170,500	156	Greater Yeomen ...	78,000
824	Lesser Yeomen ...	140,080	444	Lesser Yeomen ...	75,480
7,936	Small Proprietors	152,446	3,287	Small Proprietors	67,053
16,552	Cottagers	2,468	10,010	Cottagers	3,022
812	Public Bodies ...	60,020	501	Public Bodies ...	36,161
	Waste	12,869		Waste	254
26,648—Total.		1,247,753	14,465—Total.		593,026

	NORTHUMBERLAND.			NOTTS.	
No. of Owners.	Class.	Acres.	No. of Owners.	Class.	Acres.
9	Peers	322,722	9	Peers	156,754
53	Great Landowners	471,523	21	Great Landowners	123,313
84	Squires	*173,000	25	Squires	42,500
181	Greater Yeomen ...	90,500	109	Greater Yeomen ...	54,500
289	Lesser Yeomen ...	49,130	282	Lesser Yeomen ...	47,940
1,531	Small Proprietors	42,456	3,838	Small Proprietors	61,108
10,036	Cottagers	1,424	9,891	Cottagers	1,266
76	Public Bodies ...	39,288	344	Public Bodies ...	19,956
	Waste	30,286		Waste	1,449
12,259—Total.		1,220,329	14,519—Total.		508,786

* The Squire class in this county averages about 2,055 acres instead of 1,700.

No. of Owners.	Class.	Acres.	No. of Owners.	Class.	Acres.
	OXFORD.			**RUTLAND.**	
9	Peers	82,503	1	Peer	42,500
17	Great Landowners	84,057	5	Great Landowners	23,794
40	Squires	68,000	*5	Squires	7,471
126	Greater Yeomen ...	63,000	10	Greater Yeomen ...	4,577
342	Lesser Yeomen ...	58,140	32	Lesser Yeomen ...	5,440
2,493	Small Proprietors	45,876	458	Small Proprietors	6,782
6,833	Cottagers	876	861	Cottagers	132
317	Public Bodies ...	46,831	53	Public Bodies ...	2,392
	Waste	2,949		Waste	401
10,177—Total.		452,232	1,425—Total.		93,489

No. of Owners.	Class.	Acres.	No. of Owners.	Class.	Acres.
	SALOP.			**SOMERSET.**	
8	Peers	195,276	10	Peers	120,519
44	Great Landowners	223,429	31	Great Landowners	217,352
65	Squires	110,500	67	Squires	113,900
222	Greater Yeomen ...	111,000	270	Greater Yeomen ...	135,000
447	Lesser Yeomen ...	75,990	882	Lesser Yeomen ...	149,940
3,841	Small Proprietors	57,738	10,831	Small Proprietors	173,918
7,281	Cottagers	4,544	20,370	Cottagers	5,227
211	Public Bodies ...	13,464	304	Public Bodies ...	24,627
	Waste	19,674		Waste	31,246
12,119—Total.		811,615	32,765—Total.		971,729

* This and the two following classes are given the actual extent of their holdings ; Rutland being too small to average fairly.

	SOUTHAMPTON.			STAFFORD.	
No. of Owners.	Class.	Acres.	No. of Owners.	Class.	Acres.
13	Peers	122,091	10	Peers	164,506
55	Great Landowners	279,286	23	Great Landowners	148,100
78	Squires	132,600	37	Squires	57,400*
281	Greater Yeomen ...	140,500	137	Greater Yeomen ...	68,500
452	Lesser Yeomen ...	76,840	414	Lesser Yeomen ...	65,412†
5,102	Small Proprietors...	80,756	8,617	Small Proprietors...	105,283
21,236	Cottagers	5,749	33,672	Cottagers	4,287
255	Public Bodies ...	46,827	641	Public Bodies ...	24,595
	Waste	78,843		Waste	7,808
27,472—Total.		963,492	43,551—Total.		645,891

	SUFFOLK.			SURREY.	
No. of Owners.	Class.	Acres.	No. of Owners.	Class.	Acres.
10	Peers	132,385	12	Peers	47,946
36	Great Landowners	233,263	11	Great Landowners	60,290
65	Squires	110,500	41	Squires	69,700
297	Greater Yeomen ...	148,500	174	Greater Yeomen ...	87,000
798	Lesser Yeomen ...	135,660	318	Lesser Yeomen ...	54,060
4,965	Small Proprietors...	102,770	3,813	Small Proprietors...	49,569
12,511	Cottagers	3,673	12,712	Cottagers	2,860
594	Public Bodies ...	45,686	212	Public Bodies ...	27,322
	Waste	7,831		Waste	40,036
19,276—Total.		920,268	17,293—Total.		438,783

* As worked out. See Preface.
† At what is the real average for Staffs, viz., 158 acres instead of 170.

SUSSEX.			WARWICK.		
No. of Owners.	Class.	Acres.	No. of Owners.	Class.	Acres.
19	Peers	195,016	9	Peers	111,223
40	Great Landowners	185,374	19	Great Landowners	119,043
86	Squires	146,200	32	Squires	54,400
280	Greater Yeomen ...	140,000	143	Greater Yeomen ...	71,500
537	Lesser Yeomen ...	91,290	507	Lesser Yeomen ...	86,190
3,915	Small Proprietors...	82,024	3,519	Small Proprietors...	62,191
14,675	Cottagers	3,950	46,894	Cottagers	5,883
182	Public Bodies ...	25,569	393	Public Bodies ...	30,592
	Waste	23,738		Waste	1,833
19,734—Total.		893,161	51,516—Total.		542,855

WESTMORELAND.			WILTS.		
No. of Owners.	Class.	Acres.	No. of Owners.	Class.	Acres.
2	Peers	54,366	16	Peers	239,708
11	Great Landowners	74,064	28	Great Landowners	225,893
20	Squires	34,000	61	Squires	103,700
109	Greater Yeomen ...	54,500	209	Greater Yeomen ...	104,500
352	Lesser Yeomen ...	59,840	335	Lesser Yeomen ...	56,950
2,055	Small Proprietors...	53,205	3,485	Small Proprietors...	54,759
1,714	Cottagers	326	9,635	Cottagers	1,519
113	Public Bodies ...	4,849	244	Public Bodies ...	41,920
	Waste	114,282		Waste	1,930
4,376—Total.		449,432	14,013—Total.		830,879

No. of Owners.	Class.	Acres.	No. of Owners.	Class.	Acres.
WORCESTER.			YORK, N.R.		
7	Peers	77,480	11	Peers	200,656
18	Great Landowners	87,753	39	Great Landowners	302,319
25	Squires	42,500	80	Squires	136,000
130	Greater Yeomen ...	65,000	230	Greater Yeomen ...	115,000
475	Lesser Yeomen ...	80,750	618	Lesser Yeomen ...	105,060
4,803	Small Proprietors...	65,265	4,991	Small Proprietors...	133,340
16,008	Cottagers	4,733	10,115	Cottagers	2,113
338	Public Bodies ...	17,580	229	Public Bodies ...	36,988
	Waste	3,415		Waste	247,408
21,804—Total.		444,476	16,313—Total.		1,278,884

No. of Owners.	Class.	Acres.	No. of Owners.	Class.	Acres.
YORK, E.R.			YORK, W.R.		
6	Peers	134,619	19	Peers	236,181
27	Great Landowners	221,635	66	Great Landowners	442,031
44	Squires	74,800	101	Squires	171,700
183	Greater Yeomen ...	91,500	366	Greater Yeomen ...	183,000
486	Lesser Yeomen ...	82,620	1,119	Lesser Yeomen ...	190,230
3,602	Small Proprietors...	60,601	14,735	Small Proprietors...	228,025
15,012	Cottagers	5,398	59,496	Cottagers	13,226
216	Public Bodies ...	35,511	1,011	Public Bodies ...	67,953
	Waste	4,049		Waste	99,912
19,576—Total.		710,733	76,913—Total.		1,632,258

WELSH COUNTIES.

No. of Owners.	ANGLESEA. Class.	Acres.	No. of Owners.	BRECON. Class.	Acres.
3	Peers	31,339	1	Peer	21,722
8	Great Landowners	66,175	10	Great Landowners	106,029
*6	Squires	10,200	†34	Squires	57,800
31	Greater Yeomen ...	15,500	97	Greater Yeomen ...	48,500
86	Lesser Yeomen ...	14,620	237	Lesser Yeomen ...	40,290
955	Small Proprietors...	20,421	796	Small Proprietors...	25,001
3,015	Cottagers	234	1,195	Cottagers	248
37	Public Bodies ...	3,447	44	Public Bodies ...	2,648
	Waste	5,678		Waste	115,106
4,141—Total.		167,614	2,414—Total.		417,344

No. of Owners.	CARDIGAN. Class.	Acres.	No. of Owners.	CARMARTHEN. Class.	Acres.
1	Peer	42,890	2	Peers	48,745
8	Great Landowners	96,909	13	Great Landowners	124,830
‡48	Squires	81,600	§50	Squires	85,000
110	Greater Yeomen ...	55,000	198	Greater Yeomen ...	99,000
304	Lesser Yeomen ...	51,680	497	Lesser Yeomen ...	84,490
1,553	Small Proprietors...	61,290	2,093	Small Proprietors...	62,689
1,278	Cottagers	287	5,168	Cottagers	2,286
14	Public Bodies ...	2,030	45	Public Bodies ...	3,534
	Waste	6,971		Waste	18,077
3,316—Total.		398,657	8,066—Total.		528,651

* Inclusive of two virtual yeomen whose rents are respectively under £1,000 p. a., and under £200.

† Inclusive of twenty-five persons whose rentals are under £1,000, one having as little as £83 for 1,255 acres.

‡ Nineteen of these have less than £1,000 rental, one with 1,443 acres having but £15 p. a.

§ Inclusive of sixteen rentals under £1,000.

CARNARVON.			DENBIGH.		
No. of Owners.	Class.	Acres.	No. of Owners.	Class.	Acres.
4	Peers	102,470	0	Peers	20,812
10	Great Landowners	100,861	16	Great Landowners	130,165
*19	Squires	32,300	†38	Squires	64,600
42	Greater Yeomen ...	21,000	106	Greater Yeomen ...	53,000
96	Lesser Yeomen ...	16,320	254	Lesser Yeomen ...	43,180
1,407	Small Proprietors	23,527	1,773	Small Proprietors	31,436
4,610	Cottagers	373	3,436	Cottagers	721
52	Public Bodies ...	4,382	85	Public Bodies ...	4,503
	Waste	14,563		Waste	18,812
6,240—Total.		315,796	5,708—Total.		367,229

FLINT.			GLAMORGAN.		
No. of Owners.	Class.	Acres.	No. of Owners.	Class.	Acres.
3	Peers	25,416	6	Peers	84,549
5	Great Landowners	39,113‡	19	Great Landowners	149,830
9	Squires	15,300	§36	Squires	61,200
44	Greater Yeomen ...	22,000	106	Greater Yeomen ...	53,000
111	Lesser Yeomen ...	18,870	210	Lesser Yeomen ...	35,700
1,225	Small Proprietors	15,179	1,373	Small Proprietors	29,184
2,048	Cottagers	562	6,570	Cottagers	685
65	Public Bodies ...	5,847	106	Public Bodies ...	14,238
	Waste	4,312		Waste	47,018
3,510—Total.		146,599	8,426—Total.		475,404

* Only six of these have over £1,000 rental. † Sixteen of these have less than £1,000 p. a.
‡ Over a quarter of these belong to Mr. Gladstone. § Nine have under £1,000 rental.

MERIONETH.

No. of Owners.	Class.	Acres.
0	Peers	16,684
12	Great Landowners	128,593
*37	Squires	†68,800
96	Greater Yeomen ...	48,000
135	Lesser Yeomen ...	22,950
346	Small Proprietors	14,244
1,044	Cottagers	212
25	Public Bodies ...	3,174
	Waste	416
1,695—Total.		303,073

MONTGOMERY.

No. of Owners.	Class.	Acres.
2	Peers	61,070
9	Great Landowners	86,587
‡42	Squires	71,400
128	Greater Yeomen ...	64,000
280	Lesser Yeomen ...	47,600
1,418	Small Proprietors	43,956
1,314	Cottagers	262
48	Public Bodies ...	5,510
	Waste	6,956
3,241—Total.		387,341

PEMBROKE.

No. of Owners.	Class.	Acres.
2	Peers	24,522
19	Great Landowners	109,495
§41	Squires	69,700
130	Greater Yeomen ...	65,000
263	Lesser Yeomen ...	44,710
1,134	Small Proprietors	29,483
492	Cottagers	278
40	Public Bodies ...	12,511
	Waste	12,260
2,121—Total.		367,959

RADNOR.

No. of Owners.	Class.	Acres.
2	Peers	15,572
11	Great Landowners	62,119
‖18	Squires	30,600
65	Greater Yeomen ...	32,500
203	Lesser Yeomen ...	34,510
850	Small Proprietors	28,446
452	Cottagers	90
41	Public Bodies ...	3,557
	Waste	77,799
1,642—Total.		285,193

* Including 28 rentals under £1,000. † Average 1,860 acres instead of 1,700.
‡ Including 16 rentals under £1,000 p. a. § Including 11 rentals under £1,000.
‖ Including 12 rentals under £1,000.

SUMMARY TABLE OF ENGLAND AND WALES.

No. of Owners.	Class.	Extent in Acres.
400	Peers and Peeresses	5,728,979
1,288	Great Landowners	8,497,699
2,529	Squires	4,319,271
9,585	Greater Yeomen	4,782,627
24,412	Lesser Yeomen	4,144,272
217,049	Small Proprietors	3,931,806
703,289	Cottagers	151,148
14,459	*Public Bodies.* { The Crown, Barracks, Convict Prisons, Lighthouses, &c.	165,427
	Religious, Educational, Philanthropic, &c.	947,655
	Commercial and Miscellaneous	330,466
	Waste	1,524,624
973,011—Total.		34,523,974

These figures are compiled from those at the foot of each County in the Return of 1873. They do not harmonise exactly with the summary at the beginning of the Blue Book, but that summary itself varies from the County summaries in many instances—in Durham, for instance, by some 2,800 acres.

These tables (and the dissertation thereon) were compiled for "English Land and English Landlords," by Hon. GEORGE BRODRICK, published by the Cobden Club in 1880, the dissertation being somewhat toned down so as not to offend men of extreme Liberal views.

NOTES ON THE FOREGOING TABLES.

"STATISTICS !—why they may be made to prove anything," said an eminent civil engineer to the Compiler a few weeks ago. "The London death-rate, for instance, is the greatest lie I know ; for the bulk of the great middle class, as is well known to Doctordom, if it can possibly manage it, goes into the country to die."

A lie of this kind was the original cause of the compilation of the much-abused " Return of Landowners, 1873,"—viz., that in the census tables of 1871 some 30,000 persons only were entered under the head of " Landowners ;" which so-called fact was much gloated over by those who would fain apply Mr. Bright's " *blazing principles*" to our existing land system.   This lie vanished with the publication of the Government return of 1873, in the year 1876 ; the landowners being found to come to something like a million.

Still it was evident that, useful as this compilation might be, it was marred by several serious blots, such as the non-entry of the Metropolitan area, the omission, in some counties at least, of the woods which in 1873 were still unrated, and the occasional double entry of one and the same man, especially where he was blessed with a double-barrelled name, such as Burdett-Coutts or Vernon-Harcourt, to say nothing of grosser cases, where some four surnames are strung together, rope-of-onion fashion, like Butler-Clarke-Southwell-Wanderforde or Douglas-Montagu-Scott-Spottiswoode.

A study of the Blue Book convinced me that something like 10 per cent., if not more, of the landowners thus appeared more than once ; and, when compiling " The Great Landowners of

Great Britain," I wrote to every large owner begging a correction, the answers proved that my surmise was perfectly right. One instance may be given.

Case of CAPT. EDWARDS-HEATHCOTE, copied verbatim from the Return (his real initials being J. H.) :—

STAFFS.	Name of Owner.	Address of Owner.	Extent of Lands.			Gross Estimated Rental.	
			A.	R.	P.	£	s.
Page 19, line 19	Edwards, H. T. H.	Apedale Hall ...	962	3	0	1,587	12
Page 27, line 42	Heathcote, Capt. E.	Audley	—	—	—	9,703	16
Page 27, line 44	Heathcote, J. E,	Newcastle, Stafford	44	0	20	154	0
Page 27, line 45	Heathcote, J. H. E.	Apedale Hall ...	—	—	—	1,097	0

Capt. Heathcote's real acreage is much over the amount with which the Return credits him. The property lies in at least four parishes,—principally in Audley, in which, I believe, Apedale Hall stands ; and Newcastle is his post town.

Having considerably weeded out these double, treble, and multiple entries before compiling "The Great Landowners," I have used that work, as well as the Government returns, in compiling the foregoing tables, using only such corrections as had been sent up to Christmas, 1877, but none of later date. Curiously enough, these corrections would not materially alter the totals in each column, because the cases of over-estimation in the Return are very nearly balanced by others which tell in an opposite way.

The 3rd Class (squires), and the 4th and 5th (greater and lesser yeomen) are averaged on the scales of 1,700, 500, and 170 acres, in all cases but Cambs., Northumberland, Rutland, Staffordshire, and Merioneth, where, if the usual averages had been strictly adhered to, the result on Class 6 would have been to make a "small proprietor" in Cambs. owner of but $11\frac{2}{5}$ acres, whereas he really holds $16\frac{1}{6}$; while a Northumbrian in the same class would have been lord of nearly 50 acres. Suspecting this to be false, I worked out the actual extent of the lands held by the "squires" on Tyneside, which proved them to hold 355 acres apiece more than their fellow-squires nearer Cockaigne.

As to Staffordshire, a county very familiar to me, the staggering fact came out, after totalising the lands proper to each class, that the 6th Class landowner in Staffordshire was the pariah of his race, and not only a pariah, but one degraded so utterly as to be owner of but 11 acres ; while a semi-Cockney of the same class in Surrey, which county most nearly approached him, held 13 acres of the soil.   Still, though every statistical dodge has been tried to raise the 6th Class Staffordshire pariah from his low estate, every dodge, though it somewhat softens down his evil case, still fails to rid him of his disgrace.   He, as owner of but $12\frac{1}{5}$ acres, is still *the* pariah of England.

The fact may perhaps thus be accounted for.   At a very rural petty sessions in Northern Stafford, colloquies like the following were often taking place :—

MILD ASSAULT CASE.

Chairman of Justices loq. : " Prisoner, we have decided to convict you.   You had no business to take the law into your own hands, and to give the man (though we must own you had much provocation) two black eyes, to knock him down, kick him, kneel on his stomach, throw his hat into the fire, knock out the ashes of your pipe into his left eye, and, finally, to use very bad language towards him."

Prisoner : " Noh, sur, A knows A didna oughta a doon it—

leastways, not quoit so mooch on it : but ye see, sir, A wasna 'ardly sober at the toime."

Chairman of Justices (*severely*) *:* " Drunkenness is no excuse."

(*To Head Constable*) *:* " Shallcross ! what's this man's position ? "

Shallcross : " Milks three caaws, sir."

Prisoner : " A dunna : you're a loiar."

Chairman of Justices (*excitedly*) *:* " Really ! you mustn't," &c.

Prisoner : " But A ony milks two—t'other's a cawf."

Chairman (*after consulting Colleagues*) *:* " Very well, then, we fine you fifteen shillings, or twenty-one days."

This police case only illustrates the fact that in the humbler walks of life, in both Cheshire (a small-averaged county) and Staffordshire, the position and respectability of a man is gauged by the number of cows, or rather " caaws," he milks.

To my certain knowledge, there are hundreds, nay thousands, of colliers who hold from four to eight acres, milk two or three cows, and willingly slave in the pits or iron-works to provide the rent in case they are tenants, or the interest on the inevitable mortgage in case (as 33,000 of them are) they are freeholders.

The prevalence of this mania for cow-milking as the badge of respectability in Mercia, as contrasted with the counter mania for the same badge in the form of keeping a " servant gal " or a " one-oss shay " in Middlesex, accounts for the large number and small extent of Mercian sixth-class holdings. Rutlandshire is greedily seized upon by the host of pundits who have dilated on the Government Return as a text to preach a statistical sermon upon, viz., by *The Pall Mall Gazette* (of yore), *The Spectator*, Mr. Frederick Purdy,—Hon. Lyulph Stanley, M.P., Mr. Lambert, and others whose names have escaped me,—or at least by most of them ; 'tis a tempting text—only 4¼ pages long, as compared with 185

pages for York—but to me the sermons in figures thereon preached
seem, like the London death-rates to my host of last August, to
savour of the lie statistical. Rutlandshire folk may be estimable,
astute, or both, but somehow they have not managed to keep
possession of the acres, of all others (Leicestershire not excepted),
most glorious for a fox-hunting gallop.

For instance, among foreigners owning their soil are the
following :—

> Adderley, Sir Charles (now Lord Norton, a Warwickshire man).
> Aveland, Lord (who is classed as a Lincolnshire Peer, his principal pro-
> perty being there).
> Belgrave, Mr., of Maydwell, in Northamptonshire.
> Brooke, Sir W. de C., Bart., also of Northamptonshire.
> Hankey, Mr., of Balcombe, Sussex.
> Lonsdale, Lord, from the North Country.
> Northwick, Lord, a Worcestershire Peer.
> Richards, Mr. Westley, of Birmingham (name dear to lovers of the
> trigger).
> Exeter, Lord (who is classed as a Northamptonshire Peer).
> Pochin, Mr., of Edmondthorpe, Leicestershire.
> Pierrepoint, Mr., of Chippenham, Wilts.
> Rutland, Duke of, a Leicestershire Peer.
> Kennedy, Mr., " of London " (a somewhat vague address).
> De Stafford, Mr., a Northamptonshire man.
> Blake, Mr., of Welwyn, in Herts.
> Laxton, Mr., from Huntingdonshire.

These sixteen persons among them own nearly 37,000 acres,
or two-fifths of the whole county.

Again, the unwary statistician who can only succeed in finding
five persons ranging from 1,000 acres to 5,000 might be misled
by supposing that " *Mr. Fludyer*," who figures for 1,100 acres,
and " *Mr. Hudyer*," who owns 1,500, are two separate persons ;
whereas Sir John Fludyer tells me that he is the person aimed at
in the Returns of 1873, under both the letters F and H.

Where landowners only reach five in the third class, a mistake of one is serious, and any generalization therefore based on Rutlandshire alone would affect England as judged thereby to the extent of one-fifth at the least.

Merioneth deserves special distinction as exemplifying Class 6 in its highest stage of ownership; yet a walk through two counties would bring a wayfarer from this paradise of small proprietors into Staffordshire, its lowest type of degradation. A glimpse at the column devoted to "waste" will show the reason why— a reason in itself sufficient to prove that the parochial magnates who compiled the crude materials for the Return had many curious eccentricities. "Waste" figures for only 416 acres in Merionethshire—certainly a most bucolic part of the Queen's dominions, if not exactly (as may be said of Connaught or Wester-Ross) "west of the law." There is no doubt that a dozen spots could be picked on its wild mountain ranges where no policeman could be found within half-a-dozen miles. Contrast this with the neighbouring counties of Brecon, Denbigh, Montgomery, and Radnor, where the waste reaches a total of 215,000 acres, or say 53,000 acres each. Yet Merioneth is a wilder county than any of the four. The obvious moral is that in Merioneth all *joint* lands have been equally divided in the rate-books among the participants, while in the four neighbouring counties they figure not as *joint*, but as *waste* lands. As to waste, though no uniform system of excision from other lands has been adopted in the Return, it may be roughly taken as a fact, that generally (but by no means always) they include, in the southern counties, heaths, charts, unfenced land, and, in some cases, salt marshes; and, in the northern ones, all such land as is entered in the valuable agricultural returns published of late years annually as "mountain pasture" and "barren heath." But on what principle can one reconcile figures like the following :—Kent—waste, five thousand odd acres,

Surrey—forty thousand? Kent is more than twice the size of Surrey, and as a fact contains, though perhaps in smaller proportion to its area, quite as much "heath," "common" and "chart" as Surrey. We must guess that in the rate-books of Kent these wastes swell the estates of the local Lords of the Manor.

The northern counties contain vast areas of "waste." Much of this is "waste" only in name, being unfenced, heathery-furzy-ferny-swampy-rocky pasture, much of it at a level of some 1,000 to 2,000 feet over sea-level, and affording fair pasturage to the hardy local sheep and cattle, though useless as nourishment to a 3,000 guinea shorthorn. These "wastes" are locally divided into what are called *cattle-gates*, each *gate* representing sufficient summer feed for one beast. In Kendal, Hexham, or Carlisle such cattle-gates are as saleable as an "eligible building plot" is in Kennington, Hoxton, or Camberwell; in no sense are they wastes; they are rather the rough survivals of some fossilized communal land system.

Let me with true Tory barbarity banish a few of the south-country land-law agitators, to try the experiment of settling themselves as virtuous and contented agriculturists on five-acre plots, carved out of the braes of Skiddaw, treeless, undrained, exposed to all the winds, and handsomely fenced with rough posts and rotten colliery rope. I fear the contentment would vanish, whether or not the virtue should remain. The agitator (specially if eloquent) is a proverbially thirsty soul : picture his horror at finding the nearest beer-house eight miles off, and the friendly grog-shop another five ! Meanwhile, let him bear in mind a few simple facts—that in the northern counties he may have to keep his wife and bairns without such aids to digestion as onions, goose-berries, strawberries, carrots, apples, cherries, cabbages, and peas, none of which flourish in Northumbria over the 1,000 feet level, besides combining all trades in his own proper person—such as stonemason, waller, butcher, plasterer, shoemaker, painter, glazier, and possibly accoucheur. The case of the southern wastes is equally unpromising in a money-making or self-supporting point of view. Many a Kentish "chart," if parcelled out into ten-acre freeholds, would scarce support a four-year old baby with a healthy appetite on each of them. Their only advantage over the northern moors is their much larger allowance of bright sunshine—a commodity of which the supply is now regularly registered in the daily weather reports.

Irish ills, Irish grievances, we hear not a little of these nowadays : one grievance under which St. Patrick's protégés suffer is often overlooked, *i.e., the want of bright sunshine.*

Lord Beaconsfield, touching on matters Irish, alluded to this when he spoke of " The incessant rain-drip on shores washed by a melancholy ocean."

Ireland is Nature's buffer and umbrella to break the wild violence of the storms so oft and so unkindly sent us from New York, and the gutter to carry off the superfluous rain. England thereby benefits. Western England gets ofttimes more than it desires of rainfall. Corn-growing is but a secondary interest there. Cattle and cheese make the profits, and pay the rents. Irishmen should follow suit ; instead of increasing the numbers of a starving peasantry, and glueing them to the soil, they should leave the ungrateful soil to itself, and to the cattle whom it could, under an intelligent system of breeding and rearing, carry with ease ; or if they must continue to cultivate the soil, cultivate it where the sun does occasionally shine often enough to ripen a crop of oats—or something better.

Meanwhile, the Irish coasts swarm with fish which they seldom even try to catch. Any capitalist who introduces a new manufacture or handicraft is sure to suffer in purse, even if he escape a bullet in the head.

Why, again, may I ask, is it that an Irishman will only dig a pratie out of his own easily dug, friable peat soil? He does not care for the same job on the stiffer lands of New York, Ohio, or Illinois. No; he severely sticks to town life and its joy, the whisky-shop; he hardly even enters the country parts of Yankee land. No; the industrious Irish peasant, as I know him best in Co. Mayo, loves to work ten minutes, then to rest on his long-handled spade for another twenty, then perhaps he does a furious spurt of labour for a quarter of an hour, which deserves to be rewarded, as it generally is, by well-earned rest against the nearest cabin wall, and a pipe of tobacco as a soother, and so on *ad lib.* Irish soil for the Irish!—hurrah, t'would demean a bold peasant to delve in stiff clays, such as the East Saxon hirelings of our East Saxon agricultural prophet, Mechi, delve and moil in, from six till six, or something like seven hours more work than the most industrious Galway or Mayo man ever did in a day.

> French peasants thrive; Irish peasants don't.
> French peasants work; Irish peasants won't.

Yet, according to Roman Catholic lights, France ought to be a blighted and heaven-accursed country, where Gambetta exercises his wicked will over the priesthood, and mightily oppresses them, while our British Premier has taken the best of care to denude Erin of the only educated men who could hold their own against the rural Irish priest.

The climate of these islands, I fear, is not suitable for what the French call "the small culture." No man on an average British plot of $2\frac{1}{2}$ acres can raise and support a healthy family. I would put the smallest desirable peasant-holding at from $4\frac{1}{2}$ to 6 acres, and these only in the eastern—*i.e.*, the drier—half of Eng-

land. In the western counties, where the bulk of the land is
under permanent pasture, and corn-growing is a secondary
interest, the minimum should be raised to what would keep four
cows ; and this minimum would vary much in different counties—
say from 9 acres in the vale of Evesham, to 45 or 50 in north-
western Devonshire. Desirable as it is in every way to encourage
the subdivision of the soil on political grounds, specially from the
moderate Tory point of view, it cannot be too strongly urged that
if a man buys a small freehold (as we all hope he may be able to
do when Sir Charles Dilke carries his intended (?) measure for
the hanging of all conveyancing counsel and solicitors whose
deeds of conveyance exceed 40 lines), that man should have some
other trade or means of livelihood than the tillage of the soil.
We cannot stand an indefinite increase in the number of acres
under such crops as lettuce, radishes, cabbage, celery, and onions ;
the supply would soon exceed the demand, and the cultivator
would starve. 217,000 " small proprietors " are already in our
midst—men who own some twenty acres apiece—and it will be
well for England when the number is quadrupled. Beyond that
point it would so far do harm as to (I believe) materially reduce
the amount of food grown on the fair face of Old England. In
view of the terrible competition of American produce, large
capital, open-handed use of all manures, close-fistedness in bar-
gaining, and credit enough to avoid having to sell at bad prices,
combined with a largish area to work on, and much knowledge of
the business, are the only conditions under which the British
farmer can hold his own. Men of this stamp are far too wise to
aspire to the ownership of the lands they till.

When divided by the number of small proprietors in Class VI.,
the four million acres they hold shows the following approximate
average size of holdings in each county :—

Staffs., $12\frac{1}{5}$
Flint, $12\frac{1}{3}$
Surrey, 13
Hereford, $13\frac{1}{3}$
Worcester, $13\frac{3}{5}$
Gloucester, $13\frac{5}{7}$
Dorset, 14
Middlesex, $14\frac{1}{10}$
Cheshire, $14\frac{2}{3}$
Rutland, $14\frac{3}{4}$
Salop, 15
Lancashire, $15\frac{1}{2}$
York (W.R.), $15\frac{1}{2}$
Herts, $15\frac{2}{3}$
Wilts, $15\frac{2}{3}$
Lincoln, $15\frac{5}{7}$
Hampshire, $15\frac{4}{5}$
Derby, $15\frac{5}{6}$
Somerset, 16
Cambs., $16\frac{1}{6}$
Carnarvon, $16\frac{2}{3}$
Notts., $16\frac{2}{3}$
York (E.R.), $16\frac{3}{4}$
Huntingdon, 17
Essex, $17\frac{1}{2}$
Warwick, $17\frac{2}{3}$
Denbigh, $17\frac{3}{4}$
Oxon, $18\frac{1}{4}$
Berks, $18\frac{1}{3}$
Leicester, $18\frac{3}{4}$
Norfolk, $19\frac{1}{4}$
Kent, $19\frac{3}{4}$
Monmouth, $19\frac{5}{6}$
Bucks, 20
Sussex, $20\frac{1}{10}$
Northampton, $20\frac{1}{3}$
Glamorgan, $21\frac{1}{4}$
Anglesea, $21\frac{1}{3}$
Beds., $21\frac{1}{3}$
Suffolk, $22\frac{3}{4}$
Durham, $24\frac{3}{5}$
Westmoreland, $25\frac{1}{2}$
Pembroke, 26
Cornwall, $26\frac{1}{8}$
York (N.R.), $26\frac{3}{4}$
Devon, $27\frac{1}{4}$
Northumberland, $27\frac{2}{3}$
Cumberland, 29
Carmarthen, $29\frac{9}{10}$
Montgomery, $31\frac{1}{10}$
Brecon, $31\frac{2}{5}$
Radnor, $33\frac{1}{2}$
Cardigan, $39\frac{1}{2}$
Merioneth, $41\frac{1}{6}$

It may be noted how closely the averages of many neighbouring counties run—the four northern counties and their neighbour, the North Riding; the three cider-making counties of Gloucester, Hereford, and Worcester; Lancaster and the West Riding; Kent and Sussex; and, though divided by the "silvery Thames," it is hard to raise a distinction between a small holding in Oxon and its fellow in Berks.

The two classes of yeomen show also a few curious facts; notably, the very large proportion of them who have the prefix "Rev." to their names. Of course it may so happen that in some parts of the country the rate-collectors, following the example of the Vicar of Owston and his Diocesan of Lincoln, refuse this prefix to our non-performing clerics, and thus simplify the labour of cleric-extraction from the ranks of the yeomen; but I take it that as a rule not only "Church Parsons," but their brethren "Ministers of Religion" who so often (and wisely) are associated with them in the modern toast-list, and even "Holy Romans," are entered in the Return of 1873 as "Reverends."

Their total number is 3,185, out of a total landed yeomanry of 33,998; in other words, not far short of ten per cent. Names with the clerical prefix are thickest in Northampton, Leicester, and Rutland, where about one in five of my yeomen is a cleric. This, of course, means that the glebe-land has not been entered, as the Local Government Board directed, as the property of "The vicar of Blank," but in the vicar's name, as "Rev. J. Smith."

After all, "yeomen" is but a makeshift title for holders of between 100 and 1,000 acres. If called out for a yeomanry drill, 'twould be diverting not a little to see, dressed in line, Mr. Goschen (halting between two opinions), Sir R. Cross (smiling on his neighbour), a popular Protestant Dean, arguing a theological point with the Ex-President of the E.C.U., while his rear-rank man, Mr. Coupland, who rules in Leicestershire, might talk fox-hunting with the Poet-Laureate and an eminent Hebrew financier. Still, as no better name suggests itself, we must content ourselves with calling them "yeomen."

It is much to be hoped that, if ever a revision of the Great Return of 1873 is made, a separate volume will be given to all town properties, as it is essentially absurd to mix the rental (say 10,000*l.*) derived from a row of warehouses in Bristol, covering three acres, with 50*l.* more derived from fifty acres of Gloucestershire clay. This is always done in the present Return; thus—

Extent, 53 *acres; rental,* 10,050*l.*

Let us also hope that, ere then, our rulers, even if they do not proceed to the violent measure with which I have saddled Sir Charles Dilke, will shatter the legal bonds which fetter and prevent the free sale of land, and the expansion thereby of Class 6—a class which, if multiplied fourfold, would add greatly to the stability of our fatherland and its institutions. Could they but effect this (I could hardly say so much in 1882), I for one (Tory though I be), shall not regret that, for what I hope is but a short space, the tree-planter of Hughenden succumbed to the woodcutter of Hawarden.

JOHN BATEMAN.

Carlton Club,
    October, 1880.

ADDENDA AND CORRIGENDA.

ABERDEEN, Earl of, is (1882) Lord High Commissioner to the General Assembly of the Kirk of Scotland.

ALEXANDER, Mrs., has succeeded her father, Mr. Tucker of Pavenham.

*** ALLSOPP, Sir H., Bt., Worcester, Derby 2,522 . 5,159

| | acres. | g. an. val. |

ASHLEY, Hon. E., is now Under Secretary for the Colonies.

BACON, Sir H. B., Bt., has bought in Lincoln 680 . 901

GREAVES-BAGSHAWE, W. H., of Ford Hall, has in Derby . . . . 2,832 . 3,190

BALFOUR, B. T., died September, 1882.

BEAUMONT, Sir G., Bart., died June, 1882.

BROKE, Miss, of Livermere, has married Hon. J. SAUMAREZ.

BULLER, Col., C.B., of Downes, married, August, 1882, Lady Audrey HOWARD. Their total possessions now reach about . . . . 9,000 . 18,500

CAMPBELL, Mr., of Rum, Tenga, and Aros, figures in the Return of 1876 for 46,000 acres. Much of this has been sold, reducing the estate below the 2,000 line of rental.

CHICHESTER, Mr., of Hall, died August, 1882.

CHICHESTER, Lady, of Arlington, has sold nearly all her Montgomeryshire estate.

CHESHAM, Lord, died June, 1882.

CLENNELL, P. F., died, August, 1882, and is succeeded by Mr. J. C. FENWICK, now Mr. FENWICK-CLENNELL. His acreage now reaches . . . . . 11,411 . 10,669

CONYNGHAM, Lord, died 1882. His successor has bought, in Kent, a few acres.

CROSSLEY, Sir S., Bart., has bought, in Suffolk, about nine acres.

CUBBITT, Mr., is a misprint for CUBITT.

CUTTS, Mr. J., died July, 1882.

DEAKIN, James, has sold 2,600 acres of the Werrington estate to Mr. J. Williams, second son of the late Mr. Williams, of Caerhayes.

DICKSON, John Poynder, has the late Mr. Poynder's estates.

DUGDALE, W. S., lost his life, May, 1882, in heroically striving to save those of his colliers who were imprisoned in a burning mine.

	acres.	g. an. val.
DUKE, Sir J., Bart., has bought, in Sussex .	18 .	31

FENWICK, Mr., of Longframlington, is now Mr. FENWICK-CLENNELL.

FFYTCHE, J. L., has sold, in Derbyshire . .	753 .	750

FITZGERALD, Sir M., Bart., married 1882.

For GALE, Miss, *read*—

WADE-DALTON, Col., C.B., of Hauxwell.

GERVAIS, Francis, died July, 1882.

CONWAY-GORDON, Col., died June, 1882.

GRAFTON, Duke of, died May, 1882.

GRAY, late Lady. Mr. E. STUART-GRAY, and not Lord MORAY, has inherited her estates—they are added, in this work, to his Lordship's.

GRIERSON, Sir A., Bart., married, September, 1882.

*** GURDON, Robert Thornhagh, of Letton, Shipdham, Norfolk.

Coll. Eton, Trin. Cam.	Norfolk . . .	4,910	.	6,365
Club. Brooks' Un. Univ.	Suffolk . . .	1,211	.	1,653
b. 1829, s. 1881, m. 1st, 1862.	Northumberland .	4,971	.	740
2nd 1874. Sits for S. Norfolk.				
		11,092		8,758

HAMILTON, Duke of, has bought Westburn, Co. Lanark, for 85,000*l.*

HANBURY, Osgood, died April, 1882.

For HAWORTH, Mrs, *read—*

	acres.	g. an. val.
HAWORTH-BOOTH, Col.		
HEATHCOTE, Sir W., Bt., has sold in Hants	472	589
HOLMESDALE, Lord. The Cornwallis trustees have bought, in Kent	130	186

HOMFRAY, J. R., died August, 1882.

HORNSBY, Mr. R., has bought Burwell Park, Co. Lincoln . . . . 2,040 . 3,935

HOWARD, Lady Audrey, has married Col. Redvers BULLER, C.B.

HOWARD of Corby has sold 200 acres in Cumberland.

JAMES, Sir W., has bought, in Kent . . . . 27 . 58

KEARNEY, Cuthbert, died May, 1882.

RUCK-KEENE, Mr., does not now own any property in Suffolk.

KILMOREY, Lord, has sold in Cheshire . . 474 . 1,085

LAWSON, Rev. E., died October, 1882.

LAWSON, Sir W., Bart., has bought a few acres in Cumberland.

VAUGHAN-LEE, Major, died July, 1882.

LOMAX, Mr. T. O., of Bodfach, has bought in Montgomery. . . . . 91 . 68

MATHIAS, Lewis, died October, 1882.

SCOTT-MURRAY, C., died August, 1882.

*** PAGET, of Cranmore, Somerset . . . 4,067 . 6,346
Stafford . . . 671 . 1,514
Other particulars as before
———————————
4,738 . 7,860

acres. g. an. val.

PARES, E. H., of Hopwell, has bought, in
Derby . . . . 232 . 383
This makes his total acreage 3,202, and his rental 6,688*l.*

PONSONBY-PURDON, of Tinerana, died June, 1882.

WARDLAW-RAMSAY, of Whitehill, died June, 1882.

ROLLE, Hon. Mark, has sold, in Devon . 386 . 354

RUSHBROOKE, Miss, of Elmers, died October, 1882.

SHELLEY, Sir John, Bart., married June, 1882.

SHEPPARD, Mr., of Campsey Ashe, died 1882.

SHIRLEY, E. P., of Ettington, died September, 1882. (I was
much indebted to him for initialling all families in this book,
who could, in his opinion, claim unbroken male descent from
men of noble or gentle blood, and good estate, in the time
of Henry VII.; whence the ⚜ mark).

SHREWSBURY, Lord, married 1882. Ingestre was burnt,
October, 1882.

SMITH, Mr., is said to have purchased the Bellamont Forest
property of 5,321 acres in county Cavan, from the Coote
family, some few years ago.

STRAFFORD, Earl of, omit the second " of."

*** THORNHILL, of Diddington has—

	acres	g. an. val.
Lincoln . .	30 .	70
Middlesex .	90 .	3,900
Elsewhere .	4,710 .	6,452
	4,830 .	10,422

Other particulars in the body of the work
are right.

TUITE of Sonna. The Return gives him 11,000 acres in 1876;
the Compiler is informed that this is nearly all sold now.

TYNTE, Col., died September, 1882.

HOWARD-VYSE, H. H., married July, 1882.

WARD, W. G., died July, 1882.

WESTMINSTER, DUKE OF, married, secondly, 1882.   He has bought some house property in Chester for 3,000*l*.

WHITE, SIR T., BART., died August, 1882.

*** WICKLOW, EARL OF.   *Coll*. Rugby, Oxon.   *Clubs*, Carlton, Army and Navy, Naval and Military, Kildare Street, Sackville Street.   b. 1842, s. 1881, m. 1st 1876, 2nd 1880. Served in 60th Rifles.   Acreage, &c., as before.

WILLIAMS, MR. J. (second son of late WILLIAMS of Caerhayes), has bought Werrington from Mr. DEAKIN.

WOODWARD, R., of Arley, died June, 1882.

On page 516, *for* Wanderforde *read* Wandesforde.

„   526, „ non-performing *read* non-conforming.

HARRISON AND SONS, PRINTERS IN ORDINARY TO HER MAJESTY, ST. MARTIN'S LANE.